Series 7 License Exam Manual

2nd Edition

SERIES 7 LICENSE EXAM MANUAL, 2ND EDITION

If you find imperfections or incorrect information in this product, please visit www.kaplanfinancial.com and submit an errata report.

Published in March 2020 by Kaplan Financial Education.
Printed in the United States of America.

ISBN: 978-1-07-880373-1

CONTENTS

INTRODUCTION

INTRODUCTION

Thank you for choosing Kaplan for your educational needs and welcome to the General Securities Representative Examination (Top-Off) Series 7 License Exam Manual (LEM). This manual applies adult learning principles to give you the tools you'll need to pass your exam on the first attempt.

Why Do I Need to Pass the Series 7 Exam?

The Financial Industry Regulatory Authority (FINRA), or another self-regulatory organization, requires its members and employees of its members to pass a qualification exam to become registered as a general securities representative. You must pass the Series 7 exam to be qualified to sell all types of securities.

Are There Any Prerequisites?

No. However, in order for a Series 7 registration to become effective, an individual must pass both the Series 7 qualification exam and the Securities Industry Essentials (SIE) exam.

What Is the Series 7 Exam Like?

The exam is administered via computer. A tutorial on how to take the exam is provided prior to taking the exam. Each candidate's exam includes 10 additional, unidentified pretest items that do not contribute toward the candidate's score. The pretest items are randomly distributed throughout the exam. Each candidate's exam consists of a total of 135 items (125 scored and 10 unscored). There is no penalty for guessing. Therefore, candidates should attempt to answer all items. Candidates will be allowed three hours and 45 minutes to complete the Series 7 exam.

What Score Must I Achieve to Pass?

You need a score of at least 72% on the Series 7 exam to pass and become eligible for registration as a general securities representative. Be sure to check the Exam Tips and Content Updates link on your dashboard for any updates to the passing requirement.

What Topics Will I See on the Exam?

The questions you will see on the Series 7 exam do not appear in any particular order. The computer is programmed to select a new, random set of questions for each exam taker, selecting questions according to the preset topic weighting of the exam. Each Series 7 candidate will see the same number of questions on each topic, but a different mix of questions. The Series 7 exam is divided into four major job function areas.

Four Major Job Functions	No. of Questions	% of Exam
F1. Opens Accounts After Obtaining and Evaluating Customers' Financial Profiles and Investment Objectives	11	9%
F2. Provides Customers With Information About Investments, Makes Suitable Recommendations, Transfers Assets, and Maintains Appropriate Records	91	73%
F3. Obtains and Verifies Customers' Purchase and Sales Instructions and Agreements; Processes, Completes, and Confirms Transactions	14	11%
F4. Seeks Business for the Broker-Dealer From Customers and Potential Customers	9	7%

Test candidates should be aware that within each major job function, FINRA has identified tasks and knowledge statements that test questions are based on. The complete Series 7 General Securities Representative Qualification Examination Content Outline can be viewed on FINRA's website: www.finra.org.

When you complete your exam, you will receive a printout that identifies your performance in each of the four major job function areas.

PREPARING FOR THE EXAM

How Is the LEM Organized?

The LEM is organized into four parts corresponding to the four listed functions. Each part is divided into units. There is a glossary that can help clarify unfamiliar terms you come across, and an index makes it easy to locate content within the LEM. Look for unique features created to help you understand and comprehend the material.

There is a PDF of the LEM on your dashboard. If you open the PDF, you can then search the LEM for key words by pressing Ctrl + F.

When additional emphasis is critical to your success, the following distinctions are made.

TAKE NOTE

Each Take Note provides special information designed to amplify important points.

TEST TOPIC ALERT

Each Test Topic Alert! highlights content that is likely to appear on the exam.

EXAMPLE

Examples provide practical applications that convert theory into understanding.

Additional Study Resources

To accompany and supplement your LEM, your study package may contain additional study resources. Be sure to spend some time on your dashboard, view the best practices video, and understand all that is available to help you study.

SecuritiesPro™ QBank

Coordinating with the LEM, the SecuritiesPro™ QBank includes a large number of questions that are similar in style and content to those you will encounter on the exam. You may use it to generate tests by a specific unit or combination of units. The QBank also allows you to create weighted (simulated) mock exams that mimic your test. There is no limit on the number of QBank exams you can create.

One thing you should know about the QBank is that the answer choices are scrambled each time you take a test. That is, if the first time you saw a specific question, the correct answer was choice A, that statement might be choice D the next time. Please keep this in mind if you need to contact us regarding that question.

Practice and Mastery Exams

Depending on the study package purchased, you may also have a fixed practice exam or a fixed practice and mastery exam. These exams are designed to closely replicate the true exam experience, both in terms of the degree of difficulty and topical coverage. They provide scores and diagnostic feedback, but you will not be given access to—nor will you be able to obtain from Kaplan—correct answers or question explanations. The practice and mastery exams are sound indicators of potential actual exam scores—the better you do on these exams, the more likely you are to pass your actual exam. These may be taken just once each.

Video Library

You may also have access to various topics from our video library. These short, engaging videos cover key topics from your manual. If your package includes access to our video library, please review the topics as you complete your reading assignments in the study manual.

Exam Tips & Content Updates Link

Don't forget to monitor your Exam Tips & Content Updates. When rules and regulations change, or we want to share new information regarding your exam, it's posted there.

In addition, try as we may, in a text this large, errors are difficult to avoid. When we become aware of them, we acknowledge them in the Corrections tab, also located on your dashboard.

What Topics Are Covered in the Course?

The LEM consists of 20 units, each devoted to a particular area of study that you will need to know to pass the Series 7. Each unit is divided into lessons devoted to more specific areas with which you need to become familiar.

The Series 7 LEM's table of contents provides a listing of all the lessons.

How Much Time Should I Spend Studying?

Plan to spend approximately 75–100 hours reading the material and carefully answering the questions. Spread your study time over the three to four weeks before the date on which you are scheduled to take the Series 7 exam. Your actual time may vary depending on your reading rate, comprehension, professional background, and study environment.

What Is the Best Way to Structure My Study Time?

The first thing you should do is create a study calendar. Information on the study calendar is located on your homepage.

The following schedule is suggested to help you obtain maximum retention from your study efforts. Remember, this is a guideline only, because each individual may require more or less time to complete the steps included.

Step 1

Read a unit and complete all exercises. Review rationales for all questions whether you got them right or wrong (two to three hours per unit).

Step 2

In the SecuritiesPro™ QBank, create a minimum of QBank exams as defined by your study calendar. Carefully review all rationales. Use the reference number to locate additional or related information on the test topic in your LEM if needed (two to three hours per unit).

- Do not become too overwhelmed or bogged down in any one unit. You don't want to lose sight of the finish line because you're having trouble with one hurdle. Keep moving forward. It's a steady pace that wins the race.
- View rationales after each question initially, and spend time studying each rationale in order to learn the concepts. Later, you will want to create exam scenarios in which scores and rationales are viewed at the end of each exam.
- Perfection is not the goal during the reading phase; scores in the mid- to high-60s are good initially.

Step 3

When you have completed all the units in the LEM and their unit tests, using the SecuritiesPro™ QBank, concentrate on simulated exams covering all the material. With your comprehensive testing, it is best to view correct answers and rationales only after the test is completed. Plan to spend at least one week testing before a scheduled class (about two hours for every 100 questions).

- You should complete at least eight simulated exams before class. Review your answers and rationales. Also, review your LEM and video library as needed.
- Your goal is to consistently score in the 80s.

Step 4

Complete online practice and mastery exams. You should complete each exam, while observing the time limits for the actual exam. Upon completing the exam, you will receive a diagnostic report that identifies topics for further review (about two hours per exam). We recommend taking the practice and mastery exams after a scheduled class.

Note: After completing practice, mastery, and mock exams, be sure to review your Performance Tracker so you can identify areas of weakness. You can then create focused exams on topics as needed. Also, review your LEM and video library for additional help.

Remember, you will not see the answer keys and rationales for the practice or mastery exams, but the detailed diagnostic breakdown will provide you with clear guidance on areas where further study is required.

How Well Can I Expect to Do?

The exams administered by FINRA are challenging. You must display considerable understanding and knowledge of the topics presented in this course to pass the exam and qualify for registration.

Our practice questions were carefully crafted to simulate the actual exam. In addition, weighting was considered (i.e., the number of questions likely seen on each topic). The wording must be somewhat different, but if you understand the subject matter, you will be able to find the correct response when you sit for the test. We often add new questions to refresh our question bank, sometimes with no direct supporting information pertaining to a specific question's subject in our LEM. In that case, there will be a thorough rationale to help you capture and retain the information you need. Because complex questions require you to link different concepts together to arrive at a correct answer, dealing with questions not directly addressed in the LEM will help develop that skill.

If you study diligently, complete all sections of the course, and consistently score at least 85% on the tests, you should be well prepared to pass the exam. However, it is important for you to realize that merely knowing the answers to our questions will not enable you to pass unless you understand the essence of the information behind the question.

TEST-TAKING TIPS

Passing the exam depends not only on how well you learn the subject matter but also on how well you take exams. You can develop your test-taking skills—and improve your score—by learning a few test-taking techniques.

- Read the full question.
- Avoid jumping to conclusions—watch for hedge clauses.
- Interpret the unfamiliar question.
- Look for key words and phrases.
- Identify the intent of the question.
- Memorize key points.
- Use a calculator.
- Beware of changing answers.
- Pace yourself.

Each of these pointers is explained in the following, including examples that show how to use them to improve your performance on the exam.

Read the Full Question

You cannot expect to answer a question correctly if you do not know what it is asking. If you see a question that seems familiar and easy, you might anticipate the answer, mark it, and move on before you finish reading it. This is a serious mistake. Be sure to read the full question before answering it. Mistakes are often made when assuming too much (or too little).

Avoid Jumping to Conclusions—Watch for Hedge Clauses

The questions on FINRA exams are often embellished with deceptive distractors as choices. To avoid being misled by seemingly obvious answers, make it a practice to read each question and each answer twice before selecting your choice. Doing so will provide you with a much better chance of doing well on the exam.

Watch out for hedge clauses embedded in the question. (Examples of hedge clauses include the terms *if, not, all, none,* and *except.*) In the case of *if* statements, the question can be answered correctly only by taking into account the qualifier. If you ignore the qualifier, you will not answer correctly.

Qualifiers are sometimes combined in a question. Some that you will frequently see together are *all* with *except* and *none* with *except.* In general, when a question starts with *all* or *none* and ends with *except,* you are looking for an answer that is opposite to what the question appears to be asking.

Interpret the Unfamiliar Question

Do not be surprised if some questions on the exam seem unfamiliar at first. If you have studied your material, you will have the information to answer all the questions correctly. The challenge may be a matter of understanding what the question is asking.

Very often, questions present information indirectly. You may have to interpret the meaning of certain elements before you can answer the question. Be aware that the exam will approach a concept from different angles.

Look for Key Words and Phrases

Look for words that are tip-offs to the situation presented. For example, if you see the word *prospectus* in the question, you know the question is about a new issue. Sometimes a question will even supply you with the answer if you can recognize the key words it contains. Few questions provide blatant clues, but many do offer key words that can guide you to selecting the correct answer if you pay attention. Be sure to read all instructional phrases carefully. Take time to identify the key words to answer this type of question correctly.

Identify the Intent of the Question

Many questions on FINRA exams supply so much information that you lose track of what is being asked. This is often the case in story problems. Learn to separate the story from the question.

Take the time to identify what the question is asking. Of course, your ability to do so assumes you have studied sufficiently. There is no method for correctly answering questions if you don't know the material.

Memorize Key Points

Reasoning and logic will help you answer many questions, but you will have to memorize a good deal of information. Some memorization will be automatic as you go over the material and answer questions; some you will simply have to do systematically.

Use a Calculator

Most of the questions found on FINRA exams requiring calculations are written so that any math needed is simple in nature and function. However, using a calculator is recommended to ensure that common math errors do not lead you to incorrect answers. While test centers generally have calculators available for your use, you should have a simple function calculator with you, if needed in case of test center shortages. Test center staff will advise you as to whether or not you may use your own calculator.

Avoid Changing Answers

If you are unsure of an answer, your first hunch is the one most likely to be correct. Do not change answers on the exam without good reason. In general, change an answer only if you

- discover that you did not read the question correctly; or
- find new or additional helpful information in another question.

Pace Yourself

Some people will finish the exam early, and some do not have time to finish all the questions. Watch the time carefully (your time remaining will be displayed on your computer screen), and pace yourself through the exam.

Do not waste time by dwelling on a question if you simply do not know the answer. Make the best guess you can, mark the question for *Record for Review*, and return to the question if time allows. Make sure that you have time to read all the questions so that you can record the answers you do know.

THE EXAM

How Do I Enroll in the Exam?

To obtain admission to a FINRA-administered exam, your firm must electronically apply for and pay a fee to FINRA through its Central Registration Depository, better known as the Web CRD®. To take the exam, you must make an appointment with a Prometric Testing Center as far in advance as possible to get the date you would like to sit for the exam.

You may schedule, reschedule, or cancel your exam, locate a test center, and get a printed confirmation of your appointment 24 hours a day, 7 days a week.

- Prometric secure website at www.prometric.com, 1-800-578-6273.

You must have your Central Registration Depository (CRD) number available when scheduling your exam. This unique personal identification number should be provided to you by your employing member firm. On a cautionary note, failure to show for an examination will be permanently recorded on your examination history on the Web CRD.

What Should I Take to the Exam?

Take one form of personal identification with your signature and photograph as issued by a government agency. No personal items, food, or drink, including coffee and water, are permitted inside the testing room. Personal items include, but are not limited to, the following: pens, pagers, cellular phones, watches, hats, nonmedical electronic devices, outerwear, purses, and wallets. Personal items must be kept in your assigned locker or returned to your car before the start of your exam. Because the testing vendor is not responsible for any personal items, you are encouraged to bring only your identification into the Center.

Erasable note boards and pens will be provided to you upon admittance to the testing room. If you need additional note boards or pens, please alert your proctor. The note boards and pens must be returned at the end of your exam or continuing education session.

If you need a calculator for your testing session, please see the Test Center Administrator. You will be provided with a nonprogrammable, nonprinting calculator.

Additional Trial Questions

During your exam, you will see extra (10 for the Series 7 exam) trial questions. These are potential future exam-bank questions being tested during the course of the exam. These questions are not included in your final score and will not be identified.

Exam Results and Reports

At the end of the exam, your results will be displayed, indicating whether you passed. If you passed, no score will be given. The next business day after your exam, your results will be mailed to your firm and to the self-regulatory organization and State Securities Commission specified on your application.

ADDITIONAL INFORMATION ABOUT THE EXAM

As stated earlier in the introduction in the License Exam Manual (LEM), passing this exam is a requirement to qualify as a general securities registered representative of a Financial Industry Regulatory Authority (FINRA) member firm. What exactly does that mean? First of all, FINRA is the primary regulator of entities engaged in the business of buying and selling securities. Those businesses are known as broker-dealers. Unless qualifying for an exemption, they must become members of FINRA. Individuals, such as yourself, who represent them, must register. The category of registration is based on the type of securities they will be selling and their individual function. As a Series 7 registered representative, you will be able to sell almost any type of security. You will be doing so under the supervision of an employee of the firm. That person will be registered as a principal. Registration as a principal is required for those with a supervisory function.

You should be aware this is a top-off exam. That means you must have the Securities Industry Essentials (SIE) qualification. Alternatively, FINRA grandfathers those who, as of October 1, 2018, had an existing FINRA registration, such as a Series 6 or Series 22. FINRA expects those folks to be familiar with industry basics.

FINRA states that the SIE is a co-requisite exam. In reality, almost all of our students who are not grandfathered take the SIE before enrolling in the Series 7 Top-Off. Therefore, this course will assume that you know the basics of the industry, such as the difference between a stock and bond or an asset and a liability.

PART 1

Open Accounts After Obtaining and Evaluating Customers' Financial Profiles and Investment Objectives; Retirement Plans

Part 1 consists of two units:

Unit 1: Types of Accounts

Unit 2: Obtain Necessary Suitability Information and Approvals

In total, you will see 11 questions on material from Part 1, representing 9% of the Series 7 Top-Off Exam.

UNIT 1

Types of Accounts

LEARNING OBJECTIVES

When you have completed this unit, you will be able to accomplish the following.

- › LO 1.a **Recognize** the different types of accounts offered to clients.
- › LO 1.b **Compare** various account registration types for natural persons.
- › LO 1.c **Distinguish** between the different types of business entities capable of opening accounts.
- › LO 1.d **Explain** the requirements for opening customer accounts.
- › LO 1.e **Identify** the procedure for account registration changes and transfers.
- › LO 1.f **Contrast** qualified and nonqualified retirement plans.
- › LO 1.g **Recall** the features of individual retirement arrangements.
- › LO 1.h **Differentiate** between the different types of employer-sponsored qualified retirement plans.
- › LO 1.i **Define** ERISA and its application to private-sector retirement plans.

INTRODUCTION

As a general securities registered representative, one of the functions you might be performing is opening accounts for new clients of your employing member firm. To engage in securities transactions, investors must open an account with a broker-dealer. In concept, this is no different from opening an account at a bank if you want to have a checking account. In this unit, we will describe the different types of accounts you may see on your exam.

LESSON 1.1: TYPES OF CUSTOMER ACCOUNTS

LO 1.a Recognize the different types of accounts offered to clients.

Cash Account

There are a number of different types of accounts that may be opened at a broker-dealer. We are going to start with the two most common. Those are the *cash account* and the *margin account*.

A **cash account** is the basic investment account, and anyone eligible to open an investment account can open one. In a cash account, a customer must pay in full for any securities purchased. Although, as with almost everything in this course, there are exceptions for exam purposes. Certain accounts, all of which will be described shortly, may *only* be opened as cash accounts, including

- personal retirement accounts, such as IRAs;
- corporate retirement accounts, such as 401(k)s; and
- custodial accounts, such as Uniform Transfer to Minors Act accounts, and Coverdell Education Savings Account (ESA).

Margin Account

In a margin account, the customer can use some cash and some credit to purchase securities. The use of borrowed money is referred to as financial leverage. This is because investors can buy more securities using credit than they can using just cash. In concept, this is no different from buying a home with a mortgage; most people can't afford to pay in full so, after a down payment, they borrow the rest using the home as collateral.

In this business, the securities firm lends the necessary funds at the time of purchase, with the securities in the portfolio serving as collateral for the loan. This is called buying securities on margin. The term *margin* refers to the minimum amount of equity a customer must deposit to buy securities. The shortfall between the purchase price and the amount of money put in is a loan from the securities firm, and the customer will incur interest costs, just as with any other loan.

Anytime borrowed money is involved, there is greater risk. This is because the borrow money is a debt that must be repaid. Because of this higher risk, customers who open margin accounts must meet certain minimal suitability requirements. Leveraging can be beneficial when the security's price is moving up, but it can result in a loss greater than the original investment if the security's price goes against the investor.

This risk is the primary reason why margin transactions are not available for use within certain types of accounts, such as retirement accounts or custodial accounts for minor children.

We'll have lots more to say about margin accounts in LO 16.d.

Fee-Based Account

Many firms offer investors **fee-based accounts** that charge a single fee (either fixed or a percentage of assets in the account) instead of commission-based charges for brokerage services.

FINRA states that fee-based accounts are appropriate only for investors who engage in at least a moderate level of trading activity. Accounts with a low level of trading activity may be better off with commission-based charges. Rules require that, before opening a fee-based account, investors be given a disclosure document describing the services to be provided and the cost.

One of the benefits of fee-based accounts is that they tend to reduce the likelihood of abusive sales practices. Primary among those abuses is *churning*. Churning is the illegal and unethical practice that occurs when a broker-dealer or one of its registered representatives engages in excessive buying and selling of securities in a customer's account chiefly to generate commissions that benefit the broker. A red flag signally churning could be frequent in-and-out purchases and sales of securities that don't appear necessary to fulfill the customer's investment goals.

On the other hand, these accounts have introduced a new concept to the industry—*reverse churning*. Every year, FINRA publishes a list of regulatory priorities for that year. The 2018 report stated they were concerned about, "situations in which registered representatives recommend a switch from a brokerage account to a fee-based where that switch clearly disadvantages the customer." What that meant in simple terms is that member firms were moving low-trading activity clients into accounts where they were charged a fixed fee that turned out to be higher than what they would have paid in commissions.

Fee-based accounts are not wrap accounts. Wrap-fee accounts are accounts for which firms provide a group of services. Those might include asset allocation, portfolio management, executions, and administration. The account is charged a single fee. The fee is usually a percentage of assets being managed. Firms offering wrap accounts are generally required to register as investment advisers. This would be in addition to their registration as a broker-dealer.

Prime Brokerage Account

A **prime brokerage account** is one in which a customer—generally an institution—selects one member firm (the prime broker) to provide custody, trading, and other services, while other firms, called *executing brokers*, typically execute most of the trades placed by the customer. To open a prime brokerage account for a customer, a member (the prime broker) must sign an agreement with the customer, spelling out the terms of the agreement, as well as names of all executing brokers the customer has contracted with. The prime broker will then enter into written agreements with each executing broker named by the customer. The customer receives trade confirmations and account statements from the prime broker, who facilitates the clearance and settlement of the securities transactions. Responsibility for compliance of certain trading rules rests with the executing brokers.

The key advantage of a prime brokerage account is that it usually provides a client with the ability to trade with multiple brokerage houses while maintaining a centralized master account with all of the client's cash and securities. In essence, the prime brokerage firm is acting like a construction general contractor dealing with all of the participants in the job.

A prime brokerage account often includes a list of specialized services, such as securities lending, margin financing, trade processing, cash management, and operational support. Prime brokerage accounts are likely to be offered to a broker-dealer's more active trading clients—like hedge funds, for example—who may require a number of executing broker outlets to conduct their transactions and who can benefit by having margin requirements that are netted across all of the prime broker's positions.

PRACTICE QUESTION

1. An IRA account at a broker-dealer must be set up as
   A. a cash account.
   B. a margin account.
   C. a fee-based account.
   D. a prime broker account.

   Answer: A. IRAs can only be opened in cash accounts.

Delivery vs. Payment (DVP); Receipt vs. Payment (RVP)

In a DVP/RVP arrangement, payment for securities purchased is made to the selling customer's agent, and/or delivery of securities sold is made to the buying customer's agent in exchange for payment at time of settlement. Normally used for institutional accounts, this is a cash-on-delivery settlement. The broker-dealer handling the trade must verify the arrangement between the customer and the bank or depository, and the customer must notify the bank or depository of each purchase or sale. Later in the course, we'll cover a unique 35-day rule that applies to these transactions.

PRACTICE QUESTION

2. An institutional customer would like to use one broker-dealer to handle the administration of the account, but would like to use various other broker-dealers to execute trades for certain types of securities. Which type of account would meet the customer's needs?
   A. An advisory account
   B. A prime brokerage account
   C. A fee-based account
   D. A DVP account

   Answer: B. A prime brokerage account is one in which a customer, generally an institution, selects one member firm (the prime broker) to provide custody and other services, while other firms, called executing brokers, handle most of the trades placed by the customer.

Pattern Day Trading Account

A **day trader** is someone who buys and sells the same security on the same day to try to take advantage of intraday price movements. A **pattern day trader** is someone who executes four or more day trades in a five-business-day period. The minimum equity requirement for pattern day traders is $25,000. That means they must have on deposit at least $25,000 in the account equity on any day in which day trading occurs.

Member firms who promote day trading strategies must implement procedures to approve day trading accounts.

Before opening an account, the member must

- provide the customer with a **risk disclosure** statement that outlines all the risks associated with day trading (the statement can be furnished in writing or electronically), and
- approve the account for a day trading strategy or receive from the customer a written statement that the customer does not intend to engage in day trading.

There are special margin rules for these accounts and they will be covered later in the course.

LESSON 1.2: ACCOUNT REGISTRATIONS

LO 1.b Compare various account registration types for natural persons.

There are many different registration types available when opening an account at a broker-dealer. Let's take a look at them one at a time.

Individual Account

An **individual account** is just that—an account with one owner. The account holder is the only person who may

- control the investments within the account and
- request distributions of cash or securities from the account.

Suitability is based solely on the individual.

Multiple Owner Accounts

There are several types of accounts with multiple owners covered on the exam. These are generally referred to as joint accounts, although we do include one for which that term is not appropriate.

Joint Accounts

In a **joint account**, two or more adults are named on the account as co-owners, with each allowed some form of control over the account. In addition to filling out the appropriate new account form, a joint account agreement must be signed.

The account forms for joint accounts require the signatures of all owners. The owners are called *tenants*. Joint account agreements allow any or all tenants to transact business in the account. Checks must be made payable to the names in which the account is registered and must be endorsed for deposit by all tenants (although mail need be sent to only a single address). When securities are sold from a joint account, the certificate must be signed by all tenants.

The suitability requirements for a joint account follow the same basic rules as all accounts. You must put the interest of the client first. Because a joint account is really nothing other than a collection of individuals, suitability information must be obtained on all of the account owners. Any recommendations must be appropriate based upon that information. In other words, the suitability of recommendations must be based on the group, not on any individual within the group.

Joint Tenants With Rights of Survivorship (JTWROS)

Joint tenants with rights of survivorship (JTWROS) ownership stipulates that a deceased tenant's interest in the account passes to the surviving tenant(s). That is why JTWROS is most common for spouses. In these accounts, the ownership is equal.

Tenants in Common (TIC)

Tenants in common (TIC) ownership provides that a deceased tenant's fractional share in the account goes to that tenant's estate. TICs are most commonly used for nonspousal relatives or friends. In these accounts, the ownership can be unequal.

EXAMPLE

Suppose a TIC agreement provides for a 60% ownership interest by one owner and a 40% ownership interest by the other. If the 60% owner dies first, 60% of the account would pass into the deceased owner's estate. The TIC agreement may be used by more than two individuals.

TEST TOPIC ALERT

- JTWROS—all parties have an undivided interest in the account
- TIC—each party must specify a percentage interest in the account

Checks or distributions must be made payable to all parties and endorsed by all parties.

PRACTICE QUESTION

3. Several investors open an account as tenants in common (TIC). For suitability purposes, financial information is required on which of the following investors?
   A. Most of the investors
   B. The largest investor only
   C. Only the one authorized to trade the account
   D. All of the investors

   Answer: D. When a joint account is opened, to be able to make suitable recommendations, financial information should be obtained on all of the account owners.

Community Property

Community property is a marital property classification recognized by some, but not all states. Because it is not in universal use, it will most likely appear as a wrong answer choice on the exam. Following are some of the basics in case you do have a question. In these states, most property acquired during the marriage is considered to be owned jointly by both spouses and would be divided at the time of divorce, annulment, or death. Joint ownership is therefore automatically presumed by law in these jurisdictions. Exceptions are made for inheritances, gifts, or any property that is owned by one spouse before marriage. That is considered the separate property of that spouse, unless it was designated to be owned jointly by both spouses during the marriage.

It is important to know that community property law differs from state to state. Some states have created separate classifications called *community property with rights of survivorship* that are similar to joint tenancy with rights of survivorship property designations.

PRACTICE QUESTION

4. All of the following are true regarding community property **except**
   A. property acquired before marriage is considered to be jointly owned.
   B. community property is considered to be owned jointly by both spouses and would be divided at the time of divorce, annulment, or death.
   C. not all states are community property states.
   D. an exception to community property is for property that was inherited.

   Answer: A. Property acquired before marriage is considered to be owned separately, not jointly, as stated in the answer choice. Each of the other choices is a true statement.

Custodial Accounts

Custodial accounts are not technically joint accounts as there is only one owner but there are two names on the account. Those names are the custodian and the beneficial owner, the minor. The original format was under the Uniform Gifts to Minors Act (UGMA). That was replaced by the Uniform Transfer to Minors Act (UTMA). As of the date of this printing, only one state still uses UGMA, with all of the rest relying on UTMA. The reason for these accounts is because, under the law, a minor is not considered a legal person. That is, a minor cannot be held to contracts.

In a **custodial account**, the custodian for the minor enters all trades. UGMA and UTMA accounts require an adult to act as custodian for a minor (the beneficial owner).

The Uniform Law Commissioners adopted UGMA in 1956. The primary focus then was to provide a convenient way to make gifts of money and securities to minors. Later, it became clear that a more flexible law was desirable. The Uniform Law Commissioners adopted UTMA in 1986. UTMA expands the types of property you can transfer to a minor, and provides that you can make other types of transfers besides gifts. The essential principles of both acts are the same; the primary difference is the greater flexibility of UTMA.

Securities in an UGMA/UTMA account are managed by a custodian until the minor reaches the age of majority, or in the case of UTMA, the age determined by the specific state. The custodian has full control over the minor's account and can

- buy or sell securities;
- exercise rights or warrants; and
- liquidate, trade, or hold securities.

The custodian also may use the property in the account in any way the custodian deems proper for the minor's support, education, maintenance, general use, or benefit. However, the account is not normally used to pay expenses associated with raising a child, such as the three basic needs of food, clothing, and shelter.

Registered representatives should know the following UGMA/UTMA custodial account rules:

- All gifts, (and transfers in the case of UTMA), are irrevocable.
- An account may have only one custodian and one minor or beneficial owner.
- A donor of securities can act as custodian or appoint someone to do so.
- Unless acting as a custodian, parents have no legal control over an UGMA/UTMA account or the securities in it.

- A minor can be the beneficiary of more than one account, and a person may serve as custodian for more than one UGMA/UTMA, provided each account benefits only one minor.
- The minor has the right to sue the custodian for improper actions.
- These can only be opened as cash accounts—margin is not allowed.

PRACTICE QUESTION

5. Which of the following individuals may **not** open a joint account?
   A. Two spouses
   B. Three sisters
   C. Two friends
   D. Parent and a minor child

   Answer: D. A joint account may be opened by two or more individuals who have legal standing. A minor may not be a party in a joint account because minors are not legally considered a person. A parent (or any other adult) can be custodian for a minor, but that is a single account, not a joint account.

Transfer on Death (TOD)

Transfer on death (TOD) is a type of account registration that allows the owner of the account to pass all or a portion of it, upon death, to a single or multiple beneficiaries. No specific legal documents are needed. Furthermore, the beneficiaries and percentages can be changed as often as desired. TOD avoids probate, but the assets in the account do not avoid estate tax, if applicable.

TOD accounts are available for individual accounts. They can also be used for certain joint accounts (JTWROS, but not TIC).

PRACTICE QUESTION

6. Which type of individual account allows for investments held in that account to go straight to a named beneficiary outside of probate?
   A. A TOD account
   B. A testamentary account
   C. An account titled JTWROS
   D. An advisory account

   Answer: A. A simple way for an individual account owner to ensure that the assets in the account pass directly to the named beneficiary is to use the Transfer on Death (TOD) option. Although the assets in a JTWROS account pass to the survivor without probate, the question specifies an individual, not a joint account.

LESSON 1.3: BUSINESS ACCOUNTS

LO 1.c Distinguish between the different types of business entities capable of opening accounts.

Sole Proprietorship

Sole proprietorship is the simplest form of business organization and is treated like an individual account. Therefore, the same issues of suitability that apply to individual accounts apply to the management of sole proprietorship accounts. In a sole proprietorship, all income (or loss) is that of the individual. In fact, one of the risks of operating in this fashion is that all of the owner's assets are liable for the debts of the business—you can lose everything. Obviously, this is one of the major considerations when opening an account for this form of business.

General Partnership

A general partnership is an unincorporated association consisting of two or more individuals. In a general partnership, the partners manage and are responsible for the operation and debts of the business. Partnerships are easy to form and easy to dissolve, but are generally not suited for raising large sums of capital. Partnerships allow the business' profits and losses to flow directly through to the investors for tax purposes, thus avoiding double taxation of profits at the business and individual levels.

Because the income and losses flow through to the individual partners, an investment policy for a general partnership would have to consider the combined/collective objectives of all of the partners.

Limited Partnership

In the case of an enterprise organized as a limited partnership, the management (and liability) is assigned to the general partner(s), while the limited partner(s) are passive and have liability limited to their investment. This is the typical case with the direct participation programs (DPPs) discussed in Unit 11. Suitability decisions are similar to a general partnership except that the limited partners do not have the full liability of the general partner(s).

Limited Liability Company (LLC)

A **limited liability company (LLC)** is a business structure that combines benefits of incorporation (limited liability) with the tax advantages of a partnership (flow-through of taxable earnings or losses). The LLC owners are members (not shareholders) and are not personally liable for the debts of the LLC.

Just as with the partnership clients described above, the objectives and financial constraints of the individual members must be considered from a suitability standpoint.

S Corporation

An **S corporation**, although taxed like a partnership, offers investors the limited liability associated with corporations in general. The profits and losses are passed through directly to the shareholders in proportion to their ownership in the S corporation. Unlike an LLC, which can have an unlimited number of members, an S corporation may not have more than 100 shareholders, none of whom may be a nonresident alien, or more than one class of stock (presumably common).

Any business organization client where the entity itself has no liability and is not subject to tax, such as the partnerships, LLC, and S corporation, requires the adviser to look through the entity to the owners to properly meet the suitability standards.

C Corporation

A **C corporation** is a business structure that distinguishes the company as a separate entity from its owners. If a business expects to need significant capital, this form is almost always the preferred choice. Unlike the management of a partnership [the general partner(s)], in most cases, the corporation's officers and directors are shielded from personal liability for the corporation's debts and losses. Shareholders are also shielded from corporate creditors. That is the limited liability benefit of owning stock. Corporate income tax applies to the corporation as an entity rather than being passed through to the shareholder. If your client is a C corporation, you will only look at the corporation's financial needs and objectives when determining suitability.

TAKE NOTE

C corporation earnings are subject to double taxation. Before distribution, the earnings are taxable to the corporation and then are taxed again to the shareholder when paid out as a dividend. Distributions from LLCs and S corporations are taxed only once because there is no taxation at the business entity level.

PRACTICE QUESTION

7. Three friends plan to start a new business. It is anticipated it will be several years before the business turns a profit. Which of the following types of business organization would be best if they wish to limit their liability while, at the same time, being able to receive favorable tax treatment for the expected losses?
   A. C corporation
   B. S corporation
   C. General partnership
   D. Sole proprietorship

   Answer: B. The only way to limit liability is through a corporation (or LLC or limited partnership—neither of which is offered here as a choice). The S corporation allows for the flow-through of operating losses to the shareholders, while the C corporation does not.

LESSON 1.4: ACCOUNT OPENING REQUIREMENTS

LO 1.d Explain the requirements for opening customer accounts.

In the previous two LOs, we described the various types of accounts opened at broker-dealers. What are the legal requirements for opening up the accounts for natural persons?

New Account Form

Opening an account begins with the **new account form.** FINRA Rule 4512 requires that member firms create a record for each account with an individual customer that includes the following information:

- Customer's name and residence address
- Whether the customer is of legal age
- Name(s) of the firm's associated person(s), if any, responsible for the account
- If the customer is a corporation, partnership or other legal entity, the names of any persons authorized to transact business on behalf of the entity
- Signature of the partner, officer, or manager denoting that the account has been accepted in accordance with the member's policies and procedures for acceptance of accounts
- Subject to the Trusted Person Contact Rule, (2165), name of and contact information for a trusted contact person age 18 or older who may be contacted about the customer's account

TEST TOPIC ALERT

The customer's signature is not required on the new account form. The only signature required to open an account is a partner, officer, or manager (a principal) signifying that the account has been accepted in accordance with the member's policies and procedures for acceptance of accounts. SEC Rule 17a-3 requires delivery of a copy of the account information within 30 days of opening (and every 36 months thereafter). Customers are to verify the information and note any relevant changes to the information.

In addition to the earlier stipulations, FINRA asks that each member also make reasonable efforts to obtain, before the settlement of the initial transaction in the account, the following information to the extent it is applicable to the account:

- The customer's tax identification or Social Security number
- The occupation of customer and name and address of employer
- Whether the customer is an associated person of another member

TAKE NOTE

The firm wants to know if any person opening an account is an insider (office, director, or major shareholder) of a public company. The reasons will come up later in the course when we discuss insider trading and restricted stock.

Member firms must make a good-faith effort to obtain this information. However, if the customer neglects or refuses to provide all the information, or is unable to provide it, then the rule excuses the firm.

Customer Identification Program (CIP)

Under provisions of the USA PATRIOT Act of 2001, financial institutions, such as broker-dealers, are required to institute a customer identification program (CIP) designed to

- verify the identity of any new customer;
  - for an individual, an unexpired government-issued identification such as a driver's license, passport, military ID, or state ID;

   - for a person other than an individual, documents showing the existence of the entity, such as certified articles of incorporation, a government-issued business license, a partnership agreement, or trust instrument;
- maintain records of the information used to verify identity; and
- determine whether the person appears on the Office of Foreign Assets Control (OFAC) list of known or suspected terrorists or terrorist organizations. OFAC regulations prohibit transactions with certain persons and organizations listed on the OFAC website as *Terrorists* and *Specially Designated Nationals and Blocked Persons*, as well as listed embargoed countries and regions. Firms must check this list on an ongoing basis to ensure that potential customers and existing customers are not prohibited persons or entities and are not from embargoed countries or regions before transacting any business with them.

These rules are designed to prevent, detect, and prosecute money laundering and the financing of terrorism.

As part of its CIP, a member firm must, before opening an account, obtain the following information at a minimum:

- Customer name
- Date of birth (for an individual)
- Address, which must be:
   - for an individual, a residential or business street address
   - for an individual who does not have a residential or business street address, an Army Post Office or Fleet Post Office box number, or the residential or business street address of a next of kin or another contact individual
   - for a person other than an individual (such as a corporation, partnership, or trust), a principal place of business, local office, or other physical location
- Social Security number for an individual or Tax ID number for a business entity
- For a non-U.S. person, one or more of the following: a taxpayer identification number, a passport number and country of issuance, an alien identification card number, or the number and country of issuance of any other government-issued document evidencing nationality or residence and bearing a photograph or similar safeguard. An exception is granted to persons who do not currently have, but who have applied for, a Social Security number. In this instance, the firm must obtain the number within a reasonable period and the account card must be marked applied for.

The CIP must include procedures for responding to circumstances in which the broker-dealer cannot form a reasonable belief that it knows the true identity of a customer. These procedures should describe

- when the broker-dealer should not open an account,
- the terms under which a customer may conduct transactions while the broker-dealer attempts to verify the customer's identity,
- when the broker-dealer should close an account after attempts to verify a customer's identity fail, and
- when the broker-dealer should file a suspicious activity report in accordance with applicable law and regulation.

Opening Accounts for Other Members' Employees

Regulatory bodies have rules and special procedures regarding the establishment of accounts for certain individuals, including

- employees of member firms and
- spouses or minor children of member firm employees.

The FINRA rule requires that a person associated with a member, before opening an account or placing an initial securities order with another member, notify the employer and the executing member (where the new account is to be maintained), in writing, of her association with the other member.

Before the account can be opened, the employing FINRA member firm must grant written permission. Prior written consent from the employer is specified within the rule.

Upon written request from the employing member firm, the executing member must supply to the employing member duplicate copies of confirmations, account statements, or any other account information requested.

There are some exceptions. If the employee is purchasing mutual funds or variable annuities directly from the issuer, the rule does not apply. In addition, the rule does not apply when the employee is purchasing non-securities products, such as fixed annuities or term life insurance.

The Municipal Securities Rulemaking Board (MSRB) rule is almost the same. The major difference is that sending duplicate confirmations is required, not optional. One of the exceptions is the purchase of municipal fund securities. These are better known as 529 college savings plans.

TAKE NOTE

These rules only apply when the individual opening the account is employed by or registered with a member firm of FINRA or the MSRB.

Trusted Contact Person (Rules 2165 and 4512)

As mentioned earlier, there is a requirement to obtain trusted contact information for *specified adults*. Who is considered a specified adult?

Per FINRA Rule 2165, specified adult "is a natural person age 65 or older or a natural person age 18 or older who the member reasonably believes has a mental or physical impairment that makes the individual unable to protect his own interests."

TAKE NOTE

You might see this referred to as the FINRA **Senior Exploitation Rule**.

What do you do if a specified adult opens an account? FINRA requires members to make reasonable efforts to obtain the name of and contact information for a trusted contact person. This person must be someone age 18 or older who may be contacted about the customer's account. The rules do not require a customer to provide trusted contact information, only that the firm make the effort.

Member firms may place a temporary hold on the distribution of funds or securities from the account of a specified adult. The temporary hold is also allowed in certain circumstances where the member reasonably believes that financial exploitation of the specified adult has occurred, is occurring, has been attempted, or will be attempted. FINRA considers *temporary* to be up to 15 business days.

This rule does not require members to place temporary holds on disbursements of funds or securities from the accounts of specified adults. The rule simply gives them permission to do so.

EXAMPLE

Placing a temporary hold on a customer order to sell shares of stock in the account does not apply. However, if the customer requests that the proceeds of the sale be wired outside the account, then a temporary hold on the disbursement may take place where the customer is covered by the rule and there is a reasonable belief of financial exploitation.

PRACTICE QUESTION

8. One of your accounts is a specified adult. If the firm reasonably believes that an attempt at exploiting the person has been made, a temporary hold is permitted on disbursements for
   A. three business days.
   B. five business days.
   C. 15 business days.
   D. 30 calendar days.

   Answer: C. FINRA Rule 2165 permits firms to place a temporary hold (15 business days) on disbursements from the accounts of individuals aged 65 or older, and individuals aged 18 or older whom firms reasonably believe have an impairment that prevents them from protecting their own interests (a specified adult). Firms are permitted to place a temporary hold on funds if the firm has a reasonable belief that financial exploitation of the specified adult has or is occurring or attempted. This gives the firm time to notify a trusted contact person and to begin an internal review.

Regulation S-P (Privacy Notices)

Opening an account usually requires complying with Regulation S-P. This regulation was enacted by the SEC to protect the privacy of customer information. In particular, the regulation deals with nonpublic personal information. Examples of nonpublic personal information include a customer's Social Security number, account balances, transaction history, and any information collected through internet cookies. Your firm must provide a privacy notice describing its privacy policies to customers whenever a new account is opened, and annually thereafter.

If your firm reserves the right to disclose to unaffiliated third parties nonpublic personal information, the notice must provide customers a reasonable means to opt out of this disclosure. Reasonable opt out means include providing customers with a form with check-off boxes along with a prepaid return envelope, providing an electronic means to opt out for customers who have agreed to the electronic delivery of information, and providing a toll-free telephone number. Asking customers to write a letter to express their disclosure preferences or to opt out would not be considered reasonable under Regulation S-P.

In addition, the regulation embodies the obligation of financial institutions to safeguard customer information as related to all forms of existing and developing technology. For example, this would include, but not be limited to, securing desktop and laptop computers and encrypting email.

Regulation S-P distinguishes between a consumer and a customer. A consumer is an individual who obtains a financial product or service from a firm and has no further contact with the firm. A customer is an individual who has an ongoing relationship with a firm. Consumers are given an initial privacy notice only, while customers must be given both an initial and annual privacy notice. Only individuals, not businesses or institutions, are covered by the regulation.

TAKE NOTE

Reasonable opt-out methods available to members include providing a reply form with the opt-out notice, an electronic means to opt out if the customer has agreed to the electronic delivery of information, and a toll-free number that customers may call.

The SEC has stated that members are not providing a reasonable means to opt out if the only method to do so is by writing a letter to the member.

PRACTICE QUESTION

9. Under Regulation S-P, if a broker-dealer sends a customer an initial privacy notice that contains an opt-out provision, the firm may **not** disclose nonpublic, personal information about that customer for how many days from the mailing?
   A. 10
   B. 15
   C. 20
   D. 30

Answer: D. A broker-dealer must give a customer 30 days to implement any opt-out provision in the privacy notice.

Power of Attorney (POA)

If a person who is not named on an account is to have trading authority, the customer must file written authorization with the broker-dealer giving that person access to the account. Without this power in writing, no matter how tempting the answer on the exam, activity in the account cannot be created by anyone other than the account owner(s). Trading authorization usually takes the form of a power of attorney. Two basic types of trading authorizations are **full power of attorney** and **limited power of attorney**.

Full Power of Attorney

A full power of attorney allows an individual who is not the owner of an account to

- deposit or withdraw cash or securities and
- make investment decisions for the account owner.

Limited Power of Attorney

A limited power of attorney allows an individual to have some, but not total, control over an account. The document specifies the level of access the person may exercise.

TEST TOPIC ALERT

Limited power of attorney, also called limited trading authorization, allows entering of buy and sell orders but not the withdrawal of funds. Entry of orders and withdrawal of funds is only allowed if full power of attorney is granted.

Durable Power of Attorney

A full or limited power may be made "durable" by the grantor of the power. It is designed to provide that a specifically designated person maintains power over the account even upon the grantor's incapacitation. This could be because of physical or mental causes. Its most common use is when providing for aging parents. Upon the death of either principal to the durable power of attorney, the power is terminated.

TEST TOPIC ALERT

A durable power of attorney survives the physical or mental incompetence of the grantor but not the death of either party.

This means that orders entered after the time of death of the grantor, even if the purchase or sale was decided upon before death, are not accepted.

LESSON 1.5: ACCOUNT CHANGES

LO 1.e Identify the procedure for account registration changes and transfers.

Approval and Documentation of Changes in Account Name or Designation

Long before the airwaves were bombarding us with ads for identity theft protection or methods of keeping your accounts from being hacked, broker-dealers had concerns for the safety of their customers' accounts. It was not uncommon for one party of a married couple to call the registered representative handling their JTWROS account and ask that the other spouse's name be removed. In some instances, there was a legitimate reason for the change, but in many others, it was a preemptive strike in an upcoming divorce.

Well before the exploitation of seniors rule previously discussed was implemented, children or other relatives of a senior whose cognitive abilities were impaired would attempt (sometimes successfully) to have their names added to an account.

Under FINRA rules, no change in any account name(s) can be made unless the change has been authorized by a qualified and registered principal designated by the member. This principal must, before giving her approval of the account designation change, be personally informed of the essential facts relative thereto and indicate her approval of such change in writing. The essential facts relied upon by the person approving the change must be documented in writing and preserved with the customer account records.

Internal Transfers

A close "cousin" of the previous discussion is that of internal transfers. It is not unusual for a client to have both a cash account and a margin account. A married couple could easily have five or more accounts between them. There are many good reasons why a client might want to have funds transferred from one account to another, but there could also be cases where a party was acting without proper authority. In general, when a transfer is made to an account from an account of which the recipient is not a signatory, approvals and documentation similar to a change in designation are required.

Bulk Transfers

When customers sell securities held in their accounts, cash representing the proceeds of those sales are deposited to their accounts. In many cases, that cash is swept into a money market mutual fund where it will earn income until the money is either withdrawn or used for a new purchase. This is known as a *sweep account.*

Sometimes the broker-dealer has a reason to select a different money market fund for its clients. Contacting each of the clients individually to receive their consent is not practical. Many member firms have thousands or even millions of clients.

FINRA rules do permit member firms to make bulk exchanges at net asset value of money market mutual funds utilizing negative response letters without obtaining affirmative consent, but only when specific conditions are met.

Definitions: Negative Response Letter

A **negative response letter** generally informs the recipient of the letter of an impending action, and requires the recipient to respond or act within a specified time frame if the recipient objects to the action. If the recipient does not respond, he is deemed to have consented to the action.

Those conditions are the following:

- The bulk exchange is limited to situations involving mergers and acquisitions of funds, changes of clearing members and exchanges of funds used in sweep accounts.
- The negative response letter contains a tabular comparison of the nature and amount of the fees charged by each fund.
- The negative response letter contains a comparative description of the investment objectives of each fund and a prospectus of the fund to be purchased.
- The negative response feature will not be activated until at least 30 days after the letter was mailed.

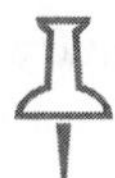

TAKE NOTE

There is a current FINRA proposal that would greatly expand the usage of negative response letters for bulk transfers. If that proposal should become effective, we will add the relevant information to the Content Updates and the q-bank.

LESSON 1.6: QUALIFIED VS. NONQUALIFIED PLANS

LO 1.f Contrast qualified and nonqualified retirement plans.

Definitions

As with so much in this course, there are similar terms with sometimes dissimilar meanings. Here is a useful list of terms used in the discussion of retirement plans in the rest of this unit:

- **Tax-deferred.** Simply, income tax is put off (deferred) to a later time. In most retirement plans, tax on the amount of the contribution is usually deferred until withdrawal. Tax on the earnings is always deferred until withdrawal.
- **Qualified plan.** An employer-sponsored plan, such as a pension, 401(k), or 403(b), where the contributions are made with pretax dollars and earnings in the account grow without

any tax (tax-deferred) until the funds are withdrawn. Qualified plans are usually governed by the Employee Retirement Income Security Act of 1974 (ERISA).

- **Qualified**. This term by itself means that contributions made with pretax dollars and earnings in the account are tax-deferred until the funds are withdrawn. This can apply to either a qualified plan or a traditional IRA.
- **Nonqualified**. An employer-sponsored plan, such as a deferred compensation plan, where there are no tax advantages other than that the pay is not received until sometime later when the individual should be in a lower tax bracket. Another advantage is that the employer can discriminate between employees. The term can also apply to an annuity purchased on an individual basis outside of a retirement plan, as described in Unit 9.
- **Deductible contribution**. The contribution made by the individual, whether an employee contribution to a qualified plan such as a 401(k) plan, or by any individual to a traditional IRA. This means the amount contributed is pretax or otherwise deductible on the tax return.
- **Nondeductible contribution**. A contribution to a qualified plan or an IRA, (traditional or Roth) which is made with after-tax dollars. The funds do grow tax-deferred, but there is no tax benefit derived from the contribution.

Employer-Sponsored Retirement Plans

An important goal for many investors is to provide themselves with retirement income. Many individuals accomplish this through corporate retirement plans, others set up their own plans, and some have both individual and corporate retirement plans.

There are two basic types of retirement plans in the United States: qualified and nonqualified. Generally speaking, qualified plans allow pretax contributions to be made, while nonqualified plans are funded with after-tax money. Both plans can allow money to grow tax-deferred until needed. There are exceptions to these basic characteristics.

Contribution limits for qualified retirement plans vary and are adjusted from time to time. Those numbers will not be tested.

A taxable distribution from any retirement plan is taxed as ordinary income, never as a capital gain.

In a qualified plan, if all of the funds were contributed by the employer, (known as a noncontributory plan), the employee's tax basis (cost) is zero. If the employee's contribution was pretax, the basis for that is *zero* as well. Because everything above the cost is taxed at the employee's ordinary income rate at the time of distribution, in most cases all funds received are fully taxable.

Nonqualified Plans

Nonqualified plans may be used to favor certain employees (typically executives) because nondiscrimination rules are not applicable to nonqualified plans. That is because these plans do not have to comply with ERISA.

Deferred Compensation Plan

A **nonqualified deferred compensation plan** is an agreement between a company and an employee in which the employee agrees to defer receipt of current income in favor of payout at retirement. It is assumed that the employee will be in a lower tax bracket at retirement age (persons affiliated with the company solely as board members are not eligible for these plans because they are not considered employees for retirement planning purposes).

Deferred compensation plans may be somewhat risky because the employee covered by the plan has no right to plan benefits if the business fails. In this situation, the employee becomes a general creditor of the firm. Covered employees may also forfeit benefits if they leave the firm before retirement.

When the benefit is payable at the employee's retirement, it is taxable as ordinary income to the employee. The employer is entitled to the tax deduction at the time the benefit is paid out.

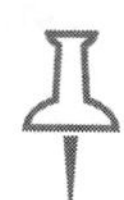

TAKE NOTE

Deferred compensation plans usually benefit highly compensated employees who are just a few years from retirement.

Payroll Deduction Plan

Payroll deduction plans allow employees to authorize their employer to deduct a specified amount for retirement savings from their paychecks. The money is deducted after taxes are paid and may be invested in any number of retirement vehicles at the employee's option.

TEST TOPIC ALERT

A 401(k) plan is not considered a payroll deduction plan. For the FINRA exams, 401(k) plans are considered salary reduction plans, not payroll deduction plans. In exam questions, assume that payroll deduction plans are nonqualified. Also note that 401(k) plans are qualified plans, whereas payroll deduction plans are not.

PRACTICE QUESTION

10. Generally speaking, nonqualified retirement plans
    A. are funded with after-tax dollars.
    B. must have a trust agreement.
    C. may not discriminate with regard to who can participate.
    D. must have IRS approval.

    Answer: A. Generally speaking, nonqualified retirement plans are funded with after-tax dollars.

11. A deferred compensation plan
    A. must allow all eligible employees to participate.
    B. is funded through a trust agreement that protects the employee in the event the company goes out of business.
    C. might not protect the employee from losing the deferred compensation should the employee leave the company before retirement.
    D. typically benefits younger employees.

    Answer: C. A provision commonly found in deferred compensation plans is that the employee might forfeit some or all of the benefit if she leaves the company before retirement.

Qualified Plans

As described earlier, most qualified plans offer several specific tax benefits differing from those in nonqualified ones. Benefits of qualified plans are that

- employer contributions are a current deductible expense,
- employee contributions are generally made with pretax money,
- all earnings and growth in the account is tax-deferred until withdrawal, and
- certain protections are offered to employees under ERISA.

We will go into greater detail on these plans in Lesson 1.8.

LESSON 1.7: ALL ABOUT IRAS

LO 1.g Recall the features of individual retirement arrangements.

TAKE NOTE

On December 20, 2019, Congress passed the Setting Every Community Up for Retirement Enhancement (SECURE) Act. The act contains a number of changes to retirement account rules.

Following are those most likely to affect your exam.

1. Effective 2020, individuals with earned income can make IRA contributions to a traditional IRA without the former **70½** age restriction. In that respect, the traditional and Roth IRAs are now the same—no upper age limit.
2. RMDs will begin after attaining age **72** rather than 70½.
3. There are two additional exceptions to the early withdrawal 10% penalty. They are:
    a. Up to **$5,000** during the first year after a child is born, or
    b. Up to **$5,000** during the first year after an eligible person is adopted
        1). "Eligible adoptee" means anybody under age 18 or who is physically or mentally incapable of self-support regardless of age.
        2). If married, each spouse can make the $5,000 penalty-free withdrawal.
4. Inherited retirement accounts for those dying in 2020 or beyond will now, with certain exceptions, require distributions to be completed in a maximum of 10 years after the original owner's death.
5. Rule 529 has added as qualified expenses, amounts paid as principal or interest on any qualified education loan for the beneficiary and any siblings. There is a maximum of **$10,000** lifetime per child.
6. ERISA eligibility for 401(k) plans, but not 403(b) and 457 plans: There is an alternative to the 1,000 hours worked per year. An employee working **500** or more hours per year for **three** years is now eligible. The purpose of this addition is to make it possible for more part-time employees to qualify for coverage.

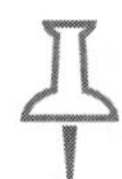

TAKE NOTE

Although *individual retirement arrangements* is the technical IRS term, (not tested), because everyone refers to these as individual retirement accounts (IRAs), we're going to use this common phrase to avoid confusion.

Individual retirement accounts (IRAs) were created to encourage people to save for their retirement. Any individual with earned income can open and contribute to an IRA. Two types of IRAs may be tested, with different contribution, tax, and distribution characteristics: traditional IRAs and Roth IRAs.

IRAs are not to be confused with retirement plans used by businesses. Later in this unit we will cover topics such as pension plans, 401(k) plans, and 457 plans.

TAKE NOTE

Although we may include some actual contribution limits, it is unlikely that you will have to know any other than the IRA and Coverdell numbers.

Traditional IRAs

The first of the IRAs we'll cover is generally referred to as the traditional IRA, although there is no such term in the IRS regulations. This was the first IRA, and as others have been introduced, this first one acquired its name. A **traditional IRA** allows a maximum *tax-deductible* annual contribution of the lesser of $6,000 per individual or $12,000 per couple, or 100% of taxable compensation for the taxable year 2019. The income and capital gains earned in the account are tax-deferred until the funds are withdrawn.

Compensation for IRA Purposes

For purposes of contributing to an IRA, the IRS considers the following to be compensation:

- Wages, salaries, and tips
- Commissions and bonuses
- Self-employment income
- Alimony[1]
- Nontaxable combat pay

Not Compensation for IRA Purposes

For purposes of contributing to an IRA, the IRS does not consider the following to be compensation:

- Capital gains
- Interest and dividend income
- Pension or annuity income

[1] The TCJA of 2017 changed the rules on alimony. For any divorce decree entered into starting January 1, 2019, alimony is no longer considered earned income. This change only applies to these new divorces and does not change the treatment for those entered into by December 31, 2018. As a test matter, the date of the divorce decree must be shown so that you can determine the status of the alimony.

- Child support
- Passive income from DPPs

Catch-Up Contributions for Older IRA Owners

The **Economic Growth and Tax Relief Reconciliation Act of 2001 (EGTRRA)** was the source of the legislation permitting certain individuals to make additional contributions to their IRAs. Individuals aged 50 and older are allowed to make **catch-up contributions** to their IRAs above the scheduled maximum annual contribution limit. This will enable them to save more for retirement. These catch-up payments can go either to a traditional IRA or to a Roth IRA. Since 2006, that catch-up amount has been $1,000.

TEST TOPIC ALERT

The exam may require you to know that EGTRRA is responsible for the catch-up provisions.

Any taxpayer of any age who reports earned income for a given tax year may contribute to a traditional IRA. If one spouse has little or no earned income and a joint tax return is filed, a spousal IRA may be opened for that person and the contribution limits and tax treatment are the same as for any other IRA.

PRACTICE QUESTION

12. One spouse of a married couple in their 30s earns an annual salary of $45,000, while the other earns $2,000 annually from a home-based business. If they file a joint tax return, their maximum IRA contribution for the year is
    A. $6,000.
    B. $8,000.
    C. $12,000.
    D. $14,000.

    Answer: C. When one spouse's annual earnings are less than $6,000, the spousal IRA benefit permits that spouse to contribute the maximum allowable contribution as long as a joint return is filed that shows combined income of at least $12,000. In this case, their income exceeds that, so they can each have an IRA with a contribution of $6,000, making for a total of $12,000. Please note that when using the spousal IRA, the higher earning spouse cannot have more than the maximum contributed to their account (currently $6,000). One can't look at this and say the couple has $12,000 to be split however they wish. If this question had stated the couple was in their 50s, then, because of the catch-up provision, $14,000 would have been the correct choice.

Earnings Limitations for Tax Benefits

As already stated, traditional participants may deduct contributions to their IRAs from their taxable income. The deductibility limits are reduced or even eliminated for individuals who are covered by employer-sponsored qualified plans.

These adjusted gross income (AGI) limits increase every year and will not be tested. Individuals who do not participate in qualified plans may deduct IRA contributions regardless of income level.

For those filing 2019 tax returns, the IRA deductibility phaseout range is expressed in the table below.

Figure 1.1 IRA Phaseout Amounts

Year	Phaseout Range: Single Filers	Phaseout Range: Joint Filers
2019	$64,000–$74,000	$103,000–$123,000

The limits are higher ($193,000—$203,000) if only one of the spouses participates in a qualified plan, but, as with all of these numbers, it is only the concept that is tested, never the numbers themselves.

These limits only deal with the deductibility of contributions. If your client earns in excess of the limits, the full contribution can still be made, but part or none of it can be deducted. The test refers to those as *post-tax* or *after-tax* contributions. The earnings still grow tax-deferred.

EXAMPLE

Two persons who are married, each of whom does not participate in a qualified plan and whose combined income is $200,000, may contribute and deduct a total of $12,000 ($14,000 if both individuals are 50 or older). No deduction is allowed for a married couple where both are covered by a qualified plan and whose combined income is $123,000 (for 2019) or more. Nevertheless, their contributions are permitted and all earnings are tax-deferred.

Time for Contributions

IRA contributions for a specific taxable year may be made anytime from January 1 of that year through the required filing date of that year's return, (generally April 15 of the next year, unless the 15th falls on a holiday or weekend). If the individual obtains a filing extension, the deadline is still April 15.

TEST TOPIC ALERT

The exam may try to trick you into thinking that you can make a contribution later than April 15 if you have received an extension to file your taxes. You can't! You should know that an extension does not give you more time to pay your taxes, it only extends the time that you have to file your return.

Excess Contributions

Annual IRA contributions exceeding the maximum allowed are subject to a 6% penalty tax if the excess is not removed by the time the taxpayer files a tax return, but no later than April 15.

Roth IRAs

The Roth IRA was created as part of the Taxpayer Relief Act of 1997. Much of what has been stated about the traditional IRA applies to the Roth IRA—what is important are the differences. The most significant difference relates to the taxation of contributions and withdrawals. Contributions to Roth IRAs, unlike those of traditional IRAs, are not tax deductible. And, earnings are not merely tax-deferred; they can be tax-free.

Earnings accumulated may be withdrawn tax-free, five years following the initial deposit, provided the

- account holder is 59½ or older;
- money withdrawn is used for the first-time purchase of a principal residence (up to $10,000); or
- account holder has died or become disabled.

Regular contributions may always be withdrawn tax-free because they are made with nondeductible contributions.

PRACTICE QUESTION

13. Among the requirements for accumulated earnings in a Roth IRA to be withdrawn free of tax is
    A. the owner of the account is at least 72.
    B. the money is withdrawn for a first-time purchase of a vacation home.
    C. the initial deposit to a Roth IRA was made at least five years ago.
    D. the owner's spouse is declared disabled.

    Answer: C. The first requirement for tax-free withdrawals from a Roth IRA is that the initial deposit to a Roth must have been made at least five years ago. The other primary requirement is that the owner must be at least 59½, not 72. If the five-year requirement is met, then owners under 59½ can receive distributions of accumulated earnings tax-free if they wish to use up to $10,000 for a first-time purchase of a primary residence, not a vacation home. The disability requirement only applies to the owner of the Roth, not a spouse.

Contribution Limits

Contribution limits to Roth IRAs are the same as those for traditional IRAs, with one important difference. Just as with a traditional IRA, there are no age limitations as long as the taxpayer has earned income.

An individual may contribute to both a traditional IRA and a Roth IRA. However, the maximum combined contribution is $6,000 (or $7,000, if 50 or older).

Eligibility Requirements

Unlike the traditional IRA, there are limits placed on Roth IRA eligibility based on income. Anyone with earned income is eligible to open a Roth IRA provided the person's AGI falls below specified income levels. The following numbers, (which are never tested), are effective for those filing a tax return for 2019. A single person with an AGI of less than $123,000 may contribute the full amount to a Roth IRA. The ability to contribute to a Roth IRA is gradually phased out if the taxpayer's AGI is between $123,000 and $137,000.

For married taxpayers who file joint tax returns, the AGI limit is $193,000, with the contribution phased out for couples whose income is between $193,000 and $203,000.

What is AGI?

Adjusted Gross Income (AGI)

Adjusted gross income, generally referred to as AGI, is computed on the bottom of the first page of your Form 1040. It might help you to take a look at yours. When you do your taxes, you begin by listing all of your earned income (salary, wages, and bonuses) plus other income such as interest and dividends, capital gains, alimony received, and profits from a business you may own. From that total, you deduct certain items to arrive at the AGI. Among the more testable items that are deductible are

- traditional IRA contribution;
- alimony paid as part of a pre-January 1, 2019, divorce decree;
- self-employment tax; and
- penalties paid on early withdrawal from a savings account.

TAKE NOTE

These numbers will not be tested because they change every year. It is the concept that important.

TEST TOPIC ALERT

Please note that although tax-exempt income from municipal securities is shown on Form 1040, it is not included in AGI.

Roth Conversions

Anyone with a traditional IRA is permitted to convert it to a Roth IRA. However, there are income tax consequences for doing so. Basically, the entire amount converted is added to the investor's ordinary income. However, as long as the funds are done in a direct rollover trustee to trustee, or, if distributed to the owner, are rolled over within 60 days, there will be no 10% early distribution tax penalty for those under age 59½. If some portion of the contributions to the traditional IRA were made with after-tax money, the IRS uses a proportionate system to determine how much is nontaxable, but that type of computation will not be tested. Conversions may also be done from any qualified employer plan such as 401(k) and 403(b) plans.

Key Points to Remember About the Roth IRA

- Contributions are not tax deductible.
- Distributions are tax-free if taken after age 59½ and a Roth account has been open for at least five years.
- Contributions can be made at any age as long as there is earned income.
- Distributions are not required to begin at age 72.
- If because of death, disability, or first-time home purchase, the distribution is qualified and not subject to tax or the 10% penalty.
- A minor can be named as beneficiary.
- The contributions (all made with after-tax money) may always be withdrawn without tax or penalty. It is only the earnings where the five years/age 59½ rules apply to avoid tax and penalties.

Let's make sure you know your IRAs:

PRACTICE QUESTION

14. The main difference between a traditional IRA and a Roth IRA is
    A. the traditional IRA is funded with after-tax dollars and the Roth IRA is funded with pretax dollars.
    B. the Roth IRA has higher contribution limits.
    C. if meeting the requirements, distributions from a Roth IRA are tax-free, while distributions from traditional IRAs are taxed as ordinary income.
    D. if the individual has too much AGI, contributions to a traditional IRA are not allowed; no such limitation exists for Roth IRAs.

Answer: C. The beauty of the Roth IRA is, if the conditions are met, they are tax-free. The contribution is funded with pretax funds for the traditional IRA. Contribution limits are the same and it is the Roth IRA where the ability to contribute phases out once the AGI gets over a certain limit.

Withdrawals From Traditional IRAs

Up until this point, we've discussed contributions; now let's look at taking the money out. When it comes to traditional IRAs, distributions without penalty may begin after age 59½ and must begin by April 1 of the year following the year an individual turns 72. Distributions before age 59½ may be subject to a tax penalty, and withdrawals less than the required minimum distributions (RMDs), after age 72 may also incur tax penalties.

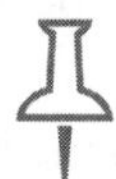

TAKE NOTE

When is the deadline for receiving a RMD from an IRA? An account owner must take the first RMD for the year in which the account owner turns 72. However, the first RMD payment can be delayed until April 1 of the year following the year in which the account owner turns 72. For all subsequent years, including the year in which the first RMD was paid by April 1, the account owner must take the RMD by December 31 of the year.

To the extent withdrawals are from tax-deductible contributions, they are taxable as ordinary income. When there are both deductible and nondeductible contributions, a formula is used whereby a portion of the withdrawal represents a nontaxable return of principal.

Taxable withdrawals before age 59½ are also subject to a 10% early withdrawal penalty unless they are because of

- death;
- disability;
- first-time purchase of a primary residence ($10,000 lifetime maximum);
- qualified higher education expenses for immediate family members (including grandchildren, but not nieces or nephews); or
- certain medical expenses in excess of an AGI limit.

These exceptions also apply in the case of a nonqualified (taxable) distribution from a Roth IRA.

PRACTICE QUESTION

15. Who of the following will not incur a penalty on an IRA withdrawal?
    A. Man who has just become totally disabled
    B. Woman who turned 59 a month before the withdrawal
    C. Woman, age 50, who decides on early retirement
    D. Man in his early 40s who uses the money to buy a second home

Answer: A. Early withdrawals, without penalty, are permitted only in certain situations (such as death or qualifying disability).

As stated, withdrawals must begin by April 1 of the year following the year in which the account owner reaches age 72, and they must meet minimum **Internal Revenue Code (IRC)** distribution requirements or incur a 50% penalty on the amounts falling short of the RMD.

One important way the Roth IRA differs from other retirement plans is that the age 72 is irrelevant. There are no RMDs and the account will continue to grow tax-free until the holder decides to take it out.

There is one other way to tap your IRA before age 59½ without penalty—through the substantially equal periodic payment exception. The **substantially equal periodic payment exception** under IRS rule 72(t) states that if you receive IRA payments at least annually based on your life expectancy (or the joint life expectancies of you and your beneficiary), the withdrawals are not subject to the 10% penalty. The IRS has tables for determining the appropriate amount of each payment at any given age.

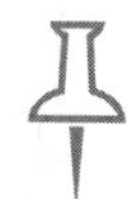

TAKE NOTE

For exam purposes, you can postpone beginning distributions until the later of

- April 1 of the calendar year after you turn age 72 or
- April 1 of the calendar year following your retirement (but only for qualified plans, not an IRA).

EXAMPLE

An IRA owner who reaches age 72 on January 1, 2020, must begin withdrawals by April 1, 2021. However, if this individual is covered by an employer-sponsored plan, there are no RMDs from that plan (but there are from any traditional IRAs) until after retirement.

Nondeductible Capital Withdrawals

IRA investors who contribute after-tax dollars to an IRA are not taxed on those funds when they are withdrawn from the account, but taxpayers are taxed at the ordinary income tax rate when they withdraw funds resulting from investment gains or income. As stated previously, if the client is in the middle part of the phaseout range resulting in some of the contribution being pretax (deductible) and the rest post-tax, the IRS has a formula to determine how much of the money withdrawn is nontaxable.

EXAMPLE

A client has invested $25,000 in after-tax dollars in an IRA currently worth $75,000. If the client were to withdraw $75,000, only $50,000 would be taxable.

TAKE NOTE

The early withdrawal penalties for all IRAs are waived in the event of death or disability.

TEST TOPIC ALERT

Assume questions are about traditional IRAs unless they specifically state ***otherwise***.

TEST TOPIC ALERT

Income and capital gains earned from investments in any IRA account are not taxed until the funds are withdrawn and, if a qualified withdrawal, are not taxed at all in the case of a Roth.

IRA Investments

Funds in an IRA account may be used to buy stocks, bonds, mutual funds, unit investment trusts (UITs), limited partnerships, REITS, U.S. government securities, and gold or silver coins minted by the U.S. Treasury Department (American Eagles), as well as certain platinum coins and certain gold, silver, palladium, and platinum bullion, annuities, and many other investments.

IRA investments should be relatively conservative and should reflect the investor's age and risk tolerance profile. Because an IRA serves as a source of retirement funds, it is important that the account be managed for adequate long-term growth.

Ineligible and Inappropriate Investments

Collectibles, including antiques, gems, rare coins, works of art, and stamps, are not acceptable IRA investments. Life insurance contracts (such as whole life and term) may not be purchased in an IRA. Tax-free municipal bonds, municipal bond funds, and municipal bond UITs are eligible, but generally considered inappropriate for an IRA (or any tax-qualified plan) because their yields are typically lower than those of other similar investments, and the income generated is taxable on withdrawal from the IRA.

Ineligible Investment Practices

No short sales of stock, speculative option strategies, or margin account trading is permitted in an IRA or any other retirement plan. Covered call writing is allowed.

Figure 1.2 Ineligible Investments and Practices

Ineligible Investments	Ineligible Investment Practices
Collectibles	Short sales of stock
Whole life insurance	Speculative option strategies
Term life Insurance	Margin account trading

PRACTICE QUESTION

16. Allowable investments within an IRA include all of the following except
    A. investment company securities.
    B. corporate stocks and bonds.
    C. certain U.S. government-minted gold and silver coins.
    D. collectibles such as postage stamps.

Answer: D. Collectibles are not permitted as investments in an IRA.

Moving IRAs

Individuals may move their funds and investments from one IRA to another IRA through one of three methods:

- 60-day rollover
- Direct rollover
- Trustee to trustee transfer

60-Day Rollovers

If you see *IRA rollover*, it will be the 60-day rollover. An IRA account owner may take temporary possession of the account funds to move the retirement account to another custodian. The account owner may do so only once per 12-month period, and the rollover must be completed within 60 calendar days of the funds' withdrawal from the original plan. However, 100% of the withdrawn amount must be rolled into the new account, or the unrolled balance will be subject to income tax and, if applicable, early withdrawal penalty.

A participant in an employer-sponsored qualified plan may move her plan assets to a rollover IRA if he leaves the company and elects to take a lump-sum distribution. If the participant does take possession of the funds, he must complete the rollover within *60 calendar days* of withdrawing the funds from the qualified plan.

When the participant takes possession of the funds from a qualified plan to make a rollover, the payor of the distribution must, by law, withhold 20% of the distribution as a withholding tax. The participant must, nonetheless, roll over 100% of the plan distribution, including the funds withheld, or be subject to income tax and, if applicable, an early withdrawal penalty.

EXAMPLE

A 50-year-old individual with $100,000 in her company retirement plan changes employers. Her pension plan may be distributed to her in a lump-sum payment, minus the mandatory 20% withholding of $20,000. She must then deposit $100,000 in an IRA rollover account within 60 days. Any portion not rolled over, including the $20,000 withheld, is considered a distribution subject to ordinary income tax and early distribution penalty. If she deposits the entire $100,000 into the IRA, she will apply on her next income tax return for a refund of the $20,000 withheld.

Direct Rollovers From Retirement Plans to IRAs

A direct rollover is a distribution from an employer-sponsored retirement plan to an IRA, either traditional or Roth. When you terminate employment (or retire), you have the option of moving your employer-sponsored plan assets to an IRA. In some cases, if you go to a new job, your new employer's plan may permit a direct rollover into the plan. The key to a direct rollover is that the money is never seen by the employee and moves directly from the current plan administrator directly to another administrator.

TAKE NOTE

There is a specific type of traditional IRA known as a *rollover* IRA. When a participant in an employer-sponsored qualified retirement plan (we'll cover those shortly) separates from the employer—whether through retirement or termination—vested assets in the company sponsored plan may be directly transferred to a separate IRA titled as a rollover IRA. There is a benefit to doing this. Because these assets have been segregated as having come from a qualified plan, should the individual obtain future employment and wish to have those assets transferred to the new employer's plan, it is a simple task to do so.

Trustee to Trustee Transfers

Sometimes simply referred to as an IRA transfer, trustee to trustee transfers are when account assets are sent directly from one IRA custodian to another, and the account owner never takes possession of the funds. Unlike the one per 12 months maximum with an IRA rollover, the number of IRA transfers an account owner may make per year is unlimited. Direct rollovers and transfers generally make better sense than 60-day rollovers because the 20% federal tax withholding does not apply to direct transfers of portfolios, and because there is no specified time limit, you don't have to rush to meet the 60-day requirement.

TAKE NOTE

How does a direct rollover differ from a transfer? A direct rollover is different from a transfer because it involves two different types of plans. For example, one would use a direct rollover to move funds from a 401(k) plan to an IRA while the transfer is from an IRA at one brokerage firm to an IRA at another.

PRACTICE QUESTION

17. How often can an IRA be rolled over to another IRA?
    A. Once every 60 days
    B. Once every 90 days
    C. Once every 12 months
    D. There are no limits on how often a rollover can occur

Answer: C. An IRA can be rolled over to another IRA once every 12 months. It is the transfers from trustee to trustee where there is no limit. Unless the question says direct rollover, or indicates that it is from a qualified plan to an IRA, *rollover* always refers to the 60-day type.

Education IRA

In addition to the Roth IRA, the Taxpayer Relief Act of 1997 also created **Education IRAs** with a $500 annual contribution limit. In 2002, these were renamed **Coverdell ESAs** and the annual contribution limit is now $2,000. ESAs allow after-tax contributions for student beneficiaries. Contributions must be made in cash and must be made on or before the date on which the beneficiary attains age 18, unless the beneficiary is a **special needs beneficiary**—an individual who because of a physical, mental, or emotional condition requires additional time to complete his education. Coverdell ESAs fund educational expenses of a designated beneficiary by allowing after-tax (nondeductible) contributions to accumulate on a tax-deferred basis.

When distributions are made from a Coverdell ESA, the earnings portion of the distribution is excluded from income when it is used to pay qualified education expenses. Withdrawn earnings are taxed to the recipient (beneficiary) and are subject to a 10% tax penalty when they are not used to pay qualified education expenses.

TAKE NOTE

If the money is not used by a beneficiary's 30th birthday (except for a special needs beneficiary), it must be distributed and the earnings are subject to ordinary income taxes and a 10% penalty.

In addition to qualified higher education expenses (postsecondary education), the account can also be used for elementary and secondary education expenses and for public, private, or religious schools.

The contribution to a Coverdell ESA may be limited, depending on the amount of AGI and filing status.

Figure 1.3 Coverdell ESA Income Limits

Allowable Contribution	Single Filers	Joint Filers
Full contribution of $2,000 at AGI of and below	$95,000	$190,000
Partial phaseout begins at	$95,001	$190,001
No contributions may be made at AGI of and above	$110,000	$220,000

TAKE NOTE

There is nothing to prevent more than one individual from contributing to a Coverdell ESA; the annual limit applies to each beneficiary. Parents and grandparents can contribute to a single account, as long as the $2,000 limit per child is not exceeded in any given year.

Other features of the ESA include

- provisions that allow contributions to continue past age 18 for beneficiaries with special needs and
- allowing Coverdell ESA contributions, for any year, to be made up to April 15 of the following year (just like contributions to your IRA).

Here are some key test points about Coverdell ESAs:

- Contributions can be made by parents and other adults; the total for one child is still $2,000.
- Contribution limit is $2,000 per year per child until the child's 18th birthday.
- Contributions are not tax deductible, but all earnings are tax-deferred.
- Distributions are tax-free if they are taken before age 30 and used for eligible education expenses.
- If the accumulated value in the account is not used by age 30, the funds must be distributed and subject to income tax and a 10% penalty on the earnings or rolled over into a different Coverdell ESA for another family member. Their definition of family is extremely broad and, in addition to the obvious, includes cousins, aunts and uncles, and even in-laws.

PRACTICE QUESTION

18. The maximum amount that may be invested in a Coverdell ESA in one year is
    A. $500 per parent.
    B. $2,000 per child.
    C. $500 per couple.
    D. $2,000 per couple.

Answer: B. Only $2,000 may be invested in each child's ESA per year. If a couple has three children, they may contribute $6,000 in total, or $2,000 per child, per year.

LESSON 1.8: EMPLOYER-SPONSORED RETIREMENT PLANS

LO 1.h Differentiate between the different types of employer-sponsored qualified retirement plans.

Tax-Sheltered Annuities (403(b) Plans)

Employer-sponsored retirement plans come in all different shapes and colors. First we will describe the most common plan for those employed by the public school system. This plan, the 403(b) plan (that is the section of the IRC), is also available to many nonprofit organizations operating under section 501(c)(3) of the Code.

Tax-sheltered annuities (TSAs) offered through 403(b) plans are available to employees of

- public educational institutions;
- tax-exempt organizations (501(c)(3) organizations); and
- religious organizations.

Qualified employees may exclude contributions from their taxable incomes provided they do not exceed limits. Qualified annuity plans offered under Section 403(b) of the IRC, sometimes referred to as **tax-sheltered annuities** (***TSAs***), are intended to encourage retirement savings. To ensure this objective, 403(b) plans, (like IRAs and other retirement plans), are subject to tax penalties if savings are withdrawn before a participant reaches age 59½.

In general, the clergy and employees of charitable institutions, private hospitals, colleges and universities, elementary and secondary schools, and zoos and museums are eligible to participate if they are at least 21 years old and have completed one year of service.

TSAs are funded by elective employee deferrals. The deferred amount is excluded from the employee's gross income, and earnings accumulate tax-free until distribution. A written salary reduction agreement must be executed between the employer and the employee. An employer can make contributions to a 403(b) solely on behalf of the covered employee or in conjunction with an employee deferral.

As with other qualified plans, distributions are 100% taxable, and a 10% penalty is applied to distributions before age 59½.

TEST TOPIC ALERT

You might see a question that asks if a student can be a participant in an educational institution's TSA. The answer is no, because the plan is only available to employees.

Tax Advantages

The following tax advantages apply to 403(b) plans:

- Contributions (which generally come from salary reduction) are excluded from a participant's gross income.
- Participants' earnings accumulate tax-free until distribution.

Investments

Historically, these plans were (and still are) referred to as TSAs because annuities were the only investment option. In 1974, a provision was made to permit the purchase of mutual funds as well, although it is estimated that more than 85% of all 403(b) money is invested in either fixed or variable annuities.

PRACTICE QUESTION

19. A retirement plan that allows the employee to make pretax contributions (within certain limits), provides for tax deferral of earnings, and is available for employees of public school systems and certain tax-exempt organizations is
    A. a 403(b) plan.
    B. a 401(k) plan.
    C. an SEP IRA.
    D. a payroll deduction plan.

    Answer: A. The giveaway here is the public school employees—the 403(b). That is their plan as well as being offered to employees of certain, but not all, tax-exempt organizations.

Section 457 Plans

A **Section 457(b) plan** is a deferred compensation plan set up under Section 457 of the tax code that may be used by employees of a state, political subdivision of a state, and any agency or instrumentality of a state. This plan may also be offered to employees of certain tax-exempt organizations (hospitals, charitable organizations, unions, and so forth, but not churches).

Even though technically a nonqualified plan, employees can defer compensation in a 457 plan, and the amount deferred is not reportable for tax purposes. Therefore, the employee receives a deduction each year for the amount deferred.

There are several important facts to know about 457 plans:

- These plans are exempt from ERISA—nongovernmental plans must be unfunded to qualify for tax benefits, while government plans must be funded.
- These plans are generally not required to follow the nondiscrimination rules of other retirement plans.
- Plans for tax-exempt organizations are limited to covering only highly compensated employees, while any employee (or even independent contractor) of a governmental entity may participate.
- Distributions from 457(b) plans of nongovernmental tax-exempt employees may not be rolled over into an IRA, but there is no 10% penalty for early withdrawal.
- It is possible to maintain both a 457 and 403(b), or a 457 and 401(k) and make maximum contributions to both. You could also have an IRA along with the 457.

PRACTICE QUESTION

20. A basic difference between a Section 457 plan established on behalf of a governmental entity and one established by a private tax-exempt organization is that
    A. a governmental plan must hold its assets in trust or custodial accounts for the benefit of individual participants.
    B. a tax-exempt plan participant does not have to include plan distributions in her taxable income.
    C. a governmental plan cannot make a distribution before the participant attains age 70½.
    D. a tax-exempt plan's distributions are not eligible for a favorable lump-sum 10-year averaging treatment.

    Answer: A. A governmental Section 457 plan must be funded—that is—it must hold plan assets in trusts or custodial accounts for the benefit of individual participants. Conversely, a tax-exempt (nongovernmental) Section 457 plan may not be funded.

21. A 457 plan
    A. is a type of deferred compensation plan for employees of state and local municipalities.
    B. will distribute money to participants, but only the earnings will be taxed.
    C. is a type of qualified plan.
    D. allows employees to defer up to 50% of income within the plan.

    Answer: A. A 457 plan is a type of deferred compensation plan for employees of state and local municipalities.

Corporate-Sponsored Retirement Plans

In this section, we will be discussing qualified plans sponsored by corporations. These include pension plans, profit-sharing plans, and the highly popular 401(k) plans.

The **Employee Retirement Income Security Act of 1974 (ERISA)** is federal legislation that regulates the establishment and management of corporate pension or retirement plans, also known as **private-sector plans.**

All qualified corporate plans must be established under a trust agreement. A trustee is appointed for each plan and has a fiduciary responsibility for the plan and the beneficial owners (the plan holders). We'll cover ERISA in greater detail later in this unit.

Defined Contribution and Defined Benefit Plans

All qualified retirement plans fall into one of two categories. Those that offer no specific end result, but, instead focus on current, tax-deductible contributions, are **defined contribution plans**. Those that promise a specific retirement benefit but do not specify the level of current contributions are **defined benefit plans**. It is important to distinguish between these two approaches.

Defined Contribution Plans

Defined contribution plans include money purchase pension plans as well as profit-sharing plans and 401(k) plans. As with other business plans (as compared to an IRA), the maximum employer contribution is significantly greater.

Defined contribution plan participants' funds accumulate until a future event—generally retirement— when the funds may be withdrawn. The ultimate account value depends on the total amount contributed, along with interest and capital gains from the plan investments. In this type of plan, the plan participant assumes the investment risk. Examples of defined contribution plans include profit-sharing plans, 401(k) plans, and money purchase pension plans.

Defined Benefit Plans

Defined benefit plans are designed to provide specific retirement benefits for participants, such as fixed monthly income. Regardless of investment performance, the promised benefit is paid under the contract terms. A defined benefit plan sponsor assumes the investment risk. The benefit is usually determined by a formula that takes into account years of service and average salary for the last five years before retirement. Older, highly compensated employees are likely to have the largest annual contributions on their behalf. Because of the expenses and complexities involved (the plan's annual return must be signed by an actuary), only 4% of workers had defined benefit plans in 2018, whereas in 1979, that number was 28%.

TAKE NOTE

Because of the actuarial assumptions and computations, the amount of the annual contributions to the plan has to be figured by an actuary.

Contributory vs. Noncontributory Plans

In a contributory plan, both the employer and employee make contributions to the account. In a noncontributory plan, only the employer makes the contributions. Probably the most common example of a contributory plan is the 401(k) plan, where the employee determines how much to contribute and the employer may match it up to a certain percentage.

Employer Deductions

The employer can usually deduct—subject to limits—contributions made to a qualified plan. The deduction limit for those contributions to a qualified plan depends on the kind of plan in place.

TEST TOPIC ALERT

Unlike an annuity payout or life insurance premium, contributions to a defined benefit plan are not affected by the participant's sex.

TEST TOPIC ALERT

Employer contributions to defined benefit or defined contribution (money purchase) pension plans are mandatory. Although profit-sharing plans and 401(k) plans are technically defined contribution plans, they are not pension plans, and employer contributions are not mandatory. In all cases, allowable employer contributions are 100% deductible to the corporation. There is no tax obligation to the employee until withdrawal.

Profit-Sharing Plans

A **profit-sharing plan** established by an employer allows employees to participate in the business's profits.

Profit-sharing plans need not have a predetermined contribution formula. Plans that do include such a formula generally express contributions as a fixed percentage of profits. In either event, to be qualified, a profit-sharing plan must have substantial and recurring contributions, according to the IRC.

Profit-sharing plans are popular because they offer employers the greatest amount of contribution flexibility. The ability to skip contributions during years of low profits appeals to corporations with unpredictable cash flows. They are also relatively easy to install, administer, and communicate to employees.

401(k) Plans

In a **401(k) plan**, an employee directs an employer to deduct a percentage of the employee's salary to contribute to a retirement account. 401(k) plans permit an employer to make matching contributions up to a set percentage of the employee-directed contributions, making this a type of defined contribution plan. All contributions are made with pretax dollars. In effect, participating employees are reducing their salary by the amount of their contribution and, therefore, their W-2 will show the actual salary less the 401(k) contribution.

TEST TOPIC ALERT

One of the benefits of investing through a 401(k) plan is that it takes advantage of dollar cost averaging, a technique described in Unit 8, which always results in a lower cost per share in a fluctuating market.

Roth 401(k) Plans

The Roth 401(k) plan is an option available to an existing 401(k) plan. This option combines features of Roth IRAs and 401(k) retirement plans. Just as with a Roth IRA, these plans require after-tax contributions but allow tax-free withdrawals, provided the retiring person is at least 59½ years old at the time of the withdrawal. Once again, paralleling the Roth IRA, the account must be at least five years old to take tax-free withdrawals.

Like a regular 401(k) plan, it has employer-matching contributions; however, the employer's match must be deposited into a regular 401(k) plan and be fully taxable upon withdrawal. Thus, the employee must have two accounts: a regular 401(k) and a Roth 401(k). Employees may contribute to either account but may not transfer money between accounts once the money has been contributed.

Unlike Roth IRAs, Roth 401(k) plans have no income limit restriction on who may participate. One may have both a Roth 401(k) plan and a Roth IRA, but the income limits would still apply to the Roth IRA. Unlike Roth IRAs, Roth 401(k) plans require withdrawals to begin no later than age 72, following the same rules that apply to all RMDs.

Required Beginning Date

We have already covered the age at which minimum distributions must begin for IRAs. We just mentioned that Roth 401(k) plans have the same 72 rule. What about in the case of all qualified corporate plans? The term used here is required beginning date. A participant must begin to receive distributions from her qualified retirement plan by April 1 of the later of the following years:

- The first year after the calendar year in which she reaches age 72.
- The first year after the calendar year in which she retires from employment with the employer maintaining the plan.
- In other words, if you are still working for that employer and are over 72, minimum distributions are not required until after you retire.

Additional Corporate Plans

Here are some other corporate-sponsored plans, but these are less likely to be tested subjects on your exam.

Simplified Employee Pension (SEP-IRA)

SEP plans are qualified individual retirement plans that offer self-employed persons and small businesses easy-to-administer pension plans. SEPs allow employers to contribute money to SEP IRAs that their employees set up to receive employer contributions.

Under IRS rules, an eligible employee is an individual (including a self-employed individual) who meets all the following requirements:

- Has reached age 21
- Has worked for the employer in at least 3 of the last 5 years
- Has received at least $600 in compensation from the employer during the year (for 2020)

Self-employed individuals may contribute up to a maximum amount each year to an SEP IRA for themselves or employees. Catch-up contributions are generally not allowed for the self-employed person. However, if an employee is enrolled in an SEP and the SEP permits non-SEP IRA contributions to be made to the SEP account, they may also make additional catch-up contributions to the SEP account if they are age 50 or older.

Generally, an employer can take an income tax deduction for contributions made each year to each employee's SEP. Also, the amounts contributed to an SEP by an employer on behalf of an employee are excludable from the employee's gross income.

Savings Incentive Match Plans for Employees (SIMPLEs)

SIMPLE plans are retirement plans for businesses with 100 or fewer employees who earned $5,000 or more during the preceding calendar year. In addition, the business cannot currently have another retirement plan in place.

The employee makes pretax contributions into a SIMPLE up to an annual contribution limit. The employer makes matching contributions. Matching contribution requirements and limits for employers are specified by the IRS and include catch-up contributions up to $3,000 for those age 50 and older. SIMPLE plans require immediate vesting.

For a small business wanting to have an inexpensive retirement plan for their employees, the SIMPLE is the way to go.

Keogh Plans

Keogh plans are retirement plans for self-employed people. They were formerly referred to as *H.R. 10 plans* after the law that first allowed unincorporated businesses to sponsor retirement plans. Because the law no longer distinguishes between corporate and other plan sponsors, the term is seldom used. However, you may still see it on your exam.

Stock Purchase Plans and Stock Options

Some publicly traded companies offer their employees the ability to purchase company stock. There are several ways this can be done, but perhaps the most straightforward method of employee stock ownership can be found in an **employee stock purchase program (ESPP)**. These plans provide a convenient method for employees to purchase company shares.

Employee **stock purchase plans** are essentially a type of payroll deduction plan that allows employees to buy company stock without affecting the transactions themselves. Money is automatically taken out of a participant's paycheck on an after-tax basis every pay period and accrues in an escrow account until it is used to buy company shares on a periodic basis, such as every six months. These plans are similar to other types of stock option plans in that they promote employee ownership of the company but do not have many of the restrictions that come with more formal stock option arrangements. Plus, they are designed to be somewhat more liquid in nature.

Here are the basics:

- Contributions should be 1%–10% of salary. The contribution is a payroll deduction. This is calculated on pretax salary but taken **after tax** (unlike with a 401(k), there is no tax deduction on ESPP contributions).
- At the end of a purchase period, usually every six months, the employer will purchase company stock for participants using contributions during the purchase period. There will be a discount on the purchase price. The employer takes the price of the company stock at the beginning of the purchase period and the price at the end of the purchase period, **whichever is lower**, and then gives a discount from that price.
- Participants can sell the purchased stock right away or hold on to the stocks longer for preferential tax treatment.

An employer may also offer **stock options** that give an employee the right to purchase a specified number of shares of the employer's common stock at a stated price over a stated time period. Unlike qualified retirement plans, there are no nondiscrimination requirements for these plans. For publicly traded stock, the *strike* price (also called the grant or exercise price) is usually the market price of the stock at the time the option is granted. In most cases, there is a minimum time the employee must remain with the company to be able to use the option (the vesting period). The hope of the employee is that the market price of the employer's stock will increase in value. Then, the employee will be able to purchase the stock by exercising the option (purchasing the stock) at the lower strike price and then sell the stock at the current market price. These are available only to employees of the issuing company. Most states require that the stock option plan be approved by the board of directors. Please note that these are not the same as the *put* and *call options* we will be covering at length in Unit 10.

We've covered a lot of material so here is your chance to see how well you understand.

PRACTICE QUESTION

22. All of the following statements regarding RMDs from a 401(k) are true **except**
    A. minimum required distributions begin by April 1 of the year following the year in which the participant turns 72.
    B. RMDs are not required if the participant is still working for that employer.
    C. RMDs not taken are subject to a 50% penalty.
    D. RMDs taken after age 72 are taxed at a more favorable long-term capital gains rate.

    Answer: D. Minimum required distributions taken after age 72 are taxed, as are all taxable distributions from retirement accounts, such as ordinary income.

23. One of the most important characteristics of a profit-sharing plan is that
    A. the employer is not required to make a contribution if the company has no profits.
    B. it favors older employees.
    C. the employer may choose who participates and who doesn't.
    D. contributions are made with after-tax dollars and therefore only the growth is taxed at distribution.

    Answer: A. One of the most important characteristics of a profit-sharing plan is the employer is not required to make a contribution if the company has no profits.

24. A type of payroll deduction plan that allows employees to purchase the company stock at a discount from the purchase price is called
    A. a preemptive right.
    B. an employee stock purchase plan.
    C. a profit-sharing plan.
    D. a money purchase plan.

    Answer: B. A type of payroll deduction plan that allows employees to purchase the company stock at a discount from the purchase price is called an employee stock purchase plan. A preemptive right does permit the purchase of stock at a discount, but is offered to existing shareholders, not employees.

25. A married 75-year-old employee, whose spouse is 55, works for a manufacturing firm and has $1 million in the firm's 401(k) plan. What is accurate regarding the RMD from the 401(k) at this point in time?
    A. RMDs should have begun by April 1 of the year following the year in which the participant turned 72.
    B. There is no required RMD at this time because the spouse is under age 59½.
    C. RMDs will begin after the employee retires.
    D. Any RMDs not taken at this time are subject to income taxes plus a 10% penalty.

    Answer: C. A participant is not required to take minimum distributions from the employer's 401(k) while still working. After retirement starts, RMDs from a qualified retirement plan must begin by April 1 of the first year after the calendar year in which the plan participant retires from employment with the employer maintaining the plan.

Unit 1

LESSON 1.9: ERISA

LO 1.i Define ERISA and its application to private-sector retirement plans.

Testable ERISA Provisions

ERISA was established to prevent abuse and misuse of pension funds. ERISA guidelines apply to private-sector (corporate) retirement plans and certain union plans—not public plans like those for government workers. Significant ERISA provisions include the following:

- **Participation.** This identifies eligibility rules for employees. All employees must be covered if they are 21 years or older and have performed one year of full-time service, which ERISA defines as 1,000 hours or more.
- **Funding.** Funds contributed to the plan must be segregated from other corporate assets. Plan trustees must administer and invest the assets prudently and in the best interest of all participants. IRS contribution limits must be observed.
- **Vesting.** Vesting defines when an employer contribution to a plan becomes the employee's money, such as an employer-matching contribution to a 401(k) plan. ERISA limits how long the vesting schedule can last before the employee is fully vested. Note that an employee is always fully vested in the employee's own contributions to a plan.
- **Communication.** The plan document must be in writing, and employees must be given annual statements of account and updates of plan benefits.
- **Nondiscrimination.** All eligible employees must be treated impartially through a uniformly applied formula.
- **Beneficiaries.** Beneficiaries must be named to receive an employee's benefits at death.

TEST TOPIC ALERT

You may see a question that asks for the type of plans that ERISA regulates. ERISA applies to private-sector plans (corporate) only. It does not apply to plans for federal or state government workers (public sector plans), nor is it applicable to nonqualified plans.

PRACTICE QUESTIONS

26. ERISA rules and regulations include all of the following **except**
    A. ERISA protects participants in private-sector retirement plans such as a pension from the creditors of the corporation.
    B. a retirement plan covered by ERISA may not discriminate against who is eligible to participate in the plan.
    C. it defines when employer contributions become the employee's money.
    D. ERISA allows the corporation to be the beneficiary of plan benefits for employees before their retirement.

Answer: D. ERISA does not allow the corporation to be the beneficiary of plan benefits for employees before their retirement.

27. Which of the following plans are covered by ERISA?
    A. A defined benefit plan offered by a manufacturing company to employees
    B. A pension plan offered to employees of the City of Detroit, Michigan
    C. A deferred compensation plan offered to select employees of a CPA firm
    D. A 457 plan

    Answer: A. A defined benefit plan offered by a manufacturing company to employees is covered by ERISA. Only private-sector plans are covered by ERISA, not state or local government plans (public sector plans).

UNIT

2

Obtain Necessary Suitability Information and Approvals

LEARNING OBJECTIVES

When you have completed this unit, you will be able to accomplish the following.

- LO 2.a **Identify** the client's current and future financial situation.
- LO 2.b **Evaluate** personal considerations other than financial.
- LO 2.c **Recall** the methods to verify customer information including sophistication and/or accredited status.
- LO 2.d **Discover** the client's goals and objectives.
- LO 2.e **Distinguish** between investment objectives and investment constraints.
- LO 2.f **Contrast** reasonable basis, customer specific, and quantitative suitability.
- LO 2.g **Identify** the documentation and approval required for different types of accounts.

INTRODUCTION

The key to **suitability** is found in the **know your customer rule (KYC)**. This rule, FINRA 2090, places an obligation on the member firm and associated persons to request information from customers. Customers are not required to provide all information asked. The KYC rule provides some flexibility when information is unavailable because the customer refused to supply it.

In this case, when some customer information is unavailable, despite a firm's request for it, limits are placed on what may be recommended. A recommendation may be made if the firm has a reasonable basis to believe it is suitable. This can be based on information that the firm knows. Both financial and nonfinancial information must be gathered before making investment recommendations.

LESSON 2.1 CUSTOMER FINANCIAL PROFILE

LO 2.a Identify the client's current and future financial situation.

Gather Financial Information

Before making a recommendation for a new customer, a registered representative must try to find out as much as possible about that person's financial and nonfinancial situation. In general, the best way to get the proper information is by completing a customer profile. This profile should contain financial and nonfinancial information.

Financial investment considerations can be expressed as a sum of money. Financial questions have answers that show up on a customer's personal balance sheet or income statement. Asking a customer, "when would you like to retire?" is not a financial question—it is nonfinancial. The answer does not show up on the customer's personal balance sheet or income statement.

Customer Balance Sheet

An individual, like a business, has a financial balance sheet—a snapshot of the individual's financial condition at a point in time. A customer's net worth is determined by subtracting liabilities from assets (assets – liabilities = net worth). Representatives determine the status of a customer's personal balance sheet by asking questions similar to the following:

- What is the value of any cash, CDs, and savings accounts (usually looked at as an emergency fund, generally considered to be a primary requirement for investing in securities).
- What are the values of tangible assets? Home? Car? Collectibles? Jewelry?
- What are the values of securities you currently own?
- Have you established long-term investment accounts, and what are the values of those accounts? Do you have an IRA, corporate pension, or profit-sharing plan, and what are the values of those plans?
- What is the cash value of your life insurance?
- What are your liabilities? How much do you owe on your mortgage? Car? Outstanding loans?
- Are there any loans against insurance cash value?
- How large is your credit card debt?

From this information, we can determine the net worth and how much of it is liquid.

Customer Income Statement

To make appropriate investment recommendations, representatives must know the customer's income situation. They gather information about the customer's marital status, financial responsibilities, projected inheritances, and pending job changes by asking the following questions:

- What is your total gross income? Total family income?
- How much do you pay in monthly expenses?

- What is your net spendable income after expenses? How much of this is available for investment?
- How secure is your employment?

TAKE NOTE

Before recommending any investment to a customer, a registered representative must, at a minimum, make a reasonable effort to obtain information concerning the customer's financial status, tax status, and investment objectives.

Taking into consideration all of this information indicates to the securities professional the extent to which the client is able to make a lump-sum investment (the balance sheet shows a large amount of net assets available), and/or periodic investments (the income statement reveals a positive cash flow—there is "money left at the end of the month").

TEST TOPIC ALERT

A family balance sheet only includes assets and liabilities, not income like salary, dividends, or interest, or amounts paid for expenses.

PRACTICE QUESTION

1. An individual's net worth is
   A. the difference between the individual's assets and the individual's liabilities.
   B. best determined by examining the individual's personal income statement.
   C. largely irrelevant in identifying the individual's investment objectives.
   D. another term for discretionary income.

Answer: A. An individual's net worth is the difference between the individual's assets and the individual's liabilities. It is determined from the personal balance sheet rather than from the personal income statement. Net worth is relevant in determining an individual's investment objectives. Clients with a negative net worth might find it preferable to reduce their debt level before beginning an investment program.

LESSON 2.2: CUSTOMER NONFINANCIAL PROFILE

LO 2.b Evaluate personal considerations other than financial.

Customer Profile: Nonfinancial Investment Considerations

Once registered representatives have an idea of the customer's financial status, they gather information on the nonfinancial status. A nonfinancial investment consideration is one that cannot be expressed as a sum of money or a numerical cash flow (risk tolerance, or tax bracket, for example). Nonfinancial considerations often carry more weight than the financial considerations and include the following:

- Age
- Marital status
- Number and ages of dependents
- Employment
- Employment of family members

- Current and future family educational needs
- Current and future family health care needs
- Risk tolerance
- Attitudes and values, such as ESG investing
- Tax status

No matter how much an analysis of a customer's financial status tells the registered representative about the ability to invest, it is the customer's emotional acceptance of investing and motivation to invest, which molds the portfolio.

To understand a customer's attitude for investment, the representative should ask questions similar to the following:

- What kind of risks can you afford to take?
- How liquid must your investments be?
- How important are tax considerations?
- Are you seeking long-term or short-term investments?
- What is your investment experience?
- What types of investments do you currently hold?
- How would you react to a loss of 5% of your principal? 10%? 50%?
- What level of return do you consider good? Poor? Excellent?
- What combination of risks and returns do you feel comfortable with?
- What is your investment temperament?
- Do you get bored with stable investments?
- Can you tolerate market fluctuations?
- How stable is your income?
- Do you anticipate any financial changes in the future?

There certainly are shades of gray when defining a customer's risk tolerance. This makes it even more critical that you and the customer are on the same page when it comes to risk tolerance. For test purposes, you can usually get the correct answer by identifying the key word.

- If you see low risk—conservative
- If you see some risk—moderate
- If you see more than average risk—moderately aggressive
- If you see high risk—aggressive

If you key on the right word, you'll get the correct answer.

PRACTICE QUESTION

2. In designing an investment portfolio for a new client, one of the first things to do is determine the client's
   A. home address.
   B. Social Security or tax ID number.
   C. risk tolerance.
   D. beneficiary.

Answer: C. One can't adequately present any investment recommendations without having an understanding of the client's risk tolerance. Home address and Social Security number are legal requirements for opening the account, but they don't enter into the decision-making process for portfolio design. Yes, you will want to know the beneficiary of any IRAs or qualified plans, but that has little to do with the nature of your recommendations.

TAKE NOTE

A registered representative's job is to assist customers in meeting their financial objectives. Responsible reps must learn all about the customers' financial situations. Securities laws prohibit unsuitable recommendations.

If a customer contacts a registered representative and wants to purchase securities that the rep feels are not suitable for the client, the registered representative has a responsibility to tell the customer that she feels the trade is not suitable. If the customer insists on the purchase, the registered representative should place the order and mark the trade unsolicited.

The following practice questions demonstrate two contrasting examples dealing with this LO.

PRACTICE QUESTION

3. All of the following are financial considerations in a customer profile **except**
   A. the balance in the 401(k) plan.
   B. wanting to retire at age 65.
   C. annual income.
   D. the remaining balance on the home mortgage.

   Answer: B. Wanting to retire at age 65 is a goal and a nonfinancial consideration. Financial investment considerations can be expressed as a sum of money (total liabilities, for example) or as a numerical cash flow (gross income of $160,000 per year, for example).

4. Which of the following would be considered nonfinancial investment considerations on a customer profile?
   A. Total fixed assets
   B. Attitude toward risk
   C. Monthly income available for investment
   D. Amount saved in a 401(k) plan

   Answer: B. Nonfinancial investment considerations are those that cannot be expressed as a concrete sum of money or as a specific monthly, yearly, or weekly cash flow. Attitude toward risk cannot be expressed in numbers at all.

LESSON 2.3: QUALIFYING THE CUSTOMER

LO 2.c Recall the methods to verify customer information including sophistication and/or accredited status.

Verification of Customer Information

How is all of the information necessary to complete the customer profile obtained? Although there is no universal method, most firms rely on a combination of tools. The first step is usually having the client complete a detailed questionnaire. Optimally, this should be followed up by a personal interview, either in the office or home, on the phone, or online with one of the various video services available. There is only so much one can learn from a form, and both the client and the registered representative benefit from the give and take of an interview, as that is the best way to discover qualitative information, such as risk tolerance and attitudes. Traditionally, data-gathering techniques involve asking clients or prospects to bring in account statements, insurance policies, 401(k) plan options, and maybe tax returns. Why is all of this information needed? Without it, there is no way to determine suitability.

Obtaining this information is critical when one needs to measure the sophistication of the investor. Viewing the types of securities previously or currently owned can provide a clue. In the case of investments requiring accredited investor status (covered extensively in Unit 20), it is even more important.

Who is an Accredited Investor?

Any individual with net worth in excess of $1 million, exclusive of the equity in a primary residence, or any individual who had an income in excess of $200,000 in each of the two most recent years or joint income with that person's spouse in excess of $300,000 in each of those years and has a reasonable expectation of reaching the same income level in the current year.

Although the legal obligation for determining accredited investor status is that of the issuer, FINRA believes that each member should take reasonable steps to verify that status where applicable. Here are some of the recommended steps:

- Tax returns or W-2s for the previous two years
- Obtaining a written representation from the purchaser that he has a reasonable expectation of reaching the income level necessary to qualify as an accredited investor during the current year
- If the purchaser is an accredited investor on the basis of the $1 million net worth, reviewing one or more of the following types of documentation dated within the prior three months:
  - Bank or brokerage account statements
  - A credit report from at least one of the nationwide consumer reporting agencies

Alternatively, the member firm can comply by doing the following:

- Obtaining a written confirmation from one of the following persons or entities that such person or entity has taken reasonable steps to verify that the purchaser is an accredited investor within the prior three months and has determined that such purchaser is an accredited investor
  - A registered broker-dealer
  - An investment adviser registered with the Securities and Exchange Commission
  - A licensed attorney who is in good standing under the laws of the jurisdictions in which she is admitted to practice law
  - A certified public accountant who is duly registered and in good standing under the laws of the place of her residence or principal office

PRACTICE QUESTION

5. A member firm wishing to verify the accredited investor status of a client would be least likely to ask for
   A. the past two years tax returns.
   B. a written confirmation from a lawyer admitted to the bar in the client's state of residence.
   C. a current paycheck stub.
   D. bank or brokerage statements.

   Answer: C. Because we need to see income for the past two years, a current paystub does not provide sufficient information.

LESSON 2.4: GOALS AND OBJECTIVES

LO 2.d Discover the client's goals and objectives.

Investment Goals

Using the information gathered about a client's circumstances and financial resources, the registered representative and client should establish financial goals. Many investors confuse goals and objectives. A goal is where you want to be (the "end game"), while objectives are the steps taken along the way to reach the goal. Some commonly specified goals include

- planning for college education;
- retirement;
- saving for a future purchase, such as a home;
- philanthropy;
- capital to start a business; and
- leaving a legacy.

Investment Objectives, Part 1

Investment objectives are the tools used to reach these goals. There are three primary objectives:

- Growth
- Income
- Stability (capital preservation)

However, in attempting to meet these objectives, there may be some obstacles, properly referred to as *investment constraints*, (covered in the next LO), which must be considered. Let's examine some objectives in greater detail.

As stated previously, when it comes to investment objectives, there are three broad classes with many shades in between:

- Growth (can be aggressive, moderate, or even conservative)
- Income (can be current, future, or high risk)
- Preservation of capital (safety)

There is a specific term for an objective that can be maximum income or maximum growth without regard to stability. That is speculation.

Figure 2.1 Matching Client Objectives

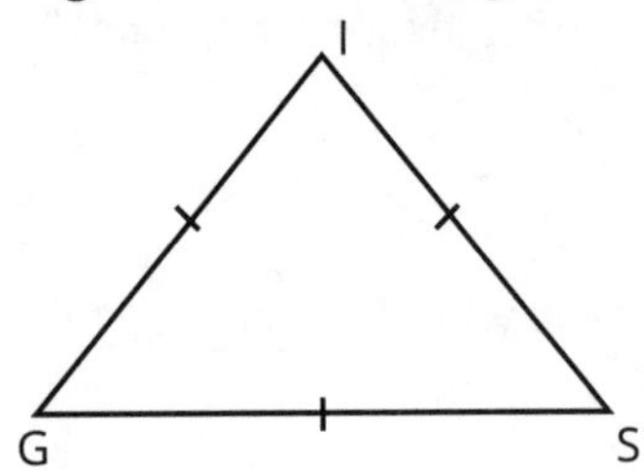

You might find the concepts of investment objectives easier to understand if we use a little geometry. The picture is of an equilateral triangle. That means each of the sides (legs) is of the same length (equal). You will notice a letter at each point. The *G* is for growth, the *I* is for income, and the *S* is for safety (preservation of capital). Borrowing another term from geometry, it is axiomatic (true) that the closer you move on the leg to one of these points (objective), the farther you move from the others.

For example, if you wish to maximize your growth, you go all the way to the G and move farther away from the I and the S. As a result, you sacrifice income and safety. Total safety, (all the way to the S), sacrifices growth and income, and maximum income sacrifices growth and safety. The role of the registered representative is to determine where in this triangle the customer's objectives lie. They can be between the G and I when the objective is growth with income. Or, if the objective is income with safety, the point will be between the I and the S. It is important to understand you can't maximize all three—something has to give.

PRACTICE QUESTION

6. Which of the following is properly referred to as an investment goal rather than objective?
   A. Current income
   B. Endowing a scholarship at your alma mater
   C. Conservative growth
   D. Speculation

Answer: B. *Goals* are what you hope to have the money for. *Objectives* are the way to get there. Remember the triangle for G, I ,and S. The S is for *stability*. The opposite of *stability* is *speculation*, and that is another one of the objectives. For some investors, that is the route they choose to take.

In Part 2 of this course, we'll discuss the various investment options used to meet these objectives.

LESSON 2.5: INVESTMENT OBJECTIVES VS. INVESTMENT CONSTRAINTS

LO 2.e Distinguish between investment objectives and investment constraints.

Investment Objectives, Part 2

As mentioned in the previous LO, investment objectives are the steps taken by investors to help them reach their stated goals. There are some potential obstacles in the way. These are called investment constraints. **Investment constraints** are limitations or restrictions that are specific to your client. Investment constraints include—among others—liquidity needs, time horizon, and personal ethical choices (no tobacco or alcohol stocks). Let's begin by going deeper into objectives.

Preservation of Capital

Many people want to avoid any drop in value of their investments. For these investors, bank insured CDs, for example, offer the safety they seek. There is a trade-off, however. By reducing risk, the investor is sacrificing the opportunity for higher income. In addition, as fixed-income investments, they are exposed to inflation (purchasing power) risk.

Income

When the investor's goal is income, a primary factor is the amount of risk the investor is willing and/or able to take. The risk/reward principle is quite clear. The more risk, the greater the potential reward. The reverse is also true. The lower the risk, the lower the potential reward. As we see in our triangle, as you move on the leg closer to *income*, you move farther away from *safety*. An example of a security suitable for an investor who wants both is one issued by the U.S. Treasury. On the other hand, one wanting to maximize income would do so at the risk of safety by investing in high-yield (junk) bonds.

Growth (Capital Appreciation)

As with income, the term *growth* refers to a broad spectrum of objectives. Some investors have a very high risk tolerance and want their portfolio to be solidly on the *G* while others are quite conservative and are closer to the *S*, while still on the "leg" toward growth rather than income. Still others might want their portfolio to be on the leg between *G* and *I*. It is the role of the registered representative to help the client understand where on the leg the portfolio should lie.

Speculation

Although a subcategory of growth, speculation is often listed as a specific objective. A customer may want to speculate—that is, try to earn much higher-than-average returns in exchange for higher-than-average risks. Investors who are interested in speculation will frequently use margin, sell short, and trade in options or penny stocks. As a registered representative, one must always determine the suitability of such recommendations.

Investment Constraints

Once we've set our objectives, we need to look out for the "bumps in the road"; those things that can cause even the best plan to take a detour. Here are the major investment constraints you may find on your exam:

Constraints	Description
Time horizon	Time frame in which goals must be attained
Liquidity	What is the cash need? High if close to goals (retirement or education); low if long time horizon
Taxes	Tax characteristics of investor and desired level of tax management
Laws and regulations	Any legal prohibitions on types of investments or transactions—is the investor accredited?
Unique circumstances and/or preferences	Investor preferences or desires to avoid particular types of assets

Time Horizon

An investor's time horizon and liquidity needs will determine the level of volatility the client should assume. Over a 20- or 30-year time frame, dramatic short-term volatility is acceptable, even to those who are risk averse. Money that will be needed within three to five years should be invested for safety and liquidity. Time horizon is a particularly important investment constraint when planning for college education and for retirement.

Liquidity

Some investors have a need for a certain sum, such as an upcoming home purchase or college tuition. Or, they might just like the idea that they can get their money literally at a moment's notice. They need liquid assets in their portfolio. A product is liquid if a customer can sell it quickly at face amount (or very close to it) or at a fair market price.

Remember that a liquid investment does not mean you won't lose money on your investment. It simply means you can get the current market value of the investment quickly. Liquid investments include

- securities listed on an exchange or Nasdaq,
- mutual funds,
- exchange-traded funds, and
- most real estate investment trusts (REITs).

Illiquid investments include

- annuities, when initially purchased and/or when the annuitant is under age 59½;
- real estate;
- securities purchased in a private placement;
- DPPs; and
- hedge funds.

Taxes

A client's tax situation is often an important factor in determining suitable investments. For exam purposes, there are two ways to reduce taxes—tax deferral and tax-free income.

- **Tax deferral.** Contributions to an IRA, a qualified retirement plan, or a TSA may be tax deductible and are not taxed until withdrawn. This gives two benefits to the investor. Firstly, the investments are made with pretax money. Secondly, there are no taxes on the income and growth until the money is paid out. That is the power of deferring taxes.
- **Tax-free income.** Municipal bonds pay interest that is free from federal taxation. There are cases where the income would be taxed on the state level; that will be covered in Unit 6. Municipal bonds generally pay interest at a lower rate than taxable bonds. That is because the interest is tax-free. Depending on the investor's tax bracket, the municipal bond may result in higher returns on an after-tax basis. As covered in Unit 1, it is also possible to generate tax-free income using a Roth IRA and the Coverdell ESA. In Unit 6, we will discuss the Section 529 plan—another way to provide tax-free income.

Laws and Regulations

An example of how laws or regulations could be an investment constraint is the case of the accredited investor. A registered representative may find the absolutely perfect investment to meet the client's objectives only to find out the client can't make the purchase because of lack of accredited investor status. Another case might be when the desired security is not registered for sale in the client's state of residence. As we've learned, there are certain investments that are illegal or inappropriate for an IRA. That is what an investment constraint is all about: we'd like to buy this, but we can't.

Unique Circumstances and/or Preferences

Investors share many common characteristics. When you speak to a customer about goals, you will notice how often the same ones keep coming up. That said, it is important to understand that these are all unique individuals with their own needs and wants. We'll take a look at how some of those are investment constraints.

The most common case on the exam is the desire to avoid investing in certain industries. The term *ESG (Environment, Social and Governance) Investing* has become more popular with each passing year. Those investors who have a strong feeling about environmental issues won't invest in companies that are considered polluters or create other health issues. A test question might ask about an investor whose parent died of lung cancer. The question might say "which stock would be least like to be attractive to this client?" You should select *tobacco companies.*

Unique cases could be receiving a large inheritance or a multi-million dollar lottery win. Objectives can change pretty quickly with those additional dollars. On the flip side, a client's business going bankrupt will cause the registered rep to rethink some recommendations. An extended period of unemployment or serious illness can do the same.

What is the takeaway? Matching your recommendations to the customer's goals and objectives takes careful thought.

PRACTICE QUESTION

7. Which of the following is an investment constraint?
   A. Retirement
   B. Income
   C. College education
   D. Time horizon

Answer: D. One of the most important investment constraints is the investor's time horizon. If you start saving for retirement (a goal) at age 55, you don't have much time to accumulate funds. A short time horizon limits how aggressive the portfolio can be. If you started at age 25, with that long a time horizon, there are many more investment options available. Income is an *objective* and college education is a *goal*. That goal is also affected by time horizon. It is much better to start saving for college when a child is very young. You don't want to wait until the teenage years.

LESSON 2.6: FINRA RULE 2111 ON SUITABILITY

LO 2.f Contrast reasonable basis, customer specific, and quantitative suitability.

Suitability

FINRA's suitability rules have always been based on a fundamental requirement to deal fairly with customers. Firms and their associated persons must have a reasonable basis to believe that a recommended transaction or investment strategy involving securities is suitable for the customer.

The more information a registered representative has about a customer's income, current investment portfolio, retirement plans, and net worth, as well as other aspects of the customer's financial situation, the better a recommendation will be. The more a customer knows about the risks and rewards of each type of investment, the better the customer's investment decisions will be.

Rule 2111

In 2009, FINRA proposed a major change to its rules on suitability. Rule 2111, which became effective in 2011, is composed of three main obligations. Those three are

- reasonable-basis suitability,
- customer-specific suitability, and
- quantitative suitability.

Reasonable-basis suitability

The registered representative has to have a reasonable basis to believe that a recommendation is suitable for at least some investors. You must recognize the potential risks and rewards associated with the recommended security or strategy. If you can't explain the risks when recommending a security or strategy, you are violating the suitability rule.

Customer-specific suitability

The registered representative has to have a reasonable basis to believe that the recommendation is suitable for a specific customer. The recommendation would be based on that customer's investment profile. For example, you have an elderly person who, in the past, was relatively sophisticated. Now, he shows signs of diminished capacity. This would require a different basis for recommendations.

Quantitative suitability

The registered representative, having control over a customer account, has to have a reasonable basis for believing that a series of recommended transactions, even if suitable when viewed in isolation, are not excessive and unsuitable for the customer when taken together. No single test defines excessive activity; however, factors such as the commissions generated, the profits-to-cost ratio, and the use of in-and-out trading in a customer's account may provide a basis for a finding that a member or registered representative has violated the quantitative suitability obligation.

PRACTICE QUESTION

8. Before making a recommendation to a client, a registered representative is
   I. required to perform a reasonable-basis suitability analysis.
   II. not required to perform a reasonable-basis suitability analysis.
   III. required to perform a customer-specific suitability analysis.
   IV. not required to perform a customer-specific suitability analysis.
   A. I and III
   B. I and IV
   C. II and III
   D. II and IV

Answer: A. FINRA requires members and their registered representative who wish to make recommendations to perform both a reasonable-basis suitability analysis and a customer-specific suitability analysis. A reasonable-basis suitability analysis is necessary to ensure that an investment is suitable for some investors as opposed to a customer-specific suitability analysis, which is undertaken on a customer-by-customer basis.

What if the client refuses to supply enough information? Look at this question:

9. A retail investor opens an account at your firm but only provides minimum information. She wants to invest for retirement in 20 years and is willing to take moderate risk. Which of the following statements best describes the responsibilities of the registered representative handling the account?
   A. Recommendations cannot be made because the customer refuses to provide income information, personal assets and liabilities, or how much can be invested.
   B. The account cannot be opened without financial and nonfinancial information.
   C. Only unsolicited trades can be made in this account.
   D. The representative is limited to what can be recommended to the customer based on the information that was provided.

Answer: D. When limited information is provided for the account, the registered representative will be limited to making recommendations that she believes are suitable based on the information she has. She is missing customer-specific suitability. It is when the customer insists on making a trade that is considered unsuitable that the order must be marked unsolicited.

LESSON 2.7: OPENING SPECIAL ACCOUNTS

LO 2.g Identify the documentation and approval required for different types of accounts.

In Unit 1, we discussed the different documents needed to open an account for a customer. That discussion was about the legal requirements, such as the CIP and Regulation S-P. In this LO, we'll dig deeper for the papers needed for options and margin and discretionary accounts.

Options Accounts

There are some unique requirements to open options accounts. In Unit 10, we will learn much more about options. This LO is only about opening an account. Trading options (puts and calls) generally involves a higher degree of risk than stocks, bonds, or mutual funds. That higher risk requires that a designated supervisory person with knowledge about options must approve the account opening. In addition, there is a special options disclosure document (ODD) that must be provided to any prospective options customer.

To get a customer's account approved for options trading, a member firm, or registered rep associated with the broker-dealer, must exercise due diligence. You must learn the essential facts relative to the customer. This is nothing new. One question asked on a new options account form that is not required when opening a regular account is investment experience and knowledge. Examples of this would be the number of years of trading and the size of the trades. You would ask about frequency and type of transactions for options, stocks and bonds, commodities, and other financial instruments. The designated supervisor uses this information to approve or disapprove the account.

The account approval will indicate

- the date the ODD is furnished to the customer;
- the nature and types of transactions for which the account is approved (e.g., buying, covered writing, uncovered writing, spreading, discretionary transactions);
- the name of the registered rep assigned to the account;
- the name of the supervisor approving the account;
- the date of approval; and
- the dates of verification of currency of account information.

There is a special options account agreement. It describes the risks of options trading and the rules the customer must follow. This agreement must be signed and returned to the member within 15 days after the account has been approved. By signing, the customer also agrees to advise the firm if any changes occur in her financial situation, investment objectives, and so forth.

PRACTICE QUESTION

10. When a registered representative opens a new options account for a client, in which order must the following actions take place?
    I. Obtain approval from a qualified supervisor.
    II. Obtain essential facts from the customer.
    III. Obtain a signed options agreement.
    IV. Enter the initial order.
    A. I, II, III, IV
    B. I, II, IV, III
    C. II, I, IV, III
    D. II, I, III, IV

Answer: C. The steps in opening an options account occur in the following order: obtain essential facts about the customer, give the customer an options disclosure document (ODD), have the manager approve the account, enter the initial order, and have the customer sign and return the options agreement within 15 days.

Margin Accounts

Opening a margin account requires more documentation than opening a regular cash account. The margin agreement includes three documents. They are

- the credit agreement (mandatory),
- the hypothecation agreement (mandatory), and
- a loan consent (optional).

FINRA rules require that the client sign the margin documents no later than the first trade in the account.

Credit Agreement

The **credit agreement** discloses the terms of the credit extended by the broker-dealer. These include the method of interest computation and situations under which interest rates may change. As stated earlier, this must be signed.

Hypothecation Agreement

Margin loans are backed by collateral. In that way, they are similar to a home mortgage or a car loan. In the case of a mortgage, the house is pledged as collateral for the loan. In the case of the car, the title shows a lien to the lender. In a margin account, the collateral is the security purchased on margin. In essence, the **hypothecation agreement** gives the broker-dealer a lien on the customer's margin securities. And, as with the credit agreement, this must be signed by the customer.

Loan Consent Form

If signed, the loan consent form gives permission to the firm to loan customer margin securities to other customers or broker-dealers, usually for short sales.

TAKE NOTE

It is mandatory that the customer sign the credit agreement and hypothecation agreement. The loan consent form is optional.

Risk Disclosure

In addition to the customer agreements, the member firm must make a special disclosure. Before opening a margin account, a broker-dealer must provide customers with a risk disclosure document. This information must also be provided to margin customers on an annual basis. The document discusses the risks associated with margin trading, some of which follow:

- Customers are not entitled to choose which securities can be sold if a maintenance call is not met.
- Customers can lose more money than initially deposited.
- Customers are not entitled to an extension of time to meet a margin call.
- Firms can increase their in-house margin requirements without advance notice.

PRACTICE QUESTION

11. When opening a margin account, it is mandatory that the customer sign
    A. the credit agreement and the loan consent agreement.
    B. the credit agreement and hypothecation agreement.
    C. the hypothecation agreement and the loan consent agreement.
    D. the credit agreement only.

Answer: B. The two documents that must be signed are the credit agreement and the hypothecation agreement. The loan consent agreement is optional.

Discretionary Accounts

In a **discretionary account,** the customer has authorized the broker-dealer or registered representative to make the investment decisions in the account.

Discretion is defined as the authority to decide

- which security,
- the number of shares or units, or
- whether to buy or sell.

Normally, an order to buy or sell a security is at the direction of the client, generally via a telephone call or online. Many clients prefer the convenience of letting their securities professional "call the shots." Being able to determine the trading activity in a client's account presents a potential conflict of interest. In the case of broker-dealers and agents, their compensation is transaction-based. The more trading in the account, the more income.

TEST TOPIC ALERT

To identify a discretionary order, try this method: an order is discretionary if any one of the **three As** is missing. The three As are

- **a**ctivity,
- **a**mount, and
- **a**sset.

FINRA rules prohibit the exercise of any discretionary power by a broker-dealer or agent in a customer's account unless

- the customer has given prior written authorization (a power of attorney) to a stated individual or individuals; and
- the account has been accepted by the brokerage firm, as evidenced in writing by the firm.

No discretionary transactions can take place without this document on file. Once authorization is given, the firm is legally empowered to make trading decisions for the account, although the customer may also continue to enter orders on his own if he wishes.

Discretion—Time or Price

There is an exception to the requirement that applies to the exercise of time or price discretion. This is discretion orally granted by the customer to purchase or sell a specific amount of a particular security (e.g., "Buy 100 shares of ABCD and get the best price you can").

An oral grant of time or price discretion is limited to the end of the business day on which the customer grants it. If the order is to be good from longer than that day, the customer must state it in writing. Any exercise of time or price discretion must be reflected on the order ticket (as is the case with regular discretion).

TAKE NOTE

Discretion does not apply to decisions regarding the timing of an investment or the price at which it is acquired.

EXAMPLE

An order from a customer worded "Buy 100 shares of ABC for my account whenever you think the price is right" is not a discretionary order because the client has specified the action (buy), the amount (100 shares) and the asset (ABC). Time or price are not considered discretion.

In addition to requiring the proper documentation, discretionary accounts are subject to the following rules:

- Each discretionary order must be identified as such when it is entered for execution.
- An officer or a partner of the brokerage house must approve each order promptly and in writing, but not necessarily before order entry.
- A record must be kept of all transactions.
- No excessive trading or churning may occur in the account relative to the size of the account and the customer's investment objectives.
- The account must be checked regularly.

Fiduciary Accounts

A fiduciary is one who has the legal power to act on behalf of another person. Common examples are

- a trustee named to administer a trust,
- an executor designated in a decedent's will to manage the affairs of the estate,

- an administrator appointed by the courts to liquidate the estate of a person who died intestate (without a will),
- a guardian designated by the courts to handle a minor's affairs until the minor reaches the age of majority or to handle an incompetent person's affairs,
- a custodian of a Uniform Gift to Minors Account (UGMA) or a Uniform Transfer to Minors Account (UTMA),
- a receiver in a bankruptcy, and
- a conservator for an incompetent person.

Opening a fiduciary account requires evidence of the individual's appointment and authority. This usually comes from a court. Someone can't claim to be the executor for a deceased person without some proof. A court appointed guardian is another case where proof of capacity must be given. No documentation is required for an individual to open an UGMA or UTMA account.

An account for a trustee must include a trust agreement detailing the limitations placed on the fiduciary. Investments in a trust account should follow the directives of the trust document. Margin accounts are only permitted if authorized by the legal documents establishing the fiduciary accounts.

TAKE NOTE

This might not be on the exam, but you should know that fiduciaries are obligated to follow the Uniform Prudent Investor Act (UPIA). UPIA currently appears on some other exams so it may soon appear on the Series 7 Top-Off Exam.

PRACTICE QUESTION

12. Which of the following accounts could be opened without any legal documents?
    A. UTMA
    B. Trust
    C. Estate
    D. Pension plan

    Answer: A. Fiduciary accounts require legal documentation establishing the power of the fiduciary. There is an exception for UTMA and UGMA accounts.

Business Accounts

The documentation for business accounts is not a commonly tested item. Here are few points that might appear.

Corporate Accounts

A registered representative who opens a corporate account must establish

- the business's legal right to open an investment account;
- an indication of any limitations that the owners, the stockholders, a court, or any other entity has placed on the securities in which the business can invest; and
- who will represent the business in transactions involving the account.

When opening an account for a corporation, a firm must obtain a copy of the **corporate charter**, as well as a **corporate resolution**. The charter is proof that the corporation does exist, and the resolution authorizes both the opening of the account and the officers designated to enter orders.

Partnership Accounts

As covered earlier, some businesses are organized as partnerships. Partnerships frequently open cash, margin, retirement, and other types of accounts necessary for business purposes.

The partnership must complete a **partnership agreement** stating which of the partners can make transactions for the account. If the partnership opens a margin account, the partnership must disclose any investment limitations.

An amended partnership agreement must be obtained each year if changes have been made.

Sole Proprietorship Accounts

This is the simplest form of business organization and is opened like an individual account.

PRACTICE QUESTION

13. If Alpha Enterprises, Inc., wants to open a cash account, a firm must have all of the following documents on file **except**
    A. a hypothecation agreement.
    B. a new account form.
    C. a copy of the corporate charter.
    D. a copy of the corporate resolution.

Answer: A. A hypothecation agreement is only needed to open a margin account. Any cash account must have a new account form on file. For corporate account, the corporation's charter must be provided as proof that the corporation exists. In addition, a corporate resolution is needed to designate the officer(s) authorized to enter orders.

Numbered Accounts

If requested, a customer's account may be identified by only a multi-digit number or symbols. The customer must sign a form certifying that he owns the account(s) identified by the number or symbols. This is not like the old Swiss bank accounts use for tax avoidance. The tax reporting is done the same as any other account.

EXAMPLE

Celebrities sometimes use numbered accounts to preserve anonymity.

PART 2

Open Accounts After Obtaining and Evaluating Customers' Financial Profiles and Investment Objectives; Retirement Plans

Part 2 consists of 13 units:

Unit 3: Equity Securities

Unit 4: Debt Securities

Unit 5: Corporate Bonds

Unit 6: Municipal Bonds

Unit 7: U.S. Treasury and Government Agency Securities

Unit 8: Investment Companies

Unit 9: Insurance Company Products

Unit 10: Options

Unit 11: Other Packaged Products

Unit 12: Other Securities Products

Unit 13: Portfolio or Account Analysis and Its Application to Security Selection

Unit 14: Types of Risk and Required Disclosures

Unit 15: Handling Customer Accounts

In total, you will see 91 questions on material from Part 2, representing 73% of the Series 7 Top-Off Exam. This is referred to as Function 3 of the FINRA exam.

UNIT 3

Equity Securities

LEARNING OBJECTIVES

When you have completed this unit, you will be able to accomplish the following.

- › LO 3.a **Identify** the types of common stock.
- › LO 3.b **Name** the characteristics of common stock.
- › LO 3.c **Consider** the rights of a common stockholder.
- › LO 3.d **Evaluate** the risks of penny stocks.
- › LO 3.e **Name** the characteristics of preferred stock.
- › LO 3.f **Compare** rights and warrants.
- › LO 3.g **Describe** the types of non-U.S. market securities.
- › LO 3.h **Examine** the different market places for equity securities.
- › LO 3.i **Differentiate** between the different kinds of tax treatment of equity securities (e.g., qualified dividends).
- › LO 3.j **Determine** the rules and regulations pertaining to the sale of equity securities.

INTRODUCTION

An important part of a registered representative's work is to make suitable investment recommendations and provide appropriate information for the customer to use in making investment decisions. In the previous part, we discussed many of the suitability requirements. Those included information gathering and understanding goals and objective. The major emphasis of this part is identifying the investment products that fit the customer's needs. In doing so, the registered representative must also understand the various forms of investment risk and the relationship between risk and reward inherent in securities investment. Recognizing how to use this information is covered in this part and will include portfolio theory, fundamental analysis, and product selection based on objectives of the customer.

Most of Part 2 is about matching the right investment products to the customer's objectives. Registered representatives must also understand the various forms of investment risk. Following that will be the relationship between risk and reward inherent in securities investment.

A security is an investment that represents either an ownership stake or a debt stake. An investor becomes part owner in a corporation by buying shares of the company's stock. That is called having an **equity** position—the topic of this unit. A debt security (Unit 4), is usually acquired by buying an issuer's (company or government) bonds. A debt investment is a loan to the issuer in exchange for interest income and the promise to repay the loan at a future maturity date. It does not confer ownership (equity) as does the purchase of stock.

Investors become owners of a corporation by purchasing stock in that company. They can participate in the company's prosperity by sharing in earnings through the receipt of dividends. Common stock holders have the opportunity to benefit from an increase in the price of the shares.

LESSON 3.1: FUNDAMENTALS OF COMMON STOCK

LO 3.a Identify the types of common stock.

Origins of Common Stock

The two primary types of equity securities are common and preferred stocks (covered in Lesson 3.2). These are considered ownership positions in a corporation. All corporations issue common stock. Each share of common stock entitles its owner to a portion of the company's profits and dividends and an equal vote on directors and other important matters. Most corporations are organized in such a way that their common stockholders regularly vote for and elect candidates to a board of directors (BOD) to oversee the company's business. By electing a BOD, stockholders have some say in the company's management but are not involved with the day-to-day details of its operations.

TAKE NOTE

An individual's common stock ownership represents her proportionate interest in a company. If a company issues 100 shares of stock, each share represents an identical 1/100, or 1%, ownership position in the company. A person who owns 10 shares of stock owns 10% of the company; a person who owns 50 shares of stock owns 50% of the company.

Common stock can be classified as

- authorized,
- issued,
- outstanding, or
- treasury.

Authorized Stock

A corporation is a legal being. Corporations are formed through the preparation of a corporate charter. In many respects, corporations can do the same things as a natural person. One of those things is opening a brokerage account as we noted in Part 1. What a corporation can do that individuals can't is raise money by issuing securities. The corporate charter specifies the number of shares the company is authorized to issue. It is a decision made by the founders of the business.

In most cases, a company does not issue all of the authorized shares. It issues enough of them to raise sufficient capital for its expected needs. The company may sell the remaining authorized shares in the future or use them for other purposes. If the company wants to issue more shares than are authorized, the charter must be amended through a stockholder vote.

Issued Stock

Issued stock is authorized stock that has been sold to investors. Those investors have bought the stock and the company has received the money. When a corporation issues or sells fewer shares than the total number authorized, it normally reserves the unissued shares for future needs, including

- raising new capital for expansion,
- paying stock dividends, or
- exchanging common stock for outstanding convertible bonds or preferred stock.

Authorized but unissued stock does not carry the rights and privileges of issued shares and is not considered in determining a company's total capitalization. Authorized but unissued stock is similar to the blank checks in your check book. They're ready to use when needed. Until then, they are just pieces of paper.

Outstanding Stock

Outstanding stock includes any shares that a company has issued and are in the hands of investors. Isn't all issued stock outstanding? Sometimes it is, but other times it is not. As we will read next, sometimes a corporation buys back its outstanding stock. Sometimes, owners of the stock will donate it to the company. However the company gets it back, that stock is no longer outstanding.

Treasury Stock

Treasury stock is stock a corporation has issued and subsequently reacquired. The corporation can hold this stock indefinitely or can reissue or retire it. Treasury stock does not carry the rights of outstanding common shares, such as voting rights and the right to receive dividends. For that reason, analysts are only concerned with outstanding shares.

TEST TOPIC ALERT

Expect to see a question on outstanding stock similar to the following.

ABC Company has authorized 1 million shares of common stock. It issued 800,000 shares one year ago. It then purchased 200,000 shares for its treasury. How many shares of ABC stock are outstanding?

The solution requires that you know a basic formula:

issued stock – treasury stock = outstanding stock

In applying this formula to our sample question, the solution is as follows:

800,000 – 200,000 = 600,000

Alternatively, treasury stock equals issued shares minus outstanding shares.

TAKE NOTE

This question illustrates a point about FINRA exams. The question provided information about the number of shares of authorized stock, but that information was not necessary for you to solve the problem. Prepare for questions that give you more information than you need. The Series 7 exam expects you to know concepts so well that you can determine both what is and what is not essential to the solution of a problem.

PRACTICE QUESTION

1. ABC Company has authorized 1 million shares of common stock. It issued 800,000 shares one year ago. It then purchased 200,000 shares for its treasury. How many shares of ABC stock are outstanding?
   A. 200,000
   B. 600,000
   C. 800,000
   D. 1 million

   Answer: B. The solution requires you to know a basic formula:

   issued stock – treasury stock = outstanding stock

Thus, 800,000 – 200,000 = 600,000.

ABC Company has 600,000 shares of common stock outstanding.

This question illustrates another point about FINRA exams. The question gives the number of shares of authorized stock, but this information is unnecessary.

LO 3.b Name the characteristics of common stock.

Common Stock Characteristics

Limited Liability

Stockholders cannot lose more than the amount they have invested to buy the stock. Those who own stock in a corporation cannot be held liable for the company's debts. That means if the business goes bankrupt, the creditors cannot come after the shareholders. That is the concept behind limited liability.

Residual Claims to Assets

If a corporation is liquidated, the common stockholder has a **residual right to claim** corporate assets. This means they come after all debts and other security holders have been satisfied. The common stockholder has the last claim (if there is anything left). Maybe that is why it is compared to the residue.

TAKE NOTE

Because common stock is last in line in a corporate liquidation, it is known as the most junior security.

Stock Splits

Investors and company executives are generally happy to see a company's stock price rise. However, a high market price may scare away investors. To make the stock price attractive to a wider base of investors—that is, small versus institutional investors—the company can declare a **stock split**.

A **forward stock split** increases the number of shares. This reduces the price without affecting the total market value of shares outstanding. An investor will receive more shares, but the value of each share is reduced. The total market value of the ownership interest is the same before and after the split. Think of a 2-for-1 stock split as nothing other than changing a $10 bill for two $5s. You have twice as many bills, but each is worth half of the previous bill.

TAKE NOTE

For an investor who owns 100 shares valued at $20 per share

- a 2:1 stock split results in that investor owning 200 shares at $10 per share; and
- the value of the investment does not change—before and after the split the value is $2,000.

To determine the number of shares after a split, multiply the number of shares owned by the first number of the split and then divide by the second number (2:1).

A **reverse split** has the opposite effect on the number and price of shares. After a reverse split, investors own fewer shares worth more per share. In the earlier example, a 1:2 reverse split would mean 50 shares at $40 each. Once again, the total value is unchanged at $2,000.

Stock Dividends

Do not confuse a stock dividend with a stock split. One option a corporation has is to pay common stockholders a dividend in additional shares of the stock. This saves the cash that would be used in a normal dividend while giving stockholders something at no cost. For example, if an investor owned 100 shares of the stock and the company declared a 20% stock dividend, that investor would receive 20 additional shares, bringing the total holding up to 120 shares. Just as with the stock split, there is no real change to the overall value. The market price of the stock drops. For example, if the stock was selling at $60 per share before the dividend, it would now be selling at $50. Check the math. Divide $60 by 120% and you get $50. The investor had 100 shares worth $6,000. The investor now has 120 shares at $50, or $6,000. There are important tax issues we will cover later in this unit.

Transferability

In almost all cases, shares of stock are freely transferrable. That means that shareholders do not need the permission of the issuer—or anyone else—to sell their stock in the open market. This is especially true in the case of shares traded on the major stock exchanges. This means that stock has good liquidity. Liquidity is the ability to get your money quickly at a fair price. One exception is restricted stock, where sales are contingent upon meeting the requirements of SEC Rule 144. Restricted stock will be covered in Unit 20.

PRACTICE QUESTION

2. An investor owning 400 shares of XYZ notices that the company will be engaging in a 3:2 stock split. As a result of this action, the investor will receive how many additional shares?
   A. 100
   B. 200
   C. 400
   D. 600

   Answer: B. This split will increase the shareholder's position by a ratio of 3 to 2. That means, after the split, the investor will own 600 shares (400 × 3/2 or 400 × 3 divided by 2). If the investor currently has 400 shares and will have 600 after the split, it means the XYZ will send this shareholder 200 additional shares. More than half of our students answer 600—that is the total, but not the additional. You have to read the questions carefully.

LO 3.c Consider the rights of a common stockholder.

Rights of Common Stock Ownership

Stockholders are owners of a company and therefore have certain rights that protect their ownership interests.

Voting Rights

As mentioned earlier, common stockholders have the right to vote. Early in this unit, we mentioned the vote for the BOD. There are other issues that can be the subject of a shareholder vote. Voting generally takes place at the company's annual meeting and could include such topics as

- issuance of convertible securities or additional common stock;
- substantial changes in the corporation's business, such as mergers or acquisitions; and
- declarations of stock splits (forward and reverse).

You probably won't have to know the reason, but here is why they get to vote on issuing convertible securities. As we will discuss in Unit 5, a convertible security gives the owner the right to swap that security for common shares of the issuer. When that happens, there are more shares outstanding (those authorized but unissued shares or treasury stock are used). The company is no larger, but the "pie" is split into more "pieces." This is a concept known as dilution. You see that happen when you put some ice cubes into a drink and come back later, after they've melted. The drink has been diluted.

Calculating the Number of Votes

A stockholder can cast one vote for each share of stock owned. Depending on the company's bylaws and applicable state laws, a stockholder may have either a statutory or cumulative vote.

- **Statutory voting.** Statutory voting allows a stockholder to cast one vote per share owned for each item on a ballot, such as candidates for the BOD. A board candidate needs a simple majority to be elected.
- **Cumulative voting.** Cumulative voting allows stockholders to allocate their total votes in any manner they choose.

EXAMPLE

XYZ Corporation will be electing three directors at its annual meeting. Each XYZ shareholder has a number of votes equal to the number of shares owned times the number of directorships up for election. Assume a shareholder owns 100 shares. Under statutory voting, the shareholder may use a maximum of 100 votes for any one seat on the board.

Under cumulative voting, the shareholder may allocate all 300 votes to one director, giving the shareholder a greater impact.

Statutory vs. Cumulative Voting

Example One: Mr. X Owns 100 Shares

Statutory Voting	
BOD Seat 1	100
BOD Seat 2	100
BOD Seat 3	100

Example Two: Mr. X Owns 100 Shares

Cumulative Voting	
BOD Seat 1	175
BOD Seat 2	50
BOD Seat 3	75

OR

Cumulative Voting	
BOD Seat 1	300
BOD Seat 2	0
BOD Seat 3	0

TAKE NOTE

Cumulative voting benefits the smaller investor, whereas statutory voting benefits larger shareholders.

TEST TOPIC ALERT

Shareholders do not vote on dividend-related matters, such as when they are declared and how much they will be. They do vote on stock splits, board members, and issuance of additional equity-related securities such as common stock, preferred stock, and convertible securities.

Proxies

Stockholders often find it difficult to attend the annual stockholders' meeting, so most vote on company matters by means of a **proxy**, a form of an absentee ballot. After it has been returned to the company, a proxy can be automatically canceled if the stockholder attends the meeting, authorizes a subsequent proxy, or dies. When a company sends proxies to shareholders, usually for a specific meeting, it is known as a proxy solicitation. A stockholder may revoke a proxy at any time before the company tabulates the final vote at its annual meeting.

Nonvoting Common Stock

Companies may issue both voting and nonvoting (or limited voting) common stock, normally differentiating the issues as Class A and Class B, respectively. Issuing nonvoting stock allows a company to raise additional capital while maintaining management control and continuity without diluting voting power.

Preemptive Rights

When a corporation raises capital through the sale of additional common stock, it may be required by law or its corporate charter to offer the securities to its common stockholders before the general public. This is known as an anti-dilution provision. Stockholders then have a **preemptive right** to purchase enough newly issued shares to maintain their proportionate ownership in the corporation.

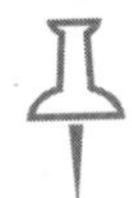

TAKE NOTE

Preemptive rights give investors the right to maintain a proportionate interest in a company's stock.

EXAMPLE

ABC has 1 million shares of common stock outstanding. Grace Billings owns 100,000 shares of ABC common stock, or 10%. If ABC issues an additional 500,000 shares, Billings will have the opportunity to purchase 50,000 of those shares. If Billings decides to exercise the rights, her proportionate ownerships remains the same. It not, she will own a lower percentage. We say that her interest in the company is *diluted* (weakened).

	Original		New		
ABC:	1 million shares	+	500,000	=	1.5 million shares
Billings:	100,000 shares	+	50,000	=	150,000 shares
	10%		10%		10%

Inspection of Corporate Books

Stockholders have the right to receive annual financial statements and obtain lists of stockholders. **Inspection rights** do not include the right to examine detailed financial records or the minutes of BOD meetings.

LESSON 3.2 OTHER EQUITY SECURITIES

LO 3.e Name the characteristics of preferred stock.

As mentioned earlier, the two basic forms of ownership in a company are common and preferred stock. We've already covered common stock. Now, it is time to learn about preferred stock.

Preferred Stock

Preferred stock represents ownership, (equity), in the corporation. However, it does not normally offer the appreciation potential associated with common stock. Not all corporations issue preferred stock.

For test purposes, **preferred stock** is always issued with a fixed (stated) rate of return. That fixed return is a fixed dividend that is being paid. As such, these securities are generally purchased for income. Although the dividend of most preferred stocks is fixed, some are issued with a variable dividend payout known as *adjustable-rate preferred stock*. Like other fixed-income assets such as bonds, preferred stock prices tend to move inversely with interest rates. On the exam, preferred stock is nonvoting.

Preferred stock does not typically have the same growth potential as common stock. That makes it subject to inflation risk. However, preferred stockholders generally have two advantages over common stockholders:

- When the BOD declares dividends, owners of preferred stock must receive their stated dividend in full before common stockholders may receive a dividend.
- If a corporation goes bankrupt, preferred stockholders have a priority claim over common stockholders on the assets remaining after creditors have been paid.

Because of these features, preferred stock appeals to investors seeking income and safety. Following are some of the key characteristics of preferred stock.

TAKE NOTE

Preferred stock has preference over common stock in payment of dividends and in claim to assets in the event the issuing corporation goes bankrupt. However, preferred stock does not get to vote.

Fixed Rate of Return

Preferred stock's **fixed dividend** is a key attraction for income-oriented investors. Normally, a preferred stock is identified by its annual dividend payment stated as a percentage of its par value. A preferred stock with a par value of $100 that pays $6 in annual dividends is known as a 6% preferred. Or the dividend could just be stated as an annual amount. In the earlier example, it would be known as a $6 preferred. If the stock had a $25 par value with a 4% dividend rate, the dividend would be $1.00. This could also be referred to as a $1.00 preferred. On the exam, assume all dividends are paid quarterly. On the $6 preferred, that would be 4 dividends of $150. On the $25 par, 4% stock, that would be 4 dividends of $0.25.

One important point about these dividends is that, just as with common stock, there is no obligation for them to be paid. This is not a debt security where interest payments are required. It takes a vote of the BOD for the dividend to be declared. What is true is that the dividend is fixed and it must be paid before common.

The stated rate of dividend payment causes the market price of preferred stock to move opposite changes in interest rates. That is, as interest rates climb, the prices of preferred stocks decline. The reverse is true when interest rates go down. If preferred stock pays dividends, not interest, why should changes to interest rates have any impact on the preferred? We'll address that in greater detail in Unit 14. The fixed dividend on preferred stock provides a fixed income in the same way as interest paid on a bond. Regardless of the source, (dividend or interest), investors demand a return comparable to current rates in the market. For the moment, perhaps the following example will make some sense.

EXAMPLE

Consider a 6% preferred. If the stock has a par value of $100, that is $6 per year. If interest rates are at 8% and you want to sell your preferred, you will not be able to get $100 for it. Why not? Why would an investor settle for a 6% return when an 8% return is the current standard? You would only be able to get about $75 for the stock. Why $75? Because a $6 dividend (remember, the amount of the dividend is fixed) on an investment of $75 equals a return of 8%. If interest rates fall to 4%, the 6% preferred will trade at a premium. Because it is offering a stream of income above the current market rate, it will command a higher price. In this case, the price would likely be $150. Check the math: $6 on an investment of $150 = 4% (6 divided by 150).

TEST TOPIC ALERT

Preferred stock represents ownership in a company like common stock, but its price is sensitive to interest rates—just like the price of a bond.

Although it is a fixed-income investment, preferred stock, unlike bonds, has no preset date at which it matures and no scheduled redemption date or maturity value.

Categories of Preferred Stock

There are several different types of preferred stock starting with straight preferred (think of *plain vanilla*). From there, it can expand, depending on which and how many adjectives we use to describe the security. However, all maintain preference over common stock. Preferred stock may have one or more of the following characteristics.

Straight (Noncumulative)

Straight preferred has no special features beyond the stated dividend payment. The year's stated dividend must be paid on straight preferred if any dividend is to be paid to common shareholders. If the company can only pay part, or none of the dividend this year, it does not have to be made up in future years. Using our $6 preferred, any payment less than $6 for the year is forever gone. In this case, obviously, nothing can be paid to the common.

TAKE NOTE

Preferred stock with no special features is known as straight preferred.

Cumulative Preferred

Buyers of preferred stock expect fixed dividend payments. We just gave an example of a company where the dividend was paid in part or skipped completely. With **cumulative preferred**, any dividends skipped must be paid before paying a common dividend. The technical term for missed dividends is dividends in *arrears*.

TAKE NOTE

Any special feature attached to preferred, such as a cumulative feature, has a price. The cost for such a benefit is less dividend income. Cumulative preferred typically has a lower stated dividend than straight preferred (less risk equals less reward).

The company keeps records of the skipped dividends. When the time comes that it is able to pay, all of the arrearage (the dividends in arrears) are paid to holders of cumulative preferred. Not only that, but the current dividend must be paid as well if the company wishes to pay a dividend on the common. For those seeking income, cumulative is safer than straight. That is why the dividend rate is somewhat lower. As we said, it is the risk/reward concept.

EXAMPLE

RST Corporation has both common stock and cumulative preferred stock outstanding.

Its preferred stock has a stated dividend rate of 5% (par value $100). Because of financial difficulties, no dividend was paid on the preferred stock last year or the year before. RST wishes to declare a dividend on its common stock this year. RST must first pay how much in dividends to the cumulative preferred shareholders?

RST must pay missed dividends to cumulative preferred (as well as the current dividend) before dividends are paid on common stock. RST must pay $5 for two years ago, $5 for last year, and $5 for this year, for a total of $15.

If this had been a straight preferred, the answer would have been $5. Only the current year's dividend would need payment before common because straight preferred is not entitled to dividends in arrears.

Convertible Preferred

A convertible preferred gives the owner the right to exchange each preferred share for shares of common stock. The conversion rate is fixed at the time of issue. It may be shown as the number of shares, such as convertible into four shares. Or, it may be shown as the price at which the investor can convert. You divide the par value by the conversion price to see the number of shares of common.

The convertible feature results in these shares having a lower dividend rate. Why is that? Because the ability to convert a preferred into common stock offers growth potential not otherwise available to a preferred stockholder. This feature causes the stock's price to track that of the common. That results in convertible preferred stock having less interest-rate risk than the others. When the underlying common stock has the same value as the convertible preferred, it is said to be at its *parity price*. This concept will be covered in detail in Unit 5.

EXAMPLE

XYZ Company's convertible preferred stock, with a par value of $100. The conversion price is $20. That means it can be exchanged for five shares of XYZ common stock ($100 ÷ $20 = 5). This is true, no matter what the current market value is of either the preferred or the common stock. Assume an investor bought the preferred for $100 per share. Sometime later, the common stock rises in price to $25 per share. Converting would give the investor 5 shares at $25. That represents a profit of $25 stemming from the conversion feature.

Participating Preferred

Like other preferred stock, there is a fixed dividend. In addition, **participating preferred** stock is eligible to receive a percentage of the common dividend. The maximum percentage is stated when the stock is issued. Before the participating dividend can be paid, a common dividend must be declared. How else could they participate?

EXAMPLE

A preferred stock is described as "XYZ 6% preferred participating to 50%." In addition to the fixed dividend, the company could pay holders of this stock up to 50% of the common dividend.

Callable Preferred

Corporations often issue **callable preferred or redeemable preferred**. This means the company can buy back the stock from investors at a stated price on the call date or any date thereafter. The call feature would most likely be used when interest rates decline. They could issue a new preferred with a lower dividend and use that money to call in the old stock. In that way, it is similar to refinancing a loan when interest rates go down. We'll discuss that more in Unit 5.

When a corporation calls a preferred stock, that stock basically ceases to exist. Dividend payments and conversion rights end on the call date. In most cases, the call price is a bit higher than the par value. An example could be $103 for a $100 par value stock. The extra money is to compensate the investors for having to look for a new investment.

TAKE NOTE

A risk in buying callable preferred stock is that the issuer may decide to redeem it. That ends dividend payments. We already mentioned that the call price is higher than the par value. This helps ease the pain of having to look for another stock. Another benefit is that callable preferred generally has a higher dividend rate than straight, noncallable preferred.

Adjustable-Rate Preferred

Some preferred stocks are issued with **adjustable/variable dividend rates**. The adjustment is made based on a chosen standard. The interest rate on U.S. government Treasury bills is one frequently used. These adjustments are generally done quarterly. The advantage to an adjustable-rate preferred stock is that it does not have the interest-rate risk of other fixed-income securities. This is because its income isn't really fixed. When interest rates go up, so does the dividend.

PRACTICE QUESTION

3. The BOD of DDC omitted dividends in 2017 on their $100 par 6% noncumulative preferred stock. In 2018, a $2 preferred dividend was paid. For DDC, 2019 has been a good year, and the board wishes to pay a common dividend. How much must be paid per share on the preferred for 2019 to pay a common dividend?
   A. $6
   B. $8
   C. $12
   D. $16

   Answer: A. A 6% dividend on a $100 par means a $6 dividend per share each year. Because this preferred stock is noncumulative, any missed dividends do not have to be paid before common dividends can be declared. If this were a cumulative issue, any dividends not fully paid would go into arrears and accumulate until paid to the preferred cumulative stockholder. During this time, common dividends cannot be declared or paid until the cumulative holders receive their full dividend amount.

4. Which of the following choices would be a suitable recommendation for an investor who likes a fixed dividend but also would like to take advantage of capital appreciation if the company's common stock rises?
   A. Cumulative preferred stock
   B. Convertible preferred stock
   C. Adjustable-rate preferred stock
   D. Participating preferred stock

Answer: B. Convertible preferred stock has a fixed-stated dividend and can be converted to the company common stock if the price of the common stock appreciates. Participating preferred stock might have an increased dividend, but no capital appreciation. The dividend on adjustable-rate preferred will change, usually semiannually. That would not meet the needs of a client who wants a fixed dividend.

LO 3.f Compare rights and warrants.

Preemptive Rights

Existing stockholders have **preemptive rights** or **stock rights.** These entitle them to maintain their proportionate ownership in a company. This is done by giving them the right to buy newly issued shares before the company offers them to the public. A **rights offering** allows stockholders to purchase common stock below the current market price. The rights are valued separately from the stock, and trade in the secondary market during the subscription period.

Although referred to as an equity security, these rights are not ownership. Only when exercised does the investor have more shares. Just like any other shares, they have voting and dividend rights. Remember that rights themselves do not pay dividends and do not vote.

A stockholder who receives rights may

- exercise the rights to buy stock by sending the rights certificates and a check for the required amount to the rights agent,
- sell the rights and profit from their market value (rights certificates are negotiable securities), or
- let the rights expire and lose their value.

Shareholders who do not wish to exercise their rights will find an active secondary market for them. Those rights generally trade on the same stock market as the common stock. Shortly, we will show you how to compute their value.

Subscription Right Certificate

A **subscription right** is a certificate representing the privilege to buy additional shares of a corporation. The corporation sends this certificate to each common stockholder. The certificate grants one right for each share of common stock they own. These rights have a short lifespan. Most rights expire within 30–45 days of issue. As you will see in our examples, it usually takes more than one right to buy one share of the new stock.

Terms of the Offering

Described in the subscription right certificate are the terms of the offering. These terms would include the number of new shares a stockholder may buy and the subscription (exercise) price. The final date for exercising the rights is shown and, in many cases, the date the new shares will be issued.

EXAMPLE

ABC Company plans to raise capital by issuing additional stock and, on April 1, declares a rights offering. Common stockholders as of May 1, the record date, can subscribe to one new share, at a price of $30, for each 10 shares of stock they own. ABC stock is currently trading at $41 per share. The rights will expire on June 18.

The corporation will issue rights to stockholders of record May 1. That means their names on the company's records as shareholders.

The common stock trades *cum* (with) rights until the *ex-* (without) date. The ex-date is the first day it is too late for investors to buy the stock and get their names on the company's records. It is generally one business day before the record date (the day the company makes the list of owners). In this case, the ex-date would be April 30. As we will cover in detail in Unit 17, it takes two business days to get your name on the company's books. An investor who buys stock **cum rights** receives the right. An investor who buys stock **ex-rights** does not.

The number of rights required to buy one new share is based on the number of shares outstanding and the number of new shares offered.

EXAMPLE

ABC will be issuing 1 million new shares. ABC has 10 million shares currently outstanding. Each share is entitled to one right. That means 10 million rights will be issued. How many rights will it take to buy one share? The math is simple. With 10 million rights to buy 1 million shares, a shareholder will need 10 rights to buy one share. We divided 10 million by 1 million to get our answer. If our example said ABC is issuing 2 million shares, how many rights would it take to buy one share? Five, because 10 million divided by two equals five.

TEST TOPIC ALERT

Many investors prefer to sell their rights rather than exercise them. Because those rights enable the holder to buy the stock at a price below the current market, they have a value. The exam may ask you to compute the theoretical value of a right. It makes a difference if it is trading cum rights or ex-rights. Let's use a case where the value is computed cum rights. Consider the following: ABC's price per share is $41; the subscription per share is $30. Ten rights are needed to purchase one share of stock. We compute the value of one right as follows:

$$\frac{\text{market price} - \text{subscription price}}{\text{number of rights to purchase 1 share} + 1}$$

$$\frac{41 - 30}{10 + 1} = \frac{11}{11} = \$1$$

On the morning of the ex-date, the market price typically drops by the value of the right. Use the ex-rights formula to determine the value of a right after the ex-date. The ex-rights formula is:

$$\frac{\text{market price} - \text{subscription price}}{\text{number of rights to purchase 1 share}}$$

TAKE NOTE

In dealing with any question on the value of a right, you will not have to adjust market price. The questions deal only with the value of the right. That makes your only decision whether to divide MP – SP by N or N + 1. The easy way to remember is this: When the question asks for the value of a right before the ex-date (cum rights), the formula is *with* 1. If it ask for the value of a right on or after the ex-date, it is *without* the 1.

Stand By Underwriter

What happens when some of the shareholders fail to exercise their rights? Perhaps they let them lapse, or maybe they didn't understand what the right was about. Maybe they just didn't have the money to exercise, or maybe they just ignored the mail carrying the notice.

In Unit 20, we will discuss the various methods of bringing a new issue to the public. Part of the discussion is the role of the investment banker or underwriter who assists the issuer. When it comes to a rights offering, there is a special role that is played by the broker-dealer serving as the underwriter of the offering. That is the role of the stand by underwriter.

When a company's current stockholders do not exercise their preemptive rights in an additional offering, a corporation has an underwriter **standing by** to purchase whatever shares remain unsold as a result of rights expiring.

Because the standby underwriter unconditionally agrees to buy all shares that current stockholders do not subscribe to at the subscription price, the offering is a firm commitment.

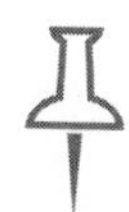

TAKE NOTE

By engaging a standby underwriter, an issuer is assured of selling all the shares being offered.

Warrants

A **warrant** is a certificate granting its owner the right to purchase securities from the issuer at a specified price. Warrants are sometimes confused with rights. We'll take a look at some of the differences and similarities.

Unlike a right, a warrant is always a long-term instrument. There is no standard length, but they generally have an expiration date at least two years after issue. A more typical length is five years. In some cases, the expiration date is much longer than that. In fact, years ago, a few companies issued perpetual warrants. Those never expire.

Unlike rights, the purchase price is always higher than the current market price on the date of issue of the warrant.

EXAMPLE

The ABC Corporation issues warrants to purchase shares of its common stock. Each warrant allows the holder to purchase $100 shares. The exercise price is $30 per share while the current market price is $25 per share.

As with rights, although referred to as an equity security, these warrants are not ownership. Only when exercised does the investor have more shares. Just like any other shares, they have voting and dividend rights. Remember that warrants themselves do not pay dividends and do not vote.

Origination of Warrants

Warrants are usually offered to the public as **sweeteners**, or inducements, in connection with an offering of other securities, such as bonds or preferred stock. This makes those securities more attractive. Most investors like the fact that they have a chance to benefit from an increase in the price of the company's stock. This attractiveness enables the issuer to reduce the interest cost of debt or the fixed dividend of preferred stock. Such offerings are often bundled as **units**.

After issuance, the warrants are detachable and may trade separately from the bond or preferred stock. When first issued, a warrant's exercise price is set somewhat above the stock's market price. If the stock's price increases above the exercise price, the owner can exercise the warrant and buy the stock below the market price or sell the warrant in the market. A logical question is, "why would anyone be interested in a warrant enabling a purchase of the underlying stock at a price above the current market?" Remember, warrants have a typical life of five years or even longer. When we cover options, you will learn about time value. In five years, a stock's market price could increase substantially, making that warrant quite valuable.

The following chart summarizes the key testable points about these securities.

Rights	**Warrants**
Short-term	Long-term
On issuance, exercise price below market price	On issuance, exercise price higher than market price
May trade with or separate from the common stock	May trade with or separate from the units
Offered to existing shareholders with preemptive rights	Offered as a sweetener for another security

PRACTICE QUESTION

5. Rank the following securities from the same issuer from most suitable to least suitable for a client whose primary objective is income with relative safety.
   I. Cumulative preferred stock
   II. Convertible preferred stock
   III. Common stock
   IV. Warrant
   A. I, II, III, IV
   B. I, III, II, IV
   C. III, I, IV, II
   D. II, III, IV, I

Answer: A. For a client seeking income with some safety, preferred stock—especially one that is cumulative—would be the most suitable of the choices given. Convertible preferred stock generally pays a lower dividend rate than other preferred stocks. This is because of the attractiveness of the convertibility. Although there are some categories of common stock (e.g., utility stocks that pay liberal dividends), unless specifically mentioned, you can assume that preferred stock dividends are higher than those for common stock of the same issuer. Warrants (and rights) never provide any income.

LO 3.g Describe the types of non-U.S. market securities.

American Depositary Receipts (ADRs)

An American depositary receipt (ADR) is simply a receipt for shares of a foreign stock deposited with a custodian. In that respect, it is similar to a stock certificate. The stock certificate shows ownership in a company's stock. The ADR shows ownership in the deposited security. Each ADR represents a specific number of shares in a foreign company held by a custodian. That custodian is typically a bank in that company's country. The stock must remain on deposit as long as the ADRs are outstanding. That is because the ADRs are the depositary bank's guarantee that it holds the stock.

ADRs are securities that trade on the U.S. securities markets. ADRs are in English and trade in U.S. dollars.

Rights of ADR Owners

ADR owners have most of the rights common stockholders normally hold. These include the right to receive dividends when declared. Most important, those dividends are in U.S. dollars. That simplifies things for the investor. It is much easier to deposit a dollar check than to have to worry about converting currency.

Generally, ADRs do not have voting rights, though some ADR issuers will pass on voting rights to the holders of ADRs. As for preemptive rights, the issuing bank sells off the rights and distributes the proceeds pro rata to holders. That point is unlikely to be tested.

PRACTICE QUESTION

6. An ADR represents
   A. a U.S. security trading in a foreign market.
   B. a foreign security trading in the United States.
   C. a U.S. security trading in both the United States and a foreign market.
   D. a foreign security trading in both the United States and a foreign market.

   Answer: A. ADR stands for American depositary receipt. ADRs are receipts issued by U.S. banks. They represent ownership of a foreign security and trade in the U.S. securities markets.

Delivery of Foreign Security

ADR owners have the right to exchange their ADR certificates for the foreign shares they represent. They can do this by returning the ADRs to the depositary banks, which cancel the ADRs and deliver the underlying stock. This is rarely done, but is an option available for the ADR holder.

Taxes on ADRs

In most countries, a withholding tax on dividends is taken at the source. In the case of investors holding ADRs, this would be a foreign income tax. The foreign income tax may be taken as a credit against any U.S. income taxes owed by the investor.

Currency Risk

In addition to the normal risks associated with stock ownership, ADR investors are subject to **currency risk**. We will cover that risk in more detail in Unit 14. Simply, the foreign company is paying dividends in its local currency. If that currency drops in value compared to the U.S. dollar, the investor receives less money, even if the dividend stays level. The same is true with the market value of the stock. The stock's price can go up in its local market, but, if the value of that currency falls, the ADR investor's value can go down.

TAKE NOTE

The custodian holding the actual shares receives dividends in the foreign currency. It then converts them to U.S. dollars. This leads to potential currency risk. Because ADRs originate outside the United States, they are also subject to political risk.

Registered Owner

ADRs are registered on the books of the U.S. banks responsible for them. The individual investors in the ADRs are not considered the stock's registered owners. ADRs are registered on the books of U.S. banks, so dividends are sent to the custodian banks as registered owners. The banks collect the payments and convert them into U.S. dollars.

Sponsored ADRs

All exchange-listed ADRs are sponsored—that is, the foreign company sponsors the issue to increase its ownership base. Issuers that sponsor ADRs provide holders with financial statements in English. Sponsored ADRs are sometimes referred to as American depositary shares (ADS). For exam purposes, we do not expect you to have to know the subtle difference between an ADR and an ADS. Nonsponsored ADRs are issued by banks without the assistance and participation of the issuer.

LESSON 3.3 TRADING PLACES

LO 3.h Examine the different market places for equity securities.

No, we are not talking about the wonderful movie of the same name. There are two terms used to describe the marketplace for securities. The **primary market** is the market in which the proceeds of sales go to the issuer of the securities sold. That is generally called the *new issues market* and will be covered in Unit 20. The **secondary market** is where previously issued securities are bought and sold. This unit will focus on secondary market trading of equity securities.

TAKE NOTE

The Securities Act of 1933 regulates activity in the primary market. That is, the market place for new issues. The Securities Exchange Act of 1934 regulates the activity in the secondary market. That is, the buying and selling of securities once they have been distributed in the primary market. Most of our discussion in this course will be about the secondary market. It is important to recognize that the SEC, under the powers granted in the Exchange Act, aims to protect investors by regulating the exchanges, the over-the-counter market, the extension of credit by the Federal Reserve Board, broker-dealers and their registered representative, insider transactions, trading activities, client accounts, and financial requirements.

Stock Exchanges

After the initial offering, many stocks are bought and sold on exchanges in a two-way auction process. The major exchanges include the New York Stock Exchange (NYSE), NYSE American LLC (formerly known as the American Stock Exchange (AMEX)), the Chicago Board Options Exchange (CBOE), and the Nasdaq Stock Market. Other trades take place in the nationwide network of broker-dealers known as the over-the-counter (OTC) market.

The **exchange market** is composed of the NYSE and other exchanges on which **listed** securities are traded. *Listed security* refers to any security that is bought and sold on an exchange. Each stock exchange requires corporations to meet certain standards before it will allow their stock to be listed for trading on the exchange. Listing requirements are not tested. Those of the NYSE are the most stringent. In terms of dollar volume, trading on the exchanges dwarfs that of the OTC markets. Many of the stocks listed on the NYSE are considered "blue-chips." The term refers to the common stock of well-known companies with a history of growth and dividend payments. A typical example would be those found in the Dow Jones 30 Industrials.

The Securities Exchange Act of 1934 requires registration of an exchange with the SEC. Under that act, the SEC has many powers including enforcement of the laws.

Historically, stock exchanges had physical trading floors. For the most part, with the notable exception of the NYSE, today's stock exchange is an electronic market. The Nasdaq Stock Market is the best example of an electronic stock exchange.

As of the date of this printing, there are 21 exchanges registered as national stock exchanges with the SEC. At one time, there some regional stock exchanges, but they have either been closed or merged into the national ones.

Historically, stock exchanges operated as **auction** markets. That is the correct answer to a possible test question. Floor brokers competed to execute trades at the most favorable prices. That process still exists on some exchanges. The designated market maker, (DMM), formerly called the specialist, conducts the auction. We will discuss this in more detail in Unit 17.

The Over-the-Counter Market (OTC)

In terms of the number of securities traded, the OTC market is the largest in the U.S. The OTC market functions as an interdealer market in which **unlisted securities**—that is, securities not listed on any exchange—trade.

In the OTC market, computers and telephones connect securities dealers across the country. Thousands of securities are traded OTC, including stocks, corporate bonds, and all municipal and U.S. government securities. One of the best known of the OTC markets is the OTC Bulletin Board where stocks that do not qualify for listing on the exchanges are traded. Another is the OTC Link, which for many years was known as the *Pink Sheets* because the quotes were printed on pink colored paper. In general, the OTC Link stocks do not trade very often. We say they are *thinly traded* stocks. Like securities traded on the exchange, these are registered with the SEC, but tend to be on the highly speculative side. In a later unit, we will learn that these stocks are not eligible for margin trading.

Unlike the NYSE, the OTC market has no central marketplace. Trading takes place over the phone, over computer networks, and in trading rooms across the country. The OTC market is an **interdealer network**. While the NYSE has the DMM to facilitate trading on the floor, the OTC market has market makers. A market maker chooses to "deal" in selected OTC stocks. This is similar in concept to an auto dealer choosing to deal in certain brands.

Just as the auto dealer maintains an inventory of that brand to sell, the market maker has its selected stocks in its inventory. Just as auto dealers are willing to buy your old car, market makers are ready to buy shares of those stocks. Just as auto dealers compete to advertise the best prices, market makers compete to post the best prices at which they are ready to buy or sell those stocks. We will cover the details of how they work in Unit 17. The correct answer to a possible test question is that the OTC market is a *negotiated* market.

Electronic Communications Network (ECN)

Technology has made many advances in the securities industry. One area of the OTC market is the electronic system known as an electronic communications network (ECN). Broker-dealers can send an order through an ECN instead of going through a market maker. An ECN is an electronic trading system that automatically matches buy and sell orders at specified prices. ECNs are SEC-sanctioned alternative trading systems (ATS). They are open 24 hours a day. There is no inventory; the ECN matches buy and sell orders as agents, not as principals. Extended hours orders are handled by ECNs.

Throughout the history of trading securities in the United States, the NYSE set the standards. Normal trading times were from 9:30 am until 4:00 pm ET Monday–Friday. However, in the latter part of the 20th century, the demand for after-hours trading grew. Now, after the closing bell, ECNs make it easy for both institutional and individual investors to trade anytime.

Dark Pools

Dark pools, sometimes referred to as *dark pools of liquidity*, is trading volume that occurs that is not openly available to the public. The bulk of this volume represents large trades engaged in by institutional traders and trading desks away from the exchange markets. Generally, these large volume transactions occur on ECNs. The orders are matched electronically for execution without routing the order to marketplace where last sale price and volume information is displayed.

Institutional choosing to use dark pools are able to execute large block orders without affecting public quotes or prices. In this way, they do not reveal their investment strategy. The public does not see what they are buying or selling. Indeed, orders can be placed anonymously so that the identity of the entity placing the order is unknown to the general investing public along with the volume and price for the transaction. The concern with dark pools is that some market participants are left disadvantaged because they cannot see the trades, volume, or prices agreed upon within the pools. This lack of transparency is why they are called dark pools.

Dark pools account for about 17% of the trading volume in the U.S. stock market.

PRACTICE QUESTION

7. The OTC market is a negotiated market. This is best described by saying that buyers and sellers
   A. bid and offer in a public place.
   B. bid and offer continuously.
   C. arrive at an agreeable price by bargaining.
   D. must accept prices set by dealers.

Answer: C. Unlike the exchanges, which are considered auction markets, prices on OTC securities are determined by negotiation (bargaining) between broker-dealers.

LESSON 3.4: TAXATION OF EQUITY SECURITIES

LO 3.i Differentiate between the different kinds of tax treatment of equity securities (e.g., qualified dividends).

As we discussed at LO 2.e, one of the investment constraints is taxes. In this lesson, we are going to focus on the tax considerations facing investors in equity securities.

Portfolio Income

Portfolio income includes dividends, interest, and net capital gains derived from the sale of securities. No matter what the source of the income, it is taxed in the year in which it is earned.

Dividends

Dividends are an important source of income for holders of equity securities. In the case of preferred stock, it is usually the main purpose of the investment. That can be true of some common stocks as well. Dividends on preferred stock are always paid in cash. Dividends on common stock may be paid in cash or as additional shares of stock (stock dividend).

Cash Dividends

On the exam, most of the cash dividends will be *qualified*. No, that does not have anything to do with the qualified retirement plans described in Part 1 of this course. As you move through your studies, you will notice that some words are repeated, but with different meanings. *Qualified* is one of them. If the dividend qualifies, the tax rates are lower than if nonqualified.

If the dividend is qualified, the tax rate is generally a maximum of 15%. It can be as high as 20% or more for taxpayers in the highest brackets, but that is unlikely to be tested. If the dividend is nonqualified, ordinary income tax rates apply. For test purposes, assume that any dividend from a U.S. corporation, including mutual funds, is qualified, unless the question states otherwise.

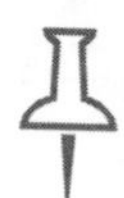

TAKE NOTE

You do not need to know the technical points that make a dividend qualify. Just know that the tax rate is lower than the ordinary income rate applied to nonqualified dividends.

Stock Dividend

When a corporation pays a stock dividend, it pays out shares of common stock rather than cash. As covered in Lesson 3.1, there is no monetary change to the investor's account. There are more shares, but each share has a lower price. This results in the total value remaining the same. The IRS does not considered stock dividends taxable when paid. What is required is an adjustment to the cost basis of the shareholding. How does that work?

EXAMPLE

We are going to use the numbers from the example used earlier in this unit. "For example, if an investor owned 100 shares of the stock and the company declared a 20% stock dividend, that investor would receive 20 additional shares, bringing the total holding up to 120 shares. Just as with the stock split, there is no real change to the overall value. The market price of the stock drops. For example, if the stock were selling at $60 per share before the dividend, it would now be selling at $50. Check the math. Divide $60 by 120% and you get $50. The investor had 100 shares worth $6,000. The investor now has 120 shares @ $50, or $6,000." That $50 per share is known as the investor's cost basis.

How does this apply to the taxation? The investor's stock now has an adjusted cost basis of $50 per share. There was no tax due when the additional 20 shares was received. Instead, when any or all of the 120 shares are sold, taxes will be based on the difference between that $50 cost and the sale price of the shares. That leads us to the next topic.

Capital Gains and Losses

The sale of a security at a price higher than its cost results in a profit. In tax language, this is a capital gain. If sold at a lower price than it cost, there is a loss. We refer to this as a capital loss. These losses and gains fit into one of two categories. They are either short-term or long-term. The dividing line is 12 months.

For any security sold within 12 month of purchase, the holding period is short-term. From 12 months plus one day, it is long-term. Why do we care? We care because the tax treatment favors long-term gains. At the end of the tax year, investors compute all of their gains and their losses. Comparing them tells us if there is a net loss or a net gain.

EXAMPLE

During 2019, an investor made the following transactions:

- Sold 100 shares of ABC at $40 per share on December 15. The shares were purchased on February 11, 2019, at $35 per share.
- Sold 200 shares of DEF at $70 per share on April 22. The shares were purchased on September 22, 2017, at $50 per share.
- Sold 100 shares of GHI at $20 per share on November 13. The shares were purchased on July 31, 2018, at $30 per share.
- Bought 1,000 shares of JKL at $30 per share. The price of JKL on December 31 was $100 per share.

What are the investor's tax consequences for 2019?

The first step is to compute the gains and losses. Trade #1 resulted in a short-term (10 month holding period) gain of $5 per share, or $500. Trade #2 results in a long-term (more than 12-month holding period) gain of $20 per share or $4,000. Trade #3 results in a long-term loss of $10 per share or $1,000. Trade #4 has not happened yet. Until the shares are sold, there is no taxable gain. This is known as an unrealized gain (we can also have an unrealized loss).

We compare our gains and losses. The only short-term transaction is the gain of $500. We have two long-term transactions. There is the gain of $4,000 and the loss of $1,000. The net long-term result is a capital gain of $3,000. For tax purposes, the investor will report a short-term capital gain of $500 and a long-term gain of $3,000. The tax rate on short-term gains is the same as ordinary income like salary. The tax on long-term capital gains is the same as that of qualified dividends, generally 15%.

What if the selling price of the stock in trade #1 was $30 instead of $40? That would have given the investor a short-term capital loss of $500. In that case, the $500 loss would have been compared the $3,000 long-term gain. For tax purposes, the investor would report a net long-term gain of $2,500.

Using this information, as well as what we discussed with stock dividends, here is the type of question you might see on your exam.

PRACTICE QUESTION

8. Florence Forte purchased 100 shares of YXC common stock for $22 per share on February 12, 2018. She received a 10% stock dividend on May 18, 2019. She sold all of her YXC at $25 per share in June of the same year. What are the tax consequences of her trades?
   A. $500 long-term gain
   B. $550 long-term gain
   C. $300 long-term gain; $250 short-term gain
   D. $500 long-term gain; $50 short-term gain

Answer: B. We compare the cost to the proceeds. Florence paid $2,200 for 100 shares. She received an additional 10 shares from the stock dividend. Then, she sold all 110 shares for $25 per share—$2,750. The difference between the cost and the proceeds is $550. The holding period was from May 2018 to June 2019—more than 12 months. That makes the gain long-term.

Net Capital Losses

When the net position is a capital gain, it is relatively simple. Short-term gains are taxed at ordinary income rates and long-term gains at 15% (unless in the highest tax brackets). It makes no difference if the gain is $100 or $1 million—all of it is taxable. The story is different when it comes to net capital losses.

Capital losses that exceed capital gains are deductible against earned income. The annual maximum is $3,000 per year. What if the losses are greater than $3,000? The excess over $3,000 may be carried forward indefinitely as a deduction to offset capital gains in future years. If the losses carried forward are short-term, they keep that status.

EXAMPLE

An investor had net capital losses in 2018 of $10,000. They were all short-term. The investor deducts $3,000 of that against earned income in 2018. That leaves $7,000 carried forward to 2019. If the investor had no transactions in 2019, the deduction would be another $3,000. The investor carries forward the remaining $4,000 to 2020 as a short-term gain. If in 2020 the investor has net gains of $2,000 short-term and $3,000 long-term, the loss carry forward of $4,000 is used first against the short-term gain. The $2,000 left reduces the $3,000 of long-term gain to a net gain of $1,000.

We will cover the taxation of the various securities products in their units. Then, in Unit 13, we'll learn about how taxes affect the recommendations you make to your clients. We will also introduce you to the wash sale.

PRACTICE QUESTION

9. Cindy Castle purchased 100 shares of XYC common stock for $19 per share on February 12, 2019. She received a 10% stock dividend three months later on May 18. She sold all of her XYC at $13 per share in June of the same year. What are the tax consequences of her trades?
   A. $470 short-term loss
   B. $575 short-term loss; $105 long-term gain
   C. $575 long-term loss
   D. $575 long-term gain, $105 short-term loss

Answer: A. Castle paid $1,900 for 100 shares. She received an additional 10 shares from the stock dividend. Then, she sold all 110 shares for $1,430 (110 at $13). Because the transactions all took place in less than a year, the transaction was a short-term loss.

LESSON 3.5: RULES APPLYING TO THE SALE OF EQUITY SECURITIES

LO 3.d Evaluate the risks of penny stocks.

Penny Stock Risks

The first step in a discussion of penny stocks is to define them. The full legal description is long and complicated. We are just going to keep it simple in Series 7. If the stock trades for less than $5 per share and is not listed on a major exchange such as the NYSE or the Nasdaq Stock Market, it is a penny stock. Many penny stocks do trade for pennies, but you can find some trading at $3 or $4 per share. As equity securities, they have the risks that any other common stock would have. In addition, we are going to investigate risks unique to penny stocks. Suffice it to say, penny stocks are highly speculative securities.

Lack of Transparency

Penny stocks trade on the OTC Bulletin Board and the OTC Link. The requirements for trading there are less stringent than the major exchanges. Coverage by analysts is spotty, so getting information is more difficult than with listed stock.

Lack of Liquidity

Penny stocks may trade infrequently, which means that it may be difficult to sell penny stock shares once you own them. There may not be a buyer—at least at the price you want—when you need to sell. They are an example of what we call *thinly traded securities*. Thinly traded securities usually have a large spread between the buy and sell price. We will cover that concept in Unit 13.

EXAMPLE

A penny stock broker-dealer may publish a quote on a penny stock as $0.54 bid, $0.65 ask. This means you can buy the stock at 65 cents or sell it at 54 cents. That 11-cent difference, called ***the spread***, means you are immediately at a loss if you have to sell.

No Track Record

Many penny stock companies are new. Some have little or no operating history. The SEC warns that investors in penny stocks should be prepared to lose all of their investment.

Pump and Dump

This is a fraudulent activity where unscrupulous firms or investors spread rumors in an attempt to "pump" up the stock's price. If enough investors bite, the price rises and the promoters then "dump" their shares. This causes the price to drop and the unknowing investor suffers a big loss.

LO 3.j Determine the rules and regulations pertaining to the sale of equity securities.

Penny Stock Rules

The highly speculative nature and risks of penny stocks carry special rules to protect investors. In the industry, they are known as the 15g rules. You can find them in Section 15(g) of the Securities Exchange Act. They go from 15g-1 to 15g-100. Following are the ones you would likely see on the exam. Although we are listing them with their rule numbers, that is not testable information.

Risk Disclosure Document

Rule 15g-2 requires that customers, before their initial transaction in a penny stock, be given a copy of the Risk Disclosure Document. The member firm must receive a signed and dated acknowledgment from the customer that the document has been received. In addition to obtaining the client's signature, the SEC requires the firm to wait at least two business days after sending the statement before executing the first trade. This is to give clients time to carefully consider their trade. Not surprisingly, the document describes penny stocks in less than flattering terms.

Disclosure of Quotations

Rule 15g-3 requires members to provide penny stock purchasers with a current bid and asked quote on the stock to prevent the practice of quoting prices that are away from the current market to customers. The quote information must be provided to the customer orally or in writing before effecting any transaction with the customer for the purchase or sale of any penny stock. This information is also sent in writing with the trade confirmation.

Disclosure of Compensation

Rules 15g-4 and **15g-5** require members to provide penny stock purchasers with information on the compensation to be earned by both the member and the registered representative as the result of the transaction. This is to prevent excessive markups.

Frequency of Customer Account Statements

Rule 15g-6 requires members to provide penny stock purchasers with monthly statements showing the estimated market value of each penny stock purchased. As we will learn in Unit 15, the normal statement frequency is quarterly.

Customer Suitability Determination

Rule 15g-9 addresses sales practices to curb abusive sales practices. This rule requires members who are soliciting new customers to make a suitability determination. The member must inquire as to the prospective customer's income, net worth, objectives, and risk tolerance. A suitability statement is prepared using this information. This suitability statement shows why the proposed penny stock trade is suitable for the customer. The member firm sends the statement to the customer for a signature. Once returned, trading in penny stocks may take place.

Established Customer Exception

A member may solicit an *established customer* without having to prepare a suitability statement. An established customer is one who has

- effected a nonpenny stock transaction or made a deposit of funds or securities in an account more than one year before the proposed penny stock trade; or
- made three unsolicited purchases of penny stocks, on three separate days, involving three separate issues. Once a customer buys three different penny stocks, he is no longer covered by the suitability statement requirement.

In addition, the suitability statement does not apply to any customer turning in an unsolicited order to trade a penny stock. These customers initiate the trade without the firm making a penny stock recommendation.

PRACTICE QUESTION

10. Under SEC rules, for an unlisted non-Nasdaq stock to avoid being defined as a penny stock, it must have a market price of at **least**
    A. $1 per share.
    B. $2 per share.
    C. $2.50 per share.
    D. $5 per share.

    Answer: D. SEC rules define penny stock as a non-Nasdaq stock with a market price of less than $5 per share.

Fair Prices and Commissions (FINRA Rule 2121)

Rule 2121, also known as the 5% policy, was adopted to ensure that the investing public receives fair treatment and is charged reasonable rates for brokerage services. It is considered a guideline—not a firm rule. Test questions try to trap students into thinking that the rule mandates markups or commissions of 5% or less. That is not true. Charges of more than 5% can be reasonable. This would be the case with the thinly traded securities we have discussed. On the other hand, there are cases where a charge of less than 5% would be unfair. The point is, disregard the number 5%—it is simply the name of the policy.

Application of the 5% Policy

The policy applies to transactions in equity securities. It applies in both the OTC and the exchange markets. It applies when customers buy or sell securities. It does not apply to prospectus offerings. If a member must give a customer a prospectus in any transaction, that transaction is outside the scope of the 5% policy (e.g., new issues, mutual funds, variable annuities, and DPPs). In Unit 13, we will cover the nuts and bolts of the policy.

TAKE NOTE

Later in the course, we will cover the rules regarding registering a security for sale. In the case of new issues, the document used to disclose the pertinent information is the prospectus.

TEST TOPIC ALERT

The 5% policy applies to both principal (dealer) and agency (broker) transactions. It applies to markups, markdowns, and commissions, but not to securities sold by prospectus.

UNIT 4

Debt Securities

LEARNING OBJECTIVES

When you have completed this unit, you will be able to accomplish the following.

- › LO 4.a **Recognize** the different types of debt securities.
- › LO 4.b **Name** the characteristics common to most debt securities.
- › LO 4.c **Examine** the different types of money market instruments.
- › LO 4.d **Identify** types and characteristics of non-U.S. market debt securities.
- › LO 4.e **Compute** the different yields relating to debt securities.
- › LO 4.f **Recognize** the relevance of a bond's rating.
- › LO 4.g **Identify** debt securities classified as alternative investments.

INTRODUCTION

The term *debt security* means a document that creates or evidences a debt obligation. The most common example on the exam is a bond. There are other debt securities, such as money market instruments. We will cover those as well. As we go through the units, we will discuss the different entities that issue bonds. There are three major issuers of debt securities. The largest issuer of debt securities is the U.S. government. Corporations borrow money to finance their operations. State governments and those political entities that are subdivisions of a state, such as cities, counties, towns, and so forth, also borrow substantial sums. These issues from state and local political entities are **municipal securities.**

We will cover the general similarities in this unit. In the units to follow, we will get into the many differences.

LESSON 4.1: WHAT IS A DEBT SECURITY?

LO 4.a Recognize the different types of debt securities.

Let us begin this adventure by explaining the different types of debt securities.

Bonds

Debt capital represents money loaned to an issuer by investors purchasing that issuer's bonds. A **bond** represents the issuer's indebtedness. There is, in essence, a contract between the borrower (the issuer) and the lender (the investor). The terms of the loan are expressed in a document known as the bond's **indenture**. The indenture, sometimes also referred to as the *deed of trust*, states the issuer's obligation to pay back a specific amount of money on a specific date. The indenture also states the issuer's obligation to pay the investor a specific rate of interest for the use of the funds as well as any collateral pledged as security for the loan and all other pertinent details. An investor purchasing a bond is lending the issuer money for a set period at a fixed annual interest rate. That rate is frequently referred to as the *coupon* rate because, years ago, bonds were issued with detachable coupons that were presented for collection of the interest. That is no longer the case, but the term *coupon* is still in common use. This rate is generally called the nominal yield on the exam. Once set, it never changes during the life of the bond. This is why bonds are the classic fixed-income investment.

It is important to understand that debt capital refers to **long-term debt** financing. Long-term debt is money borrowed for a minimum of five years, although more frequently, the length of time is 20–30 years.

Money Market Instruments

We define the **money market** as the market for buying and selling short-term loanable funds in the form of securities and loans. It is called the money market because that is what is traded there—money, not cash. The buyer of a money market instrument is the lender of the money; the seller of a money market instrument is the entity borrowing the money. In general, money market securities are of high quality (low risk). Because of their safety and high liquidity, their yields are low.

Although there are many different kinds of money market instruments, there are several common factors. For example, they all have a maturity date of one year or less. In fact, most money market instruments mature in less than six months. Another factor that most (but not all) money market instruments share is that they are issued at a discount; they do not pay interest. The principal amount of the loan is repaid at maturity. Because most money market instruments have a maturity of six months or less, the administrative costs of paying out interest would be very high. Therefore, the solution is to issue the security at a discount with the investor getting back par at maturity. The difference between the price paid and the maturity value is considered interest. Think of interest as *rent* for the use of borrowed money.

Money market instruments are safe. Some are not quite as safe as others are (e.g., commercial paper is not as safe as a Treasury bill). Institutions, including banks, insurance companies, and money market mutual funds are the primary purchasers of money market securities. The minimum denominations are generally too high for most individual investors. Industry best practices recommend the use of delivery versus payment (DVP) on the purchase of these securities.

LO 4.b Name the characteristics common to most debt securities.

Regardless of the type of debt issue, there are certain characteristics that are common to all of them.

Inverse Relationship Between Interest Rate and the Price of Debt Securities

In Lesson 3.2, we mentioned that the market price of preferred stock fluctuates inversely with current interest rates. We did not explain why that is so. We waited for this unit because the exam focuses on this concept with debt securities. Later on in the unit, when we discuss the math behind yields, this topic will be easier to follow. At this point, we want you to know that whenever interest rates in the market (the current cost of borrowing money) go up, the price of outstanding debt securities goes down. Likewise, if interest rates fall, the price of outstanding debt securities will rise. How much is something we will cover at yields.

TAKE NOTE

Although the market price of the debt security will fluctuate, the interest payments stay the same.

Structure

There are certain structural components common to most debt securities.

Indenture

As mentioned above, the indenture is the legal document describing the legal conditions of the bond. In the case of money market instruments, there is no indenture. In place of the indenture is generally a legal opinion, but that is not tested. The Trust Indenture Act of 1939 deals with corporate bonds. We will cover that act in the next unit.

Negotiability

Both bonds and money market securities are readily transferrable. This enables investors to sell their security before maturity date. Secondary market trading is less common in the money market because of the short maturities.

Specified Maturity Date

Debt securities are redeemed, (paid back), by the issuer on a specified maturity date. In the case of money market instruments, that can be as short as one day. It is never longer than one year. Bonds have longer maturities. Those can be as short as five years, but more often are 10–30 years.

Payment of Interest

In the case of bonds, interest is generally paid semiannually based on a stated coupon rate. Money market instruments are issued at a discount to their face value with the difference paid at maturity representing the interest. In Lesson 4.4 we will get into more detail on this.

Accrued Interest

What happens to an investor who sells a bond before the semiannual interest payment date? The buyer pays the seller the amount of interest that has accrued since the last interest payment. Then on the next payment date, the new owner receives the full six months of interest.

Most bonds trade and pay *interest*, meaning a buyer pays a seller a bond's market price, plus any accrued interest since the last interest payment. The buyer receives the full amount of the next interest payment, including interest that accrued while the seller owned the bond.

Most bonds pay interest every six months on either the 1st or the 15th of the specified months. The payment dates are known as coupon dates. Accrued interest affects bond transactions when settlement occurs between coupon dates. Some examples of coupon dates follow.

If the interest dates are:	The bonds are known as:
January 1 and July 1	J&J bonds
February 15 and August 15	F&A 15 bonds
March 1 and September 1	M&S bonds
April 1 and October 1	A&O bonds
May 15 and November 15	M&N 15 bonds
June 15 and December 15	J&D 15 bonds

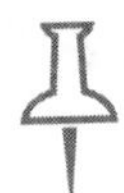

TAKE NOTE

When payment dates within the month are not specified, always assume the first of the month (e.g., J & J, assume January 1 and July 1).

We will come back to this subject in detail in Unit 6.

Paying Agent

The paying agent is usually a trust department of a bank. In some cases, it could be the treasurer of the issuers. The role of the paying agent is to transmit payments of interest and principal to the investors. Because most money market instruments are issued at a discount, the paying agent only repays the principal.

Pricing (Quotes)

In most cases, bonds are quoted as a percentage of par or face value. A quote of 100 means the bond is selling at 100% of its par, or $1,000. Sometimes bonds are selling for a price above par (we will show you why in Lesson 4.4) and sometimes at a price below par. A bond quoted at 120 is trading at 120% of $1,000, or $1,200. A bond quoted at 80 is trading at 80% of par, or $1,200. There are some differences between the way quotes for corporate, municipal, and U.S. Treasury bonds are shown. Those will be explained in the relevant units.

Trustee

The trustee is usually a financial institution, such as a trust company. The trustee represents the investors. Making sure the borrower lives up to the terms of the loan is the responsibility of the trustee. The trustee often serves as the paying agent.

Secured or Unsecured

An issuer of a debt security may choose to place specific assets as collateral for the loan. That generally adds to the safety of the security as it is now considered secured. In other cases, there is no specific asset pledged and the loan is strictly on the credit standing of the issuer.

Callable or Noncallable

Bonds can be either callable or noncallable. The call feature permits the issuer to redeem its bonds (pay off the principal) before maturity if it so desires. The call feature is most often exercised when interest rates (borrowing costs) have declined. In this case, the issuer could take advantage of the lower cost of borrowing by issuing new bonds at the lower rate prevailing in the market and using those proceeds to call in the old bonds with their higher coupons. This is similar to refinancing a home mortgage, but in this industry, we use the term *refunding*. An issuer would not be interested in redeeming its bonds when interest rates have gone up and the bond prices have gone down; the cheapest way for the issuer to retire its debt is to buy it in the open market.

Realistically, that doesn't often work, so the issuer invokes the call provision. In this case, the issuer employs an "in whole call." That is, the entire issue is called. In other cases, the issuer might have surplus funds. Rather than pay interest on the debt, it will call in a portion of the bonds (a partial call). When this is done, the bonds to be called are usually selected in a random draw. A partial call is comparable to an individual using some extra money to pay down credit card debt. There is not enough to pay the entire balance, but paying off a portion certainly saves money. More than likely, you would first pay down the accounts carrying the highest interest cost. If the issuer has several callable bonds outstanding, it would do the same thing. That is, it would call the issue with the highest coupons first.

Because of their short-term nature, it is rare to see a callable money market instrument.

Call Protection

Before purchasing a bond, determine the extent of its call protection. **Call protection** is the number of years into the issue before the issuer may exercise the call provision. The best call protection a bond may have is if a bond is noncallable; in other words, the issuer cannot call it early, and the investor has the best protection against a call.

PRACTICE QUESTION

1. A bond issue that may be retired in advance of maturity at the option of the issuer is said to have
   A. a callable feature.
   B. an optional reserve.
   C. a conversion feature.
   D. a cumulative feature.

   Answer: A. A bond that is callable has a provision that the issuer, at its option, may redeem that bond at a specified price known as the call or redemption price. As we will see later, it is the investor who can exercise the conversion feature—not the issuer.

TAKE NOTE

When the issuer calls the bond, the investors tender (sell back) their bonds at the call price.

LESSON 4.2: THE MONEY MARKET

LO 4.c Examine the different types of money-market instruments.

Types of Money Market Instruments

There are a number of different types of money market instruments. We have discussed the common elements in the previous lesson. Now it is time to drill down into the specifics.

U.S. Treasury Bills

The safest money market security is the Treasury Bill (T-bill). At the time of this printing, they are available in maturities of 4, 8, 13, 26, and 52 weeks. That can change, but what won't change is that they are never longer than 52 weeks. No security is as safe as a T-bill. In fact, later in the course, you will learn that the example of a risk-free investment is the 13 week (91 day) T-bill. These are always issued at a discount from the face value. We will discuss the features of the T-bill in Unit 7.

Commercial Paper (CP)

Commercial paper (CP) is short-term unsecured paper issued by corporations (especially finance companies), primarily to raise working capital. In other words, for current needs rather than long-term needs. The issuers of CP are usually companies with excellent credit ratings. It is possible you will see CP referred to as a promissory note. It is, after all, a promise by the issuer to repay the principal at the end of the term. In Unit 6, we will learn that municipalities sometimes issue CP. CP maturities range from one to 270 days, although most mature within 90 days. These are always issued at a discount from the face value.

Negotiable Certificate of Deposit (CD)

Please do not confuse a negotiable certificate of deposit (CD) with the ones you can buy at your local bank. The exam will frequently call these **jumbo** CDs. This is an appropriate title because the minimum size is $100,000. The most common size is $1 million, and they can be more than that. These CDs are unsecured time deposits (no asset of the bank is pledged as collateral), and the money is being loaned to the bank for a specified period. *Negotiable* means readily transferrable. A negotiable CD allows the initial investor, or any subsequent owner of the CD, to sell the CD in the open market before maturity date. Unlike the CD at your bank branch, there is no prepayment penalty. The bank that issues the CD redeems the CD at face value plus interest on maturity date. CDs are the only money market instrument issued at face value (not a discount) and that pays periodic interest, usually semiannually. Although maturities can run as long as 10 years, only those with a maturity of one year or less are considered money market instruments. FDIC insurance covers these CDs just as any other bank deposit.

TEST TOPIC ALERT

Be careful. Jumbo CDs are insured (up to the FDIC limit of $250,000), but they are not secured by any bank asset.

Brokered CDs

As the name implies, broker-dealers sell these. Brokered CDs generally have a longer holding period than the jumbo money market CDs we just discussed. Therefore, they are not part of the money market. The structure of these is such that they are generally more complex than regular bank (not jumbo) issued CDs. There are other important differences, such as the following:

- The commission or fees to buy brokered CDs are generally higher than bank issued ones.
- These may or may not be covered by FDIC insurance. The details are beyond the exam, but the concept is not.

Unlike a bank CD where the bank will redeem at face value at any time (there may be a penalty), brokered CDs are usually not redeemable before maturity. The broker-dealer offering the CD may buy it back. There would likely be fees and no assurance that the investor will receive maturity value.

Banker's Acceptance (BA)

Certain corporations in the import-export business will often use a banker's acceptance (BA) as a short-term time draft with a specified payment date drawn on a bank. BAs are essentially a postdated check or line of credit. The payment date of a BA is normally between one and 180 days and never more than 270 days.

The bank on which the instrument is drawn stamps the word *accepted* across the face of the draft. In doing so, the bank accepts the responsibility to make payment upon maturity. This is true whether or not the customer for which the acceptance was initiated has repaid the bank. This acceptance, or bank liability, makes the instrument a very marketable instrument. These are always issued at a discount from the face value.

U.S. corporations use bankers' acceptances extensively to finance international trade—that is, a BA typically pays for goods and services in a foreign country. You might see these referred to as a *bill of exchange*.

Repurchase Agreements (Repo)

A repurchase agreement (repo) is the sale of securities with an agreement to repurchase them at a higher price on an agreed upon future date. Overnight repos are those where the repurchase date is the next day. The difference between the sale price and the repurchase price represents the interest earned by the investor. That means these are always purchased at a discount. Repos trade as money market instruments. The security that is exchanged stands as collateral for the loan advanced to the seller. The most common collateral behind a repo is a Treasury security.

Reverse Repo

A reverse repo is the reverse of a repurchase agreement. In this case, the purchaser, not the seller, initiates the deal. This is a purchase of securities with an attendant agreement to resell them at a higher price on an agreed upon future date; the difference between the purchase price and the resale price represents the interest earned by the investor.

It is likely that the exam's only questions on repos/reverse repos will be about them being money market securities.

LESSON 4.3: FOREIGN DEBT SECURITIES

LO 4.d Identify types and characteristics of non-U.S. market debt securities.

Expect the exam to focus on debt instruments of U.S. issuers. However, there may be a question on debt issues from foreign entities.

Sovereign Debt Securities

The term sovereign debt applies to securities issued by national governments. In the United States, Treasury securities are the example. Probably the best known of the foreign government bonds are the *Gilts* issued in the United Kingdom. They got that name because the original certificates had a gilded edge. The sovereign bonds issued by Germany are the *Bunds*, and in France, they are the OATs.

None of these names will appear on your exam. What you do have to know is that the safety of a sovereign bond depends on the economy of the issuing country. It is not unheard of for a government to default on its bonds. Russia did in 1998. Argentina did in 2001. In fact, there have been many cases, starting with France in 1558. On the other hand, there are countries where there has never been a default and, at least for the near term, one is unlikely. One risk, unrelated to the ability of the issuer to pay, is currency risk. We will cover that in Unit 14.

Foreign Corporate Debt Securities

Foreign corporations issue debt securities in a manner similar to that of U.S.-based corporations. It is unusual to find foreign sovereign and corporate debt issues in the same portfolio of individual investors. Institutions are the most frequent purchasers of these securities. Individuals wishing foreign exposure typically do so through mutual funds and/or exchange-traded funds (ETFs). We will discuss those in Unit 8. Following are some terms you might see on the exam.

Eurobond

A **Eurobond** is any long-term debt instrument issued and sold outside the country of the currency in which it is denominated. For example, if a Swiss company issued bonds denominated in British pounds, it is a Eurobond. If the government of France issued bonds denominated in Japanese yen, it is still a Eurobond.

Eurodollar Bond

A U.S. dollar-denominated Eurobond, or **Eurodollar bond**, is a bond issued by a non-American company (or government), sold outside the United States and the issuer's country, but for which the principal and interest are stated and paid in U.S. dollars. The U.S. government does not issue Eurodollar bonds. These bonds are not limited to European issuers; that is just where they originated. For example, if an Indian bank held dollar-denominated bonds issued by a Korean company, the term *Eurodollar bond* would still apply.

TEST TOPIC ALERT

Test questions sometimes ask you to contrast Eurobonds and Eurodollar bonds. The name of the instrument tells you how principal and interest is paid. Eurodollar bonds pay in U.S. dollars; Eurobonds pay in foreign currency. Note that these instruments must be issued outside of the United States.

It is unlikely you will have to know the cute names for bonds issued outside their country but in the country's currency. *Maple* bonds are those issued in *Canadian* currency and *Matilda* bonds are those issued in *Australian* currency. The primary reason for issuing these bonds is that they are free from the requirement to register with the SEC, resulting in lower issuance costs. Because the liquidity is not as great as with U.S. domestic issues and because the political and country risks tend to be higher, yields are generally higher.

LESSON 4.4: BOND YIELDS

LO 4.e Compute the different yields relating to debt securities.

Bond Math

Please do not be frightened by that word, *math*. We are not talking trigonometry, geometry, or calculus. For the most part, you learned all of the arithmetic needed for this lesson before you left middle school. This lesson is all about the returns offered by debt securities. The primary source of return is the income from the interest payments. There are also cases where the investor might sell the security for a profit. When that happens, the investor's yield is increased.

Nominal Yield

The interest rate on a bond is always shown on the bond certificate as a percentage of the par value. That interest stated on the face of the bond is the **nominal yield**. Sometimes it is referred to as the *coupon rate*. To compute the annual interest payments in dollars, multiply this nominal yield by the face amount of the bond ($1,000 unless stated otherwise). A bond with a 5% coupon rate pays $50 per year. One with an 8% nominal yield pays $80 per year. One with a coupon of 13.5% pays $135 per year. Because, on any particular bond, this interest payment is the same every year, we refer to bonds as *fixed-income investments*.

For exam purposes, unless the question says something different, the par value of all bonds is $1,000 and the interest is paid semiannually (every six months).

TEST TOPIC ALERT

When a question states a bond pays interest at a rate of 6% semiannually, it does not mean two payments of $60 per year. The interest rate is always stated on an annual basis ($60 per year), and it is paid twice per year, $30 every six months.

Current Yield (CY)

Investors always want to know the return on their investments. The most straightforward way to do that is to place the return on the investment as follows.

$$\frac{\text{return}}{\text{investment}}$$

The return will always be the annual interest in dollars (if referring to a stock, the dividend in dollars) divided by the current market price (the amount of investment required to own the security). This calculation is called *current yield (CY)* or *current return.*

As we have stated, the face or par value of all bonds is $1,000. However, bond prices fluctuate in the secondary markets. The nominal rate is the interest rate a bond pays. How does that work? Look at this example.

EXAMPLE

The DBL 10s of '39. ***DBL*** is the name of the issuer, ***10s*** means the nominal yield is 10%, and '39 means that the bonds mature in 2039. The letter **s** is added because it is easier to say "the 10s" than to say "the 10." These bonds pay $100 a year ($50 semiannually) for each $1,000 of face value. Regardless of what the market price of the bonds may be, DBL has an obligation to pay annual interest of 10% of the $1,000 face it borrowed.

If an investor were to buy these bonds for more than $1,000 or less than $1,000, the return on the investment would not be 10%. For example, if these bonds had a current market value of $800, their CY would be 12.5% ($100 ÷ $800). Similarly, someone paying $1,200 for the bonds would receive a CY of 8.33% ($100 ÷ $1,200). Please notice, the $100 interest received is the same in all cases regardless of the current market price.

Bond prices and yields move in opposite directions; as interest rates rise, bond prices fall and vice versa. When a bond trades at a discount, its CY increases; when it trades at a premium, its CY decreases.

Discount and Premium

When a bond is selling at a price above par (or face), it is selling at a premium. When it is selling below par, it is selling at a discount. Remember these critical statements:

- If you pay more, you get less.
- If you pay less, you get more.

An investor buying a bond at a premium will always receive a rate of return less than the coupon (or nominal) yield stated on the face of the bond. As we saw in the earlier example, 8.33% is less than 10%. Conversely, any time an investor purchases a bond at a discount, the return will be more than the rate stated on the face of the bond (12.5% is greater than 10%).

TAKE NOTE

Just think of this as going shopping. The bigger the discount, the lower the price of the item. On the other hand, the bigger the discount, the more you are getting for your money. It is the same concept here.

There is another important fact to know about the par value—the amount of the loan that the issuer repays to the investor at maturity. Therefore, an investor purchasing a bond at a discount knows that holding the bond until maturity date will result in a return of the par value, an amount that will be more than her purchase price for the bond. That means a gain in addition to the interest. An investor purchasing a bond at a premium and holding it until the maturity date knows that the par value received will be less than her purchase price for the bond. That means that the total interest received is offset by a loss. We reflect this gain or loss that an investor will have at maturity by looking at another yield. This is the *yield to maturity*, or *true yield*.

TEST TOPIC ALERT

The exam may give you a quoted yield and ask you for the price relative to par. For example, if a bond with a 5% coupon is currently yielding 6%, is it selling at a discount, a premium, or par? Well, anytime you are getting a yield higher than the coupon rate, the bond has to be selling at a discount from par. Conversely, if the bond had a 5% coupon, but the current return was 4%, the bond must be selling at a premium to par. Remember, if you pay more, you get less, and if you pay less, you get more.

TEST TOPIC ALERT

One bond that is always traded at a discount is the zero coupon bond. You would see them quoted as: BCD Zr 36 @ 6.45%. BCD is the issuer, Zr is the coupon (zero), 2036 is the maturity date, and the yield to maturity (basis) is 6.45%.

Yield to Maturity (Basis)

This measurement takes into account the gain or loss the investor will have when the bonds are redeemed at maturity. The person who was mentioned earlier who buys the bonds at $800 will get back $1,000 if the bonds are held to maturity, in addition to receiving $100 per year interest (a CY of 12.5% on the $800 investment). Consequently, this investor will have a gain of $200 on top of the annual interest. The individual paying $1,200 for the bonds will have a $200 loss at maturity when receiving the face value for them at maturity.

Whenever an investor pays less (buys at a discount), there will be a profit in addition to the annual interest, and whenever the investor pays more (buys at a premium), there will be a loss if held to maturity. Try to understand these key facts:

- A bond is issued at par ($1,000) because that is how much the issuer is borrowing.
- The interest paid on the bond is always fixed as a percentage of the par (face) value.
- Regardless of changes in the market value of the bond, the interest checks remain the same.
- The current market price of a bond is determined by supply and demand.
- The current market price will fluctuate.
- The current market price may be at par, above par, or below par.
- A bond always matures at par.
- Purchasing a bond at par will always result in getting back the same as the original investment at maturity.
- Purchasing a bond at a discount (below par) will always result in getting back par, which means more (a profit) than the original investment.
- Purchasing a bond at a premium (above par) will always result in getting back par, which means less (a loss) than the original investment.

Although you will probably not have to do a yield to maturity computation on the exam, some students find that seeing the numbers played out gives them a better understanding of the concept. Try to follow this example.

EXAMPLE

An investor who buys a 10% coupon bond at 105 ($1,050 per bond) with 10 years remaining to maturity can expect $100 in interest per year. If he holds the bond to maturity, the bondholder loses $50, the amount of the premium. This loss is included in the yield to maturity (YTM) approximation.

The actual YTM calculation for this premium bond is shown below:

$$\frac{\text{annual interest} - (\text{premium} \div \text{years to maturity})}{\text{average price of the bond}}$$

A bond's average price is the price paid plus the amount received at maturity (par) divided by two. Alternatively, the average price is the price midway between the purchase price and par.

$$\frac{100 - (50 \div 10)}{1{,}025} = \frac{95}{1{,}025} = 0.093\text{, or } 9.3\%$$

The YTM of a bond bought at a premium is always lower than both the coupon rate (nominal yield) and the CY. In this example, the nominal yield is 10%, and the CY is 9.52% (100 ÷ 1,050).

If an investor buys a 10-year bond with a 10% coupon for 95 ($950 per bond), he receives $100 per year in coupon interest payments and a gain of $50 (the amount of the discount) at maturity. This gain is included in the YTM approximation.

The actual YTM calculation for this discount bond is shown below:

$$\frac{\text{annual interest} - (\text{premium} \div \text{years to maturity})}{\text{average price of the bond}}$$

$$\frac{100 + (50 \div 10)}{975} = \frac{105}{975} = 0.1077\text{, or } 10.77\%$$

The YTM of a bond bought at a discount is always higher than both the coupon rate (nominal yield) and the CY. In this example, the nominal yield is 10%, and the CY is 10.53% (100 ÷ 950).

If these calculations seem complicated, do not worry. You will have at most one question requiring a YTM calculation. Focus on the relationship between YTM and CY based on the price of the bond.

Yield to Call

A bond with a call feature may be redeemed before maturity at the issuer's option. The call price may be at par or at a premium. You will never see a bond called at a discount from par. Calling a bond makes the call date, in effect, the maturity date.

A bond's **yield to call**, similar to YTM, is the rate of return the bond provides from the purchase date to the call date and price. When the bond is selling at a premium, this calculation generates a lower return than does the YTM. That is why call protection is so important when a callable bond is trading at a premium.

TEST TOPIC ALERT

The reason why we've only referred to a bond selling at a premium being called for redemption is that it is highly unlikely that an issuer would call in a bond that was available in the marketplace at a discount. After all, if the issuer could pay less than $1,000 to buy back the debt, why would they issue a call at par or higher?

The following example and chart will help you follow the discussion of the various bond yields.

Current Yield, Yield to Maturity, and Yield to Call

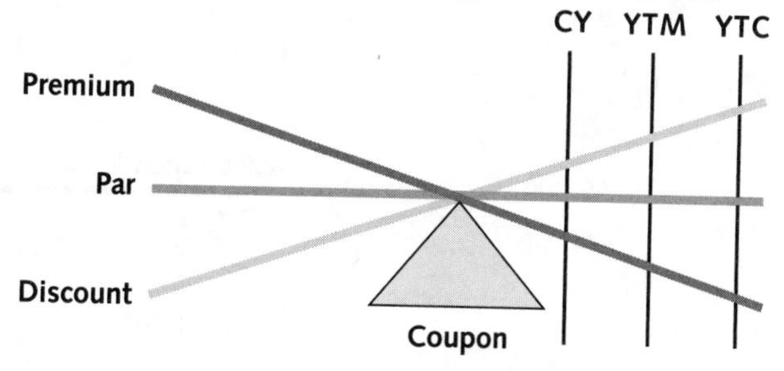

CY = Current Yield YTM = Yield to Maturity YTC = Yield to Call

1. What is the current yield of a 6% bond trading for 80 ($800)?

   Current yield = annual income / current market price

   Find the solution as follows: $60 / $800 = 7.5%. This bond is trading at a discount. When prices fall, yields rise. The current yield is greater than the nominal yield when bonds are trading at a discount.

2. What is the current yield of a 6% bond trading for 120 ($1,200)?

   Find the solution as follows: $60 / $1,200 = 5%. This bond is trading at a premium. The price is up so the yield is down. The current yield is less than the nominal yield when bonds are trading at a premium.

   It is critical to understand the inverse relationship between price and yield. An effective way to visualize it is through the chart. When bonds are at par, coupon and current yield are equal. When bonds are at a premium, the CY is less than the coupon. When bonds are at a discount, the CY is greater than the coupon.

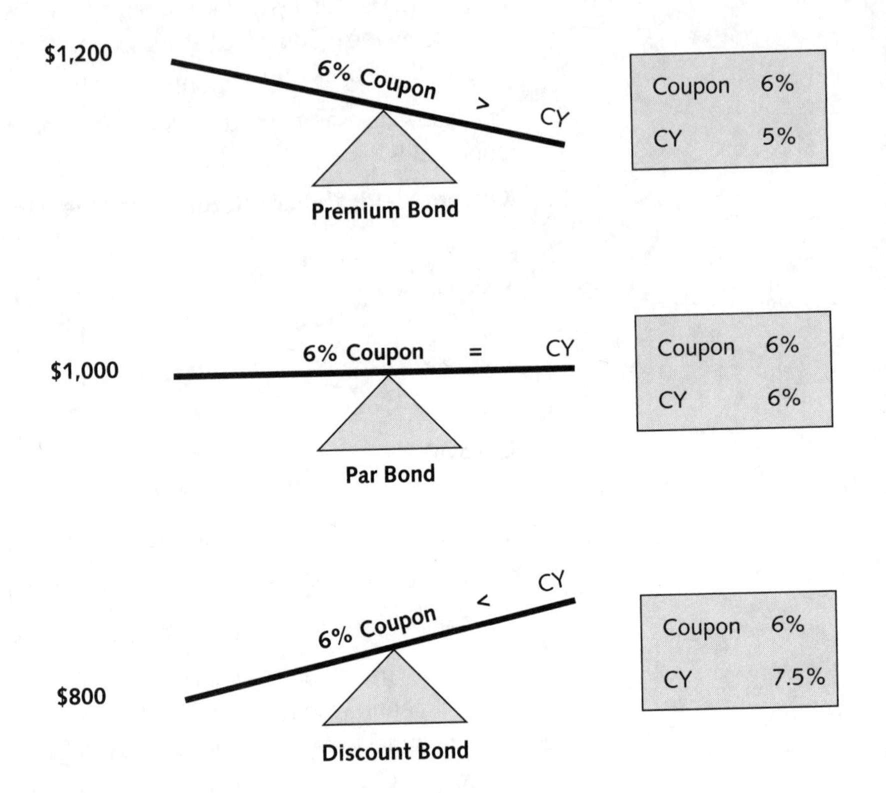

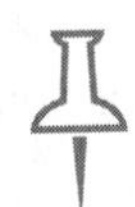

TAKE NOTE

Know how to calculate the CY of a bond or a stock. Expect to see one question on the calculation of CY.

The CY of common stock is calculated by dividing the current dividend by the current price of the stock. For instance, a stock with a $2 dividend trading on the market for $40 has a 5% CY ($2 / $40 = 5%).

EXAMPLE

Answer the following questions with **premium**, **par**, or **discount**.

1. If the bond has a YTC lower than its CY, it is trading at
2. If the bond has a YTM and CY that are equal, the bond is trading at
3. If the bond has a YTM less than its YTC, the bond is trading at
4. If a bond has a YTM greater than its coupon, the bond is trading at

The answers are: 1. premium; 2. par; 3. discount; and 4. discount.

TEST TOPIC ALERT

Memorize the following chart for the exam:

Ranking Yields from Lowest to Highest

Nominal	YTC
CY	YTM
YTM	CY
YTC	Nominal

Once you understand the yield ranking for discounts, the ranking for premium is easy—it is the exact opposite.

Price/Yield Relationship

There are many reasons interest rates rise and fall. The main concern for the exam, at this point, is the effect that interest rates have on the price fluctuations of bonds. As a rule, keep in mind that interest rates and bond prices move counter to each other. That is, when interest rates are going up, the price of older bonds will be going down. When interest rates are going down, the price of older bonds will be going up.

When most people hear this for the first time, they have difficulty understanding it. Simply stated, when newly issued bonds are paying a higher rate of interest than ones currently in the marketplace, those older bonds are not as attractive. After all, if a new bond came out with a 6% coupon, your 4% or 5% bond would not be as valuable (this always assumes equal quality or rating). Conversely, if you were holding a bond with an 8% coupon, and newly issued bonds were only offering 6%, your bond is more valuable.

PRACTICE QUESTION

2. When a bond with a 6% coupon is selling for 90, each of the following statements is correct except
   A. the current yield (CY) is approximately 6.67%.
   B. the bond is selling at a discount.
   C. the bondholder will receive two semiannual interest payments of $27 each.
   D. the yield to maturity is slightly higher than the current yield (CY).

Answer: C. A bond with a 6% coupon is going to make two semiannual interest payments of $30 each, regardless of the bond's market price. After all, the loan was $1,000 at 6% interest and that will not change. A price of 90 is 90% of the $1,000 par—clearly a discount. The CY is the $60 annual interest divided by the $900 price or 6.67%. That is a bit lower than the yield to maturity. Remember, if we hold the bond to maturity, we are going to get back the full $1,000. That will represent a $100 profit. Please see the earlier chart at the Test Topic Alert.

Duration

In Lesson 4.2, we mentioned that debt securities pay interest. There are two ways. All money market instruments, other than CDs, pay that "interest" through receiving the discount back at maturity. All bonds, with the exception of zero coupon bonds, pay semiannual interest.

In the financial industry, the term *duration* is used to measure the sensitivity of a debt security when interest rates change in the marketplace. It is a complicated computation, but, to try to simplify things, it is basically a measurement of the time it takes for the cash flow (interest payments) to repay the invested principal. The general rule is, the higher the coupon rate, the shorter the duration, and the lower the coupon, the longer the duration.

The longer the duration, the greater the market price movement, and vice versa. Long duration debt securities have greater interest-rate risk than those with a short duration.

TAKE NOTE

Coupon rate is the common term for the stated interest rate paid on a bond. A bond with 5% coupon is paying 5% of $1,000, or $50 per year. If it is a zero coupon bond, the stated interest rate is 0%. Who would lend $1,000 for 10 or more years without receiving any interest? I don't know any investors who would take that deal. The issuers of these bonds understand that so the bonds are issued at a significant discount from par. Similar to the money market instruments covered in a previous lesson, the investor receives the $1,000 face value at maturity. The difference between the purchase price, which could be as low as $300 or $400, and the maturity value is considered the "rent" (interest) for the use of the borrowed money.

The simplest duration question deals with a zero coupon bond. They are issued at a discount and mature at par. Their measured duration is always equal to the length to maturity. On the other hand, the duration of an interest-paying bond is always shorter than the time to its maturity. This is because the interest payments can be reinvested and earn additional interest. Zeroes will be covered in more detail in the next unit.

There are two components to the computation: the interest rate and the maturity date. If the maturity dates are about the same (the difference between a 20-year maturity and a 22-year one is almost insignificant), then the bond paying the highest coupon rate will always have the shortest duration and that with the lowest coupon, the longest. However, if the coupon rates are approximately the same, then the bond that will mature first will have the shortest duration, and the one that will mature last will have the longest duration.

TAKE NOTE

One way to keep things straight is to think about the zero coupon bond. With no periodic interest payments, the duration of a zero coupon bond will always equal its length to maturity. In other words, if we're trying to compute how long it will take for the income payments to return your principal, without any interest payments, you can't expect to get your money back until maturity date. If that is the case with a zero coupon bond, then as we find bonds paying interest, the more they're paying every six months, the quicker the payback.

TEST TOPIC ALERT

The general characteristics of duration follow:

- The lower the coupon rate, the longer a bond's duration; the higher the coupon rate, the shorter the duration.
- The longer a bond's maturity, the longer the bond's duration.
- For coupon bonds, duration is always less than the bond's maturity.
- Duration for a zero coupon bond is always equal to its maturity.

PRACTICE QUESTION

3. When a bond paying interest at the rate of $80 per year is quoted at 110, which of the following statements is **correct**?
   A. The nominal yield is lower than the coupon rate.
   B. The coupon rate is lower than the nominal yield.
   C. The current yield (CY) is higher than the yield to maturity.
   D. The yield to maturity is approximately 7.27%.

Answer: C. The nominal yield and the coupon rate mean the same thing. In this case, it is 8% ($80 interest on a $1,000 bond is 8%). Therefore, choices A and B cannot be correct. The CY is the $80 in interest divided by the current price of $1,100. Remember, the quote of 110 means 110% of $1,000. That computes to 7.27%. That must be higher than the yield to maturity. This bond is selling at a premium. At maturity, an investor who bought this bond will only get back the par value. That means a loss of $100 has to be part of the computation. That loss will make the YTM less than the CY. And, one more thing. Choice D could not be correct because we are missing a critical ingredient of YTM—the maturity date. Without knowing the number of YTM, we can't do the computation.

LESSON 4.5: THE RATINGS GAME

LO 4.f Recognize the relevance of a bond's rating.

Bond Ratings

The purchase of a debt security is only as safe as the strength of the borrower. That strength can be enhanced if the loan has collateral. Because safety of the bond will frequently be a very important consideration for clients, most investors consult the rating services. There are a number of different rating organizations. The following Take Note describes the ones recognized by the SEC.

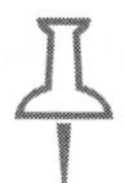

TAKE NOTE

There are seven ratings firms registered with the SEC. They are

- A.M. Best Co., Inc., (historically associated with rating insurance companies' ability to pay claims and their debt issues);
- DBRS, Ltd.;
- Fitch Ratings, Inc.;
- Japan Credit Rating Agency, Ltd.;
- Moody's Investors Service, Inc.;
- Rating and Investment Information, Inc.; and
- Standard and Poor's (S&P) Rating Service.

The most important rating organizations for the exam are S&P and Moody's. Both organizations have highly qualified personnel who analyze all the details of the debt issue and arrive at a letter rating indicating their opinion of the debt's quality (safety). The following chart should give you all the information you need for the exam.

Unit 4

Standard & Poor's Bond Ratings		Moody's Ratings	
AAA	Bonds of highest quality	Aaa	Bonds of highest quality
AA	High-quality debt obligations	Aa	Bonds of high quality
A	Bonds that have a strong capacity to pay interest and principal but may be susceptible to adverse effects	A	Bonds whose security of principal and interest is considered adequate but may be impaired in the future
BBB	Bonds that have an adequate capacity to pay interest and principal but are more vulnerable to adverse economic conditions or changing circumstances	Baa	Bonds of medium grade that are neither highly protected nor poorly secured
BB	Bonds of lower medium grade with few desirable investment characteristics	Ba	Bonds of speculative quality whose future cannot be considered well assured
B	Primarily speculative bonds with great uncertainties and major risk if exposed to adverse conditions	B	Bonds that lack characteristics of a desirable investment
CCC	Bonds in poor standing that may be defaulted	Caa	Bonds in poor standing that may be defaulted
C	Income bonds on which no interest is being paid	Ca	Speculative bonds that are often in default
D	Bonds in default	C	Bonds with little probability of any investment value (lowest rating)
Note: Plus (+) and minus (–) are used to show relative strength within a rating category.		Note: For ratings Aa through B, 1 indicates the high, 2 indicates the middle, and 3 indicates the low end of the rating class.	

You might see reference to the Fitch ratings and should note that they follow the same pattern as S&P.

PRACTICE QUESTION

4. According to Standard and Poor's (S&P) rating system, the four highest grades of bonds (from best to lowest grade) are
   A. Aaa, Aa, A, Baa.
   B. A, Aa, Aaa, B.
   C. B, A, AA, AAA.
   D. AAA, AA, A, BBB.

   Answer: D. Choice A would be correct if the question referred to Moody's.

Investment-Grade Debt

In the industry, bonds rated in the top four categories (BBB or Baa and higher) are referred to as investment grade. Investment-grade bonds are generally the only quality eligible for purchase by the institutions (e.g., banks or insurance companies) and by fiduciaries and therefore have greater liquidity than lower-grade instruments.

This is where the risk/reward concept comes into play. All other things equal, the higher the rating, the lower the yield. Think of these ratings as your personal credit score. When your score is 800, it is easy to borrow money. The rate you will be charged for the loan will be lower than for someone whose score is 600. The concept is, if the lender is going to have to take more risk that payments will not be made on time, there has to be a greater reward. That reward is in the form of a higher interest charge.

High-Yield Bonds

Lower-grade bonds, known in the industry as junk bonds, are now more commonly called high-yield bonds. Because of their lower ratings (BB or Ba or lower) and additional risk of default, high-yield bonds may be subject to substantial price erosion during slow economic times or when a bond issuer's creditworthiness is questioned. Their volatility is usually substantially higher than investment-grade bonds, but they may be suitable for sophisticated investors seeking higher returns and possible capital appreciation from speculative fixed-income investments.

Once again, think risk/reward. The less creditworthy the borrower, the more risk to the lender. That requires a greater reward to the lender to compensate for that risk. That is why lower-rated bonds carry higher rates of return.

It is important to understand that when the raters evaluate a bond they look at all the factors, including collateral. A mortgage bond is not necessarily safer than any debenture.

Finally, not all bonds are rated. Does that mean the risks are enormous? Not necessarily. The rating organizations rate those issues that either pay to be rated or have enough bonds outstanding to generate constant investor interest. The fact that a bond is not rated does not indicate its quality. Many issues are too small to justify the expense of a bond rating. In those cases, investors have to do their homework.

Money Market Ratings

The rating system for money market instruments follows the same concept as for bonds. The rating organizations attempt to measure the quality of the debt. As with bonds, the higher the quality, the lower the financing cost.

When it comes to short-term debt issues, you will need to know Moody's, S&P, and Fitch. Moody's Investment Grade (MIG) short-term note ratings are from MIG 1 (best quality) through MIG 4 (adequate quality). If a note is speculative, it is listed as SG. S&P rates notes as SP-1, SP-2, and SP-3. Fitch rates notes as F-1, F-2, and F-3.

LESSON 4.6: INVESTING IN ALTERNATIVE DEBT SECURITIES

LO 4.g Identify debt securities classified as alternative investments.

Types of Alternative Debt Financing

In the 1990s, financial advisers began introducing their wealthy clients to **alternative investments,** now generally referred to as Alts. These included, among other products, ETNs, leveraged ETFs, and new, highly sophisticated financial derivatives. They were often built "from the ground up"—another way of saying they could be created to meet the needs of a specific investor. That is why they are considered **structured** products. One thing that all of these had in common was that they were complex and not easy to understand. This was true for both the investor and the person recommending the investment.

Although investing can be complex, standard investments are fairly easy to comprehend. Even new investors understand that stocks have more risk but hold out the chance of superior returns, while bonds generally have less risk with correspondingly lower returns. All investors dream of scoring a touchdown and not getting tackled for a loss. Alternative investments try to do just that. Some are successful, but many are not. Suitability determinations need to be made on a case-by-case basis considering each customer's objectives, circumstances, and sophistication. Securities professionals must take special care in recommending these complex products to the sophisticated customer and even more so to one with less financial acumen.

Equity-Linked Notes (ELNs)

Equity-linked notes (ELNs) are debt instruments where the final payment at maturity is based on the return of a single stock, a basket of stocks, or an equity index. In the case where the note is based on the return of an index, the security would be known as an index-linked note. In the instances where the securities are traded on an exchange (most still are not), they are generally referred to as exchange-traded notes (ETNs). ELNs, exchange-traded or not, are considered alternative products with unique risks, and therefore, not suitable for most investors.

Those risks, in part, include

- credit risk (ELNs/ETNs are unsecured debt obligations);
- market risk;
- liquidity risk (although exchange-traded, a trading market may not develop);
- call, early redemption, and acceleration risk (ETNs may be called at the issuer's discretion); and
- conflicts of interest [the issuer may engage in trading activities that are at odds with note holders (shorting, for instance)].

TEST TOPIC ALERT

Don't be fooled by the name *equity-linked*. These are debt securities, not equity.

Private Placement Debt

As the name implies, this money is loaned on a private basis. These securities are not registered with any regulatory body, such as the SEC. Because of the private nature, there are no ratings to guide investors. Although the borrower can be a company in any stage of operations, these are commonly used as mezzanine debt. Just as the mezzanine in a theater is between the bottom and top floors, this is money that is borrowed at an intermediate point in the company's development. In general, the risks are high. That means the potential rewards are greater than just "leaving your money in the bank." It is not unusual for the lenders to be repaid in stock instead of cash. If the company goes on to be a roaring success, it can mean enormous returns to the investors.

Special Considerations

When comparing alternative investments, debt or equity, to traditional ones, the following factors must be considered:

- Lack of regulation
- Low transparency

- Low liquidity
- High fees
- Lack of historical data

With all of these negative risk factors, why lend money in this manner? In most cases, the investors are institutions or highly sophisticated (and wealthy) individuals. They are willing to take the risk for the higher potential rewards.

UNIT 5

Corporate Bonds

LEARNING OBJECTIVES

When you have completed this unit, you will be able to accomplish the following.

- LO 5.a **Name** the different types of corporate bonds.
- LO 5.b **Recall** the sequence of priority of claims in the event of a corporate liquidation.
- LO 5.c **Identify** the unique characteristics of convertible debt securities.
- LO 5.d **Compute** the parity price of a convertible bond.
- LO 5.e **Differentiate** between the different kinds of tax treatment of taxable debt securities.

INTRODUCTION

As we discussed in Unit 3, one way a corporation raises capital is by issuing equity securities—stock. Another way is debt financing, primarily through the issuance of bonds and debentures.

Debt capital represents money loaned to a corporation by investors who buy the issuer's debt securities. The corporation is obligated to pay back a specific sum of money (the principal) on a specific date (maturity). The corporation is also obligated to pay investors a stated rate of interest for the use of their funds. When investors buy a bond, they are lending a corporation money for a set length of time at a fixed annual interest rate.

As creditors, bondholders have several advantages. One advantage we will cover is the right of a bondholder in a corporate liquidation. One way a corporation can make its debt security more attractive is to add the convertible feature, just as we discussed with convertible preferred stock in Unit 3. In this unit, we will go further into computing parity. Another area where equity securities have an advantage is taxation, as we will discuss at the end of the unit.

LESSON 5.1: TYPES OF CORPORATE BONDS

LO5 a. Name the different types of corporate bonds.

Types of Bonds Issued by Corporations

Corporate debt securities, like any other loan, may be either secured or unsecured. **Secured debt securities** are backed by various kinds of assets of the issuing corporation. **Unsecured debt securities** are backed only by the reputation, credit record, and financial stability of the corporation. Regardless of whether secured or unsecured, the interest on debt securities is always paid before dividends on stock (preferred and common).

Mortgage Bonds

Just as the owner of a home pledges a real asset (the home and land) as collateral for the mortgage, a corporation will borrow money backed by real estate of the corporation. For example, the real estate could be the factories or office buildings the company owns. Just as a home ordinarily would have a market value greater than the principal amount of its mortgage the value of the real estate pledged by the corporation will be in excess of the amount borrowed under that bond issue. If the corporation develops financial problems and is unable to pay the interest on the bonds, those real assets pledged as collateral are generally sold to pay off the mortgage bondholders. There may be a situation where foreclosing on the property results in a sale below the outstanding mortgage balance. In that case, the mortgage holder becomes a general creditor for the unsatisfied balance.

Equipment Trust Certificates

Corporations, particularly railroads and airline companies, finance the acquisition of their rolling stock, locomotives, or airplanes by issuing an equipment trust certificate. The company makes a down payment—usually 20% of the cost of the rolling stock—and finances the balance over the course of time, for example, 15 years. Because the equipment does wear out, the railroad will pay off a portion of the loan on an annual basis. At no time, theoretically, is the value of the assets (the rolling stock, locomotives, or planes) worth less than the amount of the principal remaining on the loan. When the company has finished paying off the loan, it receives clear title to its equipment from the trustee. If the company does not make the payments, the lender repossesses the collateral and sells it for her benefit. If you have ever financed the purchase of a car, it is basically the same concept.

Collateral Trust Bonds

Sometimes a corporation wants to borrow money and has neither real estate (for a mortgage) nor equipment (for an equipment trust) to use as collateral. Instead, it deposits securities it owns into a trust to serve as collateral for the lenders. The securities it deposits can be securities in that corporation or any other securities as long as the securities are marketable, that is, readily liquidated. Obviously, the better the quality of the securities deposited as collateral, the better the quality and rating of the bond. You might see these called collateral trust certificates.

Debentures

A **debenture** is a debt obligation of the corporation backed only by its word and general creditworthiness. Debentures are written promises of the corporation to pay the principal at its due date and interest on a regular basis. Although this promise is as binding as a promise for a mortgage bond, debentures are not secured by any pledge of property. They are sold on the general credit of the company. The quality depends on the overall assets and earnings of the corporation. Although debentures are unsecured, there are issuers whose credit standing is so good that their debentures are safer than mortgage bonds of less creditworthy companies. This is similar in concept to the extension of credit on your credit cards. The better your credit score, the higher the limit and the lower the interest rate.

Guaranteed Bonds

A **guaranteed bond** is a bond that is guaranteed as to payment of interest, or both principal and interest, by a corporate entity other than the issuer. The value of the guarantee is only as good as the strength of the company making that guarantee. Guaranteed bonds were particularly popular in the railroad industry in which a major railroad seeking to lease trackage rights from a short line would guarantee that smaller company's debt. A more recent example is the ExxonMobil Corporation guaranteeing the debt issues of the Exxon Pipeline Company.

Senior

The word *senior* describes the relative priority of claim of a security. Every preferred stock has a senior claim to common stock. Every debt security has senior claim to preferred stock. Secured bonds have a senior claim to unsecured debt, such as debentures. The term senior security means bonds and preferred stock, because they have a claim senior to common stock. If an exam question described a corporation as having issued senior bonds, the answer would have to state that there were mortgage bonds and/or collateral trust bonds and/or equipment trust certificates issued by that corporation with prior claim ahead of unsecured creditors.

Subordinated

The term *subordinated* means "belonging to a lower or inferior class or rank; secondary[1]." It is usually describing a debenture. A subordinated debenture has a claim that is behind (junior to) that of any other creditor. However, no matter how subordinated the debenture, it is still senior to any stockholder.

Income Bonds

Income bonds, also known as **adjustment bonds**, are used when a company is reorganizing and coming out of bankruptcy. Income bonds pay interest only if the corporation has enough income to meet the interest payment and if the board of directors declares a payment. Because missed interest payments do not accumulate for future payment, these bonds are not suitable investments for customers seeking stable income.

1. Dictionary.com

PRACTICE QUESTION

1. A debenture is issued with the backing of
   A. the general credit of the corporation.
   B. a pledge of real estate.
   C. a pledge of equipment.
   D. the ability to levy taxes.

Answer: A. There are no pledged assets behind a debenture—merely the credit standing of the corporation. A pledge of real estate would back a mortgage bond. A pledge of equipment would back an equipment trust certificate. Only corporations issue debentures and corporations cannot levy taxes.

Zero Coupon Bond

All bonds we have discussed up to this point pay semiannual interest. **Zero coupon bonds (zeroes)** are debt obligations that do not make any interest payments. Instead, zeroes are issued, or trade, at a deep discount and mature at par ($1,000). The difference between the discounted purchase price and the full face value at maturity is the return the investor receives. That return is called accretion. We will learn about the tax treatment of accretion later in this unit.

The current market price of a zero coupon bond reflects the current interest rates for similar maturities. In addition to corporations, state and local governments, as well as the U.S. Treasury, can issue zero coupon bonds.

The major attraction of this type of investment is that it allows an investor to lock in a yield (or rate of return) for a predetermined, investor-selected time with no reinvestment risk (covered in Lesson 14.1). That is why these are often used to fund future education or retirement needs. Because all zeroes are sold at discounts and have no current return, there is a great deal of price volatility. As we learned in Unit 4, the duration of a zero coupon bond is always equal to the length to maturity. For regular bonds paying interest every six months, the duration (the payback) is shorter. Shorter duration equals less volatility.

LESSON 5.2: PRIORITY IN DISSOLUTIONS

LO 5.b Recall the sequence of priority of claims in the event of a corporate liquidation.

Liquidation Priority

When a corporation is unable to meet its obligations, it is sometimes forced to liquidate. This is generally done through a formal bankruptcy filing. The exact procedure and the different types of filings are not tested. The exam may ask you who is last, who is first, and who is in between.

At this point in your study, you are probably able to answer that question. Just to be sure, here it is.

- Secured creditors (e.g., mortgage bonds, equipment trust certificates, collateral trust bonds)
- Unsecured creditors (e.g., general creditors, including debenture holders)
- Subordinated debt holders

- Preferred stockholders
- Common stockholders

Regardless of how low on the totem pole a debt security is, such as a subordinated debenture, it still has priority in terms of payment of interest and principal ahead of any equity security. Look for a question asking, in essence, "In the event of a corporate liquidation, who comes first: A senior, prior lien preferred stock, or a junior, unsecured subordinated debenture?" Now, you may not see all of those adjectives, but no matter what, a debt security always has priority over an equity security.

In addition, the exam may want you to know about the priority of items that are not securities. Highest priority, *after the secured* creditors, such as mortgage bonds, is given to wages (up to an indexed amount earned in the 180 days before the employer's declaration of bankruptcy), followed by taxes, and then the unsecured (general) creditors, such as the debentures.

TAKE NOTE

It is possible that the exam will ask about claims from those not owning securities. The term is *administrative claims* (or something to that effect). In a bankruptcy, there are many administrative roles. They include attorneys, property appraisers, the courts, et cetera. They must be paid for doing the work and therefor have first priority. There could even be a case where the presiding judge honors claims of employees and those owed taxes before the secured creditors. We don't expect this on your exam, only the earlier list. Nevertheless, just in case something should show up, we want you to be prepared.

PRACTICE QUESTION

2. If a corporation, whose stock is publicly traded, declares bankruptcy, holders of which of the following would be most likely to recover the greatest amount of their investment?
   A. Control stock
   B. Senior preferred stock
   C. Debentures
   D. Collateral trust certificates

Answer: D. Creditors of the corporation have the first claim. Secured creditors—those with assets pledged as collateral—are at the "top of the heap." They are followed by general creditors, such as debenture holders. Regardless of the adjective employed, preferred stock is equity and all debt is ahead of equity. Control stock has no meaning here. It is common stock and, like all common stock, has the final claim.

LESSON 5.3: CONVERTIBLE DEBT

LO 5.c Identify the unique characteristics of convertible debt securities.

Convertible Debt Securities

A special type of long-term corporate debt security not covered in the previous lesson is one that is convertible. What is the convertible feature? When these are issued, the company states that lenders (the investors) may exchange (convert) the debt into shares of the company's common stock. These convertible securities are only issued by corporations. Because they may be converted or exchanged for the company's common stock, there are no convertible municipal or government bonds. The conversion privilege is exercised at the discretion of the investor. The ratio of conversion varies from one company's bond to another, according to the terms set forth in the indenture at the time the bonds are issued. The exact number of shares (or method of computing the number) that a particular bond will be convertible into at any point is printed in the bond indenture at the time of issue. Most convertibles are debentures.

Conversion Ratio

The **conversion price** is the stock price at which a convertible bond can be exchanged for shares of common stock. The **conversion ratio**, also called the **conversion rate**, expresses the number of shares of stock a bond may be converted into.

In many cases, the indenture merely tells you the number of shares into which the bond is convertible. For example, the bond may be convertible into 50 shares; thus, it would have a conversion ratio of 50:1, 50 shares for 1 bond. If a bond is convertible into 25 shares, it would have a conversion ratio of 25:1.

Frequently, instead of telling the number of shares into which the bond is convertible, the indenture will give the conversion price. That conversion price is the price per share that the corporation will sell their stock in exchange for the bond one is holding. Regardless of the current market price of the bond, the bond always represents a debt of the corporation of $1,000. Therefore, if the conversion price is given, to compute the number of shares into which the bond is convertible, always divide the par value ($1,000) by the conversion price. For example, a bond convertible at $20 per share is convertible into 50 shares ($1,000 ÷ $20 = 50 shares).

If the bond has a conversion price of $50, the conversion ratio is 20 shares ($1,000 ÷ $50 = 20 shares).

EXAMPLE

If the JRP 6s of '31, currently selling at 120, were convertible at $40, how many shares would one get when one converted the bond? The answer is not 30. The current market has nothing to do with the computation. The bond conversion is fixed at issuance, and the market fluctuates all the time. The correct answer is 25 shares ($1,000 ÷ $40 = 25 shares).

TAKE NOTE

The same concept applies to convertible preferred stock. An investor bought a share of preferred $100 par. You can derive that the investor is entitled to five shares of common—$100 ÷ the conversion price of $20 = conversion ratio of five shares.

Advantages of Convertible Securities to the Issuer

A corporation adds a conversion feature to its bonds or preferred stock to make it more marketable. This is similar to the "sweetener" concept we mentioned in Unit 3. Other facts about convertible securities include the following:

- Convertibles can be sold with a lower coupon rate than nonconvertibles because of the conversion feature.
- A company can eliminate a fixed interest charge as conversion takes place, thus reducing debt.

- Because conversion normally occurs over time, it does not have an adverse effect on the stock price, which may occur after a subsequent primary offering.
- At issuance, conversion price is higher than market price of the common stock.

Disadvantages of Convertible Securities to the Issuer

On the other hand, convertibles have potential disadvantages for a corporation and its stockholders. Most of these will be clearer as we move further into the course.

- When bonds are converted, shareholders' equity is diluted; that is, more shares are outstanding, so each share now represents a smaller fraction of ownership in the company.
- Common stockholders have a voice in the company's management, so a substantial conversion could cause a shift in the control of the company.
- Reducing corporate debt through conversion means a loss of leverage.
- The resulting decrease in deductible interest costs raises the corporation's taxable income.

Advantages of Convertible Securities to Investors

Convertible bonds offer the safety of the fixed-income market and the potential appreciation of the equity market, providing investors with the following advantages:

- As a debt security, a **convertible debenture** pays interest at a fixed rate and is redeemable for its face value at maturity, provided the debenture is not converted. As a rule, interest income is higher and surer than dividend income on the underlying common stock. Similarly, convertible preferred stock usually pays a higher dividend than does common stock.
- If a corporation experiences financial difficulties, convertible bondholders have priority over common stockholders in the event of a corporate liquidation.
- In theory, a convertible debenture's market price tends to be more stable during market declines than the underlying common stock's price. If the stock price declines to a level well below the conversion price, the debenture's price will then reflect a CY competitive with other debt securities.
- Because convertibles can be exchanged for common stock, their market price tends to move upward if the stock price moves up. The owner of a convertible debenture has all the upside potential of the common stockholder with less downside risk. That means possible inflation protection. This is a feature most fixed-income securities do not offer.
- Conversion of a senior security into common stock is not considered a purchase and a sale for tax purposes. Thus, the investor incurs no tax liability on the conversion transaction.

Disadvantages of Convertible Securities to Investors

- The primary disadvantage to an investor is the lower interest rate paid on convertibles. For test purposes, it is important to know that these are not suitable for investors with the objective of income. Specifically, if a question lists a number of different investment vehicles and it states that the investor is looking for income, do not select the convertible bond option. There will be a better choice.

- Because most convertibles are debentures, the investor's priority is lower than other debt securities. That can be a concern if the company's financial outlook is shaky.
- If the security is callable, there is the possibility the issuer will call it and force the investor to decide whether or not to convert. Once converted, the semiannual interest payments are gone. This means the investor is subject to all of the risks of owning common stock. The investor no longer receives the obligatory semiannual interest payments. As a common stockholder, the priority in liquidation is at the bottom.

Anti-Dilutive Protection

Think of the everyday definition of dilution. If you took a chemistry class in school, you couldn't use acid at its full strength. You added a solution to it and the acid was diluted (weakened). Put ice in your beverage and, as it melts, the drink is diluted. Dilution is a topic of interest in this industry.

One of the concerns of any holder of a convertible security (bond or preferred stock) is protection against the potential dilution resulting from a stock split or a stock dividend. For example, if you owned a bond convertible into 20 shares and the issuer declared a 2:1 stock split, in order for you to have the same conversion benefit, you would need to be able to convert into 40 shares. On the other hand, if the conversion privilege were expressed as a conversion price, the new price would now be half the former one, allowing you to convert into twice as many "new" shares.

PRACTICE QUESTION

3. An investor seeking to maximize current income would find which of the following investments least suitable?
   A. Callable bond
   B. Convertible debenture
   C. Equipment trust certificate
   D. Mortgage bond

Answer: B. One of the negative points about investing in convertible securities is their reduced income. Whether the dividend on a convertible preferred stock or the interest on a convertible debenture, the dividend or interest will be lower than other securities of that issuer. Investors accept the lower income in exchange for the ability to profit from the conversion feature. The key point is, do not recommend convertible securities to those investors seeking to maximize current income.

LO 5.d Compute the parity price of a convertible bond.

Computing Parity

All of the comments we've made about convertible bonds (or convertible preferred) moving in relation to the underlying common stock is because of the concept of parity. According to the dictionary, when two things are at parity, they are equal. How does that work here? If you think about it, when holding a convertible security, investors have a choice of two actions: they can either continue to hold the bond (or preferred), or, they can decide to convert it into the common. If the convertible security and the common stock we would get upon conversion are worth the same, we say they are at parity. Before we can get into the computations, we need a short lesson in corporate bond quotes.

Corporate Bond Quotes

In Lesson 4.2, we introduced you to the concept of quoting bonds as a percentage of their $1,000 par value. Let's take it one step further by showing you how those quotes can be in fractions. With a face value of $1,000, each percentage point of that face is equal to $10. That would mean a bond quoted at 99 is $990 and one quoted at 101 is $1,010. These $10 "points" are further divided into eights. Each 1/8 has a value of $1.25 (divide $10.00 by 8 and it equals $1.25).

EXAMPLE

The following may help you on some questions:

- ⅛ = $1.25
- ¼ = $3.50
- ⅜ = $3.75
- ½ = $5.00
- ⅝ = $6.25
- ¾ = $7.50
- ⅞ = $8.75

PRACTICE QUESTION

4. ABC Corporation's 4% bond is currently trading at 98⅝. That would be price of
   A. $98.625.
   B. $980.625.
   C. $985.80.
   D. $986.25.

Answer: D. We do this in two steps. First, the 98 is 98% of $1,000, or $980. Second, we add the ⅝, which is $6.25. That totals $986.25. Remember, the fraction is of $10.00, not $1.00.

A question looking for the parity price will always include mention of the conversion rate of the convertible security (debenture or preferred stock). If it is looking for the parity price of the *stock*, it will include the current market price of the *convertible*. If the question is about the parity price of the *convertible*, then it will show the current market price of the *stock*.

EXAMPLE

On the exam, there may be questions on computing the parity price. Here are two methods to help you solve the problem.

RST debenture is convertible to common at $50. If RST bond is currently trading for $1,200, what is the parity price of the common?

Method One: Parity means equal. Solve for the conversion ratio as follows:

Par value: $1,000

Conversion price: $50

Conversion ratio: 20

The parity stock price is found by dividing $1,200 by 20. The parity price of the common is $60.

Think of the phrase, "Six of one, half-dozen of the other." That means whichever you have, they are both worth the same. In this case, we are told the bond is trading at $1,200. We know you can swap it for 20 shares. If those shares are selling for $60 each, converting gets you the same $1,200 in value as just holding the bond. That is parity—equal.

Method Two: If you prefer to think in percentages, identify that the current debenture's price of $1,200 is 20% greater than the original $1,000 price. To be at equivalence, the stock price must also increase by 20%. So add 20% to 50 and the problem is solved. 20% of 50 is 10; 10 + 50 = parity price of $60.

Here is another question about parity style.

RST debenture is convertible to common at $50. If the common is trading for $45, what is the parity price of the debenture? Start by solving for the conversion ratio.

Par value: $1,000

Conversion price: $50

Conversion ratio: 20

The debenture's parity price is found by multiplying 20 × $45, which is $900. Using the percentage method, you can determine that the market price of the common stock is 10% below that of the conversion price (5 ÷ 50 = 10%). Reducing the debenture price of $1,000 by 10% results in a parity price of the debenture of $900.

It is important to remember that parity is a theoretical concept—we're looking for the price that would make the bond and stock "equal." In actuality, convertible securities, whether debentures or preferred stock, almost always have a market price that is somewhat above the parity price.

When the equity market is strong and stock prices are rising, the convertible's value rises with the underlying common stock's value. When equity prices are declining, the convertible's market price declines as well, but generally levels off when its yield becomes competitive with the yield on nonconvertible bonds. This tends to keep it from declining as much as the common stock. Convertible bonds normally sell at a premium above parity.

PRACTICE QUESTION

5. ABC Corporation has issued $100 million of convertible debentures having a nondilutive covenant. Each debenture is convertible into 40 shares of ABC's common stock. If ABC declares a 2:1 stock split,
   A. each debenture will be convertible into 20 shares.
   B. the conversion price of each debenture will be $25 per share.
   C. the conversion price of each debenture will be $12.50 per share.
   D. the total value of the debentures will increase to $200 million.

Answer: C. When a debenture is convertible into 40 shares, the conversion price is $25 per share ($1,000 divided by 40 shares). After a 2:1 stock split, the conversion rate will now be twice as many shares (80). The split will make the conversion price half of what it initially was. Instead of $25 per share, it will be $12.50 ($1,000 divided by 80 shares). The key takeaway is that anytime there is an action creating more shares (without raising more money), such as a stock split or a stock (not cash) dividend, the price per share goes down.

LESSON 5.4: TAXATION OF CORPORATE DEBT

LO 5.e Differentiate between the different kinds of tax treatment of taxable debt securities.

Just as with equity securities, corporate debt securities are subject to taxation. In this lesson we will describe the kinds of tax issues facing investors in corporate debt.

Interest

In all cases on the exam, the interest paid by corporations on their debt securities is treated as ordinary income. Unlike dividends on stock, there is no category of "qualified" interest with a reduced tax rate. In addition to federal income tax, this interest is taxable on a state and local level as well. If the bondholder lives in a state with an income tax, that just increases the tax burden. Some cities have an income tax and that adds to the total amount of taxes paid.

In the previous lesson, we discussed the zero coupon bond. Although zeroes pay no regular interest income, investors in zeroes owe income tax each year on the amount by which the bonds have accreted, just as if the investor had received it in cash. The income tax is due regardless of the direction of the market price. Let's look at an example to see how that works.

EXAMPLE

An investor buys a 10-year zero coupon corporate bond for $400. At maturity, the investor will receive the full face value of $1,000. As a result, the investor realizes $600 of interest income. Each year, however, the investor must accrete the discount and pay income tax on the annual income. This investor didn't "see" the income annually, but still has to pay taxes on it. We call that *phantom* income.

Here is how it works: The IRS requires the investor to accrete the discount annually on a straight-line basis. The total discount is $600. Because there are 10 YTM, the investor must accrete $60 annually ($600 ÷ 10 years). Each year, the investor pays income tax on $60 of interest income. The good news is that each year, the investor is permitted to adjust the cost basis of the zero upward by the amount of the annual accretion. After one year, the investor's cost basis is $460.

After two years, the cost basis is $520. After three years, it is $580, and so on. At maturity, the cost basis will be adjusted to par. Therefore, if held to maturity, there is no capital gain (cost basis is par; redeemed at par).

However, if the investor sells the zero before maturity, there may be a capital gain or a capital loss, depending on the difference between sales proceeds and the cost basis (accreted value) at time of sale.

If the same 10-year zero bought at $400 is sold five years later for $720, the investor will realize a $20 per-bond gain. At that point, the investor's cost basis is $700 ($400 plus five years of annual accretion of $60 per year).

PRACTICE QUESTION

6. An investor purchases a corporate zero coupon bond at a price of $510. The bond matures in seven years. Four years later, the bond is sold at a price of $690. What are the tax consequences of the sale?
   A. Gain of $180
   B. Loss of $100
   C. Loss of $310
   D. No gain or loss until maturity

   Answer: B. The amount of the discount is $490 ($1,000 – $510). This must be accreted over the seven years until maturity. The annual accretion is $70 ($490 ÷ 7 years). After four years, there is $280 of accretion (4 × $70). Because the annual accretion is added to the investor's cost basis, the basis is now $790 ($510 + $280). The bond's sale price of $690 is $100 below the accreted basis. That means a loss of $100.

Capital Gains and Capital Losses

The practice question we just did is a great segue into the next topic. Just as with other assets, when a bond is sold for a price higher than its cost, there is a capital gain. When sold below cost, there is a capital loss.

As we've stated, holding a zero coupon bond to maturity results in no gain or loss. That is not the case with interest-bearing bonds. There is no accretion with them. Just compare purchase and sale prices to determine a gain or a loss. When a bond is held to maturity, the sale price is par.

The tax rules are the same as we learned in Lesson 3.4. If the holding period is 12 months or less, any gain or loss is short-term. If the holding period is longer than 12 months, it is long-term. When computing net gains and losses, it makes no difference whether the transaction is in a bond or a stock. A gain is a gain and a loss is a loss. The IRS is only concerned about long-term and short-term.

UNIT 6

Municipal Bonds

LEARNING OBJECTIVES

When you have completed this unit, you will be able to accomplish the following.

- LO 6.a **Identify** the general characteristics of municipal bonds.
- LO 6.b **Describe** the purposes of the different types of municipal securities.
- LO 6.c **Compare** the methods of analyzing general obligation (GO) and revenue bonds.
- LO 6.d **Recognize** the factors affecting the marketability of municipal bonds.
- LO 6.e **Perform** the various municipal bond calculations.
- LO 6.f **Differentiate** between the different kinds of tax treatment of municipal securities.
- LO 6.g **Identify** the types of municipal fund securities.
- LO 6.h **Determine** the rules and regulations pertaining to the sale of municipal securities.

INTRODUCTION

Municipal debt financing is represented by securities issued either by a state or local government or by U.S. territories. They can also be issued by municipal authorities and special districts. Investors who buy these securities are loaning money to the issuers for the purpose of public works and construction projects (e.g., roads, hospitals, civic centers, sewer systems, and airports). Municipal securities are considered second in safety of principal only to U.S. government and U.S. government agency securities. The safety of a particular issue is based on the issuing municipality's financial stability. Most of the exam questions will deal with municipal bonds. As with the bonds we have previously discussed, these represent long-term debt. There may also be some questions about short-term financing. That is done by issuing notes, and we will cover them after the bonds. One highly tested area is that of the special tax treatment afforded the interest on these securities. After covering that, we will conclude the unit with a discussion of some of the rules issues by the MSRB.

LESSON 6.1: GENERAL CHARACTERISTICS OF MUNICIPAL BONDS

LO 6.a Identify the general characteristics of municipal bonds.

Municipal Bond Price or Basis Quotations

In a few cases, municipal bonds are quoted the same as corporate bonds (Lesson 5.3). That is, a percentage of par and in fractions of eighths. Municipal bonds are usually priced and offered for sale on a **yield to maturity (YTM)** basis rather than a dollar price. This is called a **basis quote**. In this case, the bond's basis is its YTM. If the bond is quoted at a 3.78 basis, it means the yield to maturity is 3.78%.

Each basis point is 1/100 of 1 percent. That is, if the yield on the previous bond quoted at a 3.78 basis should fall to a yield of 3.65%, we would say the yield has dropped by 13 basis points. We can also use basis points to reflect price changes. If one point on a bond is equal to $10 (1% of $1,000), then 1 basis point is 1/100 of that or 10 cents ($0.10).

In other cases, the bond quote is just a regular percentage. That would mean a bond quoted at 102.4% is trading at $1,024. When a bond is quoted as a price instead of basis (yield), it is known as a *dollar bond.*

EXAMPLE

A basis quote may be listed as 7s 35 at 7.5. This is a 7% coupon for a bond maturing in 2035 with a YTM of 7.5%. If the YTM is greater than the coupon, we can determine that the bond is trading at a discount.

A price quote may be listed as 7s 35 at 99.5. This is a 7% coupon for a bond maturing in 2035 with a price of 99.5% of par, or $995. If the bond is trading at a discount, we can determine that the YTM is greater than the coupon. This is an example of a *dollar bond*.

For those who trade bonds, it is easy to turn a basis quote into a price quote or turn a price quote into a basis quote (there is software for that). You won't have to do it, but should know the relationship between price and yield.

A zero coupon bond would be listed with *Zr*, indicating the bond pays no interest: Zr 35 at 70.

TEST TOPIC ALERT

If a question mentions a 6% bond quoted on a 6.5 basis, you should be able to determine that the coupon of the bond is 6% and its YTM is 6.5%. Because the YTM is higher than the coupon, the bond is trading at a discount.

EXAMPLE

Are the following bonds trading at premium or a discount?

1. 7% bond, 6.25% basis
2. 7% bond, 7.64% basis
3. 5% bond, 4.85% basis
4. 6% bond, 6.45% basis

Answers: 1. Premium; 2. Discount; 3. Premium; 4. Discount

Municipal Bond Quote Rules

Municipal bonds are bought and sold in the OTC market. They are not listed on the stock exchanges. Most large brokerages maintain trading departments that deal exclusively in municipal bonds. Under the Securities Acts Amendments of 1975, the MSRB was created to regulate securities professionals in the municipal securities field. In this unit, we will regularly refer to MSRB rules. It is not necessary to learn the numbers. We will start with Rule G-13 dealing with quotes.

Bona Fide (Firm) Quotes

If a municipal dealer gives, distributes, or publishes a quotation for a security, that quote must be **bona fide**. For a quote to be considered bona fide, or **firm**, the dealer must be prepared to trade the security at the price specified in the quote and under the conditions and restrictions (if any) accompanying the quote. A bona fide quote

- must reflect the dealer's best judgment and have a reasonable relationship to the fair market value (FMV) for that security and
- may reflect the firm's inventory and expectations of market direction.

In other words, a quotation need not represent the best price, but it must have a reasonable relationship to FMV. A quotation may take into consideration other factors, such as the dealer's inventory position and any anticipated market movement.

If the dealer distributes or publishes the quotation on behalf of another dealer, it must have reason to believe that the quote is bona fide and based on the other dealer's best judgment of FMV. Dealers cannot knowingly misrepresent a quote made by another municipal securities dealer.

Quotations are always subject to prior sale or change in price. Any means of communication, including print, voice, and electronic media, can be used to disseminate, distribute, or publish quotations.

TAKE NOTE

Municipal dealers can make offers to sell securities by providing quotes without owning the bonds. The dealer, however, must know where to obtain the bonds if such offers are accepted.

Other Types of Quotations

In addition to a firm quote, a municipal securities dealer can give several other types of quotations. The most common are workable indications and nominal quotes. A dealer can also hold a quote for a specified time.

- A **workable indication** reflects a bid price at which a dealer will purchase securities from another dealer. A dealer giving a workable indication is always free to revise her bid for the securities as market conditions change.
- A **nominal, or subject, quotation** indicates a dealer's estimate of a security's market value. Nominal quotations are provided for informational purposes only and are permitted if the quotes are clearly labeled as such. The rules on nominal quotes apply to all municipal bond quotes distributed or published by any dealer.
- **Holding a quote**. A municipal securities dealer may quote a bond price that is firm for a certain time. This is called an **out-firm** with recall quote. Generally, these quotes are

firm for an hour (or half hour) with a five-minute recall period. This provides time for the dealer who requested the quote to search for a better quote before selling the bonds. If, during this period, the firm that made the quote has another buyer interested in the same bonds, that firm can contact the dealer and give him five minutes to act on the quote. If no action is taken and a transaction does not take place within the five-minute recall period, he loses the right to buy the bonds at the quoted price.

TAKE NOTE

Receiving an out-firm quote allows dealers to try to sell bonds that they don't own, knowing that if they find a buyer within the allotted time, they can buy the bonds at a fixed price from the firm providing the out-firm quote.

- **BW/OW**. Municipal dealers are called upon regularly to provide current quotations for municipal securities they do not have in inventory. Municipal bonds are not listed on any exchange—they do not have the quote and price transparency of listed securities. When a customer of a municipal firm is looking for a specific bond, the dealer will actively solicit offers to sell from the marketplace. If the customer has bonds to sell, the dealer will actively solicit bids from the marketplace for those bonds.

TEST TOPIC ALERT

Under MSRB rules, any indication of interest or solicitation by a municipal dealer (such as *bid wanted* or *offer wanted*) would be considered a quotation request. The term *quotation* means any bid for or offer of municipal securities.

- **Multiple markets in the same security.** There are some very large financial organizations that have more than one broker-dealer under their control. Let's call them Affiliate X and Affiliate Y. If they publish a quote for a municipal security, it must be clear that this represents only one quote instead of two independent quotes. To do otherwise would imply a greater liquidity in the bonds.

Municipal Bond Maturities

There are three types of maturity schedules commonly found with municipal debt issues. Any of the following may be on your exam.

Term Maturity

All principal matures at a single date in the future. Term bonds are quoted by price (like corporate bonds) and, as mentioned previously, are called **dollar bonds**.

EXAMPLE

Consider the following municipal bond issue:

$200 million Illinois GO 5% debentures due November 1, 2041.

The entire $200 million matures in 2041.

To facilitate the retirement of its bonds, a corporate or municipal issuer may establish a **sinking fund** operated by the bonds' trustee. The trust indenture often requires a sinking fund, which can be used to call bonds, redeem bonds at maturity, or buy back bonds in the open market. The concept is similar to the escrow account on a home mortgage. Monthly payments are made by the homeowner to ensure that funds will be available to pay the annual insurance premium and property taxes.

To establish a sinking fund, the issuer deposits cash in an account with the trustee. Because a sinking fund makes money available for paying off the bonds, it can aid the bonds' marketability and safety.

Serial Maturity

Bonds within an issue mature on different dates according to a predetermined schedule. The following sample serial maturity structure table shows an example of a $100 million State of Illinois GO serial issue.

Figure 6.1: Sample Serial Maturity Structure

Amount	Coupon	Maturity	Price/Yield
$10 million	6%	11-1-39	5.80%
$10 million	6%	11-1-40	5.90%
$10 million	6%	11-1-41	100.00%
$10 million	6%	11-1-42	6.10%
$20 million	6%	11-1-43	6.20%
$20 million	6%	11-1-44	6.30%
$20 million	6%	11-1-45	6.40%

Serial bonds are quoted on the basis of their yield to maturity (basis), to reflect the difference of maturity dates within one issue. A price/yield of 100% indicates the yield to maturity is equal to the coupon rate, which means the bond is being offered at par. Notice that the longer the maturity, the higher the yield.

Balloon Maturity

An issuer pays part of a bond's maturity before the final maturity date, but the largest portion is paid off at maturity. The sample balloon maturity table below shows an example of a $100 million State of Georgia GO balloon maturity issue due August 1, 2045.

Figure 6.2: Sample Balloon Maturity

Amount	Coupon	Maturity	Price/Yield
$10 million	6%	8-1-40	4.80%
$10 million	6%	8-1-40	4.90%
$10 million	6%	8-1-41	100.00%
$70 million	6%	8-1-45	5.20%

TAKE NOTE

A balloon maturity is a type of serial maturity. Also note that most municipal bonds are issued serially.

PRACTICE QUESTION

1. All of the following statements are generally true about dollar bonds **except**
   A. they are term bonds.
   B. they are serial bonds.
   C. they have a sinking fund provision.
   D. they are quoted as a percentage of par.

   Answer: B. Dollar bonds are quoted as a percentage of par. That means in dollars and cents (hence the reason for their name). These are invariably term bonds because serial bonds are quoted on yield basis. With the principal payout due in a lump sum at the end of the term, a sinking fund is usually added to provide for the ultimate payoff.

Legal Opinion

Printed on the face of every bond certificate (unless the bond is specifically stamped *Ex-Legal*) is a legal opinion written and signed by the **bond counsel**, an attorney specializing in tax-exempt bond offerings. The issuer of the debt is responsible for retaining the bond counsel. The legal opinion states that the issue is legally binding on the issuer and conforms to applicable laws. If interest from the bond is tax-exempt, that too is stated in the legal opinion.

The legal opinion is issued either as a **qualified opinion** (there may be a legal uncertainty of which purchasers should be informed) or as an **unqualified opinion** (issued by the bond counsel unconditionally).

Some issuers, normally smaller municipalities, choose not to obtain a legal opinion. In such a case, the bond certificate must clearly state that the bonds are **ex-legal**. The ex-legal designation allows a bond to meet good delivery requirements without an attached legal opinion.

The Underwriter's Counsel

The managing underwriter may choose to employ another law firm as underwriter's counsel. This firm is not responsible for the legal opinion and is employed to represent the underwriter's interests.

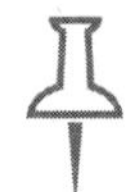

TAKE NOTE

Issuers desire an unqualified legal opinion.

PRACTICE QUESTION

2. The bond counsel's services in providing the legal opinion associated with a new issue of municipal bonds is the responsibility of
   A. the issuer.
   B. the underwriter.
   C. the investor.
   D. the MSRB.

   Answer: A. The issuer retains the bond attorneys, or the bond counsel, for a new municipal bond issue. The underwriters may also hire bond counsel, but they do not provide the legal opinion.

LESSON 6.2: DIFFERENT TYPES OF MUNICIPAL SECURITIES

LO 6.b Describe the purposes of the different types of municipal securities.

Municipal securities are defined by their maturities. Those with a maturity of less than five years are considered municipal notes. Those with longer maturities are municipal bonds. We will start with the bonds first. Two categories of municipal bonds exist:

- *General obligation bonds (GOs)* are backed by the full faith, credit, and taxing powers of the municipality. GOs issued by local (not state) government units are most often backed by ad valorem taxes.
- *Revenue bonds* are backed by the revenues generated by the municipal facility the bond issue finances. Sometimes that revenue comes from special taxes, such as excise taxes or other specified non-ad valorem taxes.

GOs Issues

GOs are municipal bonds issued for capital improvements that benefit the entire community. Typically, these projects do not produce revenues, so principal and interest must be paid by taxes collected by the municipal issuer. Because of this backing, GOs are known as **full faith and credit issues**.

Sources of Funds

GOs are backed by the issuing municipality's taxing power. Bonds issued by states are backed by income taxes, license fees, and sales taxes. Bonds issued by towns, cities, and counties are backed by property (ad valorem) taxes, license fees, fines, and all other sources of revenue to the municipality. *Ad valorem* is Latin for *according to value*. If you own a home, you are familiar with the property tax assessment. In many states, the annual motor vehicle tag is based on an assessed value. School, road, and park districts may also issue municipal bonds backed by property taxes. Because the property of the residents is being taxed, GO's frequently require voter approval. We will have more to say about ad valorem taxes in the next lesson.

PRACTICE QUESTION

3. All of the following are used to pay debt service on GOs **except**
   A. sales taxes.
   B. license fees.
   C. tolls.
   D. ad valorem taxes.

   Answer: C. For the exam, GOs are backed by taxes. There will be some exceptions in the real world, but GOs are predominately backed by tax collections. As we will soon see, tolls are a debt service source for revenue bonds.

Statutory Debt Limits

The amount of debt that a municipal government may incur can be limited by state or local statutes to protect taxpayers from excessive taxes. Debt limits can also make a bond safer for investors. The lower the debt limit, the less risk of excessive borrowing and default by the municipality.

If a municipality wishes to issue GOs that would put it above its statutory limit, a public referendum is required. Voter approval on the referendum must follow.

- **Tax limits.** Some states limit property taxes to a certain percentage of the assessed property value or to a certain percentage increase in any single year. The tax rate is expressed in mills; one mill equals $1 per $1,000, or $0.001.
- **Limited tax GOs.** A limited tax GO bond is a bond secured by a specific tax (e.g., income tax). Alternatively, the limit is place on the amount of tax that may be assesses as just described. In other words, the issuer is limited as to what tax or taxes or how much can be used to service the debt. As a result, there is more risk with limited tax GOs than with a comparable GO backed by the full taxing authority of the issuer.
- **Overlapping debt.** Several taxing authorities that draw from the same taxpayers can issue debt. Bonds issued by different municipal authorities that tap the same taxpayer wallets are known as **coterminous debt**.

TEST TOPIC ALERT

In the context of municipal securities, the term *coterminous* refers to two or more taxing agencies that share the same geographic boundaries and are able to issue debt separately. Overlapping debt occurs when two or more issuers are taxing the same property to service their respective debt.

EXAMPLE

Take the town of Smithville, located in Jones County. If Smithville issues GO debt, it will tax property in Smithville to service that debt. If Jones County issues GO debt, it will tax property in the county, which includes Smithville, to service its debt. As a result, there are two issuers taxing the same property.

TAKE NOTE

Coterminous debt only occurs in property taxing situations. Because states do not generally tax real estate, state debt never overlaps.

PRACTICE QUESTION

4. Which of the following is **not** included in the definition of coterminous debt?
   A. County
   B. City
   C. School district
   D. State

   Answer: D. Coterminous, or overlapping, debt occurs when property taxes from one property are used in support of debt issued by various municipal issuers. For instance, property taxes on a home might support county, city, and school district debt obligations. Property taxes are not assessed by states, so states are not included in the definition of coterminous or overlapping debt.

Revenue Bonds

Revenue bonds can be used to finance any municipal facility that generates sufficient income. Revenue bonds are not subject to statutory debt limits and do not require voter approval. A particular revenue bond issue, however, may be subject to an additional bonds test before subsequent bond issues with equal liens on the project's revenue may be issued. The additional bonds test ensures the adequacy of the revenue stream to pay both the old and new debt.

Feasibility Study

Before issuing a revenue bond, an issuer will engage various consultants to prepare a report detailing the economic feasibility and the need for a particular project (e.g., a new bridge or airport). The study will include estimates of revenues that will be generated and details of the operating, economic, and engineering aspects of the proposed project.

Sources of Revenue

Revenue bonds' interest and principal payments are payable to bondholders only from the specific earnings and net lease payments of revenue-producing facilities, such as

- utilities (water, sewer, and electric);
- housing;
- transportation (airports and toll roads);
- education (college dorms and student loans);
- health (hospitals and retirement centers);
- industrial (industrial development and pollution control); and
- sports.

Debt service payments do not come from general or real estate taxes and are not backed by the municipality's full faith and credit. Revenue bonds are considered self-supporting debt because principal and interest payments are made exclusively from revenues generated by the project for which the debt was issued.

Protective Covenants

The face of a revenue bond certificate may refer to a **trust indenture** (or **bond resolution**). This empowers the trustee to act on behalf of the bondholders.

In the trust indenture, the municipality agrees to abide by certain protective covenants, or promises, meant to protect bondholders. A trustee appointed in the indenture supervises the issuer's compliance with the bond covenants.

Trust Indenture

The trust indenture's provisions may vary, but a number of standard provisions are common to most bond issues, including the following:

- **Rate covenant**. A promise to maintain rates sufficient to pay expenses and debt service.
- **Maintenance covenant**. A promise to maintain the equipment and facility/facilities.
- **Insurance covenant.** A promise to insure any facility built so bondholders can be paid off if the facility is destroyed or becomes inoperable.
- **Additional bonds test**. Whether the indenture is **open-ended** (allowing further issuance of bonds with the same status and equal claims on assets or revenues if permitted under the provisions of the bond indenture) or **closed-ended** (allowing no further issuance of bonds with an equivalent lien on assets or revenues); with a closed-end provision, any additional bonds issued will be subordinated to the original issue unless the funds are specifically required to complete construction of the facility.
- **Sinking fund**. Money to pay off interest and principal obligations.

- **Catastrophe clause.** A promise to use insurance proceeds to call bonds and repay bondholders if a facility is destroyed; a catastrophe call is also called a calamity call or an extraordinary mandatory call. Bonds with a catastrophe call are not designated callable bonds on the trade confirmation.
- **Flow of funds.** The priority of disbursing the revenues collected.
- **Books and records covenant.** Requires outside audit of records and financial reports.
- **Call features.** Call date(s) and call price(s).

TAKE NOTE

Trust indentures are not required for municipal bonds per the Trust Indenture Act of 1939. Municipal issues are exempt from this act. The use of trust indentures is optional, but it greatly enhances the marketability of revenue issues. Revenue bonds have either a trust resolution or trust indentures, whereas GOs commonly have a bond resolution.

Types of Revenue Bonds

There are a number of categories of revenue bonds, depending on the type of facility the bond issue finances.

Industrial Development Revenue Bonds

A municipal development authority issues industrial development revenue bonds (IDRs or IDBs) to construct facilities or purchase equipment, which is then leased to a corporation. The municipality uses the money from lease payments to pay the principal and interest on the bonds. The ultimate responsibility for the payment of principal and interest rests with the corporation leasing the facility; therefore, the bonds carry the corporation's debt rating. Some of these bonds are subject to the alternative minimum tax (AMT). We will cover those in Lesson 6.5.

Lease-Rental Bonds

Under a typical lease-rental (or lease-back) bond arrangement, a municipality issues bonds to finance office construction for itself or its state or community.

EXAMPLE

An example of a lease-back arrangement follows.

A municipality might issue bonds to raise money to construct a school and lease the finished building to the school district. The lease payments provide backing for the bonds.

Lease payments come from funds raised through special taxes or appropriations, from the lessor's revenues, such as the school's tuition or fees, or from the municipality's general fund.

Double-Barreled Bonds

Double-barreled bonds are revenue bonds that have characteristics of GOs. Interest and principal are paid from a specified facility's earnings. However, the bonds are also backed by the taxing power of the state or municipality and therefore have the backing of two sources of revenue. Although they are backed primarily by revenues from the facility, double-barreled bonds are rated and traded as GOs.

Certificates of Participation

Certificates of participation are a form of lease revenue bond that permits the investor to participate in a stream of revenue from lease, installment, or loan payments related to the acquisition of land or the acquisition or construction of specific equipment or facilities by the municipality. Like other revenue issues, they require no voter approval. Certificates of participation are not viewed legally as debt of a municipality because payment is tied to an annual appropriation that is made by the government body. One unique feature with these certificates—though this would be a rare occurrence—is that in theory, the certificate holders themselves can foreclose on the equipment or the facility that the certificates financed in the event of default.

Special Tax Bonds

Special tax bonds are bonds secured by one or more designated taxes other than ad valorem (property) taxes. For example, bonds for a particular purpose might be supported by sales, tobacco, alcohol, fuel, or business license taxes. However, the designated tax does not have to be directly related to the project purpose. Such bonds are not considered self-supporting debt. That means that other sources may be used if the taxes generated are insufficient. You might see these called designated tax bonds.

Special Assessment Bonds (or Special District Bonds)

Special assessment bonds are issued to finance the construction of public improvements such as streets, sidewalks, or sewers. The issuer assesses a tax only on the property that benefits from the improvement and uses the funds to pay principal and interest.

New Housing Authority Bonds

New housing authority bonds are for new housing projects. Please note that new does not mean newly issued bonds. Local housing authorities issue **New Housing Authority bonds (NHAs)** to develop and improve low-income housing. NHAs are backed by the full faith and credit of the U.S. government. NHAs are sometimes called **Public Housing Authority bonds (PHAs)**. Because of their federal backing, they are considered the most secure of all municipal bonds. PHAs are backed by the rental income from the housing. If the rental income is not sufficient to service the debt, the federal government makes up any shortfall. Note that these bonds are not considered to be double-barreled. To be **double-barreled**, a bond must be backed by more than one municipal revenue source. In this case, the second backing is the federal government.

TEST TOPIC ALERT

PHAs (or NHAs) are the only municipal issues backed in full by the U.S. government. They are also called **Section 8** bonds.

PRACTICE QUESTION

5. All of the following might be used service municipal revenue debt **except**
   A. excise taxes.
   B. business license taxes.
   C. ad valorem taxes.
   D. alcohol taxes.

   Answer: C. Property taxes (ad valorem taxes) are associated with GOs. Special taxes can be used to back revenue bonds. Among them are the "sin" taxes. Those are taxes on alcohol and tobacco as well as excise taxes on fuel and business license taxes.

Moral Obligation Bonds

A **moral obligation bond** is a state- or local-issued, or state- or local-agency issued, bond. If revenues or tax collections backing the bond are not sufficient to pay the debt service, the state legislature has the authority to appropriate funds to make payments. The potential backing by state revenues tends to make the bond more marketable, but the state's obligation is not established by law; it is a moral obligation only. If a moral obligation bond goes into default, the only way bondholders can be repaid is through **legislative apportionment**. The issuer's legislature would have to apportion money to satisfy the debt but is not legally obligated to do so. Remember, the issuer has a moral but not legal obligation to service the debt.

TAKE NOTE

All moral obligation bonds are considered revenue bonds.

PRACTICE QUESTION

6. Which of the following is backed by the full faith and credit of the U.S. government?
   A. Moral obligation bonds
   B. New housing authority bonds (NHAs)
   C. IDRs
   D. Special tax bonds

   Answer: B. NHAs (or PHAs) are issued to construct, maintain, and improve low-income housing. The U.S. government guarantees the rent on these properties. They are considered the most secure of all municipal revenue bonds.

Municipal Notes

Municipal anticipation notes are short-term securities that generate funds for a municipality that expects other revenues soon. Usually, municipal notes have less than 12-month maturities, although maturities may range from three months to three years. Because of their short-term nature, interest and principal is paid at maturity. That is just another way of saying that they are issued at a discount. Municipal notes fall into several categories.

- Municipalities issue **tax anticipation notes (TANs)** to finance current operations in anticipation of future tax receipts. This helps municipalities to even out cash flow between tax collection periods.
- **Revenue anticipation notes (RANs)** are offered periodically to finance current operations in anticipation of future revenues from revenue-producing projects or facilities.
- **Tax and revenue anticipation notes** are a combination of the characteristics of both TANs and RANs.

- **Bond anticipation notes (BANs)** are sold as interim financing that will eventually be converted to long-term funding through a sale of bonds.
- **Tax-exempt commercial paper** is often used in place of BANs and TANs for up to 270 days, though maturities are most often 30, 60, and 90 days.
- **Construction loan notes (CLNs)** are issued to provide interim financing for the construction of housing projects.
- **Grant anticipation notes** are issued with the expectation of receiving grant money from the federal government.

PRACTICE QUESTION

7. Which of the following municipal securities would be **least** likely to be issued at a discount?
   A. BABs
   B. BANs
   C. CLNs
   D. RANs

   Answer: A. Build America Bonds (BABs) were issued at par. The other choices are all issued at a discount with the face value being paid at maturity. Test taking note: Ignore the fact that BABs are no longer issued. In a question like this, FINRA certainly does.

Variable Rate Municipal Securities

These are municipal debt securities with interest rates that fluctuate based on current market interest rate changes. The MSRB calls these *reset securities* because the interest rate is reset at certain intervals. The exam may ask you about two types of variable rate securities.

Variable Rate Demand Obligations (VRDOs)

The MSRB defines variable rate demand obligations (VRDOs) as floating rate obligations that typically have a nominal long-term maturity of 20–30 years, but have an interest rate that is reset periodically. The reset can be daily, weekly, monthly, semiannually, or flexible. Matching the interest rate to market conditions tends to keep the price of these relatively stable.

One of the key features of this security is the ability of the investor to demand the issuer repurchase the bonds at par value. This can be done on any reset date. In essence, this is a put option where the investor "puts" the bond and receives the face amount plus any accrued interest. This feature is why VDROs are sometimes considered money market instruments. In fact, you can find them in the portfolio of many money market mutual funds.

Auction Rate Securities (ARS)

Auction rate securities (ARS) are debt securities that have interest rates that are periodically reset through Dutch auctions, typically every 7, 14, 28, or 35 days. ARS are generally structured as bonds with long-term maturities (20–30 years). Municipalities and public authorities, student loan providers, and other institutional borrowers first began using ARS to raise funds in the 1980s. ARS were marketed to retail investors who were seeking a cash-equivalent investment that paid a higher yield than money market mutual funds or certificates of deposit, although ARS did not have the same level of liquidity as those other instruments.

Following the turmoil in the financial markets that emerged in 2007, interest-rate auctions fc ARS began to fail when the auctions attracted too few bidders. This resulted in an inability of investors to sell their ARS until there was a successful auction. The ARS market collapsed in February 2008 when lead underwriters chose not to step in to support the auctions. For investors, this meant that they were left with illiquid investments with long-term maturities. There has not been a new issue ARS since 2007, but the amount of outstanding issues is in the billions of dollars.

PRACTICE QUESTION

8. The main advantage of a variable rate municipal bond investment is that
   A. the bond is likely to increase in value.
   B. the bond's price should remain relatively stable.
   C. the bond is noncallable.
   D. the bond's interest is exempt from all taxes.

Answer: B. A variable rate municipal security does not have a fixed coupon rate. The interest rate is tied to a market rate (e.g., T-bill yields) and is subject to change at regular intervals. Because the interest paid reflects changes in overall interest rates, the price of the bond remains relatively close to its par value.

LESSON 6.3: ANALYSIS OF MUNICIPAL DEBT SECURITIES

LO 6.c Compare the methods of analyzing general obligation (GO) and revenue bonds.

Different criteria are used to evaluate the merits of GOs and revenue bonds. When analyzing GOs, investors assess the municipality's ability to raise enough tax revenue to pay its debt. Revenue bond debt service depends on the income generated from a specific facility to cover its operating costs and pay its debt.

GOs Bond Analysis

There are a number of factors that are used to analyze GOs. As you are going through this list think about how your personal credit analysis is done. A lender would look at your income, your net worth, your debt paying history, and your outstanding debt. Those are basically the first four points we are going to discuss.

Income of the Municipality

Following are the primary sources of municipal income:

- Income and sales taxes are major sources of state income.
- Real property taxes are the principal income source of counties, and school districts are the largest source of city income.
- City income can include fines, license fees, assessments, sales taxes, hotel taxes, city income taxes, utility taxes, and any city personal property tax.

General Wealth of the Community

Because GOs are backed primarily by tax revenues, their safety is determined by the community's general wealth, which includes the following demographic data:

- Property values
- Retail sales per capita
- Local bank deposits
- Diversity of industry in its tax base
- Population growth or decline

A GO issuer's taxing power enables it to make principal and interest payments through all but the most unusual economic circumstances.

Characteristics of the Issuer

A **quantitative analysis** focuses on objective information regarding a municipality's population, property values, and per capita income. A **qualitative analysis** focuses on subjective factors that affect a municipality's securities. The community's attitude toward debt and taxation, population trends, property value trends, and plans and projects being undertaken in the area are all relevant considerations.

Debt Limits

To protect taxpayers from excessive taxes, statutory debt limits may be placed on the overall amount of debt a municipality can have. Suppose a city's total debt is limited to 5% of the estimated market value of all taxable property within the city's boundary. The total value of those properties multiplied by 5% would be city's statutory debt limit. A bond's official statement discloses how close total outstanding debt, including newly issued debt, comes to its statutory debt limit.

A state constitution or city charter can also limit the purposes for which a city may issue bonds. Often, a city may issue bonds to finance capital improvements only if those bonds mature within the expected lifetimes of the improvements. This provision ensures that the city will not owe money on a facility when it becomes obsolete.

Ad Valorem Taxes

Property taxes are based on a property's assessed valuation. Assessed valuation is a percentage of the estimated market value. That percentage is established by each state or county and varies substantially. The market value of each piece of property in a county is determined by the county assessor, who relies on recent sale prices of similar properties, income streams, replacement costs, and other information.

Because the real property tax is based on the property's value, it is said to be an **ad valorem**, or per value, tax. The tax is a lien on the property, which means the property can be seized if the tax is not paid. GOs, backed by the power to tax and seize property, are considered safer than revenue bonds of the same issuer and therefore can be issued with a lower interest rate.

Property taxes are generally based on a millage rate. The assessed value is multiplied by that millage rate and the result is the amount of tax. One mill is 1⁄10 of a cent, or $0.001. Let's take a look at how this might be asked on the exam.

EXAMPLE

A taxpayer's home is currently valued at $400,000. The tax is based on a 50% assessment of market value. If the annual tax rate is 7 mills, what is the taxpayer's property tax liability?

We solve as follows: 50% of the market value is $200,000. That is multiplied by the millage rate (0.007). The result is a tax of $1,400. On the exam, you might have choices of $140, $1,400, and $14,000. This is one of the few cases where getting the decimal in the right place is critical. Try doing it in your head first. A rate of 7 mills is a bit less than 1%. You could probably figure that 1% of $200,000 is $2,000, so this will be a bit lower.

PRACTICE QUESTION

9. A couple's home has an assessed valuation of $40,000 and a market value of $100,000. What will the tax be if a rate of 5 mills is used?
   A. $200
   B. $500
   C. $2,000
   D. $5,000

   Answer: A. Taxes on real property are based on the assessed value assigned to the property by the municipality's tax assessor (in this case, $40,000). Property tax rates use the mill (or mil) as a base unit. One mill = $1 of tax per year for each $1,000 of assessed value. Five mills would equal $5 for each $1,000 of assessed value. Because there are 40,000, 40 × $5 = $200 in annual tax. A short-cut method: take the assessed value, remove the last three 0s, and multiply by the number of mills of tax ($40 × 5 mills = $200).

Analyzing the Official Statement (OS)

As we will learn in Unit 20, municipal bonds provide a form of prospectus, (disclosure document), known as an *official statement (OS)*. Analysts study the documents included in th OS to determine the issuer's financial condition at the present and in the foreseeable future.

Future Financial Needs

The municipality's financial statements should be scrutinized for signs of future debt requirements. The municipality might need to issue more debt if

- its annual income is not sufficient to make the payments on its short-term (or floating) debt,
- principal repayments are scheduled too close together,
- sinking funds for outstanding term bonds are inadequate,
- pension liabilities are unfunded, or
- it plans to make more capital improvements soon.

Issuing more debt in the near future could damage an issuer's credit rating, which would caus the current issue to trade at a lower price.

The Debt Statement

The **debt statement** is used in the analysis of GO debt. It includes the estimated full valuatio of taxable property, the estimated assessed value of property, and the assessment percentage.

To evaluate the municipality's debt structure, an analyst calculates **total debt**, the sum of all bonds issued by the municipality, and subtracts **self-supporting debt** from this figure. Although revenue bond debt is included in total debt, it is backed by revenues from the facility it financed and is not a burden on the municipality's taxpayers.

The result is the municipality's **net direct debt**, which includes GOs and short-term notes issued in anticipation of taxes or for interim financing.

Overlapping debt disclosed on the debt statement is the city's proportionate share of the debts of the county, school district, park district, and sanitary district. The city's **net total debt**, also called **net overall debt**, is the sum of the overlapping debt and the net direct debt.

Calculating a Municipality's Net Total Debt

A municipality's net total debt can be calculated as follows:

total debt (all bonds issued by the municipality)

– self-supporting debt

– sinking fund accumulations

= net direct debt

+ overlapping debt

= net total debt

TEST TOPIC ALERT

A question might ask about what is or is not included in the various categories on the debt statement. A good rule: for any category that uses the word *net*, self-supporting debt and sinking fund accumulations are not included. For instance, net total debt includes all GOs and overlapping debt but does not include the self-supporting and sinking fund accumulations.

Do not expect a calculation question on this topic. The exam will only test your understanding of the concept.

Revenue Bond Analysis

Revenue bonds are rated according to a facility's potential to generate sufficient money to cover operating expenses and principal and interest payments. Revenue bonds are not repaid from taxes, so they are not subject to statutory debt limits. Revenue bonds are meant to be self-supporting, and if the facility they finance does not make enough money to repay the debts, the bondholders, not the taxpayers, bear the risk. When assessing the quality of revenue bonds, an investor should consider the following factors:

- *Economic justification.* The facility being built should be able to generate revenues.
- *Competing facilities.* A facility should not be placed where better alternatives are easily available.
- *Sources of revenue.* The sources should be dependable.
- *Call provisions.* With callable bonds, the higher the call premium, the more attractive a bond is to an investor.
- *Flow of funds.* Revenues generated must be sufficient to pay all of the facility's operating expenses and to meet debt service obligation.

Applications of Revenues

Principal and interest on revenue bonds are paid exclusively from money generated by the facility the issuer finances. The issuer pledges to pay expenses in a specific order, called the **flow of funds**.

In most cases, a **net revenue pledge** is used, meaning that operating and maintenance expenses are paid first. The remaining funds (or net revenues) are used to pay debt service and meet other obligations.

Flow of Funds in a Net Revenue Pledge

In a net revenue pledge, total receipts from operating the facility are usually deposited in the **revenue fund**, and funds are disbursed as follows:

- *Operations and maintenance.* Used to pay current operating and maintenance expenses; remaining funds are called **net revenues.**
- *Debt service account.* Used to pay the interest and principal maturing in the current year and serves as a sinking fund for term issues.
- *Debt service reserve fund.* Used to hold enough money to pay one year's debt service.
- *Reserve maintenance fund.* Used to supplement the general maintenance fund.
- *Renewal and replacement fund.* Used to create reserve funds for major renewal projects and equipment replacements.
- *Surplus (sinking) fund.* Used for a variety of purposes, such as redeeming bonds or paying for improvements.

If the issuer has not pledged to pay operating and maintenance expenses first, debt service is the priority expense. When debt service is paid first, the flow of funds is called a **gross revenue pledge**.

The debt service includes current principal and interest due, plus any sinking fund obligations. If revenues exceed operating and other obligations, the money is usually placed in a surplus fund.

Figure 6.3: Gross and Net Revenue Pledges

Gross Revenue Pledge	Net Revenue Pledge
Issuer pays debt service first from gross revenues.	Issuer pays operations and maintenance expenses first from gross revenues.
Issuer pays operations and maintenance expenses.	Issuer pays debt service second from net revenues.

TEST TOPIC ALERT

If you see questions that require differentiating gross revenue and net revenue pledges, maybe this will help: the name of the pledge tells you how debt service is paid. In a gross revenue pledge, debt service is paid first, from gross revenues. Operations and maintenance expenses are paid after debt service. In a net revenue pledge, debt service is paid from the net revenues, meaning operations and maintenance costs are paid first. This is the more common of the two pledges. Think of this as the difference between your gross pay and your net check. Before you get anything, taxes and other items, such as 401(k) contributions and health insurance premiums, are deducted.

TEST TOPIC ALERT

When analyzing revenue bonds, one should look at the debt coverage ratio. It is the ratio of available revenues available annually to pay the debt service divided by the annual debt service requirement. The higher the ratio, the better. It looks like this:

$$\text{Coverage} = \frac{\text{Available Revenues}}{\text{Debt Service Requirement}}$$

For Example:

$$\text{Coverage} = \frac{\$10{,}000{,}000 \text{ available revenues}}{\$4{,}000{,}000 \text{ annual debt service}} = 2.5 \text{ to } 1$$

LESSON 6.4: MUNICIPAL BOND MARKETABILITY

LO 6.d Recognize the factors affecting the marketability of municipal bonds.

Municipal Bond Marketability Factors

The MSRB defines marketability as, "the ease or difficulty with which securities can be sold in the market. A municipal security's marketability depends upon many factors, including its coupon, yield, dollar price, security provisions, maturity, credit quality, and rating, if any. In the case of a new issue, marketability also depends on the size of the issue, the timing of its issuance and the volume of comparable issues being sold." We are going to look at the most tested of these including some listed by FINRA that are not in the MSRB's definition.

Rating

Simply stated, the higher the rating, the more marketable the bond. Many large institutional investors, such as banks and insurance companies, are generally limited to investment-grade debt. In some cases, they are limited to the top two grades (AA or Aa). As the number of potential investors increases, so does the marketability.

Maturity

In general, the shorter the time until maturity, the more marketable the bond.

Coupon

In general, the higher the coupon, the more marketable the bond.

Block Size

The typical block for a municipal bond trade is $100,000. Trades in smaller amounts are not as marketable.

Call Features

The longer the call protection, the more marketable the bond. That means noncallable bonds are the most marketable.

Dollar Price

In general, bonds with a lower dollar price are more marketable.

Refunding

In the securities industry, the term refunding is most like refinancing a loan, such as a mortgage. When interest rates fall, the municipality issues a new bond (at lower rates). Then they use the proceeds from the new bond to pay off the old, higher interest debt. There are two types of refunding.

Advance Refunding (Prerefunding)

This is refinancing an existing municipal bond issue before its maturity or call date by using money from the sale of a new bond issue. The proceeds of the new bond issue are used to purchase special government securities. To comply with the complex restrictions imposed by the IRS, the municipality places the proceeds of a municipal pre-refunding in an escrow account that immediately invests in **state and local government securities series**. These are U.S. government securities issued directly by the Treasury to municipal issuers only in connection with prerefundings. They are usually referred to by the acronym SLGS and pronounced "slugs". The municipality then uses these funds to pay off the original bond issue at the first call date.

Current Refunding

This differs from advance refunding in that the old bonds will be redeemed within 90 days or less from the date of issuance of the refunding bonds.

In either case, refunding increases the quality of the bonds. This leads to greater marketability.

Municipal Bond Insurance

Municipal bond issuers can insure their securities' principal and interest payments by buying insurance from a number of insurers. This will generally improve the marketability of the bond. Among those specializing in insuring municipal issues are National Public Finance Guarantee Corp. (formerly the Municipal Bond Investors Assurance Corporation—MBIA), Financial Guaranty Insurance Company, Assured Guaranty Corporation, and AMBAC Indemnity Corporation. While AMBAC is not currently insuring new municipal issues, there are many AMBAC-insured municipal bonds still outstanding.

Insured bonds are generally issued with lower coupon rates because investors will accept lower rates of return for the added safety insurance affords. In addition, the cost of insurance may also lessen the yield a municipal issuer is willing to pay. Many small issues of municipal bonds are not rated because of the cost to rate a bond can be expensive. Instead, many issuers will insure the bond for principal and/or interest. When a bond is insured, MSRB rules require of the certificates accompanied by evidence of insurance, either on the face of the certificates or in a separate document.

The effect of the bond insurance is that both interest and principal will be paid as scheduled, over time through the life of the bond. The idea is that the bondholder should not see a problem. The insurer will just take up the liability and run with it not missing a beat.

PRACTICE QUESTION

10. When the issuer of an insured municipal bond defaults, what does the insurance company do?
    A. Both principal and interest are returned over the remaining term of the bond.
    B. Principal is returned immediately and the interest is paid out based upon the normal schedule.
    C. Only the principal is returned with the bondholder losing the interest.
    D. Both principal and remaining interest payments are paid immediately to the bondholder.

Answer: A. Both interest and principal will be paid as scheduled, over time through the life of the bond. It is not paid out as a lump sum. An investor won't even notice the difference because the interest checks will come the same way they always did.

Fair Prices and Commissions Rule G-30

Just as corporate securities follow the FINRA 5% policy, municipal securities come under MSRB's Rule G-30 with similar characteristics. Remember, municipal securities are exempt from the FINRA policy. That fact is frequently tested on the exam. Similar to FINRA rules, broker-dealers cannot charge a commission and a markup or markdown on the same transaction.

You might be thinking, "Why are you covering this here?" Good question. The reason is that the marketability of a municipal bond plays a key role in determining fair prices and commissions.

The MSRB rule states the markups or markdowns or commissions that municipal securities dealers charge must be fair and reasonable and listed on the customer confirmation, taking into account all characteristics of a trade, such as:

- FMV of the securities at trade time;
- total dollar amount of the transaction;
- any special difficulty in doing the trade; and
- the fact that the dealer is entitled to a profit.

Block size certainly affects the total dollar amount of the trade as well as the ease with which the trade is made. As a general rule, the more marketable the municipal security, the lower the profit to the municipal dealer. It is similar to so many things we buy in our everyday lives. Many of the items in our grocery stores, such as milk, bread and eggs have very low markup because they move off the shelves rapidly. When it comes to items that sell rarely, like antiques and fine art, the markups are quite significant.

Reasonable compensation differs from fair pricing. A dealer could limit its profit on a transaction to a reasonable level and still violate this rule if the dealer fails to consider market value. For example, a dealer may fail to check the market value of a security when acquiring it from another dealer or customer. This could result in the firm paying a price well above market value. It would be a violation of fair-pricing responsibilities for the dealer to pass on this misjudgment to another customer, even if the dealer makes little or no profit on the trade.

Broker's Broker

There are certain firms in the municipal securities business that do not position trade (keep an inventory of) bonds. Rather, they exist to assist other firms find buyers or sellers of municipal bonds. They perform this duty in both primary and secondary market transactions. These firms are known as a broker's broker. The term is appropriate because these firms deal primarily with other municipal securities firms acting as their agents. They will also represent institutions, but never have any dealings with public customers. A major reason these firms exist is because the market for most municipal bonds is quite thin. That means not a lot of trading going on. Here is an example of how a broker's broker might perform.

EXAMPLE

Your broker-dealer specializes in mutual funds. From time to time, it has a customer wishing to make a small purchase of municipal bonds. One of your firm's clients has just inherited $500,000 in State M general obligation bonds and wishes to sell them. The size of this trade is far beyond anything your firm is capable of placing. Your firm needs help in finding buyers for these bonds so it turns to a broker's broker. Acting on behalf of your firm as its agent, the broker's broker knows the marketplace and which municipal dealers or institutions might be suitable candidates for those GO bonds. For performing in this role, the broker's broker earns a commission.

TEST TOPIC ALERT

One of the features of using a broker's broker is anonymity. Your firm does not disclose the identity of your customer and the broker's broker does not disclose the identity of the buyer of your client's bonds.

LESSON 6.5: MUNICIPAL BOND MATH

LO 6.e Perform the various municipal bond calculations.

Key Municipal Bond Calculations

Many of the municipal bond calculations are the same as those covered with corporate bonds. Those include

- nominal (coupon) yield,
- current yield (CY),
- yield to maturity (YTM),
- yield to call, and
- accrued interest.

Computing Accrued Interest

Back in Lesson 4.1, we described accrued interest and commented that we would get to it again in this unit. Computing accrued interest on a bond appears on most exams.

Rules for calculating municipal bond accrued interest are the same as they are for corporate bonds.

Unless a bond is trading flat (discussed later), the bond cost to the buyer and the proceeds to the seller include accrued interest. Accrued interest increases the bond cost to the buyer and the proceeds to the seller.

Accrued interest is calculated from the last interest payment date up to but not including the settlement date (two business days after the trade date). The buyer owns the bond on the settlement date, which means that the interest starting from that day belongs to the buyer and the previous six months interest is credited to the seller.

The Calculation

The calculation to determine accrued interest assumes all months—even February—have 30 days. All corporate and municipal bonds use the 30-day-month count. Therefore, for purposes of this calculation, the year contains 360 days.

EXAMPLE

If an F&A municipal bond is traded regular way on Monday, March 5, the number of days of accrued interest is calculated as follows:

February	30 days
March 5 trade	6 days (settles T+2 regular way March 7)
Days of accrued interest	36 days

Because the trade settles on March 7, six days of interest accrue for March. Remember: up to but not including the settlement date. There is a form of trade settlement known as *for cash*. In that case, the settlement date is the trade date. In this example, settlement for cash would be March 5. Therefore, calculating up to but not including the settlement date, the days of accrued interest for March would be four, making the total days of accrued interest 34.

TEST TOPIC ALERT

Recap for calculating accrued interest follows.

- Corporate, agencies, and municipals: use 30-day months (360-day year)
- U.S. Treasury securities: use actual day months (365-day year)

When counting days:

- Go back and include the last interest payment date.
- Go up to but not including the settlement date.

TAKE NOTE

A method using actual calendar days (365-day year) is used only on U.S. government bonds (not corporates, agencies, or municipals).

PRACTICE QUESTION

11. At settlement, accrued interest
    A. increases the amount the buyer must pay and decreases the amount the seller will receive.
    B. decreases the amount the buyer must pay and increases the amount the seller will receive.
    C. decreases the amount the buyer must pay and decreases the amount the seller will receive.
    D. increases the amount the buyer must pay and increases the amount the seller will receive.

Answer: D. Remember, at settlement, buyers pay any accrued interest due and sellers receive the accrued interest. Therefore, any accrued interest will increase the amount the buyer must pay and increase the amount the seller will receive.

Accrued Interest and the Dated Date

For a new bond issue, the date from which interest accrual begins is called the **dated date.** Even if a bond is issued at a later date, the bond starts accruing interest on the date designated as the dated date. For example, if the bond's dated date is April 1 and the interest payment dates are June 1 and December 1, the first interest payment will be on December 1 and will be for eight months of interest.

Trading Flat

When a debt security is trading flat, it means no accrued interest is included in the transaction. In most cases, this occurs when the issuer is in default of interest payments. Of course, this is also the case with zero coupon bonds because there is no interest being paid. All bonds paying semiannual interest trade flat twice each year. When the trade takes place so that it settles on an interest payment date, there is no accrued interest because the seller will receive a check from the issuer for the interest. We liken that to the broken clock that shows the correct time twice a day.

Adjusting the Cost Basis of Municipal Bonds

Upon disposition of a municipal bond, either with a sale or redemption at maturity or call, determining if an investor has a capital gain or capital loss requires knowing the cost basis. If and how cost basis is adjusted for municipal bonds depends first on if the bond was purchased at a premium or a discount.

Municipal Bonds Purchased at a Premium

The purchaser of a municipal bond at a premium must amortize the premium on a straight-line basis over the remaining life of the bond. It makes no difference if the bond was purchased as a new issue or in the secondary market. Straight-line amortization means that an equal amount of the premium will be amortized each year the bond is held.

EXAMPLE

A customer buys an 8% municipal bond with eight YTM at a price of $108. The premium of eight points ($80) must be amortized over the remaining eight YTM. The annual amortization amount is one point, or $10 per bond. After one year, the cost basis is 107; after two years, 106; and so on. If held to maturity, there is no capital loss because the cost basis at that time has been reduced to par.

Amortization

- reduces cost basis and
- reduces reported interest income.

In the example, cost basis is reduced each year by $10 per bond. In addition, interest income of $80 per bond is reduced to $70 per bond (the amount of the annual amortization). Because interest income on municipal bonds is not taxed, its annual amortization has no tax effect.

If the bond is sold before maturity, gain or loss is the difference between sales price and adjusted cost basis. Take the following example. A customer buys a five-year municipal bond at 105. Two years later, the bond is sold at 104. What is the customer's gain or loss?

The premium of five points must be amortized over a five-year period, so the annual amortization is one point, or $10 per bond. After two years, the bond's cost basis is 103. Therefore, a sale at 104 creates a one-point capital gain per bond.

Municipal Bonds Purchased at a Discount

If a municipal bond is bought at a discount, the discount is accreted. Accretion is the process of adjusting the cost basis back up to par. It is the reverse computation of amortization. However, the tax treatment is a bit more complicated. The actual tax effect of accretion depends on whether the bond was purchased as an original issue discount (OID) (i.e., a new issue being offered at a discount) or an issue purchased at a discount in the secondary market. We will cover OID bonds later in this lesson.

Accretion

- increases cost basis and
- increases reported interest income.

EXAMPLE

A customer buys a 5% municipal bond with 10 YTM at 90. The amount of the annual accretion is $10 per bond (10-point discount ÷ 10 YTM). Each year, the cost basis is adjusted upward by one point. At maturity, there is no reported capital gain.

EXAMPLE

Assume a customer buys a 5% municipal bond with a 10-year maturity at 90 in the secondary market. Five years later, the customer sells the bond at 97. What are the tax consequences? The annual accretion of $10 per bond is taxable each year as ordinary income. The customer's cost basis at the time of sale is 95. When sold at 97, the customer has a capital gain of $20 per bond.

PRACTICE QUESTION

12. An investor purchases a 5% municipal bond in the secondary market at 90. With 10 years left to maturity, the annual accretion and capital gain at maturity is
    A. zero, with no capital gain at maturity.
    B. zero, with a $100 capital gain at maturity.
    C. $10 per bond, with no capital gain at maturity.
    D. $10 per bond, with a $100 capital gain at maturity.

Answer: C. One bond point equals $10. A 10-point discount represents a $100 discount. One hundred dollars divided by 10 YTM equals $10 accretion each year. With the accretion taxed each year, there is no capital gain reported at maturity.

LESSON 6.6: MUNICIPAL BOND TAX CALCULATIONS

LO 6.f Differentiate between the different kinds of tax treatment of municipal securities.

One of the significant features of municipal bonds is how they are treated for tax purposes. We will look at all of the tax possibilities that may be on the exam.

Interest Payments

In almost every case, the interest on a municipal security is exempt from federal income tax. That is why these are called *tax-exempt* or *tax-free* investments. Because of this favorable tax treatment, municipal issuers are able to borrow at a lower interest cost. In fact, the interest is usually lower than on a U.S. government bond.

The **Tax Reform Act of 1986** restricted the federal income tax exemption of interest for municipal bonds to public purpose bonds, which are bonds issued to finance projects that benefit citizens in general rather than particular private interests. If a bond directs more than 10% of its proceeds to private parties, it is considered a private activity bond and is not automatically granted tax exemption.

TAKE NOTE

Unless stated to the contrary (unlikely), you can safely assume that any GO bond on the exam is for a public purpose (they're using your property taxes—it better be).

Calculating Tax Benefits

As stated earlier, in most cases, interest received from municipal bonds is free of federal income tax. Furthermore, if the investor resides in the issuer's state, it is generally free of state income tax as well.

Assume an investor has $2,000 to invest. If she purchases at par one corporate or government bond of standard size ($1,000) with a 10% nominal (coupon) yield, she would receive $100 per year, paid by two semiannual interest checks of $50. For purposes of this example, assume that she is in the 28% federal income tax bracket. An individual in the 28% tax bracket pays tax on any additional income earned at a rate of 28%. Therefore, on the $100 in interest she received earlier, she would pay the IRS $28 (28%) and keep the other $72.

The other $1,000 she had available to invest was used to purchase a $1,000-par value municipal bond with a 7.5% nominal yield. She would receive $75 annually on that bond paid, by two semiannual interest checks of $37.50. The 10% bonds, on which the interest is taxable, would net $72 per year after taxes. Of the $75 interest received for the 7.5% municipal, none of it is taxed—the whole amount is kept. Therefore, a client in the 28% bracket should purchase 7.5% municipals before 10% corporates. The taxable equivalent yield of a 7.5% tax-free bond for this investor in the 28% tax bracket would be the tax-free yield divided by (100% minus the tax bracket). In this case, 7.5 ÷ (100 – 28), or 0.72. That equals 10.42%, so it is obvious that the 7.5% municipal bond will provide a higher after-tax return. When answering a tax-equivalent yield question, keep in mind that the municipal yield will always be lower than the taxable bond.

TEST TOPIC ALERT

The tax-equivalent yield for a municipal bond issued by an entity within a state with a state income tax will have a higher tax-equivalent yield to a resident of that state because of the "double" tax exemption.

TAKE NOTE

The formula for computing tax-equivalent yield is municipal bond coupon divided by (100% – investor's tax bracket).

Therefore, if the coupon rate (nominal yield) of the municipal bond is 4.2% and the investor is in the 40% tax bracket, you would divide 4.2% by (100% – 40%) or 4.2% by 60% and arrive at a tax-equivalent yield of 7%. That is, to receive the same after-tax benefit, this investor would have to purchase a taxable bond (corporate or government) with a coupon of 7%. This can be easily proven by taking the 7% yield and reducing it by the 40% tax which results in 7% – 2.8% tax, or 4.2%.

PRACTICE QUESTION

13. An investor in the 27% federal income tax bracket invests in municipal general obligation (GO) public purpose bonds with a coupon yield of 4.5%. What is the tax-equivalent yield?
    A. 4.36%
    B. 2.70%
    C. 5.72%
    D. 6.16%

Answer: D. The formula for computing tax-equivalent yield is: nominal yield divided by (1 – federal income tax rate) 0.045 ÷ (1 – 0.27) = 6.16%. You can quickly eliminate the two choices less than 4.5%. The tax-equivalent yield is always higher than the municipal coupon. Then you can take the remaining choices and subtract 27% in tax to see which one comes out to 4.5%.

TEST TOPIC ALERT

For exam purposes, you never recommend municipal bonds to investors unless they are in the higher tax brackets. Any question dealing with a low tax bracket client will never have a municipal bond as a suitable recommendation.

Original Issue Discount (OID) Bonds

It is not unusual to have a municipal bond issued at a discount on its initial public offering. The reasons for this are beyond the scope of the exam. The tax consequences, however, are not. As we learned previously, when a municipal bond is bought in the secondary markets at a discount, that discount is accreted on a straight-line basis. What's more, that accretion is considered taxable income. As with any other municipal bond, the coupon interest is tax-free.

In the case of an OID bond, the IRS considers the discount to be part of the issuer's payment of interest. Therefore, the accretion on an OID bond is tax-free. Let's look at an example.

EXAMPLE

An investor buys a newly issued 5% municipal bond with 10 YTM at 90. Because the bond was purchased as an OID, the reported interest income would be $60 per bond ($50 plus the annual accretion of $10). Because interest income on municipal bonds is tax-free, the accretion has no tax effect.

Just as with the secondary market purchase of a bond at a discount, the annual accretion increases the investor's cost basis.

EXAMPLE

An investor buys a newly issued 5% municipal bond with 10 YTM at 90. Five years later, the customer sells the bond at 97. What are the tax consequences? The annual accretion of $10 per bond adds to the investor's cost basis. It is not taxable as income. Five years of $10 per year accretion brings the investor's cost basis at the time of sale to 95. When sold at 97, the customer has a capital gain of $20 per bond.

Municipal Bond Capital Gains and Capital Losses

When it comes to capital gains and losses, municipal bonds are treated like any other investment. That is, if the bond is sold for more than its cost (including those bonds where the cost basis is adjusted), there is a capital gain. If sold below cost (including those bonds where the premium is amortized), there is a capital loss. Furthermore, the gains and losses are either long-term (more than 12 months) or short-term, just like other securities.

TEST TOPIC ALERT

Because the test authors know that students tend to focus on the tax-free income of municipal bonds, they write questions hoping you will answer that the capital gains are tax-free as well. That is not so.

PRACTICE QUESTION

14. An investor purchases 100 original issue discount (OID) municipal bonds at 95 with a 10-year maturity. If the bonds are held to maturity, the investor's tax consequences are
    A. $5,000 ordinary income.
    B. $5,000 tax-free income.
    C. $5,000 long-term capital gain.
    D. $4,000 long-term capital gain and $1,000 short-term capital gain.

Answer: B. When an investor purchases OID securities and then holds them to maturity, the appreciation or accretion is treated as interest income. On a municipal security, this interest income is tax-free. However, when purchasing a municipal security in the secondary market at a discount, the accretion is taxed as ordinary income.

AMT Bonds

Technically, industrial revenue bonds are issued for a corporation's benefit. Under the **Tax Reform Act of 1986**, the interest on these nonpublic purpose bonds (or private purpose bonds) may be taxable because the act reserves tax exemption for public purposes. Because these bonds are used for a nonpublic purpose, the interest income may be subject to the **alternative minimum tax (AMT)**.

Congress enacted the AMT in 1969 to make certain that high-income taxpayers do not escape paying taxes. Certain items receive favorable tax treatment. These items must be added back into taxable income for the AMT. These **tax preference items** include

- tax-exempt interest on private purpose, nonessential government service municipal bonds;
- certain costs associated with direct participation programs (DPPs), such as research and development costs and excess intangible drilling costs;
- local taxes (e.g., state income and property) and interest on investments that do not generate income; and
- accelerated depreciation on investment property.

We will cover some of these preference items in the appropriate units. At this time, you need to know that private purpose municipal bonds are included in the list.

TAKE NOTE

The language of the Internal Revenue Code (IRC) says that taxpayers are required to add the excess of the AMT over the regular tax to determine their total tax liability.

Taxable Municipal Bonds

There are municipal bonds where the interest is not tax-exempt. The most notable case is the Build America Bonds (BABs). We don't expect any other examples to appear on your exam.

Build America Bonds (BABs)

BABs were created under the Economic Recovery and Reinvestment Act of 2009 to assist in reducing costs to issuing municipalities and stimulating the economy. While bonds to fund municipal projects have traditionally been sold in the tax-exempt arena, BABs are taxable obligations. Bondholders pay tax on interest received from BABs. However, tax credits are provided in lieu of the tax-exempt status usually afforded the interest on municipal securities. These bonds attracted investors who would normally not buy tax-exempt municipal bonds and expanded the pool of investors to include those in lower-income tax brackets, investors funding retirement accounts where tax-free securities would normally not be suitable, public pension funds, and foreign investors. There are two types of BABs issued: tax credit BABs and direct payment BABs.

Tax Credit BABs

These types of BABs provide the bondholder with a federal income tax credit equal to 35% of the interest paid on the bond in each tax year. If the bondholder lacks sufficient tax liability to fully use that year's credit, the excess credit may be carried forward.

Direct Payment BABs

Direct payment BABs provide no credit to the bondholder but instead provide the municipal issuer with payments from the U.S. Treasury equal to 35% of the interest paid by the issuer.

TEST TOPIC ALERT

The BABs program expired on December 31, 2010, without being renewed. However, in the short time that municipalities were permitted to issue BABs, billions of dollars of capital had been raised to fund municipal projects throughout the United States, and many of these issues will remain outstanding for a number of years. Finally, it should be noted that the program could be reinstated in the future, and the types of BABs offered and the credits they provide could be amended as well.

LESSON 6.7: MUNICIPAL FUND SECURITIES

LO 6.g Identify the types of municipal fund securities.

There are several investments that one would not think of as being municipal securities. These are the municipal fund securities (nothing to do with a mutual fund) as defined in Rule D-12 and are regulated by the MSRB.

Section 529 Plans

Section 529 plans are a tax-advantaged savings plan offering benefits to those saving for future education costs. These plans are generally under the auspices of states or their agencies and are technically considered municipal fund securities.

There are two basic types of 529 plans: **prepaid tuition plans** and **college savings plans**. Both plans are funded with after-tax dollars, and earnings grow tax-deferred. Withdrawals taken for qualified education expenses are generally tax-free. If the money is used for anything other than qualified education expenses, the earnings portion of the distribution will be taxable on the federal (and possibly state) income tax return in the year of the distribution. Also, there is a 10% tax penalty on the earnings portion of your distribution. There are a couple of exceptions to the 10% penalty. The penalty is usually not charged if you terminate the account because your beneficiary died or became disabled. The penalty is also waived if you withdraw funds not needed for college because your beneficiary received a scholarship. Any person can open a 529 plan for a future student; the donor does not have to be related to the student.

Prepaid tuition plans allow donors to lock in future tuition rates at today's prices, thus offering inflation protection.

The **college savings plan** allows the donor to invest a lump sum or make periodic payments. The money is typically invested into target-date funds. As the target date approaches (the date the money is needed) the portfolio gets more conservative. When the student is ready for college, the donor withdraws the amount needed to pay for qualified education expenses (e.g., tuition, room and board, and books). These plans do have investment risk. In other words, they can lose money.

Under the TCJA of 2017, starting in 2018, up to $10,000 per year can be used for K–12 tuition purposes.

Other points to note include the following:

- College savings plans (but not prepaid tuition plans) may be set up in more than one state, though the allowable contribution amount varies from state to state.
- As of the date of this printing, the total allowable contribution varies from a low of $235,000 to a high of $529,000.
- There are no age limitations for contributions or distributions.
- There are no income limitations on making contributions to a 529 plan.
- Contributions may be made in the form of periodic payments, but contributions follow the tax rules for gifts. Thus, unless willing to pay a gift tax, contributions are limited to an indexed maximum amount ($15,000 in 2019) per year per donor. Section 529 plans have a five-year election that allows a donor to contribute five times that amount in one year (a spouse can do the same to the same recipient), but then they may make no more contributions for five years.
- There are few restrictions on who may be the first beneficiary of a 529 plan. However, if the beneficiary is redesignated, the new beneficiary must be a close family member of the first.
- Just as with other municipal securities, an OS must be delivered to prospective investors.

The assets in the account remain the property of the donor, even after the beneficiary reaches legal age. However, if the account is not used for higher education, and the IRS concludes that the plan was not established in good faith, it may impose fines and other sanctions. This would generally mean the earnings in the account are taxed at ordinary income rates with an additional 10% penalty.

Plan assets remain outside the owner's estate for estate tax purposes.

TAKE NOTE

Because 529s are state-sponsored, individual states have their own version of the plan. The exam does not expect you to have knowledge of specific state plans, only characteristics of the plan in general.

Achieving a Better Life Experience (ABLE) Accounts

Achieving a Better Life Experience (ABLE) accounts are tax-advantaged savings accounts for individuals with disabilities and their families. They were created as a result of the passage of the ABLE Act of 2014. The beneficiary of the account is the account owner and income earned by the account is not taxed.

The ABLE Act limits eligibility to individuals with significant disabilities where the age of onset of the disability occurred before turning age 26. One need not be under the age of 26 to be eligible to establish an ABLE account. One could be over the age of 26, but as long as the onset of the disability occurred before age 26, the person is eligible to establish an ABLE account.

If an individual meets the age/onset criteria and is also receiving benefits either through Social Security insurance and/or Social Security disability insurance, the individual is automatically eligible to establish an ABLE account. Only one ABLE account per person is allowed.

Contributions to these accounts, which can be made by any person including the account beneficiaries themselves, as well as family and friends, must be made using after-tax dollars and is not tax deductible for purposes of federal income taxes. Some states, however, do allow income tax deductions for contributions made to an ABLE account. Contributions by all participating individuals are limited to a specified dollar amount per year, which may be adjusted periodically to account for inflation.

Local Government Investment Pools (LGIPs)

States establish local government investment pools (LGIPs) to provide other government entities—such as cities, counties, school districts, or other state agencies—with a short-term investment vehicle to invest funds. The LGIPs are generally formed as a trust in which municipalities can purchase shares or units in the LGIP's investment portfolio.

While not a money market fund, most LGIPs operate similar to one. For instance, an LGIP may be permitted to maintain a fixed $1 net asset value (NAV). Maintaining a stable NAV, similar to a money market mutual fund, facilitates liquidity and minimum price volatility.

LGIPs are not required to register with the SEC and are not subject to the SEC's regulatory requirements, given that LGIPs fall within the governmental exemption, just as municipal securities do. Therefore, investment guidelines and oversight for LGIPs can vary from state to state.

With no SEC registration required, there is no prospectus. However, LGIP programs do have disclosure documents, which generally include information statements, and investment policy and operating procedures. The information statement typically details the management fees associated with participation in the LGIP.

PRACTICE QUESTION

15. While in your office, you see that your firm is going to be holding a training session on municipal fund securities. You wish to attend because you are interested in being able to speak intelligently to your clients about
    - A. the difference between GOs and revenue bonds.
    - B. the difference between using mutual funds or UITs to invest in municipal bonds.
    - C. Section 529 plans.
    - D. Section 457plans.

Answer: C. The SEC has stated that certain Section 529 College Savings Plans established by states or local governmental entities are municipal fund securities. Accordingly, the purchase and sale of state-sponsored Section 529 plans are governed by the rules of the MSRB.

LESSON 6.8: MSRB RULES

LO 6.h Determine the rules and regulations pertaining to the sale of municipal securities.

Rules and regulations applicable to all firms and individuals having to do with municipal securities are written by the **Municipal Securities Rulemaking Board (MSRB)**. MSRB rules are heavily tested on the exam. In many cases, the rules are the same as FINRAs. Where they are different, we will note it for you. Most of the rules, as with FINRA and SEC rules, are sprinkled throughout the course and covered in the appropriate units. One other point about MSRB rules is that the rule number frequently appears in a test question. It is not required that you memorize those numbers. For example, the question might be worded: "Under MSRB Rule G-9, records of customer complaints must be preserved for at least?" The question makes it clear the topic is recordkeeping (the substance of G-9). Because of the propensity to include those numbers, we will as well, as you should have already noticed.

MSRB

The Securities Acts Amendments of 1975 established the MSRB as an independent self-regulatory organization (SRO). The MSRB governs the issuance and trading of municipal securities. The rules require municipal securities underwriters and dealers to protect investors' interests, be ethical in offering advice, and be responsive to complaints and disputes. The MSRB rules apply to all firms and individuals engaged in the conduct of municipal securities business. The MSRB does not regulate issuers.

Rule Enforcement

The MSRB has no authority to enforce the rules it makes. While the SEC oversees all securities-related rule enforcement, the MSRB rules concerning municipal securities dealers (e.g., NYSE member firms) are specifically enforced by FINRA. Much of the municipal securities business is done by dealer banks. These are commercial banks that are not members of FINRA or any exchange. For those market participants, enforcement is in the hands of various banking agencies. Those include

- the Office of the Comptroller of the Currency,
- the **Federal Reserve Board**, and
- the **Federal Deposit Insurance Corporation** (FDIC).

It is unlikely that you will have to know which banks are supervised by which banking agency.

Recordkeeping for Municipal Securities Firms

Records of Associated Persons (Rule G-7)

A municipal securities dealer must obtain and keep on file specific information about its associated persons. The MSRB defines an associated person as anyone with a securities registration. That would include representatives and principals, but not clerical help. Most of the required information (e.g., employment history, disciplinary actions, residence, and personal data) is contained on the U4 and U5 forms. Any material change must be updated within 30 days. These records must be kept for a minimum of three years after the termination of the associated person.

Books and Recordkeeping Requirements (Rules G-8 ad G-9)

Rule G-8 lists the various records to be made and Rule G-9 states the retention requirements. We think it is easier for you to learn them if we group the rules together.

Record maintenance requirements specify the length of time that various records must be kept. Generally, records are categorized into the following three maintenance periods:

- Records kept for the lifetime of the firm
- Records kept for six years
- Records kept for four years (all those not specifically designated as lifetime or six-year records)

Lifetime Records

A firm must keep the following records for its lifetime:

- Articles of incorporation (if the broker-dealer is a corporation) or partnership agreement (if the broker-dealer is a partnership)
- Minutes of board or partnership meetings
- Records of stock certificates (if the broker-dealer is a corporation)

Six-Year Records

A firm must keep the following records for at least *six years*:

- Blotters (records of original entry)
- General ledger (accounting information such as income and expense and assets and liabilities)
- Customer ledgers (statements of the customer's accounts)
- Customer account records (six years after the account is closed)
- Customer complaints (only written complaints are considered and email is *written*)
- Principal designation record (which individual supervises what)

TEST TOPIC ALERT

MSRB rules list customer complaints as a six-year record. FINRA rules only require a four-year period (Lesson 15.3). This difference is likely to be tested.

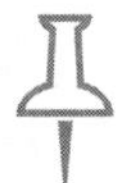

TAKE NOTE

MSRB Rule G-9 requires that designations of principals must be maintained for six years. All records must be kept readily available for two years.

EXAMPLE

A municipal securities principal who is appointed by a committee to manage the money for an LGIP must keep the documents appointing him to this role for six years.

MSRB Rule G-15

This rule requires members to provide customer with written confirmation of transactions. More of the details will be covered in Lesson 15.1. One part worth mentioning here deals with computing the yield and dollar price. We know that calling a premium bond invariably results in a lower yield to the investor than holding the bond to maturity. Therefore, this rule states that in computing yield and dollar price,

- the yield or dollar price computed and shown shall be computed to the lower of call or nominal maturity date; and
- for purposes of computing yield to call or dollar price to call, only those "in whole calls" are included.

MSRB Conduct Rule G-17

This is probably the shortest—yet one of the most important—of the MSRB rules. Here it is in its entirety:

> In the conduct of its municipal securities or municipal advisory activities, each broker-dealer and municipal advisor shall deal fairly with all persons and shall not engage in any deceptive, dishonest, or unfair practice.

This is basically saying, "Don't cheat, don't steal, and don't lie." When you are reading an exam question, always keep this in mind to help you arrive at the correct answer. And, of course, once you pass, it will help you stay out of trouble.

PRACTICE QUESTION

16. A customer of a municipal securities firm calls her registered representative to complain about the amount of commission charged on her most recent trade. The customer is irate and demands to speak with the rep's supervisor. The customer continues her tirade with the supervisor and threatens to sue if something isn't done about the charge. Under MSRB rules, a record of this complaint
    A. must be kept for four years.
    B. must be kept for six years.
    C. must be kept for the lifetime of the firm.
    D. need not be kept.

    Answer: D. Recordkeeping requirements only apply to written complaints. It can be delivered using "snail" mail or email. In this case, the complaint was only in oral form so there is no requirement to keep a record of it. That is the "test" world. You can be sure in the "real" world, your firm would make a record, but, the real world is for after you pass the exam.

MSRB Rule G-21 Advertising

Any material designed for use in the public media is considered **advertising**. This includes abstracts and summaries of the OS; offering circulars; reports; market letters; and form letters, including professional, product, and new issue advertisements.

A municipal securities principal or general securities principal of the dealer must approve all advertising before use, and a copy of each advertisement must be kept on file for three years. We will have more to say about this in Unit 19.

MSRB Rule G-22 Control Relationships

Disclosure of Control

A municipal securities firm that has a control relationship with respect to a municipal security is subject to additional disclosure requirements. A control relationship exists if the dealer controls, is controlled by, or is under common control with that security's issuer.

EXAMPLE

An officer of a municipal dealer sits on the board of directors (BOD) of an issuer.

The dealer must disclose the control relationship to the customer before it can affect any transaction in that security for that customer. Although, initially, this disclosure can be oral, the dealer must make a written disclosure at or before the transaction's completion. The disclosure is made on the confirmation. If the transaction is for a discretionary account, the customer must give express permission before the transaction can be executed.

Rule G-37 Political Contributions

Rule G-37 prohibits municipal firms from engaging in municipal securities business with an issuer for two years after any political contribution is made to an official of that issuer. In this context, municipal securities business refers to negotiated underwritings, not to competitive underwritings. The idea is to prevent firms from making large political contributions in return for being selected as underwriter for that issuer.

The rule applies to contributions by the firm, its MFPs, and by political action committees controlled by the firm or its representatives. De minimis contributions of up to $250 per election are permitted by MFPs, as long as these individuals are eligible to vote for the issuer official. This exemption does not apply to firms.

Municipal Financial Professional (MFP)

In Rule G-37, we discussed MFPs. Who are these folks? As defined by the MSRB, a municipal finance professional (MFP) is an associated person of a broker-dealer who is primarily engaged in municipal securities activities other than retail sales to individuals. The MFP designation also includes anyone who solicits municipal securities business for the broker-dealer, or is in the supervisory chain above another person with the MFP designation. This can include senior officials of the broker-dealer, or executives, or management committee members of the broker-dealer.

Of note, the MSRB is clear that anyone designated as an MFP is subject to the rules regarding political contributions and required to report those contributions to the MSRB, as well as any other payments made to a state or local political party. Be sure you know the exceptions for de minimis contributions.

The Broker-Dealer as Financial Advisor

Financial Advisors

The MSRB has established ethical standards and disclosure requirements for municipal securities dealers that act as **financial advisors** to municipal securities' issuers. A financial advisory relationship exists when a municipal dealer provides financial advisory or consulting services to an issuer with respect to a new issue for a fee or other compensation. This includes advice regarding the structure, timing, and terms of, as well as other matters concerning, the issue or issuer. Bringing a new issue public, whether it is equity or debt, is called underwriting. In Unit 20, we go into a detailed discussion of the underwriting process. In the case of municipal bonds, the disclosure document used is an official statement rather than a prospectus.

Basis of Compensation

Each financial advisory relationship must be documented in writing before, upon, or promptly after its inception. This document establishes the basis of compensation for the advisory services to be rendered.

Conflicts of Interest

Potential **conflicts of interest** arise if a firm acts as both a member of the underwriting syndicate and financial advisor for the same issue. The MSRB has the following requirements.

The MSRB simply prohibits a broker-dealer who serves as a financial advisor to a municipal issuer for any issue sold on either a negotiated or competitive bid basis from switching roles and underwriting the same issue. In other words, if a broker-dealer is acting as a financial advisor to the issuer, generally, the broker-dealer may not participate in underwriting the bonds of the issuing municipality.

However, there are some allowable exceptions. For example, a broker-dealer who has a financial advisory relationship with an issuer regarding the issuance of municipal securities, will still be permitted to assist with preparing the official statement and other similar duties normally associated with underwriting. The broker-dealer can also purchase the bonds from an underwriter either for its own trading account or for the accounts of its customers. But in all cases, if performing such functions or acting in such a capacity as described above, the broker-dealer may not receive any compensation other than for financial advisory services to the issuer. In other words, no underwriting compensation can be received by the broker-dealer who is acting in an advisory capacity.

Customers who are purchasing new securities from a broker-dealer who is acting in an advisory capacity to a municipality must be informed that the advisory relationship exists at or before confirmation of the sale.

Assistance With the Official Statement (OS)

As part of its financial advisory services to an issuer, a municipal securities dealer may help prepare the final official statement for a new issue. If it prepares the OS, the advisor must make a copy of that statement available to the managing underwriter promptly after the award is made and at least two days before the syndicate manager delivers the securities to the syndicate members.

Use of Ownership Information

While acting in a fiduciary capacity for an issuer, a municipal securities dealer often obtains confidential information about its bondholders. The dealer cannot use this information to solicit purchases or sales of municipal securities or to pursue other financial gain without the issuer's consent.

Examples of fiduciary capacities include, but are not limited to, acting as paying agent, transfer agent, registrar, or indenture trustee for an issuer.

UNIT 7

U.S. Treasury and Government Agency Securities

LEARNING OBJECTIVES

When you have completed this unit, you will be able to accomplish the following.

- › LO 7.a **Recall** the different types of securities issued by the U.S. Treasury.
- › LO 7.b **Recognize** the special characteristics of Treasury issues.
- › LO 7.c **Differentiate** between the various U.S. government agency issues.
- › LO 7.d **Recognize** the special characteristics of agency securities.
- › LO 7.e **Differentiate** between the different kinds of tax treatment of government securities.

INTRODUCTION

The U.S. Treasury issues many securities. They range from short-term money market instruments to long-term bonds.

The U.S. Treasury Department determines the quantity and types of government securities it must issue to meet federal budget needs. The marketplace determines the interest rates those securities will pay. In general, the interest that government securities pay is exempt from state and municipal taxation but subject to federal taxation.

The federal government is the nation's largest borrower, as well as the best credit risk. Interest and principal on securities issued by the U.S. government are backed by its full faith and credit, which is based on its power to tax. These securities are considered the sovereign debt of the United States.

At least for exam purposes, there is no default risk to speak of with Treasury securities, but that does not mean investors can't lose money. Government securities trade in the secondary market (OTC) and are subject to interest-rate risk just like other debt securities.

Since 1986, Treasury securities have only been available in book entry form. Book entry means that the record of ownership is kept on the "books" of the Treasury. Before the change, you would receive a beautiful certificate with engraving similar to U.S. currency.

LESSON 7.1: TYPES OF TREASURY SECURITIES AND THEIR PRICING

LO 7.a Recall the different types of securities issued by the U.S. Treasury.

Treasury Bills (T-Bills)

Treasury Bills (T-bills) are short-term obligations issued at a discount from par. Rather than making regular cash interest payments, bills trade at a discount from par value. The return on a T-bill is the difference between the price the investor pays and the par value at which the bill matures. Treasury bills are considered money market instruments. As mentioned earlier in the course, the 13-week T-bill is commonly used in quantitative analysis as the risk-free investment.

Treasury Notes (T-Notes)

Unlike Treasury bills, **Treasury notes (T-notes)** pay interest every six months. They are sold at auction every four weeks. They are considered intermediate length securities with maturities of 2, 3, 5, 7, or 10 years.

Treasury Bonds (T-Bonds)

Treasury Bonds (T-bonds) are long-term securities (10–30 years in original maturity) that pay interest every six months. Historically, the 30-year bonds were callable at par, five years before the maturity date. Callable bonds have not been issued since 1985 and none are still available in the marketplace. It is possible that the Treasury could again begin issuing callable bonds, but most industry pundits doubt this will happen.

Separate Trading of Registered Interest and Principal of Securities (STRIPS)

In 1984, the Treasury Department entered the zero coupon bond market by designating certain Treasury issues as suitable for stripping into interest and principal components.

These securities, named separate trading of registered interest and principal of securities became known by their acronym, **STRIPS**. Although the securities underlying Treasury STRIPS are the U.S. government's direct obligation, major banks and dealers perform the actual separation and trading. As zero coupon bonds, they have minimal reinvestment risk.

Treasury Receipts

Treasury receipts are not issued by the U.S Treasury. Brokerage firms can create a type of zero coupon bond known as **Treasury receipts** from U.S. Treasury notes and bonds. Broker-dealers buy Treasury securities, place them in trust at a bank, and sell separate receipts against the principal and coupon payments. The Treasury securities held in trust collateralize the Treasury receipts. Unlike Treasury securities, Treasury receipts are not backed by the full faith and credit of the U.S. government. Each Treasury receipt is priced at a discount from the payment amount, like a zero coupon bond.

TEST TOPIC ALERT

STRIPS are backed in full by the U.S. government. Receipts are not. Treasury receipts are created by broker-dealers and sold under names like Certificates of Accrual on Treasury Securities (CATS) and Treasury Income Growth Receipts (TIGRS). Both are quoted in yield to maturity and have not been issued since the late 1980s.

Treasury Inflation Protection Securities (TIPS)

A type of Treasury issue, known as **Treasury Inflation Protection Securities (TIPS)**, helps protect investors against purchasing power (inflation) risk. These bonds are issued with a fixed interest rate, but the principal amount is adjusted semiannually by an amount equal to the change in the **Consumer Price Index (CPI)**, the standard measurement of inflation.

The interest payment the investor receives every six months is equal to the fixed interest rate times the newly adjusted principal. In times of inflation, the interest payments increase, while in times of deflation, the interest payments fall. These notes are sold at lower interest rates than conventional fixed-rate Treasury notes because of their adjustable nature.

Like other Treasury securities, TIPS are exempt from state and local income taxes on the interest income generated, but they are subject to federal taxation. However, in any year when the principal is adjusted for inflation, that increase is considered reportable income for that year even though the increase will not be received until the note matures. This is the same phantom income we mentioned with zero coupon bonds.

PRACTICE QUESTION

1. A risk averse client wishes the safety of a U.S treasury backed security but is concerned about the effects of inflation on the value of the dollar. Which of the following would be most appropriate for this investor?
   A. Treasury bills
   B. Treasury notes
   C. Treasury bonds
   D. TIPS

   Answer: D. The *IP* in TIPS stands for *inflation protection*. These are the only Treasury securities where the value at maturity can be higher than the original investment if there is inflation.

LO 7.b Recognize the special characteristics of Treasury issues.

Treasury Bill Prices and Denominations

Maturities and Denominations

Treasury bills are issued in denominations of $100 to $5 million, and have original maturities of 52 weeks or less. The 52-week bills are auctioned monthly, and the others, such as the 4-week and 26-week bills, weekly.

TAKE NOTE

Maximum T-bill maturities are subject to change, but are never longer than 52 weeks.

Pricing for T-Bills

T-bills are quoted on a yield basis and sold at a discount from par. They are zero coupon securities.

EXAMPLE

Sample T-Bill Quotation

Issue	Bid	Ask
T-bills maturing 03/15/19	1.15	1.12

The *bid* reflects the yield buyers want to receive. The *ask* reflects the yield sellers are willing to accept.

TAKE NOTE

The exam will not require you to calculate the bid and ask prices of T-bills. However, it is important to be able to identify the quote as a T-bill quote.

Because T-bills are quoted in yield, a T-bill quote has a bid higher than its ask price, which is the reverse of bid-ask relationships for other instruments. Higher yield on the bid side translates into a lower dollar price. Or you could think in terms of going shopping; the bigger the discount, the lower the price.

Treasury Note Prices and Denominations

Maturities and Denominations

Treasury notes are issued in denominations of $100 to $5 million. T-notes mature at par, or they can be **refunded**. If a T-note is refunded, the government offers the investor a new security with a new interest rate and maturity date as an alternative to a cash payment for the maturing note.

Pricing for T-Notes

T-notes are issued, quoted, and traded as a percentage of par in $^1/_{32}$%.

EXAMPLE

A quote of 98.24, which can also be expressed as 98-24 or 98:24, on a $1,000 note means that the note is selling for 9824⁄32% of its $1,000 par value. In this instance, 0.24 designates $^{24}/_{32}$ of 1%, not a decimal. A quote of 98.24 equals 98.75% of $1,000, or $987.50.

Pricing of T-Notes

A bid of:	Means:	Or:
98.01	98$^1/_{32}$% of $1,000	$980.3125
98.02	98$^2/_{32}$% of $1,000	$980.6250
98.03	98$^3/_{32}$% of $1,000	$980.9375
98.10	98$^{10}/_{32}$% of $1,000	$983.1250
98.11	98$^{11}/_{32}$% of $1,000	$983.4375
98.12	98$^{12}/_{32}$% of $1,000	$983.7500

Treasury Bond Prices and Denominations

Maturities and Denominations

T-bonds are issued in denominations of $100 to $5 million and mature at least 10 years from the date of issue.

Pricing for T-Bonds

T-bonds are quoted exactly like T-notes (1⁄32% of par).

TEST TOPIC ALERT

Testable features of Treasury bills, notes, and bonds:

Marketable Government Securities

Type	Maturity	Pricing	Form
T-bills	Maximum 52 weeks	Issued at a discount; priced on discount basis	Book entry
T-notes	2–10 years (intermediate-term)	Priced at percentage of par	Book entry
T-bonds	Greater than 10 years (long-term)	Priced at percentage of par	Book entry

PRACTICE QUESTION

2. An investor purchasing a seven-year Treasury note at a price of 101.20 would be paying
   A. $101.20.
   B. $1,006.25.
   C. $1,012.00.
   D. $1,016.25.

Answer: D. A quote of 101.20 on a Treasury note means 101 20⁄32. That is equal to 101 5⁄8. The math is

101 = $1,010.

5/8 – 5 × $1.25 = $6.25

Total is $1,010 + $6.25 = $1,016.25

LESSON 7.2: U.S. GOVERNMENT AGENCY SECURITIES

LO 7.c Differentiate between the various U.S. government agency issues.

Agency Issues

Congress authorizes the following agencies of the federal government to issue debt securities:

- Farm Credit Administration
- Government National Mortgage Association (GNMA or Ginnie Mae)

Unit 7

Other agency-like organizations operated by private corporations include the following:

- Federal Home Loan Mortgage Corporation (FHLMC or Freddie Mac)
- Federal National Mortgage Association (FNMA or Fannie Mae)
- Student Loan Marketing Association (SLMA or Sallie Mae)

The term *agency* is sometimes used to refer to entities that are not technically government agencies but do have ties to the government. For example, Fannie Mae is privately owned but government sponsored.

Ginnie Mae

The **Government National Mortgage Association (GNMA)** is a government-owned corporation that supports the Department of Housing and Urban Development. Ginnie Mae are the only agency securities backed by the full faith and credit of the federal government.

3.10.8.3.1 Types of GNMA Issues

Ginnie Mae does not originate mortgage loans, nor does it purchase, sell, or issue securities. Instead, private lending institutions approved by GNMA originate eligible loans and pool them into securities, known as pass-through certificates, and sell the GNMA mortgage-backed securities (MBS) to investors. These lending institutions can include mortgage companies, commercial banks, and thrift institutions of all sizes, as well as state housing finance agencies. Ginnie Mae guarantees only MBS backed by single and multifamily home loans insured by government agencies, primarily the Federal Housing Association (FHA) and the Department of Veteran Affairs (VA), as well as others. Like the principal on a single mortgage, the principal represented by a GNMA certificate constantly decreases as the mortgages are paid down.

GNMA guarantees timely payment of interest and principal. GNMAs are backed directly by the government, so risk of default is nearly zero. GNMAs offer slightly higher interest rates than comparable Treasury securities. But, because they are government guaranteed, their rates are lower than other agency securities.

Prices, yields, and maturities fluctuate in line with general interest-rate trends. If interest rates fall, homeowners tend to pay off their mortgages early. That has the effect of accelerating the certificates' maturities. If interest rates rise, certificates may mature more slowly.

In addition to interest-rate risk (the risk that rates rise, causing the value of the underlying mortgages to fall), there are two other types of risk associated with MBS.

The first is **prepayment risk**, the risk that the underlying mortgages will be paid off earlier than anticipated. This will occur if interest rates fall, causing homeowners to refinance their mortgages at lower rates.

The second is **extended maturity risk**, the risk that the underlying mortgages will remain outstanding longer than anticipated. This will occur if interest rates rise, virtually eliminating any refinancings.

TAKE NOTE

GNMAs are backed in full by the U.S. government. Other agency instruments discussed next are not; they are backed by their own issuing authority. You should know the following GNMA features:

- $1,000 minimums
- Monthly interest and principal payments
- Taxed at all levels
- Pass-through certificates
- Significant reinvestment risk

TEST TOPIC ALERT

The exam expects you to know that MBS are susceptible to reinvestment risk. The reasons are outlined here.

When interest rates fall, mortgage holders typically refinance at lower rates. This means that they pay off their mortgages early, which causes a prepayment of principal to holders of MBS. The early principal payments cannot be reinvested at a comparable return.

Sometimes the test asks which instruments are not subject to reinvestment risk.

Of the answer choices given, the best answer is typically a zero coupon bond. No interest is paid on a current basis, so the investor has no reinvestment risk.

Farm Credit System (FCS)

The **Farm Credit System (FCS)** is a national network of lending institutions that provides agricultural financing and credit. The system is a privately owned, government-sponsored enterprise that raises loanable funds through the sale of Farm Credit securities to investors. They are not obligations of, nor are they guaranteed, by the U.S. government or any federal agency. They are backed by the Banks of the FCS.

These funds are made available to farmers through a nationwide network of four banks and 68 Farm Credit lending institutions. The Farm Credit Administration (FCA), a government agency, oversees the system. Included in the system are the Federal Land Banks, Federal Intermediate Credit Banks, and Banks for Cooperatives.

The federal FCS issues discount notes, floating rate bonds, and fixed rate bonds. The maturities range from one day to 30 years. The proceeds from the sale of securities are used to provide farmers with real estate loans, rural home mortgage loans, and crop insurance.

Freddie Mac

The **Federal Home Loan Mortgage Corporation (FHLMC)** is a public corporation. It was created to promote the development of a nationwide secondary market in mortgages by buying residential mortgages from financial institutions and packaging them into MBS for sale to investors.

FHLMC sells two types of securities: **mortgage participation certificates (PCs)** and **guaranteed mortgage certificates (GMCs)**. PCs make principal and interest payments once a month; GMCs make interest payments twice a year and principal payments once a year.

Fannie Mae

The **Federal National Mortgage Association (FNMA)** is a publicly held corporation that provides mortgage capital. FNMA purchases conventional and insured mortgages from agencies such as the FHA and the VA. The securities it creates are backed by FNMA's general credit.

Types of FNMA Issues

FNMA issues debentures, short-term discount notes, and MBS. In the case of virtually all of the agencies, there are no certificates delivered. Records of ownership are kept electronically. As mentioned earlier, this is referred to as being issued in *book entry* form.

Student Loan Marketing Association (Sallie Mae or SLMA)

Sallie Mae issues short-term and long-term securities. The proceeds from the securities sales are used to provide student loans for higher education.

Sallie Mae was once an agency issue of the U.S. government but is now privately owned with its common stock (symbol SLM) trading on Nasdaq. It might still be improperly grouped with agency issues on a test question.

Tennessee Valley Authority (TVA)

One final agency that might be tested is the TVA. The Tennessee Valley Authority is the nation's largest public power provider and a corporation of the U.S. government. TVA bonds are not backed by the U.S. government. Instead, they are backed by the revenues generated by the agencies' projects. However, credit-rating agencies perceive that there is an "implicit government guarantee of TVA bonds." If push came to shove, it's a good bet that Uncle Sam would make that guarantee explicit. One special characteristic of TVA bonds is that they are frequently issued with maturities of 50 years.

LO 7.d Recognize the special characteristics of agency securities.

Pass-Through Certificates

A pass-through security is created by pooling a group of mortgages and selling certificates representing interests in the pool. The term *pass-through* refers to the mechanism of passing homebuyers' interest and principal payments from the mortgage holder to the investors. Fannie Mae, Ginnie Mae, and Freddie Mac function this way. In some cases, such as the GNMA, the payments are monthly.

Denominations of Agency Securities

FINRA states that most agency bonds are sold in a variety of increments. The minimum is generally $10,000, with increments of $5,000. We have listed the details as supplied by the various agencies and they don't always agree with FINRA's statement. Because of the wide variety, we don't imagine this will be highly tested on the exam, even though it is included in the Content Outline. Should we learn anything specific, it will be posted to Exam Tips.

GNMA

GNMA MBS are issued in minimum denominations of $1,000 and multiples of $1 in excess of $1,000. Because few mortgages last the full term, yield quotes are based on a 12-year prepayment assumption, that is, a mortgage balance should be prepaid in full after 12 years of normally scheduled payments.

Farm Credit System (FCS)

FCSs are not pass-through securities. Denominations are $1,000 with $1,000 increments.

FHLMC

Freddie Mac offers a wide variety of increments with different minimums. For example, the discount notes with a maturity of one year or less are offered in denominations of $1,000, with $1,000 increments. FHLMC also offers reference notes with 2–10 year maturities in minimum denominations of $2,000 with $1,000 increments.

FNMA

For test purposes, know that the mortgage-backed securities are available in minimum denominations of $1,000 with $1 increments after that. Interest is paid semiannually.

SLMA

The long-term issues are generally in $10,000 minimum denominations.

PRACTICE QUESTION

3. Which statement regarding U.S. government agency obligations is **true**?
   A. They are all direct obligations of the U.S. government.
   B. They generally have higher yields than yields of Treasury securities.
   C. The FNMA interest is taxed only at the federal level.
   D. Securities issued by GNMA trade on the NYSE floor.

Answer: B. U.S. government agency debt is an obligation of the issuing agency, not the U.S. government. The only exception to that is the GNMA. This causes agency debt to trade at higher yields reflecting this greater risk. Interest on FNMA securities is taxed at all levels and no Treasury security trades on the NYSE.

LO 7.e Differentiate between the different kinds of tax treatment of government securities.

Taxation of Treasury Securities

Interest Income

The interest earned on any security issued by the U.S. Treasury is taxable on the federal level. The interest on any security issued by the U.S. Treasury is exempt from state and local taxation.

There is one taxation oddity and that deals with TIPS bonds. As we described earlier in this Unit, each six months, there is an adjustment to the principal value based on the inflation rate as measured by the CPI. Even though the investor does not receive that increase until the bond matures, it is reported as interest income each year.

Capital Gain or Loss

When an investor sells a Treasury security at a price higher than the purchase price, it is considered a capital gain. The sale at a price below cost is a capital loss. These gains and losses are no different from the others we have covered thus far. We do not expect the exam to deal with accreting the discount on T-bills.

Taxation of Agency Securities

Interest Income

The one constant about taxation of agency securities is that the interest is always subject to federal income tax. This parallels the taxation of Treasury issues. Where there are some differences is in regard to state income tax.

Taxation of Mortgage-Backed Agency Securities

Interest earned on GNMA, FHLMC, and FNMA certificates is taxable at the federal, state, and local levels. Remember that a portion of the payments on MBS is a return of principal. That is nontaxable.

Taxation of Nonmortgaged-Backed Agency Securities

Interest paid on Farm Credit System and Federal Home Loan Banks securities is taxable at the federal level and is exempt from state and local taxation in most states.

Capital Gain or Loss

In the case of non-MBS, gains and losses are computed the same way as any other security. In the case of MBS, because each payment includes principal, the computation for a gain or loss is likely too complex for the exam.

TAKE NOTE

Before we move on to the next unit, here is a summary of the tax treatment of interest:

- Interest on corporate bonds is taxable on all levels (federal, state, and local).
- Interest on municipal securities may be taxed by the municipal level (state and local governments) but not by the federal government.
- Interest on issues of the federal government (Treasury bills, notes, and bonds) is taxed by the federal government but is exempt from taxation at the state and local levels.
- Interest on mortgage-backed securities is taxed on all levels (federal, state and local).
- Interest on issues of U.S. territories, e.g., Puerto Rico and Guam, qualifies for a triple exemption (federal, state, and local).

UNIT
8 Investment Companies

LEARNING OBJECTIVES

When you have completed this unit, you will be able to accomplish the following.

- › LO 8.a **Identify** the different types of investment companies.
- › LO 8.b **Compare** the difference between the method of capitalization of open-end investment companies and closed-end investment companies.
- › LO 8.c **Identify** the difference in pricing between open-end and closed-end investment companies.
- › LO 8.d **Contrast** the different mutual fund share classes and how that relates to the different types of loads charged to fund investors.
- › LO 8.e **Recall** special features of mutual funds.
- › LO 8.f **Differentiate** between the different kinds of tax treatment of mutual funds.
- › LO 8.g **Match** the objective of the fund to that of the client.
- › LO 8.h **Recognize** the different features and types of ETFs.
- › LO 8.i **Explain** the benefits and risks of investment companies in client portfolios.
- › LO 8.j **Determine** the rules and regulations pertaining to the sale of investment company securities.

INTRODUCTION

When seeing the term *investment company*, most investors think about mutual funds. Although those represent the largest portion of the industry, there are other types that are tested. Those include closed-end funds (CEFs) and exchange-traded funds (ETFs).

An **investment company** is a corporation or a trust through which investors may acquire an interest in large, diversified portfolios of securities by pooling their funds with other investors' funds and buying shares or units of the fund. People often invest in investment companies because they believe a professional money manager should be able to outperform the average investor in the market.

Investment companies, especially mutual funds, offer many services that benefit investors. One of the challenges for any registered representative is matching the right fund to the customer's objectives.

Investment companies are subject to regulations regarding how their shares are sold to the public. The Investment Company Act of 1940 provides for SEC regulation of investment companies and their activities. It is that act that defines the types of investment companies.

LESSON 8.1: DEFINITIONS UNDER THE INVESTMENT COMPANY ACT OF 1940

LO 8.a Identify the different types of investment companies.

Types of Investment Companies

The Investment Company Act of 1940 classifies investment companies into three broad types: face-amount certificate (FAC) companies, unit investment trusts (UITs), and management investment companies.

Face-Amount Certificate (FAC) Companies

A **face-amount certificate (FAC)** is a contract between an investor and an issuer in which the issuer guarantees payment of a stated (or fixed) sum to the investor at some set date in the future. In return for this future payment, the investor agrees to pay the issuer a set amount of money either as a lump sum or in periodic installments.

The only fact you need to know about this security is that it is one of the three types of investment companies listed in the Investment Company Act of 1940.

Unit Investment Trusts (UITs)

The next of the entities meeting the definition of an investment company under the Investment Company Act is the UITs. A **unit investment trust (UIT)** is an **unmanaged investment company** organized under a trust indenture. UITs do not

- have boards of directors,
- employ an investment adviser, and
- actively manage their own portfolios (trade securities).

A unit investment trust issues only redeemable securities, known as **units** or **shares of beneficial interest,** each of which represents an undivided interest in a portfolio of specified securities. Once the specified total is raised, the trustees use the investor's money to purchase securities designed to meet the UIT's stated objective. Without an investment adviser (management), once compiled, the portfolio remains fixed. An example of a UIT is one solely invested in municipal bonds where the trust liquidates after the final bond in the portfolio matures. There are also equity trusts where, because stock doesn't mature, the portfolio is liquidated at a predetermined date and the proceeds are distributed to unit holders or reinvested into a new trust at the investor's option. UITs are sold by prospectus.

Under the Investment Company Act of 1940, the trustees must maintain secondary markets in the units, thus allowing unit holders the ability to redeem their units at NAV. Some

ETFs—covered later in this unit—are organized as UITs and trade, as the name implies, on exchanges or Nasdaq.

TAKE NOTE

Know the following features of UITs:

- UITs are not actively managed; there is no board of directors (BOD) or investment adviser.
- UIT shares (units) must be redeemed by the trust.
- UITs are investment companies as defined under the Investment Company Act.

PRACTICE QUESTION

1. Louis owns an investment that is an unmanaged portfolio in which the money manager initially selects the securities to be included in the portfolio and then holds those securities until they mature or the investment portfolio terminates. This statement best describes which type of investment?
   A. Closed-end investment company
   B. Face-amount certificate (FAC) company
   C. Open-end investment company
   D. Unit investment trust (UIT)

Answer: D. A UIT is a type of investment company, which is generally unmanaged as the money manager initially selects the securities to be included in the portfolio and then holds those securities until they mature or the UIT terminates.

Management Companies

The most familiar type of investment company is the **management investment company**, which actively manages a securities portfolio to achieve a stated investment objective. A management investment company is either closed-end or open-end. Mutual funds are open-end investment companies. Initially, both closed-end and open-end companies sell shares to the public; the difference between them lies in the way they raise capital and how investors buy and sell their shares—in the primary or secondary market. Most ETFs, covered later, are open-end investment companies. However, on the exam, when you see open-end investment company, think mutual fund. ETFs will be identified separately.

TAKE NOTE

Open-end and closed-end investment companies have far more similarities than differences. One of these is the term, *net asset value* per share, generally shown as NAV. This value is the result of the fund valuing all of its assets (the largest of which is the portfolio), subtracting its liabilities, and then dividing that by the number of shares outstanding. This NAV per share computation is critical to the purchase and sale of open-end companies, and, as we'll see, has little relationship to the buying and selling price of CEFs.

TEST TOPIC ALERT

It is important for you to know that the definition of *investment company* does not include holding companies.

PRACTICE QUESTION

2. Which of the following would not be considered an investment company under the Investment Company Act of 1940?
   A. Face-amount certificate (FAC) company
   B. Unit investment trust (UIT)
   C. Management company
   D. Holding company

   Answer: D. Holding companies are specifically excluded from the definition of *investment company*. Each of the others is a type defined in the Investment Company Act.

Diversified Management Company

There is a special term only used for management companies. The company can elect to be considered *diversified* or *nondiversified* under the Investment Company Act of 1940; a diversified investment company is one that meets the following requirements of the 75-5-10 test:

- At least 75% of the fund's total assets must be invested in cash and securities issued by companies other than the investment company itself or its affiliates.
- The 75% must be invested in such a way that
  - no more than 5% of the fund's total assets are invested in the securities of any one issuer and
  - no more than 10% of the outstanding voting securities of any one issuer is owned (by the 75%).

TEST TOPIC ALERT

Remember, for testing purposes, the 5% and 10% limitations are part of the 75% invested. There are no conditions attached to the remaining 25%.

PRACTICE QUESTION

3. An open-end investment company's net assets are $1 billion. It has elected to be treated as a diversified investment company. The company would be in noncompliance with the rules if it
   A. invested $50 million into ABC stock.
   B. invested $300 million into ABC stock.
   C. invested $350 million into ABC stock.
   D. purchased 100% of the voting shares of ABC stock.

   Answer: C. You must remember that the 5% and 10% limitations only apply to 75% of the fund's portfolio. The other 25%—in this case, $250 million—can be invested wherever the fund's management desires. Within the diversified 75%, the fund can own $50 million of a single issuer's stock (5% of the $1 billion total). Then, the other 25% can purchase $250 million, giving it a total of $300 million in one stock. That $300 million could buy 100% of the voting shares of many publicly traded companies. Remember, that 10% limit only applies to the diversified 75%.

LESSON 8.2: COMPARING OPEN-END AND CLOSED-END MANAGEMENT INVESTMENT COMPANIES

LO 8.b Compare the difference between the method of capitalization of open-end investment companies and closed-end investment companies.

Management Companies—Methods of Capitalization

As we remarked earlier, there are many similarities between open-end and closed-end companies. The most significant difference is in the way they raise capital from investors.

Open-End Investment Companies Initial Capitalization

An open-end investment company, or **mutual fund**, does not specify the exact number of shares it intends to issue. It registers an open offering with the SEC. The open-end investment company can raise an unlimited amount of investment capital by continuously issuing new shares. As we will cover in Unit 20, because the shares are always a new issue, it is required to deliver a prospectus prior to or concurrent with the sale. As a consequence, investors in mutual funds are always purchasing a new issue. The money invested goes to the issuer (the mutual fund). One other point is that open-end companies can only issue common stock. The money raised from the issuance of that common stock is then used by the portfolio manager(s) to invest in securities meeting that fund's objectives. For example, a mutual fund seeking income would likely invest a substantial portion of its capital into bonds and/or preferred stock. Don't confuse the limitation on only issuing common stock to raise capital with what it can invest with that capital—bond funds will use the proceeds from the sale of the common shares issued to buy bonds.

TAKE NOTE

An open-end investment company can buy preferred stock and bonds, but it can issue any security other than common stock.

Closed-End Investment Companies Initial Capitalization

As we stated, the primary difference between the two categories of management companies (closed-end and open-end) is the way in which they raise capital and subsequently trade. To raise capital, a closed-end investment company conducts a common stock offering. For the initial offering, the company registers a fixed number of shares with the SEC and offers them to the public for a limited time through an underwriting group in a manner the same as any corporate stock offering. The fund's capitalization is fixed unless an additional public offering is made at a later time.

Investors cannot redeem their shares back to the company. Investors close their position by selling them in the secondary market just like any publicly traded stock.

Having just said investors cannot redeem their shares of a closed-end fund, we need to mention an exception. There is a breed of closed-end funds called **interval funds**. Here are the key facts to know:

- These are closed-end investment companies, registered as such under the Investment Company Act of 1940.
- Unlike other closed-end funds, interval funds do *not* trade in the secondary market.

- They are called interval funds because at certain intervals, which may be anything from monthly to annually, investors are allowed to sell a portion of their shares back to the fund at net asset value (NAV).
- One benefit of these funds is that the portfolio manager can take certain illiquid positions a mutual fund manager might not take because there is no need for daily liquidity with an interval fund.
- In general, these would be more suitable for an investor with a longer time horizon.

Closed-end investment companies can also issue bonds and preferred stock. Therefore, the capital structure of a closed-end company can resemble that of any other corporation—common stock, preferred stock, and bonds.

PRACTICE QUESTION

4. An investor is always purchasing newly issued shares of common stock when investing in
   A. a closed-end investment company.
   B. an open-end investment company (mutual fund).
   C. a unit investment trust (UIT).
   D. a holding company.

   Answer: B. A unique characteristic of mutual funds is that they are capitalized by a continuous offering of new shares. Whenever an investor adds to her portfolio, she is buying new shares of common stock issued by that fund. UITs issue units, not shares, in a one-time offering.

Business Development Company (BDC)

Business development companies were created by an act of Congress in 1980. The purpose was to create a new vehicle to aid in the promotion and development of small businesses. A business development company (BDC) is a closed-end investment company regulated under the Investment Company Act of 1940. It does not have the flexibility of regular closed-end funds because at least 70% of its assets must be invested "eligible" assets.

The term *eligible portfolio company* includes any issuer that does not have any class of securities listed on a national securities exchange. There is an exception for issuers with a class of securities listed on a national securities exchange if they have an aggregate market value of outstanding voting and non-voting common equity of less than $250 million.

Perhaps the most significant difference between a closed-end fund and a BDC is that, with respect to the eligible assets, the BDC must make available significant managerial assistance. In other words, in addition to being an investment company, a BDC is also an operating company.

LO 8.c Identify the difference in pricing between open-end and closed-end investment companies.

Management Companies—Pricing Methods

One of the most significant differences between open-end and CEFs is the way in which they are priced. Although both types of funds compute the NAV per share, it is only the open-end company whose price is solely dependent upon that calculation. The exam will have several questions on how and why each pricing method is used. We will begin with a discussion of pricing closed-end fund shares.

Pricing of Closed-End Investment Company Shares

Closed-end investment companies are commonly known as **publicly traded funds**. After the stock is distributed, anyone can buy or sell shares in the secondary market, either on an exchange or OTC. Supply and demand determine the **bid price** (price at which an investor can sell) and the **ask price** (price at which an investor can buy). Closed-end fund shares usually trade at a premium or discount to the shares' NAV.

TEST TOPIC ALERT

Please remember the following point:

Closed-end investment companies trade in the secondary market (exchange or OTC). That makes their price based upon supply and demand for their shares. As a result, their buying and selling price does not have a direct relationship to the NAV of the shares. Put another way, the market price of a closed-end fund is independent of the fund's NAV.

Pricing of Open-End Investment Company Shares

When it comes to open-end investment companies (mutual funds), any person who wants to invest in the company buys shares directly from the company or its underwriters (or a broker-dealer with a selling agreement) at the **public offering price (POP)**. A mutual fund's POP is the NAV per share plus any applicable sales charges. A mutual fund's NAV is calculated daily by deducting the fund's liabilities from its total assets. NAV per share is calculated by dividing the fund's NAV by the number of shares outstanding. Because all buying and redeeming is done through the investment company, there is no secondary trading of shares in these companies.

An open-end investment company sells **redeemable securities**. When investors liquidate their shares, the company redeems them at their NAV. For each share an investor redeems, the company sends the investor money for the investor's proportionate share of the company's net assets. Therefore, a mutual fund's capital shrinks when investors redeem shares.

Each investor's share in the fund's performance is based on the number of shares owned. Mutual fund shares may be purchased in either full or fractional units, unlike stock, which may be purchased in full units only. Because mutual fund shares can be fractional, the investor can think in terms of dollars rather than number of shares owned. Because CEFs trade like any other corporate stock, fractional shares are not available.

EXAMPLE

If NavCo Mutual Fund shares have a POP of $15 per share, a $100 investment buys 6.667 shares ($100 ÷ $15 = 6.667).

Forward Pricing

Open-end investment companies (mutual funds) must compute their NAV per share at least once per day (very few compute more than that) as of the close of the markets (generally 4:00 pm ET). Price determination for purchases and sales is based upon the forward pricing principle. That is, whenever an order, whether to purchase or redeem shares, is received, the

Unit 8

price is based upon the next computed NAV per share. For example, any order received (and time stamped) before 4:00 pm ET will be executed at the price computed as of that day's market close. If the order is received at 4:00 pm (or later), it will be executed based upon the NAV computed as of 4:00 pm the next business day.

The following chart summarizes the testable differences between open-end and closed-end companies:

	Open-End	**Closed-End**
Capitalization	Unlimited; continuous offering of shares	Fixed; single offering of shares
Issues	Common stock only; no debt securities	May issue: common stock, preferred stock, debt securities
Shares	Full or fractional	Full only
Offering and trading	Sold and redeemed by fund only Continuous primary offering Must redeem shares	Initial primary offering Secondary trading OTC or on an exchange Does not redeem shares
Pricing	NAV + sales charge Selling price determined by formula in the prospectus; the price can never be below the NAV	Current market value + commission Price determined by supply and demand so it can be above, below, or the same as the NAV

TEST TOPIC ALERT

We said earlier that CEFs also compute NAV; however, because their price is determined by supply and demand and, as a consequence, may be more than, the same as, or less than the NAV, it does not have the relevance that it does with open-end funds. Therefore, instead of daily computation, it is generally only done once per week.

PRACTICE QUESTION

5. Daniella Martinez has a number of investment company products within her retirement portfolio. One of these investments trades on an exchange and may trade at a premium or discount to its NAV. These features are most likely found in what type of investment?
   A. Closed-end investment company
   B. Unit investment trust (UIT)
   C. Open-end investment company
   D. Face-amount certificate (FAC) company

Answer: A. A closed-end investment company (closed-end fund, or CEF) is a type of investment company whose shares trade in the secondary market. It is critical to remember for the exam that the price of a closed-end company is based on supply and demand and, therefore, can sell at, above, or below the fund's NAV.

LESSON 8.3: MUTUAL FUND SHARE CLASSES

LO 8.d Contrast the different mutual fund share classes and how that relates to the different types of loads charged to fund investors.

Introduction

FINRA Rule 2341 prohibits its members who underwrite fund shares from assessing sales charges in *excess of 8.5%* of the POP on the purchase of open-end investment company shares. The actual schedule of sales charges is specified *in the prospectus*. Sales loads, management fees, and operating expenses reduce an investor's returns because they diminish the amount of money invested in a fund. Historically, mutual funds have charged **front-end loads** of up to 8.5% of the money invested (POP). Today, few, if any, charge that much.

Alternatively, funds may charge a **back-end** load when funds are withdrawn. Some funds charge ongoing fees under section 12b-1 of the Investment Company Act of 1940. These funds deduct annual fees to pay for marketing and distribution costs.

TAKE NOTE

The term used for the expense of buying or selling mutual fund shares is called sales **charge** or sales **load**. You will see us use *charge* and *load* interchangeably.

Costs to Purchase Mutual Funds

All sales commissions and expenses for an **open-end fund** are embedded in the POP or other fees. Sales expenses include commissions for the managing underwriter, broker-dealers, and their registered representatives, as well as all advertising and sales literature expenses. Mutual fund distributors use different methods to collect the fees for the sale of shares and one to compensate sales persons on an ongoing basis (trailer commissions):

- Front-end loads (difference between POP and NAV)—Class A shares
- Back-end loads (contingent deferred sales loads)—primarily Class B shares
- Level loads (asset-based fees—provide trail commissions to the registered representative servicing the account)—generally Class C shares

Most of the exam questions will be on Class A shares, so we will start there.

Class A Shares

Shares sold with a front-end load are called Class A shares. Front-end sales loads are the charges included in a fund's POP. The charges are added to the NAV at the time an investor buys shares. Front-end loads are the most common way of paying for the distribution services that a fund's underwriter and broker-dealers provide.

EXAMPLE

An investor deposits $10,000 with a mutual fund that has a 5% front-end load.

The 5% load amounts to $500, which is deducted from the invested amount. In this example, $9,500 is invested in the fund's portfolio on the investor's behalf.

Breakpoints

The schedule of quantity purchase discounts a mutual fund offers is called the fund's *breakpoints*.

Breakpoints are available to any person. For a breakpoint qualification, *person* includes married couples, parents and their minor children, corporations, and certain other entities. Investment clubs or associations formed for the purpose of investing do not qualify for breakpoints.

The following are breakpoint considerations:

- Breakpoint levels vary across mutual fund families. There is no industry standardized breakpoint schedule.
- Mutual funds that offer breakpoints must disclose their breakpoint schedule in the prospectus and how an account is valued for breakpoint purposes.
- The SEC further encourages that breakpoint discount availability information be accessible through various means of communication, including websites.
- Discounts may be the result of a single large investment, a series of aggregated investments, or a promise to invest via a letter of intent (LOI).
- Purchases made by the same investor in various accounts can be aggregated to qualify for a breakpoint discount. Eligible accounts include traditional brokerage, accounts held directly with a fund company, 401(k), IRA, and 529 college savings.
- Shares purchased in the same fund family other than money market accounts are eligible to be aggregated together to qualify for a breakpoint discount, including those held at separate securities firms.

TEST TOPIC ALERT

You can expect a question on who is eligible for breakpoints. Married couples, parents with minor children, and corporations are eligible. Parents combined with adult children (even if they are legally considered dependents) and investment clubs are not eligible.

The discounts of sales charges are spelled out in a mutual fund's prospectus, but the following table illustrates a typical example.

Figure 8.1: Sample Breakpoint Schedule

Purchase Amount	Sales Charge
$0–$24,999	6.00%
$25,000–$49,999	5.50%
$50,000–$99,999	5.00%
$100,000–$249,999	4.00%
$250,000–$499,999	3.00%
$500,000–$999,999	2.00%
$1,000,000 +	0.00%

Breakpoint Sale

FINRA prohibits registered representatives from making or seeking higher commissions by selling investment company shares in a dollar amount just below the point at which the sales charge is reduced. This violation is known as a *breakpoint sale*, and is considered contrary to just and equitable principles of trade. It is the responsibility of all parties concerned, particularly the principal, to prevent deceptive practices.

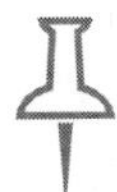

TAKE NOTE

Breakpoints offer a significant advantage to mutual fund purchasers; however, breakpoint sales are prohibited.

Letter of Intent (LOI)

A person who plans to invest more money with the same mutual fund company may immediately decrease his overall sales charges by signing a **letter of intent (LOI)**. In the LOI, the investor informs the investment company that he intends to invest the additional funds necessary to reach the breakpoint within 13 months.

The LOI is a one-sided contract binding on the fund only. However, the customer must complete the investment to qualify for the reduced sales charge. The fund holds some of the shares purchased in escrow. If the customer invests enough of the money to complete the LOI, he receives the escrowed shares. If not, he is given the choice to either pay the sales charge difference or have the underwriter liquidate enough of the escrowed shares to do so.

EXAMPLE

Refer back to the sample breakpoint schedule. A customer investing $18,000 is just short of the $25,000 breakpoint. In this situation, the customer might sign a LOI promising an amount that will qualify for the breakpoint within 13 months from the date of the letter. Investing an additional $7,000 within 13 months qualifies the customer for the reduced sales charge. The customer is charged the appropriate reduced sales charge at the time of the initial purchase.

A customer who has not completed the investment within 13 months will be given the choice of sending a check for the difference in sales charges or cashing in escrowed shares to pay the difference.

Backdating the Letter

A fund often permits a customer to sign a LOI as late as the 90th day after an initial purchase. The LOI may be backdated by up to 90 days to include prior purchases but may not cover more than 13 months in total. A customer who signs the LOI 60 days after a purchase has 11 months to complete the letter.

EXAMPLE

Purchase Amount	Sales Charge
$0–$24,999	6.5%
$25,000–$49,999	5.5%
$50,000–$99,999	5%
$100,000–$249,999	3%
$250,000–$499,999	2%
$500,000–$999,999	1%
$1,000,000 +	0%

If an investor wants to deposit $50,000 in a mutual fund over a 13-month period and puts in $25,000 when the account is opened, the investor is given a 5% sales charge on the initial and every subsequent investment if an LOI has been signed. If a letter was not signed, the sales charge on the initial amount of $25,000 would be 5.5%, based on this breakpoint schedule. The LOI allows for a discount on an installment plan purchase.

TEST TOPIC ALERT

- Letters of intent are good for a maximum of 13 months and may be backdated 90 days.
- If the LOI is not completed, the sales charge amount that applies is based on the total amount invested.
- Share appreciation and income paid by the fund do not count toward completion of the letter.

Rights of Accumulation

Rights of accumulation, like an LOI, allow an investor to qualify for reduced sales charges by reaching a breakpoint. The major differences are that rights of accumulation

- allow the investor to use prior share appreciation and reinvestment to qualify for breakpoints and
- do not impose time limits.

The customer may qualify for reduced charges when the total value of shares previously purchased plus the new purchase exceeds a breakpoint amount. For the purpose of qualifying customers for rights of accumulation, the mutual fund generally bases the quantity of securities owned on the higher of current NAV or the total of purchases made to date.

TAKE NOTE

Assume the following breakpoint schedule:

Purchase Amount	Sales Charge
$0–$24,999	6.5%
$25,000–$49,999	5.5%
$50,000–$99,999	5%
$100,000–$249,999	3%
$250,000–$499,999	2%
$500,000–$999,999	1%
$1,000,000 +	0%

An investor deposits $5,000 (paying a 6.5% sales charge) in a mutual fund but does not sign an LOI. The $5,000 grows to $10,000 over time and the investor decides to invest another $15,000. If rights of accumulation exist, the new $15,000 receives a 4.5% sales charge, which is based on the new money plus the accumulated value in the account ($15,000 + $10,000 = $25,000). If rights of accumulation do not exist, the sales charge would have been 6.5%.

Combination Privilege

A mutual fund company frequently offers more than one fund and refers to these multiple offerings as its family of funds. An investor seeking a reduced sales charge may be allowed to combine separate investments in two or more funds within the same family to reach a breakpoint.

Computing the Sales Charge Percentage

When the NAV and the POP are known, the sales charge percentage can be determined.

$$\text{POP (\$10.50)} - \text{NAV (\$10)} = \text{sales charge dollar amount (\$0.50)}$$

$$\frac{\text{sales charge dollar amount (\$0.50)}}{\text{POP (\$10.50)}} = \text{sales charge percentage (4.8\%)}$$

If the dollar amounts for the NAV and sales charges are specified, the formula for determining the POP of mutual fund shares is NAV ($10) + sales charge dollar amount ($0.50) = POP dollar amount ($10.50).

A mutual fund prospectus must contain a formula that explains how the fund computes the NAV and how the sales charge is added. The sales charge is always based on the POP, not on the NAV.

If the dollar amount of the NAV and the sales charge percentage are specified, the formula to determine POP is to divide the NAV by 100% minus the sales charge percentage.

$$\frac{\text{NAV (\$10)}}{100\% - \text{sales charge percentage (4.8\%)}} = \text{POP (\$10.50)}$$

Because of the sales charge, loaded funds should be recommended for long-term investing.

EXAMPLE

1. NAV = $20 and POP = $21. What is the sales charge percentage?

   The sales charge percentage is calculated by finding the sales charge amount ($21 – $20) and dividing by the POP. Remember, sales charge is a percentage of the POP, not the NAV:

   $1 ÷ $21 = 4.8% (when rounded)

2. Assume a NAV of $20 and a sales charge of 5%. What is the POP?

   POP is found by dividing the NAV by 100% minus the sales charge percentage:

   $20 ÷ 0.95 = $21.05

   In determining the POP when provided with the NAV, the answer has to be more than the NAV. If such a question has only one choice with a higher POP than the NAV, the correct answer should be immediately apparent.

Class B Shares

Class B shares do not charge a front-end sales charge, but they do impose a back-end charge for early redemption of shares. In addition, there is an asset-based 12b-1 fee (covered shortly) greater than those imposed on Class A shares.

The distinguishing feature of Class B shares is that they impose a contingent deferred sales charge (CDSC), also called a back-end load. The CDSC normally declines and eventually is eliminated over time. Once the CDSC is eliminated, almost all Class B shares convert into Class A shares. When they convert, they will be charged the same (lower) asset-based 12b-1 fee as the Class A shares.

Class B shares do not impose a sales charge at the time of purchase, so unlike Class A share purchases, 100 cents of the invested dollar are invested.

The following table contains a typical CDSC schedule for Class B shares.

Figure 8.2 Sample Class B Shares CDSC Schedule

Year	CDSC
1	5%
2	4%
3	3%
4	2%
5	1%
6+	0%

TAKE NOTE

Although not specifically listed as a violation, regulators scrutinize large purchases of Class B shares. A purchase large enough to reach a significant Class A share breakpoint results in a low enough sales charge that, in just a few years, the lower operating expenses of the Class A shares will more than make up the difference in front-end cost. In practice, very few firms will accept an order for Class B shares in excess of $100,000, particularly if the investor intends to maintain the position for a number of years.

Class C Shares (Level Load)

Class C shares typically have a one-year 1% CDSC, a 0.75% 12b-1 fee (discussed shortly), and a 0.25% shareholder services fee. Because these fees are relatively high and never go away, C shares are commonly referred to as having a level load. Class C shares are appropriate for investors who have short time horizons because they become quite expensive to own if investing for more than four years.

PRACTICE QUESTION

6. When discussing investment companies, the term *sales load* most commonly refers to
   A. the fund's sales charge, expressed as a percentage of the NAV.
   B. the fund's sales charge, expressed as a percentage of the public offering price (POP).
   C. the commission earned by the broker-dealer making the sale.
   D. the 12b-1 fee.

Answer: B. Class A shares of an open-end investment company, (mutual fund) have a *front-end* sales charge, or sales load, which is computed as a percentage of the POP. That is, if the fund's POP is $10 and the NAV is $9.50, the 50-cent sales charge is 5% of the $10 offering price. In general, most of the sales load is paid to the broker-dealer making the sale as compensation. The 12b-1 fee is never referred to as a *sales load* because it is not related to the sale of shares.

12b-1 Asset-Based Fees

As an asset-based fee, **12b-1 fees** are often called *asset-based distribution fees*. Named after the SEC rule that allows them, 12b-1 fees are used to cover the costs of marketing and distributing the fund to investors. These 12b-1 fees are also used to compensate registered representatives for servicing an account (trailer commissions) but shouldn't be confused with sales charges. The fee is deducted quarterly as a percentage of the fund's average total NAV.

The maximum 12b-1 fee is 0.75% for distribution and promotion. FINRA does permit funds to charge an additional 0.25% as a service fee. That makes the total 1.0%, only 0.075% of which is the 12b-1 fee.

The fee must reflect the anticipated level of distribution services.

No-Load Funds

As the name implies, this means that the fund does not charge any type of sales load. No-loads may charge fees that are not sales loads. For example, a **no-load fund** is permitted to charge redemption fees. Although a redemption fee is deducted from redemption proceeds just like a deferred sales load, it is not considered to be a sales load. Those are usually charged when an investor is going in and out of the fund too frequently. In addition, under FINRA rules, a fund is permitted to pay its annual operating expenses and still call itself *no-load*. However, the combined amount of the fund's 12b-1 fees or separate shareholder service fees cannot exceed 0.25% of the fund's average annual net assets.

Misuse of No-Load Terminology

A fund that has a deferred sales charge or an asset-based 12b-1 fee of more than 0.25% of average net assets may not be described as a no-load fund, nor can the fund have any front-end load. To do so violates the conduct rules. The violation is not alleviated by disclosures in the fund's prospectus.

EXAMPLE

Expect questions about 12b-1 fees and know the following points:

- The 12b-1 fee is expressed as an annual amount but is charged and reviewed quarterly.
- Charges covered by 12b-1 fees include advertising, sales literature, and prospectuses delivered to potential customers, not fund-management expenses.
- In order for a fund to market itself to the public as a no-load fund, the fund may not charge more than 0.25% of average net assets for 12b-1 fees.
- The maximum allowable 12b-1 charge under FINRA rules is 0.75% (75 basis points).
- FINRA does permit an additional 0.25% charge for shareholder services (25 basis points), but that is treated separate from the 12b-1 fee for marketing and promotion.

Expense Ratio

All mutual funds have expenses. It is important that you understand these expenses are not considered a cost of purchasing the fund. A fund's expense ratio expresses the management fees and operating expenses as a percentage of the fund's net assets. All mutual funds, load and no-load, have expense ratios.

The expense ratio is calculated by dividing annual operating expenses by the average dollar value of the fund's assets under management.

The sales charge is not considered an expense when calculating a fund's expense ratio.

EXAMPLE

An expense ratio of 1.72% means that the fund spends $1.72 per year for every $100 of invested assets. Typically, more aggressive funds have higher expense ratios. An aggressive growth fund's expense ratio is usually higher than that of a AAA bond fund because more trading occurs in the growth fund's portfolio. That increases the commission expense and, because the portfolio manager is generally making more decisions, the management fee tends to be higher.

PRACTICE QUESTION

7. Barbara wishes to invest in the KAPCO Growth Fund, an open-end investment company. She expects to hold the shares for at least 10 years. If she purchases KAPCO's Class A shares, each of these would be a way for her to receive a reduction on the sales charge **except**
   A. a single investment that reaches a breakpoint.
   B. joining together with her sister to make a purchase at a breakpoint level.
   C. signing a letter of intent (LOI).
   D. benefiting from the right of accumulation.

Answer: B. Reaching a breakpoint is the way in which investors can receive a "break" on the sales load charged when purchasing Class A shares. Purchases may be combined with spouses and dependent children, but not other family members—such as siblings—making the exception here choice B. The three ways to reach a breakpoint are:

- a lump-sum purchase,
- using a LOI granting 13 months to reach the breakpoint, or
- taking advantage of rights of accumulation (no time limit).

LESSON 8.4: MUTUAL FUND FEATURES

LO 8.e Recall special features of mutual funds.

Introduction

One of the reasons for the enormous popularity of mutual funds is the special features they offer to investors. We will discuss those most likely to appear on your exam.

Cost of Entry

Many mutual funds allow initial investments of as low as $1,000. Once the account is opened, additional investments may be made with as little as $25. In the case of IRAs, that initial $1,000 might be as low as $100. With this tiny sum, the investor has the diversification of a portfolio of as many as several hundred different securities. Technically, it is said that the owner of one share has an *undivided interest* in the entire portfolio of the fund. You might see that term on your exam.

Dollar Cost Averaging

The low cost of entry makes dollar cost averaging available for even the smallest of investors. One method of purchasing mutual fund shares is called **dollar cost averaging**, where a person invests identical amounts at regular intervals. This form of investing allows the individual to purchase more shares when prices are low, and fewer shares when prices are high. In a fluctuating market and over time, the average cost per share is lower than the average price of the shares. However, dollar cost averaging does not guarantee profits in a declining market because prices may continue to decline for some time. In this case, the investor buys more shares of a sinking investment.

EXAMPLE

The following illustrates how average price and average cost may vary with dollar cost averaging.

Month	Amount Invested	Price Per Share	No. of Shares
January	$600	$20	30
February	$600	$24	25
March	$600	$30	20
April	$600	$40	15
Total	$2,400	$114	90

The average price per purchase is the sum of the prices paid divided by the number of investments: $114 ÷ 4 = $28.50.

The average cost per share is total amount spent divided by the number of shares purchased: $2,400 ÷ 90 = $26.67. This lower cost is because of automatically purchasing more shares when the price was low and fewer shares when the price was high.

In this case, the average cost is $1.83 per share less than the average price.

TEST TOPIC ALERT

It is important to understand the concept of dollar cost averaging. It involves investing a fixed amount of money every period, regardless of market price fluctuation.

If the market price of shares is up, fewer shares are purchased; if the market price of shares is down, more shares are purchased. Over time, if the market fluctuates, dollar cost averaging will achieve a lower average cost per share than average price per share.

A frequent question on the exam relates a participant in a 401(k) plan regularly investing in an index mutual fund as an example of dollar cost averaging.

TAKE NOTE

Dollar cost averaging neither guarantees profit nor protects from loss. It merely results in a lower cost per share than the average price per share.

PRACTICE QUESTION

8. An investor who initially makes a small investment in a mutual fund may have the advantage of a lower sales charge on investments made over a 13-month period through
   A. a breakpoint letter.
   B. a Class A letter.
   C. a letter of intent (LOI).
   D. a sponsor's letter.

   Answer: C. Investors who sign a LOI stating they will invest a specified amount over a 13-month period are eligible for a reduced sales load if they invest enough to reach the breakpoint within that time. Breakpoints entitle investors to reduced sales charges.

Withdrawal Plans

Mutual funds are not only easy to get into; they also have plans for orderly liquidation. In addition to lump-sum withdrawals, whereby customers sell all their shares, mutual funds offer systematic withdrawal plans. Withdrawal plans are normally a free service. Not all mutual funds offer withdrawal plans, but those that do may offer the plan alternatives described here.

Fixed-Dollar

A customer may request the periodic withdrawal of a **fixed-dollar** amount. Thus, the fund liquidates enough shares each period to send that sum. The amount of money liquidated may be more or less than the account earnings during the period.

Fixed Percentage or Fixed Share

Under a **fixed-percentage** or fixed-share withdrawal plan, either a fixed number of shares or a fixed percentage of the account is liquidated each period.

Fixed-Time

Under a **fixed-time** withdrawal plan, customers liquidate their holdings over a fixed period.

Withdrawal Plan Disclosures

Withdrawal plans are not guaranteed. With fixed-dollar plans, only the dollar amount to be received each period is fixed. All other factors, including the number of shares liquidated and a plan's length, are variable. For a fixed-time plan, only the time is fixed; the amount of money the investor receives varies each period. Most mutual funds require a customer's account to be worth a minimum amount of money before a withdrawal plan may begin. Regardless of the option chosen, it is rare for a fund to permit continued investment once withdrawals start.

Because withdrawal plans are not guaranteed, the registered representative must

- never promise an investor a guaranteed rate of return,
- stress to the investor that it is possible to exhaust the account by over-withdrawing,
- state that during a down market it is possible that the account will be exhausted if the investor withdraws even a small amount, and
- never use charts or tables unless the SEC specifically clears their use.

PRACTICE QUESTION

9. An investor has arranged to receive $600 per month from a mutual fund withdrawal plan. This is an example of what type of plan?
   A. Contractual
   B. Fixed-share periodic withdrawal
   C. Fixed-dollar periodic withdrawal
   D. Fixed-percentage withdrawal

Answer: C. If the investor receives $600 a month, the dollar amount of the withdrawal is fixed. That makes this a fixed-dollar periodic withdrawal plan.

Voluntary Accumulation Plans

Mutual funds have a number of arrangements to implement an investment program. A **voluntary accumulation plan** allows a customer to deposit regular periodic investments on a voluntary basis (minimum amounts found in the prospectus). The plan is designed to help the customer form regular investment habits while still offering some flexibility. This is an easy way to take advantage of dollar cost averaging.

Voluntary accumulation plans may require a minimum initial purchase and minimum additional purchase amounts. Many funds offer automatic withdrawal from customer checking accounts to simplify contributions. If a customer misses a payment, there is no penalty because the plan is voluntary. The customer may discontinue the plan at any time.

TAKE NOTE

In a voluntary accumulation plan, once the account has been opened, contribution and frequency are very flexible.

Exchanges Within a Family of Funds

Many sponsors offer exchange or *conversion* privileges within their families of funds. A mutual fund family, (sometimes referred to as a fund *complex*), is when a single sponsor or distributor offers more than one fund. In many cases, there are more than a dozen funds with different objectives in the same fund complex. There are even a few with more than 100 funds.

Exchange privileges allow an investor to convert an investment in one fund for an equal investment in another fund in the same family without incurring an additional sales charge. A common example would be an investor who purchased the XYZ Growth Fund at age 40. Now, that investor is 62 and, as retirement approaches, needs something more conservative. The shares of the XYZ Growth Fund can be exchanged for shares of the XYZ Income Fund at no expense. Any gain or loss from the redemption of shares must be reported for tax purposes.

To have the exchange take place with no-load, the following rules apply:

- The purchase may not exceed the proceeds generated by the redemption of the other fund.
- The redemption may not involve a refund of sales charges.
- The sales personnel and dealers must receive no compensation of any kind from the reinvestment.

TEST TOPIC ALERT

The exam wants you to know that this is a taxable event. If there is a gain (or loss), it must be reported.

PRACTICE QUESTION

10. Some mutual fund families offer a conversion privilege that permits
    A. liquidation of shareholdings with an option to buy the shares back at the current net asset value (NAV) per share.
    B. the owner of the shares to convert her bonds or preferred stock in the fund to common stock of the fund at a pre-designated ratio.
    C. conversion of shares to cash at the option of the shareholder.
    D. conversion from the shares of one fund to the shares of another fund in the same family at the current NAV per share.

Answer: D. The conversion privilege is frequently referred to as the exchange privilege. You need to know that, unlike conversion of a bond or preferred stock to common stock, which is not a taxable event, converting from one fund to another is considered a sale and new purchase. If the old shares have appreciated, there would be a taxable capital gain.

LO 8.f Differentiate between the different kinds of tax treatment of mutual funds.

Introduction

Another special feature of mutual funds is the way they are taxed.

Most monies received by a taxpayer are subject to income tax. This includes salaries, bonuses, commissions, tips, dividends, and interest. These are normally taxed as ordinary income.

Receipts from selling something for more (or less) than was originally paid for it fall under the capital gains tax. If there was a gain, tax must be paid on it. If there was a loss, it can be used to offset gains and income.

Mutual funds receive income in the form of dividends from the stocks in which they invest and interest from bonds. They may also realize capital gains from the sale of securities, which were held in the portfolio, that have appreciated in price.

Mutual Fund Dividend Distributions

A mutual fund may pay dividends to each shareholder in much the same way any other corporations pay dividends to stockholders. The Investment Company Act of 1940 requires a written statement to accompany dividend payments by management companies. Every written statement made by or on behalf of a management company must clearly indicate what the payment per share is made from. Mutual fund dividends are typically paid from the mutual fund's net investment income, usually on a quarterly basis.

Dividends may be identified as qualified or nonqualified. **Qualified dividends** are taxed at the lower long-term capital gains rate. **Nonqualified dividends** are taxed as ordinary income.

Net Investment Income (NII)

Net investment income (NII) includes gross investment income—dividend and interest income from securities held in the portfolio—minus operating expenses. Advertising and sales expenses are not included in a fund's operating expenses when calculating NII, but management fees, custodian bank charges, and legal and accounting fees are included.

NII = dividends + interest – expenses of the fund

TEST TOPIC ALERT

You may see a question on the exam that asks for this calculation and gives a list of items to exclude or include in the calculation. Remember D + I – E, and it will be easy to remember which items to include. Note that capital gains are not a part of NII.

TAKE NOTE

A bond fund does not pay interest to investors. Investors buy common stock of the bond fund and, therefore, will receive a dividend if declared. Even though it is a dividend, because the source is interest it is taxed as interest. That is why you can receive a dividend from a municipal bond fund that is tax-free.

The Conduit Theory

Because an investment company is organized as a corporation or trust, you might correctly assume its earnings are subject to tax. Consider, however, how an additional level of taxation shrinks a dividend distribution value.

EXAMPLE

Triple taxation? GEM Fund, Inc., owns shares of Mountain Brewing Co. To start with, Mountain Brewing is taxed on its earnings before it pays a dividend. Then, GEM Fund pays tax on the amount of the dividend it receives. Finally, the investor pays income tax on the distribution from the fund.

Triple taxation of investment income can be avoided if the mutual fund qualifies under Subchapter M of the IRC. If a mutual fund acts as a **conduit** (pipeline) for the distribution of NII, the fund may qualify as a **regulated investment company (RIC)**. This means it is subject to tax only on the amount of NII the fund retains. The portion of the NII distributed to shareholders escapes taxation at the mutual fund level.

To avoid taxation under Subchapter M, a fund must distribute at least 90% of its NII to shareholders. The fund then pays taxes only on the undistributed amount.

EXAMPLE

If a fund distributes 89%, it must pay taxes on 100% of NII.

EXAMPLE

What are the tax consequences to a fund that distributes 98% of its NII? In this situation, the fund does not pay taxes on the 98% that is distributed; it pays taxes only on the 2% of retained earnings.

PRACTICE QUESTION

11. The concept of a mutual fund distributing its net investment income (NII) through to shareholders without first paying a tax is known as
    A. the pass-through theory.
    B. the conduit theory.
    C. tax-free passage.
    D. flow-through theory.

    Answer: B. Regulated companies under Subchapter M of the IRS Code are allowed to pass-through income to beneficial owners without a tax at the fund level on the distributed income (known as conduit or flow-through of income and taxation).

TAKE NOTE

Most closed-end companies, including BDCs, qualify as RICs for the tax benefit to investors.

Mutual Fund Capital Gains Distributions

The appreciation or depreciation of portfolio securities is unrealized capital gain or loss if the fund does not sell the securities. Therefore, shareholders experience no tax consequences. When the fund sells the securities, the gain or loss is realized. A realized gain is an actual profit made.

Capital gains distributions are derived from net realized gains. That is, the fund compares its realized gains and losses to determine the net result. The distinction between long-term and short-term is the same as for any investment. To avoid an extra level of taxation, the fund can qualify as an RIC by distributing at least 90% of the net gain. As a practical (and test relevant) matter, the fund will only distribute its long-term capital gains. Because of the conduit nature of the distribution, the IRS says investors always report these on their tax returns as long-term capital gains. This is true even if the investor purchased the fund shares only a month before the distribution. It is because it is a distribution of the fund's long-term gains. A long-term capital gains distribution may not be made more often than once per year.

What about net short-term capital gains? They are distributed along with the dividend. They are noted as a nonqualified dividend and are taxed at ordinary income rates.

TAKE NOTE

Long-term capital gain distributions may be made no more than once per year. A short-term capital gain is identified and distributed, but taxed as a dividend distribution, and taxed at ordinary income tax rates.

TEST TOPIC ALERT

The exam is fond of asking a question like this: An investor purchases shares of a mutual fund. Three months later, the fund has a long-term capital gains distribution.

This would be taxed to the investor as _______?

The answer is long-term capital gain. Why? It makes no difference how long the investor held the fund shares; this is a distribution of the fund's long-term gains being passed through to the investor.

However, when the investor sells his shares, then the holding period of those shares is important for determining long-term or short-term status.

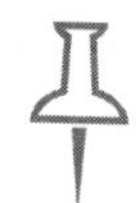

TAKE NOTE

The terms *realized gains* and *unrealized gains* can be confusing. Think of an **unrealized gain** as a paper profit and a **realized gain** as actual profit made.

EXAMPLE

If you purchased 100 shares of ABC stock at $100 per share and the market value of ABC is now $150 per share, you would experience an unrealized gain of $5,000, ($15,000 – $10,000). We call this a paper profit because the gain is only on paper. You would have no taxes to pay on this paper profit. If you sold the shares, the $5,000 would be taxable to you as a capital gain. The gain resulting from a sale is known as a realized gain. Unrealized profits are not taxable; realized profits are taxable as capital gains.

PRACTICE QUESTION

12. Which of the following factors would be used in calculating the tax due on a capital gains distribution by a mutual fund?
    A. The length of time the fund held the securities and the fund's tax bracket
    B. The length of time the investor held the securities and the fund's tax bracket
    C. The length of time the investor held the shares and the investor's tax bracket
    D. The length of time the fund held the shares and the investor's tax bracket

Answer: D. The factors used to determine the tax due on a capital gains distribution are the length of time the fund held the securities before selling them, which would identify the gain as long- or short-term, and the investor's tax bracket, which would determine the actual percentage of tax due. In virtually every case on the exam, the distribution will be of the fund's long-term capital gains.

A mutual fund portfolio that has increased in value has unrealized profits; these are not taxable to investors. But when the fund sells appreciated portfolio securities, it has realized profits. These profits are distributed as capital gains to shareholders. Shareholders can take these capital gain distributions in cash or reinvest them to purchase additional shares. In either case, these distributions are taxable as capital gains to shareholders.

Reinvestment of Distributions

Dividends and capital gains are distributed in cash. However, a shareholder may elect to **reinvest distributions** in additional mutual fund shares. The automatic reinvestment of distributions is similar to compounding interest. The reinvested distributions purchase additional shares, which may earn dividends or gains distributions.

All mutual funds formed after April 1, 2000, must offer the reinvestment of dividends and capital gains back into the fund without a sales charge (at NAV). In practice, almost all funds formed before that date do this as well. This means that investors are able to buy new shares without a sales load. This is a significant advantage resulting in faster growth to the investor.

Taxation of Reinvested Distributions

Distributions are taxable to shareholders whether the distributions are received in cash or reinvested. The IRS uses the concept of constructive receipt. That means income, such as dividends, although not actually physically received by the taxpayer, is constructively received in the taxable year during which it is created to his account or otherwise made available. All that is required is that the taxpayer could have drawn upon it during the taxable year if intention to withdraw had been given.

The fund must disclose whether each distribution is from income or capital gains. **Form 1099-DIV**, which is sent to shareholders after the close of the year, details tax information related to dividend distributions for the year. This enables the investor to enter the proper information on the investor's Form 1040.

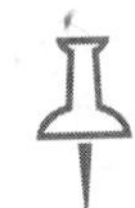

TAKE NOTE

Just as with dividend distributions, whether capital gains are taken in cash or reinvested, they are currently taxable to the shareholder. Dividends will be reported as qualified (taxed at a lower rate) or nonqualified (taxed as ordinary income).

Any short-term capital gain is distributed as a nonqualified dividend. It is the shareholder's responsibility to report all dividends and long-term capital gains distributions to the IRS and state tax agency.

PRACTICE QUESTION

13. A registered representative has recommended a growth and income fund to her client because the fund pays relatively high income and maintains strong capital appreciation. The client wishes to use the fund as the foundation of a long-term strategy for eventual retirement. The representative's recommendations and disclosures should state that
    A. the client should reinvest any dividend and capital gain distributions to accelerate the growth process through a compounding effect.
    B. the client should take any dividend and gain distributions in cash and invest them in a growth fund of another fund family for diversification.
    C. all capital appreciation of securities within the fund are distributed on an annual basis.
    D. if dividends are reinvested, they are not currently taxable, which enhances growth within the fund.

Answer: A. Because the client's goal is to use the fund as part of a long-term strategy for retirement, reinvestment of distributions should be encouraged. The compounding effect of reinvestment increases the number of shares upon which distributions are based during each period. The fact that distributions are taxable—whether taken in cash or reinvested—must be disclosed to the client. Net *realized* long-term capital gains of the portfolio are distributed annually.

LESSON 8.5: MUTUAL FUND SUITABILITY

LO 8.g Match the objective of the fund to that of the client.

Introduction

Although suitability is a requirement when recommending any investment, the exam seems to devote more questions to selecting the proper mutual fund. That is why we have a mutual fund suitability exercise for you. In this lesson, we will give you the tools to enable you to be able to select the right fund for the client. While there are literally thousands of individual mutual funds, there are only a handful of major fund categories:

- Stock funds invest in stocks
- Bond funds invest in bonds
- Balanced funds invest in a combination of stocks and bonds
- Money market funds invest in very short-term investments

Investor Objectives

Back in Lesson 2.4, we described goals and objectives and the difference between them. Here, we are going to focus on what kind of funds should be recommended to meet each objective. Following is a description of the major types of funds and where they fit into the GIS triangle (including speculation).

Stock Funds

A mutual fund, which uses stock to meet its stated objectives, can generally be referred to as a stock fund. Common stock is normally found in the portfolio of any mutual fund that has growth as a primary or secondary objective. Equity funds have historically outpaced inflation over most 10-year time horizons.

Growth/Value Funds

Growth funds invest in stocks of companies whose businesses are growing rapidly. Growth companies tend to reinvest all or most of their profits for research and development rather than pay dividends. Growth funds are focused on generating capital gains rather than income.

Growth managers may consider stocks that many feel are overvalued because there may still be upside potential. As such, funds managed for growth tend to have elevated levels of risk.

Blue-chip or conservative growth funds invest in established and more recognized companies to achieve growth with less risk. Generally, these funds own shares of companies with fairly large **market capitalization**. *Market cap*, as it is usually referred to, is the total number of shares of common stock outstanding multiplied by the current market value per share. So a listed company with 300 million shares outstanding where the share price is $50 would have a market cap of $15 billion and would be considered a large-cap stock. Funds investing in stocks like this are sometimes called **large-cap funds** (their portfolio consists of companies with a market capitalization of more than $10 billion). These types of funds can be more stable and less volatile in a turbulent market.

EXAMPLE

An investor who is willing to take moderate risk and is willing to invest for a minimum of 5–7 years may be interested in a blue-chip or large-cap growth fund.

Aggressive Growth Funds

Aggressive growth funds are sometimes called **performance funds**. These funds are willing to take greater risk to maximize capital appreciation. Some of these funds invest in newer companies with relatively small capitalization (less than $2 billion capitalization) and are called **small-cap funds**.

Mid-cap funds are somewhat less aggressive and have in their portfolios shares of companies with a market capitalization of between $2 billion and $10 billion.

Large-cap funds have market capitalization of greater than $10 billion. The lower the market cap, the greater the volatility.

EXAMPLE

An investor who is seeking high potential returns with the understanding that there can also be significant losses and is willing to invest for 10–15 years may be interested in an aggressive growth fund that focuses on small- or mid-cap companies.

Value Funds

Value funds (and, therefore, value managers) focus on companies whose stocks are currently undervalued (earnings potential is not reflected in the stock price). These undervalued companies are expected to perform better than the reports indicate, thus providing an opportunity to profit. Value stocks typically have dividend yields higher than growth stocks. Funds managed for value are considered more conservative than funds managed for growth.

EXAMPLE

An investor who is willing to take moderate risk when investing to purchase a vacation home in 7–10 years may be interested in a fund that is value-oriented.

Equity Income Funds

An income fund primarily composed of stock, also known as an **equity income fund**, stresses current income over growth. The fund's objective may be accomplished by investing in the stocks of companies with long histories of dividend payments, such as utility company stocks, blue-chip stocks, and preferred stocks. These are managed for income, not growth.

EXAMPLE

An investor who is willing to take low to moderate risk and seeks income from equity investments in the form of dividends with some capital appreciation may be interested in an equity income fund, utility fund, or preferred stock fund.

Option Income Funds

Option income funds invest in securities on which call options can be sold (known as covered calls). They earn premium income from writing (selling) the options. They may also earn capital gains from trading options at a profit. These funds seek to increase total return by adding income generated by the options to appreciation on the securities held in the portfolio. They generally have greater risk than other income funds.

Growth and Income Funds

A **growth and income fund** (combination fund) may attempt to combine the objectives of growth and current income by diversifying its stock portfolio among companies showing long-term growth potential and companies paying high dividends. Often, both value and growth management styles are utilized.

EXAMPLE

An investor seeking dividends and capital appreciation with moderate risk may be interested in a growth and income fund.

Specialized (Sector) Funds

Many funds attempt to specialize in particular economic sectors or geographic areas. These funds must have a minimum of 25% of their assets invested in their specialties. **Sector funds** offer high appreciation potential, but may also pose higher risks to the investor as a result of the concentration of investments. These funds are speculative in nature. They include gold, technology, pharmaceutical, and biotechnology funds, but can also be geographic, such as investing in companies located in the Pacific Basin or Silicon Valley.

EXAMPLE

An investor who believes the pharmaceutical industry is going to outperform the market over the next 5–10 years and is willing to speculate on the investment may be interested in a sector fund that focuses on the pharmaceutical industry.

Special Situation Funds

Special situation funds buy securities of companies that may benefit from a change within the companies or in the economy. Takeover candidates and turnaround situations are common investments. These funds are also speculative (high risk).

EXAMPLE

Investors believes the banking industry is going to be going through a phase of mergers and acquisitions. They are willing to take additional risk to possibly profit from the potential consolidation of the industry. They may be interested in a special situation fund that specializes in mergers and acquisitions.

Blend/Core Funds

Blend/core funds are stock funds with a portfolio comprising a number of different classes of stock. Such a fund might include both blue-chip stocks and high-risk/high-potential-return growth stocks. Both growth and value management styles are used. The purpose is to allow investors to diversify their investment via management and securities in a single fund.

TAKE NOTE

Value funds are considered more conservative than growth or blend/core funds.

PRACTICE QUESTION

14. An investor looking for an open-end investment company with an objective of providing current income to its shareholders would most likely choose
    A. a common stock fund.
    B. a growth fund.
    C. an income fund.
    D. a venture capital fund.

Answer: C. Income funds have the goal of producing income; that is why they are named as such. This is a case where you "don't look a gift horse in the mouth."

Index Funds

Index funds invest in securities that mirror a market index, such as the S&P 500. An index fund buys and sells securities in a manner that mirrors the composition of the selected index.

The index may be broad, such as the S&P 500, or narrow, such as a transportation index. The fund's performance should closely track the underlying index performance. Turnover of securities in an index fund's portfolio is minimal because the only trades that take place are triggered by a change in the index (one company is replaced by another company). As a result, an index fund generally has lower management costs than other types of funds.

EXAMPLE

An investor does not believe in paying for the professional stock selection of a managed fund. In other words, the belief is that it is difficult to outperform the market as a whole (or in part). Under these circumstances, recommending an index fund is appropriate.

Foreign Stock Funds

The global economy has made investing in foreign securities more attractive than ever. Many foreign businesses have become household names in the United States, and the interest in investing in those companies has followed their popularity. In Lesson 3.2, we learned about American Depositary Receipts (ADRs) for individual stock purchases. Here, we will discuss the choices with mutual funds.

International Funds

International funds invest only in the securities of foreign companies. These companied have their headquarters and principal business activities outside the United States. Long-term capital appreciation is their primary objective, although some funds also seek current income.

Global Funds

Global funds and worldwide funds invest in the securities of both the United States and foreign countries. The risks involved in a fund concentrating in foreign securities are somewhat different than those for a domestic fund. When a portfolio has a large percentage of foreign securities, currency risk and political risk becomes paramount. These risks are elevated when investing in frontier funds, which invest in pre-emerging economies, because accounting and regulatory schemes are often much less rigorous than what we are used to here in the United States.

International and global stock funds are often purchased to diversify an investor's portfolio. After all, investing inside and outside the United States provides a more diversified portfolio than just investing within the United States.

TAKE NOTE

There are two terms generally used to describe funds that invest in foreign securities.

- *International funds* have their entire portfolio invested in securities issued outside of the United States. The way to remember that is if you will be traveling internationally, you'll be outside the United States.
- *Global funds* have the portfolio invested around the globe, and that includes U.S. securities. Once again, using the travel example, if you were to travel around the globe, a portion of your trip would be in the United States.

Balanced Funds

Balanced funds, also known as **hybrid funds**, invest in stocks for appreciation and bonds for income. In a balanced fund, different types of securities are purchased according to a formula the manager may adjust to reflect market conditions.

A balanced fund's portfolio might contain 60% stocks and 40% bonds.

EXAMPLE

A balanced fund may be appropriate for an investor who seeks a conservative balance between stocks and bonds.

Asset Allocation Funds

Asset allocation funds split investments between stocks for growth, bonds for income, and money market instruments or cash for stability. Fund advisers switch the percentage of holdings in each asset category according to the performance (or expected performance) of that group. These funds can also hold hard assets, such as precious metals like gold and silver, and real estate.

A fund may have 60% of its investments in stock, 20% in bonds, and the remaining 20% in cash. If the stock market is expected to do well, the adviser may switch from cash and bonds to stock. The result may be a portfolio of 80% in stock, 10% in bonds, and 10% in cash.

Conversely, if the stock market is expected to decline, the fund may invest heavily in cash and sell stocks.

Many asset allocation funds are target funds (see the following) that target a specific goal—such as retirement—in a 5-, 10-, 15-, or 20-year period. As the target year gets closer, the mix of investments becomes more conservative.

EXAMPLE

An investor seeks an investment for retirement in 20 years that performs well under most market conditions and is diversified by purchasing multiple types of securities. An asset allocation fund that targets the year of retirement may be appropriate.

Target-Date Funds

One increasingly popular investment option is a **target-date fund**, sometimes called a **life-cycle fund**. According to a report by a large retirement plan provider, target-date funds are offered by nearly 90% of employer-sponsored defined contribution plans, such as 401(k) plans.

Target-date funds are designed to help manage investment risk. This is done by selecting a fund with a target date in mind that is closest to the year an investor anticipates needing the money (i.e., retiring in 2030). For example, a *2030 fund* gradually reduces risk by changing the investments within the fund to a more conservative mix as the target date approaches. That said, target-date funds are not risk-free, even when the target date has been reached.

FINRA is concerned that many investors surveyed do not understand that target-date funds do not provide guaranteed income. Many investors also did not realize that similar-sounding funds may, in fact, have different investments and risk profiles.

Like all investments, target-date funds can lose money if the stocks and bonds owned by the fund drop in value. And even though funds with identical target dates may look the same, they may have very different investment strategies and asset allocations that can affect how risky they are and what they are worth, at any given point in time, including when and after retirement takes place.

Bond Funds

Bond funds have income as their main investment objective. Some funds invest solely in investment-grade corporate bonds. Others, seeking enhanced safety, invest only in government issues. Still others seek to maximize current income by investing in lower-rated (junk) bonds for higher yields.

TEST TOPIC ALERT

Remember the following:

- Bonds pay interest; bond funds pay dividends if declared by the fund's BOD.
- Dividends are typically paid on a quarterly or semiannual basis, but there are income funds (both equity- and debt-oriented) that pay monthly dividends.
- When interest rates rise, the prices of bonds, and, therefore, bond funds, fall (and vice versa).

Corporate Bond Funds

Corporate bond funds, in general, have higher credit risk than various government issues but can still be classified as investment-grade (safer) or noninvestment-grade (riskier) portfolios.

As we have covered before, the greater the risk, the greater the reward. **High-yield bond funds** provide the highest yields because of their increased credit risk and are considered speculative investments.

Tax-Free (Tax-Exempt) Bond Funds and UITs

Municipal bond funds and UITs invest in municipal bonds or notes that produce income (dividends) exempt from federal income tax. These funds are appropriate for investors in a high marginal tax bracket seeking income.

EXAMPLE

The current tax system includes brackets. The tax bracket is defined as the percentage of tax due on the next dollar the individual will receive. This is called your marginal income tax bracket. An investor is in a high marginal tax bracket and seeks income. A municipal bond fund may be appropriate.

U.S. Government Funds

U.S. government funds purchase securities issued by the U.S. Treasury or an agency of the U.S. government, such as Ginnie Mae. Investors in these funds seek current income and maximum safety. **Agency security funds** are not considered quite as safe from default risk as U.S. government funds; therefore, the yields on agency security funds will be higher than U.S. government fund yields.

Agency Funds

The word agencies is a generic term used to describe two types of bonds: bonds issued or guaranteed by U.S. federal government agencies, and bonds issued by **government-sponsored enterprises (GSEs)**—corporations created by Congress to foster a public purpose, such as affordable housing.

Bonds issued or guaranteed by certain federal agencies such as the GNMA are backed by the full faith and credit of the U.S. government, just like Treasuries. This is an unconditional commitment to pay interest payments and to return the principal investment in full to you when a debt security reaches maturity.

Bonds issued by most GSEs, such as the FNMA and the FHLMC, are not backed by the same guarantee as federal government agencies.

Unit 8

EXAMPLE

An investor is risk averse and seeks income, but the U.S. government bond fund yields are too low. An agency security fund may be appropriate.

Principal-Protected Funds

Principal-protected mutual funds offer investors a guarantee of principal, adjusted for fund dividends and distributions, on a set future date (maturity) while providing opportunities for higher returns through investment in higher risk and higher expected return asset classes such as equities. The basic guarantee is that the investor's return will never be less than the original investment, less any sales load.

The guarantees are sometimes provided by third-party insurers and at other times through investments in U.S. Treasury zero coupon bonds. These appealing properties have led to considerable interest on the part of investors who have invested billions of dollars in such mutual funds in recent years. The usefulness and attractiveness of these principal-protected mutual funds is limited by three factors.

- *Guarantee principal.* Most principal-protected funds guarantee the initial investment minus any front-end sales charge even if the stock markets fall. In many cases, the guarantee is backed by an insurance policy.
- *Lock-up period.* If you sell any shares in the fund before the end of the *guarantee period*—a period of anywhere from 5 to 10 years—you lose the guarantee on those shares and could lose money if the share price has fallen since your initial investment.
- *Hold a mixture of bonds and stocks.* Most principal-protected funds invest a portion of the fund in zero coupon bonds and other debt securities, and a portion in stocks and other equity investments during the guarantee period. To ensure the fund can support the guarantee, many of these funds may be almost entirely invested in zero coupon bonds or other debt securities when interest rates are low and equity markets are volatile. Because this allocation provides less exposure to the markets, it may eliminate or greatly reduce any potential gains the fund can achieve from subsequent gains in the stock market. It also may increase the risk to the fund of rising interest rates, which generally cause bond prices to fall.

Principal-protected funds are typically front-end loaded, and their operating expense ratios tend to be higher than comparable funds.

EXAMPLE

An investor is very risk averse but wishes to invest without the possibility of losing the principal of the investment. A principal-protected fund may be appropriate.

PRACTICE QUESTION

15. If ABC Fund pays regular dividends, offers a high degree of safety of principal, and appeals especially to investors in the higher tax brackets, ABC is
    A. an aggressive growth fund.
    B. a corporate bond fund.
    C. a money market fund.
    D. a municipal bond fund.

Answer: D. Municipal bonds are considered second only to U.S. government securities in terms of safety. Furthermore, whenever you see a question about an investor in a high tax bracket, always look for the answer choice with municipal bonds; the tax-free income is the key. On the other hand, when you see growth, dividends will probably not be part of the equation.

Money Market Funds

Money market funds are no-load, open-end investment companies (mutual funds) that serve as temporary holding accounts for investors' money. As the name implies, the portfolio of a money market fund consists of money market securities. Money market mutual funds are most suitable for investors whose financial goals require liquidity above all.

The interest these funds earn and distribute as dividends is computed daily and credited to customer accounts monthly. In general, money market mutual funds offer check-writing privileges, making for extraordinary liquidity. Because all of the income is from interest, these dividends are taxed as interest.

The NAV of money market funds is generally fixed at $1 per share. Although this price is not guaranteed, a fund is managed to "break the buck," regardless of market changes. Thus, the price of money market shares does not fluctuate in response to changing interest rates.

TAKE NOTE

Money market mutual funds (MMF) for retail investors are designed to have a stable NAV of $1 per share. They are not guaranteed, nor are they protected by FDIC insurance. It is rare, but it is possible to lose money in a money market mutual fund as a retail investor.

It is not likely to be tested, but an important distinction between institutional and retail money market funds lies in the pricing of the funds. Retail money market funds are allowed to keep a NAV of $1 per share. Institutional funds, on the other hand, have a floating NAV. This means that the price can change from day to day, based on the conditions of the market.

The only other MMFs with a stable NAV are **institutional money market funds**, which are 99.5% government securities.

PRACTICE QUESTION

16. An investor has a portfolio diversified among many different asset classes. If there was an immediate need for cash, which of the following would probably be the most liquid?
    A. Cash value from a universal life insurance policy
    B. CDL Common Stock Mutual Fund
    C. QRS Money Market Mutual Fund
    D. XYZ International Stock Mutual Fund

Answer: C. Money market funds generally come with a check-writing privilege, offering investors the opportunity to convert the asset to cash at once. Although all mutual funds are readily redeemable, the fund has seven days to redeem. One must request the cash value from the insurance company and, in many cases, it can take 30 days or longer.

Unit 8

TEST TOPIC ALERT

Be aware that an investment in a money market fund is not insured or guaranteed by the FDIC or any other government agency. Although a money market fund seeks to preserve the value of the investment at $1 per share, it is possible to lose money by investing in a money market fund.

LESSON 8.6: EXCHANGE TRADED FUNDS (ETFS)

LO 8.h Recognize the different features and types of ETFs.

Types of ETFs

An ETF registers with the SEC under the Investment Company Act of 1940 either as a unit investment trust (UIT ETF) or as an open-end management company (open-end ETF).

Standard ETF

In most cases, an ETF invests in a specific index, such as the S&P 500 or the Dow Jones. Any class of asset that has a published index around it and is liquid can be made into an ETF so that there are ETFs for real estate and commodities as well as stocks and bonds. In this way, an ETF is similar to an index mutual fund. The difference is that the ETFs trades like a stock on an exchange or Nasdaq and, in this way, is similar to a closed-end investment company. The investor can take advantage of price changes that are due to the market, rather than just the underlying value of the stocks in the portfolio.

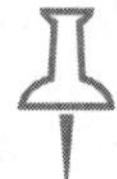

TAKE NOTE

Although, as stated, most ETFs are passive in that they are based on some index, in recent years, there has been a growth in actively managed ETFs where, instead of attempting to mirror an index, the managers select individual assets based upon expected performance. Therefore, there are ETFs that purchase equities only, fixed income securities only, or a combination. Some even purchase non-securities assets such as commodities.

ETFs can be purchased on margin and sold short (covered in Unit 16), just like any other listed stock. This is another difference between ETFs and mutual funds. Expenses tend to be lower than those of mutual funds as well, because all the adviser has to do is match up to the specified index, so the fees are minimal. In addition, there can be tax advantages to owning ETFs.

However, because there are brokerage commissions on each trade (in and out), ETFs are generally not competitive with a no-load index fund for the small investor making regular periodic investments such as in a dollar cost averaging plan.

TAKE NOTE

There are now some U.S.-listed ETFs that are available for commission-free trading on certain select platforms (these are typically proprietary funds). These products can be bought and sold without traditional brokerage commissions for investors with certain accounts and subject to certain restrictions. For exam purposes, these are the exceptions rather than the rule.

Most ETFs are open-end companies, but they cannot be referred to as mutual funds because shares are not redeemable by the issuer. Furthermore, as a result of all trading taking place in the secondary markets, delivery of a prospectus is not required. Because ETFs trade on exchanges in the same manner as CEFs, there is a tendency to equate them. As mentioned earlier, ETFs are not actively managed. CEFs are management companies with full time, active portfolio managers.

Pricing is different as well. CEFs usually trade at some distance from their NAVs. The CEF's trading price is independent of its NAV. It could be a premium or a discount because the price is determined by supply and demand. On the other hand, ETFs trade at, or very close to, their NAVs.

The exam may ask you for some of the uses of ETFs. You may not know what all of these are, but the test doesn't ask for explanations. Here are some of the uses of index ETFs:

- Asset allocation
- Following industry trends
- Balancing a portfolio
- Speculative trading
- Hedging

PRACTICE QUESTION

17. Which of the following is **not** touted as an advantage to purchasing ETFs instead of index mutual funds?
    A. Intraday trading
    B. Typically lower expense ratios
    C. Performance is generally better than the underlying index
    D. Can be purchased on margin

Answer: C. One thing that neither of these products can claim is performance better than the underlying index. Think about it—the index has no management fees. Even though the management fees on index funds are very low and those on ETFs are generally lower than that, there are still expenses making it unlikely that their performance can beat that of the index. The fact that an investor can trade the ETF during the day instead of accepting whatever the next computed price is, can be a benefit for those who are trying to time the market. And, for those who wish to add the leverage of margin trading (explained more fully in Unit 16), that can only be done with ETFs, not index mutual funds.

Leveraged ETFs

These funds attempt to deliver a multiple of the return of the benchmark index they are designated to track. For instance, a 2x leveraged fund would try to deliver two times the return of whatever index it is tracking. With leveraged funds, there are no limits by rule or regulation as to the amount of leverage that could be applied to a portfolio. Currently, there are numerous 2x and 3x leveraged funds available to investors. The risk associated with leverage is that it is always a double-edged sword; volatility is magnified. Therefore, the risk to be recognized regarding this fund strategy is that if the benchmark index is falling, then the fund's returns will be—in theory—the designated leverage amount (perhaps two or three) times the loss. In addition, most of these funds use derivatives products such as options, futures, and swaps to enable them to achieve the stated goal. Because these derivative products are not suitable for all investors, so too can it be said of the leverage fund portfolio containing them. Ultimately, as always, suitability becomes an issue when recommending these products.

Inverse (Reverse) Funds

Inverse funds, sometimes referred to as reverse or short funds, attempt to deliver returns that are the opposite of the benchmark index they are tracking. For example, if the benchmark is down 2%, the fund's goal is to be up 2%. In addition, inverse funds can also be leveraged funds, or said another way, two or three times the opposite of the indices' return. They are called short funds because they have a bearish attitude.

EXAMPLE

Consider an inverse fund tracking the S&P 500. If the index were to drop by 1%, the value of the inverse fund would rise by 1%. If this was a 3x inverse fund, then the fund's value would rise by 3%. Of course, if the index were to rise, the performance of the inverse fund would suffer, especially if it was leveraged.

TEST TOPIC ALERT

FINRA warns investors that most leveraged and inverse ETFs reset daily, meaning that they are designed to achieve their stated objectives on a daily basis. Their performance over longer periods of time—over weeks, months, or years—can differ significantly from the performance (or inverse of the performance) of their underlying index or benchmark during the same period. Therefore, in most cases, these would not be suitable investments for *buy-and-hold* investors or those with other than a very short time horizon.

For the TVIX, (VelocityShares Daily 2x VIX ST ETN), one of the risk disclosures (page 28, PS-28) reads like this:

> **The long-term expected value of your ETNs is zero. If you hold your ETNs as a long-term investment, it is likely that you will lose all or a substantial portion of your investment.**

TAKE NOTE

Both leveraged and inverse index funds (leveraged or not) can be traded on an exchange. When they are, they are known as ETFs. If the shares are exchange-traded, they are priced by supply and demand, can be purchased on margin, and bought and sold throughout the trading day, like all exchange-traded products. For those that are not exchange-traded (e.g., inverse mutual funds), they would be priced, purchased, and redeemed like all investment company shares. Neither of these fund types carry any guarantee that they will achieve the stated goal or objective.

LESSON 8.7: INVESTMENT COMPANY BENEFITS AND RISKS

LO 8.i Explain the benefits and risks of investment companies in client portfolios.

Introduction

As you have seen, there are many different types of investment companies. In the course of discussing them, we have touched on some of the benefits and risks. This lesson will summarize all of them and include a few additional ones.

Benefits of Including Investment Company Securities in Client Portfolios

When it comes to benefits in general, they all share two important characteristics:

- *Diversification.* By pooling assets with many others, investors have the opportunity to own an interest in a far greater number and range of securities than available to almost any individual investor.
- *Professional management.* In almost all cases, someone with expertise (we hope) is "minding the store." Even in the case of the UIT where there is no ongoing management, the initial portfolio is constructed by experts. And, although index funds and ETFs don't require real decision making by the fund managers, they are there making sure the portfolio is updated whenever the components of the index change.

Let's examine each of the different types of investment companies we've learned about.

Mutual Fund Benefits

In addition to the obvious diversification and professional management, there are multiple benefits to owning mutual funds.

Choice of Objectives

Whatever an investor's investment objectives are, there are mutual funds available to match. There are many shades of growth funds, from highly aggressive to very conservative. All have the goal of growing the investment. The same is true with income funds where the goal is to generate current income with varying degrees of risk from government bonds to high-yield bonds. If the objective is capital preservation, money market funds fit the bill and then there are funds that combine objectives, such as growth and income funds. There are even specialized funds (sector funds) which concentrate at least 25% of their portfolio into specific industries or geographic areas, such as a biotech fund or a Southeast Asia fund.

Convenience

With most mutual funds, buying and liquidating shares, changing reinvestment options, and getting information can be accomplished conveniently by going to the fund's website, by calling a toll-free phone number, or by mail.

Liquidity

The Investment Company Act of 1940 requires that an open-end investment company stand ready to redeem shares at the next computed NAV per share. Payment must be made within seven days of the redemption request. Although there may be a redemption charge, and, of course, the value of the shares may be less than their cost, liquidity is assured.

Minimum Initial Investment

As mentioned previously, it doesn't take a great deal of wealth to get started investing in funds and, generally, once you are a shareholder, most funds permit additional investments of $100 or even less.

Automated Investing and Withdrawal

As covered earlier in the unit, investors can start voluntary accumulation plans where set amounts are invested at regular intervals. Or, on the other end, automatic withdrawal plans are available using one of the various withdrawal options.

Convenient Tax Information

Doing the tax return is simplified because each year the fund distributes a Form 1099 explaining the taxability of distributions. The investor is told how much comes from each source. It even instructs the investor where to put each number on the tax return.

Combination Privilege

A mutual fund company frequently offers more than one fund and refers to these multiple offerings as its ***family of funds***. An investor seeking a reduced sales charge may be allowed to combine separate investments in two or more funds within the same family to reach a breakpoint.

EXAMPLE

Joe Smith has invested $15,000 in the ACE Growth Fund for retirement and $10,000 in the ACE Income Fund for his children's education. The sponsor may view the two separate expenditures as one investment totaling $25,000 when calculating the sales charge.

Exchanges Within a Family of Funds

Many investment companies offer the **exchange** or **conversion privilege** within their families of funds. **Exchange privileges** allow an investor to convert an investment in one fund for an equal investment in another fund in the same family at NAV without incurring an additional sales charge. For example, those who started investing when in their 30s or 40s by placing their money into an aggressive growth fund might consider moving into something more conservative when they reached their 50s. Once they hit their 60s and 70s, they would want to have a greater percentage of their money in income funds. By staying in the same family of funds and using the exchange or conversion privilege, all of these changes could be made free of sales loads.

TEST TOPIC ALERT

Any exchange of funds is considered a sale for tax purposes. Any gains or losses are fully reportable at the time of the exchange.

Leveraged and Inverse Funds

With 2x or 3x leverage, the investor's potential gains are higher than other funds. Inverse funds allow the investor to essentially sell short the market or an indexed segment within the framework of a mutual fund.

UIT Benefits

Income

If the UIT is composed of debt securities, it will generally provide higher income than a mutual fund with a similar portfolio. This is because there is one major fund expense not shared with a UIT. Because the UIT does not have a portfolio manager, there is no management fee.

A second benefit is the stability of the income. Because the portfolio is fixed, the income does not fluctuate. This is particularly beneficial to those who live on the fixed income generated by their portfolio.

Liquidity

While not traded in the secondary markets, the trustees are obligated to redeem units tendered by investors at the NAV of the unit. This is similar to the redemption procedure for mutual funds.

Rolling Over Proceeds

Whether a debt or an equity UIT, there is a date when the trust terminates. In most cases, investors have the option of investing the proceeds into a new trust without charge.

CEF Benefits

CEFs have all of the diversification and management benefits of open-end companies. Here are some benefits CEFs have that mutual funds don't have.

Exchange-Traded

There are a number of benefits that come along with being traded in the secondary markets. Among them is the ability to buy shares on margin and sell shares short. As with any other exchange-traded asset, there is intraday trading. That means you don't have to buy or sell based on the day's close. Another is liquidity. Instead of the seven-day redemption rule for mutual funds, proceeds from the sale of a CEF are available two business days after the trade. In fact, there is a process—covered in Unit 17—where the proceeds could be available the same day.

Pricing

We have discussed the fact that the price of CEFs is based on supply and demand. This can result in the fund selling at a premium or discount from its NAV. Investors purchasing shares of a CEF at a discount are getting the assets for less than liquidating value. A mutual fund can never be purchased at a discount from its NAV.

Leverage

CEFs can issue debt securities. That borrowed money creates financial leverage which can multiply gains.

ETF Benefits

Taxation

Most ETFs are structured such that an investor only realizes a capital gain (or loss) upon the sale. Contrast that with a mutual fund where capital gains distributions are paid annually and taxed.

Expense Ratio

For those ETFs tracking an index, (the default assumption on the exam), the management fee is low. In addition, because the portfolio is only changed when the components in the index change, trading costs (commissions) are low.

Portfolio Specificity

The large and ever growing number of ETFs contain options for almost any niche an investor desires.

Exchange-Traded

The benefits of exchange-traded ETFs are the same as indicated previously for CEFs. There is one significant difference, though. Unlike the CEFs where the price can be well above or below NAV, ETFs rarely stray far from the NAV.

Leveraged and Inverse ETFs

Leveraged and inverse ETFs have the same benefits as their mutual fund "cousins," but are ETFs instead.

TEST TOPIC ALERT

Remember that an index ETF is different from an index mutual fund in the following ways:

- Intraday trading—Investors do not have to wait until the end of a trading day to purchase or sell shares. ETF shares trade and are priced continuously throughout the day, making it easier for investors to react to market changes.
- Margin eligibility—Index ETF shares can be purchased on margin, subject to the same terms that apply to common stock.
- Short selling—Index ETFs can be sold short at any time during trading hours.

Risks of Including Investment Company Securities in Client Portfolios

Introduction

No investment is completely free of risk. Investment companies, for all of their benefits, do have risks. The amount of risk, obviously, depends on the investment objectives and the methods used to reach them. It is critical that the financial professional match the risk level of the investment to the risk tolerance of the investor. Most of the risks are common to all investment companies. We will describe those for mutual funds. Where there is something different for another investment company, that will be listed.

Mutual Fund Risks

Market Risk

Even with the benefits offered by diversification and professional management, market prices do fluctuate. Equity funds have **market risk**. As will be covered in detail in Unit 14, a risk with equity conditions is that economic conditions beyond the control of the individual company can cause stock prices to fall.

Interest-Rate Risk

Income-oriented funds, especially bond funds, may be subject to **interest-rate risk**. As we have covered several times, when interest rates rise, bond prices fall. Unlike an individual bond that ultimately repays principal at maturity, a bond fund doesn't have a maturity date. The only mutual fund that generally does not fluctuate in price is the money market fund, but there is a trade-off in lack of growth and low income. Not only that, but the income of a money market fund will vary, unlike that of a bank CD, which is fixed and insured by the FDIC.

Net Redemptions

Net redemptions is a risk unique to open-end investment companies (mutual funds). Sometimes, particularly during declining markets, there is an excess of shareholder redemptions over new share purchases. This is known as *net redemptions*. When that occurs, the portfolio manager is put in the difficult position of having to decide which assets to liquidate when prices are falling. A fund suffering with net redemptions is probably not going to deliver your clients the performance they are seeking.

As we learned in Lesson 8.2, open-end investment companies cannot issue bonds. However, there is an option available to many funds for use during periods of net redemptions. That option is short-term borrowing from banks. This occurs most often when redemption requests exceed new purchases and the portfolio manager does not want to sell portfolio assets to raise the money to meet those redemptions. There are limits on the amount that may be borrowed, but we don't expect those to be tested.

Expense Risk

There is also **expense risk**. Frequently, a fund may temporarily reduce a fee. It will notify investors when that reduction has ended, but many investors don't take the time to read the fine print. One must carefully analyze all of the costs involved. These include

- sales charges, 12b-1 fees, and possible redemption fees;
- management fees (probably the largest expense on an ongoing basis); and
- tax efficiency, as the investor has no control over the manager's timing of purchases and sales.

Tenure Risk

One of the basic tenets of communicating about securities is that past performance is no assurance of future results. That said, more often than not, a fund manager who has outperformed her peers seems to continue to enjoy better success. As we will learn in the next lesson, the contract of the fund manager has to be renewed every year. Sometimes, a successful manager gets a better offer elsewhere and leaves. That could happen shortly after you've made a large investment in the fund. The replacement might not have the same skills.

UIT Risks

Market Risk

Equity UITs have market risk like any equity security. However, there is a unique situation with UITs. Remember, there is no ongoing management and the portfolio is fixed. That means there is no way for the trust to get off a sinking ship when it is obvious that one or several of the stocks in the portfolio are losing money.

Interest-Rate Risk

Bond UITs have a similar problem as equity UITs. The nature of the fixed portfolio creates a difficult position for investors when interest rates are rising. In a bond mutual fund, the continuous inflow of new money allows the fund managers to purchase the new higher yield bonds. In a UIT, that can't be done.

CEF Risks

Pricing Risk

As we have stated many times, the price of closed-end shares is determined by supply and demand. An investor might purchase the shares at a premium over the NAV. It is beyond the scope of the exam to know why, but there are several reasons why the demand would be such that the shares would trade at a premium. For one, at a later time, the investor decides to sell the shares and now, again for reasons beyond the test, the shares are selling at a discount. Or, perhaps the NAV has gone up, but buying at a premium and selling at a discount has resulted in a loss to the investor.

This cannot happen with mutual funds or UITs because they are always redeemed at NAV. It is not likely with ETFs because they always trade very close to the NAV.

Leverage Risk

CEF's can issue bonds. That borrowed money can help increase returns when the manager guesses correctly. But, as with any leverage, if the market moves the wrong way, the losses are magnified.

ETF Risks

Index Risk

This is a risk that is conceptually similar to the fixed portfolio risk of a UIT. Remember, the portfolio mimics the composition of the specified index. If one or more of the securities in that index underperforms, the ETF is stuck with it until the index removes the security. This is a major risk to passive investing.

Tracking Risk

It is virtually impossible to have performance equal to (and never better than) the index. The index itself has no expenses. There are no trading commissions, no filings with regulatory agencies, no legal expenses, and so forth. All other things equal, you would probably want to recommend the ETF with the highest tracking reliability.

LESSON 8.8: INVESTMENT COMPANY RULES AND REGULATIONS

LO 8.j Determine the rules and regulations pertaining to the sale of investment company securities.

The Investment Company Act of 1940

Introduction

Most of the regulatory requirements for investment companies are found in this federal law. Many of the rules have been covered where relevant to the material being discussed. Here are other provisions that might be tested.

Board of Directors (BOD)

In general, management investment companies, (open-end and closed-end) cannot have a BOD that consists of more than 60% of persons who meet the definition of interested persons of the investment company.

TAKE NOTE

Another way of stating that no more than 60% of the directors may be interested persons is to say that at least 40% must be noninterested, that is, "outside" directors. These are individuals who have no connection to the fund other than a position on the board (and maybe owning some shares of the fund as would any investor).Typically outside directors are academics or prominent community members.

Prohibited Activities

Open-end investment companies are prohibited from engaging in several activities. Mutual funds may not

- purchase any security on margin;
- participate on a joint basis in any trading account in securities (i.e., an investment company cannot have a joint account with someone else);
- sell any security short; or
- acquire more than 3% of the outstanding voting securities of another investment company.

There are exceptions to these prohibitions, but, for the purposes of the exam, you may disregard any exceptions.

PRACTICE QUESTION

18. The Investment Company Act of 1940 prohibits registered open-end investment companies from engaging in any of the following practices **except**
    A. issuing common stock.
    B. selling short or purchasing securities for the company's portfolio on margin.
    C. owning more than 3% of the outstanding voting securities of another investment company.
    D. opening a joint account with another investment company.

Answer: A. The one thing that all open-end investment companies must do is issue common stock. That is the form of ownership. All of the other activities are prohibited.

Changes in Investment Policy

In order for an investment company's board to make fundamental investment policy changes, a majority vote of the outstanding voting stock is required. Examples of fundamental changes would include

- a change in subclassification, such as from an open-end to a closed-end company or from a diversified to a nondiversified company;
- deviation from any fundamental policy in its registration statement, including a change in investment objective; and
- changing the nature of its business so as to cease to be an investment company.

In other words, because the investment company is supposed to function for the benefit of the shareholders, any of these changes would require the vote of a majority of the shareholders.

Size of Investment Companies

No registered investment company is permitted to make a public offering of securities unless it has a net worth of at least $100,000.

Investment Advisory and Underwriter Contracts

A majority vote of the shareholders must approve the contract between the investment company and its investment adviser and the contract with its principal underwriter. These contracts must be in writing and provide that the contract

- precisely describes all compensation to be paid;
- will be approved at least annually by the BOD or by majority vote of the shareholders if it is to be renewed after the first two years; and
- provides that it may be terminated at any time, without penalty, by the BOD or by majority vote of the shareholders on not more than 60 days' written notice to the investment adviser.

In addition, it is unlawful for any registered investment company to enter into or renew any contract with an investment adviser or principal underwriter unless the terms have been approved by majority vote of directors who are not parties to such contract as affiliated persons (i.e., directors who are not affiliated with the adviser or the underwriter, who in the aggregate must comprise at least 40% of the directors).

TAKE NOTE

The effect of this final paragraph is that no advisory contract, whether initial or renewal, may take effect without approval of the noninterested members of the board.

Custodian

It is required that every registered investment company keeps its assets with a custodian. In most cases, that custodian is a bank, hence the common use of the term custodian bank. Although the Investment Company Act of 1940 specifies certain financial requirements for that bank, it does not require that the bank have FDIC coverage. Alternatively, the investment company may use a broker-dealer that is a member firm of a national securities exchange.

Periodic and Other Reports

All investment companies must file annual financial reports with the SEC. These reports contain an audited balance sheet and income statement. In addition, shareholders must be sent financial information semiannually. In keeping with current technology, these reports may be delivered electronically.

Knowing what is prohibited and what is required is often tested on the exam. Here are two examples expressing ideas that are likely to be tested:

PRACTICE QUESTION

19. Which of the following statements correctly expresses requirements under the Investment Company Act of 1940?
    A. A registered open-end investment company using a bank as custodian must choose one that has FDIC coverage.
    B. Shareholders must receive financial reports from the fund at least annually.
    C. No investment advisory contract may be entered into that does not provide for termination with no more than 60 days' notice in writing.
    D. No open-end investment company may offer shares to the public unless the fund has capital of at least $1 million.

Answer: C. The Investment Company Act of 1940 requires that all advisory contracts contain a provision that the contract may be terminated upon no more than 60 days' notice in writing. There is no requirement that the custodian bank have FDIC insurance. Shareholders must receive financial reports at least semiannually. The minimum capitalization of an investment company offering shares to the public is $100,000.

FINRA Rules

Most of the relevant information is found in FINRA Rule 2341. Following are the most testable portions of the rule that have not previously been covered.

Selling Dividends

Selling dividends is the prohibited practice of inducing customers to buy mutual fund shares by implying that an upcoming distribution will benefit them. What is usually not explained is that the NAV of the fund will drop by the amount of the dividend.

EXAMPLE

LMN Income Fund has declared a dividend of $0.50. A registered representative encourages a client to buy now. The rep explains that the current POP is about $10 per share (remember—forward pricing means we don't know exactly what we paid until after the trade). "This means you are going to pay $10 and get back a dividend of 50 cents. That is like an immediate 5% return on your money." What is not explained is that the fund's NAV will drop by those 50 cents. There is no benefit and, in fact, the dividend is taxable. It really would have been better to wait and buy the fund for a lower price and not have a taxable dividend.

Sales Agreement

In order for a member firm and its representatives to be able to sell a particular investment company security, the firm must have a written sales agreement with the investment company.

The agreement says that no member firm may purchase mutual fund shares from a client at a price lower than the NAV next quoted for the shares. That would be an unfair business practice because the client can redeem at NAV directly from the fund.

Another part of the agreement is designed to keep broker-dealers from receiving compensation on the sale of shares that are quickly redeemed. If any fund shares are sent in for redemption to the issuer within seven business days after the initial transaction date, the member will refund to the underwriter the full concession allowed to the firm on the original sale.

Anti-Reciprocal Rule (FINRA Rule 2341; MSRB Rule G-31)

An investment company's choice of a broker-dealer to handle portfolio transactions and investments must be based on the broker-dealer's capabilities. Any transactions must be justified on the basis of the value and quality of the brokerage services rendered, not on the basis of the dollar amount of sales of the investment company shares by that broker-dealer.

A member's retail sales of investment company shares must depend on suitability—which funds best fit the objectives of the specific clients involved. Funds should not be selected on the basis of additional brokerage commissions generated by fund portfolio transactions. In fact, a member firm may not knowingly do business with a fund it knows allocates portfolio transaction business on the basis of fund share sales.

To enforce the earlier principle, FINRA has issued the following interpretations. With respect to member retail sales of investment company shares, the member may not

- give sales personnel an incentive or additional compensation based on the amount of brokerage commissions received from any investment company (including bonuses, preferred compensation lists, sales incentive campaigns, and contests based on brokerage commissions);
- recommend specific investment companies to sales personnel or establish recommended, selected, or preferred lists if those companies are chosen on the basis of brokerage commissions received or expected;
- grant a salesperson participation in the brokerage commission generated by a portfolio transaction if participation is identified with the sale of shares of the investment company; or
- use sales of shares of an investment company in negotiating the amount of brokerage commissions to be paid on a portfolio transaction.

Noncash Compensation

In the retail distribution of investment company shares, mutual fund distributors may, in general, pay commissions and concessions to members only in the form of cash. There are exceptions to this, which may not be preconditioned on achievement of a sales target. Gifts of material value not to exceed $100 per person per year may be given, as well as occasional meals or tickets to sporting events or other entertainment. Attendance at a training or educational meeting may also be sponsored, provided records are kept of expenditures, the venue is in an appropriate—not an exotic—location, associated persons receive permission from their employers to attend the meeting, and the expenses of any guests they may bring are not reimbursed. However, if an approved meeting, there is no problem having the sponsor directly reimburse the attendee for travel expenses incurred in conjunction with attending the seminar.

This same principle applies when the noncash compensation is from the member firm to its sales personnel. Sales incentives and rewards must not favor the sale of one fund over another based on the amount of compensation received by the member. This would create a conflict of interest and make it difficult for the registered representative to honestly make the most suitable recommendations.

The Gifts Rule

Don't confuse the preceding discussion with FINRA Rule 3220 (Influencing or Rewarding Employees of Others) and MSRB Rule G-20. Better known as the Gifts Rule, it prohibits any member or person associated with a member, directly or indirectly, from giving anything of value in excess of $100 per year to any person where such payment is in relation to the business of the recipient's employer. There is no limit on the gifts or compensation that may be given to employees, as long as it isn't designed to reward or influence the sale of specific products.

UNIT 9

Insurance Company Products

LEARNING OBJECTIVES

When you have completed this unit, you will be able to accomplish the following.

- › LO 9.a **Define** variable products and their characteristics.
- › LO 9.b **Compare** the different purchase and settlement options for annuities.
- › LO 9.c **Define** the terms used to value a variable annuity.
- › LO 9.d **Differentiate** between the different kinds of tax treatment of variable annuities.
- › LO 9.e **Determine** the rules and regulations pertaining to the sale of variable products.

INTRODUCTION

Many products offered by life insurance companies are not securities. Most people have some form of life insurance, whether provided by their employer, personally owned, or both. The exam focuses on those contracts that are defined as securities. This unit will deal with variable annuities and variable life insurance.

LESSON 9.1: VARIABLE PRODUCTS OF INSURANCE COMPANIES

LO 9.a Define variable products and their characteristics.

Annuities

An **annuity** is generally a contract between an individual and a life insurance company, usually purchased for retirement income. An investor, the **annuitant**, pays the premium in one lump sum or in periodic payments. At a future date, the annuitant can either elect to surrender the policy and receive a lump-sum payout or begin receiving regular income distributions that will continue for life.

Because all earnings are tax-deferred, many individuals looking to accumulate additional funds for retirement find annuities to be a valuable tool. Unlike IRAs and qualified retirement plans (covered in Unit 24) which limit the amount that can be contributed, there is no legal limit to the amount that can be invested in an annuity (the insurance company may place a limit that it will accept, generally in the range of $1—$3 million).

Annuity contracts are classified into two major types (depending on the guarantees offered):

- Fixed annuities
- Variable annuities

Fixed Annuities

Fixed annuities are not securities. We are covering them because many of the exam questions about variable annuities (a security) compare the two products. A fixed annuity guarantees a fixed rate of return. When the individual elects to begin receiving income, the payout is determined by the account's value and the annuitant's life expectancy based on mortality tables. A fixed annuity payout remains fixed throughout the annuitant's life.

TAKE NOTE

Because the insurance company guarantees the return and the annuitant bears no risk, a fixed annuity is an insurance product and not a security. A salesperson must have a life insurance license to sell fixed annuities but does not need to be securities licensed.

Although principal and interest are not at risk, a fixed annuity risks loss of purchasing power because of inflation.

EXAMPLE

An individual who annuitized a contract in 1990 may have been guaranteed a monthly payout of $1,800. Decades later, this amount may prove insufficient to cover living expenses.

Variable Annuities

Instead of purchase payments being directed to the insurance company's general account, money deposited in a variable annuity is directed into one or more subaccounts of the company's separate account. The separate account comprises various subaccounts that behave like mutual funds (we just can't call them mutual funds). These accounts will have a variety of investment objectives to choose from, such as growth, income, and growth and income. The returns in the separate account are not guaranteed, and therefore a loss of principal is possible.

Because the separate account is registered as an investment company, as required by the Securities Act of 1933, a prospectus must be delivered prior to or concurrent with the sale (Unit 20).

Although the options include money market securities and bonds, purchase payments are most often invested in a stock portfolio, which has a better chance of keeping pace with inflation than fixed-income investments.

The greater potential gain of a variable annuity involves more potential risk than a fixed annuity because it invests in securities rather than accepting the insurance company's guarantees. Payouts may vary considerably because an annuity unit's worth fluctuates with the value of the selected subaccount(s).

The following chart covers the major differences between the two products.

Figure 9.1: Fixed vs. Variable Annuity

Fixed Annuity	Variable Annuity
Payments made with after-tax dollars	Payments made with after-tax dollars
Payments are invested in the general account	Payments are invested in the separate account
Portfolio of fixed-income securities/real estate	Portfolio of equity, debt, or mutual funds
Insurer assumes investment risk	Annuitant assumes investment risk
Not a security	Is a security
Guaranteed rate of return	Return depends on separate account performance
Fixed administrative expenses	Fixed administrative expenses
Income guaranteed for life	Income guaranteed for life
Monthly payment never falls below guaranteed minimum	Monthly payments may fluctuate up or down
Purchasing power risk	Typically protects against purchasing power risk
Subject to insurance regulation	Subject to registration with the state insurance commission and the SEC

Although annuitants of variable annuities can choose a guaranteed monthly income for life, the amount of monthly income received is dependent on the performance of the separate account. If the performance is better than assumed, the next month's payment is higher. If it is less than assumed, the next month's payment will decrease.

TEST TOPIC ALERT

Whenever you see the term *variable*, as in variable annuity or variable life (discussed later), two licenses are required for the sale. The individual needs an insurance license and a securities license. Suitability must be determined and a prospectus must be delivered before or with solicitation of the sale.

PRACTICE QUESTION

1. The key difference between a fixed annuity and a variable annuity is that the fixed annuity
   A. offers a guaranteed return.
   B. offers a monthly payment that may vary in amount.
   C. will always pay out more money than a variable annuity.
   D. attempts to offer protection to the annuitant from inflation risk.

   Answer: A. If an annuity is fixed, it means the return to the investor is guaranteed. With a variable annuity, there are no guarantees as to the amount of return. It is the variable annuity whose annuity payment will vary and, because of the growth opportunity, offers potential inflation protection.

Separate Account

The contributions that investors make to a variable annuity are kept in a **separate account** from the insurance company's general funds. Investors determine which of the subaccounts their money will be placed. Some insurance company separate accounts offer 25, 30, or even more subaccounts, from the most aggressive to the most conservative.

TEST TOPIC ALERT

The Investment Company Act of 1940 does not include variable annuities in its definition of investment companies. On the other hand, the separate account is. Most often, it is a unit investment trust (UIT).

Guaranteed Death Benefit

Most variable annuities offer an option stating that if the investor dies during the accumulation period, the beneficiary will receive the greater of the current value of the account or the amount invested. Therefore, the estate is assured of getting back at least the original investment.

Life Insurance

Life insurance provides a death benefit to a named beneficiary or beneficiaries upon the death of the insured. There are many variations of life insurance, each serving different needs. We will review these policies and focus on one considered a security. Regardless of the type of insurance, the premium for the policy is calculated according to the insured's health, age, and sex, as well as the policy's face amount at issue.

Whole life insurance is designed to last until at least age 100 or the death of the insured, whichever occurs first. These policies also accrue cash value that may be borrowed for living needs. An insurance license must sell life insurance. Whole life insurance is not a security and is not sold as an investment.

Term life insurance is protection for a specified period, hence the description term. Term insurance provides pure protection and is the least expensive form of life insurance. Unlike whole life, term does not build cash values. If the policy is surrendered before death or is not renewed, there is nothing but an expired policy.

Variable Life Insurance

Variable life insurance has a fixed, scheduled premium but differs from whole life insurance in that the premiums paid are split; part of the premium is placed in the general assets of the insurance company. These general assets are used to guarantee a minimum death benefit. The balance of the premium is placed in the **separate account** and represents the cash value of the policy. Because the cash value is invested in the separate account, which fluctuates in value, its cash value is not guaranteed. The policy's death benefit may increase above the minimum guaranteed amount as a result of investment results, but may never fall below the minimum (as long as premiums are paid).

Although the value of the separate account is calculated daily, the policyholder's cash value in a variable life contract is reported monthly.

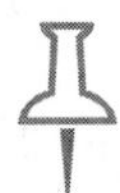

TAKE NOTE

Because a variable life insurance policy has a minimum death benefit, the premiums necessary to fund this part of the death benefit are held in the insurer's general account. Any policy benefit that is guaranteed is invested in the insurer's general account.

Any premium above what is necessary to pay for the minimum death benefit is invested in the separate account. This portion of the premium is subject to investment risk and variable life insurance and therefore is also defined as a security. As long as premiums are paid, the policy remains in force, even if the separate accounts lose money every year.

Once the premium has been determined and the expenses have been deducted, the net premium is invested in subaccounts of the separate account. Just as with variable annuities, there are number of subaccounts to choose from. Those include objectives such as

- growth,
- income,
- balanced,
- index or indices, and
- money market.

Assumed Interest Rate (AIR) and Variable Death Benefits

The death benefit payable under a variable life insurance policy is adjusted on an annual basis and can increase or decrease based on the performance of the separate account compared with an assumed interest rate (AIR). One of the benefits of variable life insurance is that the death benefit can adjust upward and possibly keep pace with inflation.

This AIR is the minimum rate of return necessary to provide the level death benefit. It is determined by the insurance company's actuaries and is stated in the policy contract. It is simply a target, not a projection.

If the separate account returns are greater than the AIR, these extra earnings are reflected in an increase in death benefit and cash value. If the separate account returns equal the AIR, actual earnings meet estimated expenses, resulting in no change in the death benefit. Should the separate account returns be less than the AIR, the contract's death benefit will decrease. It is important to note that it will never fall below the amount guaranteed at issue.

In Lesson 9.3, we are going to discuss the AIR and its effect on the valuation of a variable annuity.

TAKE NOTE

The variable death benefit is adjusted annually. Contrast this with the monthly valuation of the cash value. Some students have reported they remember this because they think about their cash all the time, but don't want to be continuously reminded about dying.

TAKE NOTE

The AIR has no effect on cash value accumulation in a variable life policy. The cash value will grow whenever the separate account has positive performance. The AIR does, however, affect the death benefit. Just remember the rules for variable annuities. The rules for the death benefits are analogous:

- If the separate account performance for the year is greater than the AIR, the death benefit will increase.
- If the separate account performance for the year is equal to the AIR, the death benefit will stay the same.

If the separate account performance for the year is less than the AIR, the death benefit will decrease (but never below the policy's face amount).

LESSON 9.2: ANNUITY PURCHASE AND SETTLEMENT OPTIONS

LO 9.b Compare the different purchase and settlement options for annuities.

Purchasing Annuities

Insurance companies offer a number of purchase arrangements for annuities. Aggregate fees include not only sales charges on the front end, but also those levied upon surrender, commonly called *conditional deferred sales loads*. In many cases, there is no-load to purchase, but if surrender—other than through annuitization—occurs during the early years of the contract, the charges can be significant.

It is important to note the key point of **FINRA Rule 2320** that deals with variable annuities sold by FINRA members. Under this rule, there is no maximum sales charge limitation in the sale of variable annuities. The only requirement is that the sales charge must be reasonable.

An investor is offered a number of options when purchasing an annuity. Payments to the insurance company can be made either with a single **lump-sum payment** or periodically on a monthly, quarterly, or annual basis.

A single premium deferred annuity is purchased with a lump sum, but payment of benefits is delayed until a later date selected by the annuitant.

A **periodic payment deferred annuity** allows investments over time. Benefit payments for this type of annuity are always deferred until a later date selected by the annuitant.

An **immediate annuity** is purchased with a lump sum, and the payout of benefits usually commences within 60 days.

TEST TOPIC ALERT

There is no such thing as a periodic payment immediate annuity.

Bonus Annuities

It is not uncommon for variable annuities to offer a bonus on top of the investor's initial contribution. For example, investing $60,000 into a single premium annuity with a 5% bonus would result in an account balance of $63,000. Usually, bonus annuities have surrender charges lasting longer than those without the bonus. Recommendations to customers must disclose the additional costs, as well as the benefits of the bonus.

PRACTICE QUESTION

2. Insurance companies selling annuities offer a variety of purchase options to owners. Which of the following definitions regarding these annuity options is **not** true?
   A. Accumulation annuity—an annuity that allows the investor to accumulate funds in a separate account before investment in an annuity.
   B. Single premium deferred annuity—an annuity with a lump-sum investment, with payment of benefits deferred until the annuitant elects to receive them.
   C. Periodic payment deferred annuity—allows a person to make periodic payments over time. The contract holder can invest money on a monthly, quarterly, or annual basis.
   D. Immediate annuity—allows an investor to deposit a lump sum with the insurance company. Payout of the annuitant's benefits starts immediately, usually within 60 days.

Answer: A. Accumulation does not refer to a purchase option. The pay-in period for an annuity is known as the accumulation stage. A single premium deferred annuity is an annuity with a lump-sum investment, with payment of benefits deferred until the annuitant elects to receive them. Periodic payment deferred annuities allow a person to make periodic payments over time. Immediate annuities allow an investor to deposit a lump sum with the insurance company payout of the annuitant's benefits starting immediately, usually within 60 days.

Settlement Options

Although there are other choices, the exam's focus is on the options available to those who choose to annuitize. When we discuss taxation later in this unit, we will cover the option surrendering the contract. We will also cover the death benefit available should the contract holder die before receiving benefits.

Annuitants wishing to receive scheduled payments for life may annuitize. In that case, a payout option must be selected. Annuity payout options, in order from largest monthly payout to smallest monthly payout, follow:

- Life annuity (also known as straight life or life only)
- Life annuity with period certain
- Joint life with last survivor annuity
- Unit refund option

This is a contractual obligation that is entered into, and once annuitized, the decision is final.

Life Annuity/Straight Life

If an annuitant selects the life income option, the insurance company will pay the annuitant for life. When the annuitant dies, there are no continuing payments to a beneficiary. Money remaining in the account reverts to the insurer. Because the option places the risk of dying too soon on the annuitant, it represents the largest monthly check an annuitant could receive for the rest of the annuitant's life. (The insurance company has no further obligation at death.)

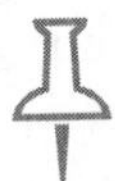

TAKE NOTE

The life annuity probably would not have been a good choice if the annuitant died after receiving only one month's payment. With the straight life option, all money accumulated that was not paid out at the time of the annuitant's death would belong to the insurer.

Life Annuity With Period Certain

The life annuity with period certain option is a little less risky because it allows for payments to a beneficiary. To guarantee that a minimum number of payments are made even if the annuitant dies, this option can be chosen. The contract will specifically allow the choice of a period of 10 or 20 years, for instance. The length of the period certain is a choice that is made when a payout option is selected. The annuitant is guaranteed monthly income for life with this option, but if death occurs within the period certain, a named beneficiary receives payments for the remainder of the period. Because there is a named beneficiary for the period certain, the size of this check will be smaller than a straight life option. (The insurance company is obligated to pay the named beneficiary an income if death occurs during the period certain.)

TAKE NOTE

To illustrate the life annuity with period certain option, assume a client selects a life annuity with a 10-year period certain. If the annuitant lives to be 150 years old, annuity payments are still made by the insurer. But, if the annuitant dies after receiving payments for two years, the beneficiary will receive payments for eight more years.

Joint Life With Last Survivor Annuity

The joint life with last survivor option guarantees payments over two lives. It is often used for spouses. Because the insurance company is obligated to pay a check over two lifetimes, this check will be smaller than a life with period certain option.

EXAMPLE

If the husband were to die first, the wife would continue to receive payments as long as she lives. If the wife were to die first, the husband would receive payments as long as he lives. Typically, the payment amount is reduced for the survivor.

Unit Refund Option

If the annuitant chooses the unit refund option, a minimum number of payments are made upon retirement. If value remains in the account after the death of the annuitant, it is payable in a lump sum to the annuitant's beneficiary. This option may be added as a rider to one of the others.

TAKE NOTE

The unit refund option is the only lifetime annuitization option that guarantees all of the money in the contract will be distributed. If unit refund is chosen for a $100,000 contract, the insurance company guarantees that a minimum of $100,000 will be distributed, and also guarantees a monthly check for life. Therefore, more than $100,000 may be distributed, but never less. Unit refund is sometimes offered as a rider.

For test purposes, this option represents the smallest check a person could receive for the rest of her life.

PRACTICE QUESTION

3. Phil and Clarissa are thinking about selecting a settlement option for their variable annuity. If their objective is to have the annuity provide income until both of them are deceased, which of the following settlement options will best meet their needs?
   A. Straight life annuity
   B. Joint and survivor annuity
   C. Installment refund annuity
   D. Life annuity with period certain

Answer: B. The joint and survivor annuity allows the couple to have the annuity provide income until both of them are deceased. The payment will be lower than on a straight life annuity because two lives are involved rather than one— there will be more risk for the insurance company but less risk for the annuitants. For a given purchase price, a straight life annuity generally provides the highest monthly payment amount because the annuity provides no payments beyond the annuitant's life. It is the old rule of the risk reward relationship—the more risk you take, the higher the reward.

LESSON 9.3: VALUING A VARIABLE ANNUITY

LO 9.c Define the terms used to value a variable annuity.

Introduction

A variable annuity has two distinct phases. The *growth* phase is its **accumulation phase**, while the *payout* phase is its annuity phase. A contract owner's interest in the separate account is known as either accumulation units or annuity units, depending on the contract phase.

Accumulation Phase

The pay-in period for a deferred annuity is known as the **accumulation stage** (**there is no accumulation period for an immediate annuity**). During the accumulation stage of an annuity contract, the contract terms are flexible. An investor who misses a periodic payment is in no danger of forfeiting the preceding contributions.

The contract holder can terminate the contract at any time during the accumulation stage, although the contract holder is likely to incur surrender charges on amounts withdrawn in the first five to 10 years after issuance of the contract.

Accumulation Units

An accumulation unit is an accounting measure that represents an investor's share of ownership in the separate account. An accumulation unit's value is determined in the same way as the value of mutual fund shares. The unit value changes with the value of the securities held in the separate account. The accumulation unit has a NAV.

The names of various purchase options are quite descriptive of how they operate and should not be difficult to follow. Just to be sure, let's try the following question.

PRACTICE QUESTION

4. Insurance companies selling annuities offer a variety of purchase options to owners. Which of the following definitions regarding these annuity options is **not** true?
   A. Accumulation annuity—an annuity that allows the investor to accumulate funds in a separate account before investment in an annuity.
   B. Single premium deferred annuity—an annuity with a lump-sum investment, with payment of benefits deferred until the annuitant elects to receive them.
   C. Periodic payment deferred annuity—allows a person to make periodic payments over time. The contract holder can invest money on a monthly, quarterly, or annual basis.
   D. Immediate annuity—allows an investor to deposit a lump sum with the insurance company. Payout of the annuitant's benefits starts immediately, usually within 60 days.

Answer: A. Accumulation does not refer to a purchase option. The pay-in period for an annuity is known as the accumulation stage. A single premium deferred annuity is an annuity with a lump-sum investment, with payment of benefits deferred until the annuitant elects to receive them. Periodic payment deferred annuities allow a person to make periodic payments over time. Immediate annuities allow an investor to deposit a lump sum with the insurance company payout of the annuitant's benefits starting immediately, usually within 60 days.

Annuity Units

When a variable annuity contract is annuitized, accumulation units are exchanged for annuity units. An **annuity unit** is a measure of value used only during an annuitized contract's payout period. It is an accounting measure, that determines the amount of each payment to the annuitant during the payout period. The number of annuity units is a key factor used to calculate the payout each month.

Figure 9.2: Annuitization

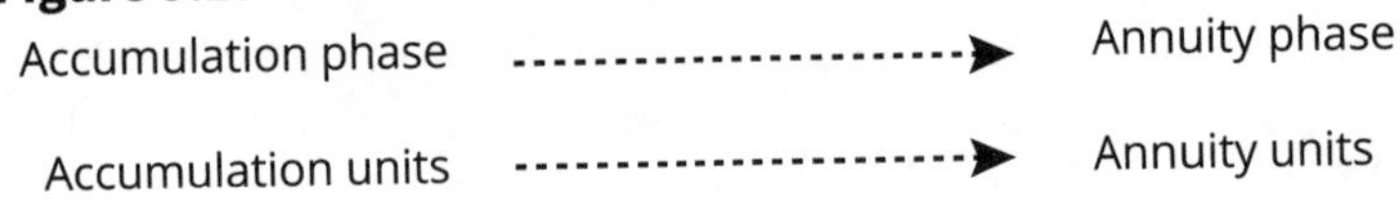

The number of annuity units is calculated when an owner annuitizes the contract. The number of annuity units liquidated each month does not change—it is fixed at the time of annuitizing based on the value of the contract when the payout period begins and on other variables (such as the payout option selected, the individual's age and sex, and AIR). The payment the annuitant will receive each month varies because each unit's value fluctuates with the separate account portfolio's value. This is, after all, a variable annuity.

Assumed Interest Rate (AIR)

The **assumed interest rate (AIR)** is a basis for determining distributions from a variable annuity. The rate, usually estimated conservatively, provides an earnings target for the separate account. Simply, if the actual earnings exceed the AIR, the annuity payments increase; if they fall short of the AIR, the payments decrease.

The actuarial department of the insurance company determines the initial value for the annuity units and the amount of the first month's annuity payment. At this time, an **AIR** is established. The AIR is a conservative projection of the performance of the separate account over the estimated life of the contract.

The value of an annuity unit and the annuitant's subsequent monthly income will vary, depending on separate account performance as compared to the AIR. To determine whether the monthly payment will increase, decrease, or stay the same as the previous month, the following rules apply:

- If separate account performance is greater than the AIR, the following month's payment is more than this month's.
- If separate account performance is equal to the AIR, the following month's payment stays the same as this month's.
- If separate account performance is less than the AIR, the following month's payment is less than this month's.

Many students have trouble catching on to this. Please try to follow this example.

EXAMPLE

Assume an AIR of 4% and that the actuaries have determined the first payment to be $1,000.

Month 2's separate account performance is 6%, greater than AIR, so the next check goes up.

Month 3's separate account performance is 4%, right at AIR. The next check received equals the last check received.

Month 4's separate account performance is 3%, which is below AIR; therefore the next check received will be less than the last check received.

Month 5's separate account performance is 3% again, which, although the same as month 4's, is still below AIR. The next check is, therefore, less than that of the last.

Month 6's separate account performance is not shown, but if separate account performance is above the AIR of 4%, the next check will be more than $950; if it is below the AIR of 4%, the next check will be less than $950.

AIR = 4%	**Month 1**	**Month 2**	**Month 3**	**Month 4**	**Month 5**	**Month 6**
Separate account return		6%	4%	3%	3%	?
Monthly payment	$1,000	$1,100	$1,100	$1,000	$950	?

TAKE NOTE

Consider this: If AIR is 4% and the separate account always returns 4%, the check would never change.

PRACTICE QUESTION

5. An insurance company offering a variable annuity makes payments to annuitants on the 15th of each month. The contract has an AIR of 3%. In July of this year, the contract earned 4%. In August, the account earned 6%. If the contract earns 3% in September, the payments to annuitants in October will be
   A. greater than the payments in September.
   B. less than the payments in September.
   C. the same as the payments in September.
   D. less than the payments in August.

Answer: C. The contract earned 3% in September. The AIR for the contract is 3%. The amount of the payment in October will not change from that of September's payment.

LESSON 9.4: TAXATION OF VARIABLE ANNUITIES

LO 9.d Differentiate between the different kinds of tax treatment of variable annuities.

Introduction

One of the most distinctive features of variable annuities is their tax treatment. We must separate the tax treatment during accumulation from that of when the funds are withdrawn.

Annuity Accumulation Stage

All growth in the value of an accumulation unit is deferred until withdrawal. For example, a grandparent gives a newborn grandchild $10,000. That money is used for a single premium deferred annuity. If the account earned 7%, when that child turned 70, it would be worth over $1.1 million. During those 70 years, not a penny of tax would be due. Shortly, we will discuss the taxation when the money is taken out.

TEST TOPIC ALERT

For exam purposes, all contributions to annuities are made with after-tax dollars, unless the annuity is part of an employer-sponsored (qualified) retirement plan or held in an IRA. Because there is no tax on the "way in," the exam will concentrate on taxation on the "way out."

Annuity Payout Stage

There are three different taxable scenarios and we will consider them one at a time.

On withdrawal, the amount exceeding the investor's cost basis is taxed as ordinary income.

Random Withdrawals

Random withdrawals from annuity contracts are taxed under the **last in, first out (LIFO)** method. Earnings are presumed by the IRS to be the last monies to hit the account. The earnings are considered to be withdrawn first from the annuity and are taxable as ordinary income. After the withdrawal of all earnings, contributions representing cost basis may be withdrawn without tax. With nonqualified annuities, it is only the earnings that are taxed. Using our grandparent example above, when that 70-year-old withdraws any money from the annuity, all $1.1 million in excess of the original $10,000 is taxed as ordinary income.

Lump-Sum Withdrawals

Lump-sum withdrawals are taken by using the LIFO accounting method. This means that earnings are removed before contributions. If an investor receives a lump-sum withdrawal before age 59½, the earnings portion withdrawn is taxed as ordinary income and is subject to an additional 10% tax penalty under most circumstances.

The penalty does not apply if the funds withdrawn after age 59½ are withdrawn because of death or disability, or are part of a life income option plan with fixed payouts.

TAKE NOTE

Remember, most variable annuities have the death benefit provision described earlier. As with any lump-sum withdrawal, everything above the cost basis is taxable at ordinary income rates. What is avoided is the 10% penalty if under 59½.

EXAMPLE

A contract with a $100,000 value consists of $40,000 in contributions and $60,000 in earnings. If the investor withdraws all $100,000 at once, the $60,000 in earnings is taxed as ordinary income and the $40,000 cost basis is returned tax-free. If the investor is at least 59½, there is no 10% tax penalty; if younger, the 10% tax penalty applies. However, the penalty only applies to the taxable portion ($60,000)—there is never a penalty tax on money that is not taxable. If the investor withdraws $10,000, (or any amount up to $60,000), under the LIFO rule, it is considered a withdrawal of earnings and will be taxed as ordinary income. There is never a capital gain with an annuity.

TEST TOPIC ALERT

Even when the distribution is from a nonqualified annuity, if it is made before the age of 59½, it is subject to the 10% additional tax (unless it meets one of the exceptions listed previously).

Assume an annuity is nonqualified unless a question specifically states otherwise. When contributions are made with after-tax dollars, these already taxed dollars are considered the investor's cost basis and are not taxed when withdrawn. The earnings in excess of the cost basis are taxed as ordinary income when withdrawn.

Any answer choice that mentions capital gains taxation on annuities or retirement plans is wrong. There is only ordinary income tax on distributions from annuities.

PRACTICE QUESTION

6. An annuity contract owner, age 45, surrenders the annuity to buy a home. Which of the following best describes the tax consequences of this action?
   A. Ordinary income taxes and a 10% early withdrawal penalty will apply to all money withdrawn.
   B. Capital gains tax will apply to the amount of the withdrawal that represents earnings; there will be no tax on the cost basis.
   C. Ordinary income taxes and a 10% early withdrawal penalty will apply to the amount of the withdrawal that represents earnings; there will be no tax on the cost basis.
   D. Ordinary income taxes apply to the amount of the withdrawal that represents earnings; the 10% early withdrawal penalty does not apply to surrendering an annuity.

Answer: C. All earnings are taxable as ordinary income. They are also subject to the 10% early withdrawal penalty when withdrawn before age 59½. The contract holder recovers the cost basis without tax.

Annuitization

Annuitized payouts are typically made monthly and are taxed according to an **exclusion ratio.** Each monthly payment consists of principal plus earnings. The portion representing principal is a return of the cost basis. That is not subject to taxes—it is simply getting your original investment back. The balance of the payment is the deferred earnings and that is what will be taxed. The exclusion ratio expresses the percentage of each monthly payment that is taxable.

EXAMPLE

An investor purchased a single premium deferred annuity with $50,000. At the time the investor annuitized, the accumulated value was $100,000. The exclusion ratio would hold that 50% of each payment will be treated as ordinary income and the other 50% of each payment will be treated (for tax purposes) as nontaxable return of basis. If the value at annuitization was $125,000, then 60% (75,000 divided by 125,000) would be taxed as ordinary income and the balance as a nontaxable return of cost basis.

There will not be a case on the exam where an investor annuitizing will be subject to the 10% penalty tax. This is true even in the unusual case where an annuitant elects to annuitize before reach age 59½.

1035 Exchange

A **1035 exchange** is a tax-free exchange between like contracts. It gets its name from Section 1035 of the IRC. The IRS allows annuity and life insurance policyholders to exchange their policies without tax current liability. For example, if a life insurance policyholder wanted to exchange his policy for one from another company, he could transfer all cash values from the old policy into the new policy without recognizing any tax consequences. Likewise, if an annuity holder decided to exchange her annuity for one offered by another company, the exchange is done without current taxation. Compare this to the mutual fund exchange privilege where there is no sales change, but, for tax purpose it is considered a sale and new purchase. This 1035 exchange provision applies to transfers of cash values from annuity to annuity, life to life, and life to annuity. It cannot be used for transfers from an annuity to a life insurance policy.

TEST TOPIC ALERT

FINRA is concerned about Section 1035 exchange abuses where the registered representative emphasizes the tax-free nature of the exchange without pointing out possible disadvantages. Those include

- possible surrender charges on the old policy,
- a new surrender charge period on the new policy, and
- possible loss of a higher death benefit that existed on the old policy.

Qualified Annuities

Back in Lesson 1.8, we learned about the tax-sheltered annuities (TSAs) available in 403(b) plans. Contributions to those annuities are made with pretax dollars. That means the investor's cost basis is zero. Therefore, with any withdrawal, everything is taxed as ordinary income. If the investor has not reached age 59½, the additional 10% tax penalty applies (unless annuitized).

LESSON 9.5: REGULATION OF VARIABLE INSURANCE PRODUCTS

LO 9.e Determine the rules and regulations pertaining to the sale of variable products.

Introduction

Many of the rules regarding sales practices for variable products are similar to those for investment companies. For example, the rules on noncash compensation are identical.

FINRA Rules

FINRA Rule 2320—Variable Contracts of an Insurance Company

We will use rule numbers from time to time, but you never have to memorize them. One key difference between the rules for funds and those for VAs is that FINRA Rule 2320 does not place a maximum sales charge on variable annuities. You might recall that FINRA Rule 2341 has a maximum load on mutual funds of 8.5% of the offering price.

Suitability of Variable Life Insurance

FINRA is concerned that the sale of variable life insurance is not misrepresented. Although legally defined as a security, it cannot be sold solely on that basis. When tested on the suitability of a recommendation for variable life, remember these three points:

- There must be a life insurance need.
- The applicant must be comfortable with the separate account and the fact that the cash value is not guaranteed.
- The applicant must understand the variable death benefit feature.

FINRA Rule 2330—Member's Responsibilities Regarding Deferred Variable Annuities

In light of the many cases involving variable annuities where there was failure to supervise and egregious unethical behavior, FINRA's Rule 2330 evolved. Please notice the title. This rule applies to recommended purchases and exchanges of deferred (not immediate) variable annuities and recommended initial subaccount allocations. On the other hand, this rule does not apply to reallocations among subaccounts made or to funds paid after the initial purchase or exchange of a deferred variable annuity. In other words, once the investor has made the initial purchase, any subsequent investments do not come under the rule. Likewise, once the initial subaccount decisions have been made, later changes are not covered by the rule.

The rule makes the obvious statement that no member or person associated with a member shall recommend to any customer the purchase or exchange of a deferred variable annuity unless the member or person associated with a member has a reasonable basis to believe that it is suitable.

TEST TOPIC ALERT

One example of egregious behavior stated in the rule (and possibly on the exam) is recommending that a client take a home equity loan and use the proceeds to fund the purchase of a deferred variable annuity.

Specific Suitability Requirements

Although there are general suitability rules that always apply, this rule specifies that, to be considered suitable, there is a reasonable basis to believe that

- the customer has been informed—in general terms—of various features of deferred variable annuities, such as the potential surrender period and surrender charge, which may include
  - potential tax penalty if customers sell or redeem deferred variable annuities before reaching the age of 59½,
  - mortality and expense fees,
  - investment advisory fees,
  - potential charges for and features of riders,
  - the insurance and investment components of deferred variable annuities, and
  - market risk;
- the customer would benefit from certain features of deferred variable annuities, such as tax-deferred growth, annuitization, or a death or living benefit; and
- the particular deferred variable annuity as a whole, the underlying subaccounts to which funds are allocated at the time of the purchase or exchange of the deferred variable annuity, and riders and similar product enhancements, if any, are suitable (and, in the case of an exchange, the transaction as a whole also is suitable) for the particular customer based on the information required by this rule.

Suitability of 1035 Exchanges

One of the specific concerns that the regulators have with variable annuities is sales personnel recommending that an investor switch from an existing contract to a new one. In the case of variable annuities, these exchanges are normally done under the provisions of IRS Section 1035 and, if done properly, are tax-free. However, it is mandatory that registered representatives and their supervisors evaluate the suitability of the exchange in light of the investor's financial condition, objectives, and the pros and cons of the switch.

Some of the negative conditions to be aware of are

- surrender charges imposed by the insurance company,
- the beginning of a new surrender period,
- possible reduction in death benefit,
- how the expenses of the new contract compare with those of the old contract, and
- the benefits included in the new contract may not be needed by the purchaser.

36-Month Rule

One of the factors in determining if the exchange is suitable is taking into consideration whether the customer has had another deferred variable annuity exchange within the preceding 36 months.

Under this provision, it must be determined whether the customer has made a variable annuity exchange using the member. It is also required that the member must make reasonable efforts to ascertain whether the customer has had an exchange at any other broker-dealer within the preceding 36 months. An inquiry to the customer as to whether the customer has had an exchange at another broker-dealer within 36 months would constitute a "reasonable effort" in this context. Members must document in writing both the nature of the inquiry and the response from the customer.

PRACTICE QUESTION

7. FINRA rules have evolved to protect investors. Which of the following products has been the subject of significant sales abuses?
   A. Fixed annuities
   B. Whole life insurance
   C. Deferred variable annuities
   D. Immediate variable annuities

Answer: C. FINRA Rule 2330 is specifically targeted at the sale of deferred variable annuities. FINRA does not have rules regarding fixed annuities and whole life insurance policies because they are not securities.

Investment Company Act of 1940 Rules for Variable Life Insurance

The SEC has no specific testable rules regarding variable annuities. The separate accounts are registered as investment companies under the Investment Company Act of 1940. The requirements of that act previously covered in Unit 8 apply here as well.

There are, however, several specific rules under federal law applying to variable life insurance contracts.

Policy Loans

Like traditional whole life insurance, a variable life insurance contract allows the insured to borrow against the cash value that has accumulated in the contract. However, certain restrictions exist. Usually, the insured may only borrow a percentage of the cash value. The minimum percentage that must be made available is 75% after the policy has been in force for three years. If the death benefit becomes payable during any period that a loan is outstanding, the loan amount is deducted from the death benefit before payment. The interest rate charged is stated in the policy.

TEST TOPIC ALERT

Several testable facts about policy loans are as follows:

- A minimum of 75% of the cash value must be available for policy loan after the policy has been in force three years.
- The insurer is never required to loan 100% of the cash value. Full cash value is obtained by surrendering the policy to the insurer.
- If the insured dies with a loan outstanding, the death benefit is reduced by the amount of the loan.
- If the insured surrenders the contract with a loan outstanding, cash value is reduced by the amount of the loan.

PRACTICE QUESTION

8. On July 15, 2015, your client purchased a variable life insurance policy with a death benefit of $500,000. The November 2017 statement showed a cash value of $30,000. If the client wanted to borrow as much as possible, the insurance company would have to allow a loan of at **least**

   A. $0.
   B. $15,000.
   C. $22,500.
   D. $27,000.

   Answer: A. Until a variable life policy is in force for a minimum of three years (this one is a bit less than 2½ years), there is no requirement to make the loan provision available. Once the three-year mark is reached, that minimum becomes 75% of the computed cash value.

Variable Life Insurance Contract Exchange

A unique feature of variable life insurance is the ability for the insured to have a change of heart. During the early stage of ownership, you have the right to exchange a variable life insurance contract for a form of permanent insurance issued by the company with comparable benefits (usually whole life). The length of time this exchange privilege is in effect varies from company to company, but under no circumstances may the period be less than 24 months (federal law).

The exchange is allowed without evidence of insurability. If a contract is exchanged, the new permanent policy has the same contract date and death benefit as the minimum guaranteed in the variable life insurance contract. The premiums equal the amounts guaranteed in the new permanent contract (as if it were the original contract).

TEST TOPIC ALERT

Three testable facts about the contract exchange provision follow:

- The contract exchange provision must be available for a minimum of two years.
- No medical underwriting (evidence of insurability) is required for the exchange.
- The new policy is issued as if everything were retroactive. That is, the age of the insured as of the original date is the age used for premium calculations for the new policy.

Sales Charges

The sales charges on a fixed-premium variable life contract may not exceed 9% of the payments to be made over the life of the contract. The contract's life, for purposes of this charge, is a maximum of 20 years. For those of you familiar with life insurance compensation, the effect of this is that renewal commissions are earned up to the 20th anniversary of policy issue.

Refund Provisions

The insurer must extend a free-look period to the policyowner for 45 days from the execution of the application, or for 10 days from the time the owner receives the policy, whichever is longer. During the free-look period, the policyowner may terminate the policy and receive all payments made.

The refund provisions extend for two years from issuance of the policy. If, within the two-year period, the policyowner terminates participation in the contract, the insurer must refund the contract's cash value (the value calculated after the insurer receives the redemption notice) plus a percentage of the sales charges deducted. After the two-year period has lapsed, only the cash value need be refunded; the insurer retains all sales charges.

TEST TOPIC ALERT

Several testable facts about sales charges and refunds are as follows:

- The maximum sales charge over the life of the contract is 9%.
- A policyowner who wants a refund within 45 days receives all money paid.
- From 45 days to two years, there is a partial refund of sale charge.
- After a variable life policy has been in effect for two years, the surrender value of the policy is the cash value; there is no sales charge refund.

UNIT 10

Options

LEARNING OBJECTIVES

When you have completed this unit, you will be able to accomplish the following.

- LO 10.a **Identify** the basic characteristics of option contracts.
- LO 10.b **Indicate** the functions of the Options Clearing Corporation.
- LO 10.c **Distinguish** between the various options values.
- LO 10.d **Recognize** the basic option strategies.
- LO 10.e **Recognize** the different spread strategies.
- LO 10.f **Recognize** the strategies combining puts and calls.
- LO 10.g **Distinguish** between the different types of nonequity options.
- LO 10.h **Calculate** profit/loss and breakeven for the various strategies.
- LO 10.i **Differentiate** between the different kinds of tax treatment of options transactions.
- LO 10.j **Determine** the CBOE rules and regulations pertaining to the sale of options.

INTRODUCTION

For many exam candidates, understanding option contracts is one of the more challenging concepts. Be sure to review each section of the unit thoroughly.

Most questions will be on equity options (options on stock), but expect some to involve nonequity options, such as index, interest rate, and foreign currency contracts.

Before we get into the details, we need to explain the term *option*. It is not new to any of use. All during our life, we have had options. Think of an option as a *choice*. When we were in school, we had choices of which electives to take, or which sports to play. When we buy a car, we make a choice. In fact, the dealer gives us a list of options we can add to the car.

In this business, an option is also a choice. One type of option gives us the choice to buy a stock if we wish. The other type of option gives us the choice to sell a stock if we wish. Those choices, and the details behind them, such as cost and when to choose, are detailed in the option contract.

LESSON 10.1: BASIC OPTIONS INCLUDING THE ROLE OF THE OCC

LO 10.a Identify the basic characteristics of option contracts.

The Options Contract

An **option** is a two-party contract that conveys a right to the buyer and an obligation to the seller. The **terms** of option contracts are standardized by the Options Clearing Corporation (OCC). This standardization allows options to be traded easily on an exchange such as the Chicago Board Options Exchange (CBOE). The underlying security for which an option contract is created may be a stock, stock market index, foreign currency, interest rate, or government bond.

Options are called **derivative securities** because their value is derived from the value of the underlying instrument, such as stock, an index, or a foreign currency. The most common type of option contract is an equity option where each contract represents 100 shares of the underlying stock.

TAKE NOTE

Because the CBOE was the first exchange to trade listed options, and is still by far the largest, most of our discussions will deal with their procedures. In may be necessary to know that the CBOE also offers option contracts known as mini-options. These contracts overlay only 10 shares of the underlying security instead of 100 shares, as is the case for standard options contracts.

With standard contracts, the multiplier is 100 (Ex: 2 premium = $200). With mini-option contracts, the multiplier is only 10. Therefore, a mini-option contract premium of 2 represents only $20.

The following terminology and concepts should be associated with the two parties to each contract: buyer and seller.

Figure 10.1: Two Parties Are Involved in an Options Contract

Buyer = Long = Holder = Owner	Seller = Short = Writer
Pays premium (the cost of the contract) to seller. There is a debit to the account of the buyer when the premium is paid. Buyers *open their position* with a debit to their account.	*Receives premium* from buyer. There is a credit to the account of the seller when the premium is received. Seller *open their position* with a credit to their account.
Has *rights* to exercise (buy or sell stock).	Has *obligation* when contract is exercised. The writer will be assigned (must buy or sell as required by contract).

Perhaps the following charts will help:

Figure 10.2: Long Position

An investor	**long a call** (bought the call)	has the right to	**buy**	the underlying asset at the strike price from a person who is short the call if the option is assigned	For agreeing to these contract provisions, the call buyer pays the premium.
	long a put (bought the put)		**sell**	the underlying asset at the strike price at any time to a person who is short the put if the option is assigned	For agreeing to these contract provisions, the put buyer pays the premium.

Figure 10.3: Short Position

An investor	**short a call** (sold the call)	is obligated to	**sell**	the underlying asset at the strike price to a person who is long the call if the option is exercised	For agreeing to these contract provisions, the call writer receives the premium.
	short a put (sold the put)		**buy**	the underlying asset at the strike price from a person who is long the put if the option is exercised	For agreeing to these contract provisions, the put writer receives the premium.

Every option contract has three specifications:

- *Underlying instrument.* Anything with fluctuating value can be the underlying instrument of an option contract. We will focus on common stock until later in the unit.
- *Price.* The contract specifies a strike or exercise price (strike price) at which purchase or sale of the underlying security will occur.
- *Expiration.* All contracts have a specified life cycle and expire on a specified date. Once a contract is issued, it can be bought or sold any time during its life cycle.
  - Standard contracts are issued with nine-month expirations and expire on the third Friday of the expiration month at 11:59 pm ET.
  - Long-term equity anticipation securities (LEAPS) have maximum expirations of 39 months. Though the maximum is 39 months, most trade with a 30-month life cycle. The length of time until the contract expires is the one contract specification that can be customized between buyer and seller when the contract first trades.

Figure 10.4: Terms of an Option Contract

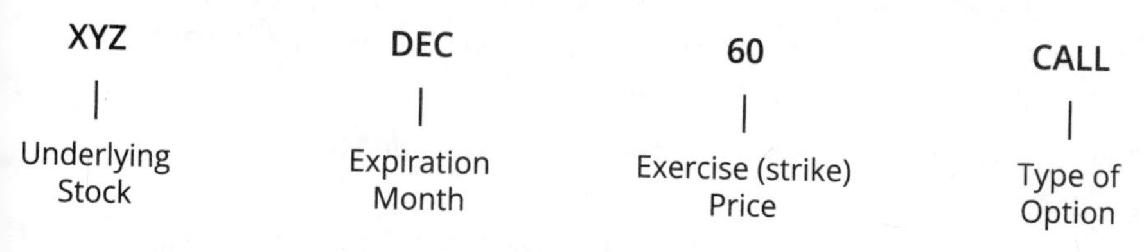

EXAMPLE

An option contract might look like this: ABC 40 NOV Call. That means the underlying asset is 100 shares of ABC common stock. The strike (exercise) price is $40 per share. The option expires in November. Another option might be an XYZ 65 JUL Put. The underlying asset is 100 shares of XYZ common stock. The strike price is 65 and the option expires in July. Let's go further by describing the difference between a call option and a put option.

Types of Options

Options are categorized by type, class, and series:

- *Type*. There are two types of options: calls and puts.
- *Class*. All options of the same type on the same underlying security are considered as being of the same class (e.g., all ALF calls make up one class of options; all ALF puts make up another class of options).
- *Series*. All options of the same class, exercise price, and expiration month are in the same series. For instance, all Jan 45 ACM puts make up one series; all Jan 50 ACM puts make up another series.

We are going to focus on the two types of options contracts: the **call** contract and the **put contract**.

Calls

An investor may buy calls (go long) or sell or write calls (go short). The features of each side of a call contract are as follows:

- **Long call**. A call buyer owns the right to buy 100 shares of a specific stock at the exercise (strike) price before the expiration if he chooses to exercise. The holder (owner) of the option can also sell the option if he desires.
- **Short call**. A call writer (seller) has the obligation to sell 100 shares of a specific stock at the strike price if the buyer exercises the contract.

Puts

An investor may buy puts (go long) or sell puts (go short). The features of each side of a put contract are noted as follows:

- **Long put**. A put buyer owns the right to sell 100 shares of a specific stock at the exercise (strike) price if she chooses to exercise. The holder (owner) of the option can also sell the option if she desires.
- **Short put.** A put writer (seller) has the obligation to buy 100 shares of a specific stock at the strike price if the buyer exercises the contract.

TAKE NOTE

Buyers of options call the shots; they are in control. They choose to exercise or not to exercise. That is why buyers pay premiums. The writer is at the mercy of the buyer's decision. Options are exercised against the writer when the buyer makes that decision. Writers do not have the opportunity to choose to exercise.

- The buyer wants the contract to be *exercised*. He wins, and the seller loses at exercise.
- The seller wants the contract to *expire*. The seller wins at expiration because he gets to keep the premium. No purchase or sale of stock is required.

You can Answer: A significant number of test questions by knowing that buyers have *rights* and sellers have *obligations*.

EXAMPLE

Following is an example of what an options trade would reflect.

Long 1 XYZ Jan 60 call at 3

Long	The investor has bought the call and has the right to exercise the contract.
XYZ	The single contract represents 100 shares of XYZ stock.
Jan	The contract expires on the third Friday of January at 11:59 pm ET.
60	The strike price of the contract is 60.
Call	The type of option is a call, and the investor has the right to buy the stock at 60 because he is long the call.
3	The premium of the contract is $3 per share. Contracts are for 100 shares, so the total premium is $300. The investor paid the premium to buy the call. The seller (writer) received the $300 premium for selling the option.

Opening and Closing Positions

When an investor establishes the option position by buying or writing calls or puts, the order ticket and confirmation are marked *Opening Purchase* or *Opening Sale*. The key is the first step—to **open**. A customer who buys an option generally may sell that option at any time before it expires. This offsetting transaction is known as a **closing sale**, and the ticket memorandum and confirmation are marked *Closing Sale*. Therefore, as with much that we buy, we *open* with a purchase and *close* (unload it) with a sale.

A customer who sold an option as an opening transaction may, at any time before the option expires, buy back the option. This transaction is known as a **closing purchase**, and the ticket and confirmation are marked *Closing Purchase*.

Because the price of the underlying stock will change over the life of the option, an investor may not be able to make a closing transaction at the same price as his opening transaction. Gains or losses on closing transactions result from the difference between premiums paid and received.

Settlement Dates

When options are bought and sold, the settlement is the next business day. We refer to that as T+1 in the industry. Unlike stocks and bonds, there are no certificates for options. That makes settlement much quicker. An investor purchasing an option on Tuesday must pay for it by the close of business Wednesday. Investors selling an option on Tuesday will have the proceeds credited to their account by the closed of business Wednesday.

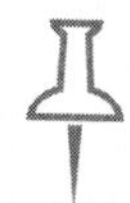

TAKE NOTE

Without a certificate, how does the client prove ownership? The investor's proof of ownership of an option is the trade confirmation.

LO 10.b Indicate the functions of the Options Clearing Corporation.

Role of the OCC

The **Options Clearing Corporation (OCC)** is the issuer of listed options contracts. It is owned by the exchanges that trade options. Its primary functions are to standardize, guarantee the performance of, and issue option contracts. The OCC determines when new option contracts will be offered to the market. It designates the strike prices and expiration months for new contracts within market standards to maintain uniformity and liquidity. It is important to note that the OCC does not determine option premiums. Supply and demand in the trading markets determines the premium for the contracts.

One of the important guarantees of the OCC is the exercise of options contracts. That means, if for some reason a seller is unable to perform, the OCC does. If a holder of an option wishes to exercise, her broker-dealer notifies the OCC. The OCC then assigns exercise notice against a broker-dealer with a customer who has written that option. The broker-dealer then assigns that exercise noted to a customer with a short position.

PRACTICE QUESTION

1. A listed ABC May 35 call option is issued by
   A. the ABC Corporation.
   B. the seller of the call option.
   C. the exchange on which the option is traded.
   D. the Options Clearing Corporation (OCC).

   Answer: D. The OCC is the issuer of all listed options. There are unlisted options, but we don't expect you will see anything about them on the exam.

Assignment of Exercise Notices

As we have learned, an investor who is long an option contract (the holder or owner), can choose to exercise that option. In the case of a call, that would be exercising the right to buy at the strike price. In the case of a put, that would be exercising the right to sell at the strike price.

When the OCC is notified by a broker-dealer that one of its customers wants to exercise, the OCC randomly selects a firm with a short position in that option to which it assigns the exercise. The OCC assigns exercise notices on a random basis. Then, it is up to the assigned broker-dealer to determine which of its clients is going to be obligated.

Customer Notification of Allocation Method

Broker-dealers have three ways to allocate exercise assignments. They may allocate to customers on

- a random basis;
- a first in, first out (FIFO) method; or
- any other method that is fair and reasonable.

Commonly referred to as the notification of allocation method, each member firm must inform its options customers in writing of how it allocates exercise notices (assignments) and the consequences of the method of allocation used.

One method that is not considered fair and reasonable (and is often tested) is selecting based on the size of the writer's position. Although those who have written 100 contracts are more likely to be selected randomly than a client who is short one contract, the firm cannot deliberately choose the client with the largest short position.

Delivery After Exercise

Upon exercise of an option, the parties are now required to make settlement. The assigned party (the writer) must either deliver the stock within two business days (for a call) or buy the stock within two business days (for a put) from notification of exercise. This is the same T+2 settlement requirement as any stock trade.

Wait a minute. Didn't we say just a bit earlier in this unit that option trades settle T+1 (next business day)? Yes, we did. Follow this Test Topic Alert.

TEST TOPIC ALERT

The exam will try to trick you with settlement dates. The settlement date for equity options is the next business day. That is, when an option is bought or sold, that option trade settles T+1. If an equity option is exercised, what happens? Stock is either bought (call) or sold (put) and that is treated as any other equity transaction. That means T+2 settlement date.

LESSON 10.2: VALUING OPTIONS

LO 10.c Distinguish between the various options values.

Introduction

How does an investor know if an option is fairly priced? We need to learn the factors evaluated by investors that influence the price of an option contract.

Factors in Options Valuation

Intrinsic Value

Probably the most important item is the option's intrinsic value. Understanding intrinsic value requires that we learn several terms. We are going to look at both calls and puts.

In the Money

A call is in the money when the market price of the underlying asset exceeds the strike price of the option. Buyers want options to be in the money; sellers do not. It is critical to understand that the term *in the money* (or out of the money) refers to the option, not to the investor.

EXAMPLE

An ABC 50 call is in the money by 7 points when the price of ABC stock is 57.

A put option is **in the money** when the market price of the underlying asset is less than the strike price of the option. Buyers generally benefit when contracts are in the money, whereas sellers do not.

EXAMPLE

An ABC 50 put is in the money by 4 points when ABC stock is at 46.

At the Money

A call or a put is **at the money** when the market price of the underlying asset equals the strike price of the option.

EXAMPLE

An ABC 50 call is at the money when the price of ABC stock is 50.

An ABC 50 put is at the money when the price of ABC stock is 50.

Out of the Money

A call option is **out of the money** when the market price of the underlying asset is less than the strike price of the option. A buyer will not exercise calls that are out of the money at expiration. Out of the money contracts are advantageous to sellers. The options expire and sellers keep the premium without obligations to perform.

EXAMPLE

An ABC 50 call is out of the money by 4 points when the price of ABC stock is 46.

A put option is out of the money when the market price of the underlying asset is greater than the strike price of the option. A buyer will not exercise puts that are out of the money. Sellers benefit when contracts are out of the money.

EXAMPLE

An ABC 50 put is out of the money by 7 points when the price of ABC stock is 57.

TAKE NOTE

We did not consider the premium in any of the three examples because we are only considering the option, not the investor.

Did you notice how puts and calls are opposite each other? When the call was in the money (the stock's price went up), the put was out of the money by an equal amount. Many students have found the following phrase (which we will use several times) to be quite helpful.

Call UP and *Put DOWN.*

That is, calls become beneficial to the owner when the price of the stock goes up. Puts become beneficial to the owner when the price of the stock goes down.

Now we can come back to intrinsic value. **Intrinsic value** is the same as the amount a contract is in the money. A call has intrinsic value when the market price of the stock is above the strike price of the call. Options never have negative intrinsic value; intrinsic value is always a positive amount or zero. Options that are at the money or out of the money have an intrinsic value of zero. Buyers like calls to have intrinsic value; sellers (writers) do not. An option that has intrinsic value at expiration will be exercised or sold by the buyer. An option that has no intrinsic value at the expiration date will simply be allowed to expire.

During the lifetime of an option contract, buyers want the contract to move in the money; sellers want the contract to move out of the money.

EXAMPLE

In, at, and out of the money—An option is in the money by the amount of its intrinsic value.

Calls: in the Money, at the Money, Out of the Money

Ex: Calls	Intrinsic Value	In, Out, at the Money
40 Call, stock @ 42	2 points	In the money 2 points
40 Call, stock @ 40	0 points (strike price = stock)	At the money
40 Call, stock @ 38	0 points (strike price > stock)	Out of the money

Puts: in the Money, at the Money, Out of the Money

Ex: Puts	Intrinsic Value	In, Out, at the Money
40 Put, stock @ 37	3 points	In the money 3 points
40 Put, stock @ 40	0 points (strike price = stock)	At the money
40 Put, stock @ 44	0 points (strike price < stock)	Out of the money

Time Value

The second component in valuing an option is its time value. Quite simply, time value is a function of the time remaining before the option expires. On the expiration date, the time value is zero—there isn't any more time left. An option expiring in nine months has more time value than one expiring in six months. The option expiring in six months has more time value than one expiring in one month.

How do you compute time value? That will likely be a question on your exam. An option has time value anytime the option's premium exceeds its intrinsic value.

The amount an option buyer will pay (and a seller will accept) above an option's intrinsic value is the time value. An option expires on a preset date; the further away that date is, the more time there is available for a change in the price of the underlying stock. The amount of time in the contract, therefore, has value to the option buyer. You can expect buyers to pay more for a contract that has a long time to run than for a contract that is about to expire.

TEST TOPIC ALERT

Remember these three points:

Intrinsic value. Amount by which the option is in the money

Time value. The market's perceived worth of the time remaining to expiration

PIT. Premium minus intrinsic value equals time value

As the option's expiration date approaches, time value will diminish. That is known as **time decay**. On the last trading day before expiration, the option no longer has time value and the premium usually equals the intrinsic value.

TAKE NOTE

An option premium is composed of two components: intrinsic value and time value. To compute time value, subtract intrinsic value from the premium. If an option is at or out of the money, the entire premium is time value. For example, an XYZ NOV 40 put has a premium of 1.25 when XYZ stock is selling at 41. With the market price above the strike price (41 is higher than 40), the option is out of the money. That means no intrinsic value. Therefore, the entire premium of $1.25 ($125) is time value.

PRACTICE QUESTION

2. Which of the following option contracts has no time value?
   A. ABC OCT 50 call @ 2 with ABC at 51
   B. DEF NOV 60 call @ 2 with DEF at 62
   C. GHI DEC 50 put @2 with GHI at 49
   D. JKL JAN 60 put @ 2 with JKL at 62

Answer: B. An option's time value is the difference between the premium and the intrinsic value. In choice B, the call option has 2 points of intrinsic value. It is in the money because the strike price is below the market. Therefore, the premium of 2 is equal to the intrinsic value. That means the option is selling a parity and had no time value. In choice A, the option is 1 point in the money. With a premium of 2, the other point represents time value. In choice C, the option is 1 point in the money. With a premium of 2, the other point represents time value. In choice D, the option is 2 points out of the money so the entire premium is time value.

Trading at Parity

An option is trading at **parity** when the premium equals the intrinsic value of the contract (e.g., a May 35 call is at parity when the market price is 40 and the premium is 5. A May 35 put is at parity when the market price is 5 and the premium is 5).

Options generally trade at parity just before the expiration date. Why is that? If the premium is equal to the intrinsic (in the money) value, what pricing component is missing? We are missing the time value. When is there no time value to an option? When there is no time—just before the option expires.

LESSON 10.3: BASIC OPTION STRATEGIES

LO 10.d Recognize the basic option strategies.

Introduction

Understanding why investors buy or sell options is an important part of the exam. In this lesson, we will cover the basic strategies.

Single Option Strategies

There are four basic strategies available to options investors:

- Buying calls
- Writing calls
- Buying puts
- Writing puts

Figure 10.5: The Four Basic Options Transactions

	Calls	
	Buy a Call	Write a Call
Buy		**Sell**
	Buy a Put	Write a Put
	Puts	

Buying Calls

Here is how the exam might describe an investor's position:

The investor is long 1 XYZ Jan 60 call at 3.

We need to be sure we know exactly what that means.

Long	The investor has bought the call and has the right to exercise the contract.
XYZ	The contract includes 100 shares of XYZ stock.
Jan	The contract expires on the third Friday of January at 11:59 pm ET.
60	The exercise (strike) price of the contract is 60.
Call	The type of option is a call, and the investor has the right to buy the stock at 60 because she is long the call.
3	The premium of the contract is $3 per share. Contracts are issued with 100 shares, so the total premium is $300. The investor paid the premium to buy the call.

Buyers of calls want the market price of the underlying stock to rise. The investor who owns this call hopes that the market price will rise above 60. She then has the right to buy the stock at the strike price of 60, even if the market price is higher (e.g., 80). We know that is the strategy because when it comes to buying a call, *Call UP* is the phrase we remember.

Selling Calls

Here is the way the exam might describe an investor's position:

Short XYZ Jan 60 call at 3

We need to be sure we know exactly what that means.

Short	The investor has sold the call and has obligations to perform if the contract is exercised.
XYZ	The contract includes 100 shares of XYZ stock.
Jan	The contract expires on the third Friday of January at 11:59 pm ET. If expiration occurs, the writer keeps the premium without any obligation.
60	The strike price of the contract is 60.
Call	The type of option is a call, and the investor is obligated to sell the stock at 60, if exercised, because she is short the call.
3	The premium of the contract is $3 per share. Options contracts are issued with 100 shares, so the total premium is $300.

Writers (sellers) of calls want the market price of the underlying stock to fall or stay the same. The investor who owns this call hopes that the market price will rise above 60. The contract will not be exercised if the market price is at or below 60 at expiration, and the writer keeps the premium of $300 with no obligation.

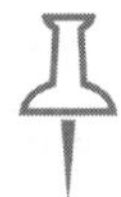

TAKE NOTE

A call ***buyer*** is a bullish investor because he wants the market to rise. That way the option gets in the money—it has value. The call may be exercised or sold and the buyer may make a profit.

A call ***writer*** is a bearish or neutral investor because she wants the market to fall. Alternatively, she will be happy if the stock's price does not rise above the strike price. If, at expiration, there is no intrinsic value, the option expires and the seller has earned the premium.

TEST TOPIC ALERT

It is critical that you recognize that only one side wins. The amount that a buyer makes when the stock price goes up is the amount the seller loses. If the stock price falls or stays at the strike price, the amount the buyer loses is the amount the seller makes. You will see this vividly later in this unit.

Long Call Option Strategies

Call buyers are *bullish* on the underlying stock. By purchasing calls, an investor can profit from an increase in a stock's price while investing a relatively small amount of money. There are many reasons why investors purchase calls.

Speculation

Speculation is the most common reason for buying calls. Investors can speculate on the upward price movement of the stock by paying only the premium. Buying the actual stock would require a far greater investment. This is a form of leverage as shown in the following example.

EXAMPLE

If ABC is trading at $40 (for a cost of $4,000) and an ABC 40 call is trading at 4 ($400 per contract), the investor can buy either the call or the stock. If he buys the ABC stock and its price goes up to $50 a share, he makes a $1,000 profit—a 25% return on the original $4,000 investment.

The same movement in the stock will make the ABC 40 call worth at least its intrinsic value of 10 ($1,000). If the investor instead buys the ABC 40 call for $400, he can realize a $600 profit ($1,000 less the $400 premium)—a 150% return on a $400 investment. The option strategy provides the investor with greater leverage (a higher potential percentage return).

However, if the stock price falls, the investor risks the entire $4,000 purchase price (the stock can fall to zero and become worthless). The option owner can lose the entire investment, but a $400 loss is less painful than a $4,000 loss.

Deferring a Decision

An investor can buy a call on a stock and lock in a purchase price until the option expires. This allows him to postpone making a financial commitment other than the premium until the expiration date of the option. This is often used when an investor has funds coming due in the future and wants to preserve today's price. An example would be a maturing CD with a penalty for early withdrawal.

Diversifying Holdings

With limited funds, an investor can buy calls on a variety of stocks and possibly profit from any rise in the options premium.

Protection of a Short Stock Position

Investors can use calls to protect a short stock position. The option acts as an insurance policy against the stock rising in price. Investors who short stock lose when the price of the stock rises. Because there is theoretically no limit as to how high that price can go, these investors face a potentially unlimited loss. A popular way to hedge (protect) against that loss is to buy a call on the stock. That way, short sellers knows the most they would have to pay to cover their short stock position.

Short Call Option Strategies

Call writers are *bearish* or neutral on the price of the underlying stock. An investor who believes a stock's price will decline or stay the same can write calls for any of the following reasons.

Covered vs. Uncovered Call Writers

Before we go further, it is necessary to distinguish between a *covered* and an *uncovered* call option. First of all, the terms are only related to short calls. There is no such term as a covered (or uncovered) long call. When a call option is covered, it means the investor owns the number of shares "covered" by the option contract. For example, if the writer is selling 3 contracts, 300 shares of the stock is in the writer's account. Instead of having the actual stock, the option can be covered by a security convertible, at no cost, into the appropriate number of shares. That would include convertible debentures or preferred stock.

A second way to cover a short call is with a long call with the same or lower strike price and an expiration date no sooner than that of the short call. For example, if an investor who does not own the stock sells an LMN OCT 45 call and buys an LMN OCT 40 call, she has *covered* the short call. If the price of the LMN stock goes up, say to 60, the 45 call will be exercised. The investor does not have the stock, but, instead of having to go into the marketplace and buy LMN at 60, the long 40 call will be exercised and the stock purchased at 40 will be used to deliver against the exercise of the 45 call.

A call option is uncovered when an investor writes a call option without owning the underlying stock or other related assets that would enable the investor to deliver the stock should the option be exercised. You may also see this referred to as a *naked* write.

Remember, the seller of an option has an obligation. The OCC, who stands behind all options exercise, wants to be sure that, if exercised, the writer can perform. In the case of a call, the obligation is to deliver stock. If the writer already has the stock (or something convertible into it), we know the obligation can be met. When the option is uncovered, that protection does not exist. In that case, a specified cash deposit (not tested) must be made by the seller to be sure there will be funds available to buy the stock to deliver.

TAKE NOTE

A corporation cannot write calls on common stock it has issued.

TEST TOPIC ALERT

Naked call writers face unlimited potential risk of loss. Remember, the obligation of a call writer is to deliver stock at the exercise price. A call option will be exercised when the market price is above the strike price. When that happens to an uncovered writer, he must buy the stock in the market, paying whatever the going price is. As we have discussed previously, there is no theoretical limit as to how high a stock's price can go. You will need to know for the exam the two strategies in the investment business that have the potential for an unlimited loss:

- Writing (selling) an uncovered call option
- Selling stock short

Increasing Returns

Writing options is an income strategy, whether covered or naked. If the option is covered, the premium adds to any dividend on the underlying stock. This generates additional income for the portfolio. Investors hope for expiration of the calls so they can keep the premiums.

Speculation

By writing calls, an investor can profit if the stock's price falls below or stays at the strike price. The investor will then earn the premium. This is most often the strategy of the uncovered writer.

Locking in a Sale Price

If an investor has an unrealized profit in a stock and is interested in selling it, a call can be written at an exercise price that will attempt to lock in that profit.

EXAMPLE

An investor owns 100 shares of RFQ purchased at $50 per share. The stock is now selling at $75 per share. He is sitting with an unrealized profit of $25 per share, but is concerned the market may turn the other way. If the investor writes an RFQ 75 call for 4 points and the stock goes up to $85 per share, the option is 10 points in the money. That means the holder (owner) of the call will certainly exercise and the writer will wind up selling his stock at the $75 exercise price. Yes, it would have been nice to still own the stock, but he did make that $25 per share profit plus the 4-point premium.

Protection of a Long Position

The premium collected from writing a call provides limited downside protection to the extent of the premium received. Using the above example, that premium of 4 points would keep the investor from losing money until the stock dropped below 71 (75 – 4). Shortly, we will show you a better way to protect the long stock position from a severe drop in the market price.

Ratio Call Writing

Ratio call writing involves selling more calls than the long stock position covers. This strategy generates additional premium income for the investor, but also entails unlimited risk because of the short uncovered calls.

EXAMPLE

An investor who is long 100 shares of HIJ common stock writes 2 HIJ OCT 45 calls. This is a 2:1 ratio write because the ratio of total calls to covered calls is 2:1. The 100 shares in the account is enough to cover one of the calls. The other call is uncovered and that means the potential loss is unlimited.

Long Put Option Strategies

Put buyers are bearish on the underlying stock. By purchasing puts, an investor can profit from a decrease in a stock's price while investing a relatively small amount of money. The following are reasons that investors purchase puts.

Speculation

Investors can speculate on the downward price movement of the stock by paying only the premium. If the market price of the stock falls below the strike price, the option is in the money and may result in a profit to the buyer. This is a low risk alternative to selling a stock short (to be covered in Unit 16).

Deferring a Decision

An investor can buy a put on a stock and lock in a sale price until the option expires. This allows her to postpone a selling decision until the expiration date of the option. With this strategy, an investor not only locks in an acceptable sales price for stock that is owned, but also protects its appreciation potential until the expiration date. As we will learn later in this unit, this technique might have beneficial tax advantages.

Protection of a Long Stock Position

Investors can use puts to protect a long stock position. The option acts as an insurance policy against the stock declining in price. This is the perfect hedge for a long stock position. For the cost of the premium (like any insurance policy), the owner of the stock knows he can sell his position at the strike price, no matter how far the market price falls.

Short Put Option Strategies

Covered vs. Uncovered Put Writers

Before we go further, it is necessary to distinguish between a covered and an uncovered put option.

Covered puts work like covered calls, except that the "covering" equity position is a short stock position instead of long. There are two ways to cover a put:

- Taking a short position in the stock underlying the short put
- A cash-covered put

The obligation of the put writer is to pay the exercising holder the exercise price. That requires money. A deposit of cash into the writer's account ensures that the money is there, if needed. The concept of the short sale covering the put is a bit more complicated. Just accept the fact that it works.

Put writers are bullish or neutral on the price of the underlying stock. An investor who believes a stock's price will increase or stay the same can write puts for the following reasons.

Speculation

By writing puts, an investor can profit if the stock's price rises above or stays at the strike price. The investor can earn the premium.

Increasing Returns

As with call writers, the premium is a source of income. Additional income can be earned for a portfolio by writing puts. Investors hope for expiration of the puts so that they can keep the premium.

Buying Stock Below Its Current Price

The premium received from writing puts can be used to offset the cost of stock when the put is exercised against the writer. The writer's actual cost becomes the strike minus the premium received. This is a popular technique for investors who believe a stock's current price is too high.

Open Interest

One of the tools used to determine strategy is the put-call ratio. It uses the open interest in puts and calls. The open interest in an option is the number of contracts outstanding. The higher the open interest, the more liquid the option. As an option approaches expiration, open interest begins to decline as investors close out or exercise existing positions.

Put-Call Ratio

The **put-call ratio** reflects the current open interest in the trading of put options to call options. The ratio can be used as a gauge of investor sentiment (bullish or bearish) and can be calculated to measure broad sectors of the market across many underlying securities or indexes, or it can be used to gauge investor sentiment for just one underlying security.

The ratio is calculated by dividing the number of traded put options by the number of traded call options. The higher the ratio, the more bearish investors have been up to that point in time. For instance, as the ratio increases, it can be interpreted as an indication that investors felt the market sector or underlying security would move lower and were buying more puts, or investors were purchasing puts to hedge existing long portfolios in anticipation of a downward move.

However, it should also be noted that the ratio can be used as a contrarian indicator by traders. For example, the higher the ratio becomes, it is likely that traders may feel it is time to close or cover short positions in favor of long positions. In other words, the ratio may have become so high that the continued bearish sentiment begins to diminish, indicating that a reversal may be near.

ESSON 10.4: ADVANCED OPTIONS STRATEGIES

LO 10.e Recognize the different spread strategies.

Introduction

As investors become more familiar with options, they recognize there are advanced strategies that can offer them opportunities to improve their portfolio results. The first of these strategies is spreading. The first thing to understand is that the word *spread* always refers to a difference. When we were quoting securities, the spread was the difference between the bid and ask price. With options, a spread always involves some difference. As we will cover, it could be a difference in exercise prices, it could be a difference in expiration dates, or it could be a difference in both.

Spreads

A **spread** is the simultaneous purchase of one option and sale of another option of the same class:

- A *call spread* is a long call and a short call.
- A *put spread* is a long put and a short put.

You may see questions on the exam that ask you to identify what position the investor has established. The following master options chart will give you the answer. The horizontal ovals shown in the chart identify the two types of spreads: call spreads and put spreads.

As you solve questions, point at the investor's options positions on your chart. You will easily identify what type of position has been created.

Figure 10.6: Master Options Chart

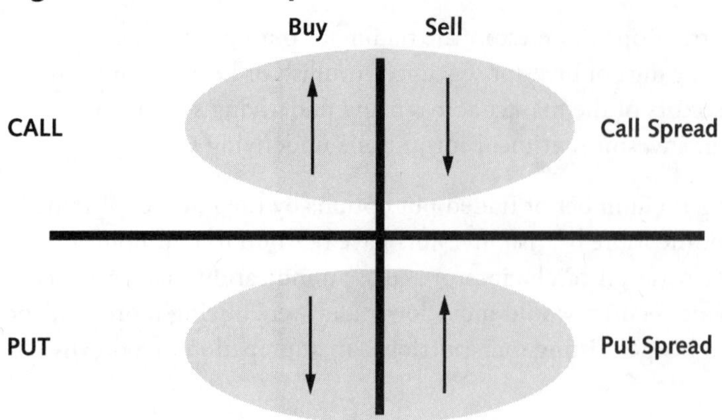

Types of Spreads

Investors can buy or sell three types of spreads: a price or vertical spread, a time or calendar spread, or a diagonal spread.

Price or Vertical Spread

A **price spread** or **vertical spread** is one that has different strike prices but the same expiration date. It may be called a vertical spread because strike prices on options reports are reported vertically.

EXAMPLE

Example of a price or vertical spread:

Long RST Nov 50 call for 7

Short RST Nov 60 call for 3

This is a price or vertical spread because the difference in the two options is the 50 and 60 strike prices (not the premiums).

TAKE NOTE

The most common spread, and the one most likely to occur on the exam, is the price spread or vertical spread, in which the two options have the same expiration date but different strike prices.

Time or Calendar Spread

A **time spread** or **calendar spread,** also known as a **horizontal spread,** includes option contracts with different expiration dates but the same strike prices. Investors who establish these do not expect great stock price volatility. Instead, they hope to profit from the different rates at which the time values of the two option premiums erode. Thus, their outlook is neutral. Time spreads are called horizontal spreads because expiration months are arranged horizontally on options reports.

EXAMPLE

Example of a time or calendar spread:

Long RST Nov 60 call for 3

Short RST Jan 60 call for 5

This is a time or horizontal spread because the difference in the two options is the Nov and Jan expiration dates (time).

Diagonal Spread

A **diagonal spread** is one in which the options differ in both time and price. On an options report, a line connecting these two positions would appear as a diagonal.

EXAMPLE

Example of a diagonal spread:

Long RST Jan 55 call for 6

Short RST Nov 60 call for 3

This is a diagonal spread because both the strike prices and expiration dates are different.

Bull and Bear Spreads

As we have learned, a spread is an investor buying one option and selling another of the same class. Although there are spreads where the outlook is neutral (the investor profits if the stock's price is stable), most of the exam questions deal with bull and bear spreads. The easiest way to identify these is to remember that bulls always buy low and sell high. That is, a bull spread is created when the investor buys the option with the low *strike* price and sells the option with the high *strike.*

Please note, this is the strike or exercise price we are looking at, not the premium. If a bull spread is buying low and selling high, then a bear spread is buying high and selling low.

Debit and Credit Spreads

Spreads are categorized as **debit spreads** or **credit spreads**. A spread is a debit spread if the long option has a higher premium than the short option; a spread is a credit spread if the short option has a higher premium than the long option. Put into practical terms, if the option you buy costs more than the one you sell, you must pay the difference. In essence, your account is debited (charged) for the net cost. If the option you sell brings in more than the one you buy, your account is credited with the difference. That makes it a credit spread.

The simplest way to determine a debit or a credit is to use a T-chart. This is done by drawing a chart with DR for debit on the left side and CR for credit on the right side. Here are four examples.

EXAMPLE

An investor establishes a call spread by going long one RST Jan 55 call for a premium of 6 and short 1 RST Jan 65 call for a premium of 2:

DR	CR
6	
	2
4	

This spread is a debit spread because the premium paid was more than the premium received. We see that clearly with the 6 in the debit column and the 2 in the credit column. The net outlay was 4 points.

EXAMPLE

An investor establishes a call spread by going long one RST Jan 55 call for a premium of 2 and short 1 RST Jan 45 call for a premium of 6:

DR	CR
2	
	6
	4

This spread is a credit spread because the premium received was more than the premium paid. We see that clearly with the 6 in the credit column and the 2 in the debit column. The net amount received was 4.

One thing you should notice with these two examples—the lower the strike price, the higher the premium. After all, with a call option, the ability to buy stock at 45 is certainly more valuable than having the option to buy it at 55. To show you how that might appear on the exam, look at this example:

EXAMPLE

An investor establishes a call spread position buy going long an ABC 60 call and short an ABC 65 call. Is this a debit or a credit spread? How can we tell? There are no premiums to put into our T-chart. How do we know if we are paying more or receiving more?

You can expect to see at least one question where the premiums are not given. What you do know is the lower the strike price on a call, the higher the premium. Therefore, in this example, it must be a debit spread because we would be paying more to buy the 60 call than we would receive when selling the 65 call.

Debit Call Spreads

Bullish investors use **debit call spreads** to reduce the cost of a long option position. There is, however, a trade-off, because the investor's potential reward is limited (as we will learn later in this unit).

EXAMPLE

An investor establishes a spread by going long 1 RST NOV 55 call at a premium of 6 and short 1 RST NOV 60 call at a premium of 3. Here is how this looks on a T-chart:

DR	CR
6	
	3
3	

Instead of paying $600 to buy the call, the investor's cost was reduced to $300 by also selling a call.

Because this is a debit spread, the investor profits if exercise occurs. The difference in premiums on the two options widens as exercise becomes likely. Investors always want net debit spreads to widen.

TEST TOPIC ALERT

The following tips will be helpful with spread questions:

debit = widen = exercise (When you begin to widen, you need to exercise.)

This reminds you that debit spreads are profitable if the difference between the premiums widens or if the options are exercised. The test may ask you about which type of spread the investor wants the premiums to widen. Look for the debit spread.

credit = narrow = expire (When you become too narrow, you may expire.)

This reminds you that credit spreads are profitable if difference between the premiums narrow or the options expire. This is logical because sellers want the options they write to expire, and option premiums decline as expiration approaches. In which type of spread does the investor want premiums to narrow? Look for the credit spread.

PRACTICE QUESTION

3. An investor has established the following spread position. Long XYZ 50 call at 9 and short XYZ 60 call at 5. This investor will benefit if
   A. the options expire unexercised.
   B. the premiums widen.
   C. the premiums narrow.
   D. none of these.

   Answer: B. As we can see in the following T-chart, this is a debit spread and investors want the spread (difference) between the premiums to widen.

DR	CR
9	
	5
4	

Unit 10

Credit Call Spreads

Bearish investors use **credit call spreads** to reduce the risk of a short option position. Look at this credit call (bear) spread.

EXAMPLE

An investor establishes a call spread by going long 1 TRS Nov 55 call for 2 and short 1 TRS Nov 45 call for 9.

DR	CR
2	
	9
	7

The T-chart shows us the difference between the money "in" (CR) and the money "out" (DR) is 7 points. The investor reduced the unlimited risk of being short a naked call by also purchasing a call. As we learned earlier, a short call is covered with a long call having a lower strike price and the same or longer expiration. The long call gives the investor the right to purchase the stock at 55 if forced to sell at 45. The investor in this situation is bearish. If the stock price declines below the lower strike price of 45, both options will expire worthless and the investor keeps the net premium.

Because this is a credit spread, the investor profits when the options expire. The difference in premiums on the two options narrows as the options are about to expire. Investors always want net credit spreads to narrow.

Put Spreads

Debit put spreads are used by investors to reduce the cost of a long put position. The investo who establishes a debit put spread is bearish.

EXAMPLE

Buy 1 RST Nov 55 put for 6

Sell 1 RST Nov 50 put for 3

DR	CR
6	
	3
3	

Instead of paying $600 to buy the put, the investor's cost is reduced to $300 by also selling a put.

This is a debit spread, so the investor profits if exercise occurs. The difference in premiums on the two options widens as exercise becomes likely. Investors always want net debit spreads to widen or be exercised.

Credit Put Spreads

Bullish investors use **credit put spreads** to reduce the risk of a short put position.

EXAMPLE

Buy 1 RST Nov 55 put for 2

Sell 1 RST Nov 65 put for 9

DR	CR
2	
	9
	7

The investor reduced the substantial risk of the being short a naked put by also purchasing a put. As we learned earlier, one of the ways to cover a short put is with a long put. The long put gives the investor the right to sell stock if necessary to provide cash the investor needs to buy stock when the short put is exercised. The investor in this situation is bullish. If the stock price rises above the higher strike price of 65, both options will expire worthless and the investor keeps the net premium.

This is a credit spread, so the investor profits when the options expire. The difference in premiums on the two options narrows as the options are about to expire. Investors always want net credit spreads to narrow.

PRACTICE QUESTION

4. An investor who has entered into a debit spread will profit if
   A. the spread widens.
   B. the spread narrows.
   C. the spread remains unchanged.
   D. both contracts expire unexercised.

Answer: A. The key to a debit spread is that the investor wants the options to be exercised or for the difference in premiums to widen.

Determining a Spread Investor's Market Attitude (Bull or Bear)

The **market attitude** of a spread investor is determined by the option that is the more costly of the two—the one with the higher premium.

For **call** spreads, the option contract with the lower strike price has the higher premium. Whether the spread is a debit or credit spread will depend on if the investor purchased or sold the option with the lower strike price.

It is a *debit* if the investor purchased the one with the lower strike price (higher premium). It is a *credit* if the investor sold the one with the lower strike price (higher premium).

EXAMPLE

Long 1 July 40 call

Short 1 July 45 call

Purchasing the one with the lower strike price (higher premium) is a *debit*, and debit call spreads are *bullish*.

Long 1 Aug. 40 call

Short 1 Aug. 30 call

Selling the one with the lower strike price (higher premium) is a *credit*, and credit call spreads are *bearish*.

For *put* spreads, it is just the opposite. The option with the *higher strike price* has the *higher premium*. Whether the spread is a debit or credit spread depends on if the investor purchased or sold the option with the higher strike price.

It is a *debit* if the investor purchased the one with the higher strike price (higher premium). It is a *credit* if the investor sold the one with the higher strike price (higher premium).

EXAMPLE

Long 1 Sept. 40 put

Short 1 Sept. 30 put

Purchasing the one with the higher strike price (higher premium) is a *debit*, and debit put spreads are *bearish*.

Long 1 Dec. 20 put

Short 1 Dec. 25 put

Selling the one with the higher strike price (higher premium) is a *credit*, and credit put spreads are *bullish*.

TAKE NOTE

You might see the term *short spread* instead of bear spread. That comes from the concept that selling stock short is a bearish strategy.

TEST TOPIC ALERT

You may be asked to determine whether a spread is bullish or bearish. Using the premiums shown, use a T-chart to determine debit or credit. If no premiums are shown, it is up to you to determine which of the options is more valuable. Expect to see one or two questions on this concept.

A quick way to determine whether a spread is bullish or bearish is the following: in any spread, put or call, if you are buying the lower strike price, you are a bull. Think of it this way: "a bullish investor *buys low and sells high*." Take the first letters of the key words and you have *BLSH* (that even sounds bullish).

- Buy XYZ Jan 20 call at 7; sell XYZ Jan 30 call at 3: bull call spread—debit spread
- Buy ABC Aug 35 call; sell ABC Aug 25 call; bear call spread—credit spread (no premiums shown, but the 25 call will have a higher premium than the 35)
- Buy DEF Mar 70 put at 6; sell DEF Mar 90 put at 17; bull put spread—credit spread
- Buy LRK Sep 30 put at 9; sell LRK Sep 20 put at 3; bear put spread—debit spread

PRACTICE QUESTION

5. In which of the following cases would the investor want the spread to widen?
   I. Write 1 May 25 put; buy 1 May 30 put
   II. Write 1 Apr 45 put; buy 1 Apr 55 put
   III. Buy 1 Nov 65 put; write 1 Nov 75 put
   IV. Write 1 Jan 30 call; buy 1 Jan 40 call
   A. I and II
   B. I and IV
   C. II and III
   D. III and IV

Answer: A. Choices I and II are debit spreads. An investor wants a debit spread to widen. As the distance between the premiums increases, the investor's potential profit also increases.

LO 10.f Recognize the strategies combining puts and calls.

Introduction

Our initial venture into advanced strategies involved using puts or calls, but not both in the same transaction. Here, we are going to combine the two types of options.

Strategies Combining Puts and Calls

The exam will test on three different strategies using both puts and calls:

- Straddles
- Combinations
- Collars

Straddles

A **straddle** is composed of a call and a put with the same exercise (strike) price and expiration month. Straddles can be long or short and are used by investors to speculate on the price movement of stock.

TAKE NOTE

Like spreads, straddles can also be identified easily with the master options chart. Straddles are identified by vertical ovals rather than horizontal ovals on the chart.

Straddles Chart

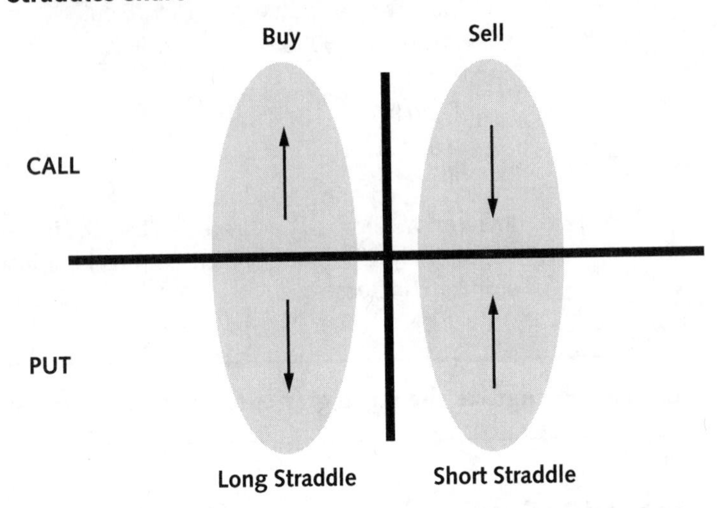

The chart also provides a tip about the strategy behind straddles. Notice the market attitude arrows pushing away from each other on the long straddle. This reminds you that the investor who buys a straddle expects a large amount of movement in the price of the stock.

The arrows on the short side are pointing toward each other. That signifies little or no market price movement. That is the objective of the seller of the straddle.

Long Straddles

An investor who uses a **long straddle** expects substantial volatility in the stock's price but is uncertain of the direction the price will move. To be ready for either occurrence, the investor purchases both a call and a put.

EXAMPLE

An investor establishes a long straddle position by going long 1 ABC JAN 50 call at 3 and going long 1 ABC JAN 50 put at 4.

The investor has created a long straddle by purchasing a call and a put with the same strike price and expiration date. With a straddle, everything about the contracts are identical except that one is a put and the other a call. If the market price of the stock rises sufficiently, the call will be profitable and the put will expire.

If the market price of the stock falls substantially instead, the put will be profitable and the call will expire. As long as the stock's price moves, regardless of the direction, this investor can make money.

Short Straddles

An investor who writes a short straddle expects that the stock's price will not change or will change very little. The investor collects two premiums for selling a straddle.

EXAMPLE

An investor establishes a short straddle position by going short 1 XYZ FEB 45 call at 4 and 1 XYZ FEB 45 put at 3.

The investor has created a short straddle by selling a call and a put with the same strike price and expiration date. Just as with the long straddle, the contract terms are identical except that one option is a put and the other a call. If the market price of the stock changes little or not at all, the call and put will expire. The investor's maximum profit is the two premiums collected.

If the market price of the stock rises or falls substantially, either the put or call will be exercised against the investor. The investor's maximum loss in this position is unlimited because of the short naked call.

Combinations

A **combination** is composed of a call and a put with different strike prices, expiration months, or both. Combinations are similar to straddles in strategy. Investors typically use combinations because they are cheaper to establish than long straddles if both options are out of the money.

EXAMPLE

An investor could establish a long combination by buying an XYZ Jan 40 call and buying an XYZ Jan 45 put. If the investor were to write both options, a short combination would result. As with straddles, the holder of a long combination makes money if the underlying stock price moves up or down far enough. The writer of a short combination makes money if the stock stays relatively stable.

PRACTICE QUESTION

6. Your customer sells a DOH Mar 35 call. To establish a straddle, he would
   A. sell a DOH Mar 40 call.
   B. buy a DOH Mar 35 put.
   C. sell a DOH Mar 35 put.
   D. buy a DOH Mar 40 call.

   Answer: C. Straddles involve options of different types, but both options must be long or both must be short. They must have the same expiration date and strike price.

Collars

A **collar** is an option strategy generally used to protect an unrealized gain on a long stock position.

EXAMPLE

An investor bought 1,000 shares of XYZ at $22 and the stock is now trading at $30. To collar the stock, the customer could write an out of the money call and buy an out of the money put. Here is what it would look like:

Long 1,000 XYZ now at $30

- Write 10 XYZ 32.50 calls
- Buy 10 XYZ 27.50 puts

With these options in place, the writer has collared the gain. If the stock were to decline sharply, the writer can always sell the shares at $27.50 by exercising the puts. If the stock were to rise sharply, the customer's calls would be exercised and he would then sell at $32.50. The investor has protected a profit (remember, the stock was purchased at 22), but has limited the upside potential.

A **cashless collar** is one where the premium received on the short call is the same amount or higher than the premium paid for the long put.

EXAMPLE

The client is long 1,000 MNO at 50.

- Short 10 MNO JAN 55 calls at 4
- Buy 10 MNO Jan 45 puts at 4

Because we have a 4-point credit and a 4-point debit, the collar is established with no out of pocket cash.

LESSON 10.5 NONEQUITY OPTIONS

LO 10.g Distinguish between the different types of nonequity options.

Introduction

Most of the exam questions will deal with equity options. There will be some on those known as *nonequity options*. In a few cases, the solutions are the same as with equity options. In others, they differ noticeably and we will point those out. The three types of nonequity options likely to be tested are

- index,
- interest rate, and
- foreign currency.

Index Options

Options on indexes allow investors to profit from the movements of markets or market segments and hedge against these market swings. They may be based on broad-based, narrow-based, or other indexes with a particular focus.

Broad-based indexes reflect movement of the entire market and include the S&P 100 (OEX), S&P 500, and the Major Market Index.

Narrow-based indexes track the movement of market segments in a specific industry, such as technology or pharmaceuticals.

The Volatility Market Index (VIX)

Some indexes have a very particular focus, such as the Volatility Market Index (VIX). This index is a measure of the implied volatility of the S&P 500 Index options traded on the CBOE. VIX options, also traded on the CBOE, are designed to reflect investor expectations of market volatility over the next 30 days. It is often referred to as the *fear gauge* or *index*. High readings are not bullish, nor are they bearish, but instead are a measure of the expectation (fear) that the market will be volatile. The expectation of greater volatility generally translates into higher premiums for options contracts.

The VIX rises when put option buying increases and falls when more calls than puts are being bought. Put buying is bearish, so when the "bears" are more active, market participants get scared. On the other hand, call buying is bullish, so when the "bulls" are in command, anxiety levels decrease.

Therefore, one could say that a higher VIX is a contrarian signal.

PRACTICE QUESTION

7. A VIX option contract is based on the expected movements of
   A. the Dow Jones Industrial Average index (DJIA).
   B. the Standard & Poor's 500 index (SPX).
   C. the Standard & Poor's 100 index (OEX).
   D. the Dow Jones Utility index (DJU).

Answer: B. A VIX option contract, often referred to as the fear index, is based on the expected movements of the Standard & Poor's 500 index (SPX).

Index Option Features

Index options share many features with equity options. Let's look at those along with a few that are unique.

Premium Multiplier

Index options typically use a multiplier of $100. The premium amount is multiplied by $100 to calculate the option's cost, and the strike price is multiplied by $100 to determine the total dollar value of the index. This is essentially the same as multiplying an equity option contract by 100 shares.

EXAMPLE

Index	Index Premium	Index Multiplier		Cash Value of Premium
S&P 100 (OEX)	16.50	× 100	=	$1,650
S&P 500 (SPX)	8.05	× 100	=	$805

Trading

Purchases and sales of index options—like equity options—settle on the next business day. Index options stop trading at 4:15 pm ET if they are broad-based. Narrow-based index options stop trading at 4:00 pm ET.

Exercise

Unlike an equity option, the exercise of an index option settles in cash rather than in delivery of a security. Furthermore, settlement, if the option is exercised, requires the cash to be delivered on the next business day, (T+1). If the option is exercised, the writer of the option delivers cash equal to the intrinsic value of the option to the buyer. If an index option is in the money by 5 points, the owner of a put can exercise and receive $500 from the assigned seller.

PRACTICE QUESTION

8. When an investor exercises an OEX option, she receives
   A. common stock.
   B. cash equal to the strike price.
   C. cash equal to the intrinsic value.
   D. nothing, because index options cannot be exercised.

Answer: C. Exercise settlement on index options is in cash, not stock. When the owner of an option exercises, the person who has a short position must deliver cash equal to the intrinsic value (the in the money amount). This is computed on the basis of the closing value of the index on the day the option is exercised.

Settlement Price

When index options are exercised, their settlement price is based on the closing value of the index on the day of exercise, not the value at the time of exercise during the trading day.

Expiration Dates

Index options expire on the third Friday of the expiration month.

TEST TOPIC ALERT

With regard to settlement, there is one major difference between index options and equity options. The exercise of an index option settles the next business day, whereas the exercise of an equity option settles the regular way (two business days). With regard to trading (i.e., buying or selling), settlement is the next business day for both.

EXAMPLE

A customer buys 1 OEX Jan 460 call at 3.20 when the OEX index is trading at 461.

What is the premium?	$320 (3.20 × $100)
What is the intrinsic value?	$100 (461 – 460)
What is the time value?	$220 ($320 – $100)

One month later, with the index at 472 and the Jan 460 call trading at 13.70, the customer elects to exercise.

How much cash will the customer receive from the writer?	$1,200, the intrinsic value of the option (472 – 460)
How much profit did the customer make?	$880, which is the cash received from the writer less the premium paid ($1,200 – $320)

Now, instead of exercising, assume the customer closes the position.

How much profit would the customer make?	$1,050, which is the difference between the premium received on selling ($1,370) and the premium paid to open the position ($320)

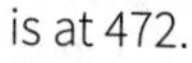

Note that instead of making $880 by exercising, the customer would have made $1,050 by closing the position. Why the $170 difference? As long as there is time value in the option, the customer will always make more by closing an index option, (or any other option), rather than by exercising. The time value of the 460 call trading at 13.70 is $170 when the index is at 472.

PRACTICE QUESTION

9. An investor writes an OEX Oct 900 put at 5 when the OEX is at 902. If the OEX then closes at 890 and the put is exercised, how much cash must the writer pay to the holder of the put?
   A. $10
   B. $100
   C. $1,000
   D. $0; option is out of the money

Answer: C. The put writer pays the holder 10 points worth of cash ($1,000) because the put is in the money by 10 points.

Index Options Strategy

Index options may be used to speculate on movement of the market overall. If an investor believes the market will rise, she can purchase index calls or write index puts. If an investor believes the market will fall, she can purchase index puts or write index calls.

Hedging a portfolio is an important use of index options. If a portfolio manager holds a diverse portfolio of equity, he can buy puts on the index to offset loss if the market value of the stocks fall. This use of index puts is known as **portfolio insurance**. Index options protect against the risk of a decline in the overall market. That risk is known as **systematic risk** and will be covered in Unit 13.

EXAMPLE

A customer has a broad-based stock portfolio worth $920,000 and is concerned about a possible market downturn. To hedge, the customer could buy broad-based index puts (e.g., the OEX). If the market does turn downward, the loss on the portfolio would be offset by a gain on the puts. Remember, a put increases in value as the underlying security or portfolio goes down in value. If the OEX is trading at 460, each contract has a value of $46,000 (460 × $100). Therefore, to hedge a $920,000 stock portfolio, the customer would buy 20 OEX 460 puts (20 × $46,000 = $920,000).

TAKE NOTE

Weekly index options contracts provide an efficient way to trade options around certain news or events, such as economic data or earnings announcements. New options series are listed on Thursday and expire the Friday of the following week. Other than the expiration date and time to expiry, weeklies have the same contract specifications as standard options.

Portfolio managers may also choose to write index options to generate income.

PRACTICE QUESTION

10. Your client owns a portfolio of blue-chip stocks. She tells you she believes the securities will provide good, long-term appreciation but also believes that the market will decline over the short-term. Which index options strategy should you recommend that will protect against the expected decline and still allow for long-term capital appreciation?
    A. Buy puts
    B. Buy calls
    C. Sell covered puts
    D. Sell covered calls

    Answer: A. Because your client is long stock, her position would be hurt by a drop in the market. To hedge against that risk, she must take an option position that appreciates in value as the market declines—long puts or short calls. Because your client also wishes to benefit from any appreciation, the long put is the better hedging vehicle. If the market averages increase, the put position will lose only the premium, and your client could still gain on the portfolio.

Interest Rate (Yield-Based) Options

Interest rate options are yield-based (i.e., they have a direct relationship to movements in interest rates). These options are based on yields of T-bills, T-notes, and T-bonds. A yield-based option with a strike price of 35 reflects a yield of 3.5%. Assume an investor believes that rates on T-notes—currently at 3.5%—will rise in the near term. The investor could purchase a call option with a 35 strike price (at the money). If rates rise to 4.5%, the investor could exercise and receive cash equal to the intrinsic value of the option.

Rates have gone up by 10 points—35 to 45—so the investor would receive $1,000 because each point is worth $100. Profit would be the $1,000 received on exercise less the premium paid. On the other hand, the investor could have closed her position, profiting from the difference between the premium paid and the premium received on closing.

The strategy is straightforward. It is the Call UP/Put DOWN logic, only applied to interest rates rather than prices. If a portfolio manager believes rates will fall, the manager will buy puts or write calls. If the manager believes rates will rise, buying calls and writing puts would be appropriate.

TEST TOPIC ALERT

We don't expect many questions on this topic. What can be confusing is it is the opposite of what you learned earlier (and will be tested heavily on) regarding bond prices and interest rates. Back in Lesson 4.1, we studied how bond prices fell as interest rates rose. Here, when interest rates rise, the value of a call option also goes up. The key is that yield-based options allow the investor to "bet" on the movement of interest rates, not prices.

General Characteristics of Yield-based Options

Yield-based options have a few characteristics in common with index options, such as

- a contract size multiplier of $100 and
- settlement is the next business day in cash rather than in delivery of the underlying security.

EXAMPLE

An investor who believes interest rates are rising buys a yield-based call with a strike price of 65. Interest rates rise to 7.5%, and the investor receives, in cash, the difference between the strike price of 65 and the exercise settlement value of 75, times the multiplier of $100. Ten points × $100 = $1,000.

An investor who is bearish on interest rates buys a yield-based put with a strike price of 75 for a premium of 3.5. Interest rates decline to 6.5%, and the investor receives, in cash, the difference between the strike price of 75 and the exercise settlement value of 65 (10 × $100 = $1,000).

To calculate the investor's profit, find the difference between the strike price and the exercise settlement value, and subtract the premium paid. The strike price is 75 and the exercise settlement value is 65, for a difference of 10. Multiply by $100 to find the amount received at settlement ($1,000), and subtract the premium paid ($350) to find the put buyer's profit—$650.

PRACTICE QUESTION

11. When exercised, yield-based options settle on
    A. the exercise date plus three business days with the delivery of the underlying debt securities required.
    B. the exercise date plus three business days with the delivery of cash required.
    C. the exercise date plus one business day with the delivery of the underlying debt securities required.
    D. the exercise date plus one business day with the delivery of cash required.

Answer: D. When exercised, yield-based debt options settle on the next business day in cash.

Foreign Currency Options (FCOs)

Currency options allow investors to speculate on the performance of currencies other than the U.S. dollar or to protect against fluctuating currency exchange rates against the U.S. dollar. Currency options are available for trading on U.S.-listed exchanges on the Australian dollar,

British pound, Canadian dollar, Swiss francs, Japanese yen, and Euro. Importers and exporters frequently use currency options to hedge currency risk.

Features of FCOs

When purchased, sold or exercised foreign currency options contracts are cash settled in U.S. dollars with no physical delivery of foreign currency.

Contract Sizes

Currency options contract sizes are small enough to accommodate retail investors. A British pound contract, for instance, covers 10,000 pounds. Each currency has its own contract size as follows:

Figure 10.7: Foreign Currency Contracts

Currency		Options Contract Size
Australian $	(XDA)	10,000
British £	(XDB)	10,000
Canadian $	(XDC)	10,000
Euro €	(XDE)	10,000
New Zealand $	(XDZ)	10,000
Swiss Fr	(XDS)	10,000
Japanese ¥	(XDN)	1 million

TEST TOPIC ALERT

You should know that the only FCO with a contract size other than 10,000 units is the Japanese yen.

PRACTICE QUESTION

12. Which of the following currency options is **not** traded on United States options exchanges?
    A. British pound
    B. Japanese yen
    C. Canadian dollar
    D. U.S. dollar

Answer: D. These are called *foreign currency options* (FCOs) because they are only available in the U.S. on foreign currencies.

Strike Prices

Strike prices of most FCOs are quoted in U.S. cents. The Japanese yen is an exception and is quoted in 1/100th of a cent.

EXAMPLE

Strike price of 85 = 85 U.S. cents ($0.85), except for Japanese yen, where a strike price denoted as 121 = 1.21 U.S. cents (121 × 1/100).

Premiums

Currency options are quoted in cents per unit. Just as with equity options, one point of premium = $100. The total premium of the contract is found by multiplying the premium by the number of units. If a Swiss franc contract (10,000 units) is quoted with a premium of 1.5, the cost of the contract is 10,000 × $0.015, or $150.

PRACTICE QUESTION

13. An investor purchases 2 Dec .56 Swiss franc calls at 2.5. One Swiss franc contract includes 10,000 units. How much does he pay for the position?
    A. $250
    B. $500
    C. $5,000
    D. $25,000

Answer: B. Swiss francs options are quoted in cents per unit. One call at 2.5 cents multiplied by 10,000 units (0.025 × 10,000) equals $250. Because the investor has purchased 2 contracts, the total premium is $500.

Trading

Listed currency options are primarily traded on the Nasdaq OMX PHLX (formerly the Philadelphia Stock Exchange). Trading hours are 9:30 am – 4:00 pm ET.

Expiration Date

Currency options expire on the third Friday of the expiration month just as equity options do.

Settlement

Currency options settle, like equity options, on the next business day. When a foreign currency option is exercised, settlement occurs on the next business day as well. Delivery is made in U.S. dollars.

Strategies

If an investor believes the value of a currency is going to rise, she will buy calls or sell puts on the currency. If an investor expects the value of a currency to fall, she will buy puts or sell calls on the currency. Currency options are measured relative to the U.S. dollar, and an inverse relationship exists between their exchange rates. Therefore, if the U.S. dollar is rising relative to other currencies, then those currencies are falling. Conversely, if the U.S. dollar is falling against other currencies, then those currencies are rising.

EXAMPLE

A U.S. importer must pay for Swiss chocolates in Swiss francs within three months. The importer is fearful that the value of the dollar will fall. Using FCOs, what should this investor do?

If the importer believes the U.S. dollar will fall, then foreign currency values will rise. The investor should buy calls on the Swiss franc to lock in the purchase price for the francs needed in three months.

TAKE NOTE

As a rule, importers buy calls on the foreign currency to hedge; exporters buy puts to hedge. We call that the EPIC rule, (*exporters* buy *puts; importers* buy *calls*).However, keep in mind that there are no options available on the U.S. dollar. As an example, consider a Japanese company that exports stereos to the United States. The company will be paid in dollars upon delivery. The risk to the Japanese company is that the dollar will decline between now and the delivery, which means $1 will be worth fewer yen. How should this company hedge this risk?

The rule of thumb is that exporters should buy puts on the foreign currency. However, because there are no options on the U.S. dollar, the Japanese company should buy calls on its own currency, the yen. In other words, EPIC works in reverse if the question is dealing with a foreign company. Then it is IPEC.

PRACTICE QUESTION

14. A British company is exporting sweaters to the United States. How should the company hedge its foreign exchange risk?
    A. Buy BP calls
    B. Sell BP calls
    C. Buy BP puts
    D. Sell BP puts

    Answer: A. Because options on the U.S. dollar are not available, exporters to the United States should buy calls on their own currency. Had this been a U.S. company exporting to England, it would buy BP puts.

15. All of the following statements are true regarding listed options trading on U.S. exchanges **except**
    A. foreign currency options (FCO) settle in their respective foreign currency.
    B. index options settle in U.S. dollars.
    C. equity options settle in U.S. dollars.
    D. yield-based (debt) options settle in U.S. dollars.

    Answer: A. All options trading on U.S. exchanges, including FCOs, settle in U.S. dollars.

LESSON 10.6: OPTIONS MATH

LO 10.h Calculate profit/loss and breakeven for the various strategies.

Introduction

The exam will have a number of questions dealing with options calculations. Those will deal with maximum gain, maximum loss, and breakeven points. They take a bit of practice, but once you have the concept down, they are quite simple.

Options contracts may have various characteristics that are unique to the options marketplace Some terms used to describe options contracts—such as *in the money, at the money, out of the money, intrinsic value,* and *breakeven*—have meanings that are specific to options trading. In case you don't remember our coverage of *in, at,* and *out of the money*, you might want to go back to Lesson 10.2 and review.

Breakeven

The **breakeven point** is the point at which the investor neither makes nor loses money. It is expressed in terms of a price of the underlying asset.

Breakeven—Call Options

In the case of calls, the *breakeven* is the strike price plus the premium (Call UP). For the call buyer, the contract is profitable above the breakeven. For the call seller, the contract is profitable below the breakeven.

TAKE NOTE

An option that is in the money is not necessarily at breakeven. Options that are in the money are not always profitable.

TAKE NOTE

These concepts are applicable whether the contract is long or short. The words *Call UP* will help you remember the call concept. A call has intrinsic value (or is in the money) when the market price of the underlying asset is *up* above the strike price of the option, whether it is long or short. Also, the call breakeven is up above the option's strike price (strike price + premium).

Breakeven—Put Options

In the case of puts, the *breakeven* is the strike price of the option minus the premium (Put DOWN). For the put buyer, the contract is profitable below the breakeven. For the put seller, the contract is profitable above the breakeven.

TAKE NOTE

These concepts are applicable whether the contract is long or short. The words *Put DOWN* will help you remember put definitions. A put has intrinsic value (or is in the money) when the market price of the underlying security is down below the strike price, regardless whether a position is long or short. Also, the put breakeven is down below the strike price (strike price – premium).

EXAMPLE

Put definitions are the opposite of what they are for calls. Options are a game of opposites. Calls are opposites of puts, and buyers are opposites of sellers.

The following table summarizes the basic definitions for calls and puts.

CMV = Current Market Value SP = Strike Price

Calls		Puts
CMV > SP	In the Money	CMV < SP
CMV = SP	At the Money	CMV = SP
CMV < SP	Out of the Money	CMV > SP
CALL UP	Intrinsic Value	PUT DOWN
SP + Premium	Breakeven	SP – Premium

Summary of Basic Concepts

The following chart will help you remember the basics of options.

Figure 10.8: Basic Options Chart

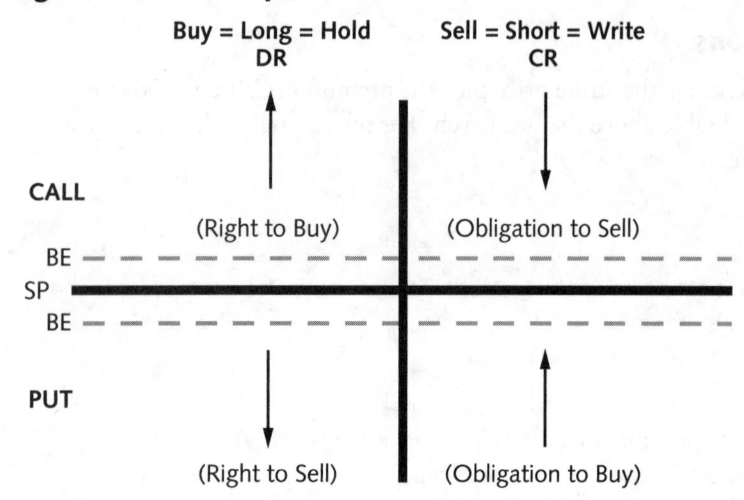

Each quadrant represents one of the four basic options positions.

- Buyers are on the left side; sellers are on the right side.
- The arrow identifies the market attitude—up arrows represent bullish investors; down arrows represent bearish investors.
- Information in parentheses identifies what occurs at exercise of the option.
- The solid horizontal line represents the strike price.
- Dashed horizontal lines represent the breakeven points.
  - For calls, the breakeven is strike price + premium, long or short.
  - For puts, the breakeven is strike price – premium, long or short.
- Calls are above the horizontal line because they are in the money when the market price is above the strike price, long or short (call up).
- Puts are below the horizontal line because they are in the money when the market price is below the strike price, long or short (put down).

Breakeven—Spreads

Finding the breakeven point on a spread uses the same Call UP and Put DOWN formula. With 2 calls or 2 puts, the trick is knowing which strike price to use. In the case of a call spread, the net credit or debit is always added to the lower strike price. In the case of a put spread, you always subtract the net credit or debit from the higher strike price. As you do questions, you will notice that the breakeven point is always a number between the two strike prices.

EXAMPLE

An investor establishes a call spread by going long 1 RST NOV 55 Call at a premium of 6 and short 1 RST NOV 60 call at a premium of 3 (this should look familiar—we set it up a couple of lessons ago). What is the breakeven point?

DR	CR
6	
	3
3	

As you can see, there is a net debit of 3 points. The breakeven on a call spread is always found by adding the debit (or credit) to the lower strike price. In this case, the lower strike is 55. We add the 3 point debit to 55 and the breakeven point is 58. We know for sure that we don't add to the 60 because that would give us a breakeven of 60. On a spread, the breakeven point is always between the strike prices—in this case between 55 and 60.

Let us try another one.

An investor establishes a call spread by going long 1 RST NOV 55 Call at a premium of 3 and short 1 RST NOV 50 call at a premium of 7.

If we use the T-chart, we see that 3 points goes out (a debit) and 7 points comes in (a credit). That gives us a net credit of 4 points. This is a credit call spread. The breakeven is determined by adding the net credit to the lower strike price. That would be 50 + 4 giving the investor a breakeven point of 54. Once again, you notice this is between strike prices of 50 and 55.

How about a couple of put spreads?

EXAMPLE

An investor establishes a put spread by going long 1 RST NOV 55 put at a premium of 6 and short 1 RST NOV 50 put at a premium of 3.

DR	CR
6	
	3
3	

Note that we purchased the put with the higher strike price (the more you can put the stock for, the higher the premium) and that made this a debit spread. On a put spread, the breakeven follows the Put DOWN rule. We take the net debit (or credit) and subtract it from the higher strike price. In this case, we subtract the 3 point net debit from the strike of 55 and have a breakeven point of $52. As a debit put spread, this is a bearish strategy and the investor profits when the price goes below breakeven.

EXAMPLE

An investor establishes a put spread by going long 1 QED DEC 55 put at a premium of 2 and short 1 QED DEC 65 put at a premium of 9.

DR	CR
2	
	9
	7

By selling the more valuable option, (the one with the higher strike price), the investor created a credit spread. As we see, the net credit is 7 points. The breakeven for this bullish spread follows the Put DOWN method and is 65 – 7, or 58. As is always the case with spreads, the breakeven point is somewhere in between the two strike prices.

Breakeven—Straddles and Combinations

This looks a bit different, but is really the same: Call UP and Put DOWN. There are two breakeven points because there are two options. The breakeven for the call is the strike price plus both premiums paid. The breakeven for the put is the strike price minus both premiums paid. A couple of examples should help make this clear. Remember, when you are long a straddle, you want the stock's price to move up or down. It has to move enough to get past th breakeven in order for the investor to make money.

EXAMPLE

An investor establishes a long straddle by going long 1 ABC JAN 50 call at a premium of 3 and long 1 ABC JAN 50 put at a premium of 4.

Because the investor has purchased both options, there is an investment cost of 7 points. The breakevens are the call strike plus the 7 points and the put strike minus the 7 points. That gives us 57 and 43. The stock's price will have to go above 57 or below 43 for this investor to profit. Of course, if it stays within that range, the selling is the winner.

We will visit few more of these as we move on to maximum gain and loss computations.

Breakeven—Index Options

Breakeven follows the Call UP and Put DOWN rule, but it helps to see an example.

EXAMPLE

A customer buys 1 OEX Jan 460 call at 3.20 when the OEX index is trading at 461.

What is the premium?	$320 (3.20 × $100)
What is the breakeven point?	463.20 (strike price + premium)
What is the intrinsic value?	$100 (461 – 460)
What is the time value?	$220 ($320 – $100)

One month later, with the index at 472 and the Jan 460 call trading at 13.70, the customer elects to exercise.

How much cash will the customer receive from the writer?	$1,200, the intrinsic value of the option (472 – 460)
How much profit did the customer make?	$880, which is the cash received from the writer less the premium paid ($1,200 – $320)

Instead of exercising, assume the customer closes the position.

How much profit would the customer make?	$1,050, which is the difference between the premium received on selling ($1,370) and the premium paid to open the position ($320)

Note that instead of making $880 by exercising, the customer would have made $1,050 by closing the position. Why the $170 difference? As long as there is time value in the option, the customer will always make more by closing an index option rather than by exercising. The time value of the 460 call trading at 13.70 is $170 when the index is at 472.

Maximum Gains and Losses

Investors who open an option position should understand the following three scenarios: the maximum amount they can gain, the maximum amount they can lose, and the point at which the investment will break even. We have already discussed breakeven so we will move ahead to gains and losses.

Long Calls

Maximum gain

As stock prices rise above the breakeven point, the potential gain on a call option generally increases point for point with the stock's value. Theoretically, the potential gains available to call owners are unlimited because a rise in stock price is unlimited.

Maximum loss

On a long call, investors risk losing 100% of the premium paid, which happens when the stock's market price is at or below the option's exercise price at expiration, making the option worthless. Just as with any security, when you buy something, the most you can lose is what you pay for it.

Short Calls

Maximum gain

Bearish call writers anticipate that the stock's price will drop. If it drops below the exercise price by the expiration date, the call will be worthless to the buyer and will expire unexercised. The writer then keeps the entire premium, with no further risk exposure. No matter how low the stock price falls (even if it drops to zero), the writer's gain is limited to the amount of the premium originally received.

Maximum loss

The greatest risk assumed by call writers is that a call they wrote will be assigned and they will have to deliver stock they do not own. If the option is uncovered (naked), the potential loss is unlimited. If a naked call writer has to go out into the open market to buy the stock, he may end up paying a price much higher than the option's exercise price. As the stock price rises, so does the call seller's potential loss. If he decides to enter a closing purchase, he can stop his losses from increasing. Otherwise, there is no theoretical limit on his potential loss. If the call is covered, the loss is limited based on the writer's cost of the underlying stock and the premium received.

PRACTICE QUESTION

16. An investor buys 100 shares of CDL stock at $50. Two months later, with CDL selling for $48, the investor writes a CDL APR 45 call for a premium of $4. If the option is exercised, the investor's maximum potential loss is
    A. zero.
    B. $100.
    C. $400.
    D. unlimited.

    Answer: B. The investor paid $5,000 for the stock and received a premium of $4. That means the net cost of the position is $4,600. Regardless of how high the price of CDL goes, when assigned an exercise notice, the investor will deliver the stock currently owned and receive the strike price of 45, or $4,500. That results in a loss of $100.

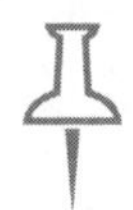

TAKE NOTE

While breakeven is the same number for both call buyers and sellers (strike price + premium), consider that call buyers (bullish) want to see the underlying stock above the breakeven to be profitable, while call sellers (bearish) want to see the stock below the breakeven to be profitable.

Call Summary

Position	Maximum Gain	Maximum Loss	Breakeven
Long call	Unlimited	Premium	Strike price + premium
Short call	Premium	Unlimited	Strike price + premium

PRACTICE QUESTION

17. An investor selling 1 KLP Dec 45 call at 3 has a maximum potential gain of
    A. $300.
    B. $4,200.
    C. $4,800.
    D. unlimited.

    Answer: A. The maximum gain on a short call is equal to the premium received by the seller. One contract represents 100 shares, and the seller received a $3 per share premium. 100 × $3 = $300.

Long Puts

Maximum gain

The typical put buyer is bearish, and the maximum gain will occur when the price of the underlying stock reaches the lowest possible market price, which is zero. If an investor could buy the stock for no money, she could sell it at the strike price by exercising the option. This gain would be reduced by the premium paid in the opening transaction.

Maximum loss

A put buyer's maximum potential loss is the premium he paid. On all long options, the investor pays (and risks) the premium. The worst that can happen to a put buyer is that his option expires before it is worth exercising, which can occur at any market price at or above the strike price.

Short Puts

Maximum gain

The writer of a put receives a premium in the opening transaction. His greatest potential gain is the premium. When the stock price is at or above the exercise price, the put has no intrinsic value and will not be exercised by the holder. If the stock price stays at or above the exercise price, the put will expire worthless and the writer will keep the premium.

Maximum loss

A put seller's maximum potential loss occurs if the stock price drops to zero. In this case, the put owner will exercise the option. The put seller will have to take delivery of the stock, and because it has no market value, she is out the exercise price minus the premium received in the opening transaction.

TAKE NOTE

While breakeven is the same number for both put buyers and sellers (strike price – premium), consider that put buyers (bearish) want to see the underlying stock below the breakeven to be profitable, while put sellers (bullish) want to see the stock above the breakeven to be profitable.

Put Summary

Position	Maximum Gain	Maximum Loss	Breakeven
Long put	Strike price – premium	Premium	Strike price – premium
Short put	Premium	Strike price – premium	Strike price – premium

PRACTICE QUESTION

18. If an investor buys 1 ALF Jan 50 put at 2, the maximum potential gain is
    A. $200.
    B. $4,800.
    C. $5,200.
    D. unlimited.

    Answer: B. The maximum gain on a long put is calculated by subtracting the premium paid from the strike price. Subtract the premium of 2 from the strike price of 50 and multiply by the number of shares to determine the maximum potential gain. Because a contract represents 100 shares, the buyer's maximum gain is $4,800.

Spreads

Calculating the maximum gain, loss, and breakeven on spreads will appear on several questions on the exam. We will begin by reviewing a few key points:

- If it is a debit spread, the investor wants the difference between the premiums to widen. If they widen enough, the options will be exercised and the investor will profit.
- If it is a credit spread, the investor wants the difference between the premiums to narrow. If they narrow to zero, the options will expire and the investor will profit.
- The breakeven point is always somewhere between the two strike prices.
- When the underlying asset's price moves beyond the breakeven point, the investor begins to profit.

- In finding breakeven points on spreads, remember CAL and PSH:
  - For **C**all spreads: **A**dd the net premium to the **L**ower SP.
  - For **P**ut spreads: **S**ubtract the net premium from the **Hi**gher SP.

Debit Call Spreads

Maximum gain

An investor establishing a debit call spread is bullish. That is because the option purchased has the low strike and the one sold has the high strike. Buy low and sell high (BLSH) is a bullish strategy. If the market price of the underlying asset reaches or goes above the higher strike price, the investor's gain is maximized. Here is an example of what this means.

EXAMPLE

An investor establishes a debit call spread by going long 1 RST NOV 55 for a premium of 6 and short 1 RST NOV 60 call for a premium of 3.

DR	CR
6	
	3
3	

We see in our T-chart that the debit is 3 points. What happens if the stock price goes to $60? The long 55 call is 5 points in the money. It can either be exercised at 55 and the stock sold at 60 or sold for its intrinsic value. In either case, there is a profit of $5 per share. The short 60 call expires [there is no point in calling (exercising) stock at 60 when the market price is 60.]

If we were to enter this on the T-chart, we would see a credit of 5. That would make the total credits 8 and that means the spreader made a 2 point gain.

Using this example, what if the stock's price goes to 70? After all, this investor is bullish and the higher the better, right? Not really so for a spread position. At 70, the long 55 call is 15 points in the money and, at expiration, could be sold for that amount. But, the 60 call the investor is short is 10 points in the money and will surely be exercised. The spreader uses the stock purchased at 55 to deliver against the exercise of the short call and receives 60.

That spread, the difference between the two exercise prices, never changes. Regardless of how high the price of the underlying stock goes, there is always that 5 point difference and that limits the investor's gain to the difference between the debit paid and the strike price spread. In this example, with a debit of 3 and a price spread of 5 points, the most this investor can ever make is 2 points, (5 – 3).

Maximum loss

The maximum loss in any debit spread is the debit. In our example, the spread was established at a cost of 3. If the stock's price falls, the most this investor can lose is the 3 points paid. Both options expire worthless.

PRACTICE QUESTION

19. An investor establishes a spread position by going long 1 LMN OCT call at 8 and short 1 LMN OCT 90 call at 2.75. What is the maximum gain and the maximum loss?
    I. Maximum gain, $475
    II. Maximum gain, $525
    III. Maximum loss, $475
    IV. Maximum loss, $525
    A. I and III
    B. I and IV
    C. II and III
    D. II and IV

    Answer: B. The first step is to compute the debit (or credit). In this case, the long option cost 8 while the short option brought in 2.75. That is a 5.25 debit. The maximum gain is $475. The maximum gain on a debit spread is the difference between the strike prices minus the net debit: 10 – 5.25 = 4.75; 4.75 × 100 shares = $475. The maximum loss is $525. The maximum loss on a debit spread is the net debit. Notice that the maximum gain and maximum loss always add up to the spread.

Debit Put Spreads

A bearish investor who establishes a debit put spread buys the put with the higher strike price and sells the put with the lower strike price. A put with a higher strike price will be worth more to investors (and will have a higher premium) than a put with a lower strike price, so more money will be flowing out of the account (for the put purchased) than will be flowing into the account (from the put sold).

A bearish investor buys a put or put spread expecting that the price of the underlying stock will fall. If it does, he can exercise the long put of the spread (the one with the higher strike price) and sell stock above the current market price. If the short put (the one with the lower strike price) is exercised, he will have to buy the stock, but by having exercised the option he owns, he keeps the difference between the strike prices less the net debit. As with single option strategies, the investor can close out his option positions and keep the profits (or take the losses) rather than exercise.

Maximum gain

Debit put spreaders will realize their maximum gain any time the stock's market price is at or below the strike price of the lower option. At that point, they will have to buy stock at the low strike price, but they can sell the stock at the higher strike price and keep the difference between the two prices, minus the net premium (net debit).

Maximum loss

If the stock's price rises to or above the strike price of the higher option, both puts will expire worthless. No investor will exercise a put when the stock can be sold in the market for more than the strike price of the option. At any price above the higher strike price, the investor will sustain the maximum loss because both puts will expire worthless. The general rule is that the maximum loss on a debit spread is the net premium (net debit). The maximum gain is the difference in strike prices less the net debit (maximum loss).

EXAMPLE

An investor establishes a spread by going long 1 AAJ NOV 90 put at 7 and short 1 AAJ NOV 80 put at 2.

DR	CR
7	
	2
5	

The maximum gain is $500, which will occur if the stock is at 80 or below. In this instance, both contracts will be exercised. The investor will be forced to buy at 80 but holds the right to sell at 90 for a $1,000 gain. The gain on the stock is reduced by the net premium paid of $500. Therefore, maximum potential gain is $500. The maximum loss is $500, which will occur if, at expiration, the stock is at 90 or above. In this instance, both contracts will expire worthless and the investor will lose the net debit of $500.

Breakeven occurs at 85 (90 – 5). At this price, the investor will exercise the 90 put for a $500 gain (which offsets the net debit exactly). Below 85, the customer makes money, up to a maximum of $500. Above 85, the customer loses money, up to a maximum of $500.

Credit Call Spreads

Bearish investors establish credit call spreads. To do so, they buy the call with the higher strike price and sell the call with the lower strike price. The call with a higher strike price will have a lower premium than the call with a lower strike price, so the investor will be paying out less money for the purchase than she is taking in from the sale. When more money flows into an account than out, there is a net credit.

Bearish investors sell calls and call spreads because they expect the underlying stock's price to go down. If it does, both options will expire worthless and the investor may keep the net premium (the net credit).

If the investor is wrong and the stock goes up, the long option can be exercised to buy the stock, which then must be delivered against the short option. The investor will lose the difference between the two strike prices, less the net credit. The investor can close out the positions and keep the profits (or take the losses) rather than exercise.

Maximum gain

The maximum gain on a credit call spread, as with any position established for a credit, is the net premium, (the net credit). The maximum gain will occur when the stock price is at or below the lower strike price.

Maximum loss

The maximum loss on a credit call spread is the difference between strike prices less the net premium. This occurs when the stock's price is at or above the higher strike price.

Breakeven

The breakeven point is the lower strike price plus the net premium.

EXAMPLE

An investor establishes a spread position by going long 1 AAJ AUG 65 call for a premium of 1 and short 1 AAJ AUG 60 call for a premium of 3.

DR	CR
1	
	3
	2

On a credit spread, the maximum gain is always the net credit. In this example, the maximum gain is $200. This will occur if the stock is at 60 or below. In this instance, both contracts will expire worthless and the investor will keep the net credit.

The maximum loss is $300, which will occur if the stock is at 65 or above. In this instance, both contracts will be exercised. The investor will buy at 65 and be forced to sell at 60 for a $500 loss. The loss is offset by the $200 credit received, which results in an overall loss of $300 (the difference in strike prices less the net credit).

Breakeven occurs at 62 (60 + 2). At 62, the customer will be exercised on the 60 call and be forced to sell, at 60, stock that cost him 62, resulting in a $200 loss on the stock. This amount is offset exactly by the $200 net credit received. Above 62, the customer loses money, up to a maximum of $300. Below 62, the customer makes money, up to a maximum of $200.

Credit Put Spreads

Bullish investors establish credit put spreads. They buy the put with the lower strike price and sell the put with the higher strike price. The put with the lower strike price will have a lower premium than the put with the higher strike price, so the investor will be spending less money on the option with the low strike price than he is taking in on the sale of the option with the higher strike price.

Bullish investors sell puts and put spreads expecting the stock's price to go up. If it does, both options will expire worthless and the investor will keep the net premium.

If the investor is wrong and the stock price goes down below the lower strike price, the investor will have to buy the stock at the high strike price but can then exercise the other put with the lower price to sell the stock. The investor will lose the difference between the strike prices, less the net credit. The investor can close out the positions and keep the profits (or take the losses) rather than exercise.

Maximum gain

The maximum gain on a credit put spread is the net premium (net credit), which occurs when the stock price is at or above the higher strike price.

Maximum loss

The maximum loss on a credit put spread is the difference between strike prices minus the net premium, which occurs when the stock's market price is at or below the lower strike price.

Breakeven

The breakeven point on a put spread is the higher strike price minus the net premium.

EXAMPLE

An investor establishes a spread by going long 1 XYZ MAR 30 put for a premium of 2 and short 1 XYZ MAR 40 put at 9.

DR	CR
2	
	9
	7

The maximum gain is $700, which will occur if, at expiration, the stock is at 40 or above. In this instance, both contracts will expire worthless and the customer will keep the net premium (net credit) of $700.

The maximum loss is $300, which will occur if, at expiration, the stock is at 30 or below. In this instance, both contracts will be exercised; the customer will buy at 40 and exercise his right to sell at 30. The $1,000 loss on the stock is offset by the $700 credit received, which results in an overall loss of $300.

Breakeven occurs at 33 (40 – 7). At 33, the customer will be assigned and forced to buy stock at 40 that is worth 33. This $700 loss is offset exactly by the net credit received. Above 33, the customer begins to profit, up to a maximum of $700. Below 33, the customer begins to lose, up to a maximum of $300.

Closing Positions—Gains and Losses

Remember, with spreads, it is the premiums of the two options that changes, not the strike prices. All of our examples thus far have assumed gain or loss at expiration date. At that point, at least for exam purposes, all options are only worth intrinsic value; there is no time value.

Instead of waiting until expiration, investors can close out their spread positions at any time. That is, they sell their long position (closing sale) and buy back the short position (closing purchase). A debit spread is profitable if it can be closed out at a greater credit than the initial debit. That is, the spread between the sale price of the long and the purchase price covering the short must be greater (wider) than the initial debit. That is why we say that investors with debit spreads want the spread between premiums to widen.

A credit spread will be profitable when the difference to close out the short position (closing purchase) and the long position (closing sale) is a smaller debit than the initial credit when the position was opened. That is why investors with credit spreads want the spread to narrow. These sound a bit confusing at first, but a few examples here (and questions in the q-bank) will help you get on the right path.

EXAMPLE

An investor establishes a spread position buy going long 1 XYZ JAN 70 call at a premium of 3 and going short 1 XYZ JAN 60 call at a premium of 9. Immediately, we see that the premium for the option sold is greater than that for the one purchased. That tells us this is a credit spread. The T-chart confirms this:

DR	CR
3	
	9
	6

A month before expiration date, XYZ is trading at $64 per share. If the stock were to fall to $59, the premiums on both contracts would fall. At that price, they are out of the money. Assume the premium on the 60 call is now 5 and the premium on the 70 call is now 1 (it is now trading at a $4 credit).

If the customer closes both positions, the customer would have a $200 profit. On the T-chart, we close the 60 call with a purchase at 5 and the 70 call with a sale at 1.

DR	CR
3	
	9
5	1
8	10

The net is a credit of 2 points or $200 profit. The spread between the premiums narrowed from the original 6 points to 4 points (5 minus 1) and that gave the investor a $200 profit. If both options expire worthless, then the spread is zero and the investor makes the entire $600. If the spread widens (the stock price rises), the investor could lose the balance of the spread (10 minus 6) or $400. Let's look at another example.

EXAMPLE

With PRS common stock selling at 34, an investor establishes a spread by going long 1 PRS JAN 30 call at 8 and short 1 PRS JAN 40 call at 3. If the price of PRS goes to 39 and the premium of the 30 call rises to 13 and that of the 40 call to 5, what is the investor's profit or loss if both positions are closed at the current prices?

We notice this is a debit spread because the investor is paying more than receiving. The T-chart confirms that.

DR	CR
8	
	3
5	

There are two ways to answer the question. The quickest is to remember that investor with debit spreads want the premium spread to widen. The difference between the premiums is now 8 points (13 – 5). By widening from 5 to 8, the investor's profit is 3 points ($300).

Or, by using the T-chart, we have the 30 closed at 13 (13 into the credit column) and the 40 closed at 5 (put 5 into the debit column). The totals now are 13 debit (money out) and 16 credit (money in) for a profit of 3 points ($300).

DR	CR
8	13
5	3
13	16

How about trying one with a credit spread.

PRACTICE QUESTION

20. An investor establishes a spread by going long 1 DEF FEB 60 put at 3 and short 1 DEF FEB 70 put at 7. Before expiration, DEF is selling for 68 and both positions are closed out at their intrinsic value. As a result, the investor has
    A. a loss of $200.
    B. a gain of $200.
    C. a loss of $600.
    D. a gain of $600.

Answer: B. Using the T-chart, we see this is a credit spread with a net credit of $400. With the price of DEF at $68, the 60 put is out of the money and would be closed by a sale at zero. The 70 put is 2 points in the money and the closing purchase at intrinsic value would cost $200. As the premium spread has narrowed from 4 points to 2 points, the investor made $200.

DR	CR
3	7
2	0
5	7

As a bull spread, if the DEF reached 70 or higher, both options would expire unexercised and the entire 4 point would be profit to the investor. On the other hand, if DEF's price drops to 60, the 70 put would be exercised at a 10-point loss which, once subtracting the initial 4-point credit, would give this investor a net loss of $600. But, we knew that would be the maximum loss because, with a maximum gain of 4 of the 10-point difference between 60 and 70, the maximum loss is the rest of the spread.

Here is a question similar in format to one that is frequently used on the exam.

PRACTICE QUESTION

21. An investor establishes a spread position by going long 1 GHI 30 MAR call and short 1 GHI 35 MAR call. The investor will profit if
    I. the spread narrows.
    II. the spread widens.
    III. GHI is at 30 or below.
    IV. GHI is at 35 or above.
    A. I and III
    B. I and IV
    C. II and III
    D. II and IV

Answer: D. This is a *bull call* spread. We know that because the investor bought the lower strike price and sold the higher strike price. Buy low, sell high (BLSH) is bullish. We also know that this is a debit spread. We can tell because there are no premiums. We know that because when it is call options, the lower the strike, the higher the premium. Regardless of the numbers, the premium to buy a 30 call will always be higher than the premium received from selling a 35 call.

Bull spreads benefit when the price goes up. The investor's maximum profit is reached when the stock is at 35 (or higher). As a debit spread, we want the premium spread to widen.

Straddles and Combinations

The maximum gain of the long straddle is unlimited because the potential gain on a long call is unlimited. The maximum loss of the long straddle is both premiums paid. There are two breakeven points because there are two options. The breakeven for the call is the strike price plus both premiums paid; the breakeven for the put is strike price minus both premiums paid. The investor does not experience profit unless the market price is above the breakeven of the call or below the breakeven of the put.

EXAMPLE

An investor establishes a long straddle by going long 1 ABC Jan 150 call at 5 and long 1 ABC Jan 150 put at 6. What is the maximum gain, loss and breakeven points?

maximum gain = unlimited

maximum loss = $1,100

breakevens = 161, 139 (150 + 11; 150 – 11)

Let's look at an example of a short combination.

EXAMPLE

With XYZ trading at 25, a customer writes 1 XYZ Jan 20 call at 6 and writes 1 XYZ Jan 30 put at 7. This is an example of a short combination where both contracts are in the money. Both the call and the put are in the money by 5 points. The exam could ask you the following question:

Just before expiration, with XYZ now trading at 27, the customer closes his positions at intrinsic value. How much did the customer make or lose?

In this example, closing means buying back the original two options sold. What will be the cost of buying back both options? The answer is their intrinsic value. With XYZ now at 27, the call is in the money by 7 points and the put is in the money by 3 points. Now it is just a simple computation. The call was sold for 6 and bought back for 7, a loss of $100. The put was sold for 7 and bought back for 3, a gain of $400. Overall, the gain is $300. Another way to come up with the same result is to note that the position opened with a credit of 13 (6 + 7). It is closed with a debit of 10 (7 + 3) for a gain of $300.

The *maximum gain* is the total credit minus the difference in strike prices. That is 13 – 10 = 3 points. In a short combination, the investor makes money if the stock stays inside the breakeven points. Those follow the Call UP and Put DOWN rule and are 20 +13 (33) and 30 – 13 (17). Once the stock goes above 33 or below 17, the investor will lose money.

The *maximum loss* is unlimited because of the short call.

Options Hedge Positions

As mentioned earlier in this unit, options can be used to hedge (protect) a long or a short position. The computation of the breakeven point does not follow the Call UP and Put DOWN rule.

Long Stock, Long Put (Protective Put)

An investor buys 100 shares of RST at 53 and buys an RST 50 put for 2 as protection. Should the stock price fall below the strike price of 50, the investor will exercise the put to sell the stock for 50. In this scenario, the investor loses $3 per share on the stock and has spent $2 per share for the put. The total loss equals $500. The breakeven point is reached when the stock rises by the amount paid for the put; in this case, 53 + 2 = 55.

In this example, no matter how far the stock falls, the investor can get out at 50 by exercising the put. Therefore, the most the investor can lose on the stock position is $3 per share. The cost of this protection is $2 per share. Therefore, maximum potential loss is $5 per share, or $500. On the other hand, maximum gain is unlimited because the stock price could rise infinitely. To break even, the stock must rise by the cost of the put option purchased. The breakeven point for long stock-long put is the cost of stock purchased plus premium. In our example, the breakeven is $55.

TAKE NOTE

Protective put strategies are most often employed with equity positions, as in the previous example, or with index options to protect an entire portfolio.

Long Stock, Short Call (Covered Call)

Another way to protect a long stock position is with a covered call. As you will discover, it does not offer the complete protection of a long put. A covered call has limited risk protection. The protection is the premium received, so the breakeven is the stock price purchased minus the premium. A covered call writer has a neutral to slightly bullish sentiment. If the price of the underlying stock declines, the option will expire and the writer keeps the premium. As that price is declining, the long stock position is losing money. Once the decline exceeds the premium received, the maximum loss is all the way to zero. That is, if the stock was purchased at $50 per share and a 50 call was sold for 4 points, anything below $46 per share results in a loss. If the stock becomes worthless, the investor loses $46 per share. So, this is only a partial hedge.

If the stock appreciates in above the strike price, the option will be exercised. This is not necessarily a bad thing, as the trade will generally be profitable. If the appreciation is less than the amount of the premium received, the profit will exceed what you would have made by buying the stock and selling it at the appreciated price. In our earlier example, if the stock rises to $53 per share, the call will be exercised and the writer will receive a total of 50 for the stock plus 4 for writing the call. That is $54 compared to selling the stock at $53.

EXAMPLE

An investor buys 100 shares of RST at 53 and writes 1 RST 55 call for 2. The maximum gain equals $400. If the stock price rises above 55, the call will be exercised; thus, the investor will sell the stock for a gain of $200, in addition to the $200 premium received. The maximum loss is $5,100. Should the stock become worthless, the $200 premium reduces the loss on the stock. The breakeven point is reached when the stock falls by the amount of the premium received. Therefore, 53 – 2 = 51.

In this example, the customer is protected only on the downside by the amount of the premium received for writing the call. Thus, the stock could fall to $51, at which point the customer breaks even; the $2 loss on the stock is offset exactly by the premium received. Below $51, losses begin. If the stock becomes worthless, the customer could lose $5,100 (which is maximum loss). If the stock rises above $55, the option will be exercised and the customer will be assigned, and forced to sell stock at $55 for a $2 per share gain. Combined with the $2 per share premium received, the maximum potential gain is $400.

TAKE NOTE

One of the drawbacks of writing calls against a long stock position is that it limits upside potential. Therefore, covered call writing is normally done in a stable market. The breakeven point for long stock-short call is cost of stock purchased minus premium.

Short Stock, Long Call

An investor sells short 100 shares of RST at 58 and buys an RST 60 call for 3. The investor's maximum gain is $5,500. If the stock becomes worthless, the investor gains $5,800 from the short sale minus the $300 paid for the call. The maximum loss is $500. If the stock price rises above $60, the investor will exercise the call to buy the stock for 60, incurring a $200 loss on the short sale, in addition to the $300 paid for the call. The breakeven point is the stock's sale price minus the premium paid in this case, 58 – 3, or 55.

In a short stock sale, the potential loss is unlimited. One who sells stock short is obligated to replace the borrowed stock, regardless of how high the price has risen. In this example, no matter how high the stock rises, the investor can buy back the borrowed stock at 60 by exercising the call. Therefore, the most the investor can lose on the short stock position is $2 per share. The cost of this protection is $3 per share. That makes the maximum potential loss $5 per share, or $500. On the other hand, maximum gain will occur if the stock becomes worthless. If the stock falls to zero, the customer will make $5,800 on the short stock position less the $300 paid to buy the call. Overall, maximum potential gain is $5,500. The breakeven point for short stock-long call is short sale price minus premium.

Short Stock, Short Put (Covered Put)

Just as writing a call can offer partial protection to a long stock position, writing a put can do the same for an investor with a short stock position. This is one of the ways to cover a short put. It is unlikely your exam will go deep into this strategy. Most often, you need to know that a short put can be covered by a long put (the short put is no longer naked) and that this strategy offers limited protection for a short stock seller. Just in case there is a surprise, here is an example of the math involved.

EXAMPLE

An investor sells short 100 shares of ABC at $52 per share. At the same time, the investor sells 1 ABC DEC 50 put at 2. The investor's breakeven point is the proceeds of the short stock sale plus the proceeds from the sale of the put. That is 52 + 2 = $54.

Maximum gain is $400. Short stock sellers want the price of the stock to fall. As the stock falls below the $50 strike price, the option gets in the money and exercise is likely. Therefore, there is a dollar-for-dollar offset as the price falls. For each dollar made on the short stock sale, a dollar is lost on the short put option. The profit is capped at $400 for all prices below 50, (i.e., $200 on the stock positon plus the $200 collected when selling the put).

Maximum loss is unlimited. Even though there are two points of price protection against an increase in the stock price, that doesn't do much when the price of the stock has no upper limit.

Losses could be unlimited if the stock price continues to increase, but they will always be $200 less than the stock trade alone. That still is considered unlimited on an exam question.

LESSON 10.7: OPTIONS TAXATION

LO 10.i Differentiate between the different kinds of tax treatment of options transactions.

Introduction

In most instances, the taxation of options transactions is similar to that of any other security. There are a few quirks and this lesson will explain those.

Tax Rules for Options

Because options are capital assets, capital gains tax rules apply. The tax consequences will vary depending on what the investor does with the option position.

Expiration, Close, or Exercise

There are three ways to handle an existing (open) option position. An open positon can expire, be closed in the open market, or be exercised by the party who is long (owner).

Expiration

At the expiration of an options contract, the buyer loses the premium; the seller profits from the premium. The buyer reports a capital loss equal to the premium amount; the seller reports a capital gain equal to the premium amount.

The tax treatment for LEAPS writers at expiration is unique. Although investors may have held the contract for more than 12 months, LEAPS writers must report **short-term capital gains** at expiration. LEAPS buyers will report long-term losses and gains if the contact is held for more than 12 months. Essentially, LEAP contracts for buyers are handled like most other securities regarding long- and short-term gains and losses. For sellers, they are treated as any other short sale.

Closing Out

Closing sales or purchases generate a capital gain or loss equal to any price difference. This gain or loss must be reported on the basis of the date of the closing transaction. This is true for both buyers and sellers. For example, if an investor sells an option for a premium of 4 and then enters a closing purchase transaction at 6, there is a 2-point short-term capital loss. If the closing purchase was at 1, there would be a 3-point short-term capital gain. Likewise, an investor taking a long position in an option at 4 and entering a closing sale transaction at 6, there is a 2-point short-term capital gain (we're excluding LEAPS—on the exam it will have to specify LEAPS; otherwise all options are 9 months maximum life). If the closing sale is at 1 point, there is a 3-point short-term capital loss.

As always, notice that whatever the writer makes is what the buyer loses, and the reverse.

Exercise

The exercise of options does not generate a capital gain or loss until a subsequent purchase or sale of the stock occurs. If a long call is exercised, the option holder buys the stock. Because the investor paid a premium for the stock, the total cost basis for the stock includes the premium and strike price. The following chart identifies the tax consequences of these options strategies. In the case of a long put, exercise will result in a taxable event. Stock is being sold (put) at the strike price and that, minus the premium, must be compared to the purchase price to determine the amount of gain or loss.

TEST TOPIC ALERT

Possible Tax Consequences of Options Strategies

Strategy	Option Expires	Option Exercised	Position Closed
Buy a call	Capital loss	Strike price + premium = cost basis	Capital gain or loss
Sell a call	Capital gain	Strike price + premium = sale proceeds	Capital gain or loss
Buy a put	Capital loss	Strike price – premium = sale proceeds	Capital gain or loss
Sell a put	Capital gain	Strike price – premium = cost basis	Capital gain or loss

Stock Holding Periods

The IRS does not allow the use of options to postpone the sale of stock to generate long-term capital gains treatment. Options that allow an investor to lock in a sale price are long puts. If stock's holding period is 12 months or less before the purchase of a put, the gain will be classified as short-term.

EXAMPLE

An investor bought XYZ 11 months ago at 50. It now trades for 70. If the investor were to sell it now, the gain would be classified as short-term.

Assume the investor buys a 70 put that will expire in three months. Even though the sale of the stock is postponed until up to 14 months have elapsed, the IRS still requires the holding period to be classified as short-term for tax purposes. Furthermore, purchasing the put eliminates the existing holding period. It does not begin aging all over again until the put expires. If the XYZ stock had been purchased more than 12 months before the purchase of the put, its holding period would not be affected and any gains or losses would be long-term.

Married Put

If, on the same day, a customer buys stock and buys a put option on that stock as a hedge, the put is said to be **married** to the stock. For tax purposes, irrespective of what happens to the put, the cost basis of the stock is adjusted upward by the premium paid. Even if the put expires worthless, there is no capital loss on the put. Rather, the premium paid is reflected in the cost basis of the stock, which is the breakeven point for long stock/long put (cost of stock purchased plus premium).

EXAMPLE

If, on the same day, a customer buys 100 XYZ at 52 and buys 1 XYZ Jan 50 put at 2, the customer's cost basis in the stock is 54.

TEST TOPIC ALERT

Expect to see about five to seven questions on options taxation. Many of these questions are a matter of finding the profit or loss, so use a T-chart. Remember that option exercise alone does not create a taxable event.

PRACTICE QUESTION

22. On May 1, 2018, an investor purchased 100 shares of XYZ for $50 per share. On November 10 of the same year, after XYZ's price has rise to $54, the investor bought 1 XYZ Aug 55 put for 3. In August 2019, the put expires and in December of that year, the investor sells the XYZ stock for $55 per share. Based on this information, it would be correct to state that this investor realized
    A. a long-term capital gain of $500.
    B. a long-term capital gain of $200.
    C. a short-term capital gain of $500.
    D. a short-term capital gain of $200.

    Answer: D. Because the investor bought the put on a stock with a short-term holding period (less than 12 months), the holding period of the stock is erased and does not start to age again until the put expires. That aging begins at day one in August, so when the stock is sold in December, is it only four months old. That makes the sale of the stock short term. We determine the gain or loss by comparing the cost to the proceeds. The cost of the stock is $50 plus the premium of $3 ($53) and the proceeds are $55. That is a gain of $200.

Wash Sale Rule

In Lesson 13.5, we will learn the details of the wash sale rule. One of the provisions of that rule deals with substantially identical securities. When applying that rule to call options, different options series are not substantially identical. That is, the ABC JAN 50 puts are a different security from the ABC MAR 50 puts. Keep this in mind when you get to that lesson.

LESSON 10.8: RULES AND REGULATIONS OF THE OPTIONS MARKET

LO 10.j Determine the CBOE rules and regulations pertaining to the sale of options.

Introduction

We have covered some of the rules where appropriate, such as delivery of the options disclosure document (ODD). In this final LO of Unit 10, we will discuss the remaining rules that are relevant to your exam.

Rules for Opening an Options Account

We covered the basic rules for opening an options account in Lesson 2.7. We will repeat som of them here and add details.

New Account Form

When opening an options account, an options new account form or similar record must be completed. In addition to standard new account information required of every customer, the broker-dealer must seek to obtain the following information from customers who want to trade options:

- Investment objective(s) (e.g., safety of principal, income, or growth)
- Employment status (name of employer, self-employed, or retired)
- Estimated annual income from all sources
- Estimated net worth (exclusive of residence)
- Estimated liquid net worth (cash, securities, etc.)
- Marital status and number of dependents
- Legal age (whether the customer has reached the age of majority in that state)

In addition, the customer's account record may contain the following information (if applicable):

- Investment experience and knowledge (e.g., number of years, size, frequency, and types of transactions for options, stocks, bonds, other)
- Source(s) of background and financial information for the customer
- Date the ODD was furnished to the customer (not later than the date the account is approved for options trading)
- Nature and types of transactions for which the account is approved (e.g., buying, uncovered writing, or spreading)
- Whether this a retail (natural person) account or institutional account
- Signature of the registered representative introducing the account
- Signature of the registered options principal (ROP) or the general sales supervisor approving the account and the date of approval

Written Approval by the ROP

Once the new account form is completed, a ROP or branch office manager must review and approve the account in writing at or before the initial trade. The approver bases the approval on review of the information provided on the new account form. According to FINRA Rule 2360, "based upon such information, the branch office manager, a Registered Options Principal [Series 4] or a Limited Principal—General Securities Sales Supervisor [Series 10] shall specifically approve or disapprove in writing the customer's account for options trading. ... If the branch office manager is not a Registered Options Principal or a Limited Principal—General Securities Sales Supervisor, account approval or disapproval shall within ten (10) business days be submitted to and approved or disapproved by a Registered Options Principal or a Limited Principal—General Securities Sales Supervisor." In the meantime, trading can take place while waiting for the final approval. The approval indicates the nature and types of transactions the firm will permit in the account.

PRACTICE QUESTION

23. A customer first discusses options trading with a registered representative on July 3. On July 7, the customer is approved for trading listed options, and on July 12, she enters the first trade. The investor must receive an options disclosure document (ODD) no later than
    A. July 3.
    B. July 7.
    C. July 12.
    D. July 13.

    Answer: B. The ODD of the OCC must be given to the customer no later than at the time the account is approved for options trading.

Investment Strategies and Different Levels of Approval

Many option strategies are speculative and designed to capitalize on movements in the price of the underlying asset. Investors also use options to enhance returns or limit risks. Investment strategies that involve multiple option positions include spreads, straddles, and combinations, and all are strategies in which an investor buys or sells more than one option at a time.

A basic level of option trading is buying options. Additional approval may be required if the customer wishes to engage in option writing (including writing covered calls), uncovered option writing, ratio writing, spreads and straddles, and other strategies.

Using the customer information gathered to facilitate opening the account, the ROP will determine which of the different levels of options trading might be appropriate and meet suitability standards; the account will be approved accordingly. While levels of approval may differ from member firm to member firm, they are generally similar in that there may be four or five levels, with each level to include the strategies of the previous level, and similar in the specific strategies allowed for each level as well. A typical example might be as follows:

- Level I—Covered options (calls and puts)
- Level II—Long calls, puts, straddles, and combinations
- Level III—Spreads (calls and puts)
- Level IV – Uncovered (naked calls and puts), short straddles, combinations, and ratio spreads

For customers approved to write uncovered calls or puts, the firm must have written procedures in place covering

- specific criteria used in approving such accounts,
- specific minimum equity requirements for such accounts, and
- the requirement to provide the customer with a special written document describing the risks involved in uncovered writing (Special Statement for Uncovered Options Writers). This document must be provided to the customer before the initial uncovered sale.

Verification by the Customer

Within 15 days of account approval, the firm must obtain from the customer a signed written agreement (customer option agreement) that the account will be handled under the rules of the OCC and the CBOE and that the customer will not violate position or exercise limits. The signature also verifies the accuracy of the information provided on the new account form.

TEST TOPIC ALERT

If the signed option agreement is not returned within 15 days of account approval, the firm can permit closing transactions only.

TAKE NOTE

In the event that the OCC should revise the ODD, all existing options account holders must receive the revised ODD no later than by the date the customer's next option transaction confirmation is delivered.

Figure 10.9: Options Account Diagram

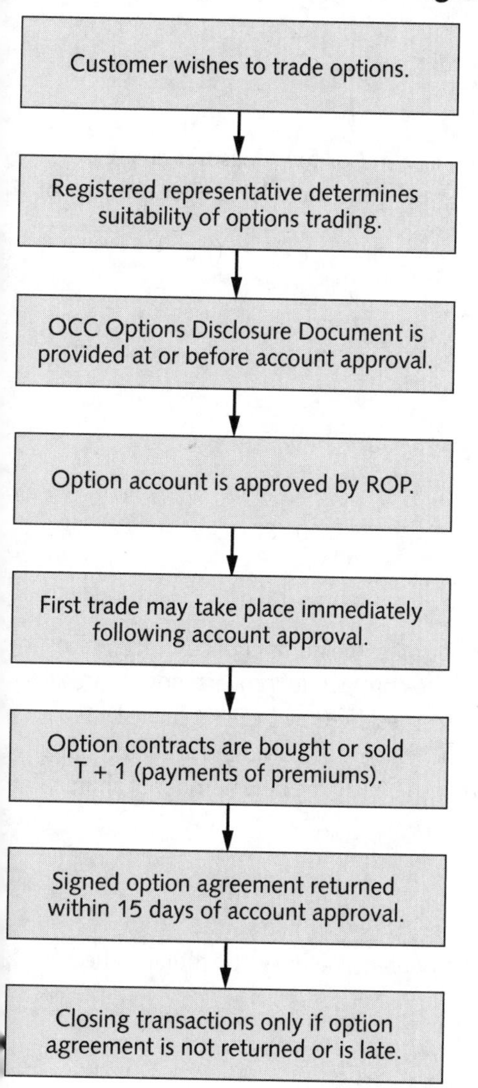

Options Contract Adjustments

The rules require adjusting options contracts for stock splits, reverse stock splits, stock dividends, and rights offerings. Adjustments are not made for ordinary cash dividends. Adjustments to the number of shares are rounded down to the next whole share. First, we will look at the concept and examine some examples. An investor bullish on ABC stock buys 1 ABC 50 call. The contract is good for 100 shares at $50 per share and, if the stock rises, the investor stands to make a profit. What happens if ABC has a 2:1 split? We know there will now be twice as many shares at half the price. How does that impact our call buyer? Surely buying 100 of the new shares at 50 isn't fair. Recognizing this, the rules provide that this investor's position will change to reflect the split. Instead of 1 contract for 100 shares at 50, there will now be 2 contracts for 100 shares at 25.

When *even* stock splits occur, additional options contracts are created. An even split ends in 1—such as a 2:1, 3:1, or 4:1 split.

EXAMPLE

After a 2:1 split, 1 ALF 60 call becomes 2 ALF 30 calls. A 2:1 creates 200 shares instead of 100, so the owner has twice as many contracts as before, at half the exercise price.

The total exercise value remains the same:

Original contract: 100 × 60 = $6,000

New contracts: 200 × 30 = $6,000

An **uneven split,** also known as a **fractional split**, such as a 3:2 or 5:4, does not create additional options contracts. Contracts adjusted for uneven splits include a larger number of shares and will receive a new option contract symbol.

EXAMPLE

After a 3:2 split, 1 FLA 60 call will effectively be represented by 1 FLA 40 call with 150 shares in the contract.

The total exercise value effectively remains the same as before:

Original contract: 100 × 60 = $6,000

New contract when closed or exercised: 150 × 40 = $6,000

EXAMPLE

Note that stock dividends are treated as uneven splits; the number of contracts remains the same, strike price is adjusted, and the contract now covers more shares. After a 20% stock dividend, 1 LFA 60 call will be represented by 1 LFA 50 call with 120 shares in the contract. How did we do the math? A 20% stock dividend is an additional 20 shares. Dividing the original exercise value of $6,000 by the new number of shares (120) results in a strike price of $50 per share.

Original contract: 100 × 60 = $6,000

New contract when closed or exercised: 120 × 50 = $6,000

It is important to note that whatever the adjustment, monetary value remains the same.

The Functioning of the Listed Options Market

Options trade on several U.S. exchanges and OTC. Exchange-traded options are **listed options** and have standardized exercise prices and expiration dates. OTC options are called conventional options and are not standardized. As a result, little secondary market activity exists because contract terms are individually negotiated between the buyer and seller; no two contracts are the same. As stated earlier, we don't expect anything on OTC options on the exam.

The most likely tested locations for trading listed options are:

- The CBOE
- The NYSE
- The Nasdaq Stock Market
- The PHLX (the Philadelphia Stock Exchange, technically the Nasdaq PHLX, specializing in foreign currency options)

TAKE NOTE

If a security is subject to a trading halt on its trading market, options on that security stop trading as well.

Standard Features of Options Trading and Settlement

The key to the listed options market is the standardization. That allows for active secondary trading.

Trading Times

Listed stock options trade from 9:30 am to 4:00 pm ET (3:00 pm CT). Note that broad-based index options trade until 4:15 pm ET (3:15 pm CT).

Exercise

The latest time for turning in an exercise notice is 5:30 pm ET (4:30 pm CT).

Expiration

Listed stock options expire on the third Friday of the month at 11:59 pm ET. The final time for trading an option is 4:00 pm ET on the final day of trading (expiration). Why is there a difference between the exercise deadline and the middle of the night expiration? The hours between 5:30 pm (the latest an option can be exercised) and 11:59 pm on the third Friday of the expiry month allow firms time to clear their books of option transactions by notifying the OCC.

Settlement

Listed options transactions settle on the next business day. Stock delivered as a result of exercise is settled on a **regular way basis** (two business days).

Automatic Exercise

Contracts that are in the money by at least 0.01 at expiration are automatically exercised as a service to the customer unless other instructions have been given. Automatic exercise applies to both retail customer and institutional accounts. Customers may give *do not exercise* instructions for any contract in the money if they do not want to have their contract exercised. All instructions must be received by the OCC no later than 5:30 pm ET on the third Friday of the expiration month (last day of trading).

Figure 10.10: Exercise, Trading, or Expiration of Options

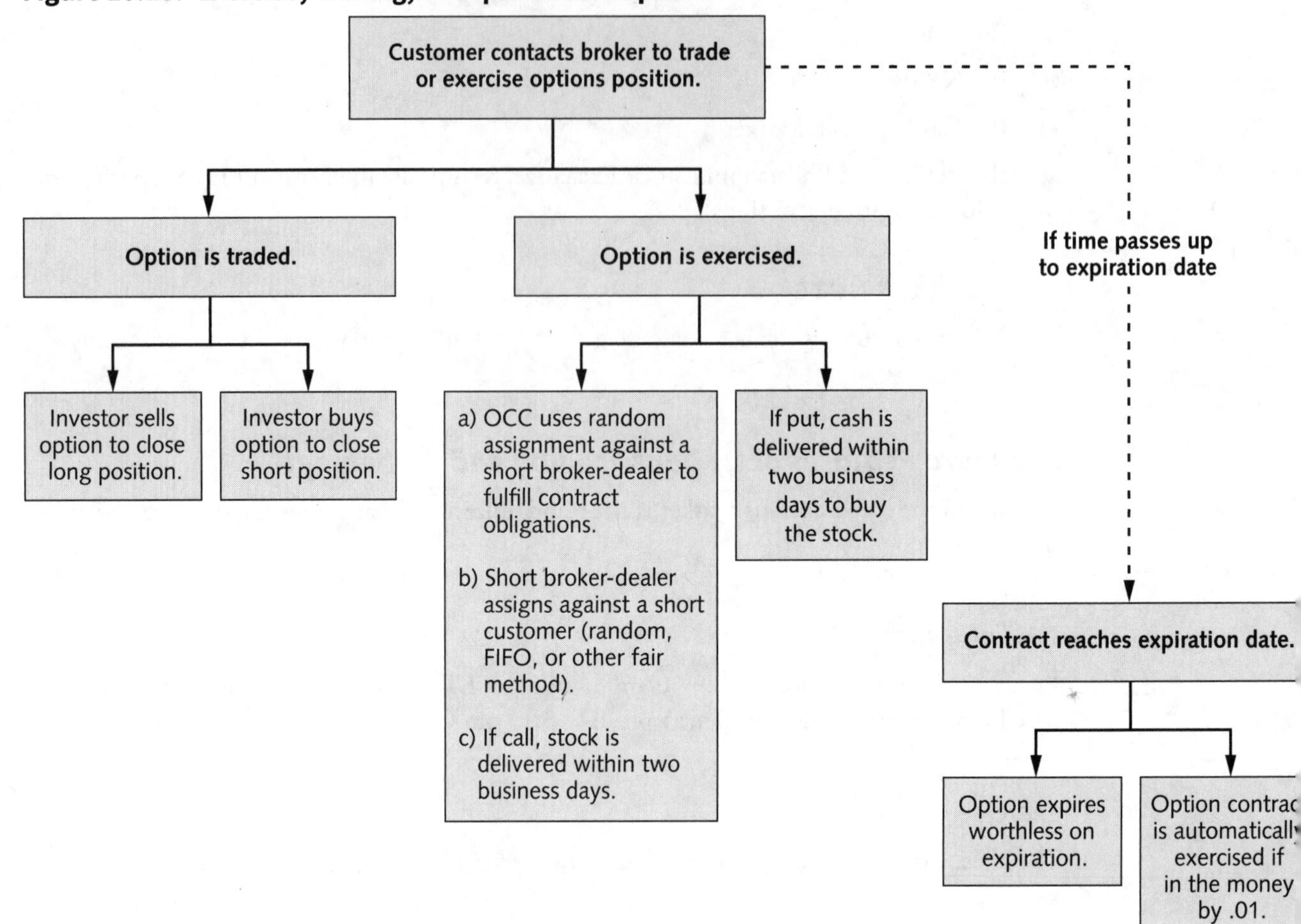

Position Limits

For the most heavily traded equity options contracts, position limits are 250,000 contracts o the same side of the market. This limit is subject to frequent adjustment.

Position limits apply to individuals, registered representatives acting for discretionary accounts, and individuals *acting in concert* (acting together as one person). A group of investors cannot avoid the position restrictions by intentionally splitting a large position to circumvent the limits. The aggregate position of individuals acting in concert applies in determining whether there is a breach of position limits. LEAPS are added to traditional options to determine whether a violation of the position limit rules has occurred.

EXAMPLE

WRJ Corporation is in the lowest tier and subject to a position limit of 25,000 contracts. If two individuals, acting in concert, each were long 13,000 WRJ calls, both would be in violation of exchange rules.

In determining whether individuals are acting in concert, the CBOE looks for **control**, whic indicates the ability to make investment decisions for an account or influence the investment decisions made for an account. Control is presumed when

- all parties to a joint account have authority to act on behalf of the account and
- a person has the authority to execute transactions in an account.

Therefore, the following accounts will be presumed to be acting in concert unless evidence to the contrary is given to and accepted by an exchange:

- An individual account (for example, for one spouse) or a joint account (for example, for a married couple)—a spouse clearly exercises control over his account and has the authority to act in a joint account. In this case, positions in both accounts would be aggregated to determine whether a violation of position limits exists.
- An individual who has discretion over an account and the account itself—the option position in the account of the person holding third-party trading authority is aggregated with positions in the account over which this individual has discretion to determine whether a position violation exists.

Position limits are measured by the number of contracts on the same side of the market. There are two sides: the bull side and the bear side. Long calls and short puts represent the former; long puts and short calls represent the latter.

Take for example a company subject to a 250,000-contract limit. If a customer were long 140,000 calls and 140,000 puts, there would be no violation. However, if the same customer were long 140,000 calls and short 140,000 puts, the customer would have 280,000 contracts on the bull side of the market—a violation. In determining whether a violation has occurred, long calls are aggregated with short puts and long puts are aggregated with short calls.

Exercise Limits

OCC exercise limits are the maximum number of contracts that can be exercised on the same side of the market within a specified period. Currently, the period is five consecutive business days. For the most heavily traded equity options contracts, no more than 250,000 contracts on the same side of the market may be exercised within a five-business-day period. As with position limits, the maximum number applicable to exercise limits can vary from one underlying security to another, and to determine if a violation has occurred, long calls and short puts (bullish contracts) are aggregated, and short calls and long puts (bearish contract) are aggregated.

Like position limits, exercise limits apply to individuals, individuals acting in concert, and registered representatives acting for discretionary accounts, among others.

American- or European-Style Contracts

Investors with a long position can exercise their contract anytime before expiration if the contract is an American-style option. European-style options can be exercised on expiration day (last day of trading) only. Nearly all equity options are American style. FCOs may be either American style or European style, and most index options are European-style contracts, including weekly index contracts. Yield-based options are European-style contracts.

TAKE NOTE

A tool for remembering the difference between American and European exercise is to look at the first letter.

A for American means *anytime*.

E for European means *expiration date*.

Summary of Key Options Terms

Please be sure you are familiar with each of these terms.

Figure 10.11: Summary of Basic Options Terms

Term	Definition
American style	Contracts exercisable any time until expiration.
European style	Contracts only exercisable at expiration.
Call	A contract to buy stock or another underlying instrument or asset at a specified price for a limited time.
Call buyer	Pays a premium for an option contract and receives the right to buy, during a specified time, the underlying asset at the specified price.
Call writer	Receives a premium and takes on, for a specified time, the obligation to sell the underlying asset at the specified price at the call buyer's discretion.
Covered	Position of an options writer with an offsetting position in the underlying instrument that assures the ability to perform if the option contract is exercised by the option holder.
Expiration date	Specified date on which the option becomes worthless and the buyer no longer holds the rights specified in the contract.
Naked (uncovered)	Position of an options writer without an offsetting position in the underlying instrument guaranteeing the ability to perform if the option is exercised by the holder.
Option	Contract giving the buyer the right to buy or sell an asset (such as stock) and requiring the writer to sell or buy the underlying item if the option buyer chooses to exercise the contract.
Parity	When the premium equals the intrinsic value of the contract (e.g., a May 35 call is at parity when the market price is 40 and the premium is 5).
Premium	Cash price the option buyer pays to the option writer.
Put	Right to sell stock or another underlying instrument or asset at a specified price for a limited time.
Put buyer	Pays a premium for an option contract; has, for a specified time, the right to sell the underlying asset at the specified price.
Put writer	Receives a premium and takes on, for a specified time, the obligation to buy the underlying asset at the specified price at the put buyer's discretion.
Strike price (exercise price)	Price at which the underlying asset is bought or sold if the option buyer exercises his rights in the contract.
Underlying asset	Security (or other asset) on which an option is based.

TEST TOPIC ALERT

Here are some options terms you might see on the exam as incorrect answers:

- Butterfly
- Condor or Condor spread
- Iron butterfly or iron condor
- Strangle

UNIT 11

Other Packaged Products

LEARNING OBJECTIVES

When you have completed this unit, you will be able to accomplish the following.

- › LO 11.a **Identify** the types and characteristics of real estate investment trusts.
- › LO 11.b **Recall** the tax treatment of REITs.
- › LO 11.c **Recognize** the structure of a DPP.
- › LO 11.d **Differentiate** between the roles of the general partners and the limited partners in a DPP.
- › LO 11.e **Name** the different types of DPPs and how they are offered.
- › LO 11.f **Identify** the tax ramifications of investing in DPPs.
- › LO 11.g **Recognize** the importance of proper evaluation of DPPs.
- › LO 11.h **Determine** the rules and regulations pertaining to the sale of DPPs.

INTRODUCTION

The most common example of a packaged product is the mutual fund. There are many others, and those are the subject of this unit. A packaged product is an investment that relieves the investor of daily decision making. In the case of real estate investment trusts (REITS), investors do not have to find the properties or manage them. That is taken care of for them by the management of the trust. The same is true with a direct participation program (DPP). The program handles the details, not the investors.

LESSON 11.1: REAL ESTATE INVESTMENT TRUSTS (REITS)

LO 11.a Identify the types and characteristics of real estate investment trusts.

Types of REITS

A **real estate investment trust (REIT)** (pronounced reet) is a company that manages a portfolio of real estate investments to earn profits and/or income for its shareholders. Like many other pooled investment vehicles, REITs offer professional management and diversification. REITs are normally publicly traded and serve as a source of long-term financing for real estate projects. A REIT pools capital in a manner similar to an investment company. There are three basic types of REITs:

- **Equity REITs**. Own commercial property.
  - They take an ownership position in the properties. They receive rental income and possible capital gains upon a future sale of the properties.
- **Mortgage REITs**. Own mortgages on commercial property.
  - They make real estate loans (mortgages). Their earnings come from the interest payments on those loans.
- **Hybrid REITs**. Own commercial property and own mortgages on commercial property.
  - They are, as the name implies, a combination of both mortgage and equity REITs.

REITs are organized as trusts in which investors buy and sell shares either on stock exchanges or in the OTC market. They are not redeemable as is the case with mutual funds or UITs, but have the liquidity of listed stocks. REITs do compute a NAV per unit. As you can imagine, the valuation of real estate is not as exact as the price of publicly traded stock. Therefore, the NAV is only an approximation. Because REITs are not redeemed by the issuer, the prices are based on supply and demand. Just as with CEFs, the price an investor pays can be more, less, or the same as the NAV.

TAKE NOTE

In recent years, there has been substantial growth in the number of nontraded REITs (limited liquidity). However, for exam purposes, assume the REIT is publicly traded unless the question states otherwise.

What are the benefits of including REITs in a client's portfolio?

- REITs allow investors the opportunity to invest in real estate without incurring the degree of liquidity risk historically associated with real estate because REITs trade on exchanges and OTC.
- Properties are selected by professionals with greater negotiating power than an individual.
- There is a negative correlation to the general stock market because real estate prices and the stock market frequently move in opposite directions.
- There is reasonable income and/or potential capital appreciation.

In doing so, the client would be incurring the following risks:

- The investor has no direct control over the portfolio and relies on professional management to make all purchase and sale decisions. While the expectation of having a professionally managed portfolio should be considered advantageous, the quality of the portfolio lies with the quality of the professional management.

- REITs generally have greater price volatility than direct ownership of real estate because they are influenced by stock market conditions.
- If the REIT is not publicly traded, liquidity is very limited. As a result, there is the need for more stringent suitability standards and the regulators give greater scrutiny to trades in unlisted REITs.
- Problem loans in the portfolio could cause income and/or capital to decrease.

Later in this unit, we will discuss the limited partnership offerings known as direct participation programs (DPPs). The exam will require you to know that REITs are not DPPs. We will discuss the difference in the DPP section.

LO 11.b Recall the tax treatment of REITs.

REIT Taxation

REITs enjoy a unique hybrid status for federal income tax purposes. A REIT shareholder generally is taxed only on dividends paid by the REIT and on gains upon the disposition of REIT shares. A REIT is a corporation for U.S. tax purposes. The REIT is generally not subject to corporate tax if it distributes to its shareholders substantially all of its taxable income for each year

How much is ***substantially all***? Under the guidelines of Subchapter M of the IRC, a REIT can avoid being taxed as a corporation by receiving 75% or more of its income from real estate and distributing 90% or more of its taxable income to its shareholders.

Shareholders receive dividends from investment income. In most cases, those dividends are taxed at ordinary income rates rather than as qualified dividends. If there are capital gains distributions, they are generally taxed at the favorable long-term capital gains rate. Please note that with the advent of the Tax Cut and JOBS Act of 2017 (TCJA), there are some complex tax issues with REITs and those are not likely to be tested.

A tax-related concern for investors is that failure to meet the distribution rules could cause the REIT to be taxed. That would lead to another level of taxation before the income gets to the investor.

TEST TOPIC ALERT

Important points to remember about REITs:

- An owner of REITs holds an undivided interest in a pool of real estate investments.
- REITs are liquid because they trade on exchanges and OTC.
- REITs are not investment companies (mutual funds).
- REITs offer dividends and gains to investors but do not offer flow-through losses like limited partnerships, and therefore are not considered direct participation programs.
- REITs are not investment companies.
- REITS must distribute 90% or more of income to shareholders to avoid taxation as a corporation.
- Dividends from REITs are not qualified; they are taxed as ordinary income.

PRACTICE QUESTION

1. In order for a REIT to avoid being taxed like a corporation, it must distribute at **least**
   A. 75% of its taxable income.
   B. 90% of its taxable income.
   C. 95% of its taxable income.
   D. 100% of its taxable income.

   Answer: B. To qualify under IRS regulations, REITs must distribute at least 90% of their taxable income in the form of dividends to shareholders. At least 75% of the REIT's income must come from real estate investments.

LESSON 11.2: DPPS AND THEIR INVESTORS

LO 11.c Recognize the structure of a DPP.

Direct participation programs (DPPs) are investments that pass income, gains, losses, and tax benefits (such as depreciation, depletion, and tax credits) directly to the limited partners. There are some unique tax concepts and suitability issues associated with DPPs. Limited partnerships are one of the most common types of DPPs. They can also be set up as an S corporation or limited liability companies (LLCs).

Because the exam focuses on the limited partnership, so will we.

Structuring a Limited Partnership

The concept of a partnership for our purposes is based upon tax law. An unincorporated organization with two or more members is generally classified as a partnership for federal tax purposes if its members engage in a trade, business, financial operation, or venture and divid its profits. However, a joint undertaking merely to share expenses is not a partnership. For example, co-ownership of property maintained and rented or leased is not a partnership unle the co-owners provide services to the tenants.

In the case of a limited partnership, one of those members is the limited partner (LP) and th other the general partner (GP). We will get into the details of their roles later in this lesson.

An organization is classified as a **partnership** for federal tax purposes if it has two or more members and is none of the following:

- An organization that refers to itself as incorporated or as a corporation
- An insurance company
- A REIT
- An organization classified as a trust or otherwise subject to special treatment under the IRC

To qualify as a partnership, the business entity must avoid corporate characteristics such as continuity of life. This is the easiest of the corporate characteristics to avoid because partnerships have a predetermined date of dissolution when they are established, whereas corporations are expected to exist in perpetuity.

TEST TOPIC ALERT

Exam questions may test avoidance of corporate characteristics. For example:

1. Which of these characteristics is the **most** difficult to avoid?

Centralized management—no business can function without it.

2. Which of these characteristics is the easiest to avoid?

Continuity of life—there is a predetermined time at which the partnership interest must be dissolved.

3. Which two corporate characteristics are most likely to be avoided by a DPP?

Continuity of life and *freely transferable interests*—interests cannot be freely transferred; GP approval must transfer shares.

Issuing Limited Partnership Interests

Limited partnerships may be sold through private placements or public offerings. If sold privately, investors receive a **private placement memorandum** for disclosure. Generally, such private placements involve a small group of investors, each contributing a large sum of money. These investors must be **accredited investors**—that is, they must meet certain net worth or income standards. The general public does not meet this description.

In a public offering, partnerships are sold with a prospectus to a larger number of investors, each making a relatively small capital contribution, such as $1,000–$5,000.

The **syndicator** oversees the selling and promotion of the partnership. The syndicator is responsible for the preparation of any paperwork necessary for the registration of the partnership. Syndication or finders fees are limited to 10% of the gross dollar amount of securities sold.

Required Documentation

Three important documents are required for limited partnerships to exist:

- The certificate of limited partnership
- The partnership agreement
- The subscription agreement

Certificate of Limited Partnership

For legal recognition, the certificate of limited partnership must be filed in the home state of the partnership. It includes

- the partnership's name;
- the partnership's business;
- the principal place of business;
- the amount of time the partnership expects to be in business;
- the conditions under which the partnership will be dissolved;
- the size of each LP's current and future expected investments;
- the contribution return date, if set;
- the share of profits or other compensation to each LP;

- the conditions for LP's assignment of ownership interests;
- whether the limited partnership may admit other LPs; and
- whether the business can be continued by remaining GPs at death or incapacity of a GP.

Partnership Agreement

Each partner receives a copy of this agreement. It describes the roles of the GPs and LPs and guidelines for the partnership's operation.

Subscription Agreement

All investors interested in becoming LPs (passive investors) must complete a subscription agreement. The agreement appoints one or more GPs to act on behalf of the investors and is only effective when the GPs sign it. Along with the subscriber's money, the subscription agreement must include

- the investor's net worth,
- the investor's annual income,
- a statement attesting that the investor understands the risk involved, and
- a power of attorney appointing the GP as the agent of the partnership.

In addition to a cash contribution, subscribers may assume responsibility for the repayment of a portion of a loan made to the partnership. This type of loan is called a **recourse loan.** Frequently, partnerships also borrow money through **nonrecourse loans**; the GPs have responsibility for repayment of nonrecourse loans (not the LPs).

TEST TOPIC ALERT

LPs are liable for a proportionate share of recourse loans assumed by partnerships. LPs have no liability for nonrecourse loans and only in real estate DPPs does the nonrecourse loan add to the investor's basis.

PRACTICE QUESTION

2. The rights and liabilities of general partners (GPs) and limited partners (LPs) are listed in
   A. the certificate of partnership.
   B. the Uniform Limited Partnership Act.
   C. the partnership agreement.
   D. the partnership title.

   Answer: C. The partnership agreement is the contract between the partners and contains each entity's rights and duties.

Dissolving a Limited Partnership

Generally, limited partnerships are liquidated on the date specified in the partnership agreement. Early shutdown may occur if the partnership sells or disposes of its assets or if a decision is made to dissolve the partnership by the LPs holding a majority interest. When **dissolution** occurs, the GP must cancel the certificate of limited partnership and settle accounts in the following order:

- Secured lenders
- Other creditors
- LPs
  - First, for their claims to shares of profits
  - Second, for their claims to a return of contributed capital
- GPs
  - First, for fees and other claims not involving profits
  - Second, for a share of profits
  - Third, for capital return

Figure 11.1: DPP Life Cycle Diagram

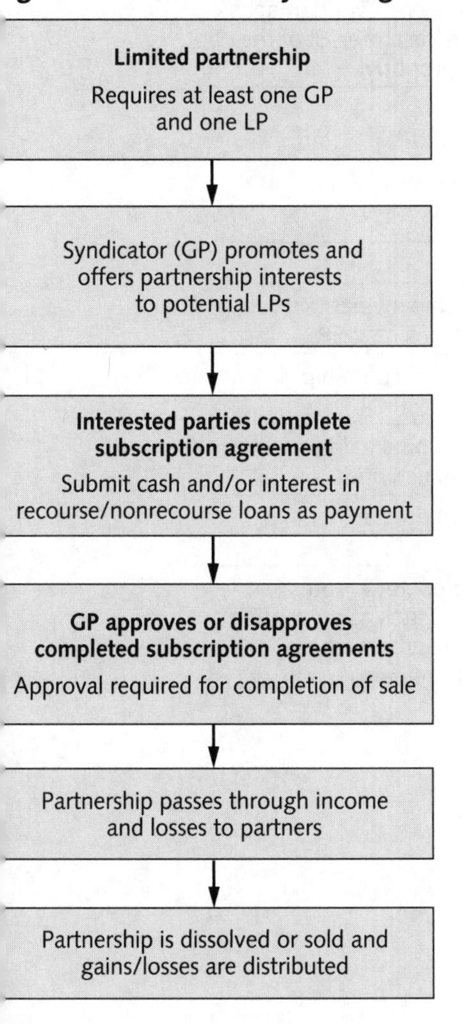

LO 11.d Differentiate between the roles of the general partners and the limited partners in a DPP.

Investors in a Limited Partnership

As state previously, the limited partnership form of DPP involves two types of partners: the GP(s) and the LP(s). Limited partnerships must have at least one of each.

Figure 11.2: GPs vs. LPs

GPs	LPs
Unlimited liability: Personal liability for all partnership business losses and debts	Limited liability: Can lose no more than their investment and proportionate interest in recourse notes
Management responsibility: Assumes responsibility for all aspects of the partnership's operation	No management responsibility: Provides capital for the business but may not participate in its management; known as a passive investor
	Attempting to take part in a management role jeopardizes limited liability status
Fiduciary responsibility: Morally and legally bound to use invested capital in the best interest of the investors	May sue the GP: Lawsuits may recover damages if the GP does not act in the best interest of the investors or uses assets improperly

The following tables compare other activities of GPs and LPs.

Figure 11.3: GPs and LPs: Allowed Activities

GPs can:	LPs can:
Make decisions that legally bind the partnership	Vote on changes to partnership investment objectives or the admission of a new GP
Buy and sell property for the partnership	Vote on sale or refinancing of partnership property
Maintain a financial interest in the partnership (must be a minimum of 1%)	Receive cash distributions, capital gains, and tax deductions from partnership activities
Receive compensation as specified in the partnership agreement	Inspect books and records of the partnership
	Exercise the partnership democracy (vote under special circumstances, such as permitting the GP to act contrary to the agreement, to contest a judgment against the partnership, or admit a new GP)

ure 11.4: GPs and LPs Cannot: Prohibited Activities

Ps cannot:	LPs cannot:
ompete against the partnership for ersonal gain	Act on behalf of the partnership or participate in its management
orrow from the partnership	Knowingly sign a certificate containing false information
ommingle partnership funds with personal ssets or assets of other partnerships	Have their names appear as part of the partnership's name
dmit new GPs or LPs or continue the artnership after the loss of a GP unless pecified in the partnership agreement	

PRACTICE QUESTION

3. In a direct participation program (DPP), liability for the debts of the business falls upon
   A. the general partner(s) (GPs).
   B. the limited partner(s) (LPs).
   C. the shareholder(s).
   D. the agent(s) selling the program.

Answer: A. DPPs consist of at least one GP and one LP. The liability of the LPs is limited to their investment, including commitments made but not yet fulfilled. On the other hand, the GPs bear the liability for the debts of the entity.

ESSON 11.3: TYPES OF DPPS

LO 11.e Name the different types of DPPs and how they are offered.

Introduction

As with so many of the investment products we've discussed, DPPs come in many different "flavors." It is important to recognize that DPPs are one way to structure a business. We commonly see huge corporations and single person sole proprietorships. As we go through the different types of DPPs, remember, these are just businesses using the limited partnership structure as a way to raise capital.

Real Estate Partnerships

Real estate DPPs are by far the most popular type. There are five different kinds and, as you will see in the following tables, some offer income, some offer potential growth, and some offer both.

The five types of real estate programs and their features are the following.

Raw Land

Partnership Objective	Purchase undeveloped land for its appreciation potential
Advantages	Appreciation potential of the property
Disadvantages	Offers no income distributions or tax deductions
Tax Features	No income or depreciation deductions Not considered a tax shelter
Degree of Risk	Most speculative real estate partnership

New Construction

Partnership Objective	Build new property for potential appreciation
Advantages	Appreciation potential of the property and structure; minimal maintenance costs in the early years
Disadvantages	Potential cost overruns; no established track record; difficulty finding permanent financing; inability to deduct current expenses during construction period
Tax Features	Depreciation and expense deductions after construction is completed and income is generated
Degree of Risk	Less risky than new land; more risky than existing property

Existing Property

Partnership Objective	Generate an income stream from existing structures
Advantages	Immediate cash flow; known history of income and expenses
Disadvantages	Greater maintenance or repair expenses than for new construction; expiring leases that may not be renewed; less than favorable rental arrangements
Tax Features	Deductions for mortgage interest and depreciation
Degree of Risk	Relatively low risk

Government-Assisted Housing Programs

Partnership Objective	Develop low-income and retirement housing
Advantages	Tax credits and rent subsidies
Disadvantages	Low appreciation potential; risk of changing government programs; high maintenance costs
Tax Features	Tax credits and losses
Degree of Risk	Relatively low risk

Historic Rehabilitation

Partnership Objective	Develop historic sites for commercial use
Advantages	Tax credits for preserving historic structure
Disadvantages	Potential cost overruns; no established track record; difficulty finding permanent financing; inability to deduct current expenses during construction period
Tax Features	Tax credit and deductions for expenses and depreciation
Degree of Risk	Similar to risk of new construction

PRACTICE QUESTION

4. All of the following would generally be associated with an existing real estate DPP **except**
   A. immediate income stream.
   B. high appreciation potential.
   C. known history of income and expenses.
   D. lower risk than other types of real estate programs.

   Answer: B. High appreciation potential is generally not associated with existing real estate programs. Investors looking for larger gains prefer new construction. The other choices are clear benefits. Buying an existing office building or apartment has very few surprises.

Oil and Gas Partnerships

Oil and gas programs include speculative drilling programs and income programs that invest in producing wells. We will list them from the most risk to the least risk.

Three types of oil and gas programs are exploratory, developmental, and income.

Exploratory (Wildcatting)

Partnership Objective	Locate undiscovered reserves of oil and/or gas
Advantages	High rewards for discovery of new reserves
Disadvantages	Few new wells produce
Tax Features	High intangible drilling costs for immediate tax sheltering
Degree of Risk	High; most risky oil and gas program

Developmental

Partnership Objective	Drill near existing fields to discover new reserves (called step-out wells)
Advantages	Less discovery risk than exploratory
Disadvantages	Few new wells produce
Tax Features	Medium intangible drilling costs, immediate tax sheltering
Degree of Risk	Medium to high risk

Income

Partnership Objective	Provide immediate income from sale of existing oil
Advantages	Immediate cash flow
Disadvantages	Oil prices; well stops producing
Tax Features	Income sheltering from depletion allowances
Degree of Risk	Low

Equipment Leasing Programs

Equipment leasing programs are created when DPPs purchase equipment leased to other businesses. Investors receive income from lease payments and also a proportional share of write-offs from operating expenses, interest expenses, and depreciation. Tax credits were once available through these programs but were discontinued by tax law changes. The primary investment objective of these programs is tax-sheltered income.

Issuing Partnership Investments

DPPs may be offered either as private placements, qualifying for an exemption from registration under state and federal law, or publicly registered either with the SEC, the state(s) or both. Most are sold in private placements. When sold privately, they are usually limited to accredited investors.

Unlike most securities, sales are conditioned upon acceptance of subscribers. That means that just because the investor wants to buy, he may not be accepted by the GP. Many offerings use wholesalers. These are individuals or firms paid to serve as an interface between the issuer and broker-dealers and their sales force. It is legal for them to be compensated for their services. That compensation is usually on the basis of sales of program interests.

One of the most important requirements is performing **due diligence.** FINRA defines that as "the exercise of reasonable care to determine that the offering disclosures are accurate and complete." This helps the broker-dealer avoid fraud charges. Investigating the background of the management is one action taken in performing due diligence. For those who have a track record, checking it is an important step. Finally, the broker-dealer will evaluate all fees and other distribution of the offering's proceeds. At the end of this unit, we'll go a bit deeper into some of FINRA's rules on offering compensation.

LESSON 11.4: DPP TAXATION

LO 11.f Identify the tax ramifications of investing in DPPs.

Introduction

It is important to understand that a DPP is just a different way to invest in a business rather than buying the company's stock. There are certain tax advantages to being structured as a partnership with the flow-through of income or loss being one of them. That aside, this is merely an investment in a business, whether it be a Real Estate Limited Partnership, an oil and gas drilling program, or a movie production company. Important tax concepts associated with DPPs include the following:

- DPPs were formerly known as tax shelters because investors used losses to reduce or shelter ordinary income (by writing off passive losses against ordinary income).
- Tax law revisions now classify income and loss from these investments as passive income and loss. Current law allows passive losses to shelter only passive income, not all ordinary income as before. Many programs lost their appeal because of this critical change in tax law.
- As we learned in Unit 1, passive income is not considered earned income for the purpose of making an IRA contribution.
- The IRS considers programs without any economic viability to be abusive tax shelters. The promoters and investors can face severe penalties.

Flow-Through

The key tax benefit of DPPs is that they allow the economic consequences of a business to flow-through to investors. Any income or loss to the investor is considered passive because the investor does not take an active role in the management of the business—that is the role of the GP. Unlike corporations, limited partnerships pay no dividends. Rather, they pass income, gains, losses, deductions, and credits directly to investors. While each of the DPPs covered offer flow-through, some of the details are unique to each program. Let's look at them one at a time.

Real Estate Program Taxation

As we know, the tax benefit from all DPPs is that operating losses flow-through to investors. When a corporation loses money, there is no tax benefit to the shareholders. When a DPP shows a loss, that loss can be used to offset passive income and save on taxes. The exam wants you to know the specific source of those tax losses for each of the programs.

In the case of a real estate program, expenses creating the losses are

- mortgage interest expense,
- depreciation allowances for the "wearing out of the building," and
- expenses for improvement to the property.

In addition, there are two other benefits unique to real estate programs:

- Nonrecourse debt adds to the investor's cost basis. We will get to this shortly.
- **Tax credits are offered** for government-assisted housing and historic rehabilitation projects. The advantage of a tax credit is that is reduces tax liability dollar-for-dollar.

EXAMPLE

An individual in the 30% tax bracket receives a tax deduction of $1,000. By lowering her income by $1,000, she saves $300 in tax. But, if she received a $1,000 tax credit, she lowers her taxes by $1,000.

Oil and Gas Program Taxation

Unique tax advantages associated with oil and gas programs include intangible drilling costs (IDCs) and depletion allowances.

Intangible Drilling Costs

Write-offs for the expenses of drilling are usually 100% deductible in the first year of operation. These include costs associated with drilling such as wages, supplies, fuel costs, and insurance. **Intangible drilling costs (IDCs)** can be defined as any cost that, after being incurred, has no salvage value.

Tangible Drilling Costs

Tangible drilling costs are those costs incurred that have salvage value (e.g., storage tanks and wellhead equipment). These costs are not immediately deductible; rather, they are deducted (depreciated) over several years.

Depletion Allowances

The IRS allows allowances in the form of tax deductions that compensate the partnership for the decreasing supply of oil or gas (or any other resource or mineral). Depletion is only allowed for natural resource programs. That includes timber and mining DPPs.

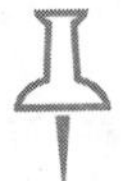

TAKE NOTE

Depletion allowances may be taken only once the oil or gas is sold. There are two forms of depletion, **cost** and **percentage**. Other than knowing these two terms, we do not expect any detail on these to be on the exam.

Oil and Gas Sharing Arrangements

The costs and revenues associated with oil and gas programs are shared in a variety of ways. A description of these arrangements follows:

- **Overriding royalty interest.** The holder of this interest receives royalties but has no partnership risk. An example of this arrangement is a landowner who sells mineral rights to a partnership.
- **Reversionary working interest.** The GP bears no costs of the program and receives no revenue until LPs have recovered their capital. LPs bear all deductible and nondeductible costs.
- **Net operating profits interest.** The GP bears none of the program's costs but is entitled to a percentage of net profits. The LPs bear all deductible and nondeductible costs. This arrangement is available only in private placements.
- **Disproportionate sharing.** The GP bears a relatively small percentage of expenses but receives a relatively large percentage of the revenues.
- **Carried interest.** The GP shares tangible drilling costs with the LPs but receives no IDCs. LPs receive the immediate deductions, whereas the GP receives write-offs from depreciation over the life of the property.
- **Functional allocation.** This is the most common sharing arrangement. The limited partnerships receive the IDCs, which allow immediate deductions. The GP receives the tangible drilling costs, which are depreciated over several years. Revenues are shared.

PRACTICE QUESTION

5. Which of the following sharing arrangements is the **most** common in an oil and gas DPP?
   A. Net operating profits interest
   B. Carried interest
   C. Functional allocation
   D. Overriding royalty interest

   Answer: C. Functional allocation is most commonly used because it gives the best benefits to both parties. The LPs receive the immediate tax write-offs from the IDCs, whereas the GPs receive continued write-offs from the tangible costs over the course of several years. Both share equally in the revenues.

Tax Features Applicable to All DPPs

As described, a partnership distributes income, losses, and gains to the LPs because of their flow-through nature. Limited partnerships, as with other businesses, are able to apply certain deductions and tax credits to income as described here.

Business Deductions

Expenses of the partnership, such as salaries, interest payments, and management fees, result in deductions in the current year to the income of the business. Principal payments on property are not deductible expenses. Compare that to a home mortgage. The interest is deductible, but that portion of the mortgage payments applied to reduce the loan is not.

Cost recovery systems offer write-offs over a period of years as defined by IRS schedules. **Depreciation write-offs** apply to cost recovery of expenditures for equipment and real estate (land cannot be depreciated). **Depletion allowances** apply to the using up of natural resources, such as oil and gas. Depreciation and depletion allowances may be claimed only when income is being produced by the partnership. Also, recognize that some assets are not depreciable, nor can they be depleted. For example, farm crops fall into this category and are generally known to be renewable assets.

TAKE NOTE

Depreciation may be taken on a straight-line (i.e., the same amount each year) or accelerated basis. Accelerated depreciation, known as a modified accelerated cost recovery system, increases deductions during the early years and decreases them during the later years.

TAKE NOTE

The crossover point is the point at which the program begins to generate taxable income instead of losses. This generally occurs in later years when income increases and deductions decrease.

Tax Basis

An investor's tax basis represents the upper limit on deductibility of losses. LPs must keep track of their **tax basis**, or amount at risk, to determine their gain or loss upon the sale of their partnership interest. An investor's basis is subject to adjustment periodically for occurrences such as cash distributions and additional investments.

TAKE NOTE

A LPs basis consists of

- cash contributions to the partnership,
- noncash property contributions to the partnership,
- recourse debt of the partnership, and
- nonrecourse debt for real estate partnerships only.

Partners must adjust their basis at year-end. Any distributions of cash or property and repayments of recourse debt (also nonrecourse debt for real estate only) are reductions to a partner's basis. Partners are allowed deductions up to the amount of their adjusted cost basis.

TAKE NOTE

With nonrecourse debt, other than any collateral pledged, the lender has no other option to pursue the borrower. With recourse debt, if the pledged collateral is not sufficient to satisfy the obligation, the lender can file a suit to recover the balance. As a lender, you would prefer recourse debt. As a borrower, you would prefer a nonrecourse loan.

EXAMPLE

If a partner's basis is $25,000 at year-end and the investor has losses of $35,000, only $25,000 of the losses may be used to deduct against passive income. The remaining $10,000 may be carried forward.

Computing Tax Basis

Tax basis is computed using the following formula:

> investment in partnership + share of recourse debt (+ nonrecourse debt in real estate DPPs) – cash or distributions = basis

It is important to note that any up-front costs incurred by the investor will not affect beginning basis. Assume that an LP invests $50,000 in a partnership unit, and the broker-dealer selling the unit takes a commission of $3,000. Therefore, only $47,000 of the investment goes into the partnership. However, the investor's beginning basis is $50,000, not $47,000.

PRACTICE QUESTION

6. A customer invests $10,000 in a DPP and signs a recourse note for $40,000. During the first year, the investor receives a cash distribution from the partnership for $5,000. At year-end, she receives a statement showing that her share of partnership losses is $60,000. How much of that $60,000 can she deduct on her tax return?

   Answer: The investor cannot deduct losses in excess of her year-end basis, $45,000, computed as follows:

investment	$10,000
+ recourse debt	$40,000
	$50,000
– cash distributions	$5,000
year-end basis	$45,000

TAKE NOTE

If a partnership interest is sold, the gain or loss is the difference between sales proceeds and adjusted basis at the time of sale. If, at the time of sale, the customer has unused losses, these losses may be added to the cost basis. If a customer has an adjusted cost basis of $22,000 and unused losses of $10,000 and sells her partnership interest for $20,000, her loss on the sale would be $12,000.

Tax Filing Requirements

Limited partnerships do not file a formal tax return because everything flows through to the investors. An information return is filed on Form 1065, with a Schedule K-1 sent to the partners indicating the amount of income or loss attributable to each of them. Remember, the business entity pays no income tax—all reportable income/loss flows through to the partners. Form 1065 is due on March 15 of the following year. The year-end for these businesses is typically December 31. Taxes are due on April 15, when the individual partners file their Form 1040s showing their share of the business's income or loss that was reported on the Schedule K-1.

LESSON 11.5 EVALUATING THE DPP

LO 11.g Recognize the importance of proper evaluation of DPPs.

Introduction

In selecting a limited partnership interest to participate in, an investor should first consider whether the partnership matches his investment objectives and has economic viability. **Economic viability** means that there is potential for returns from cash distributions and capital gains. Although tax benefits may be attractive, they should not be the first consideration in the purchase of an interest in a DPP.

Measuring Economic Soundness

There is an old saying in the real estate business. When valuing a property, what are the three most important factors? The answer is location, location, location. When it comes to evaluating a DPP, there are also three factors: *economic soundness, economic soundness,* and *economic soundness.* How is the economic soundness or viability measured? Two methods applied to the analysis of DPPs are cash flow analysis and internal rate of return.

- *Cash flow analysis* compares income (revenues) to expenses.
- *Internal rate of return* determines the present value of estimated future revenues and sales proceeds to allow comparison to other programs.

Cash Flow

Cash flow is defined as net income or loss plus noncash changes (such as depreciation).

EXAMPLE

Revenue:	$300,000
Less costs:	
Selling	$50,000
Interest	$70,000
Operating	$160,000
Depreciation	$50,000
	$330,000
Net loss:	($30,000)

This example shows a loss of $30,000. However, when we add back in depreciation, the cash flow is a positive $20,000.

net income or loss	($30,000)
+ depreciation	$50,000
cash flow	+$20,000

Internal Rate of Return

The internal rate of return (IRR) is the discount rate (r) that makes the future value of an investment equal to its present value.

You will not have to do any calculations with IRR. All you need to know is that it takes into consideration the time value of money and is a favorite method of evaluating a DPP.

Other Evaluation Factors

Here are additional factors that investors should consider in their overall analysis of these investments:

- Management ability and experience of the GP in running other similar programs
- **Blind pool** or nonspecific program—in a blind pool, less than 75% of the assets are specified as to use; however, in a specified program, at least 75% have been identified
- Time frame of the partnership
- Similarity of start-up costs and revenue projections to those of comparable ventures
- Lack of liquidity of the interest

Partnership interests are not for all investors. Careful consideration must be given to the overall safety and lack of liquidity of these programs before investing.

The DPP investor enjoys several advantages, including

- an investment managed by others;
- flow-through of income and certain expenses; and
- limited liability—the most the investors can lose is the amount of their investment plus any funds committed for, but not yet remitted.

The exam will probably give more attention to the following disadvantages:

- **Liquidity risk.** The greatest disadvantage for a DPP investor is lack of liquidity. Because the secondary market for DPPs is limited, investors who want to sell their interests frequently cannot locate buyers.
- **Legislative risk.** When Congress changes tax laws, new rules can cause substantial damage to LPs, who may be locked into illiquid investments that lose previously assumed tax advantages.

- **Leverage risk.** It is common for DPPs to use borrowed funds. Although the leverage can boost returns, it can have the same effect on losses. The risk is even higher when partnership uses recourse debt.
- **Risk of audit.** Statistics from the IRS indicate that reporting ownership of a DPP results in a significantly higher percentage of returns selected for audit.
- **Depreciation recapture**. One of the tax benefits is the ability to depreciate most fixed assets, especially when that depreciation can be accelerated. The effect of the depreciation deduction is to lower the tax basis of the asset. If that asset is then sold for more than that basis, the excess is recaptured and subject to tax, possibly at ordinary income tax rates. You won't need to know anything more than the concept.

LESSON 11.6: DPP REGULATION

LO 11.h Determine the rules and regulations pertaining to the sale of DPPs.

Introduction

As with the other investments we've discussed, there are common and specific regulations relating to the issuance and sale of DPPs.

FINRA Rules Dealing with DPPs

FINRA Rule 2310 is specifically titled Direct Participation Programs. Many of the requirements placed upon member firms and their representatives have been included where relevant in this unit.

FINRA Rule 2310

Before participating in a DPP offering, member firms must have reasonable grounds for believing, based on the information provided in the prospectus, that all material facts are adequately disclosed and that these facts provide a framework for customers to evaluate the program.

DPP Suitability

Under FINRA Rule 2310, all DPPs must have clearly stated standards of suitability in the prospectus. In recommending a DPP to a customer, a member firm must be certain that the program is consistent with the customer's objectives and that the customer

- is in a position to take full advantage of any tax benefits generated by the DPP; and
- has a net worth sufficient to sustain the risks of the DPP, including loss of investment.

The member, after making a suitability determination, must maintain documents in its files describing the basis on which the determination of suitability was made. In addition, no member is permitted to execute a DPP transaction in a discretionary account without the prior written consent of the customer.

DPP Compensation Restrictions

The rule places limits on the overall expenses and amount of broker-dealer compensation considered fair and reasonable. Specifically, if the organization and offering expenses exceed 15% of the gross proceeds, FINRA considers that too high. A subset of those expenses is the compensation to the member firm. That cannot exceed 10% of the gross proceeds. Included in the 10% is any compensation to wholesalers.

EXAMPLE

A DPP offering is sold in units of $10,000. It is prohibited for any member firm to participate in the offering if less than $8,500 is received by the issuer. Member compensation, including all participants in the sales chain, cannot exceed $1,000.

Noncash Compensation

The rules on noncash compensation are the same as covered previously in Unit 8. For example, gifts cannot exceed $100 per year. An occasional meal or ticket to a sporting event would be permitted.

DPP Roll-Up

A **roll-up** is a transaction involving the combination or reorganization of one or more limited partnerships into securities of a successor corporation. The lure to investors is the possibility of turning an illiquid DPP into a more liquid security.

Disclosure documents prepared in connection with a proposed roll-up transaction must

- disclose all the risk factors;
- disclose the GP's belief concerning fairness of the transaction; and
- include all reports, opinions, and appraisals received by the GP in connection with the transaction.

Failure to provide adequate disclosure of a negative opinion rendered by an investment banker or financial adviser concerning fairness constitutes fraud.

Under FINRA rules, members are prohibited from soliciting votes from LPs in connection with a proposed roll-up unless any compensation to be received by the member

- is payable and equal in amount regardless of whether the LPs vote affirmatively or negatively and
- does not exceed 2% of the value of the securities to be received in the exchange.

PRACTICE QUESTION

7. Under FINRA rule 2310, which of the following DPP compensation arrangements would be prohibited?
   A. Organization and offering expenses not exceeding 15% of the gross proceeds
   B. Compensation to a selling member firm not exceeding 15% of the gross proceeds
   C. Compensation to a selling member firm not exceeding 10% of the gross proceeds
   D. Roll-up compensation not exceeding 2% of the securities received

Answer: B. The maximum compensation to a member firm involved in the sale of a DPP is 10% of the gross proceeds. The rule permits an additional 5% for administrative, organization, and offering expenses. That brings the total maximum to 15%.

SEC Rules Dealing With DPPs

Most DPPs are private offerings under Regulation D of the Securities Act of 1933. That will be covered in detail in Unit 20. Generally, purchasers must be accredited investors as defined in SEC Rule 501. DPPs that are offered to the public must meet the SEC's registration requirements. We will discuss those in Unit 20.

UNIT 12

Other Securities Products

LEARNING OBJECTIVES

When you have completed this unit, you will be able to accomplish the following.

- LO 12.a **Determine** the structure of hedge funds.
- LO 12.b **Recognize** the special characteristics of hedge funds.
- LO 12.c **Recall** the different types of asset-backed securities.
- LO 12.d **Recognize** the special characteristics of asset-based securities (ABS).

INTRODUCTION

When the subject is securities, we tend to limit ourselves to stocks and bonds, and perhaps mutual funds as well. There are many other securities, but most of them tend to be limited to sophisticated or high wealth investors. That is certainly true of the hedge fund. For those investors with a higher level of sophistication, collateralized mortgage obligations (CMOs) and collateralized debt obligations (CDOs) can be attractive alternatives to bonds.

LESSON 12.1: HEDGE FUNDS

LO 12.a Determine the structure of hedge funds.

Hedge Fund Structure

Hedge fund structures are a form of fund generally organized as a limited partnership with no more than 100 investors. That keeps the fund from having to register with the SEC. Because there is no registration requirement, one of the differences between a mutual fund and a hedge fund is the hedge fund's lack of transparency. A mutual fund is offered via a prospectus filed with the SEC, while a hedge fund's prospectus is generally referred to as a private placement memorandum containing significantly less information.

It is important to recognize that hedge funds are not investment companies under the Investment Company Act of 1940. Their structure is such that they qualify for an exemption from the definition. This allows them flexibility that would not be possible as an investment company.

TEST TOPIC ALERT

Most hedge funds are organized as limited partnerships with the portfolio managers investing, along with the investors. As they say in the industry, they have "skin in the game" so they have a greater motivation to succeed. The partnership is the issuer of the ownership units.

PRACTICE QUESTION

1. Which type of fund is **most** often organized as a limited partnership?
   A. Face-amount certificate (FAC) company
   B. Exchange-traded fund (ETF)
   C. Hedge fund
   D. Unit investment trust (UIT)

   Answer: C. For various legal reasons, mostly related to the need to avoid registration with the SEC, hedge funds are generally structured as limited partnership entities with the organizers invariably sinking their own funds into a few units.

LO 12.b Recognize the special characteristics of hedge funds.

Hedge Fund Characteristics

Hedge Fund Strategies

Hedge funds are similar to mutual funds in that investments are pooled and professionally managed, but they differ in that the fund has more flexibility in the investment strategies employed, and are unregulated by U.S. securities laws. They are aggressively-managed portfolios of investments that use advanced investment strategies. Generally, these investment vehicles are considered suitable for sophisticated investors—those meeting the standard of accredited investors. While hedging is the practice of attempting to limit risk, most hedge funds specify generating high returns as their primary investment objective. Some of the more common strategies employed by hedge funds are

- highly leveraged portfolios,
- the use of short positions,
- utilizing derivative products such as options and futures,
- currency speculation,
- commodity speculation, and
- investing in politically unstable international markets.

Because hedge funds—unlike mutual funds or investment companies—are unregulated, the very nature of the investment is almost always considered speculative. Most also require that investors maintain the investment for a minimum length of time (e.g., one year) and to that extent they can be considered illiquid. These requirements are known as *lock-up provisions.*

TAKE NOTE

Although hedge funds are unregulated, U.S. laws do require that most investors meet the test of a sophisticated investor. They should be considered accredited investors, having a minimum annual income and net worth, and have considerable investment knowledge.

Hedge Fund Lock-Up Provisions

This provision provides that during a certain initial period, an investor may not make a withdrawal from the fund. The period when the investor cannot withdraw investment dollars is known as the lock-up period—the investor's capital is locked up. Generally recognized as one way the manager of the hedge fund portfolio can have capital retained in the fund, it is also seen to be another factor adding to the unique risk of hedge funds—in this case, shares being illiquid for that specified length of time.

Lock-up periods are generally associated with new or start-up hedge funds and can differ in length from one fund to another. The length of the lock-up period will largely be dependent on what the investment strategy of the fund is and how long the portfolio manager anticipates it will take to implement the strategy and then see results of that implementation.

Hedge Fund Management Fees

Another important feature of hedge funds is that management fees tend to be considerably higher than with other investments. Almost all hedge funds charge performance-based fees. The typical fee structure is known by the vernacular 2 & 20—most funds take a 2% management fee and 20% of any profits. This creates a strong incentive for the manager to attempt to generate higher returns. As is true with all investments, the higher the potential return, the greater the risk.

Therefore, because of the higher risk, investment in these vehicles is limited to institutional clients and wealthy individuals, known as accredited investors.

PRACTICE QUESTION

2. Which of the following characteristics do hedge funds share with mutual funds?
   - A. A high degree of transparency
   - B. Relatively low management costs
   - C. A pooled investment with other investors
   - D. High liquidity

Answer: C. From what we've covered, you should have seen that hedge funds do not offer the transparency of mutual funds. The key to getting that point is that they are not registered with the SEC, so the disclosures that must be made are limited. The management fees for hedge funds are much higher than mutual funds and, because of the lock-up period, their liquidity is questionable. However, the common characteristic is that they are pooled investments.

Funds of Hedge Funds

Though hedge funds discussed in this unit are generally available to and suitable for highly qualified or sophisticated (accredited) investors, there are registered mutual funds available to all investors that invest primarily in unregistered hedge funds known as **funds of hedge funds**. They can target and diversify among several hedge funds and, in this way, give non-accredited investors access to hedge funds. These funds share some of the benefits and risks associated with hedge funds.

One benefit is that lower initial investments are required than when investing directly in a hedge fund. In contrast, one risk to note is that like all mutual funds, the shares are not traded in the secondary markets. Selling your shares can only occur if the mutual fund company redeems them. Because the underlying assets are not liquid, this fund is not as liquid as other mutual funds. Another point to discuss with clients is that, in addition to the high hedge fund fees, investors also pay a management fee to the fund, just as with any mutual fund. Recommendations of funds of hedge funds would need to disclose the specific risks associated with hedge funds and the transfer of those risks that occurs when mutual funds invest in hedge funds.

Blank-Check or Blind-Pool Hedge Fund

Some hedge funds target blank-check companies to invest in. Blank-check companies, sometimes known as special purpose acquisition companies (SPACs), carry their own unique risks. Blank-check companies are companies without business operations that raise money through IPOs in order to have their shares publicly traded for the sole purpose of seeking out a business or combination of businesses. When a business is located, they will present proposals to holders of their shares for approval.

Some hedge funds target blind-pool companies. Similar to blank-check companies, these issuers raise capital by selling securities to the public without telling investors what the specific use of the proceeds will be, but might target a particular industry or sector.

Some characterize blank-check companies as a type of blind pool, with one discernable difference. While the blind-pool company will usually provide at least some indication of what general industry the funds will be invested in, blank-check offerings do not identify any proposed investment intent.

While some hedge funds target these types of holdings for their portfolios, it should be noted that they might be included within any hedge fund portfolio and, in both cases, should be considered when assessing risk and determining suitability.

LESSON 12.2: ASSET-BACKED SECURITIES

LO 12.c Recall the different types of asset-backed securities.

Types of Asset-Backed Securities (ABS)

There are number of different types of asset-backed securities (ABS), but they all have one thing in common: their value and income payments are derived from or backed by a specific pool of underlying assets. These pools of assets can include expected payments from different types of loans such as mortgages—as is the case with CMOs—auto loans, or other types of loans. In some instances, ABS can pool expected cash flow from credit cards, leases, or even royalty payments.

Pooling the assets into financial instruments allows them to be sold to general investors more easily than selling them individually. This process is called *securitization*, and it allows the risk of investing in the underlying assets to be diversified, because each security will now represent only a fraction of the total value of the diverse pool of underlying assets. The common theme among all ABS is the contractual obligation to pay the debt.

TAKE NOTE

This is probably beyond the exam, but, this is for just in case FINRA decides to go deeper. The securitization process involves the creation of a special purpose entity (SPE). The title to the assets is transferred to the SPE. The SPE then issues the ABS using those assets as collateral.

Collateralized Mortgage Obligations (CMOs)

CMOs pool a large number of mortgages, usually on single-family residences. CMOs are issued by private-sector financing corporations and are often backed by Ginnie Mae, Fannie Mae, and Freddie Mac pass-through securities. As a result, CMOs backed by government agency securities have historically been highly rated.

Collateralized Debt Obligations (CDOs)

CDOs are complex ABS. CDOs do not specialize in any single type of debt. In almost all cases, their portfolios consist of nonmortgage loans or bonds. The assets backing the CDOs can be a pool of bonds, auto loans, or other assets such as leases, credit card debt, a company's receivables, or even derivative products of any of the assets listed. While the individual assets may be small and not very liquid, pooling the assets facilitates them being sold to individual investors in the secondary markets.

Amortizing and Nonamortizing CDOs

An amortizing loan is one in which regular payments are made against the principal. This results in an investor's return consisting of principal along with interest. At the end of the term, the principal has been repaid. The most common examples of this in our everyday lives are the mortgages on our homes or the loans on our automobiles. An auto loan CDO is the classic example of an amortizing ABS.

A nonamortizing CDO is one backed by debt obligations without a fixed ending date. The classic example of a nonamortizing ABS is the credit card CDO.

LO 12.d Recognize the special characteristics of asset-backed securities (ABS).

Characteristics of ABS

CMOs and CDOs have many similar characteristics. The exam tends to focus on CMOs, so we will start there. If you find this confusing, FINRA understands that. In fact, any client of a member firm wishing to invest in CMOs must complete a special suitability form. As you work your way through our SecuritiesPro q-bank, you'll catch on to the most tested items.

Characteristics of CMOs

CMOs pool a large number of mortgages, usually on single-family residences. A pool of mortgages is structured into maturity classes called **tranches** (the French word for *slice*). A CMO pays principal and interest from the mortgage pool monthly; however, it repays principal to only one tranche at a time.

In addition to interest payments, investors in a short-term tranche must receive their entire principal before the next tranche begins to receive principal repayments. Principal payments are made in $1,000 increments to randomly selected bonds within a tranche. Changes in interest rates affect the rate of mortgage prepayments, and this, in turn, affects the flow of interest payment and principal repayment to the CMO investor.

TAKE NOTE

As you will learn, there are many different varieties of CMOs. We have just described the *plain vanilla* CMO. As we stated, each of the tranches receives interest payment simultaneously. However, it pays principal to only one tranche at a time until it is retired. Subsequent principal payments are made to the next tranche in line until it is paid off, and so on.

A CMO's yield and maturity are estimates based on historical data or projections of mortgage prepayments from the Public Securities Association (PSA). The particular tranche an investor owns determines the priority of her principal repayment. The time to maturity, amount of interest received, and amount of principal returned are not guaranteed. The model developed by the PSA compensates for the fact that prepayment assumptions will change during the life of an obligation and that this will affect the yield of the security.

Figure 12.1: Sample CMO Tranche Structure

Tranche	Interest Rate	Estimated Life in Years
1	5.125%	1.5
2	5.25%	3.5
3	5.5%	6.0
4	5.875%	8.5
5	6.125%	11.0

PRACTICE QUESTION

3. CMOs are generally backed by which of the following assets?
   A. Mortgages
   B. Real estate
   C. Auto loans
   D. Bonds

   Answer: A. The *M* in CMO stands for mortgages. It isn't the real estate (that is what backs the mortgage).

Classes of CMOs

In addition to the standard CMOs discussed, some CMOs have been structured to suit specific needs of investors. Common CMO types include

- principal only,
- interest only,
- planned amortization class, and
- targeted amortization class.

Principal Only CMOs (POs)

The flow of income from underlying mortgages is divided into principal and interest streams and directed to the **principal only CMOs (POs)** owners and **interest-only CMOs (IOs)**, respectively. For a PO, the income stream comes from principal payments on the underlying mortgages—both scheduled mortgage principal payments and prepayments. Thus, the security ultimately repays its entire face value to the investor.

A PO sells at a discount from par; the difference between the discounted price and the principal value is the investor's return. Its market value, like all deeply discounted securities, tends to be volatile. POs, in particular, are affected by fluctuations in prepayment rates. The value of a PO rises as interest rates drop and prepayments accelerate, and its value falls when interest rates rise and prepayments decline.

Interest-Only CMOs (IOs)

IOs are by-products of POs. Whereas POs receive the principal stream from underlying mortgages, IOs receive the interest. An IO also sells at a discount, and its cash flow declines over time, just as the proportion of interest in a mortgage payment declines over time. Unlike POs, IOs increase in value when interest rates rise, and they decline in value when interest rates fall because the number of interest payments changes as prepayment rates change. Thus, they can be used to hedge a portfolio against interest-rate risk.

When prepayment rates are high, the owner of an IO may receive fewer interest payments than anticipated. Because the entire CMO series receives more principal sooner, and therefore less overall interest, the IO owner does not know how long the stream of interest payments will last.

Planned Amortization Class CMOs (PACs)

PACs have targeted maturity dates; they are retired first and offer protection from **prepayment risk** and **extension risk** (the chance that principal payments will be slower than anticipated) because changes in prepayments are transferred to companion tranches, also called support tranches.

Targeted Amortization Class CMOs (TACs)

A TAC structure transfers prepayment risk only to a companion tranche and does not offer protection from extension risk. TAC investors accept the extension risk and the resulting greater price risk in exchange for a slightly higher interest rate.

Zero-Tranche CMO (Z-Tranche)

A Z-tranche CMO receives no payment until all preceding CMO tranches are retired. These are the most volatile CMO tranches.

TEST TOPIC ALERT

Z-tranche CMOs would not be suitable for an investor needing funds in a specified amount of time, because of the unpredictable nature of when payment will be received.

CMO Risks

Because mortgages back CMOs, they are considered relatively safe. However, their susceptibility to interest rate movements and the resulting changes in the mortgage repayment rate mean CMOs carry several risks:

- The rate of principal repayment varies.
- If interest rates fall and homeowner refinancing increases, principal is received sooner than anticipated (prepayment risk).
- If interest rates rise and refinancing declines, the CMO investor may have to hold his investment longer than anticipated (extended maturity risk). This is sometimes called extension risk.

Other CMO Characteristics

Returns on CMOs

CMOs yield more than Treasury securities and normally pay investors interest and principal monthly. Principal repayments are made in $1,000 increments to investors in one tranche before any principal is repaid to the next tranche.

Taxation

Interest from CMOs is subject to federal, state, and local taxes.

Liquidity

There is an active secondary market for CMOs. Trading is done OTC. However, the market for CMOs with more complex characteristics may be limited or nonexistent. Certain tranches of a given CMO may be riskier than others, and some CMOs in certain tranches carry the risk that repayment of principal may take longer than anticipated.

Denominations

CMOs are issued in $1,000 denominations.

Suitability

Some varieties of CMOs, such as PAC companion tranches, may be particularly unsuitable for small or unsophisticated investors because of their complexity and risks. The customer must sign a **suitability statement** before buying any CMO. Potential investors must understand that the rate of return on CMOs may vary because of early repayment. Also note that the performance of CMOs may not be compared with any other investment vehicle.

TEST TOPIC ALERT

It will be useful to know the following summary:

- CMOs are not backed by the U.S. government; they are corporate instruments.
- Interest paid is taxable at all levels.
- CMOs are backed by mortgage pools.
- CMOs yield more than U.S. Treasury securities.
- CMOs are subject to interest-rate risk.
- CMOs are issued in $1,000 denominations and trade OTC.
- PACs have the least prepayment and extension risk.
- TACs are protected against prepayment risk but not extension risk.

Because of the lower risk, PACs have lower yields than comparable TACs.

PRACTICE QUESTION

4. Which of the following debt securities does **not** have a fixed maturity date?
   A. Collateralized mortgage obligation (CMO)
   B. General obligation (GO) bond
   C. Treasury STRIPS
   D. Subordinated debenture

   Answer: A. CMOs are mortgage-backed securities (MBS). Because mortgages are often paid off ahead of the scheduled maturity, the exact maturity date of a CMO is uncertain.

General Characteristics of CDOs

Similar in structure to CMOs, CDOs represent different types of debt and credit risk. Like CMOs, the different types of debt and risk categories are often called *tranches*. Each tranche has a different maturity and risk associated with it. The higher the risk, the more the CDO pays. In practice, investors will choose a tranche with a risk-and-return combination that is suitable for them.

Cautions when investing with CDOs should include the following:

- Some CDOs are so complex that individual investors may not fully understand the product and, therefore, do not understand what they are purchasing. While the securitization of the assets easily enables their sale to individual investors, the product is recognized as being more suitable to institutional or sophisticated investors.
- The sale of the individual assets from the originators of the loans to those who are repackaging them allows the originators to avoid having to collect on them when they become due because they are now owned by someone else. In this case, the issuer of the

CDO owns the assets. In turn, this may lead to originators of loans being less judicious and disciplined in adhering to sound lending practices when the loans are made.

- FINRA has found that a significant percentage of registered representatives selling CDOs do not understand them. Member firms have been fined for failure to supervise and the reps are often fined and/or suspended. If this is a product you will be recommending, please be sure to learn the ins and outs of the product.

PRACTICE QUESTION

5. The term *tranche* is associated with which of the following investments?
   A. Mortgages and ELNs
   B. ETNs and ETFs
   C. CDOs and CMOs
   D. Fannie Mae and Freddie Mac

Answer: C. The different maturities of CDOs and CMOs are called tranches.

UNIT 13

Portfolio or Account Analysis and Its Application to Security Selection

LEARNING OBJECTIVES

When you have completed this unit, you will be able to accomplish the following.

- › LO 13.a **Discriminate** between the major asset classes used in an asset allocation program and how that diversifies a portfolio.
- › LO 13.b **Identify** the components and goals of the modern portfolio theory.
- › LO 13.c **Recognize** balance sheet and income statement items and their use in fundamental analysis.
- › LO 13.d **Calculate** key measurements of financial health.
- › LO 13.e **Recall** market analysis considerations and their use in technical analysis.
- › LO 13.f **Identify** the specific market analysis considerations for municipal securities.
- › LO 13.g **Analyze** the importance of costs and fees when selecting investments.
- › LO 13.h **Define** the tax considerations applied when selecting investments.

INTRODUCTION

By analyzing an investment portfolio and analyzing an account, products may be selected to fit the needs of the customer. One of the important items to consider is the performance of various securities that are recommended.

The securities and performance measures will depend on the information gathered and the customer's investment experience. Aggressive investors may try timing the market and seek capital appreciation.

EXAMPLE

A customer may like moving in and out of the market. If trading a lot, it would be important to know whether market prices are going up, have started to slide, or seem to have reached a plateau. On the other hand, a buy-and-hold investor may be more concerned about the stock's value 15–20 years in the future, and is likely to be more interested in whether it has a pattern of earnings growth and seems to be well-positioned for future expansion.

With a conservative investor or one who is approaching retirement, the primary concern may be the income your investments provide. An examination of the interest rate that bonds and CDs are paying in relation to current market rates would be important. An evaluation of the yield from stock and mutual funds bought for the income they provide is important. Of course, if market rates are down, reinvestment opportunities may disappoint as existing bonds mature. There may be a temptation to buy investments with a lower rating in expectation of getting a potentially higher return. In either event, a performance measure that assesses the risk to the results would be helpful when making investment decisions.

In **measuring investment performance,** be sure to avoid comparing apples to oranges. Finding and applying the right evaluation standards for investments is important. Otherwise, the wrong conclusions may result.

EXAMPLE

There's little reason to compare yield from a growth mutual fund with yield from a Treasury bond, because they don't fulfill the same role in a portfolio. Instead, one measures performance for a growth fund by comparing it to other growth-oriented investments, such as a growth fund index or an equity market index

LESSON 13.1: ASSET ALLOCATION AND MODERN PORTFOLIO THEORY

LO 13.a Discriminate between the major asset classes used in an asset allocation program and how that diversifies a portfolio.

Asset Classes

Diversification, with its emphasis on variety, allows the spreading of assets around. In short, don't put all your investment eggs in one basket. Where your spread those assets is critical. That is what asset allocation is all about.

Asset allocation (more accurately, but rarely stated, asset *class* allocation) refers to the spreading of portfolio funds among different asset classes with difference risk-and-return characteristics, based on the investment policy statement. Proponents of asset allocation feel that the mix of assets within a portfolio, rather than individual stock selection or marketing timing, is the primary factor underlying the variability of returns in portfolio performance. There are three major types (each with subclasses) of asset classes:

- Stock, with subclasses based on market capitalization, value versus growth, and foreign equity
- Bonds, with subclasses based on maturity (intermediate versus long-term), and issuer (Treasury versus corporate versus non-U.S. issuers)
- Cash, focusing mainly on the standard risk-free investment, the 91-day (13 week) Treasury bill, but also including other short-term money market instruments

Proper asset allocation takes into consideration the investor's desire for preservation of capital income, capital growth, or a combination of all of these.

In some instances, tangible assets, such as real estate (usually in the form of REITs), precious metals, and other commodities, and certain collectibles (think fine art), are part of the asset allocation because these types of assets tend to reduce inflation risk. Increasingly, institutional investors (and some very high net worth individuals because of the high cost of entry) are using such alternative investment asset classes as ETNs, private equity, and venture capital. It is important to understand that asset allocation is not simply spreading the money around helter-skelter to different asset classes—there is a process.

One form of diversification popular with municipal bond investors is geographic. That is, the portfolio is constructed with bonds issued from different areas of the country.

Strategic Asset Allocation

Strategic asset allocation refers to the proportion of various types of investments composing a long-term investment portfolio. This is a passive strategy.

EXAMPLE

A standard asset allocation model suggests subtracting a person's age from 100 to determine the percentage of the portfolio to be invested in stocks. According to this method, a 30-year-old would be 70% invested in stocks and 30% in bonds and cash; a 70-year-old would be invested 30% in stocks with the remainder in bonds and cash.

Over time, the portfolio is **rebalanced** to bring the asset mix back to the target allocations. If the stock market should perform better than expected, the client's proportion of stocks to bonds would be out of balance. So, on some timely basis (perhaps quarterly), stocks would be sold and bonds would be purchased (or funds would be placed in cash) to bring the proportions back to the desired levels.

Tactical Asset Allocation

Tactical asset allocation refers to short-term portfolio adjustments that adjust the portfolio mix between asset classes in consideration of current market conditions. This is an active strategy.

TEST TOPIC ALERT

In Lesson 1.1, we discussed the fee-based account. Those who practice tactical asset allocation, buying and selling to try to "time the market," are candidates for that type of account. A fee-based account is likely to be unsuitable for one using strategic asset allocation.

LO 13.b Identify the components and goals of the modern portfolio theory.

Modern Portfolio Theory (MPT)

Managing risk is about the allocation and diversification of holdings in a portfolio. Investments should be chosen with an eye to what is already owned and how the new investment helps achieve greater balance.

For example, an investment strategy might include some investments that may be volatile because they have the potential to increase dramatically in value, when other investments in your portfolio are unlikely to have the same potential.

Modern portfolio theory (MPT) employs a scientific approach to measuring risk and, by extension, to choosing investments. It involves calculating projected returns of various portfolio combinations to identify those that are likely to provide the best returns at different levels of risk. It is the concept of minimizing risk by combining volatile and price-stable investments in a single portfolio.

Harry Markowitz, the founder of MPT, explained how to best assemble a diversified portfolio and proved that the portfolio with a lower amount of volatility would do better than a portfolio with a greater amount of volatility. This concept appeals to those with a lower risk tolerance, i.e., risk averse.

MPT focuses on the relationships among all the investments in a portfolio. This theory holds that specific risks can be diversified by building portfolios of securities whose returns are not correlated. MPT seeks to reduce the risk in a portfolio while simultaneously increasing expected returns.

Holding securities that tend to move in the same direction as one another does not lower an investor's risk. Diversification reduces risk only when assets whose prices move inversely, or at different times, in relation to one another are combined.

In other words, MPT wants securities in a portfolio to have **negative correlation**, not **positive correlation**. Perfect negative correlation is –1.0 and would indicate that if one security goes up, the other security would go down the same amount. Obviously, this is not an exact science, but it is an indication of the movement of the portfolio.

Some analysis tools that are used in MPT include the following terms.

Capital Asset Pricing Model (CAPM)

The capital asset pricing model (CAPM) is used to calculate the return that an investment should achieve based on the risk that is taken. The more risk taken, the higher the potential returns. Investors should be rewarded for the risk they take. CAPM calculates a required return based on a risk multiplier called the *beta coefficient.*

A portfolio's **total risk** is made up of nonsystematic (unsystematic) risk and systematic risk. Those risks are covered in the next unit—you might want to take a quick look at them now. If an investor has a diversified portfolio, nonsystematic risk is reduced to almost zero. Therefore, the only real risk is systematic risk, and this is the risk that needs a required return.

Investors with a well-diversified portfolio will find that the risk affecting the portfolio is wholly systematic (markets moving together). Individual investments have both systematic and unsystematic risk; however, in a portfolio that is diversified, only the systematic risk of a new security would be relevant.

In other words, if an individual investment becomes part of a well-diversified portfolio, the unsystematic risk can be ignored.

PRACTICE QUESTION

1. Which of the following types of risk cannot be eliminated through diversification under the modern portfolio theory?
   A. Interest-rate risk
   B. Systematic risk
   C. Business risk
   D. Liquidity risk

Answer: B. Market risk, sometimes referred to as systematic risk, cannot be diversified away. The risk of investing in a single industry or sector can be diversified away by investing in several industries with returns not correlated to one another. A general downturn in the market, however, cannot be eliminated through diversification.

Beta Coefficient

Beta and **beta coefficient** mean the same thing. In the securities industry, the word *coefficient* is ordinarily dropped for purposes of convenience. A stock or portfolio's beta is a measure of its volatility in relation to the overall market (systematic risk). The overall market is typically based on the S&P 500. A security that has a beta of one moves in line with the market. A security or portfolio with a beta of greater than one is generally going to be more volatile than the overall market. The reverse is true when the beta is less than one.

A security that does not move in relation to market movement would have a beta of zero. For example, a money market security or money market mutual fund would have a beta of close to zero.

TAKE NOTE

If the S&P 500 rises or falls by 10%, a stock with a beta of one rises or falls by about 10%, a stock with a beta of 1.5 rises or falls by about 15%, and a stock with a beta of 0.75 rises or falls by about 7.5%.

PRACTICE QUESTION

2. Adding investments with a negative beta to a well-diversified portfolio that currently has a beta of +1.0 will cause
   A. the expected performance of the portfolio to improve in declining markets.
   B. the expected performance of the portfolio to decline in declining markets.
   C. the portfolio to experience more volatility in times of a rising market.
   D. the portfolio to experience more volatility in times of a declining market.

Answer: A. A negative beta means that the investment will move in an opposite direction from the overall market. Therefore, if the market is declining, then the asset should increase in value, thereby increasing the expected performance of the portfolio.

Alpha

Analysts advise when to buy, sell, or hold securities. The CAPM is a method that analysts may use to make these decisions. Based on its beta, an analyst would calculate the expected return for the security. **Alpha** is the extent to which an asset's or portfolio's return exceeds or falls short of its expected return. A positive alpha would indicate a buy recommendation.

EXAMPLE

If an investment has a beta of 1.5, it is 50% more volatile than the market. Therefore, if the market goes up 10%, it is expected that the investment with a beta of 1.5 will go up 15%.

However, if the investment only goes up 11%, the investor took a greater risk for less return on their money. So the return of 11% is less than the 15% expected return (negative alpha).

If the investment increased by 17%, the investor received a greater return than the risk taken. So the return of 17% is greater than the expected return of 15% (positive alpha).

The CAPM calculation of alpha would replace the expected return with the required return. You will not have to compute alpha on the exam. Just understand the concept.

TAKE NOTE

A positive alpha, rather than a negative one, is desirable.

PRACTICE QUESTION

3. When looking at the alpha of a particular investment, you notice it is a negative number, and that indicates
   A. the investment lost money.
   B. the investor took more risk than the return received.
   C. the investment is not volatile.
   D. a very efficient portfolio manager.

Answer: B. Alpha measures the extent to which the return exceeded or fell below the expected return for the risk taken. When the alpha is negative, the investor's return was too low for the risk taken.

LESSON 13.2: FUNDAMENTAL ANALYSIS WITH FINANCIAL STATEMENTS

LO 13.c Recognize balance sheet and income statement items and their use in fundamental analysis.

Introduction

Fundamental analysis is the study of the business prospects of an individual company within the context of its industry and the overall economy. They do this by examining the company in detail, including the **financial statements** and company management. We could compare this to an individual receiving a full physical examination that, in addition to all kinds of tests, would include a detailed family medical history. With a company, the financial statement analysis is like the blood tests, x-rays, stress tests, and so forth, and the evaluation of the company's management is like the medical history.

Financial Statements

A corporation's **financial statements** provide a fundamental analyst with the information needed to assess that corporation's profitability, liquidity, financial strength (ability of cash flow to meet debt payments), and operating efficiency. By examining how certain numbers from one statement relate to prior statements, and how the resulting ratios relate to the company's competitors, the analyst can determine how financially viable the company is.

Companies issue quarterly and annual financial reports to the SEC. A company's balance sheet and income statement are included in these reports.

What is a Balance Sheet?

The balance sheet provides a snapshot of a company's financial position at a specific point in time. It identifies the value of the company's assets (what it owns) and its liabilities (what it owes). The difference between these two figures is the corporation's owners' equity, or net worth.

The balance sheet equation is

- assets – liabilities = owners' equity; or
- assets = liabilities + owners' equity.

Although it is useful in determining a company's current value, the balance sheet does not indicate whether the company's business is improving or deteriorating. The balance sheet gets its name from the fact that its two sides must balance. The balance sheet equation mathematically expresses the relationship between its two sides. Simply stated, everything that is owned (assets) minus everything that is owed (liabilities) is equal to the net worth (owners' or shareholders' equity) of the entity.

Assets

Assets appear on the balance sheet in order of liquidity, which is the ease with which they can be turned into cash. Assets that are most readily convertible into cash are listed first, followed by less liquid assets. Balance sheets commonly identify three types of assets: current assets (cash and assets easily convertible into cash), fixed assets (physical assets that could eventually be sold), and other assets (usually intangible and only of value to the corporation that owns them).

Current Assets

Current assets include all cash and other items expected to be converted into cash within the next 12 months, including the following:

- Cash and equivalents include cash and short-term safe investments, such as money market instruments that can be readily sold, as well as other marketable securities.
- Accounts receivable include amounts due from customers for goods delivered or services rendered, reduced by the allowance for bad debts.
- Inventory is the cost of raw materials, work in process, and finished goods ready for sale.
- Prepaid expenses are items a company has already paid for but has not yet benefited from, such as prepaid advertising, rents, insurance, and operating supplies.

Fixed Assets

Fixed assets are property, plant, and equipment. Unlike current assets, they are not easily converted into cash. Fixed assets, such as factories, have limited useful lives because wear and tear eventually reduce their value. For this reason, their cost can be depreciated over time or deducted from taxable income in annual installments to compensate for loss in value.

Other Assets

Intangible assets are nonphysical properties, such as formulas, brand names, contract rights, and trademarks. Goodwill, also an intangible asset, reflects the corporation's reputation and relationship with its clients.

TAKE NOTE

Although intangible assets may have great value to the corporation owning them, they generally carry little value to other entities.

Liabilities

Total liabilities on a balance sheet represent all financial claims by creditors against the corporation's assets. Balance sheets usually include two main types of liabilities: current liabilities and long-term liabilities.

Current Liabilities

Current liabilities are corporate debt obligations due for payment within the next 12 months. These include the following:

- *Accounts payable.* Amounts owed to suppliers of materials and other business costs.
- *Accrued wages payable.* Unpaid wages, salaries, commissions, and interest.
- *Current long-term debt.* Any portion of long-term debt due within 12 months.
- *Notes payable.* The balance due on equipment purchased on credit or cash borrowed.
- *Accrued taxes.* Unpaid federal, state, and local taxes.

Long-Term Liabilities

Long-term liabilities are financial obligations due for payment after 12 months. Examples include bonds and mortgages.

TAKE NOTE

Long-term debts include mortgages on real property and outstanding corporate bonds.

What is an Income Statement?

The **income statement**, sometimes called the profit and loss or P&L statement, summarizes a company's revenues (sales) and expenses for a fiscal period, usually quarterly, year to date, or the full year. It compares revenue against costs and expenses during the period. Fundamental analysts use the income statement to judge the efficiency and profitability of a company's operation. Just as with the balance sheet, technical analysts generally ignore this information—it is not relevant to their charting schemes.

Components of the Income Statement

A discussion of the various operating and nonoperating expenses on the income statement follows.

Revenues indicate the firm's total sales during the period (the money that came in).

The **cost of goods sold (COGS)** is the costs of labor, material, and production (including depreciation on assets employed in production) used to create finished goods. Subtracting COGS from revenues shows the gross operating profit. The two major methods of accounting for material costs are the first in, first out method (FIFO) and last in, first out method (LIFO). Under LIFO accounting, COGS normally will reflect higher costs of more recently purchased inventory (last items in). As a result of higher reported production costs under LIFO, reported income is reduced. The opposite is true if the FIFO method is used.

Pretax margin is determined by subtracting COGS and other operating costs (rent and utilities) from sales to arrive at net operating profit. The resulting figure is earnings before interest and taxes (EBIT).

Interest payments on a corporation's debt is not considered an operating expense. However, interest payments reduce the corporation's taxable income. **Pretax income**, the amount of taxable income, is operating income less interest payment expenses.

If dividends are paid to stockholders, they are paid out of net income after taxes have been paid. After dividends have been paid, the remaining income is added to retained earnings and is available to invest in the business.

TEST TOPIC ALERT

Please note the previous three terms in boldface. Revenue (or sales), COGS, and pretax income are the three primary components of an income statement.

Think of it simply like this: the income statement shows (1) what came in, (2) what went out, and (3) how much is left (before taxes).

TAKE NOTE

Interest payments reduce a corporation's taxable income, whereas dividend payments to stockholders are paid from after-tax dollars. Because they are taxable as income to stockholders, dividends are taxed twice, whereas interest payments are taxed once as income to the recipient.

Accounting for Depreciation

As mentioned earlier, when reviewing the balance sheet, fixed assets are shown at their cost minus accumulated **depreciation**. For these assets, which wear out over time, tax law requires that the loss of value be deducted over the asset's useful life, longer for some assets, shorter for others (you won't have to know depreciation schedules). On the income statement, the allowable portion for the year is shown as an expense and, for our purposes, will generally be part of COGS. Remember, if the company uses accelerated depreciation, the expenses will be higher in the early years, resulting in lower pretax income (and lower-income taxes) but higher income later on.

LO 13.d Calculate key measurements of financial health.

Balance Sheet Computations

Figure 13.1: Sample Balance Sheet

Balance Sheet
Amalgamated Widget
as of Dec. 31, 2018

ASSETS			
Current assets	Cash and equivalents	$ 5,000,000	
	Accounts receivable	15,000,000	
	Inventory	19,000,000	
	Prepaid expenses	1,000,000	
	Total current assets		$ 40,000,000
Fixed assets	Buildings, furniture, and fixtures (at cost less $10 million accumulated depreciation)	$40,000,000	
	Land	15,000,000	
	Total fixed assets		$55,000,000
Other (intangibles, goodwill)		$5,000,000	
Total assets			$100,000,000
LIABILITIES AND NET WORTH			
Current liabilities	Accounts payable	$5,000,000	
	Accrued wages payable	4,000,000	
	Accrued taxes payable	1,000,000	
	Total current liabilities		$10,000,000
Long-term liabilities	8% 20-year convertible debentures		$50,000,000
Total liabilities			$60,000,000
Net worth	Preferred stock $100 par ($5 noncumulative convertible 200,000 shares issued)	$20,000,000	
	Common stock $1 par (1 million shares)	1,000,000	
	Capital in excess of par	4,000,000	
	Retained earnings	15,000,000	
Total net worth			$40,000,000
Total liabilities and net worth			$100,000,000

Shareholder Equity

Shareholder equity, also called net worth or owners' equity, is the stockholder claims on a company's assets after all its creditors have been paid. Shareholder equity equals total assets less total liabilities. On a balance sheet, three types of shareholder equity are identified: capital stock at par, capital in excess of par, and retained earnings.

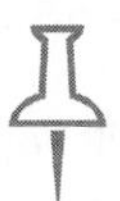

TAKE NOTE

net worth = total assets – total liabilities

Capital Stock at Par

Capital stock includes preferred and common stock, listed at par value. Par value is the total dollar value assigned to stock certificates when a corporation's owners (the stockholders) first contributed capital. Par value of common stock is an arbitrary value with no relationship to market price.

Capital in Excess of Par

Capital in excess of par, often called additional paid-in capital or paid-in surplus, is the amount of money over par value that a company received for issuing the stock in a primary offering. The par value is an arbitrary amount selected when the company is formed. In virtually all instances, the price of the stock when it is initially issued is above the par.

Retained Earnings

Retained earnings, sometimes called earned surplus or accumulated earnings, are profits that have not been paid out in dividends. Retained earnings represent the total of all earnings held since the corporation was formed, less dividends paid to stockholders. Operating losses in any year reduce the retained earnings from prior years.

Capital Structure

A company's **capitalization** is the combined sum of its long-term debt and equity securities. The **capital structure** is the relative amounts of debt and equity that compose a company's capitalization. Some companies finance their business with a large proportion of borrowed funds; others finance growth with retained earnings from normal operations and little or no debt.

Looking at the balance sheet, a corporation builds its capital structure with equity and debt, including the following four elements:

- Long-term debt (bonds and debentures)
- Capital stock (common and preferred)
- Capital in excess of par (paid-in or capital surplus)
- Retained earnings (earned surplus)

EXAMPLE

The total capitalization on the sample balance is $90 million ($50 million in long-term debt, $20 million in preferred stock, and $20 million in common shareholders' equity). Remember, capital stock + capital surplus + retained earnings = net worth (shareholders' equity).

LT debt	$50 million
+ Pfd.	$20 million
+ Common	$1 million
+ Cap. surplus	$4 million
+ Ret. earnings	$15 million
Total capitalization	$90 million

If a company changes its capitalization by issuing stock or bonds, the effects will show up on the balance sheet.

Liquidity Calculations

The following computations help a financial analyst determine the ability of a company to meet its current obligations.

Working Capital

Working capital is the amount of capital or cash a company has available. Working capital is a measure of a firm's liquidity, which is its ability to quickly turn assets into cash to meet its short-term obligations.

The formula for working capital is:

current assets – current liabilities = working capital

Factors that affect working capital include

- increases in working capital, such as profits, sale of securities (long-term debt or equity), and sale of noncurrent assets; and
- decreases in working capital, such as declaring a cash dividend, paying off long-term debt and net loss.

Current Ratio

Knowing the amount of working capital is useful, but it becomes an even better indicator when paired with the **current ratio**. This computation uses the same two items—current assets and current liabilities—but expresses them as a ratio of one to the other. Simply divide the current assets by the current liabilities, and the higher the ratio, the more liquid the company is.

Quick Asset Ratio (Acid-Test Ratio)

Sometimes it is important for the analyst to use an even stricter test of a company's ability to meet its short-term obligations (such as, "pass the acid test"). The quick asset ratio uses the company's quick assets instead of all of the current assets. Quick assets are current assets minus the inventory. Then divide these quick assets by the current liabilities to arrive at the quick ratio.

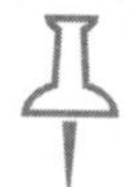

TAKE NOTE

Liquidity measures a company's ability to pay the expenses associated with running the business.

Leverage

Financial leverage is a company's ability to use long-term debt to increase its return on equity. A company with a high ratio of long-term debt-to-equity is said to be highly leveraged.

Stockholders benefit from leverage if the return on borrowed money exceeds the debt service costs. But leverage is risky because excessive increases in debt raise the possibility of default in a business downturn.

In general, industrial companies with debt-to-equity ratios of 50% or higher are considered highly leveraged. However, utilities, with their relatively stable earnings and cash flows, can be more highly leveraged without subjecting stockholders to undue risk. If a company is highly leveraged, it is also affected more by changes in interest rates.

Debt-to-Equity Ratio

The best way to measure the amount of financial leverage being employed by the company is by calculating the **debt-to-equity ratio**. It is really a misnomer—it should be called the debt-to-total capitalization ratio because that is what it is. For example, using the numbers in the capitalization example, we see that the total capital employed in the business is $90 million. Of that, $50 million is long-term debt. So, we want to know how much of the $90 million total is represented by debt capital. The answer is simple: $50 million of the $90 million, or 55.55%. That is the debt-to-equity ratio, and it indicates that this is a highly leveraged company (over 50%).

Book Value Per Share

A fundamental analyst is described as one who focuses on the company's books. Therefore, one of the key numbers computed is the **book value per share**. The calculation is almost identical to one we have already studied—net asset value (NAV) per share of an investment company.

In the case of a corporation, it is basically the liquidation value of the enterprise. That is, let's assume we sold all of our assets, paid back everyone we owe, and then split what is left among the stockholders. But remember, before we can hand over anything to the common shareholders, we must take care of any outstanding preferred stock. So, from the funds that are left after we pay off all the liabilities, we give the preferred shareholders back their par (or stated) value and the rest belongs to the common stockholders.

But, there is one more thing. In the case of liquidation, some of the assets on our books might not really be worth what we're carrying them at—in particular, those that are known as intangible assets (goodwill, patents, trademarks, copyrights, etc.). That is why the analyst uses only the tangible assets, computed by subtracting those intangibles from the total assets.

Expressed as a formula, book value per share is:

$$\frac{\text{tangible assets} - \text{liabilities} - \text{par value of preferred}}{\text{shares of common stock outstanding}} = \text{book value per share}$$

Balancing the Balance Sheet

Balance sheets, by definition, must balance. Every financial change in a business requires two offsetting changes on the company books, known as double-entry bookkeeping. For example, when a company pays a previously declared cash dividend, cash (a current asset) is reduced while dividends payable (a current liability of the same amount) is eradicated. This results in no change to working capital or net worth because each side of the balance sheet has been lowered by the same amount.

Depreciating Assets

Because fixed assets (e.g., buildings, equipment, and machinery) wear out as they are used, they decline in value over time. This decline in value is called **depreciation**. A company's tax bills are reduced each year the company depreciates fixed assets used in the businesses.

Depreciation affects the company in two ways: accumulated depreciation reduces the value of fixed assets on the balance sheet, and the annual depreciation deduction reduces taxable income on the income statement.

Companies may elect either straight-line or accelerated depreciation. By use of the straight-line method, a company depreciates fixed assets by an equal amount each year over the asset's useful life. A piece of equipment costing $1 million with a 10-year useful life will generate a depreciation deduction of $100,000 per year.

Accelerated depreciation is a method that depreciates fixed assets more during the earlier years of their useful life and less during the later years.

TAKE NOTE

Compared with straight-line, accelerated depreciation generates larger deductions (lower taxable income) during the early years and smaller deductions (higher taxable income) during the later years.

Footnotes

Footnotes to the financial statements identify significant financial and management issues that may affect the company's overall performance, such as accounting methods used, extraordinary items, pending litigation, and management philosophy.

Typically, a company separately discloses details about its long-term debt in the footnotes. These disclosures are useful for determining the timing and amount of future cash outflows. The disclosures usually include a discussion of the nature of the liabilities, maturity dates, stated and effective interest rates, call provisions and conversion privileges, restrictions imposed by creditors, assets pledged as security, and the amount of debt maturing in each of the next five years.

Also disclosed in the footnotes would be off-the-books financing arrangements, such as debt guarantees.

TEST TOPIC ALERT

Footnotes are generally found on the bottom of the financial statements and can be several pages long.

TAKE NOTE

The balance sheet reports what resources (assets) a company owns and how it has funded them. How the firm has financed the assets is revealed by the capital structure—for example, long-term debt and owners' equity (preferred stock, common stock, and retained earnings).

Income Statement Computations

There are a number of important ratios that can be computed using information from the income statement. We'll take a look at several of them.

Earnings Per Share (EPS)

Among the most widely used statistics, earnings per share (EPS) measures the value of a company's earnings for each common share:

$$EPS = \frac{\text{earnings available to common}}{\text{number of shares outstanding}}$$

Earnings available to common are the remaining earnings after the preferred dividend has been paid. EPS relates to common stock only. Preferred stockholders have no claims to earnings beyond the stipulated preferred stock dividends.

Figure 13.2: Simplified Income Statement

Net revenues (sales)	$10 million
- COGS (including $500,000 of depreciation)	5.5 million
= gross profit	4.5 million
- other operating expenses (rent, utilities)	500,000
= operating profit (EBIT)	4 million
- interest expense	750,000
= income after interest expense (pretax income)	3.25 million
- income tax	1 million
= net income	2.25 million
EPS (1 million common shares outstanding)	2.25
Dividends per share ($1.50)	1.5 million
Credited to retained earnings	750,000

EPS After Dilution

EPS after dilution assumes that all convertible securities, such as warrants and convertible bonds and preferred stock, have been converted into the common. Because of tax adjustments, the calculations for figuring EPS after dilution can be complicated and will not be tested.

Current Yield (Dividend Yield)

A common stock's **current yield (CY)**, like the CY on bonds, expresses the annual income payout (dividends rather than interest) as a percentage of the current stock price:

$$\text{CY} = \frac{\text{annual dividends per common share}}{\text{market value per common share}}$$

Dividend Payout Ratio

The **dividend payout ratio** measures the proportion of earnings paid to stockholders as dividends:

$$\text{dividend payout ratio} = \frac{\text{annual dividends per common share}}{\text{EPS}}$$

In general, older companies pay out larger percentages of earnings as dividends. Utilities as a group have an especially high payout ratio. Growth companies normally have the lowest ratios because they reinvest their earnings in the businesses. Companies on the way up hope to reward stockholders with gains in the stock value rather than with high dividend income.

Statement of Cash Flow

The **statement of cash flow** reports a business's sources and uses of cash and the beginning and ending values for cash and cash equivalents each year. The three components generating cash flow are

- operating activities,
- investing activities, and
- financing activities.

TEST TOPIC ALERT

Most financial professionals add revenues and expenses that do not involve cash inflows or outflows (e.g., cost allocations, such as depreciation and amortization) back to the company's net income to determine the cash flow. As described previously, the cash flow statement will also reflect money from operations, financing, and investing, but not accounting changes.

EXAMPLE

Sometimes, using numbers makes this concept much easier. If you take a look at the income statement we reviewed a few pages ago, you will see that this company's net income (bottom line, to use the vernacular) was $2.25 million. Among the $6 million in expenses deducted from the total revenues was $500,000 of depreciation. However, the company never "wrote a check" for that money; it is the amount of the original cost that it is allowed to be written off as an expense each year as the fixed assets wear out. So, not only does the company have the net income remaining after all expenses and taxes, but also it had another $500,000 in funds it could use, giving the company a total cash flow of $2.75 million.

Earnings Before Interest and Taxes (EBIT)

EBIT helps a fundamental analyst to evaluate a company's performance without incorporating interest expenses or income tax rates. Without accounting for interest or taxes that are variables for every company, the fundamental analyst can focus on operating profitability as a single measure of success.

This is very important when comparing companies within an industry that have different debt obligations or tax obligations.

It is calculated from information found on the income statement.

Example: ABC Corp.	
Sales revenue	$10 million
Expenses	8 million
EBIT	2 million
Interest paid	500,000
Earnings before taxes	1.5 million
Income taxes	60,000
Net income	$1.44 million

Earnings Before Taxes (EBT)

With EBIT, the analyst has taken out the tax structure when evaluating a company in an industry—once again, making it easier to compare companies within an industry. Note that a highly leveraged company will have a relatively higher interest expense, and a lower EBT to a company with less debt obligations.

Price-to-Earnings Ratio

The widely used **price-to-earnings (P/E) ratio** provides investors with a rough idea of the relationship between the prices of different common stocks compared with the earnings that accrue to one share of stock.

$$\text{P/E ratio} = \frac{\text{current market price of a common share}}{\text{EPS}}$$

Growth companies usually have higher P/E ratios than cyclical companies. Investors are willing to pay more per dollar of current earnings if a company's future earnings are expected to be dramatically higher than earnings for stocks that rise and fall with business cycles. Companies subject to cyclical fluctuations generally sell at lower P/Es; declining industries sell at still lower P/Es. Investors should beware of extremely high or extremely low P/Es. Speculative stocks often sell at one extreme or the other.

If a stock's market price and P/E ratio are known, the EPS can be calculated as follows:

$$\text{EPS} = \frac{\text{current market price of common stock}}{\text{P/E ratio}}$$

Growth vs. Value

One of the longest running arguments in investment analysis is, "which is more successful, the growth style or the value style?" The father of value investing was Benjamin Graham and his text *Security Analysis* (co-authored with David Dodd) is still widely read today. The exam won't ask you about Graham and Dodd, but will want you to know the essential features of both styles.

Growth Style

Portfolio managers using the growth style of portfolio management focus on stocks of companies whose earnings are growing faster than most other stocks and are expected to continue to do so. Because rapid growth in earnings is often priced into the stocks, growth investment managers are likely to buy stocks that are at the high end of their 52-week price range. Therefore, in the eyes of some, they might be buying stocks that are overvalued.

Value Style

Portfolio managers using the value style of management concentrate on undervalued or out-of-favor securities whose price is low relative to the company's earnings or book value and whose earnings prospects are believed to be unattractive by investors and securities analysts. In fact, sometimes value managers think they can find a bargain with companies that are currently operating at a loss (no earnings, hence no P/E ratio). Value investment managers seek to buy undervalued securities before the company reports positive earnings surprises. Their primary source of information is the company's financial statements. Value investment managers are more likely to buy stocks that are at the bottom of their 52-week price range.

TEST TOPIC ALERT

Growth managers expect to see high P/E ratios (price to earnings ratios) or high price-to-book ratio with little or no dividends. On the other hand, value managers expect to see a low P/E ratio or low price-to-book ratio and dividends offering a reasonable yield.

LESSON 13.3: TECHNICAL ANALYSIS

LO 13.e Recall market analysis considerations and their use in technical analysis.

Introduction

Both technical and fundamental analyses attempt to predict the supply and demand of markets and individual stocks. As shown earlier, **fundamental analysts** concentrate on broad based economic trends; current business conditions within an industry; and the quality of a particular corporation's business, finances, and management.

Technical analysis attempts to predict the direction of prices on the basis of historic price an trading volume patterns when laid out graphically on charts.

Technical Market Analysis

Trading Volume

Technical analysts view changes in the trading volume of a stock to be an important predictor of future price movements. A significant change to the trading volume (up or down) sends a signal to the technician that a trend may be starting.

Support and Resistance Levels

Stock prices may move within a narrow range for months or even years. The bottom of this trading range is known as the **support level**; the top of the trading range is called the **resistance level**.

Figure 13.3: Support and Resistance Levels

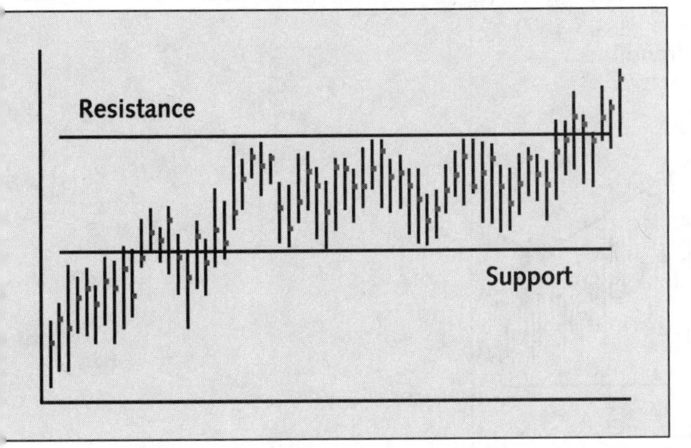

When a stock declines to its support level, the low price attracts buyers, whose buying supports the price and keeps it from declining farther. When a stock increases to its resistance level, the high price attracts sellers, whose selling hinders a further price rise. Stocks may fluctuate in trading ranges for months, testing their support and resistance levels. If a particular stock's price penetrates either the support or the resistance level, the change is considered significant.

A decline through the support level is called a **bearish breakout**; a rise through the resistance level is called a **bullish breakout**. Breakouts usually signal the beginning of a new upward or downward trend.

Advances/Declines

The number of issues closing up or down on a specific day reflects **market breadth**. The number of advances and declines can be a significant indication of the market's relative strength. When declines outnumber advances by a large amount, the market is bearish even if it closed higher. In bull markets, advances substantially outnumber declines. Technical analysts plot daily advances and declines on a graph to produce an **advance/decline line** that gives them an indication of market breadth trends.

Tools of Technical Analysis

Charting Stocks

In addition to studying the overall market, technical analysts attempt to identify patterns in the prices of individual stocks.

Trendlines

Although a stock's price may spike up or down daily, over time its price tends to move in one direction. Technical analysts identify patterns in the **trendlines** of individual stocks from graphs as they do patterns in the overall market. They base their buy or sell recommendations on a stock's price trendline. An upward trendline is bullish; a downward one is bearish.

Figure 13.4: Upward and Downward Trendlines

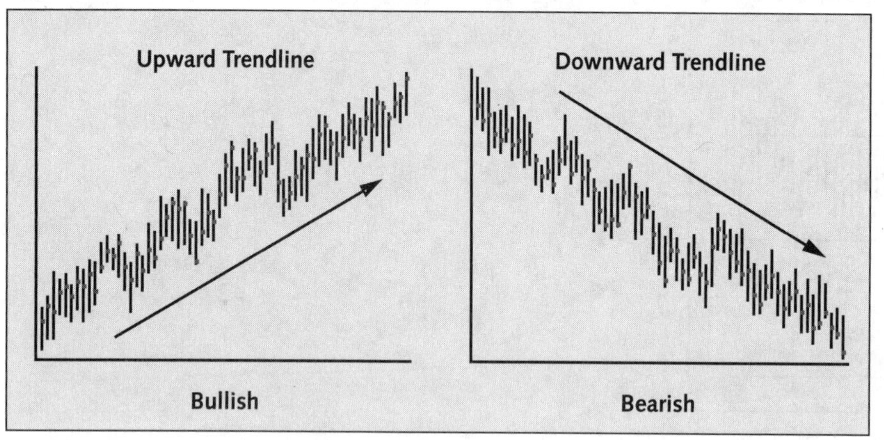

A trendline connects the lows in an uptrend and the highs in a downtrend. Three common patterns in stock price trendlines are consolidations, reversals, and support and resistance levels.

Consolidations

If a stock's price stays within a narrow range, it is said to be **consolidating**. When viewed on a graph, the trendline is horizontal and moves sideways, neither up nor down.

Reversals

A **reversal** indicates that an upward or a downward trendline has halted, and the stock's price is moving in the opposite direction. Between the two trendlines, a period of consolidation occurs, and the stock price levels off. A genuine reversal pattern can be difficult to recognize because trends are composed of many rises and declines, which may occur at different rates and for different lengths of time.

Because of its gently curving shape, an easily identifiable reversal pattern is called a **saucer** (reversal of a downtrend) or an **inverted saucer** (reversal of an uptrend). A similar reversal pattern is the **head-and-shoulders** pattern, named for its resemblance to the human body.

The **head-and-shoulders top** pattern indicates the beginning of a bearish trend in the stock. First, the stock price rises, then it reaches a plateau at the neckline (left shoulder). A second advance pushes the price higher, but then the price falls back to the neckline (head). Finally, the stock price rises again, but falls back to the neckline (right shoulder) and continues downward, indicating a reversal of the upward trend.

When reversed, this pattern is called a **head-and-shoulders bottom**, or an **inverted head-and-shoulders**, and indicates a bullish reversal.

Figure 13.5: Head-and-Shoulders Top and Bottom Trendlines

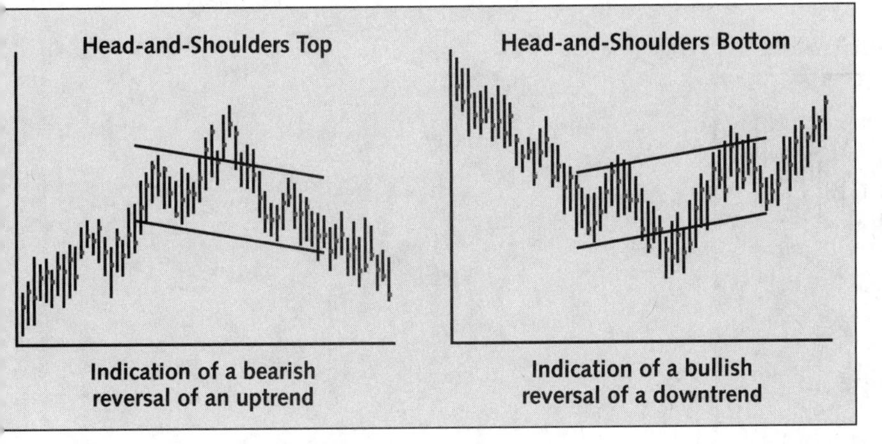

Overbought and Oversold

If market indexes such as the S&P 500 and the Dow are declining, but the number of declining stocks relative to the number of advancing stocks is failing (fewer stocks declining), the market is said to be oversold and is likely to reverse itself. This is considered to be a *bullish* sign.

Conversely, if market indexes are rising, but the number of declining stocks relative to the number of advancing stocks is rising (fewer stocks rising), the market is said to be overbought and is ready for a correction. This is considered to be a *bearish* sign.

Technical Market Theories

Technical analysts follow various theories regarding market trends. Some of them are outlined next.

Dow Theory

Analysts use the **Dow theory** to confirm the end of a major market trend. According to the theory, the three types of changes in stock prices are **primary trends** (one year or more), **secondary trends** (3–12 weeks), and **short-term fluctuations** (hours or days).

In a bull market, the primary trend is upward. However, stock prices may still drop in a secondary trend within the primary upward trend, even for as long as 12 weeks. The trough of the downward secondary trend should be higher than the trough of the previous downward trend. In a bear market, secondary upward trends may occur, but the highs reached during those secondary upward movements are successively lower.

According to the Dow theory, the primary trend in a bull market is a series of higher highs and higher lows. In a bear market, the primary trend is a series of lower highs and lower lows. Daily fluctuations are considered irrelevant.

A primary upward trend interrupted by secondary downward movements is shown in the following chart. The chart illustrates a series of successively higher highs and lows, conforming to the definition of a primary upward trend.

Any change in direction is considered deceptive unless the Dow Jones Industrial and Transportation Averages reflect the change. However, using this average lacks precision and is sometimes slow in confirming changes in market trends.

Figure 13.6: Dow Theory of Market Trends

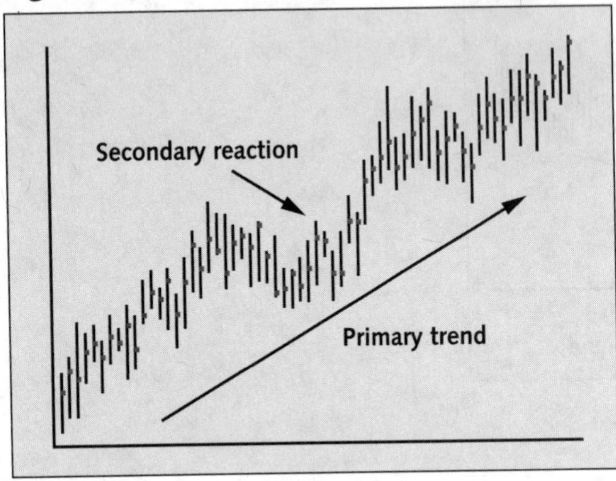

Odd-Lot Theory

Typically, small investors engage in **odd-lot trading**. Followers of the odd-lot theory believe that these small investors invariably buy and sell at the wrong times. When odd-lot traders buy, odd-lot analysts are bearish. When odd-lot traders sell, odd-lot analysts are bullish.

This theory goes way back in time. Think of the 1930s when a house might have cost $4,000. People took out mortgages for that kind of money. If a stock is priced at $40, and a round lot of that stock cost $4,000, most people didn't have that kind of money. So they bought one or two shares because that is what they could afford. They were not necessarily well-informed investors and often traded on emotion—buying when they should have sold, and selling when they should have bought.

TEST TOPIC ALERT

The standard trading unit for equity securities is a round lot. A round lot is 100 shares. An odd-lot is something less than 100 shares. If a trade is made for 550 shares of common stock, the trade was for five round lots (500 shares) and one odd-lot (50 shares).

Short-Interest Theory

Short interest refers to the number of shares that have been sold short. Because short positions must be repurchased eventually, most analysts believe that short interest reflects mandatory demand, which creates a support level for stock prices. High short interest is a bullish indicator, and low short interest is a bearish indicator.

LESSON 13.4: ANALYZING MUNICIPAL SECURITIES

LO 13.f Identify the specific market analysis considerations for municipal securities.

Introduction

A number of publications and services offer information on proposed new issues and secondary market activity for municipal issues. These include *The Bond Buyer* and *Thomson Muni News*, which publishes the *Thomson Muni Market Monitor* (formerly known as *Munifacts*). These are used to analyze the current market for municipal securities. Here are the most testable items.

The Bond Buyer

The Bond Buyer is published every business day and serves as an authoritative source of information on primary market municipal bonds. The Bond Buyer publishes the **30-day visible supply** (the total dollar volume of municipal offerings—not including short-term notes—expected to reach the market in the next 30 days) and the **placement,** or **acceptance, ratio indexes** (the percentage of the total dollar value of new issues sold versus the total dollar value of new issues offered for sale the prior week). Although not a term you'll see on the exam, think of this as the *success ratio*. It reports how well the underwriters did in moving the week's new issues.

TAKE NOTE

If the visible supply is exceptionally large, interest rates are likely to rise to attract investors to the larger number of bonds available. A small visible supply is an indication that interest rates are likely to fall.

If the placement ratio is high, the market for municipal bonds is strong. If it is low, dealers will likely exhibit concern about bidding on new issues. A placement ratio of 90% means that market has absorbed 90% of the dollar volume of bonds issued for the week, with 10% left in the dealer's inventory.

The Bond Buyer also compiles the 40 Bond Index, 20 Bond Index, 11 Bond Index, and the Revdex 25.

Figure 13.7: Bond Buyer Compiled Indexes (Updated Weekly)

40 Bond Index
Daily price index of 40 GO and revenue bonds with an average maturity of 20 years. A rise in the index indicates bond prices are rising and yields are falling.
20 Bond Index
Weekly index of 20 GOs with 20 YTM, rated A or better.
11 Bond Index
Weekly index of 11 of the 20 bonds from the 20 Bond Index, rated AA or better.
Revdex 25
Weekly index of 25 revenue bonds with 30 YTM, rated A or better.

TAKE NOTE

The yields on the Revdex are always higher than the yields on the GO 20 Bond Index because revenue bonds have higher risk. The yields on the 11 Bond Index are lower than the yields on the 20 Bond Index because the 11 Bond Index contains the more highly rated bonds.

Thomson Muni Market Monitor (Formerly *Munifacts*)

Thomson has been offering wire services, such as *Thomson Muni News* and the *Thomson Muni Market Monitor* (formerly *Munifacts*), used by numerous municipal dealers for many years. Current news items pertaining to the secondary municipals market appear in these wire services throughout the day along with current municipal offerings. Comparatively, these wire services should be considered a source for bonds already trading in the municipal secondary markets, while The *Bond Buyer* is a source for new issue municipal bonds (primary market).

PRACTICE QUESTION

4. Test your knowledge of information sources on the municipal bond market.
   1. Which municipal publication includes the 30-day visible supply index?
   2. Which municipal publication provides the most up-to-the-minute information relevant to the secondary municipal bond market?

   Answers: 1. *The Bond Buyer*; 2. *Thomson Muni Market Monitor*

Newspaper Listings

Tax-exempt bonds are listed in financial publications such as *The Bond Buyer* and *The Wall Street Journal.*

Tax-Exempt Bond Transactions

Figure 13.8: Newspaper Listing of Municipal Bond Quotes

Tax-Exempt Bonds

Representative prices for tax-exempt revenue and GO bonds based on institutional trades. Changes rounded to nearest 1/8. Yield is YTM.

Issue	Coupon	Maturity	Price	Chg	Bid Yld
Alaska Hsg Fin Corp	6.600	12-01-33	97 1/2	- 1/4	6.79
Cal Dept of Wtr Res	6.125	12-01-23	95 3/4	- 1/2	6.50
Charlotte Hosp Auth	6.250	01-01-30	95 3/8	+ 1/2	6.62
Farmington NM Util Sys	5.750	05-15-23	91 1/4	- 1/8	6.53
Ill State Toll Hwy Auth	6.375	01-01-25	96	+ 3/8	6.72
Kenton Co KY Airport	6.300	03-01-25	95 1/4	- 1/2	6.71

*** This sample comprises formats, styles, and abbreviations from a variety of currently available sources and has been created for educational purposes.**

EXAMPLE

Examine the Kenton County, Kentucky, Airport bond. The name of the bond appears in the left column under the *Issue* column. The entries in the *Coupon* and *Maturity* columns indicate that the bond pays 6.3% interest and matures on March 1, 2025. The bond was traded at 95¼, or $952.50, per $1,000 bond.

The price represents a half-point ($5) decrease from the last trade, as reported under the *Chg* (change) column. The 6.71 yield is the bid yield and the YTM. Because the bond is selling at a discount, the YTM is higher than the CY.

LESSON 13.5: INVESTMENT COSTS, FEES, AND TAX CONSIDERATIONS

LO 13.g Analyze the importance of costs and fees when selecting investments.

Introduction

In addition to all of the analytical tools presented in the unit, the registered representative must be cognizant of the costs involved in selecting a security or portfolio of securities. Furthermore, there are a number of tax considerations that come into play.

Costs and Fees Associated With Investments

Many of costs and fees associated with investments have already been covered. Examples include markups, markdowns, and commissions. We have also covered the different mutual fund share classes and how their charges work. Another charge for mutual funds is the 12b-1 asset-based charge. Variable annuities usually carry surrender charges. Some clients open up fee-based accounts where, for a flat fee, trading is commission-free. Following are some costs we haven't dealt with yet.

Mortality and Expense Charges

An important consideration in determining the appropriate variable insurance product (annuity or life), is the company's mortality and expense charges. Just as mutual funds have an expense ratio where all of the operating costs are viewed as a percentage of the net assets, variable insurance companies have expense ratios, too. Some of these charges, such as for portfolio management, are similar to those found with mutual funds. But, insurance companies have some specific costs unique to their products.

The most significant of those is the mortality expense. Because this is not an actuarial science exam, we'll keep it very simple. Annuities and life insurance have certain guarantees. In the case of the annuity, once annuitization begins, the insurance company guarantees payments for life. In the case of life insurance, it guarantees a death benefit. In both cases, mortality tables are used to compute life expectancy.

For example, if life expectancy changes and annuitants live longer than originally anticipated, the insurance companies assume the increased mortality cost. Or, if life expectancy moves the other way and people don't live as long as expected, life insurance premiums will be too low. The mortality expense is a charge collected by the insurance companies as a form of insurance protecting them against mortality risk.

TEST TOPIC ALERT

The mortality risk fee covers the risk that the insured may live for a period shorter than assumed. The expense risk fee covers the risk that the costs of administering and issuing the policy may be greater than assumed. And, of course, the investment management fee is the cost of the management of the chosen separate account subaccounts.

Death Benefit Fee

Most variable annuities offer an option stating that if the investor dies during the accumulation period, the beneficiary will receive the greater of the current value of the account or the amount invested. Therefore, the estate is assured of getting back at least the original investment. There is a cost for this benefit which is usually sold as a rider to the policy. Regardless of whether this option is chosen, annuities, like all other insurance products, provide for a designation of beneficiary. One important benefit of a named beneficiary is that probate is avoided.

Waiver of Premium

A popular option available for insurance policies is the waiver of premium. If the insured becomes disabled or otherwise unable to work, the premiums are waived.

The 5% Markup Policy (FINRA Rule 2121)

The 5% markup policy was adopted to ensure that the investing public receives fair treatment and pays reasonable rates for brokerage services in both exchange and OTC markets. It is considered a guideline only and is not a firm rule for markups and markdowns. A firm charging a customer more or less than a 5% markup may or may not be in violation of fair and equitable trade practices. The markup may be considered excessive once all the relevant factors are taken into account.

A broker-dealer can fill a customer order in the following three ways:

- If the broker-dealer is a market maker in the security, it will (as principal) buy from or sell to the customer, charging a markup or markdown.
- If the firm is not a market maker in the security, it can fill the order as agent, without taking a position in the security, and charge a commission for its execution services.
- An order can be filled as a riskless and simultaneous transaction.

Markup Based on Representative Market Prices

The 5% markup or markdown is based on the price representative of prevailing (inside) market prices at the time of a customer transaction. The 5% markup policy applies to all transactions in nonexempt listed or unlisted securities traded on an exchange or OTC, regardless of whether the transactions are executed as agency or principal trades.

EXAMPLE

	Bid	Ask/Offer
MMA	17.50	17.95
MMB	17.58	17.99
MMC	17.62	18.01

This inside quote is 17.62 – 17.95. That is, the highest any market maker is willing to pay (bid) for the stock is 17.62 and the lowest any market maker is willing to sell the stock (ask/offer) is 17.95. Using the inside quotes always gives us the narrowest spread. It is from these inside quotes that a dealer's markup or markdown is computed for compliance with the 5% policy.

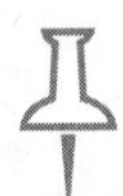

TAKE NOTE

The 5% policy applies to markups, markdowns, and commissions.

Fixed Public Offering Price Securities

The 5% markup policy does not apply to mutual funds, variable annuity contracts, or securities sold in public offerings, all of which are sold by a prospectus, nor does it apply to municipal securities.

Dealer's Inventory Costs

If a customer's buy order is filled from a broker-dealer's inventory, the net price to the customer is based on the prevailing inside market (highest bid and lowest ask), regardless of whether the BD selling to the customer is also making a market in the stock and what the firm's quote might be.

The price at which the broker-dealer acquired the stock being sold to the customer has no bearing on the net price to the customer; the price to the customer must be reasonably related to the current market.

Riskless and Simultaneous Transactions

A riskless and simultaneous transaction is an order to buy or sell stock in which the firm receiving the order is not a market maker. The dealer has the following two options for filling the order:

- As agent for the customer, it could buy or sell on the customer's behalf and charge a commission, subject to the 5% policy.
- It could buy or sell for its riskless principal account, then buy or sell to the customer as principal, charging a markup or markdown subject to the 5% policy.

When the order is filled as a principal transaction, the BD must disclose the markup to the customer.

Proceeds Transactions

When a customer sells securities and uses the proceeds to purchase other securities in a proceeds transaction, the BD's combined commissions and markups must be consistent with the 5% markup policy. In other words, member firms must treat proceeds transactions as one transaction for markup and markdown purposes.

EXAMPLE

A member firm acting as agent sells 100 shares of stock for a customer and charges a commission of $87.50. The customer directs that the proceeds of the sale be invested in 100 shares of WXYZ, which the member sells to the customer at 21 net. At the time of sale, the inside market for WXYZ was 20 – 20.25. Under FINRA rules, the percent markup for this proceeds transaction is

A. 4.32%.
B. 7.16%.
C. 8.02%.
D. 9.37%.

The answer is 8.02%. In a proceeds transaction, markup is computed by combining the amounts earned on both the sell side and buy side and applying the total against the inside market on the buy side. $87.50 (sell side) + $75.00 (buy side) = $162.50. Divide the total by the inside market on the buy side (20.25/share or $2,025) and the percentage markup is 8.02%.

Markup Policy Considerations

While the policy is applicable to all account types, in assessing the fairness of a BD's commission and markup practices, the following factors are considered:

Type of Security

In general, more market risk is associated with making markets and trading common stocks than is associated with dealing in bonds. The policy gives guidance to markups specific to both stock and bond transactions, including government securities. The more risk a BD assumes, the greater the justification for higher markups.

Inactively Traded Stocks

The thinner the market for a security, the more volatile the stock and the greater the market risk to anyone dealing in the stock. Thus, a BD is justified in charging higher markups on inactively traded stocks. For inactive stocks and situations where no prevailing market quotes are available, a BD may base a markup on its cost in the stock.

Selling Price of Security

Commission and markup rates should decrease as a stock's price increases.

Dollar Amount of Transaction

Transactions of relatively small dollar amounts generally warrant higher percentage markups than large-dollar transactions.

Nature of the BD's Business

This standard pertains to full-service brokers versus discount brokers. In most cases, a general securities firm has higher operating costs than does a discount broker and thus may justify higher commissions and markups.

Pattern of Markups

Although the regulators are concerned primarily with detecting cases where BDs have established patterns of excessive markups, a single incident could still be considered an unfair markup.

TEST TOPIC ALERT

The 5% markup policy is peculiarly named for two reasons:

1. It applies to markups, markdowns, and commissions, meaning it is applicable to principal and agency transactions.
2. Five percent is not the limit. A transaction charge of more than 5% might be fine if it is reasonably based on the circumstances of the trade.

Examples of subject transactions are REITS, closed-end company shares, ADRs, third-market trades, listed and unlisted stocks, bonds, and government securities.

New issues sold by prospectus and municipal securities are not subject to this policy.

Remember that all computations must be based on the inside quote (the best available from all the market makers), not the firm's quote.

Net Transactions

A net transactions is sometimes called a hidden fee. When a broker-dealer sells to a client on a net basis, it means there is no commission charge. This occurs when the member acts as a principal in the trade. Does that mean the broker-dealer isn't making anything? FINRA wants to be sure that clients understand that in a net trade, there is either a markup or a markdown. It is against the conduct rules for a member to misrepresent the costs in a net trade.

LO 13.h Define the tax considerations applied when selecting investments.

Introduction

Tax planning is an essential component of investment planning. This is especially true for those in the higher income tax brackets, but it also impacts investors at all tax levels. As we end this unit, we will go into depth on some of the tax issues that may appear on your exam.

Wash Sales

No, we're not talking about a special at your local laundromat. As we learned earlier in the course, if an investor has net capital losses, up to $3,000 of that loss can be taken as a deduction against ordinary income. The wash sale rule of the IRS applies to investors who take a loss on the sale of a security and repurchase that same security within a specific time.

Capital losses may not be used to offset gains or income if the investor sells a security at a loss and purchases the same or a substantially identical security within 30 days before or after the trade date. The sale at a loss and the repurchase within this period is a **wash sale.**

The rule disallows the loss or tax benefit from selling a security and repurchasing the security or one substantially identical to it in this manner. The term *substantially identical* refers to any other security with the same investment performance likelihood as the one being sold.

Examples are

- securities convertible into the one being sold,
- warrants to purchase the security being sold,
- rights to purchase the security being sold, and
- call options to purchase the security being sold.

TAKE NOTE

The wash sale rule covers 30 days before and after the trade date. Including the trade date, this is a total period of 61 days.

EXAMPLE

An investor buys 100 shares of ABC for $50 per share. One year later, the investor sells those shares for $40 per share. Fifteen days after the sale, 100 shares of ABC are repurchased for $42 per share. The investor's new cost basis is $52 because the $10 loss that was disallowed is added to the repurchase price of $42.

TAKE NOTE

The wash sale rule applies only to realized losses—not to realized gains.

TEST TOPIC ALERT

The interpretation of the wash sale rule does not consider different options series to be substantially identical securities. For example, an options investor who is long an XYZ OCT 40 call sells the contract at a loss. Immediately after the sale, the investor purchases an XYZ NOV 40 call. The IRS does not consider this a wash sale and, therefore, the loss is deductible.

Tax Swapping

A tax swap is the sale of a bond and the simultaneous purchase of a different bond in a like amount. The technique is used to control tax liability, extend maturity, or update investment objectives. This is often confused with a wash sale. When done properly, the loss is not disallowed.

The IRS compares three qualities of debt securities in determining whether they are substantially identical: the maturity, coupon, and issuer. A bond is substantially identical if all three qualities of the bond sold at a loss and the newly purchased bond are the same.

After selling a bond, an investor can buy another bond with a different maturity, coupon, or issuer without violating the wash sale rule.

EXAMPLE

An investor could sell an ABC 8% bond that matures in 2030 at a loss and buy back an XYZ 8% bond that matures in 2031 and claim the loss. Even though the coupons are the same, the issuers and maturity dates are different. This is commonly called *tax swapping*.

Determining Which Shares to Sell

An investor holding identical securities, each with a different acquisition date and cost basis, may determine which shares to sell by electing one of three accounting methods: FIFO, share identification, or average cost basis. If the investor fails to choose, the IRS assumes the investor liquidates shares on a FIFO basis.

When FIFO shares are sold, the cost of the shares held the longest is used to calculate the gain or loss. In a rising market, this method normally creates adverse tax consequences.

When using the **share identification** accounting method, the investor keeps track of the cost of each share purchased and uses this information to liquidate the shares that would provide the lowest capital gain. Share identification is used to identify the specific per-share cost basis when shares are sold. The investor keeps track of the cost of each share purchased and specifies which shares to sell on the basis of that investor's specific tax needs.

A shareholder may elect to use an **average cost basis** when redeeming mutual fund shares (but not shares of specific stocks). The investor would calculate average basis by dividing the total cost of all shares owned by the total number of shares. The shareholder may not change the decision to use the average basis method without IRS permission.

TAKE NOTE

Share identification may result in more advantageous tax treatment, but most accountants prefer the convenience of the averaging method for mutual fund shares. Share identification is most commonly used with stock sales.

PRACTICE QUESTION

5. On April 10, 2019, when DEF stock was trading at 31, Sara Park purchased 10 DEF OCT 30 puts at a premium of 3 points each. By September 12, the stock had dropped to 27 and Park bought 5 more OCT 30 puts at a premium of 4½ each. On October 2, Park closed out 5 of her 15 contracts at a price of 7 each. Using IRS assumptions, she
   A. realized a short-term capital gain of $2,000.
   B. realized a short-term capital gain of $750.
   C. made $2,000 in ordinary income.
   D. realized a $1,250 short-term capital gain.

   Answer: A. The IRS assumes FIFO, so Park was selling 5 of the initial purchase made at a price of $300 each. The sale at $700 realized a short-term capital gain of $400 per contract for a total of $2,000. She could have used the identified cost basis and selected the 5 puts from the second purchase. In that case, the gain would have been $250 per contract (7 – 4½), or a total of $1,250. Although this example uses options, it would be the same for any other security.

Cost Basis of Shares Inherited/Gifted

The **cost basis of inherited property** is either stepped up or stepped down to its fair market value (FMV) at the date of the decedent's death. In the case of open-end investment companies, this would be the NAV. Shares inherited are always considered to have a holding period that is long-term for tax purposes. Therefore, the sale of inherited shares are subject to more favorable long-term tax rates, no matter how long (or short) they have been held by the beneficiary.

When a gift of securities is made, the donor's cost basis becomes the donee's cost basis.

EXAMPLE

Grandpa bought $10,000 of stock 20 years ago; it is currently valued at $50,000.

If inherited, the cost basis of shares received equals the FMV at Grandpa's death: $50,000.

If Grandpa instead gave it to Susie, who received the stock as a gift, the cost basis remains unchanged at $10,000 and his holding period continues.

TEST TOPIC ALERT

The step up provision does not apply when inheriting an annuity.

PRACTICE QUESTION

6. A client purchases 1,000 shares of the ABC Global Growth Fund when the NAV is $8.75 and the POP is $9.21. Three years later, the client makes a gift to her daughter when NAV is $9.50 and POP is $10.00, and the daughter elects to receive all distributions in cash. Two years later, she sells all shares when the NAV is $14.25 and POP is $15.00. What are the tax consequences of this sale?
   A. Long-term capital gain of $5,040
   B. Long-term capital gain of $4,750
   C. Long-term capital gain of $5,000
   D. Long-term capital gain of $5,500

   Answer: A. In the case of a gift of securities, the donee acquires the donor's cost basis—$9.21 per share. Sale (redemption) takes place at the NAV ($14.25) for a profit of $5.04 per share (times 1,000 shares).

Estate and Gift Taxes

Taxes can be levied upon the estate of a deceased person and upon those gifting securities to others. This section discusses these specific scenarios.

Donor Taxes

When a person dies, tax is due on the estate. This tax is payable by the estate, not by heirs who inherit the estate (although certain other taxes may apply to heirs). Likewise, if a person gives a gift, tax is due on the gift. Gift tax is payable by the donor, not the recipient. Estate and gift taxes are progressive taxes. For tax purposes, the valuation of the estate is the date of death; the valuation of a gift is the date it is given.

Annual Gift Tax Exclusion

Individuals may give gifts up to $15,000 per year to any number of individuals without incurring gift tax. The amount of the exclusion is subject to change depending on inflation. Gifts between spouses, no matter the size, are not subject to tax. If a gift tax is due, it is paid by the donor.

Estate Tax Exclusion

The estate of a deceased person is allowed to exclude some of that person's estate from taxation. The amount of the exclusion is subject to change depending on current tax law.

TAKE NOTE

Estate and gift taxes are progressive taxes that increase with the size of the estate or the gift. Income taxes are another example of a progressive tax. Flat taxes, such as sales tax, are considered regressive taxes because they impact lower-income families and individuals to a greater degree.

Unlimited Marital Deduction

Married couples are allowed to transfer their entire estate to the surviving spouse at death. This unlimited marital deduction results in taxes being owed at the death of the survivor.

Unified Credit

Taxation of estates and gifts are unified. That means that whatever is used of the lifetime gift exclusion before death reduces the estate tax exclusion. Both have a lifetime exclusion (2019) of 11.4 million and both have a progressive structure with rates beginning at 18% and reaching a maximum tax rate (2019) of 40%. There are two testable differences:

1. The annual gift tax exclusion ($15,000 in 2019).
2. Gift taxes are due at the same time as the individual tax return (April 15) while estate taxes are due nine months after death.

TEST TOPIC ALERT

The concept of taxation relating to gifts and inheritances can be confusing. There are two separate taxable situations; taxes due on the proceeds of a sale of gifted or inherited property; and taxes due based on the amount of the gift or the estate.

The following should help:

1.) A client has received a gift of securities from someone, or has inherited securities.

a. Gift: The client's cost basis for determining if there is a taxable capital gain is that of the donor. The client is considered to have acquired the security on the donor's purchase date and at the donor's purchase price.

b. Inheritance: The client's cost basis for determining if there is a taxable capital gain is the FMV as of the date of death. Holding period is not a consideration because any gains are considered long-term.

2.) Your client made a gift of securities to someone, or has died.

a. Gift: The obligation to pay a gift tax is that of the donor. Anything over the annual exclusion (currently $15,000) may be subject to the gift tax. The amount of the gift for tax purposes is the FMV as of the date of the gift.

b. Estate: The obligation to pay an estate tax is that of the deceased's estate. The value used to determine if there is an estate tax liability is the FMV.

PRACTICE QUESTION

7. One of your ultra-high net worth clients would like to give some low cost basis stock as gifts to her adult grandchildren. It would be prudent for you to tell her that
   A. she should use a TOD account to avoid probate.
   B. for purposes of the gift tax, her cost basis will be used.
   C. unlike an inheritance, there is no stepped-up cost basis.
   D. making the gift under the Uniform Transfer to Minors Act (UTMA) is generally the most advantageous for the child.

Answer: C. One of the benefits of inheriting low cost basis securities is the stepped-up basis, and that does not apply to gifts. Although the donor will not be the one subject to capital gains tax, letting her know that the donees (her grandchildren) will be receiving the stock at her cost basis would be the right thing to do. TOD would not apply to stock that is the subject of a gift; it is only when the stock remains in the grandmother's name and has been designated for the grandchildren after her death. When computing the value of a gift to determine if there is a gift tax obligation, it is the FMV of the gift that is used. Finally, the question states these are adult grandchildren—UTMA would not apply to them.

UNIT 14

Types of Risk and Required Disclosures

LEARNING OBJECTIVES

When you have completed this unit, you will be able to accomplish the following.

- › LO 14.a **Contrast** systematic and nonsystematic risks.
- › LO 14.b **Identify** the required risk disclosures.
- › LO 14.c **Determine** if senior exploitation is happening in an account.
- › LO 14.d **Recall** the safe harbor provisions of Section 28(e) of the Exchange Act.

INTRODUCTION

The concepts discussed in this unit are types of risk that both businesses and investors bear. Though not a comprehensive list, they are among the most common.

Although we routinely use the term *risk*, we often have difficulty defining it precisely. In finance, **risk** is defined as the uncertainty that an investment will earn its expected rate of return. There are two basic categories of risk: systematic and unsystematic. We will address both of them and their subcategories one at a time.

After that, we will look into some customer-specific risks, such as exploitation of seniors and the possible conflicts of interest resulting from an investment adviser receiving soft dollar compensation from a broker-dealer based on the commission business generated by the adviser's clients.

LESSON 14.1: TYPES OF RISK

LO 14.a Contrast systematic and nonsystematic risks.

Systematic Risk

Systematic risk is the risk in the return of an investment that is associated with the macroeconomic factors that affect all risky assets. Stated another way, systematic risk is the risk that changes in the overall economy will have an adverse effect on individual securities regardless of the company's circumstances. It is generally caused by factors that affect all businesses, such as war, global security threats, or inflation. Primary examples would include market risk, interest rate risk, and purchasing power risk, each of which will be dealt with separately. You might also see this referred to as nondiversifiable risk because, as we'll learn, systematic risk cannot be avoided through diversification.

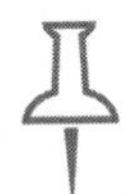

TAKE NOTE

Systemic risk is not a synonym for *systematic* risk. It has a totally different meaning and is not relevant to the exam.

Market Risk

The first example of systematic risk that generally comes to mind is *market risk*. When the market tanks, virtually all securities lose value. This is a classic example of a nondiversifiable risk because, regardless of the number of different stocks in your portfolio, when you encounter a stock market such as the one we had from late 2007 until early 2009, chances are most of those assets will have declined in price. In the previous unit, we discussed correlation. One way to protect against market risk is to have some negatively correlated securities in your portfolio. Remember, they go up when the others go down.

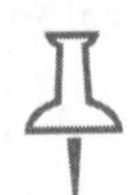

TAKE NOTE

Market risk is measured by a security's beta.

EXAMPLE

Should a war break out between two major oil-producing countries, the stock market could decline dramatically. The stocks of individual companies would likely decline as well, regardless of whether the war directly affected their businesses.

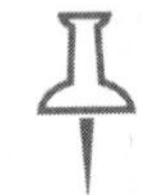

TAKE NOTE

Market risk cannot be diversified away. As we discussed in Unit 10, options can be used to hedge against market risk.

Interest-Rate Risk

Interest rates fluctuate in the market all the time. If market conditions or the Federal Reserve push interest rates higher, the market price of all bonds will be affected. When interest rates rise, the market price of bonds falls and that is why this is a systematic risk. This risk is sometimes referred to as the market risk for bonds. Rising interest rates can be bearish for some common stock prices as well, particularly those of highly leveraged companies such as public utilities. Having a diversified portfolio of bonds won't help because an increase in interest rates will cause all bonds to decline in price.

TAKE NOTE

Interest rate risk is intrinsic to all types of fixed-income investments, such as debt securities and preferred stock, whether from an emerging market issuer or a triple-A issuer. It is the risk that a security's value will decline because of an increase in market interest rates.

EXAMPLE

If the Federal Reserve increases interest rates dramatically, the market price of all bonds, regardless of credit quality, will decline.

TEST TOPIC ALERT

There are even some common stock investments with interest-rate risk. For exam purposes, it is the common shares of public utility companies. There are two reason for those stocks being interest-rate sensitive:

- Public utility stocks are known for their liberal dividend policies. When a stock's price is largely determined by its dividend yield (the case with most utilities), as interest rates go up, their stock prices go down. This is true of public utility stocks more than any other common stock.
- Public utility companies are highly leveraged. That is, they are regularly borrowing money. As interest rates go up, so does the utility's borrowing cost. That will have the effect of lowering the income and possibly a reduction to the dividend.

Method of Reducing Interest-Rate Risk

A popular way of reducing interest-rate risk is by laddering a bond or CD portfolio. Picture a ladder. You see rungs at set intervals going from bottom to top. That is the concept behind a laddered portfolio. In a laddered strategy, the bonds are all purchased at the same time but mature at different times (like the steps on the ladder). As the shorter maturities come due, they are reinvested and now become the long-term ones. This has also been a very common strategy with those purchasing CDs at their local bank.

Reinvestment Risk

A variation of interest-rate risk is reinvestment risk. There is reinvestment risk as to interest and reinvestment risk as to principal.

An investor receiving a periodic cash flow from an investment—such as interest on a debt security—may be unable to reinvest the income at the same rate as the security itself is paying. For example, if an investor purchased a bond with a 10% coupon and several years later comparable securities were only paying 7%, the investor would not be able to compound the investment at the original rate. Zero coupon bonds avoid this risk because there is nothing to reinvest.

This risk also occurs at maturity. If the fixed-income investor was enjoying a 10% return on the earlier bond, when it matured, the investor was only able to reinvest the principal in a 7% security. That is one of the advantages of purchasing bonds with a longer term to maturity—you're assured the fixed return for that length.

Inflation Risk (Purchasing Power Risk)

Inflation risk is another systematic risk. Inflation reduces the buying power of a dollar (or whatever currency is used where you live). A modest amount of inflation is inherent in a healthy, growing economy. Uncontrolled inflation causes uncertainty among individual investors as well as corporate managers attempting to evaluate potential returns from projects. TIPS are one investment vehicle designed to protect against inflation risk.

Fixed-income securities are the most vulnerable to this risk; equity securities are historically the least susceptible. In Lesson 13.1 of this course, we learned that tangible assets—such as real estate and precious metals like gold—are also good inflation hedges.

EXAMPLE

As we stated, purchasing power risk is a systematic risk, meaning that diversifying your portfolio is of little or no help. Let's assume that an individual nearing retirement took $1 million and, seeking income with safety, invested $100,000 into each of 10 different corporate bonds, all maturing in 20 years. For sure, this diversification does give protection against financial risk (if one of the bonds defaults because of bankruptcy of the issuer, the other nine should still pay off). However, if the cost of living rises, 20 years from now, when each of those bonds pays back the $100,000 principal, the investor will have $1 million. How much do you think that $1 million purchase compared to what it would have 20 years earlier?

Nonsystematic (Unsystematic) Risk

Unlike systematic risk, which is nondiversifiable, nonsystematic risks can be reduced through diversification. They are risks that are unique to the specific industry or business enterprise and would include things such as labor union strikes, lawsuits, and product failure. We will cover the most testable examples next.

Business Risk

Business risk is an operating risk, generally caused by poor management decisions (e.g., Edsel, New Coke, or more recently, Blackberry's former developers failing to pay attention to the success of the iPhone). At best, earnings are lowered; at worst, the company goes out of business and common stockholders probably lose their entire investment.

Financial Risk

Often confused with business risk (it is similar), financial risk relates primarily to those companies that use debt financing (leverage). An inability to meet those debt obligations could lead to bankruptcy and, once again, total loss for the stockholders. For that reason, this is sometimes called **credit risk** or **default risk**.

TEST TOPIC ALERT

Nonsystematic risk can be minimized through portfolio diversification. For example, a client long 1,000 shares of XYZ selling those shares and investing the proceeds into an S&P Index fund eliminates (or greatly reduces) business risk (but not market risk). In similar fashion, owning a diversified portfolio of bonds, such as is offered in a bond fund, offers protection against financial risk.

TEST TOPIC ALERT

Business risk is highest for investors whose portfolios contain stock in only one issuer or in lower-rated bonds.

Regulatory Risk

A sudden change in the regulatory climate can have a dramatic effect on the performance or risk of a business and entire business sectors. Overreaching bureaucrats and court judgments that change the rules a business must comply with can devastate individual companies and industries almost overnight. A very common example of this is rulings by the Environmental Protection Agency, which can sometime play havoc with the oil and gas industry.

Legislative Risk

It is common to lump together regulatory and legislative risk, but there is a difference. Whereas regulatory risk comes from a change to regulations, legislative risk results from a change in the law. And, because there is frequently a political agenda behind legislation, this risk is sometimes referred to as political risk, although most consider political risk to be of its own making. A governmental, state, or federal agency may pass certain regulations, but only a legislature can pass a law. Changes to the tax code are the most obvious legislative risks.

Political Risk

It might seem like we are splitting hairs here, but each of these, although potentially interrelated, does have a different basis in the source of the risk. In the case of political risk, most attribute this to potential instability in the political underpinnings of the country (think of a coup). This is particularly true in emerging economies, but, as history has shown, political insurrections can occur even in highly developed societies.

Sovereign Risk

Sovereign risk ratings capture the risk of a country defaulting on its commercial debt obligations. Headlines were made several years ago when the credit rating of the United States was reduced from AAA (at the time of this printing, the United States was back up to AAA). That is an example of the perceived increased sovereign risk that existed at the time. We discussed other examples in Lesson 4.3 when covering sovereign bonds.

EXAMPLE

Investments that could be affected by regulatory changes include "green" industries (and those that tend to pollute), oil and gas exploration, airlines, and pharmaceutical manufacturers. The most common regulatory risk comes from governmental agency attempts to control or influence product prices or the competitive structure of a particular industry through the passage and enforcement of regulations.

EXAMPLE

An example of legislative risk is how the domestic boat-building business in the United States was nearly wiped out in the early 1990s after the government instituted a luxury tax for yacht purchases.

EXAMPLE

A recent example of political risk was the actions of the Chavez government in Venezuela several years ago, where nationalization took place in many industries, ranging from cement to supermarkets. Those investors, in what were previously privately owned (not government) businesses saw most, if not all, of their investment lost.

Liquidity Risk

Liquidity measures the speed or ease of converting an investment into cash without causing a price disruption. **Liquidity risk** is the risk that when an investor wishes to dispose of an investment, no one will be willing to buy it, or that a very large purchase or sale would not be possible at the current price. Although there is technically a difference, for exam purposes, you may also refer to this as **marketability risk**.

EXAMPLE

The Treasury bill market is a highly liquid market because investors can sell a Treasury bill within seconds at the quoted prices. Real estate investments, however, can take months or years to sell if you want to get close to your asking price. The longer it takes to convert an investment into cash without having a fire sale, the greater the liquidity risk.

TAKE NOTE

Listed stocks and mutual funds have virtually no liquidity risk. Thinly traded stocks, many municipal bonds, and most tangible assets have a greater degree of inability to liquidate rapidly at your price.

PRACTICE QUESTION

1. Which of these risks would be reduced the **most** by diversification?
   - A. Business risk
   - B. Interest rate risk
   - C. Inflation risk
   - D. Market risk

   Answer: A. Diversification works best with nonsystematic (unsystematic) risks. Business risk, the possibility of losing money when a specific company underperforms, is a common case where spreading the risk around (diversifying), reduces risk. The other choices are all systematic risk, and diversification is not very useful for them.

Currency or Exchange Rate Risk

Purchasers of foreign securities, whether through direct ownership or American depository receipts (ADRs), face the uncertainty that the value of either the foreign currency or the domestic currency will fluctuate. For example, as of the date of publication, the Euro (€) is up over 13% against the U.S. dollar in the past 12 months. As a result, someone who invested one year ago in the stock of a company domiciled in the eurozone will find that, even if the stock has remained level or slightly lower on its local market, in terms of dollars, the value has increased. On the other hand, if your funds are in domestic cash or cash equivalents, you have little if any exposure to currency or exchange rate risk.

EXAMPLE

On an individual level, the exam may ask you about exchange rates and vacationers. For example, you take a trip to Country A and purchase a dinner on your credit card for 200 units of the local currency. Then, on the final night of your stay, you go to the same restaurant, order the same meal and, once again, the bill is for 200 units. When you get home, you check your credit card statement and see that you were billed $100 for the first meal and $110 for the second. What happened? The value of the foreign currency rose against the U.S. dollar from $0.50 ($100/200) to $0.55 ($110/200). Even though no prices changed in the foreign country, you encountered currency risk.

TEST TOPIC ALERT

You may need to know that the three primary systematic risks are

- market,
- interest rate, and
- inflation or purchasing power.

And, there are five primary unsystematic risks:

- Business
- Financial
- Liquidity
- Political
- Regulatory

PRACTICE QUESTION

2. All of the following risks are considered diversifiable **except**
   A. currency risk.
   B. liquidity risk.
   C. purchasing power risk.
   D. sovereign risk.

   Answer: C. Purchasing power risk, also known as inflation risk, is a systematic risk and, as such, is one that cannot generally be lessened through diversification.

ESSON 14.2: DISCLOSURE OF RISKS

LO 14.b Identify the required risk disclosures.

Introduction

It was once said at a FINRA conference the "The religion of the SEC is disclosure." The point being that full disclosure of all material facts and risks is the only way to operate in this business.

As with so many of the lessons, where appropriate, material relating to later lessons has been discussed. That certainly is true with risk disclosures. We'll mention some of those for ease of going back to review.

Risk Disclosures

The first risk disclosure document we discussed was at Lesson 3.5. That was for penny stocks. If you don't remember what those requirements are, please take a glance back at that lesson. At Lesson 8.4, we pointed out the need to disclose the risks in a mutual fund withdrawal plan. Shortly after that, at Lesson 8.6, we gave you a quote from a risk disclosure statement regarding a leveraged ETF. Near the end of Lesson 11.4, we listed the disclosure requirements for DPP roll-ups.

Control Relationships

Control relationships can lead to significant conflicts of interest. A control relationship exists when a broker-dealer is owned by, is under common ownership with, or owns an entity that issues securities. It could be thought of as being part of the same family. When it comes to a recommendation, one would have a natural bias toward that entity. There are no problems with this relationship as long as it is disclosed.

There are similar types of relationships where a conflict of interest could exist. That could affect the ability of the member or its representatives to give totally unbiased information. The best way to avoid these conflicts of interest is to disclose them so that the customer can decide what to do. Some examples of potential conflicts of interest are

- offering a proprietary product, such as a house fund (a mutual fund where the underwriter or adviser is affiliated with the broker-dealer);
- offering a limited partnership offering (DPP) where the sponsor is an affiliate of the broker-dealer;
- program sponsors, such as investment companies or insurance companies, providing incentives or rewards to agents for selling the sponsors' products;
- a securities professional having a financial interest in any security being recommended;
- a broker-dealer going public and placing shares of its own stock into discretionary accounts; and
- a broker-dealer publishing a favorable research report after underwriting the issuer's stock offering.

This is just a sample. The key point is, if there is any doubt about the transparency of the recommendation or transaction, be sure to make full disclosure.

PRACTICE QUESTION

3. A conservative customer is invested in a large-cap, value-managed equity fund. The stock market drops 10% because of a poor economic forecast for the country. Your customer is upset that his conservative mutual fund lost almost as much as the stock market. What risks does your customer need to understand?
   A. The investor should be aware that the size of a mutual fund, if smaller, may result in greater losses than mutual funds that have more money to invest. This is known as capitalization risk.
   B. The investor should be aware that when the stock market goes down, all securities trading will decline proportionately.
   C. The investor should know that mutual funds tend to be diversified, but that does not protect the portfolio from systematic risk.
   D. The investor should know that if he wants to liquidate the position, mutual funds have liquidity risk.

Answer: C. Both stocks and bonds involve some degree of market risk—the risk to investors is they may lose some of their principal because of price volatility in the overall market (also known as systematic risk). The size of a mutual fund has no bearing or protection from market risk. Mutual funds are liquid; they can be turned into cash quickly. Federal law requires redemption at NAV within seven days. However, that does not mean an investor can't lose money.

TEST TOPIC ALERT

Suppose you were selling shares of a company where your sister was the CEO. Do you think you'd have to disclose that potential conflict to your clients? Yes!

Regulation Full Disclosure (FD)

Regulation Full Disclosure (FD) is an SEC rule dealing with issuers disclosing information that can affect the price of the stock. Before passage of this rule, there was always a risk to the individual investor that an issuer might disclose material nonpublic information (MNPI) to certain institutional investors. Or, perhaps disclosure would be made to analysts at a broker-dealer who was a market maker in the company's stock. This put the "little guy" at a distinct disadvantage.

These disclosures are rarely made intentionally today. That would require an immediate public disclosure of the information. Almost all Regulation FD disclosures are for unintentional leaks. When that happens, the issuer must make prompt disclosure (defined as before the next trading day).

The SEC has agreed that public conference calls, press releases or press conferences, and webcasts are FD-compliant methods of public disclosure.

Tender Offers

It is not uncommon for one company to attempt to takeover another by acquiring a significant percentage of its voting shares. This is called a **tender offer**. A tender offer may also be made by an issuer of noncallable bonds when interest rates have fallen. Without the call feature, this would be the best way to retire the old high interest-rate bonds.

The SEC defines tender offer as "an active and widespread solicitation by a company or third party (often called the bidder or offeror) to purchase a substantial percentage of the company's securities. Bidders may conduct tender offers to acquire equity (common stock) in a particular company or debt issued by the company."

In general, tender offers for equity securities need shareholder approval. The nature of these offers requires adequate disclosures to clients. Usually, the tender offer is at a premium to the most recent trade so it can be a good deal for the client. There is a time limit and, if the client is not aware of that and misses it, not only will the client be unhappy, but it could lead to an arbitration case against the firm and/or the registered representative.

Here are some testable dates:

- The tender offer, unless withdrawn, under Regulation 14E, must remain open for at least 20 business days from the date the offer is first announced.
- If the terms of the offer are changed, the revised offer must remain open for at least 20 business days from the commencement and 10 business days from the date the terms are changed.

- The target company, within 10 business days of the announcement, must provide its shareholders with a statement:
  - accepting or rejecting the offer,
  - expressing no opinion on the offer, or
  - that it is unable to take a position on the offer.

There is one important prohibited action: short-tendering.

Shareholders of the target company are permitted to tender shares only to the extent of their net long position. That means shareholders cannot sell shares back to the company that they do not own.

EXAMPLE

A customer is long 400 shares of ABCD in a cash account and short 100 shares of the stock in a margin account. If ABCD becomes the target of a tender offer, the customer would be permitted to tender 300 shares, the net long position. If the customer were permitted to tender the 400 shares in the cash account and the tender offer was successful in acquiring all the outstanding shares, the customer would be short 100 shares with no way to cover.

A customer is considered **long a stock** if the customer owns

- the stock,
- a convertible security and has issued conversion instructions, or
- a call option and has issued exercise instructions.

TAKE NOTE

There is a special rule for a *partial* tender. If a tender offer is for less than 100% of the outstanding shares or is contingent on a minimum number of shares being tendered, holders of convertible securities can tender without first converting. They will only be required to convert if their tender is accepted.

PRACTICE QUESTION

4. An investor is long 300 shares of ABCD in a cash account and short 300 shares of ABCD in a margin account. A tender offer for ABCD is announced. How many shares may be tendered by the investor?
   A. 0
   B. 300
   C. 600
   D. 900

Answer: A. Only the investor's net long position may be tendered. The investor's long position of 300 shares is fully offset by the short position of 300 shares. No shares can be tendered in this situation.

SEC Rule 10b-18

SEC Rule 10b-18 appears in the FINRA Content Outline, but we don't expect any exam questions on it. Just in case there is a surprise, this rule deals with an issuer buying back its own stock in the open market. If an issuer wants to buy back its own securities in the open market, SEC Rule 10b-18 applies. If it is ever tested, these are the most likely candidates:

- Transactions cannot affect the opening or closing of the security. To be safe, the issuer can't be involved in the first trade at the opening or do any purchasing in the final 30 minutes of the trading day (3:30–4:00 pm ET).
- Transactions can be executed at prices no higher than the highest independent bid or the last reported sale price, whichever is higher.

Margin Risk Disclosure Document

When a client opens a margin account, the risk disclosure document covered in Lesson 2.7 must be furnished. Because that document is highly testable, we urge you to go back and review it. You might wait until after our coverage of *margin math* in Unit 16 because some of the concepts may be easier to understand at that point.

LESSON 14.3: COMPLIANCE WITH THE SENIOR EXPLOITATION RULES

LO 14.c Determine if senior exploitation is happening in an account.

Introduction

In Lesson 1.4, we went over the *trusted contact* requirements when opening an account for a *specified adult*. We also reviewed Rule 4512 on temporary holds. In this short lesson, we will look at some of the steps to be taken by a registered representative to determine if exploitation is taking place in a client's account.

Senior Exploitation

Member firms and their associated persons must pay close attention to the accounts of specified adults. They are frequently easy targets for scam artists. Amazingly, a very high percentage of the financial abuse is committed by their own family members. What exactly does FINRA consider financial exploitation? Financial exploitation is considered

- the wrongful or unauthorized taking, withholding, appropriation, or use of a specified adult's funds or securities; or
- any act of omission taken by a person, including through the use of a power of attorney, guardianship, or any other authority, regarding a specified adult to
  - obtain control through deception, intimidation, or undue influence, over the specified adult's money, assets, or property; or
  - convert the specified adult's money, assets, or property.

Prevention

Here are some suggested steps that member firms might want to take to prevent exploitation of their senior clients.

1. There should be clear, written procedures specifically addressing the needs of these clients.
2. Personnel should be given a plan showing what to do when exploitation is suspected. That would include how to escalate the concern.
3. Keep up with the regulations. Although the exam will only deal with the FINRA rules, the states have similar rules and there is the federal Senior Safe Act.
4. Training and more training. Rule 2165 provides for a safe harbor, but only when the member can document proper training of personnel. The training should point out the red flags to look for, such as cognitive decline and unusual activity in the account.
5. Take preemptive action. When a registered representative notices changes, reach out to the trusted person contact before anything happens.

LESSON 14.4: EXCHANGE, BROKER-DEALER COMMISSIONS, AND BROKERAGE AND RESEARCH SERVICES

LO 14.d Recall the safe harbor provisions of Section 28(e) of the Exchange Act.

Introduction

Broker-dealers typically provide a bundle of services to investment advisers. These include research and execution of transactions. The research provided can be either proprietary (created and provided by the broker-dealer) or third party (created by a third party but provided by the broker-dealer). Because commission dollars pay for the entire bundle of services, the practice of allocating certain dollars to pay for the research component is called *soft dollars*. The SEC has defined soft dollar practices as arrangements under which products or services other than execution of securities transactions are obtained by an investment adviser from or through a broker-dealer in exchange for the direction by the investment adviser of client brokerage transactions to the broker-dealer.

Safe Harbor

The original use of the term *safe harbor* had a maritime connotation, in that it referred to a safe place for a ship to enter, especially during a storm or a war. In the business world, it has come to mean a method of behavior which avoids running afoul of the law. In our case, the Section 28(e) safe harbor term describes compensation to an investment adviser from a broker-dealer that will generally not be considered unethical.

Because of the conflict of interest that exists when an investment adviser receives research, products, or other services as a result of using the commissions generated by client trades, the SEC requires advisers to disclose soft dollar arrangements to their clients.

Here is an example of a statement found in one adviser's brochure:

> We may direct transactions for your account to registered broker-dealers in return for research products and services that assist us in making decisions about investments. The research products will be used to generally service all of our clients,

so the brokerage commissions you pay may be used to pay for research that is not used in managing your account.

Finally, the SEC believes that an adviser accepting soft dollar benefits must explain that

- the adviser benefits because it does not have to produce or pay for the research or other products or services acquired with soft dollars; and
- the adviser has an incentive to select or recommend brokers based on the adviser's interest in receiving these benefits, rather than on the client's interest in getting the most favorable execution.

TEST TOPIC ALERT

What this all comes down to is knowing what is and what is not included in the safe harbor provisions. Here are some of the items that, if received as soft dollar compensation, would likely fall under Section 28(e)'s safe harbor provisions:

- Research reports analyzing the performance of a particular company or stock
- Financial newsletters and trade journals could be eligible research if they relate with appropriate specificity
- Quantitative analytical software
- Seminars or conferences with appropriate content
- Effecting and clearing securities trades

On the other hand, likely to fall out of the safe harbor would be the following:

- Telephone lines
- Office furniture, including computer hardware
- Travel expenses associated with attending seminars
- Rent
- Any software that does not relate directly to analysis of securities
- Payment for training courses for this exam
- Internet service

PRACTICE QUESTION

5. Which of the following would not be included in the safe harbor provisions of Section 28(e) of the Securities Exchange Act of 1934?
   A. Proprietary research
   B. Third-party research
   C. Rent
   D. Seminar registration fees

   Answer: C. Section 28(e) provides a safe harbor for those expenses paid with soft dollars that offer a direct research benefit. Rent is not included in the list of acceptable items coming under that safe harbor.

UNIT 15

Handling Customer Accounts

LEARNING OBJECTIVES

When you have completed this unit, you will be able to accomplish the following.

- LO 15.a **Recognize** the components and delivery requirements of customer confirmations.
- LO 15.b **Determine** the account information to be disclosed to customers.
- LO 15.c **Recall** the requirements for updating customer account records.
- LO 15.d **Identify** the steps in transferring accounts to another broker-dealer.
- LO 15.e **Name** the books and records retention requirements.
- LO 15.f **Determine** the rules and regulations pertaining to the handling of customer accounts.

INTRODUCTION

Books and records are an essential part of a broker-dealer's life. It could be the account records, with all of the details about the customer. It could be the details of a transaction, as shown on the confirmation. It could be the records relating to the internal operations of the firm. There are loads of them. Those records, and their retention requirements are delineated in SEC Rules 17a-3 and 17a-4.

LESSON 15.1: CUSTOMER CONFIRMATIONS AND ACCOUNT RECORDS

LO 15.a Recognize the components and delivery requirements of customer confirmations.

Introduction

It is FINRA's contention that customer confirmations help protect investors by allowing them to verify the terms of their transactions, alerting them to potential conflicts of interest, safeguarding against fraud, and providing them with information to evaluate the costs of their transactions and the quality of their broker-dealer's execution.

Customer Confirmations

There are two principal tested items on this topic:

- What is included on a customer confirmation?
- When is the confirmation sent?

Confirmation Contents

A **trade confirmation** is a document that confirms a trade of a security. It applies if the customer is buying or selling a security. On the face of the confirmation is the amount of money due from or owed to the customer. It will also include the date the money changes hands. That is the settlement date. The basic requirements for confirmation are found in SEC Rule 10b-10 and FINRA Rule 2232.

Appropriate to the specific trade, those rules require the confirmation to contain

- whether the member acted as agent or principal (capacity);
- whether the member acted as dual agent (dual agency occurs when a firm represents customers on both sides of the trade—the buyer and the seller—and charging each side a commission);
- the source and amount of commission in an agency trade;
- whether a control relationship exists between the issuer and member;
- a description of the deferred sales load, if any;
- the markup or markdown charged retail customers when acting in a principal capacity (it is unlikely the exceptions will be tested);
- the identity of the shares or units as well as the price and number of shares (if the trade price on the confirmation is incorrect, the actual price prevails);
- the total par value of the trade of debt securities;
- the accrued interest in a trade of debt securities;
- if the member is a market maker in the security;
- the date and time of the transaction execution or a statement that it will be furnished upon request; and
- the lower of yield to call or yield to maturity when a transaction in a debt security is done on a yield or dollar basis.

Confirmation Delivery

SEC Rule 10b-10 includes the requirements for confirmation deliveries. For each transaction, the customer must be sent or given a written confirmation of the trade at or before the completion of the transaction (settlement date).

When-, As-, and If-Issued Contracts (When-Issued Trades)

Typically, new municipal bond issues are sold to investors before the bonds are issued and available for delivery. An investor receives a when-issued confirmation describing the bonds. The confirmation does not include a total dollar amount or settlement date because, until the settlement date is known, the accrued interest cannot be calculated to determine the total dollar amount. Once the bonds are issued, the investor receives a new confirmation stating the purchase price and settlement date.

A when-issued transaction confirmation must include

- a description of the security;
- the purchase price (dollar bond) or yield (serial bond); and
- the trade date.

Because the settlement date is unknown, a when-issued confirmation for bonds cannot include accrued interest. That means it will not show the total dollar amount due.

Electronic Delivery of Information

In keeping with today's digital age, FINRA allows members to electronically send documents, such as confirmations and account statements, to customers as long as certain conditions are met. To do so, the firm must have procedures in place to show that the information sent has been delivered as intended and that the confidentiality and security of personal information are protected. Furthermore, customers must provide written consent to electronic delivery.

In addition, a customer who consents to receive information and documents electronically must be provided with the information in paper form, upon request.

TAKE NOTE

Copies of customer confirmations must be retained for three years.

LO 15.b Determine the account information to be disclosed to customers.

Customer Account Statements

Members are required to send statements to customers at least quarterly. You should remember from Lesson 3.5 that, in the case of penny stocks, statements are sent monthly even when there is no account activity. Account activity includes, but is not limited to, purchases, sales, interest credits or debits, charges or credits, dividend payments, transfer activity, securities receipts or deliveries, and/or journal entries relating to securities or funds in the possession or control of the member. In addition to the obvious activity just mentioned, there are some other requirements that might be tested.

For most securities, the positions are shown at current market value. But, what if the customer's account contains illiquid investments?

The FINRA rule specifically refers to DPPs and unlisted REITs. A general securities member must include in a customer account statement a per share estimated value of a DPP or unlisted REIT security, developed in a manner reasonably designed to ensure that the per share estimated value is reliable.

There are several methods that can be used to estimate the value. It is unlikely any of these will be on the exam, but, just in case, they follow.

Net Investment

Net investment is based on the "amount available for investment" percentage in the *Estimated Use of Proceeds* section of the offering prospectus. When the issuer provides a range of amounts available for investment, the member may use the maximum offering percentage unless the member has reason to believe that such percentage is unreliable, in which case the member must use the minimum offering percentage.

Appraised Value

At any time, the member may include a per share estimated value reflecting an appraised valuation, which must be

- based on valuations of the assets and liabilities of the DPP or REIT performed at least annually, by, or with the material assistance or confirmation of a third-party valuation expert or service and
- derived from a methodology that conforms to standard industry practice.

Disclosures

"Any account statement that provides a per share estimated value for a DPP or REIT security shall disclose that the DPP or REIT securities are not listed on a national securities exchange, are generally illiquid and that, even if a customer is able to sell the securities, the price received may be less than the per share estimated value provided in the account statement." —from FINRA Rule 2231.

In January of each year, members must send statements to customers showing a summary of all interest and dividends credited to the account as well the gross proceeds of all sales made the prior year. The statement is sent to the account owner and to the IRS on Form 1099.

With respect to joint accounts, the statement is sent to the person whose Social Security number is on the account. Although the member collects information on all parties in a joint account, each account has a primary Social Security number.

Customer account statements must include a statement advising customers to promptly report any discrepancy or inaccuracy to the brokerage firm and, if applicable, the clearing firm. It is the same concept as your bank or credit card statements where you are told to promptly report any errors.

LESSON: 15.2: CUSTOMER RECORDS INCLUDING ACCOUNT TRANSFERS

LO 15.c Recall the requirements for updating customer account records.

Introduction

Common with other financial institutions, broker-dealers have many recordkeeping requirements. The exam focuses on those relating to customers.

Updating Customer Account Information

As we learned in Lesson 1.4, each retail customer who opens a new account must, within 30 days of the opening of the account, be furnished with a copy of the account record. This is to ensure that the information obtained by the firm, particularly suitability information, is correct.

For updating purposes, the member firm must send a copy of the account record to customers at least every 36 months thereafter. Supervisors always must, however, look for red flags, which may indicate something has changed in the circumstances of the customer.

If the customer should notify the firm of any changes to the account record, such as change in name, address, or investment objectives, the firm must send a copy of the updated account record within 30 days of receiving notice of the change. Another important update is when the client's employment situation changes. There are two reasons for that.

First, it may have an effect on suitability. A promotion would likely enable the client to take somewhat more aggressive actions. A demotion or unemployment would have the opposite effect. Therefore, it may become necessary to revise the client's investment objectives.

Second, broker-dealers always have to be aware of client's being employed by publicly traded companies. That dramatically increases the possibility of the client acquiring MNPI. That raises a red flag if the client makes a trade in that stock.

A broker-dealer must retain records of all of the identification information obtained from the customer for five years after the account is closed.

By contrast, records made about the information verifying a customer's identity have to be retained for only five years after the record is made.

TAKE NOTE

Accounts that are acquired through acquisition of another member firm are not subject to customer identification procedures. It can be presumed that the other member fulfilled its obligation.

LO 15.d Identify the steps in transferring accounts to another broker-dealer.

Introduction

An important process is the transferring of customer accounts from one member firm to another. Customers can have all kinds of reasons for making the change. It can also happen when a registered representative leaves one firm and goes to another. In many cases, clients follow the rep to the new firm. We'll cover the special FINRA rule dealing with registered representatives "taking" clients with them. In other cases, an older client passes away and the children who inherit the account wish to move it to the firm handling their account. The industry recognizes that "you win some and you lose some," and these transfers must be fluid. That is what the Automated Customer Account Transfer Service (ACATs) is all about.

Transferring Customer Accounts Between Member Firms

When a customer whose securities account is carried by a member (the carrying member) wants to transfer the account to another member (the receiving member), the customer must sign an account transfer form. This form is called the Transfer Initiation Form (TIF). The **Automated Customer Account Transfer Service (ACATS)** automates and standardizes the procedure for the transfer. The TIF is sent to ACATS by the receiving firm. For purposes of this rule, customer authorization could be the customer's actual signature or an electronic signature.

TAKE NOTE

It may help your understanding to think of the carrying firm as the losing firm (it is losing the account) and the receiving firm as the winning firm (it is gaining the new account).

Once forwarded and received by the carrying firm, it has one business day to validate the securities listed on the TIF or take exception to the transfer instructions. If there are no exceptions, within three business days following validation, the carrying firm must complete the transfer of the account.

No member may interfere with a customer's request to transfer an account in connection with the change in employment of the customer's registered representative when the account is not subject to any lien for monies owed by the customer or other bona fide claim.

Following a Registered Representative From One Member Firm to Another

When registered representatives move to a new firm and try to convince former customers to move with them, FINRA Rule 2273 requires certain disclosures to be made. Those disclosures are provided in educational material outlining things for the customer to consider, including financial incentives that could rise to a conflict of interest for the rep.

The FINRA required educational communication highlights the following potential implications of transferring assets to the new firm:

- Whether financial incentives received by the representative may create a conflict of interest
- That some assets may not be directly transferrable to the recruiting firm and, as a result, the customer may incur costs to liquidate and move those assets or account maintenance fees to leave them with his current firm
- Potential costs related to transferring assets to the recruiting firm, including differences in the pricing structure and fees imposed by the customer's current firm and the recruiting firm
- Differences in products and services between the customer's current firm and the recruiting firm

The rule states that a member who hires a registered person must provide to a former customer (a natural person), in paper or electronic form, the educational communication when

- the member, directly or through that registered person, individually contacts the former customer to transfer assets; or
- the former customer, absent individualized contact, transfers assets to an account assigned to the registered person associated with that member firm.

The communication is required at the time of contact with a former customer by the registered person or the member firm regarding transferring assets.

Contacting the customer may be done with written, electronic, or oral communication. Electronic communication may include a hyperlink directly to the educational communication. If the contact is oral, the member or registered person must notify the former customer that an educational communication that includes important considerations in deciding whether to transfer assets to the member will be provided not later than three business days after the contact.

If a former customer attempts to transfer assets, but no individualized contact with the former customer by the registered person or member occurs before the former customer seeks to transfer assets, the member must deliver the educational communication with the account transfer approval documentation.

The delivery of the communication applies for three months following the date the registered person begins employment or associates with the member.

FINRA Rule 2273 is not applicable when a former customer who is contacted to transfer assets expressly states that she is not interested in transferring assets to the member. If the former customer later decides to transfer assets to the new member without further individualized contact within three months following the date the registered person begins employment with the member, then the educational material must be sent. This rule is also not applicable to institutional accounts; it is solely for natural persons.

LESSON 15.3 HANDLING CUSTOMER ACCOUNTS INCLUDING RETENTION REQUIREMENTS

LO 15.e Name the books and records retention requirements.

Introduction

We have covered many of these in the appropriate lessons so this will be more of a summary than anything else.

Records to Be Made

The rules dealing with recordkeeping are SEC Rules 17a-3 and 17a-4 and FINRA Rule 4511. Rule 17a-3 lists the records to be kept. If you were taking a principal's exam, you would need extensive knowledge of this. For this exam, it is just the basics.

SEC Rules 17a-3 and 17a-4

SEC Rules 17a-3 and 17a-4 address what records must be prepared by members, when such records must be prepared, and for how long such records must be retained. For retention purposes, records are either lifetime records, six-year records, or three-year records. One exception is customer complaints; complaints are a four-year record.

Figure 15.1: Recordkeeping Periods

Lifetime Records	Six-Year Records	Three-Year Records
Stock Certificate Book	**Blotters**—Records of original entry receipts and deliveries	Virtually all other records:
Partnership Agreement or Articles of Incorporation	**General Ledger**—Accounting records of assets, liability, and net worth; prepared at least monthly	FOCUS Reports
Minutes of Board or Partnership Meetings	**Stock Ledger**—Stock owned by the firm and where held; posted the business day after settlement	Trial balances—prepared at least monthly
	Customer Ledgers—Statements for cash and margin accounts held by customers; posted no later than settlement date	Forms U-4 and U-5
	Customer Account Records—New account forms, margin agreements, and other customer information and agreements	Fingerprint cards
	Designated Principals—A record for each office listing, by name or title, of each person at that office who, without delay, can explain the types of records the firm maintains at that office and the information contained in those records.	Confirmations of trades
		Order tickets
		Security and cash loan records
		Failed-to-receive and failed-to-deliver records
		Long and short securities differences

TAKE NOTE

Customer complaints are a four-year record.

Whether a record retention requirement is six, four, or three years, records for the two most recent years must be in a readily accessible location.

TEST TOPIC ALERT

Trade blotters are a daily record of all activity, including cash received and disbursed, securities received and delivered, and identification of securities bought and sold that day. The daily blotter would **not** contain client information or settlement dates. Blotters must be posted no later than the first business day following the activity.

LO 15.f Determine the rules and regulations pertaining to the handling of custome accounts.

Most of the FINRA and SEC rules regarding the handling of customer accounts have been mentioned in one unit or another. This learning objective is contains several items that have not been covered.

Death of an Account Holder

With regard to individual accounts, once a firm becomes aware of the death of the account owner, the firm must cancel all open orders, mark the account *deceased*, and freeze the assets in the account until receiving instructions and the necessary documentation from the executo of the decedent's estate. If the account has a third-party power of attorney, the authorization i revoked.

TAKE NOTE

Discretionary authority ends at the death of the account owner.

Depending on the type of account, the documents necessary to release the assets of a decedent are

- a certified copy of the death certificate,
- inheritance tax waivers, and
- letters testamentary.

If one party in a **joint tenants with rights of survivorship (JTWROS)** account dies, the account cannot be transferred to the name of the new owner (the other party) until a certified copy of the death certificate is presented to the member firm. The other documents noted earlier are not needed to transfer ownership at death in a JTWROS account.

If one party in a tenants in common (TIC) account dies, the decedent's interest in the account goes to the decedent's estate. The executor for the decedent must present the proper documents before the assets belonging to the decedent can be released. In some states, the death of a tenant in a TIC account requires that the executor present an affidavit of domicile to the member that shows the decedent's estate will be handled under the laws of that state.

Also note that in TIC accounts, the death of a tenant requires that the member firm freeze the account and acceptance of orders until the required documents are presented. Compare this with a JTWROS account, for which the death of one tenant does not preclude the remaining tenant from entering orders.

With regard to partnership accounts, if one partner dies, the member needs written authority from the remaining partners before executing any further orders. This written authorization generally takes the form of an amended partnership agreement.

TEST TOPIC ALERT

Three basic steps apply at the death of a customer:

- Cancel open orders
- Freeze the account (mark it deceased)
- Await instructions from the executor of the estate

Holding Customers' Mail

A customer gives specific mailing instructions when opening a new account. Statements and confirmations may be sent to someone who holds power of attorney for the customer if the customer requests it in writing and if duplicate confirms are also sent to the customer.

FINRA rules permit member firms to hold mail for a customer (e.g., statements and confirmations) who will not be receiving mail provided that

- the member firm receives written instructions that include the time period the request is being made for up to three months (requests may be granted for periods longer than three months for an acceptable reason such as safety or security concerns but not merely for the sake of convenience);
- the member firm informs the customer of any alternate methods that the customer may use to receive or monitor account activity such as email or through the member firm's

website (the member must obtain customer confirmation that this information regarding alternate methods was received); and

- the member verifies at reasonable intervals that the customer's instructions still apply.

Additionally, during that time that a member firm is holding mail for a customer, the firm must be able to communicate with the customer in a timely manner to provide important account information. The firm must take actions reasonably designed to ensure that a customer's mail is not tampered with or used in a manner that would violate FINRA rules or federal securities laws.

While holding mail is a courtesy that firms may extend to customers, the rule does not require them to. If extending the courtesy is consistent with the broker-dealer's in-house rules, the written request by the customer to do so implies that the customer is also giving the broker-dealer permission to do so.

Approval and Documentation of Changes in Account Name or Designation

FINRA Rule 4515 says: "Before any customer order is executed, there must be placed upon the order form or other similar record, the name or designation of the account (or accounts) for which such order is to be executed. No change in such account name(s) (including related accounts) or designation(s) shall be made unless the change has been authorized by a registered principal."

Anti-Money Laundering (AML) Compliance

FINRA Rule 3310 requires member firms to develop, implement, and monitor anti-money laundering (AML) programs designed to achieve compliance with the **Bank Secrecy Act** and related regulations. The firm's anti-money laundering (AML) program must be approved in writing by a member of senior management. If the approving senior manager leaves the member firm, the AML program should be reapproved by the new manager. Specifically, the rules would require member firms to

- establish and implement policies and procedures that can be reasonably expected to detect and cause the reporting of transactions that raise a suspicion of money laundering;
- establish and implement policies, procedures, and internal controls reasonably designed to achieve compliance with the Bank Secrecy Act;
- designate to FINRA an individual or individuals responsible for implementing and monitoring the day-to-day operations and internal controls of the program; and
- provide ongoing training for appropriate personnel.

Currency Transaction Report (CTR)

The Bank Secrecy Act requires broker-dealers to report on Form 112 any currency deposited or received in excess of $10,000 on a single day. This requirement applies to cash transactions used to pay off loans, the electronic transfer of funds, or the purchase of certificates of deposit, stocks, bonds, mutual funds, or other investments. The act also requires the reporting of wire transfers of $3,000 or more.

Though paying for purchased securities with currency is not prohibited, many firms do not permit this. Failure to report can result in fines of up to $500,000, 10 years in prison, or both. The record retention requirements for Form 112 are five years.

Form 112 must be E-filed within 15 days of receipt of the currency. This rule is part of the regulatory effort to deal with money laundering. The two federal agencies empowered to deal with this abuse are the Federal Reserve and the Department of the Treasury.

AML Compliance Program

Broker-dealers are required to establish internal compliance procedures to detect abuses. There are signs—or red flags—that might suggest the possibility of money laundering. If one of these is detected, prompt reporting to the appropriate principal is required. Examples of red flags include a customer

- exhibiting a lack of concern regarding risks, commissions, or other transaction costs;
- attempting to make frequent or large deposits of currency or cashier's checks;
- making a large number of wire transfers to unrelated third parties;
- engaging in excessive transfers between unrelated accounts; and
- designing currency deposits or withdrawals to fall under the $10,000 cash transaction report filing threshold. This is a practice known as *structuring*.

PRACTICE QUESTION

1. A broker-dealer would have to complete a Form 112 when a customer
   A. deposits $10,000 in cash to his account.
   B. deposits $10,000.01 in cash to her account.
   C. wires $3,500 to an offshore bank.
   D. and child deposits a personal check for $11,000 into their TIC account.

Answer: B. The cash reporting requirements for Form 112 apply when the cash transaction exceeds $10,000. This is true when the excess is only a penny. Wires of more than $3,000 must be reported, but not on Form 112. Personal checks, regardless of the amount, are not recorded.

PART 3

Obtains and Verifies Customers' Purchases and Sales Instructions and Agreements; Processes, Completes, and Confirms Transactions

Part 3 consists of 3 units:

Unit 16: Types of Orders and Quotations

Unit 17: Processing Transactions

Unit 18: Complaint Resolution

In total, you will see 14 questions on material from Part 3, representing 11% of the Series 7 Top-Off Exam.

UNIT 16 Types of Orders and Quotations

LEARNING OBJECTIVES

When you have completed this unit, you will be able to accomplish the following.

- › LO 16.a **Name** the different types or orders available to customers.
- › LO 16.b **Name** the different types of quotes.
- › LO 16.c **Define** short sale strategies and requirements.
- › LO 16.d **Compute** margin requirements.
- › LO 16.e **Determine** the rules and regulations pertaining to trading securities.

INTRODUCTION

As a general securities registered representative, one of the functions you might be performing is entering orders for customers. Understanding the different types of orders and their applications is necessary when acting in this role. Likewise, recognizing securities quotations is critical. Perhaps some of your clients will engage in more aggressive strategies, such as margin trading and short selling. You may be called upon to explain how the calculations behind these strategies work. That is why this exam tests you on them.

LESSON 16.1: TYPES OF CUSTOMER ORDERS

LO 16.a Name the different types of orders available to customers.

Price-Restricted Orders

Some orders, such as limit and stop-limit, restrict the price of the transaction. Typical orders include the following:

- *Market.* Executed immediately at the market price.

- *Limit.* Limits the amount paid or received for securities.
- *Stop.* Becomes a market order if the stock reaches or goes through the stop (trigger or election) price.
- *Stop-limit.* Entered as a stop order and changed to a limit order if the stock hits or goes through the stop (trigger or election) price.

PRACTICE QUESTION

1. Which of the following types of orders does **not** restrict the price at which an order is executed?
   A. Limit
   B. Stop
   C. Market
   D. Stop-limit

   Answer: C. A market order does not reflect or restrict the price at which a security is executed. A limit order limits the amount to be paid or received for securities. A stop order becomes a market order if the stock reaches or goes through the stop price. A stop-limit order becomes a limit order if the stock hits or goes through the trigger price.

Market Orders

Market orders are sent immediately to the trading floor for execution without restrictions or limits. They are executed immediately at the current market price and have priority over all other types of orders. A market order to buy is executed at the lowest offering price available; a market order to sell is executed at the highest bid price available. Those prices are usually referred to as the *inside market* or *inside quote*. As long as the security is trading, a market order guarantees execution. When the objective of the client is immediate execution, use a market order.

Limit Orders

In a **limit order**, a customer limits the acceptable purchase or selling price. A limit order can be executed only at the specified price or better. If the order cannot be executed at the limit price immediately, it is placed on the designated market maker's (DMM's) book and executed when and if the market price meets the order limit price. Buy limit orders are placed below the current market, whereas sell limit orders are placed above the current market. Buy limit orders are used by investors who believe a stock is currently overpriced, but would like to buy on a dip in the market. Investors who own a stock and believe it is currently undervalued turn in sell limit orders getting them out of the position should the stock rise to the desired level.

Length of Limit Orders

Limit orders can be turned in with one or two different time restrictions. They can be good for the day entered (day order), or good 'til canceled (GTC), sometimes referred to as an open order. We will discuss these a bit later.

Risks of Limit Orders

A customer who enters a limit order risks missing the chance to buy or sell, especially if the market moves away from the limit price. The market may never go as low as the buy limit price or as high as the sell limit price. Sometimes limit orders are not executed, even if the stock trades at the limit price.

Why would that happen? A term you should be aware of is **stock ahead**. Limit orders on the DMM's book for the same price are arranged according to when they were received. If a limit order at a specific price was not filled, chances are another order at the same price took precedence—that is, there was stock ahead.

TAKE NOTE

Limit orders stand in time priority. There may be multiple orders to buy a stock at a particular price. Once the stock begins trading at that price, those limit orders that were entered first will be filled first.

Stop Orders

A **stop order**, also known as a **stop loss order**, is designed to protect a profit or prevent a loss if the stock begins to move in the wrong direction.

The stop order becomes a market order once the stock trades at or moves through a certain price, known as the stop price. Stop orders are left with and executed by the DMM. There is no guarantee the executed price will be the stop price, unlike the price on a limit order. Buy stop orders are entered above the current market, whereas sell stop orders are entered below the current market.

A trade at the stop price triggers the order, which then becomes a market order. A stop order takes two trades to execute, which are as follows:

- **Trigger**. The trigger transaction at or through the stop price activates the trade.
- **Execution**. The stop order becomes a market order and is executed at the next price, completing the trade.

Buy Stop Order

A buy stop order protects a profit or limits a loss in a short stock position. The buy stop is entered at a price above the current market and is triggered when the market price touches or goes through the buy stop price.

EXAMPLE

A customer has shorted 1,000 shares of XYZ stock at $55, and the stock is now at $48. The customer would like to hang on for more gain but is concerned the stock will reverse itself and begin to rise, eroding some of the unrealized profit. To deal with this, the customer could place the following order: buy 1,000 XYZ 49 stop. If the stock does start to head north, once it trades at or through the stop price of 49, the order becomes a market order to buy 1,000 XYZ.

Buy stop orders are also used by technical traders who track support and resistance levels for stocks. For instance, collect on delivery (COD) stock trades between 38 and 42. It never seems to go above 42 or below 38. Technicians believe that if the stock breaks through resistance, it will continue to move upward at a rapid pace. Therefore, they will not buy at 40 because there is little upside potential. However, they may place a buy stop order above the resistance level, knowing that if the stock breaks resistance and begins to move up, they will buy the stock before it develops upward momentum.

An investor might place a stop order to buy 100 COD at 42.25 stop when the market is at 40 if she believes 42 represents a technical resistance point, above which the stock price will continue to rise.

Figure 16.1: COD Buy Stop Order

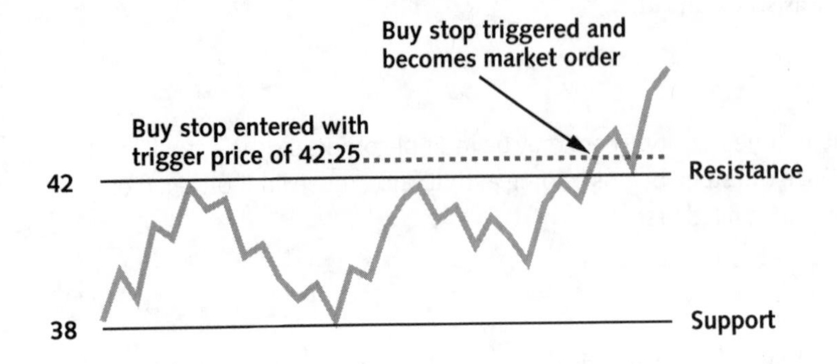

Sell Stop Order

A **sell stop order** protects a profit or limits a loss in a long stock position and is entered at a price below the current market.

EXAMPLE

A customer is long 1,000 shares of XYZ at $32, and the stock is now at $41. The customer would like to hang on for more gain but is concerned the stock will reverse itself and begin to fall, eroding some of the unrealized profit. To deal with this, the customer could place the following order: sell 1,000 XYZ 40 stop. If the stock does start to head south, once it trades at or through the stop price of 40, the order becomes a market order to sell 1,000 XYZ.

Technical traders also use sell stop orders. They believe that if a stock breaks through support, it will fall like a rock. Therefore, they will not short the stock at 40 because there is little downside potential. Historically, the stock has not traded below 38.

However, they may place a sell stop order just below the support level, knowing that if the stock breaks through support and begins to move down, they will short the stock before it develops downward momentum.

An investor who is long stock might place a stop order to sell 100 COD at 37.75 stop when the market is at 40 if he believes 38 represents a technical support point below which the stock will continue to fall.

Figure 16.2: COD Sell Stop Order

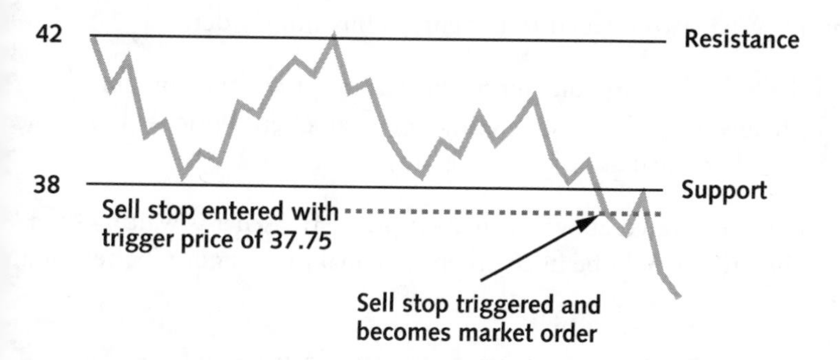

If a large number of stop orders are triggered at the same price, a flurry of trading activity takes place as they become market orders. This activity will accelerate the advance or decline of the stock price.

Stop-Limit Order

A **stop-limit order** is a stop order that once triggered, becomes a limit order instead of a market order.

EXAMPLE

A customer calls you and says, "I want to sell my ABC stock if it falls to $30, but I don't want less than $29.95 for my shares." So you enter the following order: sell 1,000 ABC 30 stop 29.95. Once ABC trades at or below 30, the order becomes a limit order to sell at 29.95 or better. The problem here is that the market could leapfrog between the stop price and the limit price. As a result, the customer will not get an execution.

Assume once the order is entered, the stock trades as follows: 30.01, 29.97, 29.94, 29.92, and so on. The trade at 29.97 triggers the order, at which point the order becomes a limit order to sell at 29.95 or better (higher). In this scenario, the customer does not sell. The moral of this example is if you are concerned that a stock is heading south, place a market order to sell or a stop order. A stop-limit may leave you without an execution.

Figure 16.3: Stop and Limit Orders

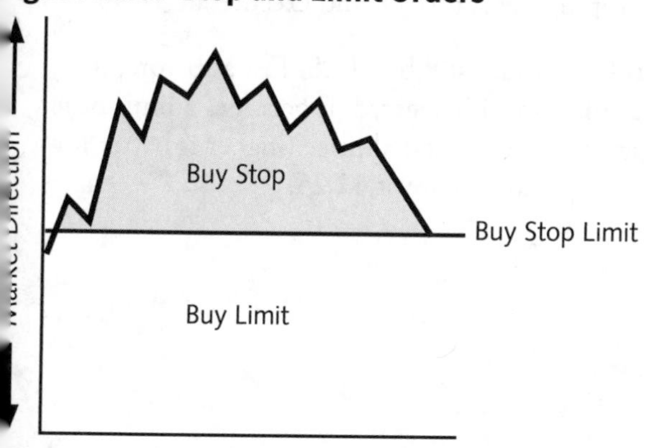

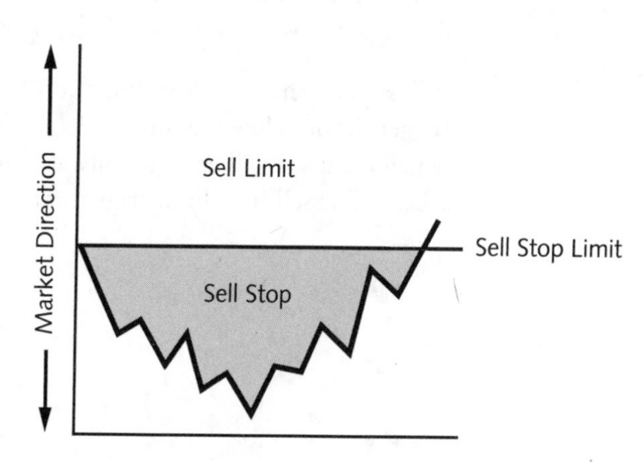

TEST TOPIC ALERT

Be prepared for two to four questions regarding limit and stop orders. Use the chart to solve some problems, starting with limit orders.

Let's take a walk through some of the possibilities.

XYZ is currently trading at 52. Where would a customer enter a buy limit order?

Refer to the chart. Think of the horizontal middle line as the current price. The buy limit would be entered somewhere below 52. The investor wants to buy at a better price—a lower price for a buyer. The order would be filled at or below the order price.

A sell limit order for XYZ would be entered above the market price. The seller is waiting for a price that is better than 52. The order would be filled at a price equal to or higher (better for a seller) than the order price.

Stop orders are a little trickier because they have two parts: trigger (election) and execution. Consider a buy stop at 52 entered when the market is 51. Based on the ticks below, at what price would this order be executed?

51.88 51.99 52.13 52.13 51.88

Look at the chart. The chart shows you that a buy stop is entered above the market price. This reminds you that it is only elected or triggered at the first price where the market is at or above the order price. Stops become market orders when triggered, so it executes at the price immediately following the trigger. Based on this example, this buy stop triggers at 52.13 and could execute at 52.13.

If this had been a buy stop-limit at 52, the trigger would still be 52.13. Just as before, it triggers at or above the order price. When a stop-limit is triggered, it becomes a limit order, which means it will execute only at a price at or below the stated price (lower is better for a buyer).

Based on this example, this buy stop-limit triggers at 52.13 and could execute at 51.88.

Consider a sell stop at 52 entered when the market is 53. Based on the ticks shown below, at what price could this order be executed?

52.50 51.88 51.50 51.75 52.25

The chart shows you that a sell stop is entered below the market price. This reminds you that it is only elected or triggered when the market is at or below the order price. Stops become market orders when triggered, so it executes at the next available price immediately following the trigger. Based on this example, this sell stop triggers at 51.88 and executes at 51.50.

If this had been a sell stop-limit at 52, the trigger would still be 51.88. Just as before, it triggers at or below the order price. When a stop-limit is triggered, it becomes a limit order, which means it will execute only at a price at or above the stated price (higher is better for a seller). This sell stop-limit triggers at 51.88 and could execute at 52.25.

PRACTICE QUESTION

2. UZEW is trading at 40.63. Your customer, who owns 100 shares of the stock, places an order to sell UZEW at 39.87 stop-limit. The tape subsequently reports the following trades:

   UZEW 40.63 40.75 40.05 39.83 39.80 39.93

   Your customer's order could first be executed at

   A. 39.80.
   B. 39.83.
   C. 39.93.
   D. 40.63.

   Answer: C. The sell stop-limit order is elected (triggered) at the trade of 39.83. That is the first time the stock trades at or below the stop price of 39.87. The order then becomes a sell limit order at 39.87. The order can be executed at that price or higher (the limit placed by the customer). The next trade reported after the trigger is reached (39.80) is below the limit price. The order could be executed at the next trade of 39.93.

When drawing your order reference chart, think of the phrase, *SLoBS over BLiSS*. It stands for *Sell Limits and Buy Stops over Buy Limits and Sell Stops*. SLoBS tells you the orders placed above the current market price (The *o* reminds you that the orders are over the market price. BLiSS refers to orders placed below the current market price. *B* in BLiSS reminds you of *B* in below.).

Why use stop orders?

Buy stop orders

- protect against loss in a short stock position,
- protect a gain from a short stock position, and
- establish a long position when a breakout occurs above the line of resistance.

Sell stop orders

- protect against loss in a long stock position,
- protect a gain from a long stock position, and
- establish a short position when a breakout occurs below the line of support.

There is no guarantee that if a stop order is elected (triggered), the investor will pay or receive the stop price. Because it is a marker order that is entered after being triggered, the price can be more, less, or the same as the stop price. If the investor wants a specified price (or better), then it must be a stop-limit order. With that, you have the risk that the order might be triggered, but never executed.

Reducing Orders

Certain orders on the DMM's order book are reduced when a stock goes ex-dividend. All orders entered below the market are reduced on the ex-dividend date (or ex-date)—the first date on which the new owner (purchaser) of stock does not qualify for the current dividend. On the ex-date, the stock price opens lower by the amount of the distribution. Orders reduced include buy limit and sell stops, including sell stop-limit orders. These orders are reduced by the dividend amount. Without this reduction, trading at the lower price on the ex-dividend date could cause an inadvertent execution.

EXAMPLE

ABC closes at 35.00. The following day is the ex-date for a $0.31 cash dividend.

ABC stock should open at 34.69. Without the reduction, a sell stop order at 35 could be triggered even though the lower price is not due to market forces.

Do Not Reduce (DNR)

A do not reduce (DNR) order is not reduced by an ordinary cash dividend. In this case, the customer does not care if there is an execution due solely to the ex-date reduction.

TEST TOPIC ALERT

You are likely to be asked which orders are reduced for cash dividends. Only those placed below the market price are automatically reduced. Remember that BLiSS (buy limits and sell stops) orders are placed below the market price and are reduced for cash dividend distributions. All orders are adjusted for stock dividends and stock splits, whether placed above or below the market.

Reductions for Stock Splits

If there is a stock dividend or stock split, the DMM will adjust all open orders.

EXAMPLE

There is an open (GTC) order to sell 100 XYZ at 50 stop. If there is a 2:1 split, the order becomes sell 200 XYZ at 25 stop.

EXAMPLE

There is an open order to buy 500 XYZ at 30. If there is a 20% stock dividend, the order becomes buy 600 XYZ at 25.

EXAMPLE

There is an open order to buy 100 XYZ at 30. If there is a 20% stock dividend, the order becomes buy 100 XYZ at 25. Common sense says the order size should be 120 shares. However, only round lots are allowed on the order book. The additional 20 shares are in the customer's account but cannot be part of an open order. For reverse splits, all open orders are canceled.

TAKE NOTE

The standard trading unit for stocks is normally 100 shares. We call that a *round* lot. Any quantity less than a round lot is known as an *odd-lot*. Lesson 17.3 will delve further into the topic of round lots and odd lots.

PRACTICE QUESTION

3. A company is about to pay a dividend of $0.70. On the ex-dividend date, an open order to sell at 46 stop would
   - A. be automatically adjusted to 45.30 stop.
   - B. be automatically adjusted to 45.38 stop.
   - C. be automatically adjusted to 45.50 stop.
   - D. remain at 46 stop.

Answer: A. When a stock goes ex-dividend, the price of the stock falls by the amount of the dividend. A dividend of $0.70 would reduce the stop price by that amount.

Time-Sensitive Orders

Orders based on time considerations include the following:

- Day
- Good until canceled
- At-the-open and market-on-close
- Not held
- Fill-or-kill
- Immediate-or-cancel
- All-or-none
- Alternative, which provides two alternatives, such as sell a stock at a limit or sell it on stop

Day Orders

Unless marked to the contrary, an open order (stop or limit) is assumed to be a day order, valid only until the close of trading on the day it is entered. If the order has not been filled, it is canceled at the close of the day's trading.

Good Til Canceled (GTC) Orders

GTC orders are valid until executed or canceled. However, all GTC orders are automatically canceled if unexecuted on the last business day of April and the last business day of October. If the customer wishes to have the order remain working beyond those specific days, the customer must reenter the order. An example would be, *Buy 20M GGZ 9% Debentures at 95 AON GTC.* This is a GTC order that also has an all-or-none specification.

At-the-Open and Market-on-Close Orders

At-the-open orders are executed at the opening of the market. Partial executions are allowable. They must reach the post by the open of trading in that security or they will be canceled. Market-on-close orders are executed at or as near as possible to the closing price in the OTC market. On the NYSE, however, a market-on-close order must be entered before 3:40 pm ET and will be executed at the closing price.

Not Held (NH) Orders

A **market order** coded NH (not held) indicates that the customer agrees not to hold the floor broker or broker-dealer to a particular time or price of execution. This provides the floor broker with the authority to decide the best time or price at which to execute the trade. Market NH orders may not be placed with the NYSE DMM.

TAKE NOTE

Under FINRA Rule 3260, market NH orders in which a retail customer gives you authority over price or timing, are limited to the day the order is given. In other words, they are day orders. An exception is granted if the customer, in writing, states that the order is GTC.

Fill-or-Kill (FOK) Orders

The commission house broker is instructed to fill an entire fill-or-kill (FOK) order immediately at the limit price or better. A broker who cannot fill the entire order immediately cancels it and notifies the originating branch office.

Immediate-or-Cancel (IOC) Orders

Immediate-or-cancel (IOC) orders are like FOK orders except that a partial execution is acceptable. The portion not executed is canceled.

All-or-None (AON) Orders

All-or-none (AON) orders must be executed in their entirety or not at all. AON orders can be day or GTC orders. They differ from the FOKs in that they do not have to be filled immediately.

Alternative Orders (OCO)

Assume a customer is long stock at $50 that was purchased six months earlier at $30. To protect his unrealized gain, the customer might enter a sell stop at $48. Alternatively, if the stock continues to rise, he wants out at $53. What he might do is enter both orders with the notation, *one cancels the other* (OCO). If one of the orders is executed, the other is immediately canceled.

TAKE NOTE

Exchanges can limit the order types they will accept. For instance, the NYSE and Nasdaq do not accept GTC or stop orders (stop loss or stop-limit) or AON or FOK orders to be entered in their equity markets. Because these different order types are also used in the bond market, students should still be familiar with them and be able to distinguish them from other order types. Additionally, though an exchange might not accept them, broker-dealers are still able to do so if they wish to. However, they would need to manually monitor the status of the order if entered on an exchange that does not accept them.

gure 16.4: Comparison of Order Characteristics

rder Type	Description	Exchange Orders	OTC Orders
arket	Buy or sell at the best available market price	Most common order type on all exchanges	Most common OTC order type
imit	Minimum price for sell orders; maximum price for buy orders	Can be handled by a specialist (DMM) or floor broker as a day order. GTCs may not be acceptable, depending on the exchange	Acceptable on either a day or GTC basis if GTCs are accepted
top	Buy orders entered above the market; sell orders entered below the market	May or may not be acceptable, depending on the exchange	Acceptable by some dealers
top-limit	Stop order that becomes a limit order once the stop price has been reached or exceeded (triggered)	May or may not be acceptable, depending on the exchange	Acceptable by some dealers

Unit 16

PRACTICE QUESTION

4. An IOC order
   A. allows for several attempts to be executed in its entirety.
   B. makes one attempt to fill the order, and must be filled in its entirety.
   C. makes one attempt to fill the order; partial executions are okay.
   D. allows for several attempts to be executed; any outstanding part of the order is canceled at the end of the day.

Answer: C. An immediate-or-cancel (IOC) order is one in which the firm handling the order has one attempt to fill the order, but a partial execution is binding on the customer.

ESSON 16.2: QUOTATIONS

LO 16.b Name the different types of quotes.

Introduction

In many cases, before customers place an order, they want to know the approximate price they will be paying or receiving. The information is relayed to the client by furnishing a quotation or quote. This lesson will describe the various quotes supplied by securities firms.

Bids, Offers, and Quotes

Quotations are available for both listed and unlisted securities. In the case of stocks traded on the NYSE, the quotes come from the DMM. These are available electronically, even to retail investors. In the case of the OTC market, the quotations originate with the market makers. Exam questions are more likely to focus on them than on the DMM, at least when it comes to understanding the types of quotes.

The OTC market has no DMMs. Instead, firms wishing to make a market in a particular security must register with, and receive approval from, FINRA. They buy and sell for their own inventories, for their own profit, and at their own risk. A broker-dealer acting as a market maker, buying and selling for his own account rather than arranging trades, acts as a principal, not an agent. Another way to describe this is proprietary trading.

A full quote consists of a bid price and an offer (ask) price. When coming from the market maker, it will also include the size.

The current bid is the highest price at which the market maker will pay to buy, and the current offer is the lowest price at which the market maker will accept to sell. The difference between the bid and ask is known as the spread. A typical quote might be expressed as bid 63–offered 63.07. The highest price the dealer will pay is 63, and the lowest price the dealer will accept is 63.07. The spread is 0.07 of a point between the bid and ask. The firm could also say 63 bid–63.07 ask or 63 to 0.07.

Figure 16.5: The Customer's and the Market Maker's Relationship to the Quote

	Bid-63	**Ask/Offer-63.07**
Quoting dealer	Buys	Sells
Customer	Sells	Buys

When a customer buys a stock from a firm acting as principal, the broker marks up the ask price to reach the net price to the customer. Likewise, when a customer sells stock to a firm acting as principal, the dealer marks down from the bid price to reach the net proceeds to the customer.

Students are often confused by these terms, so let's try to simplify. If you ever go to an auction (even on eBay), and you want to buy something, you turn in a *bid*. That is what you are willing to pay to buy the item. That is exactly what the market maker is doing. The firm is announcing to the investment world, "This is how much we are willing to pay to buy this stock from another FINRA member firm."

What about the ask price? Have you ever gone to a flea market or some other selling scene where the prices are not marked on the item? If you are interested in buying it, you will say, "How much are you *asking* for this?" That is what the market maker is saying: "We have this stock in our inventory and are asking $X for it." The market maker could also say, "We are offering the stock at $X." That is why the terms ask price and offer price are interchangeable.

When a customer of a FINRA member firm enters an order to buy a stock, the firm has two ways of acting. If the firm acts as a principal (the *dealer* part of broker-dealer), it buys the stock from the market maker at the asking or offering price. Then, following the FINRA 5% policy (covered in Lesson 13.5), it adds a markup to its cost. Alternatively, it can act as an agent (the *broker* part of broker-dealer), and charge the customer the same price it paid plus commission.

If the customer enters a sell order, things work in reverse. The firm, acting as a principal, buys from the customer and sells to the market maker at the bid price. The price paid to the customer by the member firm is less than what it receives from the market maker. That difference is the markdown. The broker-dealer can also act in an agency capacity by crediting the customer with the market maker's bid price, less a commission.

TEST TOPIC ALERT

A broker-dealer can never charge a markup (or markdown) and a commission on the same trade. One or the other, but never both.

EXAMPLE

If the market maker in WXYZ is quoting 43.25 to 0.50, (short hand for 43.25 bid-43.50 ask or offer), and the customer's broker-dealer wants a half-point for the trade, a customer buying would pay 44 net, and a customer selling would receive 42.75 net. The additional half-point (added to the ask or offer, or subtracted from the bid) is the firm's markup and markdown, respectively. When you see the term net after a price, it means no commission (but there was a markup or markdown).

Types of Quotes

As mentioned earlier in the course, we refer to the OTC market as a negotiated market. As a negotiated market where broker-dealers are trading with other broker-dealers, there are several different types of quotes. We will review those most likely to appear on your exam.

Firm Quote

A firm quotation is the price at which a market maker stands ready to buy or sell at least one trading unit—100 shares of stock or five bonds—at the quoted price with other member firms. When a FINRA member firm makes a market in a security, the broker-dealer must be willing to buy or sell at least one trading unit of the security at its firm quote. All quotes are firm quotes unless otherwise indicated. In almost all cases, the quote size will be more than 1 round lot.

EXAMPLE

A market maker in ABCD common stock is quoting

52.15 – 52-27, 4 × 6

That means the bid is $52.15 and the ask is $52.27. At those prices, the dealer is willing to buy as many as 400 shares and sell as many as 600 shares. If a member calls to sell 100 on behalf of its customer, the market maker will sell 100 at 52.15 and revise the quote to 52.15 – 52.27, 3 × 6 to reflect the fact that it has already purchased 100 shares.

One function of an employee of a broker-dealer is that of OTC trader. This individual is responsible for taking customer orders received in the trading department and getting them executed at the best possible price. This trader may attempt to negotiate a better price with a market maker by making a counteroffer or a counterbid, especially if the spread between the market maker's bid and ask is fairly wide. However, the only way to guarantee an immediate execution is to buy stock at the market maker's ask price or sell at the bid price.

In a typical bond transaction, a trader at one broker-dealer (a market maker) calls a trader at another to buy a specific bond. A market maker might give another broker-dealer a quote that is firm for an hour with five-minute recall. This is a firm quote that remains good for an hour. If, within that hour, the market maker receives another order for the same security, the trader calls the broker-dealer back and gives it five minutes to confirm its order or lose its right to buy that security at the price quoted. You might recall the term *out-firm* from Lesson 6.1.

On the exam, you may have to identify the language of a firm quote. Examples would be, "it is 40 -41," or "we are quoting 40 – 41." The phrasing indicates that the quote is actual.

Backing Away

A market maker can revise a firm quote in response to market conditions and trading activit but a market maker who refuses to do business at the price(s) quoted is backing away from t quote. Backing away is a violation of trading rules. If you see this on the exam, remember, it a bad thing to back away from a firm quote.

Subject Quote

One could think of a subject quote as being the opposite of a firm quote. Whereas the firm quote represents the prices the dealer will honor, a subject quote requires further confirmation. It would be very rare to get a subject quote from a market maker. The most common case is when a customer calls her registered representative and asks, "How is ABCD doing today?" The representative could respond, "Last time I looked, it was 38 to a half," or think it is about 38–38.50." The statement is clear that the prices might have changed. As we showed you phraseology used to indicate a firm quote, the phrasing used to indicate a subjec quote might be tested as well.

Qualified Quotes

A quote will often be given with qualifiers intended to allow the dealer to back away if mark conditions change.

Workout Quote

The term *workout quote* is usually reserved for situations where a market maker knows that special handling will be required to accommodate a particular trade. Either the order size is too big for the market to absorb without disruption, or the market is too thin or temporarily unstable.

A **workout quote** is an approximate figure used to provide the buyer or the seller with an indication of price, not a firm quote.

Figure 16.6 Type of Quotes

Subject or Workout Market	Firm Market
"It is around 40–41."	"The market is 40–41."
"Last I saw, it was 40–41."	"It is currently 40–41."
"It is 40–41 subject."	
"40–42.50 workout."	

Nominal Quote

A **nominal quote** is someone's assessment of where a security might trade in an active marke Nominal quotes may be used to give customers an idea of the market value of an inactively traded security, but they are not firm quotes. Nominal quotes in print must be clearly labeled as such. These are common with municipal bonds (see Lesson 6.1) because the market for so many of them is very thin.

PRACTICE QUESTION

5. A broker-dealer is looking for a Nasdaq security for a customer and calls a market maker for a quote and is told that the quote is 20,000 shares at $20.22 for the next 10 minutes. What kind of quote would this be defined as?
   A. Nominal
   B. Firm
   C. Workout
   D. Subject

Answer: B. This quote is firm. The market maker has extended the quote with a given size, price, and time for how long the quote is good for. If the broker making the call decides to purchase the security in the next 10 minutes, the broker can buy 20,000 shares at the designated price of $20.22. Why is the quote not two-sided (bid and ask)? Because we know the broker-dealer's customer is interested in purchasing the security; only the asking price (and size) is necessary.

Quotation Spread

The difference between a security's bid and offer (ask) price is known as the *spread.*

Spread Factors

Many factors influence a spread's size, including

- the issue's size,
- the issuer's financial condition,
- the amount of market activity in the issue, and
- the market conditions.

TEST TOPIC ALERT

A phrase worth remembering is, "The more active a security, the narrower the spread." The reverse would be true as well.

Best Execution of Customer Orders

In any transaction for or with a customer, a member must use reasonable diligence to find the best market for the subject security. Once completed, the trade should be executed so that the resultant price to the customer is as favorable as possible under prevailing market conditions. FINRA Rule 5130 considers the following factors in determining whether a member has used "reasonable diligence":

- The character of the market for the security (e.g., price, volatility, relative liquidity, and pressure on available communications)
- The size and type of transaction
- The number of markets checked
- Accessibility of the quotation
- The terms and conditions of the order that result in the transaction, as communicated to the member and persons associated with the member

Orders Involving Securities With Limited Quotations or Pricing Information

Although the best execution requirements in Rule 5310 apply to orders in all securities, markets for securities differ dramatically. One of the areas in which a member must be especially diligent in ensuring that it has met its best execution obligations is with respect to customer orders involving securities for which there is limited pricing information or quotations available. This is not an issue for stocks traded on the NYSE or the Nasdaq Stock Market. On the other hand, for stocks traded on the OTC Link, the pricing information is frequently quite limited. In addition, the specified security's quotes or trades might not be shown for weeks at a time.

Furthermore, when there is a quote, it is often from a single market maker. Without competition, it is just like a store selling something that no one else has—it can set the price wherever it wants. In these instances, a member should generally seek out other sources of pricing information or potential liquidity, which may include obtaining quotations from other sources (e.g., other firms that the member has traded that security with in the past).

Interpositioning

When acting in an agency capacity for a customer, a member firm cannot place a third party between itself and the best available market (members cannot route an order through another firm). They must go directly to the best available market (to a firm at the inside market). That is the practice of *interpositioning*.

Generally, interpositioning results in a less-favorable price to the customer, as the third party will trade at the inside market and then add additional costs for itself.

TEST TOPIC ALERT

The only time interpositioning can be justified is if it results in a better execution for the customer. *Better* means a lower price than the inside offer or a higher price than the inside bid.

TEST TOPIC ALERT

Failure to maintain or adequately staff an OTC order room or other department assigned to execute customers' orders cannot be considered justification for executing away from the best available market. Channeling orders through a third party—as described earlier—as reciprocation for service or business generated, cannot operate to relieve a member of its obligations under this rule.

TEST TOPIC ALERT

Following is a list of important test points about OTC quotes:

- Markups and markdowns are charged when a market maker is acting as a principal (dealing from inventory with financial risk).
- Unless stated otherwise, firm quotes are good for a round lot only. A quote of 11 – 11.50, 3 × 5 is firm between dealers for 300 shares at the bid price of 11 and 500 shares at the ask price of 11.50.
- Nominal quotes can be given for informational purposes and can be printed only if clearly labeled as such.

- A relatively wide spread indicates a thin trading market for the security.
- Securities identified as OTC non-Nasdaq may not always have last sale information readily available. That is because that information may be difficult to find for these thinly traded securities.

LESSON 16.3: SHORT SALES

LO 16.c Define short sale strategies and requirements.

Introduction

The term *short sale*, or *selling short*, has been mentioned several times, but other than in the glossary, no explanation has been given. As you may recall from the course introduction, we have written our material primarily for those who have recently completed the SIE exam. For those of you who are grandfathered, or those who don't remember your SIE material, here is a short (no pun intended) refresher on selling short.

Selling a security one does not own is known as being short or having a short position in the securities. Unlike a long position, where the investor is bullish, a short seller is taking the view that the price of the security will decline. This is a bearish strategy. A profit is made when the short seller is able to replace the borrowed security at a price below that at which it was initially sold.

The risk to a short seller is that the price of the borrowed security increases. This means the price the seller will have to pay to replace it will be higher than the sale price. Because there is theoretically no limit on how high a security's price can go, the short seller has unlimited loss potential. Purchasing the security to replace the borrowed one is known as covering the short or closing the short position. Because short selling involves borrowing, all short sales must be done in a margin account.

Short Sale Rules

A **short sale** involves the sale of a security that the customer does not own. To make delivery, the broker-dealer lends the security to its customer. After settlement of the trade, the broker-dealer credits the proceeds to the customer's account. Short selling is the buy low-sell high principle, but in reverse, where the sale is made before the purchase.

The short seller profits if the stock declines in value, but has a potentially unlimited loss if the stock appreciates. The short seller ultimately has to replace the borrowed stock. There is no limit as to how high the market price can reach. This is why selling a stock short is so risky.

EXAMPLE

A customer sells 100 shares of ABC stock at $40 = $4,000. The broker-dealer lends the customer the shares so that delivery can be made to the purchaser. The customer owes the broker-dealer 100 shares of ABC stock.

To profit, the stock must decline in value. The short seller buys the stock to replace the borrowed shares the customer sold. If the stock's price declines to $25 per share, the customer will buy 100 shares of ABC stock at $25 = $2,500.

The investor profits ($1,500) because the purchase price ($2,500) is less than the sale price ($4,000).

If the price goes up, there is no limit to how high the price can go and, therefore, there is unlimited loss potential. On the other hand, the maximum profit is limited. The price of a security can never fall below worthless. That makes the maximum profit the difference between the sale price and $0.

All short sales must be done in a short margin account, and the broker-dealer must make su the customer who sells short understands the risk and that opening the account is suitable. Short sales may occur anytime during the trading day, including at the opening and closing of the day. The only requirement is that the broker-dealer has or is able to locate the shares lend.

PRACTICE QUESTION

6. A customer is interested in selling securities short. The most important disclosure t the customer is that
   A. the customer has unlimited financial risk.
   B. the customer profits when the price of the stock goes up.
   C. the safest securities to short are municipal securities.
   D. the best time to sell short is in a bull market.

   Answer: A. The most important disclosure when selling short is that if the stock gc up instead of down, the customer is losing money. Theoretically, there is no limit to how high the price can go before the position is closed. Therefore, the customer is exposed to unlimited financial risk.

Regulation SHO

Regulation SHO mandates a locate requirement. That means that before the short sale of any equity security, firms must locate the securities for borrowing to ensure that delivery will be made on the settlement date. Not doing so is known as naked short selling and is no permitted.

Insider Short Sale Regulations

The Securities Exchange Act of 1934 prohibits directors, officers, and principal stockholders (insiders) from selling short stock in their own companies.

Sell Order Tickets

The SEC requires that all sell orders be identified as either long or short. No sale can be marked long unless the security to be delivered is in the customer's account or is owned by t customer and will be delivered to the broker by the settlement date.

A person is long a security if he

- has title to it,
- has purchased the security or has entered into an unconditional contract to purchase the security but has not yet received it,
- owns a security convertible into or exchangeable for the security and has tendered such security for conversion or exchange, or
- has an option to purchase the security and has exercised that option.

Unless one or more of these conditions are met, the SEC considers any sale of securities a short sale.

TAKE NOTE

When a customer is both long and short shares of the same stock simultaneously, the positions must be netted out to determine if the customer is net long or net short.

For example, if a customer is long 500 shares of XYZ and short 200 shares of XYZ, the net position is long 300 shares. In this case, if the customer wished to sell 400 shares of XYZ, the sell order ticket must read "SELL 300 shares long and 100 shares short," because the customer is only long 300 shares (net).

Borrowing Securities

Investors cannot sell short if they are not able to borrow the security they are selling. Securities can be borrowed from

- the member firm executing the short sale on behalf of the customer;
- margin customers of that member firm;
- other member firms; and
- institutional investors, such as pension plans and custodial banks.

When opening a margin account, customers often sign a loan consent agreement that allows custodians to lend customer margin securities from the portfolio. Certain sophisticated investors and institutional customers, such as pension funds, lend securities (this is especially useful for hard-to-find-securities) to generate additional income in their portfolios by charging for the loan.

Mark to Market

Mark to market, sometimes called marking to the market, is simply making daily adjustments to the customer's margin account as the price of the underlying security changes. In a short position where the stock's price increases, the equity in the account goes down. Of course, when the price of the short security drops, the effect on the account's equity is positive. Remember, short sellers profit when the price of the stock goes down.

Shorting Bonds

Some securities, such as listed stocks, have many equivalent securities trading at any time. For instance, it is easy to short 100 shares of an NYSE listed stock because an equivalent 100 shares of that stock can be purchased on the NYSE at any time. It is not easy to cover shorts for most municipal bonds because the limited number of bonds available in each issue could make it difficult to buy back the short position. In other words, the municipal market is too thin.

TEST TOPIC ALERT

You may be required to know that short selling municipal bonds is almost never done.

PRACTICE QUESTION

7. All the following statements regarding the short sale of a listed security are true **except**
   A. the order ticket must indicate that the sale is short.
   B. short sales may take place at the opening.
   C. the buyer must be advised that she is purchasing borrowed shares.
   D. short sales may take place at the closing.

Answer: C. A buyer has no idea that shares purchased were sold short, but the orde ticket prepared by the brokerage firm representing the seller must indicate that the sale is short. Short sales may be executed at any time during the trading day, including the opening and closing.

LESSON 16.4: EXTENSION OF CREDIT IN THE SECURITIES INDUSTRY

LO 16.d Compute margin requirements.

Introduction

Margin accounts allow investors to leverage their investment dollars. Through margin accounts, investors can borrow money through brokerage firms by pledging securities as collateral. The Federal Reserve Board regulates margin transactions.

FINRA member firms are required to impose initial and maintenance requirements on all margin accounts. They must mark to market all positions daily to ensure account equity mee the minimum requirements.

Although this unit involves substantial calculation and accounting scenarios, students should expect that only about one-third to one-half of the margin test questions involve computations, with the rest dealing with concepts.

Types of Margin Accounts

There are two types of margin accounts: long and short. In a **long margin account**, custome purchase securities and pay interest on the money borrowed until the loan is repaid. In a **short margin account**, the stock is borrowed and then sold short, enabling the customer to profit if its value declines. All short sales must be executed through and accounted for in a margin account.

In long margin accounts, customers borrow money; in short margin accounts, customers borrow securities.

Advantages of margin accounts for customers are that they can

- purchase more securities with a lower initial cash outlay and
- **leverage** the investment by borrowing a portion of the purchase price.

Leveraging magnifies the customer's rate of return, or rate of loss in adverse market conditions.

Figure 16.7: Cash/Margin Purchase

	Cash Purchase	Margin Purchase
Purchase of 1,000 shares of ABC for $20	Customer pays $20,000 for purchase	Customer borrows 50% ($10,000) from broker-dealer, deposits equity of $10,000
Return after increase from $20 to $30 per share	Customer experiences 50% return (gain/initial investment: $10,000 ÷ $20,000 = 50%)	Customer experiences 100% return (gain/initial investment: $10,000 ÷ $10,000 = 100%)
Return after decrease from $20 to $15 per share	Customer experiences 25% loss (loss/initial investment: –$5,000 ÷ $20,000 = –25%)	Customer experiences 50% loss (loss/initial investment: –$5,000 ÷ $10,000 = –50%)

The advantages of margin accounts for broker-dealers are

- margin account loans generate interest income for the firm and
- margin customers typically trade larger positions because of increased trading capital, generating higher commissions for the firm.

Margin Account Agreements

Customers who open margin accounts must sign a **margin agreement** before trading can begin. The agreement consists of three parts: the credit agreement, the hypothecation agreement, and the loan consent form.

Credit Agreement

The **credit agreement** discloses the terms of the credit extended by the broker-dealer, including the method of interest computation and situations under which interest rates may change.

Hypothecation Agreement

The **hypothecation agreement** gives permission to the broker-dealer to pledge customer margin securities as collateral. The firm hypothecates customer securities to the bank, and the bank loans money to the broker-dealer on the basis of the loan value of these securities. All customer securities must be held in **street name** (registered in the name of the firm) to facilitate this process. When customer securities are held in street name, the broker-dealer is known as the *nominal*, or *named, owner*. The customer is the *beneficial owner*, because he retains all rights of ownership.

After customers pledge their securities to the broker-dealer by signing the hypothecation agreement, the broker-dealer **rehypothecates** (repledges) them as collateral for a loan from the bank. Regulation U oversees the process when a bank lends money to a broker-dealer based on customer securities that have been pledged as collateral.

Broker-dealers are limited to pledging 140% of a customer's debit balance as collateral. Any customer securities in excess of this amount must be physically segregated. The firm cannot commingle customer securities with securities owned by the firm.

Firms can only commingle one customer's securities with another customer's securities for hypothecation if customers have given specific permission by signing the hypothecation agreement.

Figure 16.8: Rehypothecation of Customer Securities

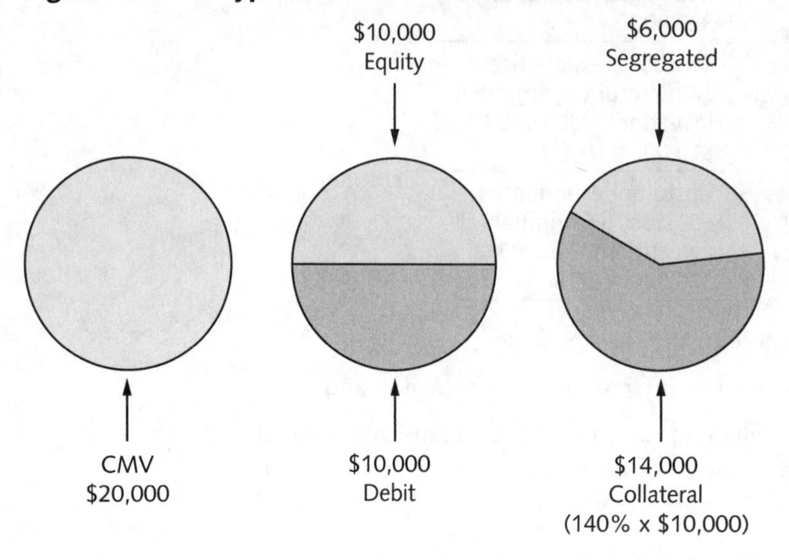

Loan Consent Form

If signed, the **loan consent form** gives permission to the firm to lend out customer margin securities to other customers or broker-dealers, usually for short sales.

TAKE NOTE

It is mandatory that the customer sign the credit agreement and hypothecation agreement. The loan consent form is optional.

TEST TOPIC ALERT

The interest paid by margin customers on money borrowed is a variable rate based on the broker call rate.

Risk Disclosure

Before or at the time of opening a margin account, a member firm must provide customers with a margin disclosure statement. This information must also be provided to margin customers on an annual basis. The document discusses the risks associated with margin trading, some of which follow:

- Customers can lose more money that initially deposited.
- Customers are not entitled to choose which securities or other assets in their account(s) are liquidated or sold to meet a call for additional funds.
- Customers are not entitled to an extension of time to meet a margin call.
- Firms can increase their in-house margin requirements without advance notice.

Here is a summary of the margin documents:

Figure 16.9: Margin Account Agreements

Credit Agreement	Discloses the terms under which credit is extended, including the use of the client's securities as collateral for the margin loan. SEC Rule 10b-16 requires firms to disclose the method of computing interest and the conditions under which interest rates and charges will be changed. Firms must send customers an assurance that statements accounting for interest charges will be sent with the same frequency that interest is charged (monthly or quarterly).
Hypothecation Agreement	Gives the firm permission to pledge (hypothecate) securities held on margin to a lending institution; a mandatory part of a margin agreement.
Loan Consent (optional)	Gives the firm permission to lend securities held in the margin account to other brokers, usually for short sales. It is not mandatory for customers to sign the loan consent agreement.
Margin Disclosure Statement	FINRA Rule 2264 requires a margin disclosure statement be furnished before or at the time of opening a margin account. The document focuses on the risks of margin trading.

PRACTICE QUESTION

8. To open a margin account, it is mandatory that the customer sign
   A. the credit agreement and the loan consent agreement.
   B. the credit agreement and hypothecation agreement.
   C. the hypothecation agreement and the loan consent agreement.
   D. the credit agreement, the hypothecation agreement, and the margin disclosure statement.

Answer: B. Only the credit and hypothecation agreement must be signed. The loan consent agreement is optional and there is no signature on the margin disclosure statement.

Regulation T

The Securities Exchange Act of 1934 gives the Federal Reserve Board the authority to regulate the extension of credit in the securities industry. For margin accounts, Regulation T states that customers must deposit a minimum of 50% of the price of the transaction within two additional business days of regular way settlement (T+2 for most securities). This is sometimes expressed as S+2, (settlement plus 2). Therefore, the deposit must be done within four business days of the transaction.

TAKE NOTE

The Regulation T time limit applies to both cash and margin accounts. Customers have two business days after settlement to make their required payment, regardless of the account type. Broker-dealers expect their customers will pay on the settlement date. The industry views the Regulation T rule as a two-day cushion.

Marginable Securities

Regulation T also identifies which securities are eligible for purchase on margin and which may be used as collateral for loans for other purchases.

TAKE NOTE

Differentiate between use of the terms *margin* and *marginable*:

- **Margin** is the amount of equity that must be deposited to buy securities in a margin account.
- **Marginable** refers to securities that can be purchased on margin and can be used as collateral in a margin account.

The following should be helpful in keeping things in order.

May be purchased on margin and used as collateral:

- Exchange-listed stocks, bonds
- Nasdaq stocks
- Non-Nasdaq OTC issues approved by the Federal Reserve Board
- Warrants

Cannot be purchased on margin and *cannot* be used as collateral:

- Put and call options
- Rights
- Non-Nasdaq OTC issues *not* approved by the Federal Reserve Board
- Insurance contracts

Cannot be bought on margin but *can* be used as collateral after 30 days:

- Mutual funds
- New issues

Deadlines for Meeting Margin Calls

As previously discussed, Regulation T requires margin account customers to meet initial margin deposit requirements no more than two business days after the settlement date. The deposit may be made in cash or in fully paid *marginable* securities valued at twice (200%) th amount of the Regulation T cash call. We will show you shortly where that number comes from.

If payment is late, the broker-dealer may apply to its **designated examining authority (DE** for an extension. The DEA for a broker-dealer can be either FINRA, an exchange, or, in som cases, the Federal Reserve Bank. For introducing broker-dealers, (those who do not clear the own trades), the request is made by the firm that does their clearing (back-office work).

A broker-dealer may, at its option, disregard any sum due from the customer not exceeding $1,000. That does not mean the firm ignores the debt. It means the sell out and freeze described in the next paragraph does not have to take place.

If no extension is received by the morning of the third business day after the settlement date (one day after the deposit must be made), the firm must sell out the securities purchased and freeze the account for 90 days. If the customer wants to purchase securities in a frozen account, the customer must have full payment in the account before order entry.

Freeriding is a term used when securities are purchased and then sold without making payment for the purchase on settlement date. Freeriding is generally prohibited in both cash and margin accounts. As a penalty, the account will be frozen for 90 days and no new transactions can occur unless there is cash or marginable securities in the account before the purchase is made.

EXAMPLE

An example of *freeriding* is a customer buying 100 shares of ABC at 25 on Monday and then selling it on Tuesday at 27. Instead of settling the trade on Wednesday (T+2) with a $2,500 deposit, the customer tells the broker-dealer to use the $2,700 that will be coming in on Thursday and credit the account with the $200 profit. Although the client is entitled to that profit, the account will be frozen because the purchase was not paid for before the sale.

What about day traders? They buy and sell on the same day. There are two ways to avoid the freeze:

- They can have sufficient funds in their account before making the trade.
- "Swap" checks on settlement date. That is, pay the broker-dealer and then receive payment for the sale.

PRACTICE QUESTION

9. When a client's cash account is frozen, the client
   A. must deposit the full purchase price no later than the settlement date for a purchase.
   B. must deposit the full purchase price before a purchase order may be executed.
   C. may make sales with the firm's permission.
   D. may not trade under any circumstances.

Answer: B. When an account is frozen, funds equal to the full purchase price must be in the client's account before a broker-dealer can accept any buy orders.

Exempt Securities

Certain securities are exempt from Regulation T margin requirements. When purchased in a margin account, they are subject to the firm's determination of an initial requirement. Firms must follow maintenance requirements established by FINRA or their SRO rules. Other than knowing which securities are exempt, it is unlikely you will be asked anything else about them.

Securities exempt from Regulation T include

- U.S. Treasury bills, notes, and bonds;
- government agency issues; and
- municipal securities.

Initial Requirements

Customers are required to deposit a minimum amount of equity for their **first purchase** in a margin account. Although Regulation T states that a deposit of 50% of the market value of the purchase is required, FINRA rules require that this initial deposit cannot be less than $2,000, unless paid in full.

Figure 16.10: Initial Requirements Example

Customer Purchase	Regulation T Requirement	FINRA Minimum Rule	Customer Deposit Required
100 shares at $50/share	$2,500	$2,000	$2,500
100 shares at $30/share	$1,500	$2,000	$2,000
100 shares at $15/share	$750	$1,500	$1,500

The customer must deposit the greater of the Regulation T requirement or the FINRA minimum. The exception occurs when the customer's initial purchase is less than $2,000; the customer is not required to deposit $2,000, only the full purchase price.

There is another way to look at this: if the customer's first purchase in a margin account is less than $2,000, deposit 100% of the purchase price. If the first purchase is between $2,000 and $4,000, deposit $2,000. If the first purchase is greater than $4,000, deposit 50%.

TAKE NOTE

The FINRA minimum rule also applies to short margin accounts. However, because short transactions are more speculative, the minimum of $2,000 is never waived. If a short sale margin requirement is less than $2,000, the required deposit is still $2,000. For example, a short sale of 100 shares of XYZ at $18 per share would require a $2,000 deposit. On the other hand, a purchase of 100 shares of XYZ at $18 per share would requires $1,800 (full payment). Note that we are only talking about initial transactions. As we go on in this lesson, you will see that things can be different in an established margin account.

TAKE NOTE

The Federal Reserve Board can change Regulation T, but the current requirement has been in place since January 1, 1974. Assume Regulation T equals 50% in test questions.

PRACTICE QUESTION

10. An investor opens a new margin account and buys 200 shares of DWQ at 50, with Regulation T at 50%. What is the investor's initial margin requirement?
    A. $2,500
    B. $3,000
    C. $5,000
    D. $10,000

Answer: C. The initial margin requirement is calculated by multiplying the market value of $10,000 by the Regulation T requirement of 50%, which equals $5,000.

Margin Accounting

For active margin accounts, broker-dealers must verify that equity in the account still meets minimum requirements following fluctuations in market value.

The practice of recalculation to check the status of the equity in the account is called **marking to the market**. It is typically done every business day on the basis of the closing price of the stock. This concept applies to both long and short margin accounts, which will be discussed separately.

Long Margin Accounting (The Customer Owns the Security)

The exam uses the following terms to describe activity in long margin accounts:

- *Long market value (LMV).* The current market value of the stock position the investor purchased.
- *Debit register (DR).* The amount of money borrowed by the customer.
- *Equity (EQ).* The customer's net worth in the margin account; it represents the portion of the securities the customer fully owns.

The amount of equity in the account is determined by this equation:

LMV – DR = EQ

To simplify long margin accounts, think of them as a house with a mortgage. If the market value of a house goes up or down, the mortgage amount does not change, but the equity goes up or down. The same is true in a margin account; when the market value of securities goes up, the debit balance (what the customer owes the broker-dealer) stays the same, while the equity increases. When market value of securities goes down, the debit balance stays the same and the equity decreases.

Continuing the analogy, consider a house payment. The payment does not affect the market value of the house, but reduces the debit balance and consequently increases the equity. When money is paid into a margin account, the debit balance is decreased, and the equity is increased.

Analyzing Long Margin Accounts

To analyze long margin account activity, a simplified balance sheet will be used, as shown as follows. The LMV is an asset, the DR is a liability, and the difference between them is the equity.

LMV	DR
	EQ

TAKE NOTE

Draw a chart whenever you are asked to compute equity in a margin account. Remember the master margin account equation: **LMV – DR = EQ**. Be sure that your account is balanced before going to the next step.

EXAMPLE

A customer purchases 1,000 shares of XYZ at 60 on margin and borrows the maximum 50% from the broker-dealer.

The margin chart is set up as follows:

LMV	DR
60,000	30,000
	EQ
	30,000

In this instance, the customer must deposit $30,000 (50% of $60,000). The customer may deposit cash or fully paid securities. Meeting the margin requirement in securities requires double the necessary cash margin when Regulation T is 50%. For a margin requirement of $30,000, the customer may pay $30,000 in cash, or deposit $60,000 of fully paid securities to meet the Regulation T requirement.

Earlier, we said we would explain where the 200% deposit came from. In the earlier example, we stated that the margin requirement could be met by double the cash requirement (200%). In this example, instead of depositing $30,000 cash, the client could have deposited $60,000 in fully paid marginable securities. Before we go the chart to prove that, we need to understand the concept.

We continuously state that Regulation T requires a 50% deposit when buying (or selling short) on margin. Well, that is correct, but not really what Regulation T says. The regulation assigns a loan value to securities. In the case of the stocks we will be dealing with, that loan value is 50%. That means that a customer walking into a brokerage office with marginable stock worth $20,000 can borrow $10,000 by leaving that stock as collateral (hypothecating). The customer can walk out with a check for the money or can have it put into a special memorandum account (SMA) where it can be withdrawn later.

Suppose a customer purchases $20,000 worth of stock in a margin account, but has no money. The cash call would be for $10,000. As we just described, if the customer has $20,000 of stock, it can be deposited into the account. The broker-dealer can lend $10,000—exactly what is needed for the call. What does that look like on our balance sheet?

LMV	DR
20,000	20,000
20,000	
	EQ
	20,000

The first $20,000 is the stock purchased. The second $20,000 is the stock deposited. Because there was no cash paid by the customer, the entire $20,000 is borrowed money making, the DR $20,000. That leave us $20,000 of equity, and that happens to be exactly the amount of fully paid stock deposited.

The takeaway here is that any margin requirement can be met with marginable stock worth twice (200%) the amount of the call.

PRACTICE QUESTION

11. A margin account is restricted by $2,000. Which of the following actions may the customer take to bring the account to the Regulation T requirement?
    A. Withdraw $2,000 of SMA
    B. Deposit $1,000 cash
    C. Deposit $4,000 of fully paid marginable stock
    D. Deposit $2,000 of fully paid marginable stock

    Answer: C. Keep it simple. Saying the account is restricted is just to make it seem more difficult. The question asks how to get the account off restriction? The customer needs $2,000 in cash to do so. However, there is no answer of $2,000. We just learned another way to get money—deposit fully paid marginable securities. How much? The deposit should be 200% or twice the amount of cash needed. That would be $2,000 × 2, or $4,000.

When the market value of securities changes, the broker-dealer must **mark to market the positions** to ensure that enough equity remains in the account. The customer's account must always meet the **maintenance requirement** of FINRA. In a long margin account, minimum maintenance is 25% of the LMV.

Marking to the market identifies the status of the customer's account. The determination of the status requires the computation of two benchmarks:

- Regulation T (50% of LMV)
- Minimum maintenance (25% of LMV)

Using the previous example, if XYZ declines to 50, we compute both of these benchmarks based on the new market value of the account, as shown as follows:

LMV	DR
	30,000
~~60,000~~ 50,000	
	EQ
	~~30,000~~ 20,000

Regulation T = 25,000 (50% × 50,000). This account is restricted (see next topic).

Minimum maintenance required = 12,500 (25% × 50,000). This account is well above the minimum maintenance level.

Here are some helpful tips in long margin accounting:

- When the market value of securities goes up or down, the DR does not change.
- When marking to the market, the calculation of Regulation T and minimum maintenance is based on the new LMV.

Restricted Accounts

If the equity in the account is less than the Regulation T requirement but greater than or equal to the minimum maintenance requirement, the account is **restricted**. We saw an example of that on the previous chart.

TAKE NOTE

If an account becomes restricted, there is no requirement for the customer to take any action to remove the account from the restricted status. A maintenance call will be sent only if the account falls below the minimum maintenance requirement.

Restricted Account Rules

If an account is restricted, the following rules apply.

- To purchase additional securities, put up 50%.
- To withdraw securities from the account, the customer must deposit cash equal to 50% of the value of the securities to be withdrawn.
- If securities are sold in a restricted account, at least half the proceeds must be retained in the account to reduce the debit balance. This is called the **retention requirement**. Also, 50% of the proceeds are credited to SMA.

TAKE NOTE

SMA is used much like a line of credit with a bank. SMA preserves the customer's right to use excess equity (discussed later in the unit.) Please also note that even though we are referring to an account, in practice and on the exam, it is always referred to simply as *SMA*, not *an SMA*.

EXAMPLE

Let's go back to our earlier example. After the purchase at $60 per share, the value has dropped to $50 per share. That makes our numbers:

LMV $50,000; DR $30,000; EQ $20,000

This account is restricted by $5,000 because 50% of the LMV is $25,000 and the account's equity is only $20,000.

The customer contacts the firm to state that she wants to sell $10,000 worth of stock.

Initially, the firm applies all of the proceeds against the debit balance and credits SMA with $5,000. Her account now looks as follows:

LMV $40,000; DR $20,000; EQ $20,000; SMA $5,000

What if the customer wishes to withdraw some of the proceeds of the $10,000 sale instead of leaving it all in the account? Because the account is restricted, automatically 50% of the proceeds go to reduce the debit balance. That would mean $5,000 to reduce the DR and the other $5,000 to the customer. That would make the account look like this:

LMV $40,000; DR $25,000; EQ $15,000; SMA 0

Why is the SMA zero? Remember, it was created because all $10,000 was retained in the account to reduce the debit balance. 50% of that $10,000 was put into SMA as money that could be withdrawn in the future. In this example, the SMA was initially created based on retaining all of the proceeds. When the customer changes her mind, from a margin accounting standpoint, the 50% she takes out comes from that SMA.

The reason all the proceeds of the sale are initially applied against the debit balance is this. What if the customer does not want any of the proceeds to be sent to herself? In this case, the firm has the obligation to reduce the debit and thus her interest charges.

PRACTICE QUESTION

12. If securities are sold in a restricted account, which of the following is **not** affected?
    A. LMV
    B. DR
    C. EQ
    D. SMA

Answer: C. All but equity are affected. Equity is affected only if the customer elects to remove a portion of the proceeds.

Maintenance Requirements

When the equity in the account falls below the minimum maintenance requirement, the customer receives a **maintenance margin call**. Maintenance calls are a demand that the customer make a payment to bring the account back to minimum. Failure to meet the call immediately requires the broker-dealer to liquidate enough securities in the account to bring the account back to minimum. There are two ways to meet the margin maintenance call:

- Depositing cash
- Fully paid marginable securities

TAKE NOTE

A firm can impose a maintenance level higher than the FINRA minimum maintenance rule levels. This is a **house minimum**. Many firms today impose 30%–35% minimum maintenance requirements.

TEST TOPIC ALERT

It is critical to remember that Regulation T imposes margin requirements for new securities transactions and for withdrawals of cash or other collateral. Regulation T does not otherwise establish any requirements relating to the amount of margin that must be maintained in a customer's account after it has bought (or sold short) one or more securities. The rules on maintenance equity are solely those of the self-regulatory organizations (SROs).

Consider the previous example we have been working with. By evaluating the amount of equity in the account relative to the Regulation T and minimum maintenance benchmarks, it can be determined that the account is in **restricted status.**

The new equity of $20,000 is less than the Regulation T requirement of $25,000, but more than the minimum maintenance of $12,500.

LMV	DR
	30,000
~~60,000~~ 50,000	
	EQ
	~~30,000~~ 20,000

Regulation T = 25,000 (50% × 50,000)

minimum maintenance = 12,500 (25% × 50,000)

TAKE NOTE

When calculating the equity in a margin account using a T-chart, be sure to follow these steps:

- Calculate the equity after a market value change: LMV – DR = EQ.
- Calculate the new Regulation T: 50% of the new LMV.
- Calculate the new minimum maintenance: 25% of the new LMV.

Maintenance Call

Assume that the market value of the securities falls from $50,000 to $36,000. To find the status of the account, the chart would be adjusted as follows:

LMV	DR
	30,000
~~50,000~~ 36,000	
	EQ
	~~20,000~~ 6,000

Regulation T level = 18,000 (50% × 36.000)

minimum maintenance requirement = 9,000 (25% × 36,000)

Note the adjustment to the LMV. The LMV has fallen to $36,000, so the EQ must be changed to $6,000 ($36,000 – $30,000 = $6,000). After adjusting EQ in the account, the new Regulation T and minimum maintenance levels are calculated. (Regulation T = 50% of $36,000, or $18,000; minimum maintenance = 25% of $36,000, or $9,000).

This account is subject to a **maintenance call** because the equity is below the minimum requirement by $3,000 ($9,000 required – $6,000 actual). If the call is not met promptly, the broker-dealer will liquidate securities in the customer's account as needed.

A formula can be applied to calculate the market value to which securities can fall before there is a maintenance call. This formula is known as the **market value at maintenance formula** and is calculated as follows:

DR ÷ 0.75

EXAMPLE

A customer buys $90,000 worth of stock on margin and meets the initial Regulation T requirement by depositing $45,000. The debit balance is $45,000. To what level would the market value have to fall in order for the account to be at minimum maintenance?

Divide the debit balance of $45,000 by 0.75, which results in a maintenance market value of $60,000. If the market value does fall to $60,000, the account will look like this: LMV $60,000; DR $45,000; EQ $15,000. At this point, the account is exactly at 25% equity.

As with most computations, there is more than one way to do this. For some, it is more comfortable to multiply the debit balance times 4/3 (or 1⅓). It will still come out to $60,000.

TAKE NOTE

If an account falls below the minimum, the broker-dealer sends a maintenance call demanding an amount sufficient to bring the account back to the minimum.

PRACTICE QUESTION

13. A customer has a long margin account with a market value of $12,000 and a debit balance of $10,000. The customer would receive a maintenance call for
    A. $0 because the account meets the minimum equity requirement of $2,000.
    B. $1,000.
    C. $2,000.
    D. $4,000.

Answer: B. The equity in the account is $2,000, which is approximately 16% of the market value, ($2,000 divided by $12,000). To bring the account back to the minimum, which is $3,000 (25% × $12,000), the customer will receive a maintenance call for $1,000. After meeting the call, the account will look like this: LMV $12,000; DR $9,000; EQ $3,000.

Excess Equity and the SMA

Excess equity (EE) in a margin account is the amount of equity exceeding the Regulation T requirement.

To illustrate, return to the example account:

LMV	DR
60,000	30,000
	EQ
	30,000

Assume that the market value of the securities increases to $80,000. After marking to the market, the account appears as follows:

LMV	DR	
	30,000	(2) SMA = 10,000
~~60,000~~ 80,000		
	EQ	
	~~30,000~~ 50,000	(1) EE = 10,000

Regulation T = 40,000 (50% × 80,000)

minimum maintenance = 20,000 (25% × 80,000)

The increase in market value creates equity of $50,000 because the DR does not change. The new Regulation T requirement is $40,000 (50% of $80,000), and the new minimum maintenance is $20,000 (25% of $80,000). Because the equity exceeds Regulation T, this account has EE of $10,000 ($50,000 – $40,000 = $10,000).

In the example, (1) refers to the excess equity and (2) refers to the SMA, which we are now going to discuss.

TAKE NOTE

A rule to determine SMA is as follows: for every $1 increase in market value, $0.50 of SMA is created. In the previous example, market value increased by $20,000, which created SMA of $10,000.

EE creates **SMA**, or **buying power**, in the account.

SMA is a line of credit that a customer can borrow from or use to purchase securities.

It is perhaps the most complicated margin concept. The house analogy can also help simplify SMA. Assume that a house has increased substantially in value. Homeowners with large amounts of equity sometimes borrow against their equity through home equity loans. When they take a loan, the amount they owe on their house is more than before, and the equity falls. SMA is like a home equity loan. It is created because of increased equity in the account and is an additional line of credit. When the SMA line of credit is used, the debit balance in the customer's account is increased and the equity falls.

TAKE NOTE

The amount of SMA in the account is equal to the greater of the EE or the amount already in SMA.

Until this transaction, our example account had no EE. The EE of $10,000 generated SMA of $10,000.

What happens to the SMA if the market value of the securities falls? The following example depicts the market value falling to $70,000:

LMV	DR	
~~80,000~~	30,000	(2) SMA = 10,000
70,000		
	EQ	
	~~50,000~~	(1) EE = 5,000
	40,000	~~10,000~~

Regulation T = 35,000 (50% × 70,000)

minimum maintenance = 17,500 (25% × 70,000)

The decrease in market value creates equity of $40,000. The new Regulation T requirement is $35,000 (50% of $70,000), and the new minimum maintenance is $17,500 (25% of $70,000). Because the equity exceeds Regulation T, this account has EE of $5,000 ($40,000 – $35,000 = $5,000).

What is the new SMA amount? Regulation T states that the SMA amount is equal to the greater of the EE or the SMA already in the account. Because the SMA of $10,000 is greater than the EE of $5,000, the SMA remains at $10,000. In summary, remember that although SMA increases when the market value in the account increases, it does not decrease as a result of a market value decline.

TAKE NOTE

SMA may be more than EE and may exist even if there is no EE in the account.

TAKE NOTE

Although the SMA is not reduced by a decline in market value, there is a certain condition where it cannot be used. SMA can always be used in a restricted account, as long as its use does not bring the account below the minimum maintenance level.

The following is one last example in calculating the SMA balance. Assuming the market value of securities rises to $100,000, what is the new SMA balance?

LMV	DR	
~~70,000~~ 100,000	30,000	(2) SMA = ~~10,000~~ 20,000
	EQ	
	~~40,000~~ 70,000	(1) EE = ~~5,000~~ 20,000

Regulation T = 50,000 (50% × 100,000)

minimum maintenance = 25,000 (25% × 100,000)

The increase in market value creates equity of $70,000. The new Regulation T requirement is $50,000 (50% of $100,000), and the new minimum maintenance is $25,000 (25% of $100,000). Because the equity exceeds Regulation T, this account has EE of $20,000 ($70,000 – $50,000 = $20,000). This affects the amount of SMA. The SMA rule explains that the SMA amount is equal to the greater of the EE or the SMA already in the account. Because the EE of $20,000 is greater than the existing SMA of $10,000, the SMA balance becomes $20,000.

We have shown you that SMA is increased by EE from market value increases. Any of the following also generate SMA:

- *Nonrequired cash deposits.* If a customer deposits cash that is not required to meet a margin call, the full amount reduces the debit and is also credited to SMA.
- *Dividends.* Dividends received on securities in the margin account are added to SMA. The customer can withdraw these income distributions, even if the account is restricted.

TAKE NOTE

Customers wishing to remove cash dividends coming into their margin accounts must do so within 30 days of receipt. Otherwise, the cash dividend is applied against the debit balance, thereby increasing the equity in the account.

- *Loan value.* If a customer makes a nonrequired deposit of marginable stock, the stock's loan value is credited to SMA. Because the loan value is 50% of the current market value, the credit is equal to half what would be gained by a deposit of an equal amount of cash.
- *Sale of stock.* When stock is sold, 50% of the sales proceeds is credited to SMA.

Using SMA

SMA is a line of credit; therefore, the investor can use it to withdraw cash or meet the margin requirement on stock purchases.

Assume a margin account appears as follows:

LMV	DR	
70,000	30,000	SMA = 20,000
	EQ	
	40,000	

Regulation T = 35,000 (50% × 70,000)

minimum maintenance = 17,500 (25% × 70,000)

The customer can withdraw cash by borrowing against the credit line of $20,000, which will increase the debit balance by $20,000. If the full $20,000 is withdrawn, the account will appear as follows:

LMV	DR	
70,000	~~30,000~~ 50,000	SMA = ~~20,000~~ 0
	EQ	
	~~40,000~~ 20,000	

Regulation T = 35,000 (50% × 70,000)

minimum maintenance = 17,500 (25% × 70,000)

The use of $20,000 of SMA reduces the SMA balance to zero. The debit balance is increased to $50,000, because SMA is a loan. The equity balance falls to $20,000, and the account is in restricted status. The customer can use SMA as long as it does not cause a maintenance call.

SMA can be used when the account has EE or is in restricted status. SMA can also be used to meet the initial margin requirements on stock purchases. SMA gives the investor buying power. Assume a margin account appears as follows:

LMV	DR	
70,000	30,000	SMA = 20,000
	EQ	
	40,000	

Regulation T = 35,000 (50% × 70,000)

minimum maintenance = 17,500 (25% × 70,000)

The SMA of $20,000, when used as the margin requirement, allows the customer to purchase $40,000 of stock. In other words, for every $1 of SMA, the customer can purchase $2 of stock. SMA has a buying power of 2:1. After the purchase of $40,000, the account appears as follows:

LMV	DR	
~~70,000~~	~~30,000~~	SMA = ~~20,000~~
110,000	70,000	0
	EQ	
	40,000	

Regulation T = 55,000 (50% × 110,000)

minimum maintenance = 27,500 (25% × 110,000)

The $40,000 purchase was paid for by a debit balance increase of $40,000. Anytime SMA is used to buy stock, the debit balance increases by the full amount of the purchase.

The use of SMA to meet the purchase price is like borrowing on a credit card. The customer owes more money. This account is in restricted status after the purchase of $40,000 of stock.

TEST TOPIC ALERT

Here is a quick review of critical long margin account concepts:

- The first transaction in a margin account requires a deposit of the greater of 50% of the LMV or $2,000. The $2,000 minimum is waived if 100% of the transaction is less than $2,000 [e.g., 100 shares at $15 requires $1,500 (full payment)].
- The basic margin equation is: LMV – DR = EQ.
- Regulation T = 50% of the LMV.
- Minimum maintenance = 25% of the LMV (SRO rules).
- SMA can be borrowed from the account, dollar-for-dollar.
- Utilizing SMA increases the debit balance.
- The buying power of SMA is 2:1.
- EE and SMA are not necessarily equal.
- SMA cannot be used to meet a maintenance margin call.
- The market value at maintenance equation for long margin accounts is DR ÷ 0.75. or DR × 4/3. This calculates what the market value can fall to before a maintenance call is sent.
- Exempt securities are not subject to Regulation T but are subject to the maintenance requirements of FINRA.

PRACTICE QUESTION

14. Which of the following will **not** change the SMA balance in a long account?
    A. Sale of securities in the account
    B. Market appreciation of securities in the account
    C. Interest and cash dividends deposited in the account
    D. Decrease in value of securities in the account

Answer: D. The sale of securities in the account results in an automatic release of funds to SMA. Nonrequired cash deposits, such as interest and dividends, are also automatically credited to SMA. An increase in the value of the securities will increase SMA if the EE becomes greater than the existing SMA. A decrease in the market value of the securities will not increase or decrease SMA in a long margin account. It will, however, increase the SMA in a short margin account.

SMA Review

The following table reviews how various activities in a long margin account affect SMA.

Figure 16.11 SMA Review Table

Activity	Effect on SMA	Remarks
Rise in market value	Increase	SMA increases only if the new EE is higher than the old SMA.
Sale of securities	Increase	The client is entitled to EE in the account after the sale, or up to 50% of the sale proceeds, whichever is greater.
Deposit of cash	Increase	The full amount of the deposit is credited to SMA.
Deposit of marginable securities	Increase	SMA is increased by the loan value of the securities deposited, as prescribed by Regulation T at the time of the deposit (50%).
Dividends or interest	Increase	100% of a cash dividend or interest (a nonrequired deposit) is credited to SMA.
Purchase of securities	Decrease	The margin requirement on new purchases is deducted from SMA. If SMA is insufficient to meet the charge, a Regulation T call is issued for the balance.
Withdrawal of cash	Decrease	The full amount of the cash withdrawal is deducted from SMA. Remaining equity may not fall below FINRA rules or house equity requirement.
Fall in long account market value	No effect	After the SMA balance is established, it is not affected by a fall in market value in a long account.
Interest charges to account	No effect	SMA remains the same.
Stock dividend or split	No effect	SMA remains the same.

Pattern Day Traders

A **day trader** is someone who buys and sells the same security on the same day to try to take advantage of intraday price movements. A **pattern day trader** is someone who executes four or more day trades in a five-business-day period.

We are not hearing anything about this on the exam, but, because it is in FINRA's content outline, we are presenting you with the basics. If we hear of any new information, it will be posted in Exam Tips and Content Updates.

The minimum equity requirement for pattern day traders is $25,000; they must have on deposit at least $25,000 in the account equity on any day in which day trading occurs. The minimum maintenance margin requirement for pattern day traders is 25%, the same as for regular customers.

Pattern day traders are also treated differently when it comes to **buying power**. Buying power for day traders is four times the maintenance margin excess. **Maintenance margin excess** is defined as the equity in the account above the 25% minimum requirement. For regular customers, buying power is two times SMA.

Margin rules also prohibit day trading accounts from using **account guarantees,** which are otherwise permitted. A **cross guarantee** is one for which another customer, in writing, agrees to the use of money or securities in her account to carry the guaranteed accounts (i.e., to meet any margin calls).

Approval for Day Trading Accounts

Member firms who promote day trading strategies must now implement procedures to approve day trading accounts.

Before opening an account, the member must

- provide the customer with a **risk disclosure** statement that outlines all the risks associated with day trading (the statement can be furnished in writing or electronically) and
- approve the account for a day trading strategy or receive from the customer a written statement that the customer does not intend to engage in day trading.

Short Sales and Margin Requirements

Short sales are always done in a short margin account. In a short sale, there is a **short seller**, a **stock lender** (from whom the shares are borrowed), and a **buyer** who purchases the shares being sold short. One of the basic requirements of short selling is that the short seller, on the dividend payment date, must make good to the stock lender for the dividends the lender is no longer receiving from the issuer. The buyer of the shares is receiving the dividends directly from the issuer. Therefore, on the dividend payment date, the short seller's account is debited the amount of the cash dividend for remittance to the stock lender.

Margin Deposits

To borrow shares for short sales, an investor must make **margin deposits**. Regulation T specifies that the initial margin for short sales can be met with either cash or marginable securities, just as in long margin transactions. Because the short seller is obligated to replace the borrowed shares, sufficient cash (or buying power) must be in the account at all times to enable the broker-dealer to purchase the necessary shares if the customer is unable to do so.

The Series 7 exam uses the following terms to describe activity in short margin accounts:

- *Short market value (SMV).* The current market value of the stock position the investor sells short.
- *Credit register (CR).* The amount of money in the customer's account; equal to the sales proceeds plus the margin deposit requirement. Think of this as a credit balance in the account.
- *Equity (EQ).* The customer's net worth in the margin account; the amount by which the credit balance exceeds the current SMV of the securities in the account.

The amount of equity in the account is determined by this equation:

CR – SMV = EQ

Analyzing Short Margin Account Activity

To analyze short margin account activity, a simplified balance sheet will be used, just as we did with long margin accounts:

CR	SMV
	EQ

When establishing a short margin account, there is a minimum deposit of $2,000. This minimum must be met even if the customer sells short less than $2,000 worth of securities. The Regulation T requirement for short sales is the same as it is for long purchases: 50%.

Figure 16.12: Customer Sells Short

Customer Sells Short	Regulation T Requirement	FINRA Minimum Rule	Customer Deposit Required
100 shares at $50 per share	$2,500	$2,000	$2,500
100 shares at $30 per share	$1,500	$2,000	$2,000
100 shares at $15 per share	$750	$2,000	$2,000

TAKE NOTE

Shorting stock that is below $5 per share requires an initial deposit of $2,000 or $2.50 per share, whichever is greater.

Minimum Maintenance

FINRA **minimum maintenance requirement** rules on short positions are 30%, compared with 25% on long positions. As with long margin accounts, the firm may impose a higher house minimum.

PRACTICE QUESTION

15. What is the minimum initial dollar requirement in a short margin account?
16. What is the Regulation T requirement in a short margin account?
17. What is the minimum maintenance requirement in a short margin account?

Answers: 15. $2,000; 16. 50%; 17. 30%

Short Margin Account Math

To illustrate how a short margin account works, assume the following.

A client sells short 1,000 shares of ABC at $70,000 and meets the Regulation T requirement. The market value of securities falls to $60,000. What is the new equity in the account? The accounting in the short margin chart should appear as follows.

CR	SMV
105,000 (3)	70,000 (1)
	EQ
	35,000 (2)

- The market value of the securities sold short is entered as the SMV.
- The Regulation T requirement of 50% of the SMV is entered as equity.
- The credit balance (CR) is the stock sales proceeds plus the equity deposited (SMV + EQ).

The **credit balance** (**CR**) provides assurance to the broker-dealer that there will be cash available for the customer to purchase the securities if the market value of the securities rises. The risk of a short account is a stock price increase; a short seller profits only if the market value of the securities declines.

TEST TOPIC ALERT

For short margin accounting questions: once you get the credit balance by adding the SMV and EQ together, do not change it. Use it to compute equity after a market value change with the basic equation: CR – SMV = EQ.

The following illustrates the accounting for the market value decline and the resulting new equity:

CR	SMV
105,000	~~70,000~~ 60,000 (1)
	EQ
	~~35,000~~ 45,000 (2)

The market value of the securities sold short declines to $60,000.

The equity increases to $45,000 as a result of the decline. This is determined as follows: CR – SMV = EQ ($105,000 – $60,000 = $45,000).

PRACTICE QUESTION

18. A customer sells short 100 shares of ABC at $80 per share and meets the minimum Regulation T requirement. Two months later, she covers the short position by buying ABC at $70 per share. This was the only transaction in the account. What is the maximum amount she can withdraw from the account after closing the short position (Regulation T is 50%)?
   A. $1,000
   B. $4,000
   C. $5,000
   D. $12,000

   Answer: C. The customer originally sold the stock at $80 per share and deposited $4,000 per the Regulation T requirement ($8,000 × 50%). She now has SMV of $8,000 and a credit balance of $12,000 ($8,000 sale proceeds + $4,000 deposit). The market value of the stock is now down to $7,000. The customer may withdraw the equity of $5,000 when the position is closed. The simple way to do this is: she deposited $4,000 and made $1,000. That gives her $5,000—all of which is all her money.

Short positions, like long positions, are marked to market daily to reflect any change in position value.

What is the status of this investor's account? Just as in long margin accounts, the short margin account statuses are as follows:

- *Excess equity*. Equity in excess of Regulation T (50% of the current SMV).
- *Restricted*. Equity less than Regulation T, and greater than or equal to minimum maintenance.
- *Maintenance call*. Equity less than minimum maintenance (30% of the SMV).

By calculating the Regulation T benchmark, we can see that this account has EE and has created SMA of $15,000, as shown:

CR	SMV	
105,000	~~70,000~~ 60,000 (1)	SMA = 15,000
	EQ	
	~~35,000~~ 45,000 (2)	EE = 15,000

Regulation T = 30,000 (50% × 60,000)

minimum maintenance = 18,000 (30% × 60,000)

TAKE NOTE

Multiply the decrease in SMV by 1.5 to arrive at the EE and the amount that is credited to the SMA.

The EE and SMA of $15,000 are available because the equity in the account ($45,000) exceeds the Regulation T requirement ($30,000) by $15,000. Now assume that the market value of the securities in this account rises to $80,000. How much cash must the customer deposit?

CR	SMV	
	~~60,000~~ 80,000	The increase of short market value to $80,000 causes the equity to fall to $25,000 (CR – SMV = EQ).
		The new Regulation T requirement is $40,000 (50% of $80,000); the new minimum maintenance is $24,000 (30% of $80,000).
105,000	**EQ**	
	~~45,000~~ 25,000	Because the equity of $25,000 exceeds the minimum maintenance of $24,000, there is no cash deposit required.

Regulation T = 40,000 (50% × 80,000)

minimum maintenance = 24,000 (30% × 80,000)

To find the maximum market value to which a short sale position can increase before a maintenance call is issued, apply the following formula:

total credit balance ÷ 130% (1.3)

This is known as the **SMV at maintenance**.

Minimum Maintenance in a Short Account

The minimum maintenance margin requirement for short accounts is 30%. However, there are exceptions based on price per share:

- For stock trading under $5 per share, a customer must maintain 100% of SMV or $2.50 per share, whichever is greater.
- For stock trading at $5 per share and above, the minimum requirement is the greater of $5 per share or 30% or the short market value. As a practical matter, only when the SMV exceeds $16.67 will the requirement be 30%.

EXAMPLE

A customer sells short 1,000 shares of stock at $4 per share. The margin deposit would be $4,000, not $2,000.

A customer sells short 1,000 shares at $2 per share. The margin deposit would be $2,500.

In both cases, the minimum maintenance margin requirement exceeds the initial requirement. Therefore, each customer must deposit the higher amount.

PRACTICE QUESTION

19. A customer has a short margin account. In it, there is one stock currently trading at $10 per share. The minimum maintenance requirement for this account is
    A. 100%.
    B. 30%.
    C. $5 per share.
    D. $2.50 per share.

Answer: C. With the stock at $10, $5 per share is greater than 30% of the SMV.

Combined Margin Accounts

A client who has a margin account with both long and short positions in different securities has a **combined account**. In combined accounts, equity and margin requirements are determined by calculating the long and short positions separately and combining the results.

The following example shows the use of the long and short margin charts in calculating combined equity.

An investor has the following margin account positions:

LMV = $50,000; SMV = $40,000; CR = $60,000; DR = $20,000

SMA = $5,000 (The combined equity in this example is $50,000.)

LMV	DR
	20,000
50,000	**EQ**
	30,000

CR	SMV
	40,000
60,000	**EQ**
	20,000

The basic equation for the calculation of combined equity is:

LMV + CR – DR – SMV = EQ

The formula above shows combined equity, but questions may ask for the combined Regulation T requirement or combined minimum maintenance requirements. As with questions asking about the combined equity, to calculate combined Regulation T or minimum maintenance requirements, first calculate the long, then the short, and add the two together.

PRACTICE QUESTION

20. The combined net equity for an investor having both a long and short margin account is calculated as
    A. SMV + LMV – DR – CR = EQ.
    B. SMV – LMV – DR – CR = EQ.
    C. LMV – CR + DR + SMV = EQ.
    D. LMV + CR – DR – SMV = EQ.

Answer: D. Using our mini-balance sheet, each margin account has, in essence, an asset and a liability. In the case of a long margin account, the asset is the LMV, the value of the stock held in the account. The liability is the debit balance, the money owed to the broker-dealer. In a short margin account, the asset is the credit balance. That consists of the cash proceeds from the sale plus the margin deposit. The liability is the cost to buy back the stock, the SMV. We know that the equity in any account is the difference between what the investor owns and what is owed. One option is to compute the equity separately for each account and add the totals together. Another is to take all four numbers and add together the two assets (the LMV + the CR balance) and then subtract the two liabilities (the DR balance + the SMV).

Options and Margin

With the exception of LEAPS options, options are not marginable securities. When buying options, customers must deposit 100% of the premium. When buying a stock on margin and then writing a covered call, there is no Regulation T requirement for the call option. All the customer must do is have 50% of the purchase price of the stock in the account. If you see a margin question on covered call writing, be sure to focus on what is being asked: Is it the Regulation T requirement, or is it the margin deposit? Consider the following examples.

EXAMPLE

If a customer buys stock and receives a premium by writing a call, the premium received for the call reduces the margin deposit that would be required.

Question: A customer purchases 100 ABC at 62 and simultaneously writes an ABC 65 call at 3 in her margin account. What is the margin deposit?

Answer: The Regulation T requirement for establishing the long stock position is $3,100 (50% × $6,200). The margin deposit is $2,800, which is the Regulation T requirement reduced by the premium received. Because options trades settle T+1, the $300 from the sale will be in the account ahead of the settlement date (T+2) for the stock purchase. With $300 already in the account, the investor need only deposit $2,800 to meet the Regulation T requirement of $3,100.

Question: A customer purchases 100 ABC at 62 and simultaneously writes an ABC 65 call at 3 in his cash account. What is the required deposit?

Answer: In a cash account, the Regulation T requirement is 100% of the purchase price of the stock—that is, $6,200. The required deposit, however, is $5,900. Once again, the option sale settles T+1, so the $300 is in the account ahead of the settlement date for the stock purchase. That reduces the required deposit. Conceptually, this is no different from making a $6,200 purchase on your charge card and receiving a $300 credit for something you returned. Your end of the month statement will show a balance due of $5,900.

If, in a margin account, a customer buys stock and simultaneously buys an option, the customer must deposit 50% of the purchase price of the stock and 100% of the premium.

EXAMPLE

Question: A customer purchases 100 ABC at 62 and at the same time, buys an ABC 60 put at 3. What is the margin deposit?

Answer: The margin deposit is $3,400. The 50% requirement on the stock is $3,100. Because options require full payment, the customer must pay the entire premium of $300.

TAKE NOTE

LEAPS options with more than nine months to expiration are marginable. The initial (and maintenance) requirement is 75%. But, unless the question specifically refers to LEAPS, no borrowing is allowed to purchase options.

EXAMPLE

A customer buys 10 XYZ LEAPS at $4.50 each. The LEAPS expire in 24 months. What must the customer deposit?

The customer must deposit $3,375, which is 75% of the total cost of $4,500. When the time remaining to expiration reaches nine months, the maintenance requirement is 100% of the current market value.

With regard to option spreads, Regulation T requires customers to deposit the maximum loss. In debit spreads, the net debit represents the maximum loss. In credit spreads, subtract the net credit from the difference between the strike prices to determine maximum loss.

EXAMPLE

Question: A customer buys 1 XYZ Jan 60 put at 8.50 and writes 1 XYZ Jan 50 put at 2.25. What must the customer deposit?

Answer: This is a bear put spread established at a net debit of 6.25. Because the net debit represents maximum loss, the customer must deposit $625.

EXAMPLE

Question: A customer buys 1 XYZ 60 call at 2.25 and writes 1 XYZ 50 call at 8.50. What is the required deposit?

Answer: This is a bear call spread established at a net credit of 6.25. The maximum loss is the difference between the 10-point spread of the strike prices and the 6.25 credit. That is 3.75 and makes the required deposit $375.

Customer Portfolio Margining (CPM)

As with some other points we've made throughout the course, this topic is in FINRA's content outline, but we have not run across it in the exam. We will post to Exam Tips and Content Updates when we learn anything new.

Customer portfolio margining (CPM) is a different way to calculate margin requirements for an account based on the net risk of an entire portfolio of securities rather than a standardized percentage applied to each individual position. Margin requirements calculated this way are generally lower than those that are calculated conventionally. Broker-dealers must meet certain requirements if they wish to offer portfolio margining to customers. Among those are the following:

- The customer must be approved to engage in uncovered short option transactions.
- Depending on the firm's capabilities, customer accounts must have a minimum equity of $100,000 or even more.
- REITs, even those listed on the NYSE, can be included.

LESSON 16.5: RULES OF THE SECURITIES MARKETPLACES

LO 16.e Determine the rules and regulations pertaining to trading securities.

NYSE Euronext

The **NYSE** is the most widely known stock exchange. Although exchanges are called stock markets, other securities, such as bonds and/or options, may trade there as well. Often called the **Big Board**, the NYSE is the largest of all U.S.-listed exchanges. Stocks listed on the NYSE can also be listed on regional exchanges, such as the Chicago Stock Exchange. It should be noted that the exchange does not influence or determine the price of securities traded there.

Exchange Listing Requirements

Securities traded on the NYSE, known as **listed securities**, must satisfy the exchange's listing requirements. Generally, a corporation that wants its securities listed must have a minimum number of publicly held shares and a minimum number of shareholders, each holding 100 shares or more. Although the minimum numerical criteria are not tested, it is important that you recognize that only companies of significant size and public ownership qualify for listing on the NYSE.

Only NYSE members (individual seat owners) can trade on the floor.

The NYSE is not the only exchange; regional exchanges tend to focus on the securities of companies within their regions, although they also offer trading in many securities listed on the NYSE. This is known as *dual listing*. Listing requirements on regional exchanges are often less stringent than those of the national exchanges, and the companies they list are usually among the smallest and newest in their industries.

Designated Market Maker (DMM)

DMMs facilitate trading in specific stocks, and their chief function is to maintain a fair and orderly market in those stocks. In fulfilling this function, they act as both brokers and dealers. They act as dealers when they execute trades for their own accounts and as brokers when they execute orders other members leave with them. The specialist (DMM) acts as an auctioneer. In return for providing this service to the exchange, DMMs receive rebates on fees charged by the exchange whenever their quotes result in trades.

Auction Market

Exchange securities are bought and sold in an **auction market**. Exchange markets are also sometimes called **double-auction markets** because both buyers and sellers call out their best bids and offers in an attempt to transact business at the best possible price.

To establish the best bid, a buying broker-dealer must initiate a bid at least $0.01 higher than the current best bid. The best offer by a selling broker-dealer must be at least $0.01 lower than the current best offer.

EXAMPLE

A quote might look like this:

Last	Bid	Ask	Size
$46.71	$46.66	$46.74	30 × 14

Several bids at the same price and several offers at the same price may occur. To provide for the orderly transaction of business on the floor, the highest bids and lowest offers always receive first consideration.

Priority, Precedence, and Parity

When more than one broker enters the same bid or offer, the specialist (DMM) awards the trade in the following order:

1. Priority—first order in
2. Precedence—largest order of those submitted
3. Parity—spin the *parity wheel* (random)

Volatile Market Conditions Rule 80B

Rules known as the *market-wide circuit breaker rules* protect against rapid, uncontrolled drops in the market. A market-wide trading halt will be triggered if the S&P 500 Index declines in price by specified percentages from the prior day's closing price of that index. Those triggers are currently set at three circuit breaker thresholds as follows:

Level 1 halt = **7%** decline in S&P 500

- Before 3:25 pm—15 minutes;
- At or after 3:25 pm—trading may continue, unless there is a Level 3 halt

Level 2 halt = **13%** decline in S&P 500

- Before 3:25 pm—15 minutes;
- At or after 3:25 pm—trading may continue, unless there is a Level 3 halt

Level 3 halt = **20%** decline in S&P 500

- At any time—trading will halt and not resume for the rest of the day

A Level 1 or 2 halt cannot occur more than one time per day. In other words, if a Level 1 halt has already occurred, it would take a Level 2 halt to stop trading again.

Finally, trading halts for listed securities trading on an exchange will generally be initiated by the exchange itself or by the SEC. For OTC stocks, either FINRA or specific trading venues such as Nasdaq can initiate a trading halt.

TAKE NOTE

During a market halt, while no trading can occur, investors can still cancel existing (open) orders that had been entered previously.

PRACTICE QUESTION

21. If the S&P 500 is down 13% by 11 am at the NYSE, what happens?
    A. This is a Level 1 halt and the market will halt trading for 15 minutes.
    B. This is a Level 2 halt and the market will halt trading for 15 minutes.
    C. This is a Level 3 halt and the market will halt trading for 30 minutes.
    D. Nothing happens until the S&P 500 drops 15%, then trading will halt for 30 minutes.

Answer: B. A Level 2 halt occurs when the S&P 500 drops 13% from the opening. Trading will halt for 15 minutes.

Arbitrage

Arbitrage is a trading strategy that specialized traders, called **arbitrageurs**, use to profit from temporary price differences between markets or securities. In general, arbitrageurs look for ways to profit from temporary price disparities in the same or equivalent securities. This term frequently appears in questions about market manipulation. Unlike the examples of market manipulation, arbitrage is a perfectly legal activity.

Market Arbitrage

Some securities trade in more than one market—on two exchanges, for instance—creating the possibility that one security may sell for two different prices at the same time. When that happens, arbitrageurs buy at the lower price in one market and sell simultaneously at the higher price in the other. Arbitrage is not a type of market manipulation.

Convertible Security Arbitrage

Arbitrage trades are also possible in equivalent securities—convertible bonds and the underlying stock, for instance. If conditions are right, an arbitrageur may be able to convert bonds to stock and sell the stock for a profit.

PRACTICE QUESTION

22. During a trading halt, an investor can
    A. cancel an order that was placed before the halt.
    B. execute a market order.
    C. execute a limit order.
    D. close an existing position.

Answer: A. Once there is a trading halt, it stops all trading in the security until the halt expires. Canceling an order does not involve any trading. Please do not confuse this with something similar we learned in Lesson 10.1. Although trading in a security stops, options on that security may still be exercised.

COD Trades

In Lesson 1.1, we described the delivery versus payment (DVP) and receipt versus payment (RVP) accounts. Those are accounts, primarily for institutional clients, where the delivery of securities purchased is made to a third party acting as an agent for the purchaser. This third party is usually a bank and holds the institution's money. Payment is made upon delivery to the agent. RVP is the opposite—the agent delivers the securities concurrent with the payment by the purchaser.

FINRA Rule 11860 refers these as collect on delivery (COD) and payment on delivery (POD) transactions. Members cannot accept an order on a COD or POD basis unless members follow all of the FINRA rule procedures, as follows:

- The member shall have received from the customer prior to or at the time of accepting the order, the name and address of the agent and the time and account number of the customer on file with the agent and institution number, where appropriate.
- Each order accepted from the customer pursuant to such an arrangement has noted thereon the fact that it is a POD or COD transaction.
- The member shall deliver to the customer a confirmation, or all relevant data customarily contained in a confirmation with respect to the execution of the order, not later than the close of business on the next business day after any such execution.
- The member shall have obtained an agreement from the customer that the customer will furnish its agent instructions with respect to the receipt or delivery of the securities involved in the transaction promptly upon receipt by the customer of each confirmation.

Trades in these accounts qualify for a special rule under Regulation T. If a broker-dealer purchases for or sells to a customer a security in a delivery against payment transaction, the broker-dealer has up to 35 calendar days to obtain payment if delivery of the security is delayed because of the mechanics of the transaction and is not related to the customer's willingness or ability to pay.

UNIT 17

Processing Transactions

LEARNING OBJECTIVES

When you have completed this unit, you will be able to accomplish the following.

- › LO 17.a **Recall** the information required to be on an order ticket.
- › LO 17.b **Define** the function and procedures of securities trading and reporting in the secondary market.
- › LO 17.c **Identify** the various components that make up good delivery of securities.
- › LO 17.d **Determine** the rules and regulations pertaining to processing transactions.

INTRODUCTION

Since the Great Depression, the securities industry has been closely regulated in the interest of protecting the investor. To that end, the processes of issuing securities and trading them once issued are subject to careful regulatory procedures. It is also recognized that investing money is inherently risky. The laws cannot eliminate all risks. Instead, they require that investors receive enough information to be able to assess the risk accurately and be able to make sound investment decisions. To apply an understanding of the disclosure requirements, the registered representative must recognize regulatory standards. Think of this unit as a view of the "back-office" directives. It covers the mechanics of what happens when the customer decides to implement a decision to buy or sell securities and follows it through to settlement.

LESSON 17.1: THE ORDER TICKET

LO 17.a Recall the information required to be on an order ticket.

Order Memorandum

Although the term you will use in everyday work is *order ticket*, technically, the SEC uses the term **order memorandum**. Traditionally, when entering a customer order, the registered representative has manually filled out an order ticket. Increasingly, representatives are enterin orders electronically.

After the representative prepares the order ticket, it is sent to the wire room or trading desk, where the order is routed to the proper market for execution. A registered principal must approve the order promptly after execution. FINRA's interpretation of the term *promptly afte execution* is no later than the end of the trading day. Approval consists of checking for errors and—especially for discretionary accounts or trades in high-risk securities—suitability. Error do happen.

A customer order is most susceptible to error at two points: communication of the order between customer and broker and transmission of the order from broker to wire operator.

Breakdowns in communication in the ordering process most often occur because of inaccura information on a ticket. For example, a buy limit order is entered as a buy stop order. Or, a market order is entered as a limit order. Sometimes, when a customer has more than one account, the order ticket is written for the wrong account. This can happen when there is a married couple and each has their own account and they also have a joint account. In the rus to get the trade done, the registered representative may "hit the wrong button."

The information required on the order ticket includes

- customer account number;
- registered representative identification number;
- whether the order is solicited or unsolicited;
- whether the order is subject to discretionary authority;
- description of the security (symbol);
- number of shares or bonds to be traded;
- action (buy, sell long, or sell short);
- options (buy, write, covered, uncovered, opening, or closing);
- order restrictions and price qualifications (e.g., market, GTC, or day order);
- type of account (cash or margin); and
- the time the order was received, the time of entry, and the price at which it was executed

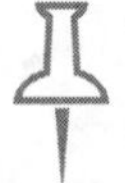

TAKE NOTE

The account name or number must be on an order ticket before order execution.

TEST TOPIC ALERT

Two items that would not be on an order ticket are the current market price of the security and the client's name or address.

If a mistake is made (e.g., a wrong account number), no change to the order can be made without the approval of a principal or the branch manager. All the facts surrounding the change must be put in writing and retained for three years.

Report of Execution

The registered representative receives a report after a trade is executed. He first checks the **execution report** against the order ticket to make sure that everything was done as the customer requested. If everything is in order, he reports the execution to the customer. If an error exists, the representative must report it to the branch office manager or principal immediately. As stated earlier, changing an account number on an order ticket (cancel and rebill) requires manager approval.

Incorrect Trade Reports

Sometimes the details of a trade are reported to a customer incorrectly. Even when the reporting mistake was made by the firm, the actual trade is binding on the customer. However, if execution takes place outside the customer's instructions, the trade is not binding. For example, if the customer order was for 200 shares and the trade was reported as 300 shares, the customer is not obligated for the extra 100 shares.

Reporting an Error

FINRA rules require that a record of any errors be reported to the person designated to receive such error reports by the firm. At a broker-dealer, that individual would always be a manager or someone who holds a principal's license. All such reports should be made immediately in writing and retained for three years under the general record retention rules.

These reports may be referred to as error reports, error records, trade correction reports, or any number of generic names a firm might assign to such records.

TEST TOPIC ALERT

If justified, a supervisory person with the broker-dealer, but not a registered representative, may correct a bona fide error. A rep of a broker-dealer cannot do this because of the concern that any such payment may conceal individual misconduct.

PRACTICE QUESTION

1. As with all businesses, mistakes happen. What document is checked by the registered representative to verify the accuracy of a trade?
    A. The customer confirmation
    B. The broker-dealer confirmation
    C. The execution report
    D. The order flow report

Answer: C. It is the execution report that is reviewed by the registered representative to verify the trade matched the submitted order. The confirmations come later and we want to make sure they are accurate.

Unit 17

LESSON 17.2: ORDER FLOW

LO 17.b Define the function and procedures of securities trading and reporting in the secondary market.

When things work the way they are supposed to, this is the way the flow of an order looks.

Figure 17.1: Order Process Diagram

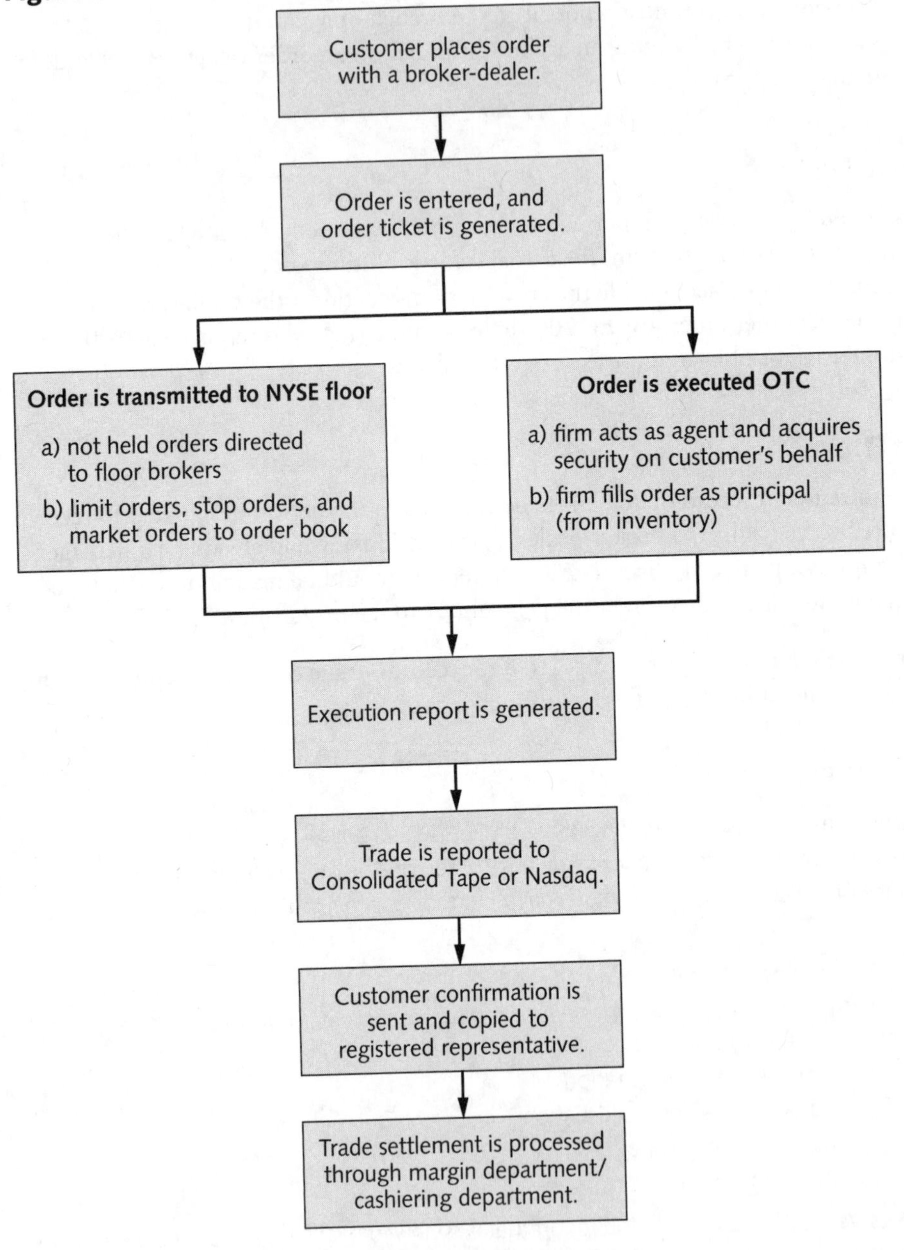

These are the basic steps taken once the order leaves the broker-dealer's hands. As would be true when we are shopping anywhere, the final step is the cashier. In our business, if the trade is on margin, then there is a quick stop at the margin department to determine the final bill (the amount of the call).

PRACTICE QUESTION

2. Which department in a brokerage firm handles all customer transactions using credit?
   A. Margin
   B. Cashiering
   C. Purchases and sales
   D. Reorganization

Answer: A. Yes, there will be questions this simple on the real exam. Margin is using credit so, obviously, it is the margin department that handles credit. Students miss questions like this because they think there is a trick.

FINRA has established an "alphabet" of systems and processes to help the flow of transactions move. We will look at them in no specific order.

Nasdaq Quotation Service

Orders generally begin by getting a quote for the security. Nasdaq provides a computer link between broker-dealers that trade OTC. The system provides three levels of stock quotation service to the securities industry.

- **Nasdaq Level 1** is available to registered representatives through a variety of public vendors. Level 1 displays the inside market only, the highest bids and the lowest asks for securities included in the system, and other basic information such as last sale and volume. Normal market price fluctuations prevent a registered representative from guaranteeing a Level 1 price to a client.
- **Nasdaq Level 2** is available to approved subscribers only. Level 2 provides the current quote and quote size available from each market maker in a security in the system. To list a quote on Level 2, a market maker must guarantee that the quote is firm for at least 100 shares.
- **Nasdaq Level 3** provides subscribers with all the services of Levels 1 and 2 and allows registered market makers to input and update their quotes on any securities in which they make a market.

igure 17.2: Levels of Nasdaq Service

DWAQ 35 – 35.13

evel 1: The inside quote

DWAQ 35 – 35.13

DWAQ	Bid	Ask
Serendip	35	35.25
Tippec	34.88	35.13
Cheath	35	35.13

Level 2: The inside quote plus quotes from all market makers

DWAQ 35 – 35.13

DWAQ	Bid	Ask
Serendip	35	35.25
Tippec	34.88	35.13
Cheath	35	35.13
Enter	BID:	ASK:

Level 3: The inside quote, all other quotes, plus ability to enter or change your own quote

Nasdaq Reporting

Nasdaq is the computerized information system that tracks OTC equities trading is called the National Association of Securities Dealers Automated Quotation service (Nasdaq). Most of the services we are going to discuss apply largely or exclusively to Nasdaq.

TAKE NOTE

Not all OTC securities are listed on Nasdaq. For instance, government and municipal securities, while traded OTC, are not listed on Nasdaq.

Order Audit Trail System (OATS)

Order audit trail system (OATS) is an automated computer system created to record information relating to orders, quotes, and other trade information from all equities that are traded on Nasdaq. OATS helps to ensure that all the time-sensitive information relating to the sequence of events throughout the order execution process is recorded accurately. OATS tracks orders from the time of order entry until execution or cancelation, and in doing so provides an accurate audit trail. For example, one detail required by the system is that all computer clocks and time stamps be synchronized and capable of providing time to the hour, minute, and second. OATS reports are made on an order-by-order basis to FINRA.

Dark Pools of Liquidity

Dark pools, sometimes called **dark pools of liquidity** or simply *dark liquidity*, is trading volume that occurs or liquidity that is not openly available to the public. The bulk of this volume represents trades engaged in by institutional traders and trading desks away from the exchange markets. Generally, these are large volume transactions that occur on crossing networks or alternative trading systems (ATS) that match buy and sell orders electronically for execution without routing the order to an exchange or other market where the quote, last sale price, and volume information is displayed.

Institutional trading desks that choose to utilize dark pools are able to execute large block orders without affecting public quotes or price, or revealing their investment strategy regarding any of their holding accumulations or divestitures. Additionally, orders can be placed anonymously so that the identity of the entity placing the order is unknown to the general investing public, along with the volume and price for the transaction. The concern with dark pools is that some market participants are left disadvantaged because they cannot see the trades, volume, or prices agreed upon within the pools, and thus market transparency is darkened.

Trade Reporting and Compliance Engine (TRACE)

The Trade Reporting and Compliance Engine (TRACE) is the FINRA-approved trade reporting system for corporate and government agency bonds trading in the OTC secondary market. Reporting to TRACE enables better market transparency as trade details are disseminated immediately to the investing public.

TRACE is a trade reporting system only. It is not an execution system. It does not accept quotations, nor does it provide settlement and clearance functions. Following are the reporting rules for TRACE:

- Both sides of the transaction must report.
- Trades must be reported as soon as practicable and no later than 15 minutes after execution.
- Execution date, time of trade, quantity, price, yield, and if price reflects a commission charged are all reportable and displayed.

While most corporate debt securities, asset-backed securities (ABS), Treasury securities, and collateralized mortgage obligations (CMOs) are TRACE eligible, there are exclusions. The following is a list of exclusions to know:

- Debt of foreign governments
- Money market instruments
- Debt securities that are not depositary trust eligible

Trade Reporting Facilities (TRFs)

Trade reporting facilities (TRFs) are facilities through which members report transactions in stocks listed on the NYSE and the Nasdaq Stock market when the trades are made off the exchange, (OTC). All OTC transactions in equity securities to which a FINRA member is a party must be reported to FINRA, unless expressly excepted from the trade reporting rules. Reportable transactions include OTC trades in OTC equity securities and transactions in restricted equity securities effected pursuant to Securities Act Rule 144A. These 144A trades are made by qualified institutional buyers. This even includes secondary transactions in unlisted DPP and REIT securities.

The "normal market hours" are from 9:30:00:000 a.m. until 4:00:00:000 p.m. Eastern Time, and trades with an execution time outside of this period are considered "outside normal market hours." The FINRA Facilities support milliseconds. Thus, for example, a trade executed at 4:00:00:001 is considered "outside normal market hours" and must be modified accordingly.

PRACTICE QUESTION

3. TRACE can best be described as
   A. an execution system.
   B. an order display and execution system.
   C. a quotation system.
   D. a trade reporting system.

Answer: D. TRACE is a FINRA trade reporting system. If you remembered that the acronym stands for Trade Reporting and Compliance Engine, the answer is obvious. Subscribers can access last sale information on eligible fixed income such as corporate bonds and U.S. agency debentures transactions in the OTC market.

Role of the NYSE DMM

After almost 100 years of domination on the floor of the NYSE, the era of the specialist ended as 2008 came to a close. Replacing the specialist (and doing essentially the same work) is the DMM. As of the date of print, all of the DMMs work for one of seven NYSE member firms.

A DMM is a person who represents a member firm of the NYSE. The DMM's primary role is to facilitate trading in certain stocks. DMMs must make a market in the stock they trade by displaying their best bid and ask prices to the market during trading hours. They also are required to maintain a *fair and orderly market* in the stocks they trade. They do this by stepping in with their own capital to help reduce market volatility when there is an imbalance of buy and sell orders. While the number of stocks a DMM trades depends on how active the stock trades, most DMMs are responsible for trading 5–10 stocks.

In addition to maintaining an orderly market, a secondary function of the DMM is to minimize price disparities that may occur at the opening of daily trading. They do this by buying or selling (as a dealer) stock from their own inventory only when a need for such intervention exists. Otherwise, the DMM lets public supply and demand set the market's course. Maintaining a market in a stock requires considerable financial resources. Therefore, the DMM must have enough capital to maintain a substantial position in the security.

A DMM must abide by certain NYSE floor rules in the daily conduct of her business. The DMM

- must maintain a fair and orderly market;
- must stand ready to buy and sell for her own account, if necessary, to maintain a fair and orderly market;
- is expected to transact business for her own account in such a way as to maintain price continuity and minimize temporary price disparities attributable to supply and demand differences;
- must avoid transacting business for her own account at the opening or reopening of trading in a stock if this would upset the public balance of supply and demand;
- must file the reports and keep the books and records the NYSE requires; and
- may trade for her own account in between the current bid and ask quotes in its book.

Agent and Principal

The DMMs are both agents and principals. On the NYSE floor, they can act in the following ways:

- As **agents**, they execute all orders brokerage firms leave with them. They accept certain kinds of orders from members, such as limit and stop orders, and execute these as conditions permit.
- As **principals**, or dealers, they buy and sell in their own accounts to make markets in assigned stocks. They are expected to maintain continuous, fair, and orderly markets—that is, markets with reasonable price variations. However, a DMM may not buy stock f her own account at a price that would compete with the current market. In other words, specialist cannot buy, as principal, at a price that would satisfy a customer order to buy.

Municipal Bond Reporting

Electronic Municipal Market Access (EMMA)

The electronic municipal market access (EMMA) website is funded and operated by the Municipal Securities Rulemaking Board (MSRB). EMMA is a centralized online site used to locate key information about municipal securities. The information on EMMA is presented for retail, nonprofessional investors. It is free of charge. EMMA makes available official statements (OSs) (the municipal equivalent of a prospectus) for most new municipal bond offerings, 529 college savings plans, and other municipal securities. Ratings information is also available. In fact, if an issuer's rating changes, the information surrounding the change is posted. EMMA also provides real-time access to prices, as well as prices and rates from remarketing agents regarding auction rate securities (ARS).

Real-Time Transaction Reporting System

The MSRB operates the Real-Time Transaction Reporting System (RTRS). The system collects and disseminates transaction data in municipal securities for market transparency, surveillance purposes, and analytics. Broker-dealers and municipal securities dealers must report transactions in municipal securities pursuant to MSRB Rule G-14. Firms may employ agents for the purpose of submitting transaction data. However, the primary responsibility for timely and accurate submission remains with the firm that effected the transaction. The data is captured and made available to the marketplace within 15 minutes of a trade.

For regulatory purposes, RTRS maintains an audit trail and provides regulators with transaction data and related information to enhance surveillance capabilities. The RTRS surveillance database stores each trade report submitted by, or on behalf of, a dealer, and audit trail reports provide, among other things, information about trades effected by a dealer, modifications and cancelations reported by, or on behalf of, a dealer, and trades in specific municipal securities shown by their CUSIP numbers.

One notable exception from the reporting requirements are municipal fund securities (e.g., Section 529 plans).

PRACTICE QUESTION

4. Information about which of the following is available on EMMA but not on RTRS?
   A. Auction rate securities (ARS)
   B. General obligation (GO) bonds
   C. Municipal fund securities
   D. Revenue bonds

Answer: C. Municipal fund securities (i.e., Section 529 plans) are included in EMMA but not RTRS.

Third Market/Fourth Market

Following are two market terms that might appear on the exam. Let's define them for you.

Third Market

The **third market** is a trading market in which exchange-listed securities are traded in the OTC market. Broker/dealers registered as OTC **market makers** in listed securities can do transactions in the third market. All securities listed on the NYSE and most securities listed on the regional exchanges are eligible for OTC trading as long as the trades are reported within 90 seconds of execution.

Fourth Market

The **fourth market** is a market for institutional investors in which large blocks of stock, both listed and unlisted, trade in transactions unassisted by broker/dealers. These transactions take place through **electronic communications networks (ECNs)**. ECNs are open 24 hours a day and act solely as agents.

LESSON 17.3: GOOD DELIVERY UNDER FINRA'S UNIFORM PRACTICE CODE (UPC)

LO 17.c Identify the various components that make up good delivery of securities.

The Uniform Practice Code (UPC)

"The Uniform Practice Code (UPC) is a series of rules, interpretations and explanations designed to make uniform, where practicable, custom, practice, usage, and trading technique in the investment banking and securities business, particularly with regards to operational and settlement issues. These can include such matters as trade terms, deliveries, payments, dividends, computation of interest, and marking to the market." —FINRA's Market Transparency Reporting Tools

FINRA created the UPC so that the transaction of day-to-day business by members may be simplified and facilitated, that business disputes and misunderstandings, which arise from uncertainty and lack of uniformity in such matters, may be eliminated, and that the mechanisms of a free and open market may be improved and run smoothly.

All OTC transactions in securities by members, except transactions in securities that are exempted the Securities Exchange Act of 1934, including municipal securities, are subject to the provisions of the UPC.

For exam purposes, the most tested portion of the UPC deals with delivery and payment of securities transactions.

Making Good Delivery

Good delivery is a delivery where everything is in good order such that a transaction settles satisfactorily. There are a number of requirements, such as the proper time, size, and documentation. We will look at those most likely to be on your exam, starting with time and size. That will be followed by explaining good delivery form. It is the registered representative's responsibility to ensure that a security is in good deliverable form when a customer sells it.

Time for Delivery

The **settlement date** is the date on which ownership changes between buyer and seller. It is the date on which broker-dealers are required to exchange the securities and funds involved in a transaction and customers are requested to pay for securities bought and to deliver securities sold. There are several specified good delivery times.

Regular Way Settlement

Unless otherwise specified at the time of the trade, all settlements are made the regular way. Regular way settlement for most securities transactions is the second business day following the trade date, known as T+2.

EXAMPLE

If a trade occurs on a Tuesday (trade date), it will settle regular way on Thursday.

If a trade takes place on a Thursday, it will settle the following Monday.

Knowing that not all securities settle T+2 is equally important, and a summary of settlement rules is included later in this section. Corporate securities, municipals, and government agency securities settle T+2. U.S. government T-bills, T-notes, T-bonds, and options settle next business day—T+1. Money market securities transactions settle the same day. In trades between dealers, if the seller delivers before the settlement date, the buyer may either accept the security or refuse it without prejudice.

TAKE NOTE

Interdealer trades in government securities settle in federal funds. Interdealer trades in all other securities settle in clearinghouse funds. Federal funds represent payments that have same day availability. The most common examples of clearinghouse funds are personal (or business) checks. Those take time to *clear* and are not considered immediately available funds.

Cash Settlement

Cash settlement, or same day settlement, requires delivery of securities from the seller and payment from the buyer on the same day a trade is executed. Stocks or bonds sold for cash settlement must be available on the spot for delivery to the buyer.

Cash trade settlement occurs no later than 2:30 pm ET if the trade is executed before 2:00 pm. If the trade occurs after 2:00 pm, settlement is due within 30 minutes.

Seller's Option Contracts

Seller's option contracts are a form of settlement that are available to customers who want to sell securities but know they cannot deliver the physical securities in time for regular way settlement. A seller's option contract lets a customer lock in a selling price for securities without having to make delivery on the second business day. Instead, the seller can settle the trade as specified in the contract. Or, if the seller elects to settle earlier than originally specified, the trade can be settled on any date from the third business day through the contract date, provided the buyer is given a one-day written notice.

A buyer's option contract works the same way, with the buyer specifying when settlement will take place. The exam does not ask, "Why would someone do this?" You only need to know what the terms mean.

When-, As-, and If-Issued Contracts (When-Issued Trades)

Typically, new municipal bond issues are sold to investors before the bonds are issued and available for delivery. An investor receives a when-issued confirmation describing the bonds. The confirmation does not include a total dollar amount or settlement date because, until the settlement date is known, the accrued interest cannot be calculated to determine the total dollar amount. Once the bonds are issued, the investor receives a new confirmation stating the purchase price and settlement date.

A when-issued transaction confirmation must include

- a description of the security;
- the purchase price (dollar bond) or yield (serial bond); and
- the trade date.

Because the settlement date is unknown, a when-issued confirmation for bonds cannot include accrued interest. That means it will not show the total dollar amount due.

TAKE NOTE

As we discussed in Lesson 16.4, Regulation T specifies the date customers are required to pay for purchase transactions. The settlement date, however, is the date customers are requested to deliver payment or the securities involved in transactions. Under Regulation T, payment is legally due two business days after settlement date. Failure to make payment on time can lead to an account freeze, unless the broker-dealer has received an extension from its designated examining authority (DEA).

TEST TOPIC ALERT

The following table gives a summary of the trade settlements and delivery times for different securities and different types of settlement choices.

Figure 17.3: Summary of Settlement Rules

Regular way—Equity (including exercise of equity options)	2 business days
Regular way—Corporate and municipal bonds	2 business days
Regular way—When trading options	Next business day
Regular way—When trading or exercising nonequity options	Next business day
Regular way—T-bills, T-notes, and T-bonds	Next business day
Regular way—U.S. government agency	2 business days
Seller's option	No sooner than T+3
Cash settlement	Same day
Regulation T	2 business days after regular way

Assume a question is asking about the normal customer settlement terms, regular way, unless the question specifically mentions Regulation T.

In addition, here is a hint on municipal when-issued settlements. A probable question will a either what is not included or what is included on a when-issued confirmation. To discern th correct answer, remember SAT, which identifies what is not included:

- Settlement date
- Accrued interest
- Total dollar amount due at settlement

If a question asks when customer confirmations must be sent, the answer is no later than the settlement date. However, if the question asks when broker-to-broker confirmations must be sent, the answer is no later than the business day following the trade date (T+1).

Don't Know (DK) Notice

In an interdealer trade, each side electronically submits its version of the transaction to the Automated Confirmation Transaction System. If one side does not recognize the other side's details of the transaction (e.g., the number of shares is wrong, or the price is wrong), it will electronically DK (don't know) the trade.

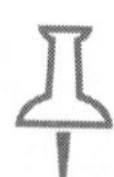

TAKE NOTE

DKs are used in interdealer trades for which one party to the transaction does not recognize the trade or, if it does, disagrees with the terms of the trade as submitted by the other party.

The term can also be used within a member firm when an order or wire room does not recognize the account number or other information on an order ticket.

The exam is not likely to get into the procedures followed after the DK notice is sent. That is for coverage on principal's exams.

Due Bills

If one of your customers buys a stock before the ex-dividend date, the customer is entitled to the dividend. However, if the trade is somehow mishandled and does not settle until after the record date, the seller will receive the dividend in error. In this case, your firm should send a due bill to the seller's firm stating, "Our customer is due the dividend—kindly remit."

TAKE NOTE

Broker-dealers send *due bills* when the wrong party receives a dividend, interest, or rights from the issuer.

PRACTICE QUESTION

5. A confirmation of each customer trade must be given or sent
   A. on the trade date.
   B. before the trade date.
   C. on or before the settlement date.
   D. before the settlement date.

Answer: C. SEC rules require that a confirmation must be given or sent to a customer at or before the completion of the transaction (the settlement date).

Good Deliverable Form

Good delivery describes the physical condition of, signatures on, attachments to, and denomination of the certificates involved in a securities transaction. Good delivery is normally a back-office consideration between buying and selling brokers. In any member-to-member transaction, the delivered securities must be accompanied by a properly executed uniform delivery ticket. Every issue has a transfer agent. The transfer agent is the final arbiter of whether a security meets the requirements of good delivery.

Overdelivery and Underdelivery

In settling customer sell transactions in which the securities delivery matches the exact number of shares or bonds sold, the first rule of good delivery is met. But if the customer overdelivers or underdelivers, the transaction is not good delivery.

EXAMPLE

Overdelivery: A customer sells 300 shares and brings in one certificate for 325 shares.

Underdelivery: A customer sells 100 shares and brings in one certificate for 80 shares.

Partial Delivery

A member-to-member partial delivery is acceptable under Uniform Practice Rules if the amount remaining to be delivered does not include an odd-lot.

EXAMPLE

Delivering 200 shares to satisfy a 300-share sale would be good delivery (the amount remaining is a round lot). However, delivering 250 shares in the same scenario would not be good delivery, because it would be a mix of two round lots and an odd-lot.

Good Delivery Clearing Rule (100-Share Uniform Units)

Please pay attention to the good delivery clearing rule because is it highly tested. When one broker-dealer delivers stock certificates to another broker-dealer, the firm separate round lot and odd lots. Round lot certificates are good delivery as long as they are in 100s or multiple of 100s. In simple terms, as long as the certificate ends in 00 (e.g., 400, 1,200, 8,500), it meets the conditions of the UPC. When it comes to odd lots, members can make round lot deliveries of them if the odd lots add up to a single round lot.

EXAMPLE

Using odd lots to make round lots:

The trade is for 200 shares. If the firm delivers four certificates of 50 shares each, that is good delivery. Why? Because taking two of the certificates together equals 100 shares. That can be done twice to total 200 shares. Another alternative would be 1-70 share certificate, 1-share certificate, 1-40 share certificate, and 1-30 share certificate. How so? Take the 70 and the 30 and we have 100. Then take the 60 and the 40 and we have the next 100.

If the trade has an odd-lot, any number of certificates adding up to that odd-lot is acceptable. For example, a trade for 67 shares can be a 50 plus a 17, or a 25, plus a 30, plus a 12. Here is another example.

EXAMPLE

For a 300-share sale, the seller could deliver

- one 300-share certificate;
- three 100-share certificates;
- six 50-share certificates;
- two 100-share certificates, one 60 share certificate, and one 40 share certificate; or
- three 60-share certificates and three 40-share certificates.

Each of these deliveries meets the requirements of the rule. However, delivering four 75-share certificates would not be good delivery. Think of it this way: can you take the certificates and make piles of 100 shares? If the answer is yes, it is good delivery. There is no way to get stacks of 100 shares if you only have certificates of 75 shares. Remember, the fact that 4 × 75 = 300 is irrelevant. The rule states that certificates of less than 100 shares can only be used if you can make separate piles of 100 each.

Good Delivery for Bonds

The rules for good delivery are the same for corporate and municipal bonds. Delivery of bonds in coupon or bearer form should be made in denominations of $1,000 or $5,000. Fully registered bonds are delivered in denominations of $1,000 or multiples of $1,000, but never larger than $100,000. Municipal bonds may settle in bearer or registered form and be delivered in the denominations stated earlier.

Missing Coupons

If coupons are missing from a bond, it is not good delivery. If an issuer is in default on a coupon bond, all of the unpaid coupons must be attached for it to be good delivery.

TAKE NOTE

From a practical standpoint, with coupon bonds not issued since the mid-1980s, there are very few of these left. Once again, we remind you that we are in the "test" world and not necessarily the "real" word.

PRACTICE QUESTION

6. All of the following would be good delivery for 470 shares **except**
   A. two 100-share certificates and three 90-share certificates.
   B. four 100-share certificates and one 70-share certificate.
   C. eight 50-share certificates, one 40-share certificate, and one 30-share certificate.
   D. 47 10-share certificates.

Answer: A. We want to know which of these does not follow the rule.

In choice A, we have two 100-share certificates—that's great for 200 shares. We also have three 90-share certificates. How do we make two stacks of 100, plus an additional 70 shares for the odd-lot? We can't. Yes, 3 × 90 = 270 (the remaining shares), but we need stacks of 100. With a 90-share certificate, you need a 10 to make 100 and we don't have that.

Look at the others to see how they meet the rule.

B. Four stacks of 100 and one stack of 70—perfect.

C. Eight 50s. We take two of the 50s and have 100 and can do that four times. Then, we add the 40 and the 30 and we have our odd-lot.

D. Forty-seven 10-share certificates. This is sort of like paying a $470 purchase with 47 $10 bills—the cashier doesn't like it, but it works. Here, we take 10 of the 10s and that is 100. We can do that four times. That leaves over seven 10-share certificates, which is our 70-share odd-lot.

LESSON 17.4: TRANSACTION PROCESSING RULES AND REGULATIONS

LO 17.d Determine the rules and regulations pertaining to processing transactions.

Legal Requirements for Good Delivery

In addition to the proper time and size, having the necessary documentation is a critical part of good delivery. In order for ownership to change hands, the certificate representing ownership must be negotiable. In a way, it is similar to depositing a check. If the check is not made out properly or signed (endorsed) with the proper name, the bank might not process it. Here are the major criteria that determine negotiability of certificates.

Assignment

Each stock and bond certificate must be assigned (endorsed by signature) by the owner(s) whose name is registered on the certificate's face. Certificates registered in a joint name require all owners' signatures.

Endorsement by a customer may be made on the back of a certificate on the signature line or on a separate stock or bond power of substitution. One stock or bond power can be used with any number of certificates for one security, but a separate power is required for each security.

Stock or Bond Power

A **stock power** or **bond power**, often called a *security power*, is a legal document—separate from a securities certificate—that investors can use to transfer or assign ownership to another person. "Securities powers typically are used either: (1) as a matter of convenience when an owner cannot sign the actual certificates, or (2) for safety (such as sending unsigned certificates in one envelope and signed powers in another). Physically, a securities power looks like the backside of a securities certificate, and it can be completed in the same manner. Market professionals typically attach a customer's signed powers to the related unsigned certificates for processing purposes." —U.S. Securities and Exchange Commission

Alteration

If an alteration or a correction has been made to an assignment, a full explanation of the change signed by the person or firm who executed the correction must be attached.

Signature Guarantee

When customers hold securities in physical certificate form and want to transfer or sell them, they will need to sign the certificates or the securities powers mentioned earlier. In most cases, the signature(s) will need to be guaranteed before a transfer agent will accept the transaction. Although it is an inconvenience to get signatures guaranteed, the process protects customers by making it harder for people to steal their money by forging a signature on the securities certificates or powers.

Medallion Signature Guarantee

An investor can obtain a signature guarantee from a financial institution, such as a commercial bank, savings bank, credit union, or broker-dealer that participates in one of the Medallion signature guarantee programs.

A Medallion imprint or stamp indicates that the financial institution is a member of a Medallion signature guarantee program and is an acceptable signature guarantor. By participating in the program, financial institutions can guarantee customer signatures with the assurance that their guarantees will be immediately accepted for processing by transfer agents.

Figure 17.4: Example of Medallion Signature Guarantee

SIGNATURE GUARANTEED
MEDALLION GUARANTEED
COMPANY INC
Authorized Signer, V.P. Operations
AUTHORIZED SIGNATURE
(004) X0002011
NYSE, INC. MEDALLION SIGNATURE PROGRAM

Signature Requirements

A customer's signature must match exactly the name registered on the security's certificate.

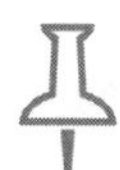

TAKE NOTE

Regarding signature requirements for purposes of good delivery, the only two acceptable abbreviations within a signature are Co. for the word *company*, and & for the word *and*. No other abbreviations, such as *Inc.*, or *Corp.*, are permitted.

Legal Transfer Items

Any form of registration other than an individual or joint ownership may require supporting guarantees or documentation to render a certificate negotiable.

For business registrations involving sole proprietorships or partnerships, a simple guarantee by a broker-dealer is usually sufficient. For corporate registrations and certificates in the names of fiduciaries, a transfer agent may require a corporate resolution naming the person signing a certificate as authorized to do so. Fiduciaries must supply either a certified copy of a trust agreement or a copy of a court appointment, depending on the type of fiduciary involved.

Invalid Signatures

If a broker-dealer guarantees a forged signature, such as that of a deceased person, the firm becomes liable. The executor or administrator of the estate must endorse the certificate or furnish a stock power and transfer the securities to the name of the estate before they can be sold. Minors' signatures are invalid for securities registration purposes.

Good Condition of Security

If a certificate is mutilated or appears to be counterfeit, appropriate authentication must be obtained before a transfer agent can accept the security for replacement. If the damage is so extensive that the transfer agent doubts the certificate's authenticity, it will require a surety bond from the seller. This is a form of insurance protecting the transfer agent from claims.

CUSIP Regulations

Committee on Uniform Securities Identification Procedures (CUSIP) numbers are used in all trade confirmations and correspondence regarding specific securities. A separate CUSIP number is assigned to each issue of securities; if an issue is subdivided into classes with differing characteristics, each class is assigned a separate CUSIP number. In general, a CUSIP number will aid in identifying and tracking a security throughout its life.

Legal Opinion: Municipal Securities

Unless a municipal bond is traded and stamped ex-legal (without a legal opinion), the **legal opinion** must be printed on or attached to the bond as evidence of the bond's validity. Securities traded ex-legal are in good delivery condition without the legal opinion.

Fail-to-Deliver

A **fail-to-deliver** situation occurs when the broker-dealer on the sell side of a contract does not deliver the securities in good delivery form to the broker-dealer on the buy side on the settlement date.

As long as a fail-to-deliver exists, the seller will not receive payment.

In a fail-to-deliver situation, the buying broker-dealer may buy-in the securities to close the contract and may charge the seller for any loss caused by changes in the market. If a customer fails to deliver securities to satisfy a sale, the firm representing the seller must buy-in the securities after 10 business days from the settlement date.

Reclamation

Reclamation occurs when a buying broker-dealer, after accepting securities as good delivery, later discovers that the certificates were not in good deliverable form (e.g., certificates are mutilated). The securities can be sent back to the selling broker-dealer with a Uniform Reclamation Form attached within specific time frames, depending on the reason reclamation is being made.

TEST TOPIC ALERT

There are two types of bond deliveries that are never subject to reclamation:

(1) bond certificates subject to an in-whole call and

(2) bonds where the issuer goes into default after the trade date.

PRACTICE QUESTION

7. Instead of signing on the back of a certificate representing a security sold, the registered owner could sign on a separate paper called
   A. an endorsement.
   B. a stock (or bond) power.
   C. a proxy.
   D. a stock split.

Answer: B. If the client were to assign the back of the certificate, that security would now be completely negotiable. If lost, it would be the same as losing an endorsed check. To minimize problems, make the assignment on a stock power, which is a separate piece of paper, and when put together with the actual certificate, it is treated as if the certificate itself had been signed.

UNIT 18

Complaint Resolution

LEARNING OBJECTIVES

When you have completed this unit, you will be able to accomplish the following.

- › LO 18.a **Identify** Form U-4 reporting requirements.
- › LO 18.b **Relate** the procedure for addressing customer complaints.
- › LO 18.c **Determine** the methods of resolution.
- › LO 18.d **Determine** the rules and regulations pertaining to complaint resolution.

INTRODUCTION

As the old saying goes, "You can please some of the people all of the time, you can please all of the people some of the time, but you can't please all of the people all of the time." It is rare that even the most cautious registered representative doesn't receive at least one customer complaint during the many years of being registered. FINRA has established a lengthy procedure for dealing with those complaints and the reporting obligations of member firms and their associated persons.

LESSON 18.1: REPORTING DISCIPLINARY INCIDENTS AND HANDLING CUSTOMER COMPLAINTS

LO 18.a Identify Form U-4 reporting requirements.

Form U4

Registration as an associated person of a FINRA member firm requires the filing of Form U4. The information required on Form U4 is extensive and includes

- name, address, and any aliases used;
- five-year residency history;

- 10-year employment history (verify the past three years); and
- disclosure of an arrest or conviction for any felony or any securities-related misdemeanor.

A *yes* answer to the final bullet point requires a detailed explanation on a DRP (disclosure reporting page).

Any changes to this information require filing an amended form with the Central Registration Depository no later than 30 days after the member becomes aware of these changes.

Qualifications Investigated

Before submitting an application to register an individual with FINRA as a registered representative, a member firm must certify that it has investigated the person's business reputation, character, education, qualifications, and experience, and that the candidate's credentials are in order.

If, during its routine review of Form U4, FINRA discovers that any portion of the information submitted, especially relating to personal history and past disciplinary or law enforcement encounters, is misleading or omits material information, disciplinary action may be taken, resulting in a bar to the individual. In addition, the principal signing the application may be liable as well.

TAKE NOTE

It is not necessary to update Form U4 to note educational achievements or changes to marital status.

DRPs

The DRPs can be the scariest part of Form U4. Depending on your personal history, they can contain nothing, or can be many pages long. The disclosures are not limited to the securities industry. FINRA breaks them down into these six categories:

- Criminal disclosure
  - Felony and certain financially related misdemeanors
- Regulatory action disclosure
  - SEC, state regulators, SRO
- Civil judicial disclosure
  - Civil cases not involving securities
- Customer complaint/arbitration/civil litigation disclosure
  - Customer complaints
- Termination disclosure
  - Terminations for cause
- Financial disclosure
  - Bankruptcy
  - Payment on surety bond
  - Unsatisfied judgments and liens

Failure to make FD can lead to serious disciplinary action including a permanent bar from the industry.

PRACTICE QUESTION

1. Which type of historical information is required on Form U4?
   I. 5-year residency
   II. 10-year residency
   III. 5-year employment
   IV. 10-year employment
   A. I and III
   B. I and IV
   C. II and III
   D. II and IV

Answer: B. Form U4 requires an applicant to provide a 5-year residency history and a 10-year employment history.

LO 18.b Relate the procedure for addressing customer complaints.

Customer Complaint Procedures

Although each member firm must establish its own procedures, there are common elements to all. First of all, we need to define a customer complaint. Here is FINRA's definition:

> For purposes of Rule 4513, "customer complaint" means any grievance by a customer or any person authorized to act on behalf of the customer involving the activities of the member or a person associated with the member in connection with the solicitation or execution of any transaction or the disposition of securities or funds of that customer.

FINRA then describes the proper recording of the complaint like this:

"Each member shall keep and preserve a separate file of all written customer complaints and action taken by the member, if any. Customer complaint records shall be preserved for a period of at least four years."

The key takeaways are

- a complaint is only a complaint if it is in writing, and
- complaint records are retained for a minimum of four years.

When Complaints are Received

If the complaint is received by the registered representative, it must be immediately brought to the attention of the person designated in the member's written procedures manual. That could be the branch manager or perhaps someone in the firm's legal department.

If a complaint about a registered representative is received by the broker-dealer, the most common procedure is to discuss it with the rep first before contacting the customer. Efforts are made to solve the complaint without taking it through FINRA's formal procedures. If that can't be done, mediation or arbitration is usually the next step.

PRACTICE QUESTION

2. There are different record retention requirements for different records. Under FINRA Rule 4513, how long must a FINRA member firm keep a record of written customer complaints?
   A. One year
   B. Four years
   C. Six years
   D. Lifetime of the customer's account

Answer: B. According to FINRA Rule 4513, written customer complaints and any correspondence related to the complaints have a record retention requirement of four years.

LESSON 18.2: FINRA'S COMPLAINT RESOLUTION METHODS AND RULES

LO 18.c Determine the methods of resolution.

Code of Arbitration Procedure

Arbitration is an alternative to going to court to resolve disputes. According to the American Bar Association, "Arbitration is a private process where disputing parties agree that one or several individuals can make a decision about the dispute after receiving evidence and hearing arguments."

The FINRA Code of Arbitration Procedure was originally established to arbitrate unresolved industry disputes. It was mandatory in controversies involving

- a member against another member or registered clearing agency,
- a member against an associated person, and
- an associated person against another associated person.

Over time, customer complaints became subject to mandatory arbitration resulting in two codes: the *Customer Code* and the *Industry Code*.

Today, virtually all new account forms contain a predispute arbitration clause that must be signed by customers before account opening. Thus, assuming the customer has signed the arbitration agreement or the new account form containing the predispute arbitration agreement, unresolved customer complaints must be arbitrated under the Code of Arbitration

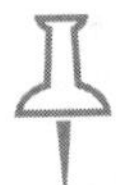

TAKE NOTE

In the absence of a signed arbitration agreement, a customer can still force a member to arbitration, but a member cannot force a customer to arbitration.

Class action claims are not subject to arbitration. In addition, claims alleging employment discrimination brought against a member firm by its own employees, including sexual harassment claims, are not required to be arbitrated unless the parties agree.

The advantages of arbitration over suits in state or federal courts are savings of time, money, and the fact that all decisions are final and binding; no appeals are allowed. One party may not like the result, but the dispute is settled.

TEST TOPIC ALERT

If a customer requests to see the predispute arbitration agreement she has signed, a member firm must supply her with a copy within 10 business days of the request.

Initiation of Proceedings

Any party to an unresolved dispute may initiate proceedings by filing a claim with the director of arbitration of FINRA. The statement of claim must describe in detail the controversy in dispute, include documentation in support of the claim, and state the remedy being sought (a dollar amount). The claimant must also include a check for the required claim filing fee. The director will then send a copy of the claim to the other party (respondent).

The respondent then has 45 calendar days to respond to both the director and the claimant. The answer must specify all available defenses and any related counterclaim the respondent may have against the claimant. A respondent who fails to answer within 45 days may, at the sole discretion of the director, be barred from presenting any matter, arguments, or defenses at the hearing.

If the dispute involves irreparable injury to one of the parties, that party may seek an interim injunction or a permanent injunction. The party seeking relief must make a clear showing that its case is likely to succeed on its merits and that it will suffer permanent harm unless immediate relief is granted.

Mediation

An alternate dispute resolution process and a reasonable, inexpensive first step is mediation.

If both parties agree, before the opening of hearings, a meeting may be held in an attempt to work out a settlement. A mediator is selected to preside over the discussions and to assist the parties, if possible, in reaching their own solution. If mediation is unsuccessful, a hearing is conducted. A mediator is prohibited from serving on an arbitration panel regarding any matter in which that person served as mediator. Sometimes, parts of a dispute settle in mediation, leaving fewer differences to be settled in arbitration, which can translate into savings of time and money. The issue is settled when the memo of understanding is signed.

TAKE NOTE

Once mediation begins, either party may withdraw at any time without the consent of the mediator or the other party.

Selection of Arbitrators

FINRA maintains a list of arbitrators divided into two categories: nonpublic and public.

Nonpublic arbitrators are as follows:

- Any persons who worked in the financial industry for any duration during their careers, including persons associated with a mutual fund or a hedge fund, and persons associated with an investment adviser, will always be classified as nonpublic arbitrators.
- Any financial industry professional who regularly represents or provides services to investor parties in disputes concerning investment accounts or transactions including attorneys, accountants, or other professionals whose firms earned significant revenue from representing individual and/or institutional investors relating to securities matters are classified as nonpublic arbitrators. However, for these individuals, waiting five years

Unit 18

(cooling-off period) after ending the affiliation based on their own activities, or two years after ending an affiliation based on someone else's activities, reclassifies and allows them to serve as public arbitrators.

Public arbitrators are as follows:

- Any persons who do not meet the definition of a nonpublic arbitrator may serve as a public arbitrator.

Arbitration Thresholds and Simplified Arbitration

For both the customer and the industry codes, the following threshold rules apply:

- $50,000 or less—one arbitrator
- $50,000–$100,000—one arbitrator unless both parties agree to three
- Greater than $100,000—three arbitrators unless both parties agree to one

Any dispute involving a dollar amount of $50,000 or less is eligible for simplified arbitration. In this instance, a single arbitrator reviews all of the evidence and renders a binding decision within 30 business days.

Composition of the Panel

We don't expect the exam to get this deep, but when the case involves a member of the public, the case is heard by a public arbitrator if only one. If there are three, a majority will be public. And, if requested, the panel can be three public arbitrators.

If the case is strictly between members and does not involve a statutory discrimination claim, all panel members are nonpublic. In cases involving an associated person, public arbitrators are on the panel as well.

Awards

All monetary awards must be paid within 30 days of the decision date. Any award not paid within this time will begin to accrue interest as of the decision date. In addition, all awards and details on the underlying arbitration claim are made publicly available by FINRA.

Statute of Limitations

No claim is eligible for submission to arbitration if six years or more have elapsed from the time of the event giving rise to the claim.

PRACTICE QUESTION

3. A dispute involving a dollar amount of $50,000 or less is eligible for
   A. remediation.
   B. a panel of three arbitrators.
   C. an appeal.
   D. simplified arbitration.

Answer: D. Any dispute involving a dollar amount of $50,000 or less is eligible for simplified arbitration. In this instance, a single arbitrator reviews all the evidence and renders a binding decision within 30 business days. It would be eligible for mediation, not remediation. It is too small for a panel of three arbitrators. One of the features of arbitration is that there are no appeals; the decision is final and binding.

LO 18.d Determine the rules and regulations pertaining to complaint resolution.

The Code of Procedure (COP)

For trade practice violations, FINRA follows the Code of Procedure (COP). Unlike the Code of Arbitration Procedure that deals with disputes, the initials *COP* in a test question are a clue that there has been a violation of the rules—someone has broken the law. As we will learn next, penalties for violating the rules can be severe.

Availability of Manual to Customers

Customers might not know their rights, so FINRA Rule 8110 has an interesting requirement. Members must make available a current copy of the FINRA Manual for examination by customers upon request. It used to be that firms had to maintain an inventory of the FINRA manuals. In keeping with modernity, members may comply with this rule by maintaining electronic access to the FINRA Manual and providing customers with such access upon request. This is done by having a hyperlink to the FINRA website.

Reporting Requirements

The reporting requirements of FINRA Rule 4530 demand that a member firm promptly report to FINRA, but in any event not later than 30 calendar days, after the member knows (or should have known) that members or associated persons of the member

- have been found to have violated federal securities law;
- are subject to a customer complaint alleging theft, misappropriation of customer assets, or forgery;
- have been suspended or expelled by another SRO;
- are indicted, convicted, or plead guilty or no contest to any criminal offense (other than traffic violations);
- become a defendant or respondent in any securities- or commodities-related litigation or arbitration settled for an amount in excess of $15,000 ($25,000 if the defendant/respondent is the member firm itself);
- become subject to a statutory disqualification; or
- are the subject of in-house disciplinary action involving suspension, termination, withholding of commissions, or fines in excess of $2,500.

Sanctions

Sanctions against a member or associated person found in violation of securities laws and rules are included with the written decision. Under FINRA Rule 8300, sanctions could include one or more of the following:

- Censure
- Fine
- Suspension of the membership of a member or suspension of the registration of an associated person for up to two years
- Expulsion of the member, cancelation of the membership of the member, or revocation or cancelation of the registration of an associated person
- Barring a member or associated person from association with all members
- Any other fitting sanction

If an associated person is suspended, that person cannot remain associated with the member in any capacity, including a clerical or administrative capacity (during the suspension period, that person cannot remain on the member's premises). The member is prohibited from paying a salary, commission, or other remuneration that the person might have earned during the suspension period. The suspended person may be paid monies earned before the suspension period. When a member firm is suspended, the firm is treated like a nonmember in any dealings with members. Essentially, this means no participation in underwritings and no member-to-member pricing.

Appeals

If either side is displeased with the decision, an appeal may be made to the National Adjudicatory Council (NAC). Any appeal must be made within 25 days of the decision date; otherwise, the decision is final. If no satisfaction is received from the NAC, the appealing party may take the case to the SEC. Again, if turned down, the appealing party has the right to continue the appeal process by taking its case to the federal court system. Appealing a decision stays the effective date of any sanctions other than a bar or expulsion.

PRACTICE QUESTION

4. As a result of a disciplinary infraction, FINRA has suspended a member for 3 months. During this period, the member shall
   A. have no securities dealings of any kind.
   B. be treated as a nonmember by other members.
   C. restrict activities with customers solely to investment companies.
   D. restrict activities with member firms solely to investment banking.

Answer: B. A suspended member is considered a nonmember firm while the suspension is in effect. There is no restriction on activity, but everything is done on a retail basis, substantially reducing any income for the firm.

Clearly Erroneous Transactions

Under Rules 11892 and 11893, Nasdaq has the authority to declare any interdealer trade null and void or adjust the terms of any interdealer trade if the terms of the trade are clearly in error (e.g., obvious error in price, number of shares). Nasdaq can take these actions on its own or in response to a complaint from a member.

If a member wants to have a trade nullified or adjusted, it must notify Nasdaq Market Operations within 30 minutes of the execution and provide all the details surrounding the trade. After review, Nasdaq will make a decision to

- void the trade,
- adjust the terms of the trade, or
- take no action.

The rules apply to any OTC transaction involving an exchange-listed security (11892) and any transaction involving an OTC equity security (11893). FINRA notes that it is less likely to take action when the report is about an OTC equity security because aberrant trading in the OTC equity market is often due to issues other than systems problems or extraordinary events.

PRACTICE QUESTION

5. If a member wishes to appeal an adverse decision in a Code of Procedure (COP) hearing, the member must appeal to the National Adjudicatory Council (NAC) within how many days of the decision date?
   A. 25
   B. 30
   C. 40
   D. 45

Answer: A. If either side is displeased with a COP decision, an appeal must be made within 25 days of the decision date.

PART 4

Seeks Business for the Broker-Dealer From Customers and Potential Customers

Part 4 consists of two units:

In total, you will see nine questions on material from Part 4, representing 7% of the Series 7 Top-Off Exam.

UNIT 19

Communications With the Public

LEARNING OBJECTIVES

When you have completed this unit, you will be able to accomplish the following.

- › LO 19.a **Compare** the three main types of communications with the public, their characteristics, and definitions.
- › LO 19.b **Recall** other communications by characteristics and definitions.
- › LO 19.c **Classify** the required approvals of public communications including reviews and education of personnel.
- › LO 19.d **Identify** procedures for product-specific advertisements and disclosures required for public use.
- › LO 19.e **Determine** the rules and regulations relevant to communications with the public.

INTRODUCTION

Broker-dealers communicate with the public for two major reasons. First, as with most businesses, it pays to advertise. That is, if potential clients don't know who you are, they won't come knocking on your door. Then, once you have obtained the clients, good communications are necessary to keep them. On the exam, both objectives are addressed. Having gotten this far in the course, we do not expect you to be surprised that there are many regulations covering these communications. Almost everything in this unit is drawn from FINRA Rule 2210. It is doubtful you will need to remember that number.

LESSON 19.1: TYPES OF COMMUNICATIONS WITH THE PUBLIC

LO 19.a Compare the three main types of communications with the public, their characteristics, and definitions.

In Rule 2210, FINRA has taken the federal requirements on communications with the public and expanded on them in its conduct rules. These rules require that all members observe high standards of commercial honor and just and equitable principles of trade. It is strictly prohibited to make use of any manipulative, deceptive, or other fraudulent devices or contrivances when conducting business with the public.

FINRA and SEC rules deal with communications concerning a member's investment banking or securities business. A registered principal must be familiar with the standards for content, supervisory review and approval, and recordkeeping for such material.

FINRA provides definitions and categories that differentiate the various types of communications for which the principal is responsible.

TAKE NOTE

When we get to the specific review and approvals, you will need to know that general securities principals (Series 24) may review and/or approve communications for all securities except options. Limited securities principals (Series 26) may only review and/or approve communications for investment company products. Options communications generally need review or approval from an ROP (Series 4).

The definitions of communication with the public are classified into correspondence, retail communications, and institutional communications.

The application of the rules differs depending on the category of a particular communication. For this reason, you must be able to determine what fits where.

Correspondence

Correspondence is written or electronic communication that is distributed or made available to 25 or fewer retail investors within any 30 calendar-day period. FINRA means this to include current and prospective customers.

Each member must establish written procedures that are appropriate to its business, size, structure, and customers for the review of incoming and outgoing correspondence with the public. This includes procedures to review incoming correspondence directed to registered representatives. Firms need to be able to properly identify and handle customer complaints and to ensure that customer funds and securities are handled in accordance with firm procedures. Procedures may allow for either pre- or post-review of correspondence by a principal. When pre-review is not required, the firm must include a provision for the education and training of associated persons as to the firm's procedures governing correspondence. These procedures must include documentation of such education and training, and surveillance and follow-up to ensure that such procedures are implemented and adhered to. Evidence that these supervisory procedures have been implemented and carried out must be maintained and made available to FINRA upon request.

Retail Communication

Retail communication is defined in FINRA Rule 2210 as "any written (including electronic) communication that is distributed or made available to more than 25 retail investors within any 30 calendar-day period." What would commonly be thought of as *advertisements* and *sales literature* generally fall under this definition. Some specific examples of retail communication would include

- telemarketing or other sales scripts (if expected to be used with more than 25 noninstitutional investors within a 30-day period);
- posts to an interactive electronic forum (e.g., social media updates);
- a storyboard of a television or video ad; and
- independently prepared reprints.

What is a retail investor? Any person—other than an institutional investor—regardless of whether the person has an account with any firm is considered a retail investor. With a few exceptions (which will follow), an appropriately qualified registered principal of the member must approve each retail communication before the earlier of its use or filing with FINRA's Advertising Regulation Department.

The requirement to have a principal approve retail communication does not apply if, at the time that a member intends to distribute it

- another member has filed it with FINRA's advertising department and has received a letter from the department stating that it appears to be consistent with applicable standards,
- the member using it in reliance upon the letter has not materially altered it and will use it in a manner that is consistent with the conditions of the department's letter,
- if it is a post to an interactive electronic forum.

The requirement of prior principal approval generally will not apply with regard to any retail communication that does not make any financial or investment recommendation or otherwise promote a product or service of the member.

FINRA may also grant an exception from the approval rule for good cause. Notwithstanding any other exception, an appropriately qualified registered principal of the member must approve each retail communication before the earlier of its use or filing with FINRA.

TEST TOPIC ALERT

Please note that the term ***retail customer*** refers to any customer—existing or prospective—that does not fit into the definition of *institutional client.*

Institutional Communication

Institutional communication is any written communication that is distributed or made available only to institutional investors but does not include a member firm's internal communications.

Keep in mind that when regulators talk about written communication, they always include electronic communications, too.

The following is a list of those included in FINRA's definition of institutional investor:

- FINRA member firm or registered person of the member firm
- Bank

- Savings and loan
- Insurance company
- Registered investment company
- Registered investment adviser
- Any entity with $50 million or more of total assets, including natural persons
- Governmental entity
- Employee benefit plan (e.g., 401(k), 403(b), 457) that has at least 100 participants
- Person acting solely on the behalf of an institutional investor

This definition is important because any entity that isn't defined as an institution is retail. The rule specifically excludes the individual participants of employee benefit plans from the definition of institutional investors.

If a member has reason to believe that a communication or excerpt of the communication intended for institutional investors will be forwarded to or made available to a person who is not an institutional investor, the communication must be treated as a retail communication until the member reasonably concludes the improper practice has ceased.

Each member must establish written procedures that are appropriate to its business, size, structure, and customers for the review of institutional communications used by the member and its associated persons by an appropriately qualified, registered principal. Such procedures must be reasonably designed to ensure that institutional communications comply with applicable standards. When such procedures do not require review of all institutional communications before first use or distribution, they must include provision for the education and training of associated persons as to the firm's procedures governing institutional communications, documentation of such education and training, and surveillance and follow-up to ensure that such procedures are implemented and adhered to. Evidence that these supervisory procedures have been implemented and carried out must be maintained and made available to FINRA upon request.

PRACTICE QUESTION

1. Institutional communication is defined as sales material
   A. received from a mutual fund or other institutional investor.
   B. sent only to an institutional investor.
   C. sent to both institutional investors and the general public.
   D. sent to an institutional investor for forwarding to its public clients.

   Answer: B. To qualify as institutional communication, the material can only be seen by institutions. If the broker-dealer receives any hints that the communication may be passed on from the institution to a retail investor, it will likely fall out of the definition and require approvals.

LO 19.b Recall other communications by characteristics and definitions.

Other Communications

In addition to the three primary types of communications with the public, there are several other types of communications you should be aware of.

Public Appearance

A **public appearance** is participation in a seminar, webinar, radio or television interview, or other public appearance or public-speaking activity. To qualify, it must be an activity that is unscripted and could not be classified as correspondence, retail, or institutional communication.

Members must establish written procedures that are appropriate to their business, business's size, structure, and customers to supervise their associated persons' public appearances. Therefore, preapproval of a principal may be required but is not mandated. Such procedures must provide for the education and training of associated persons who make public appearances as to the firm's procedures, documentation of such education and training, and surveillance and follow-up to ensure that such procedures are implemented and adhered to. Evidence that these supervisory procedures have been implemented and carried out must be maintained and made available to FINRA upon request.

Any scripts, slides, handouts, or other written (including electronic) materials used in connection with public appearances are considered communications for purposes of this rule, and members must comply with all applicable provisions of this rule based on those communications' audience, content, and use. If the material will be seen by more than 25 investors in a 30-day period, it is considered retail communication. In that case, it must have preapproval from a principal unless meeting one of the exceptions mentioned previously.

If an associated person recommends a security in a public appearance, the associated person must have a reasonable basis for the recommendation. The associated person also must disclose any conflicts of interest that may exist, such as a financial interest in any security being recommended. This disclosure is not required when the security recommended is a mutual fund or variable contract of an insurance company. If past performance of a mutual fund or variable contract is shown, it must be for no less than the previous 12 months.

PRACTICE QUESTION

2. Which of the following would meet FINRA's definition of a public appearance?
   A. A carefully scripted presentation in an online interactive electronic forum, such as a chat room or in an online seminar
   B. An unscripted presentation in an online interactive electronic forum, such as a chat room or in an online seminar
   C. An unscripted presentation to over 1,000 registered representatives through the member firm's internal broadcasting facilities
   D. A brochure describing the features offered by the member firm that includes a link to a specially prepared video on the member's website

Answer: B. To be a public appearance, it must be unscripted and for the public, not a group of registered representatives. Brochures, even those with video links, are invariably going to be retail communications.

Independently Prepared Reprint

Independently prepared reprints are retail communications and have some special characteristics that generate exam questions. An **independently prepared reprint (IPR)** consists of any article reprint that meets certain standards. A key requirement is that the reprint was prepared by an independent publisher and was not materially altered by the member. A member may alter the contents of an IPR only to make it consistent with applicable regulatory standards or to correct factual errors.

An article reprint qualifies as an IPR under the rules only if, among other things, its publisher is not an affiliate of the member using the reprint or any underwriter or issuer of the security mentioned in the reprint. Also, neither the member using the reprint nor any underwriter or issuer of a security mentioned in the reprint may have commissioned the reprinted article. IPRs must be preapproved by a principal and are exempted from the FINRA filing requirements.

Research Reports

A **research report** is a document prepared by an analyst or strategist, typically as a part of a research team for an investment adviser or broker-dealer. The report may focus on an individual stock or sector of the economy and generally, but not always, will recommend buying, selling, or holding an investment.

FINRA has established rules designed to improve the objectivity of research reports and provide investors with more useful and reliable information when making investment decisions.

Members must take steps to ensure that all research reports reflect an analyst's honest view and that any recommendation is not influenced by conflicts of interest, such as investment banking business (see Unit 20) with the issuer. If a member issues a report or a research analyst renders an opinion that is inconsistent with the analyst's actual views regarding a subject company, FINRA considers such action fraudulent.

To ensure the investing public receives objective information from the media and publications, the FINRA rules require the following:

- Firms must clearly explain their rating systems, use rating terms according to their plain meaning, note the percentage of all ratings they have assigned to each category (e.g., buy/sell/hold), and document the percentage of investment banking clients in each category.
- Analysts' compensation may not be tied to the firm's investment banking revenues.
- Analysts must disclose in their research reports and public appearances whether they or any member of their households have a financial interest in the subject security and whether their employer firms owned 1% or more of any class of a subject company's equity securities at the close of the previous month.
- Research reports must disclose whether, within the last 12 months, the firm has received fees for investment banking services from—or managed or co-managed—a public offering for a company that is the subject of a research report. They must also disclose whether the firm expects to receive or intends to seek in the three months following publication of a research report any investment banking fees from any company that is the subject of a report.
- An investment adviser or a broker-dealer may not present to a client research reports, analyses, or recommendations prepared by other persons or firms without disclosing the fact that the adviser or broker-dealer did not prepare them. An investment adviser or a broker-dealer may base a recommendation on reports or analyses prepared by others, as long as these reports are not represented as the investment adviser's or broker-dealer's own.

Quiet Period

A member firm, acting as manager or co-manager of a securities offering, may not publish research nor may an analyst make a public appearance regarding the subject company for 40 days following an initial public offering (IPO), or for 10 days following an additional issue offering.

FINRA interprets the date of the offering to be the later of the effective date of the registration statement or the first date on which the securities were bona fide offered to the public.

TAKE NOTE

The following items fall outside the definition of research reports:

- Discussions of broad-based indices
- Commentaries on economic, political, or market conditions
- Technical analyses concerning the demand and supply for a sector, index, or industry based on trading volume and price
- Statistical summaries of multiple companies' financial data, including listings of current ratings
- Notices of ratings or price target changes

PRACTICE QUESTION

3. Which of the following requires that the communication was issued by an independent publisher and **not** materially altered by the member?
   A. A research report
   B. An independently prepared reprint (IPR)
   C. A website article
   D. A script for a public appearance

   Answer: B. An IPR consists of any article reprint that meets certain standards designed to ensure that the reprint was issued by an independent publisher and was not materially altered by the member.

Electronic Communications With the Public

Although not classified as a specific type of communication, with the growth of the internet and the rise of **electronic communications** in general, it has been necessary for FINRA to bring electronic communications in the securities industry into the regulatory framework.

Websites, whether sponsored by the company itself or set up by an individual registered representative, are considered retail communications and are subject to applicable filing and recordkeeping rules. They must be reviewed and approved by a principal before first use and must contain no exaggerated claims or misleading information, and if materially altered since the last filing, must be reapproved and refiled. There must also be nothing in the website that suggests business affiliation with or approval by FINRA.

Members may indicate FINRA membership on a member's website, provided that the member provides a hyperlink to FINRA's homepage—www.finra.org—in close proximity to the member's indication of FINRA membership. This provision also applies to a website relating to the member's investment banking or securities business maintained by or on behalf of any person associated with a member.

Electronic bulletin boards are also considered retail communications, but a registered representative using one, or a chat room, need not identify himself as a registered person. Use of an online interactive forum by a registered representative must be approved by a principal, although each post does not require principal approval. The communications must be held to normal standards of accuracy and completeness.

Individual emails to customers fall under the definition of correspondence and are subject to the appropriate standards of conduct and supervision. Instant messaging could qualify as retail communication or correspondence, depending on the size of the audience.

FINRA has released several notices dealing with the use of social media, such as Facebook and Twitter. We have learned of a few questions on the topic and they are included in our QBank.

TAKE NOTE

Regulations are clear—firms must have established procedures to maintain, review, and supervise communications transmitted via blogs, email, instant messaging, texts, Twitter, Facebook, and whatever new communication forum is coming our way.

Recently, a firm and some representatives were fined when it was discovered that reps had used outside electronic sources for securities-related business. In other words, there was no supervision, no review, and no record of the communication. FINRA does not look kindly on that.

SEC Advertising Rules

The SEC has two rules regarding advertising that can appear on the exam. They are Rule 135a dealing with generic advertising and Rule 156, titled Investment Company Sales Literature.

Generic Advertising SEC Rule 135A

Generic advertising promotes securities as an investment medium, but does not refer to any specific security. Generic advertising often includes information about

- the securities investments that companies offer,
- the nature of investment companies,
- services offered in connection with the described securities,
- explanations of the various types of investment companies,
- descriptions of exchange and reinvestment privileges, and
- where the public can write or call for further information.

All generic advertisements must contain the name and address of the sponsor of the advertisement but never include the name of any specific security. A generic advertisement may be placed only by a firm that offers the type of security or service described.

TAKE NOTE

Firms must have available for sale the type of security or service they advertise. For example, a brokerage firm is not permitted to advertise no-load mutual funds if it does not sell them.

EXAMPLE

A broker-dealer may place an advertisement announcing mutual funds are now offered, but may not provide the name of the mutual fund family or families offered. In other words, if the advertisement states that the broker-dealer now offers FLY FAR mutual funds, this would not be defined as a generic advertisement.

PRACTICE QUESTION

4. If a firm wanted to promote securities as an investment medium but does not refer to any specific security, it would likely use which of the following?
   A. Generic advertising
   B. An independent generic research report
   C. A generic website post
   D. A public correspondence

Answer: A. All generic advertisements must contain the name and address of the sponsor of the advertisement but never include the name of any specific security.

Rule 156

Under federal law, it is unlawful for any person, directly or indirectly, by the use of any means or instrumentality of interstate commerce or of the mails, to use sales literature which is materially misleading in connection with the offer or sale of securities issued by an investment company. Under these provisions, sales literature is materially misleading if it (1) contains an untrue statement of a material fact or (2) omits to state a material fact necessary to make a statement made, in the light of the circumstances of its use, not misleading.

Performance Reporting

Probably the most common offense deals with performance. Representations about past or future investment performance could be misleading because of statements or omissions made involving a material fact. Per SEC Rule 156, examples of these would include

- representations implying that future gain or income may be inferred from or predicted based on past investment performance;
- portrayals of past performance, made in a manner which would imply that gains or income realized in the past would be repeated in the future;
- failure to disclose, if a sales load or any other nonrecurring fee is charged, the maximum amount of the load or fee. If the sales load or fee is not reflected, a statement that the performance data does not reflect the deduction of the sales load or fee, and that, if reflected, the load or fee would reduce the performance quoted.

In any sales literature for an investment company, other than a money market fund, that contains performance data, average annual total return (after taxes on distributions, as well as after taxes on distributions and redemption) for one-, five-, and 10-year periods must be shown. If the fund has been in operation for a shorter period, the life of the fund must be used. Longer periods may be shown in five-year increments up to the life of the fund.

If the sales literature refers to yield, it must include the total return figures and show the CY in no greater size or prominence than total return. The quotation must also identify the length of the period quoted and the last day in the base period used in the computation.

Some municipal bond funds like to advertise a tax-equivalent yield. To do so, they must show both the CY and total return as earlier in addition, and the tax-equivalent yield may be set out in no greater prominence. And, as stated previously, if the fund carries a sales load, performance data must indicate the effect of the load.

Names Rule

Rule 156 also addresses certain broad categories of investment company names that are likely to mislead investors about an investment company's investments and risks. The name rule requires a registered investment company with a name suggesting that the company focuses on a particular type of investment (e.g., an investment company that calls itself the ABC Stock Fund, the XYZ Bond Fund, or the QRS U.S. Government Fund) to invest at least 80% of its assets in the type of investment suggested by its name.

In addition, under SEC Rule 482, any advertisement, pamphlet, circular, form letter, or other sales literature addressed to or intended for distribution to prospective investors is considered materially misleading unless the sales literature includes the following information.

> An investment in the Fund is not insured or guaranteed by the Federal Deposit Insurance Corporation or any other government agency. Although the Fund seeks to preserve the value of your investment at $1.00 per share, it is possible to lose money by investing in the Fund.

LESSON 19.2: REVIEW, APPROVAL, AND FILING OF COMMUNICATIONS

LO 19.c Classify the required approvals of public communications including reviews and education of personnel.

Required Approvals of Public Communications

A principal of your firm may be required to approve or review communications to the public. Here are the requirements.

- Institutional—No preapproval of a principal is required. When such procedures do not require review of all institutional communications before first use or distribution, they must include provision for the education and training of associated persons as to the firm' procedures governing institutional communications.
- Retail—Preapproval of a principal is required (before use).
- Correspondence—Pre- or post-review of a principal is required (reviewed before or after use).
- Public appearance—Preapproval of a principal may be required but is not mandated.
- Independently prepared reprints—These must be preapproved by a principal if the communication meets the definition of a retail communication.
- Research reports—Approval requirements are based on how they are defined (e.g., institutional, retail). Research reports must be preapproved by a principal if the communication meets the definition of a retail communication.
- Electronic communications
  - Website preapproval of a principal is required.
  - Electronic bulletin boards—Use of an online interactive forum by a registered representative must be approved by a principal, although each post does not require principal approval.

- Emails and instant messaging—Approval requirements are based on how they are defined (institutional, retail, or correspondence).
- Generic advertising—Preapproval of a principal is required.

Filing Requirements

There is a special filing requirement for new members of FINRA. During its first year of operation, the new member must file *any* retail communication with FINRA at least 10 business days before first use. This is called prefiling. When FINRA says *any*, they mean any retail communication published or used in any

- electronic or other public media, including any generally accessible website;
- newspaper;
- magazine or other periodical;
- radio, television, telephone or audio recording;
- video display, signs or billboards, motion pictures; or
- telephone directories (other than routine listings).

After the first year of registration, a member firm is now established. From this point, the firm may file retail communications within 10 business days of first use (postfiling).

TEST TOPIC ALERT

Whether a first-year firm or not, retail communications for investment companies (including mutual funds, variable contracts, and unit investment trusts) that include a ranking or a comparison that is generally not published or is the creation of the investment company or the member must be filed with FINRA at least 10 business days before first use (prefiling).

In addition, there is a 10-day prefiling requirement for any retail communication involving option contracts (for all members).

If the ranking or comparison is generally published or is the creation of an independent entity (e.g., Lipper or Morningstar), the usual filing rules for filing will apply (i.e., within 10 business days of first use [postfiling]).

Retail communications must be kept on file for three years from last use. This includes electronic as well as paper format.

PRACTICE QUESTION

5. When comparing the types of communication, which of the following require prior principal approval before use?
   A. Sending a letter to a pension plan with a recommendation for the purchase of a security
   B. The broker-dealer sending a letter to all existing clients promoting a new service it offers
   C. Sending a summary of a recent meeting to an institutional client
   D. Notifying all existing clients of a change of location

Answer: B. Sending notification to all existing clients at a broker-dealer would involve more than 25 retail investors in a 30-calendar-day period. This would define it as *retail communication* and require prior principal approval. It is the best answer from the choices given. Institutional communications don't require prior principal approval and notifying clients of a change of address is not considered a retail communication requiring approval.

LESSON 19.3: PRODUCT SPECIFIC COMMUNICATIONS

LO 19.d Identify procedures for product-specific advertisements and disclosures required for public use.

Product-Specific Advertisements and Disclosures

All of a member's communications with the public—institutional, retail, and correspondence—must be based on principles of fair dealing and good faith and provide a sound basis for evaluating the facts in regard to any particular security or type of security, industry discussed, or service offered.

No material fact or qualification may be omitted if it could cause the communication to be misleading. Although most of these standards apply to all forms of communications with the public, the principal should be aware of the nuances.

Exaggerated or misleading statements are prohibited. In determining whether a communication is misleading, FINRA calls for consideration of the following:

- Overall context of the statement—a statement that is misleading in one context may be appropriate in another. An essential test in this regard is the balanced treatment of risks and potential returns.
- Different levels of explanation or detail may be needed, depending on the audience and the ability of the member to control who might come in contact with the communication.
- Overall clarity of the communication—FINRA warns that unclear statements can create serious misunderstandings to the point of constituting a rules violation.

EXAMPLE

Overly technical explanations or material disclosures buried in footnotes are likely to confuse the reader and could be construed as misleading.

Use of Investment Company Rankings in Retail Communications

For purposes of this rule, the term **ranking entity** refers to any entity that provides general information about investment companies to the public, that is independent of the investmen company and its affiliates, and whose services are not procured by the investment company o any of its affiliates to assign the investment company a ranking.

Members may not use investment company rankings in any retail communication other thar

- rankings created and published by Ranking Entities or
- rankings created by an investment company or an investment company affiliate but base on standard performance measurements.

Required Disclosures of Investment Company Rankings

A headline or other prominent statement must not state or imply that an investment company or investment company family is the best performer in a category unless it is ranked first in the category.

Other disclosures include

- the name of the category (e.g., growth);
- the name of the ranking entity and, if applicable, the fact that the investment company or an affiliate created the category or subcategory;
- criteria on which the ranking is based (e.g., total return, risk-adjusted performance);
- the fact that past performance is no guarantee of future results; and
- a ranking based on total return must be accompanied by rankings based on total return for one year, five years, and 10 years, or since inception, if shorter.

Requirements for the Use of Bond Mutual Fund Volatility Ratings

The term **bond mutual fund volatility rating** is a description issued by an independent third party. The rating relates to the sensitivity of the net asset value (NAV) of a portfolio of an open-end management investment company that invests in debt securities to changes in market conditions and the general economy. The rating is based on an evaluation of objective factors, including

- the credit quality of the fund's individual portfolio holdings;
- the market price volatility of the portfolio;
- the fund's performance, and specific risks, such as
  - interest rate risk,
  - prepayment risk, and
  - currency risk.

These ratings may not describe volatility as a risk rating.

Required Disclosures of Bond Mutual Fund Volatility Ratings

The name of the entity that issued the rating must be disclosed, along with

- the date of the current rating;
- a link to a website that includes the criteria and methodology used;
- a statement that there is no standard method to determine the rating;
- a description of the types of risk the rating measures (e.g., short-term volatility); and
- a statement that there is no guarantee the fund will continue to have the same rating or perform in the future as rated.

CMO Suitability

CMOs are multi-class debt instruments backed by a pool of mortgages, such as Ginnie Maes. They are far more complex than stocks and bonds. Even the registered representative may have a difficult time understanding how these work.

FINRA Rule 2216 states that before a member can sell a CMO to a retail customer (anyone other than an institutional investor), the firm must be sure the representative is trained and must offer the customer educational material that includes information and a discussion on

- the characteristics and risks of CMOs, including prepayment rates and average lives;
- the interest rates, including their effect on value and prepayment rates;
- tax considerations;
- transaction costs and liquidity;
- the structure of CMOs, including the different tranches that are offered and the risks pertaining to each;
- the relationship between mortgage loans and mortgage securities;
- questions an investor should ask before investing; and
- a glossary of terms.

Any retail communication concerning CMOs

- may not compare CMOs to any other investment vehicle, including bank CDs;
- must disclose, if applicable, that a government agency backing applies only to the face value of the CMO and not to any premium paid; and
- must disclose that a CMO's yield and average life will fluctuate depending on the prepayment rate and changes in interest rates.

PRACTICE QUESTION

6. A member firm is selling CMOs. Which of the following statements regarding membe advertising for this security are ***true***?
   A. The member may state that the CMO is guaranteed by the federal governmen
   B. The member may state that the CMO is similar to a mortgage REIT.
   C. The member may compare the CMO to a bank CD.
   D. The member must state that the CMO's yield and average life will fluctuate depending on the prepayment rate.

Answer: D. A communication with the public may never compare a CMO to any other investment vehicle. Furthermore, retail communication must state that yield and average life will fluctuate depending on the prepayment rate and changes in interest rates.

Options Communications

The three categories we've been discussing in this unit also apply to communications about options. A registered options principal (ROP) is responsible for advance approval of retail communications.

With regard to retail communication relating to options, the member must file copies with FINRA at least 10 days before first use (prefiling) if the OCC Disclosure Booklet (ODD) has not been delivered. Firms have two methods of filing with FINRA's Advertising Regulation Department: (1) electronically using a web-based filing system, or (2) in hard copy.

Options advertising is limited to

- a general description of the security being offered and its issuer, the Options Clearing Corporation (OCC);

- a description of the nature and functions of the options markets; and
- the name and address of the person at the member firm placing the advertisement from whom a current *OCC Disclosure Booklet* may be obtained.

The advertising may include advertising designs and devices, including borders, scrolls, arrows, pointers, multiple and combined logos and unusual type faces and lettering as well as attention-getting headlines and photographs and other graphics, provided such material is not misleading.

Recommendations, past performance, and projected performance are not permitted in options advertising.

PRACTICE QUESTION

7. Retail communications describing bull put spreads must be approved by
   A. a branch manager.
   B. an advertising principal.
   C. the chief compliance officer.
   D. a registered options principal (ROP).

Answer: D. When it comes to approval of communications dealing with options, approvals can only be done by a ROP.

LESSON 19.4: FINRA FILING RULES INCLUDING VARIABLE LIFE

LO 19.e Determine the rules and regulations relevant to communications with the public.

Summary of FINRA Filing Requirements for Communications With the Public

This unit has covered most of the FINRA filing requirements at the point of discussing the specific product. It will be helpful for you to have all of these in one place. Don't confuse *filing* with *principal approval.*

Principal Approval

Please review Lesson 19.2.

Prefiling

Filing with FINRA at least 10 business days before the use of any retail communication is required for

- a new member for a one year starting on the day its FINRA membership became effective,
- retail communications concerning registered investment companies that include a custom ranking, and
- retail communications concerning options if the ODD has not been previously delivered (filing with FINRA must first be done at least 10 *calendar* days in advance).

Postfiling

Filing with FINRA within 10 business days of first use is required for

- retail communications that promote or recommend a specific registered investment company or family of registered investment companies;
- retail communications concerning public DPPs;
- retail communications concerning collateralized mortgage obligations (CMOs) registere under the Securities Act; and
- if a member has filed a draft version or storyboard of a television or video retail communication pursuant to a filing requirement, then the member also must file the fir filmed version within 10 business days of first use or broadcast.

Exclusions From the Filing Requirement

Here are some of the most likely exclusions to be tested:

- Retail communications that previously have been filed with FINRA and that are to be used without material change
- Retail communications that do not make any financial or investment recommendation otherwise promote a product or service of the member
- Retail communications that do no more than identify a national securities exchange symbol of the member or identify a security for which the member is a registered marke maker
- Retail communications that do no more than identify the member
- Correspondence
- Institutional communications
- Communications that refer to types of investments solely as part of a listing of products or services offered by the member
- Retail communications that are posted on an online interactive electronic forum

Communications Regarding Variable Contracts

The following standards apply to all communications related to variable life and variable annuities, in addition to the general FINRA standards governing communications. These standards are applicable to advertisements and sales literature, as well as individualized communications such as personalized letters and computer-generated illustrations, whether printed or made available on-screen.

Product Communications

All communications must clearly describe the product as either variable life or a variable annuity, as applicable. Proprietary names may be used in addition to these descriptions. The may be no implication that the product being offered or its underlying account is a mutual fund.

Liquidity

Because variable life insurance and variable annuities frequently involve substantial charges and/or tax penalties for early withdrawal, there may be no representation or implication that these are short-term, liquid investments. Any statement about the ease of liquidation of these products must be accompanied by the negative impact of factors such as contingent deferred sales loads, tax penalties, and impact on cash value and death benefits.

Guarantees

Although insurance products contain a number of specific guarantees, the relative safety of the product from these guarantees may not be overemphasized because it depends on the claims-paying ability of the insurance company. There may be no representation or implication that a guarantee applies to the investment return or principal value of the separate account. Also, it may not be represented or implied that an insurance company's financial ratings apply to the separate account.

Although the rating firms S&P and Moody's Investor Service offer ratings on the financial health of insurance companies, the primary source used by almost everyone in the industry is A.M. Best. An A or A+ rating from them signifies substantial ability to meet their claim obligations.

Fund Performance Predating Inclusion in a Variable Product

Illustrations are sometimes used to show how an existing fund would have performed as an investment option within a variable life or variable annuity policy. Performance that predates a fund's inclusion may be used only if no significant changes occurred to the fund at the time or after it became a part of the variable product.

Single Premium Variable Life

Communications regarding single premium variable life may only emphasize investment features of this product if an adequate explanation of the life insurance features is also provided.

When a life insurance policy is funded with too much money within a seven-year period, it is defined as a *modified endowment contract (MEC)*. MECs have restricted access to cash values and also lose some tax advantages that other cash value polices have. Therefore, few single premium life insurance policies are issued.

Hypothetical Illustrations of Rates of Return in Variable Life Insurance

Hypothetical illustrations showing assumed rates of return may be used to demonstrate the performance of variable life policies. Rules that apply to the use of these illustrations include the following:

- Hypothetical illustrations may not be used to project or predict investment results.
- Illustrations may use any combination of assumed investment returns up to and including a gross rate of 12%, provided that one of the returns is a 0% gross rate. The maximum

rate illustrated should be reasonable, considering market conditions and the available investment options.

- Illustrations must reflect the maximum mortality and expense charges associated with the policy for each assumed rate of return illustrated. Current charges may also be illustrated.

In general, variable life product performance may not be compared with other investment products. However, comparison of variable life with a term insurance product is permitted to demonstrate the concept of tax-deferred growth resulting from investment in the variable product.

PRACTICE QUESTION

8. Communications related to variable life and variable annuities must meet specific standards. All of the following standards are required **except**
   A. all communications must clearly describe the product as either variable life or variable annuity.
   B. explaining that the policy's cash values will never be less than the total of the premiums paid.
   C. hypothetical illustrations showing assumed rates of return may be used to demonstrate the performance of variable life policies.
   D. communications regarding single premium variable life may only emphasize investment features of this product if an adequate explanation of the life insurance features is also provided.

Answer: B. Even with excellent performance of the separate account, it generally takes a number of years before the cash value equals the amount of the premiums paid. Furthermore, there are no guarantees to the cash value. It could be more, less, or the same as the total of premium payments. Remember that hypothetical projections must always include a return of 0% and cannot show more than 12%.

UNIT 20

The New Issues Market

LEARNING OBJECTIVES

When you have completed this unit, you will be able to accomplish the following.

- LO 20.a **Identify** characteristics of the primary market.
- LO 20.b **Recall** the process for bringing new issues to market.
- LO 20.c **Contrast** prospectus requirements.
- LO 20.d **Differentiate** official statements, preliminary official statements (POS), and notice of sale for issuing municipal securities.
- LO 20.e **Distinguish** exempt transactions rules and rules regarding restricted securities.
- LO 20.f **Determine** the rules and regulations pertaining to the new issues market.

INTRODUCTION

We have learned about the many different types of securities available in the marketplaces. Many issued by corporations, others by governments, federal, state and local. In all cases, the purpose of issuing these securities is to raise money and capital to work for the benefit of the issuer.

In general, investors purchase securities as new issues from a corporation, municipality, or the federal government. After the initial sale, those securities trade in the secondary market as trades between investors. This unit begins the process for bringing new issues to market. It then continues with the many legal requirements related to raising capital publicly and privately.

LESSON 20.1: MARKETING NEW ISSUES

LO 20.a Identify characteristics of the primary market.

The Primary Market

The term **primary market** does not refer to a market place such as an exchange or the OTC market. The primary market describes the sale of securities to the investing public in what are known as issuer transactions. That means the issuer receives the proceeds generated by th sale of those securities. In all cases, these are shares that have never been issued to the public before. The most common example is the **initial public (or primary) offering (IPO)**. Thos shares represent the first time any shares have been issued to raise new capital for the issuer.

Can an issuer have more than one primary offering? Yes, it happens with mutual funds every day. As you learned in Unit 8, open-end investment companies are constantly issuing new shares. They have a primary every day. However, they, like any other issuer, can only have on IPO. Whenever a corporation wishes to raise additional equity capital, it can issue additiona new shares. These shares generally come from the authorized but unissued shares we discusse in Unit 3. There are several terms used for these additional primary offerings, such as *follow-offering* or **additional primary offering (APO)**.

The easiest way to identify a primary offering is to "follow the money." If the funds wind up in the coffers of the issuer, it is a primary offering or a primary distribution.

TEST TOPIC ALERT

There is one case where the issuer receives the proceeds and it is not a primary offering. When a company resells treasury stock, it receives the proceeds. Because those shares were previously owned, it cannot be called a primary offering.

PRACTICE QUESTION

1. An initial public offering (IPO) is always
   A. an issuer transaction.
   B. a nonissuer transaction.
   C. of treasury stock.
   D. a follow-on offering.

Answer: A. An issuer transaction is one where the money goes to the issuer. An IPO is the first time the issuer is raising funds from the public. A nonissuer transaction is when the money goes to investors rather than the issuer. A sale of treasury stock is a issuer transaction, but it cannot be an IPO because those shares were already sold. follow-on offering is an offering of new shares, but it "follows" after an IPO.

The Secondary Market

Discussed in detail in Lesson 3.3, once a new issue has been distributed, all further buying and selling takes place in the secondary market. As pointed out much earlier, these are the exchanges, Nasdaq, and the OTC market. Transactions in the secondary market are largely nonissuer transactions. That is, the proceeds of the sale do not go to the issuer; they go to th selling shareholder (or bondholder).

LO 20.b Recall the process for bringing new issues to market.

Participants in a New Issue

The main participants in a new issue are the entity selling the securities and the broker-dealer acting as the underwriter (investment banker). The exam will focus on both corporate and municipal underwritings. Most of the industry participants play similar roles for both. Where there is an important difference, we will note it.

The Issuer

Unless the issue is exempt from registration (coming up in the next lesson), the issuer (the entity), selling the securities to raise money, must file a registration statement with the SEC. This document requires that the issuer supply sufficient information about the security and the corporation and its officers to allow an investor to make a sound investment decision. When the SEC reviews this document, during what is known as the 20-day cooling-off period, it looks for sufficiency of investment information rather than accuracy, though upon completion of the review, it does not guarantee adequacy of the prospectus.

Near the end of the cooling-off period, the underwriter holds a **due diligence** meeting. The preliminary studies, investigations, research, meetings, and compilation of information about a corporation and a proposed new issue that go on during an underwriting are known collectively as *due diligence.*

The underwriter must conduct a formal due diligence meeting to provide information about the issue, the issuer's financial background, and the intended use of the proceeds. Representatives of the issuer and the underwriter attend these meetings and answer questions from broker-dealers, securities analysts, and institutions.

When underwriting municipal revenue bonds, this due diligence investigation relies on a **feasibility study**. This study focuses on the projected revenues and costs associated with the project and an analysis of competing facilities.

As part of the due diligence process, investment bankers must

- examine the use of the proceeds,
- perform financial analysis and feasibility studies,
- determine the company's stability, and
- determine whether the risk is reasonable.

TAKE NOTE

The issuer knows a lot about manufacturing, accounting, software, or whatever it is they do. They don't know a lot about what it takes to sell securities to the public. That is why an investment banking firm is used.

Underwriter

A business (or municipal government) that plans to issue securities usually works with an **underwriter**, a broker-dealer specializing in investment banking—the process of underwriting new issues. An investment bank's functions may include

- advising corporations on the best ways to raise long-term capital,
- raising capital for issuers by distributing new securities,
- buying securities from issuers and reselling them to the public,
- distributing large blocks of stock to the public and to institutions, and
- helping issuers comply with securities laws.

The investment banker who negotiates with the issuer is known as the **underwriting manager** or **syndicate manager**. The underwriting manager directs the entire underwriting process, including signing the underwriting agreement with the issuer and directing the due diligence meeting and distribution process. A syndicate may have more than one manager.

TAKE NOTE

Investment bankers help issuers raise money through the sale of securities. They do not loan money. They are also called *underwriters*. All underwriters of corporate securities must be FINRA member firms. Underwriters of municipal securities must be members of the MSRB.

Forming a Syndicate

The MSRB defines the syndicate (sometimes called a selling syndicate) as "a group of underwriters formed to purchase (underwrite) a new issue of municipal securities from the issuer and offer it for resale to the general public. The syndicate is organized for the purposes of sharing the risks of underwriting the issue, obtaining sufficient capital to purchase an issue and broadening the distribution channels of the issue to the investing public."

Underwriting syndicate members make a financial commitment to help bring the securities public. In a firm commitment offering, all syndicate members commit to purchase from the issuer and then distribute an agreed-on amount of the issue (their participation or bracket). Syndicate members sign a **syndicate agreement**, or **syndicate letter,** that describes the participants' responsibilities and allocation of syndicate profits, if any. Syndicate and selling groups may be assembled either before or after the issue is awarded to the underwriter.

In a **negotiated underwriting**, the issuer and the investment banker negotiate the offering terms, including the amount of securities to be offered, offering price or yield, and underwriting fees.

Negotiated underwritings are standard in underwriting corporate securities because of close business relationships between issuing corporations and investment banking firms.

Competitive bid underwriting arrangements are the standard for underwriting most municipal securities and are often required by state law. In a competitive bid, a state or municipal government invites investment bankers to bid for a new issue of bonds. The issuer awards the securities to the underwriter(s) whose bid results in the lowest net interest cost to the issuer.

After the issuing municipality meets with the municipality's attorneys and accountants to analyze each bid, it awards the municipal bond issue to the syndicate that offers to underwrite the bonds at the lowest net interest cost or true interest cost to the issuer.

Net interest cost (NIC) is a common calculation used for comparing bids and awarding the bond issue. It combines the amount of proceeds the issuer receives with the total coupon interest it pays. **True interest cost (TIC)** provides the same type of cost comparison adjusted for the time value of money.

TAKE NOTE

NIC is a straight mathematical interest-rate calculation. The lowest NIC is the winner. TIC weights early interest payments more heavily to give greater value to dollars of today over dollars to be paid in the future, consistent with present value calculations.

Selling Group Formation

Although the members of an underwriting syndicate agree to underwrite an entire offering, they frequently enlist other firms to help distribute the securities as members of the selling group. **Selling group** members act as agents with no commitment to buy securities.

The managing underwriter is normally responsible for determining whether to use a selling group and, if so, which firms to include. If the securities to be issued are attractive, broker-dealers will want to participate. If the securities are not attractive, the manager may have to persuade broker-dealers to join.

Selling group members sign a **selling group agreement** with the underwriters, which typically contains

- a statement that the manager acts for all of the underwriters,
- the amount of securities each selling group member will be allotted and the tentative public offering price (POP) at which the securities will be sold (this price is firmed up just before the offering date),
- the portion of the underwriting spread (called the concession) to be received on sales made by selling group members (this is usually the largest portion of the spread);
- provisions as to how and when payment for shares is to be made to the managing underwriter, and
- legal provisions limiting each selling group member's liability in conjunction with the underwriting.

TEST TOPIC ALERT

Syndicate members take on financial liability and act in a principal capacity. Selling group members have no financial liability and act as agents because they have no commitment to buy securities from the issuer.

PRACTICE QUESTION

2. On a negotiated underwriting, the investment banker who negotiates with the issuer is known as
   A. the investment banker.
   B. the selling group manager.
   C. the syndicate manager.
   D. the negotiating manager.

Answer: C. The term used to describe the investment banker who leads the negotiations is the *syndicate* or *underwriting manager*. It is possible the term *lead underwriter* could be used as well.

Types of Underwriting Agreements

An agreement among underwriters details each underwriter's commitment and liability, particularly for any shares that remain unsold at the underwriting syndicate's termination.

The agreement designates the syndicate manager to act on behalf of the syndicate members. The manager's authority to manage the underwriting, which includes establishing the offering price with the issuer, deciding the timing of the offering, controlling advertising, and making all required filings, comes via this agreement.

Firm Commitment

The **firm commitment** is the most commonly used type of underwriting contract. Under its terms, the underwriter(s) [investment bank(s)] commit to buy the securities from the issuer and resell them to the public. The underwriters assume the financial risk of incurring losses in the event they are unable to distribute all the shares to the public.

A firm commitment underwriting can be either a negotiated underwriting contract or a competitive bid arrangement. Negotiated underwriting contracts are used in most corporate issues. The issuer selects an underwriter and negotiates the conditions of the underwriting contract. A competitive bid arrangement is the standard for new issue offering in the municipal securities market. Sales begin on the effective date of the offering.

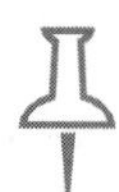

TAKE NOTE

In a firm commitment underwriting, the managing underwriter takes on the financial risk because he purchases the securities from the issuer. Because he purchases and resells the shares, he is acting in a principal (dealer) capacity.

TEST TOPIC ALERT

Syndicates are usually formed to spread the risk of an offering among several underwriters instead of one underwriter taking all the risk.

PRACTICE QUESTION

3. Because the firm commitment is the most commonly used type of underwriting contract, which of the following can be said of this type of underwriting?
   A. A firm commitment underwriting must be used with a negotiated underwriting contract.
   B. A firm commitment underwriting can be either a negotiated underwriting contract or a competitive bid arrangement.
   C. In a firm commitment all the underwriting risk is shifted to the issuer.
   D. A firm commitment may be added to a best efforts for the sake of securing the underwriting commitment.

Answer: B. A firm commitment can be used with either type of underwriting. The risk is shifted from the issuer to the underwriter(s).

Standby

Standby is a form of firm commitment unique to corporate rights offerings. When a company's current stockholders do not exercise their preemptive rights in an additional offering, a corporation has an underwriter **standing by** to purchase whatever shares remain unsold as a result of rights expiring.

Because the standby underwriter unconditionally agrees to buy all shares that current stockholders do not subscribe to at the subscription price, the offering is a firm commitment.

TAKE NOTE

By engaging a standby underwriter, an issuer is assured of selling all the shares being offered, even if the shareholders do not exercise their rights.

Best Efforts

In a **best efforts** arrangement, the underwriter acts as an agent for the issuing corporation. The deal is contingent on the underwriter's ability to sell shares to the public. In a best efforts underwriting, the underwriter sells as much as possible, without financial liability for what remains unsold. The underwriter is acting in an agency capacity with no financial risk.

All-or-None

In an **all-or-none (AON) underwriting**, the issuing corporation has determined that it wants an agreement outlining that the underwriter must either sell all of the shares or cancel the underwriting. Because of the uncertainty over the outcome of an AON offering, any funds collected from investors during the offering period must be held in escrow pending final disposition of the underwriting.

Broker-dealers engaged in an AON distribution are prohibited from deceiving investors by stating that all the securities in the underwriting have been sold if it is not the case.

Mini-Max

A **mini-max offering** is a best efforts underwriting setting a floor or minimum, which is the least amount the issuer needs to raise to move forward with the underwriting, and a ceiling or maximum on the dollar amount of securities the issuer is willing to sell. The underwriter must locate enough interested buyers to support the minimum (floor) issuance requirement. Once the minimum is met, the underwriter can expand the offering up to the maximum (ceiling) amount of shares the issuer specified. Mini-max underwriting terms are most frequently found in limited partnership program offerings, and funds collected from investors during the offering period must be held in escrow pending final disposition of the underwriting.

PRACTICE QUESTION

4. An underwriting syndicate has a firm commitment with an issuer to sell $5 million of common stock to the public. The syndicate has four selling groups. What is each selling group's financial responsibility for the sale?
   A. Each shares a firm commitment with the issuer to sell all the securities in the offering.
   B. Each selling group is responsible for $1 million of the $5 million offering.
   C. Selling groups take no financial responsibility in the offering.
   D. Each member of the selling group is responsible for its proportionate share of the offering.

Answer: C. The primary difference between the selling syndicate and the selling group is the financial commitment. Selling group members only get paid for what they sell. Selling groups are not limited to selling to institutional buyers.

TEST TOPIC ALERT

Be prepared for a question that requires an understanding of underwriter risk in firm commitment and best efforts underwriting.

Underwriting Municipal Securities

There are a number of testable procedures and terms relating to municipal securities. Although similar in concept to corporate securities, the exam will relate these to municipal securities. One significant difference between corporate and municipal underwritings to note is the need for a legal opinion, covered in Lesson 6.

Formation of the Municipal Underwriting Syndicate

As we know, a syndicate is an account that helps spread the risk of underwriting an issue among a number of underwriters. Although the bidding process for municipal bonds is competitive, successive offerings of a particular municipality are often handled by the same syndicate, which is composed of the same members.

A firm makes the decision to participate as a syndicate member after it considers

- the potential demand for the security,
- the existence of presale orders,
- the determination and extent of liability,
- the scale and spread, and
- the ability to sell the issue.

Participants formalize their relationship by signing a **syndicate letter,** or **syndicate agreement,** in a competitive bid or a **syndicate contract,** or **agreement among underwriters** in a negotiated underwriting. About two weeks before the issue is awarded, the syndicate manager sends the syndicate letter or contract to each participating firm for an authorized signature. The member's signature indicates that the member agrees with the offering terms. Syndicate letters include

- each member firm's level of participation or commitment;
- priority of order allocation;
- duration of the syndicate account;
- appointment of the manager(s) as agent(s) for the account;
- fee for the managing underwriter and breakdown of the spread; and
- other obligations, such as member expenses, good-faith deposits, observance of offering terms, and liability for unsold bonds.

TAKE NOTE

Syndicate letters are not legally binding until the syndicate's submission of the bid. Firms may drop from the group until this point.

Types of Syndicate Accounts

The financial liability to which each underwriter is exposed depends on the type of syndicate account. Underwriting syndicates use two arrangements: Western accounts and Eastern accounts.

Western Account

A **Western account** is a divided account. Each underwriter is responsible only for its own underwriting allocation.

Eastern Account

An **Eastern account** is an undivided account. Each underwriter is allocated a portion of the issue. After the issue has been substantially distributed, each underwriter is allocated additional bonds representing its proportionate share of any unsold bonds. Thus, an underwriter's financial liability might not end when it has distributed its initial allocation.

TAKE NOTE

When remembering the difference between Western and Eastern, divided and undivided accounts, try this phrase: "The continental *divide* is in the *West*." It helps remind you that Western accounts and divided accounts are the same, as are Eastern and undivided accounts.

EXAMPLE

A syndicate is underwriting a $5 million municipal bond issue. There are five syndicate members, each with equal participation, including your firm. Your firm sells its entire allocation, but bonds worth $1 million remain unsold by the other syndicate members.

If this is a Western account, what is your firm's liability?

In a Western account, your firm would have no remaining liability because its entire share was sold. However, if your firm had sold only $700,000 of its $1 million allocation, it would have to purchase the remaining $300,000 for its own inventory.

If this is an Eastern account, what is your firm's liability?

In an Eastern account, the unsold amount is divided among all syndicate members based on their initial participation. In this example, your firm would be allocated 20% of the remaining amount, or $200,000. The responsibility for any unsold bonds continues until the entire bond issue is sold.

PRACTICE QUESTION

5. An investment banker is a member of the selling syndicate of a new issue of municipal bonds. The member commits to $500,000 of bonds out of a total offering of $5 million in an undivided syndicate and sells $300,000 of the bonds. Of the total offering, $1 million of the bonds are unsold. What is the syndicate member's remaining liability?
   A. $100,000
   B. $200,000
   C. $300,000
   D. $500,000

Answer: A. An Eastern or undivided syndicate means joint and several liability for any unsold portion. This firm's original commitment was for 10% of the issue. Therefore, the liability is for 10% of the unsold portion. With $1 million unsold, 10% is $100,000.

The Syndicate Bid

A syndicate will present a bid to the issuer to win the right to represent the new issue in the primary market. If a syndicate wins the bid they will be selling the bonds to the public in the IPO.

Establishing the Bid

The syndicate arrives at its competitive bid over a series of meetings during which member dealers discuss the proposed reoffering scale and spread for the underwriters. Their goal is to arrive at the best price to the issuer while still making a profit. At a preliminary meeting, the manager seeks a tentative agreement from members on the prices or yields of all maturities in the issue as well as the gross profit or underwriting spread (the difference between what the public pays and what the issuer receives).

A final bid price for the bond is set at a meeting conducted just before the bid is due. If the member dealers cannot all agree on a final bid, the syndicate can go ahead with its bid as long as the syndicate members agree to abide by the majority's decision.

TAKE NOTE

To win the bid, the syndicate must resolve this question: What is the lowest interest rate that can win the bid and provide a competitive investment to public buyers as well as provide a profit for the underwriter?

The process of establishing the reoffering yield (or price) for each maturity is called **writing the scale**. A scale is the list of the bond issue's different maturities. If the coupon rate has already been determined, each maturity listed is assigned a yield. If the rate has not been set, each maturity is assigned a coupon. A normal scale has higher yields for long-term bonds.

Once the underwriters have written a scale that allows them to resell the bonds, they prepare the final bid. Put another way, writing the scale involves first determining what prices (yields are necessary to be able to sell the various serial maturities and then backing off a little to arrive at a bid. Before they submit the bid, the underwriters must ensure that they have met any unique specifications the issuer has set.

Competitive bids are submitted as firm commitments. This means that the underwriters are committing to sell all the bonds. If any are left unsold, the underwriters must take them for their own accounts. Therefore, bids must be carefully written to be competitive yet profitabl Underwriters receive no profit guarantee. Note that syndicates bidding on the proposed issu must bid on the entire amount being offered for sale.

Disclosure of Fees

Fees to be paid to a clearing agency and the syndicate manager must be disclosed to syndica members in advance. Normally, this disclosure is part of the syndicate letter or the agreeme among underwriters. Management fees include any amount in the gross spread that is paid the manager alone and not shared with syndicate members.

Awarding the Issue

After the issuing municipality meets with the municipality's attorneys and accountants to analyze each bid, it awards the municipal bond issue to the syndicate that offers to underwrite the bonds at the lowest NIC or true interest cost to the issuer.

When the issuer makes its choice, it announces the successful bidder and returns the good-faith deposits to the remaining syndicates.

The successful syndicate has a firm commitment to purchase the bonds from the issuer and reoffer them to the public at the agreed on offering price. The issuer keeps the successful bidder's good-faith deposit to ensure that the syndicate carries out its commitment.

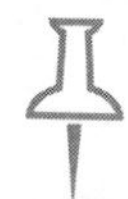

TAKE NOTE

While the amount of the good-faith deposit can differ from one issue to another, it is usually 1%–2% of the total par value of the offering.

Syndicate Account

The **syndicate account** is created when the issue is awarded. The **syndicate manager** is responsible for keeping the books and managing the account. All sale proceeds are deposited to the syndicate account, and all expenses are paid out of the account. Settlement of syndicate accounts is 30 calendar days after the issuer delivers the securities to the syndicate. Therefore, the maximum length of time for the syndicate to exist is 30 calendar days from the time the issuer delivers the securities to the syndicate.

Breakdown of the Spread

The price at which the bonds are sold to the public is known as the **reoffering price** (or **reoffering yield**). The syndicate's compensation for underwriting the new issue is the **spread**, or the difference between the price the syndicate pays the issuer and the reoffering price. Each participant in the syndicate is entitled to a portion of the spread, depending on the role each member plays in the underwriting.

EXAMPLE

A corporation issues stock to the public at $20 per share. It is done through a firm commitment and the syndicate manager's fee is $0.25 per share. The underwriting fee is $0.40 per share and the selling concession is $0.50 per share. The issuer will receive

A. $19.75 per share.
B. $19.60 per share.
C. $19.10 per share.
D. $18.85 per share.

Answer: D. The proceeds to the issuer are the offering price less the spread. The spread consists of all of these pieces ($0.25 + $0.40 + $0.50) and is a total of $1.15. The $20 offering price less the $1.15 spread results in the issuer receiving $18.85 per share.

TEST TOPIC ALERT

Just as with mutual funds, the offering price, or public offering price, is the price paid by investors and includes the spread. That is, using the above example, the investors do not pay the $20 per share plus something else. Everything is included.

TAKE NOTE

The term *production* refers to the total dollar sales earned from a municipal issue. The production less the amount bid for the issue results in the spread.

Syndicate Management Fee

Syndicate managers receive a per-bond fee for their work in bringing the new issue to market.

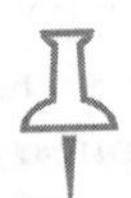

TAKE NOTE

The manager might receive ⅛ point ($1.25) as a management fee from a total spread of 1 point ($10).

Total Takedown

The portion of the spread that remains after subtracting the management fee is called the **total takedown**. Members buy the bonds from the syndicate manager at the takedown.

In the following example, for a 1-point spread with a management fee of ⅛ point, the takedown is ⅞ point ($8.75). A syndicate member that has purchased bonds at the takedown can sell its bonds either to customers at the offering price or to a dealer in the selling group below the offering price.

Unlike syndicate members, firms that are part of the selling group do not assume financial risk. They are engaged to help the syndicate members sell the new issue. Their compensation for each bond sold is termed the **selling concession.**

Selling Concession and Additional Takedown

A syndicate member can buy bonds from the manager for $991.25, sell them to the public for $1,000, and earn the takedown of ⅞ point ($8.75). If the firm chooses instead to sell bonds to a member of the selling group, it does so at a price less than $1,000, or, $995 in the following example. The discount the selling group receives from the syndicate member is called the selling **concession.** This $5 is equal to ½ point.

Selling group members buy bonds from syndicate members at the concession. The syndicate member keeps the remainder of the total takedown, called the **additional takedown**. The additional takedown in this example is ⅜ point ($3.75).

Figure 20.1: Additional Takedown

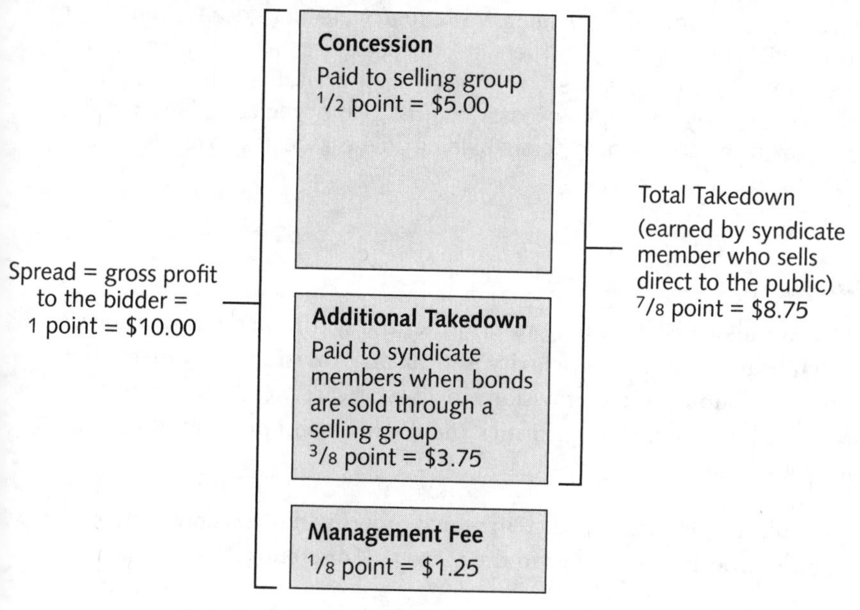

Cost to investor	=	$1,000
Spread	=	$10
Amount bid for the issue	=	$990

The syndicate manager may notify other firms that are not syndicate or selling group members of the new issue through *The Bond Buyer*. Interested firms may buy the bonds from the syndicate at a small discount from the reoffer price. This discount is termed a **reallowance,** which is generally half of the concession amount.

TEST TOPIC ALERT

Municipal spread questions are generally asked in terms of points, not dollars. One bond point equals $10.

Be ready for a question that asks you to rank parts of the spread in order of their size. Remember that the manager's fee is typically the smallest, and the total takedown is the largest. The additional takedown is a part of the total takedown amount, even though the name is a bit misleading.

You may see a question that asks under what circumstances a syndicate member can receive the full spread when a bond is sold. The answer is that the syndicate member receives the full spread if the member is also the syndicate manager. Also, be ready to define total takedown as the concession plus the additional takedown.

PRACTICE QUESTION

6. A dealer should consider all of the following factors when determining the spread on a new issue **except**
   A. the prevailing interest rates in the marketplace.
   B. the amount bid on the issue.
   C. the type and size of the issue.
   D. the amount of the good-faith check.

Answer: D. The spread is the difference between the reoffering price and the amount bid on an issue in competitive bidding. MSRB rules state that a dealer is entitled to make a profit in an underwriting. Therefore, the dealer can take into account such factors as market conditions, the type and size of the issue, the dollar volume of the transaction, and any extraordinary costs incurred by the syndicate. The amount of the good-faith check deposited before bidding on the issue has no relevance to the bid or to the reoffering price.

Order Allocation

Municipal bond orders are allocated according to priorities the syndicate sets in advance. The MSRB requires syndicates to establish **priority allocation provisions** for orders. The managing underwriter must submit these provisions to all syndicate members in writing. Normally, the manager includes allocation priorities and confirmation procedures in the syndicate agreement.

The syndicate must establish a definite sequence in which orders will be accepted and cannot simply state that the order priority will be left to the manager's discretion.

Syndicate members must signify in writing their acceptance of the allocation priorities. In addition, the manager must notify the members in writing of any change to the set priorities.

Order Period

The MSRB has established a timeline for municipal underwritings. The **order period** is the time set by the manager during which the syndicate solicits customers for the issue and all orders are allocated without regard to the sequence in which they were received. The order period usually runs for an hour on the day following the award of the bid.

Allocation Priorities

A syndicate's **allocation priorities** become especially important when a bond issue is oversubscribed. The normal priority follows.

Presale Order

A **presale order** is entered before the date that the syndicate wins the bid, which means that a customer is willing to place an order without knowing the final price or whether the syndicate will even win the bid. A presale order takes priority over other types of orders, and individual syndicate members are not credited with any takedown on presale orders. The takedown is split among all syndicate members according to participation.

Group Net Order

A group order is placed after the bid is awarded. A syndicate member that wants a customer's order to receive priority enters the order as a **group net order**. The takedown on a group net order is deposited in the syndicate account, and upon completion of the underwriting, it is split among all syndicate members according to participation.

Designated Order

The next highest priority for orders received during the order period is assigned to **designated orders**. These orders are usually from institutions that wish to allocate the takedown to certain syndicate members.

Member Order and Member-Related Order

The lowest priority for orders goes to member and member-related orders. A member firm enters such an order for its own inventory or related accounts, such as for a dealer-sponsored unit investment trust (UIT). The easiest way to remember the priority of the various types of orders is that the highest priority is given to those orders that benefit the most members. The lowest priority is given to orders that benefit a single member.

Under MSRB rules, a syndicate member placing an order for a related account must disclose this fact to the syndicate manager when the order is placed. Therefore, the manager will know to accord these orders the lowest priority.

Within two business days of the sale date, the syndicate manager must send a written summary of how orders were allocated to the other syndicate members.

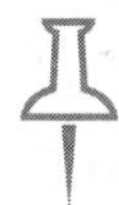

TAKE NOTE

A simple way to remember the normal order allocation priority found in the syndicate letter is *Pro Golfers Don't Miss*. PGDM stands for Presale, Group, Designated, and Member.

PRACTICE QUESTION

7. An order confirmed for the benefit of the entire underwriting syndicate placed after the bid is awarded is called
   A. a group net order.
   B. a net designated order.
   C. a presale order.
   D. a member at the takedown order.

   Answer: A. A municipal group net order is credited to syndicate members according to their percentage participation in the account. This order type is given priority over designated or member takedown orders, but not over presale orders. By placing this type of order, syndicate members are stipulating that they want those bond orders to have the highest priority still available. Note that presale orders are also confirmed for the benefit of the entire syndicate, but these are placed before the time the winning bid is awarded.

LESSON 20.2: REGISTRATION REQUIREMENTS

LO 20.c Contrast prospectus requirements.

The Securities Act of 1933

Investigation of the conditions that led to the stock market crash of 1929 determined that investors had little protection from fraud in the sale of new issues of securities. Rumors, exaggerations, and unsubstantiated claims led to excessive speculation in newly issued stock. Congress passed the **Securities Act of 1933** to require issuers of new securities to file registration statements with the SEC to provide investors with complete and accurate information in the form of a prospectus when soliciting sales. Think of the Securities Act of 1933 as the *Paper Act* because of the registration statement and prospectus. It will remind you of the paperwork requirements for full and fair disclosure.

New securities that are subject to the act's requirements are called nonexempt issues. Exempt securities are not subject to these requirements.

Exempt Issuers and Securities

The Securities Act of 1933 provides specific exemptions from federal registration provisions.

Among the exemptions are the following issuers:

- The U.S. government
- U.S. municipalities and territories
- Nonprofit religious, educational, and charitable organizations
- Banks and savings and loans
- Public utilities and common carriers whose activities are regulated as to rates and other items by a state or federal regulatory body (e.g., railroad equipment trust certificate)

The following securities are exempt from the Securities Act of 1933:

- Commercial paper—maturity less than 270 days
- Bankers' acceptances—maturity less than 270 days
- Securities acquired in private placements—Regulation D

When a security is exempt from federal registration, there is no registration statement, no prospectus. In some cases, a security might have to register solely with the state (e.g. Rule 147 at LO 20.e) or with the state as well as the SEC.

State Registration

State securities laws, also called **blue-sky laws**, also require registration of securities, broker-dealers, and registered representatives. An issuer or investment banker may blue-sky an issue by one of the following methods.

- Qualification—The issuer registers only with the state. There is no federal registration because the issue is sold strictly intrastate. The requirements are those of the specific state.
- Coordination—The issuer registers simultaneously with the state and the SEC. Both registrations become effective on the same date.
- Notice filing—Securities listed on the major stock exchanges and on Nasdaq, as well as investment companies registered under the Investment Company Act of 1940, are known as federal covered securities. State registration is not required, but most states require the filing of a notice that the issuer intends to offer its securities for sale in that state and the state may assess a filing fee.

The Registration Process

Although we tend to think of new issues when discussing registration, that is not the only time registration is required. There could be a registered **secondary distribution**. This is a distribution, with a prospectus, that involves securities owned by major stockholders (typically founders or principal owners of a corporation). The sale proceeds go to the sellers of the stock, not to the issuer. There could also be a combined or **split offering**. This is a public offering of securities combining both a primary and a secondary offering. A portion of the issue is a primary offering, the proceeds of which go to the issuing corporation. The remainder of the issue is a secondary offering, the proceeds of which go to the selling stockholders.

After an issuer files a registration statement with the SEC, a 20-day **cooling-off period** begins. During the cooling-off period, the SEC reviews the security's registration statement and can issue a stop order if the statement does not contain all of the required information.

Figure 20.2: The Three Phases of an Underwriting

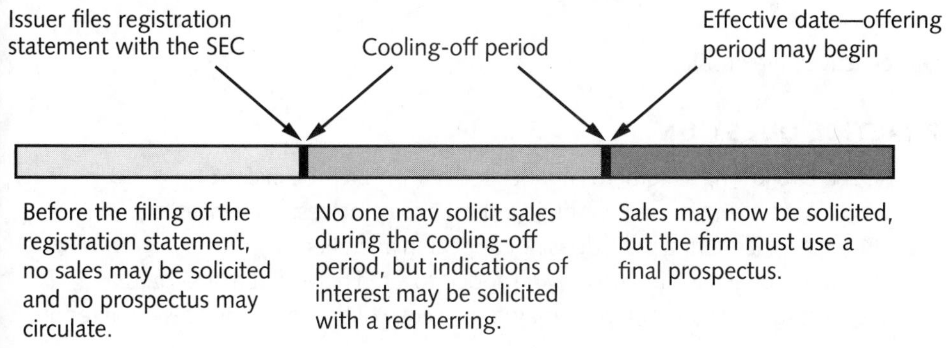

Red Herring

The **red herring** (preliminary prospectus) is used to gauge investor reactions and gather indications of interest for corporate securities. A registered representative may discuss the issue with prospects during the cooling-off period and provide them with preliminary information through the red herring. It must carry a legend, printed in red, that declares that a registration statement has been filed with the SEC but is not yet effective. The final offering price and underwriting spread are not included in the red herring.

Figure 20.3: Allowable Activity During the Cooling-Off Period

May:	May Not:
Distribute red herrings	Offer securities for sale
Publish tombstone advertisements	Distribute final prospectuses
Gather indications of interest	Disseminate advertising material
	Disseminate sales literature
	Take orders
	Accept postdated checks

SEC rules prohibit the sale of public offering securities without a prospectus, which means that no sales are allowed until the final prospectus is available.

Tombstone Advertisements

During the cooling-off period, sales of the security and related activities are prohibited. Nonbinding indications of interest may be gathered with a preliminary prospectus. In addition, tombstone advertisements are allowed to be published. These announcements, typically published after the offering has been cleared for sale, offer information to investors.

However, they do not offer the securities for sale. Issuers are not required to publish tombstones, but they may appear either before or after the effective date of the sale.

TAKE NOTE

The term *tombstone advertisement* is derived from the bare-bones, minimum information they provide. Information found in a tombstone advertisement published on or after the effective date includes

- name of issuer,
- type of security,
- underwriter,
- price, and
- effective date of sale.

PRACTICE QUESTION

8. All of the following statements about a red herring are true **except**
   A. a red herring is used to obtain indications of interest from investors.
   B. the final offering price does not appear in a red herring.
   C. additional information may be added to a red herring at a later date.
   D. registered representatives may send a copy of the company's research report with it.

Answer: D. Because the preliminary prospectus may be used for gathering indications of interest only, it may not be used to solicit sales. No other form of communication may be attached to or accompany it.

Pricing the New Issue of Publicly Traded Securities

During the cooling-off period, the underwriter advises the issuing corporation on the best price at which to offer securities to the public. The following variables may be considered when pricing new issues:

- Indications of interest from the underwriter's book
- Prevailing market conditions, including recent offerings and the prices of similar new issues
- Price that the syndicate members will accept
- Price-to-earnings (P/E) ratios of similar companies and the company's most recent earnings report (at what price the shares must be offered so that the P/E ratio is in line with the P/E ratios of other similar publicly traded stocks)
- The company's dividend payment record (if any) and financial health
- The company's debt ratio

An issue's price or yield must be determined by the effective date of the registration. The effective date is when the security begins to trade.

FINRA on Size of the Spread

FINRA reviews underwritings to determine if the compensation earned by the underwriter(s) is fair and reasonable. There are a number of factors considered. The amount of the spread varies by issue and can be influenced by any of the following:

- Type of commitment—A firm commitment earns a larger spread than a best efforts agreement because of the risks the underwriter assumes.
- Security's marketability—A bond rated AAA has a smaller spread than a speculative stock.
- Issuer's business—A stable utility stock usually has a smaller spread than a more volatile stock.
- Offering size—In a very large offering, the underwriter can spread costs over a larger number of shares; thus, the per share cost may be lower.

The Final Prospectus (Effective, Statutory Prospectus)

When the registration statement for corporate securities becomes effective, the issuer amends the preliminary prospectus and adds information, including the final offering price and the underwriting spread for the final prospectus. Registered representatives may then take orders from those customers who indicated interest in buying during the cooling-off period.

A copy of the final prospectus must precede or accompany all purchase confirmations. However, if the prospectus has been filed with the SEC and is available through its website, access to the prospectus equals delivery of the prospectus.

The prospectus must include

- a description of the offering;
- the offering price;
- selling discounts;
- the offering date;
- use of the proceeds;
- a description of the underwriting, but not the actual contract;
- a statement of the possibility that the issue's price may be stabilized;
- a history of the business;
- risks to the purchasers;
- a description of management;
- material financial information; and
- the SEC disclaimer.

SEC Disclaimer

The SEC reviews the prospectus to ensure that it contains the necessary material facts, but it does not guarantee the disclosure's accuracy. Furthermore, the SEC does not approve the issue but simply clears it for distribution. Implying that the SEC has approved the issue violates federal law. Finally, the SEC does not pass judgment on the issue's investment merit.

The front of every prospectus must contain a clearly printed **SEC disclaimer** specifying the limits of the SEC's review procedures. A typical SEC disclaimer clause reads as follows:

> *These securities have not been approved or disapproved by the SEC or by any State Securities Commission nor has the SEC or any State Securities Commission passed upon the accuracy or adequacy of this prospectus. Any representation to the contrary is a criminal offense.*

The information supplied to the SEC becomes public once a registration statement is filed. If, at any time, the SEC believes that the registration statement is incomplete or has other problems, it may issue a **stop order**. This is not to be confused with the buy stop and sell stop orders discussed in Lesson 16.1. This stop order "stops" the registration process. Typically, a deficiency letter is sent, and if the deficiency is not cured by the stated deadline, the issue may be permanently halted.

TEST TOPIC ALERT

Anything that says the SEC approves or disapproves an issue of securities is wrong. The SEC does not approve or disapprove—it clears or releases issues of securities for sale. When the SEC has completed its review, the registration becomes effective.

Issuers and underwriters are responsible for the information found in the prospectus and will conduct due diligence meetings to ensure that the prospectus is true and accurate.

TAKE NOTE

Access equals delivery does not apply to registered investment companies. Physical delivery must be made before or concurrent with the sales presentation.

PRACTICE QUESTION

9. All of the following are true statements **except**
   A. before the filing of the registration statement, the SEC will set up a cooling-off period to ensure all registration requirements have been fully met.
   B. the front of every prospectus must contain the SEC disclaimer.
   C. the preliminary prospectus may be used to gather indications of interest.
   D. the Securities Act of 1933 required nonexempt issuers of new securities to file registration statements with the SEC.

Answer: A. The 20-day cooling-off period begins after the registration statement has been filed, not before. The SEC disclaimer is printed on the front of the prospectus and indications of interest may be gathered through the use of a preliminary prospectus. Unless the issue qualifies for an exemption, it must register with the SEC.

Summary Prospectus—SEC Rule 498

When it comes to open-end investment companies, the physical delivery requirements can be met by delivery of a summary prospectus. A mutual fund can provide a **summary prospectus** to investors that may include an application investors can use to buy the fund's shares.

The summary prospectus is a standardized summary of key information found in the fund's statutory (full) prospectus. Investors who receive the summary have the option of either purchasing fund shares using the application found therein or requesting a statutory prospectus. An investor who purchases fund shares on the basis of the summary prospectus must be able to access a statutory prospectus online. Remember, customers can always reques and receive a paper copy. If requested, the statutory prospectus must be sent within three business days of receipt of the written request.

The summary must provide specific information in a particular sequence. Following is a list of required disclosures:

- Risk/return summary: investments, risks, and performance
- Risk/return summary: fee table
- Investment objectives, principal investment strategies, related risks, and disclosure of portfolio holdings
- Management, organization, and capital structure
- Shareholder information
- Distribution arrangements
- Financial highlights information

Statement of Additional Information (SAI)

Although a prospectus is always sufficient for the purpose of selling shares, some investors may wish to have additional information not found in the prospectus. This additional information is not necessarily needed to make an informed investment decision but may be useful to the investor.

An SAI must be available to investors upon request without charge. Investors can obtain a copy by calling or writing to the investment company via a company website, contacting a broker that sells the investment company shares, or contacting the SEC. If requested, a paper copy must be sent within three days of the request.

The SAI affords the fund an opportunity to have expanded discussions on matters such as the fund's history and policies. It will also typically contain the fund's consolidated financial statements.

TAKE NOTE

The SAI must be available for open-end and closed-end companies. Exchange-traded funds (ETFs) also have SAIs, but not unit investment trusts (UITs).

Trust Indenture Act of 1939

The Trust Indenture Act of 1939 applies to corporate bonds (nonexempt) with the following characteristics:

- Issue size of more than $50 million within 12 months
- Maturity of nine months or more
- Offered interstate

This act was passed to protect bondholders and requires that issuers of these bonds appoint a trustee to ensure that promises (covenants) between the issuer and the trustee who acts solely for the benefit of the bondholders are carried out. The document is filed at the office of a custodian so that investors may review it if they choose.

PRACTICE QUESTION

10. The Trust Indenture Act of 1939 covers which of the following securities transactions?
    A. An offering of an issue of $5 billion worth of Treasury bonds maturing in 2040
    B. A public issue of debentures worth $40 million sold by a single member firm throughout the United States
    C. A corporate bond issue worth $55 million sold interstate
    D. The sale of an industrial revenue development bond issue of $62 million sold in the tri-state area

Answer: B. The Trust Indenture Act of 1939 requires all corporate debt issues of $50 million or more sold interstate to have a trust indenture; U.S. Treasury issues and municipal bonds (IDRs) are not corporate issues. That makes them exempt from the provisions of this act.

LESSON 20.3: MUNICIPAL BOND DOCUMENTATION

LO 20.d Differentiate official statements, preliminary official statements (POS), and notice of sale for issuing municipal securities.

Official Statement (OS)

The MSRB defines an OS as:

> A document prepared by or on behalf of the issuer of municipal securities in connection with a primary offering that discloses material information on the offering of such securities. Official statements typically include information regarding the purposes of the issue, how the securities will be repaid, and the financial and economic characteristics of the issuer, conduit borrower or other obligated person with respect to the offered securities. Investors and market intermediaries may use this information to evaluate the credit quality of the securities and potential risks of the primary offering.

From a practical standpoint, it is the equivalent of an SEC registered issuer's prospectus, just with a different name.

Municipal securities are exempt from the filing requirements of the Securities Act of 1933. However, like all other securities, they are subject to the anti-fraud provisions of the Securities Exchange Act of 1934. Therefore, a full and fair disclosure of material facts of the offering is still required.

The full and fair disclosure document for municipal securities is called the **official statement (OS)** (there is no prospectus). There is no preliminary prospectus either for municipal securities, but there is a **preliminary official statement**. Just as with the red herring for an equity issue, underwriters use a preliminary OS to determine investors' and dealers' interest in the issue.

Prepared by the issuer, the OS identifies the issue's purpose, the source from which the interest and principal will be repaid, and the issuer's and community's financial and economic backgrounds. The OS also has information relating to the issue's creditworthiness.

A typical OS includes

- the offering terms;
- the summary statement;
- the purpose of the issue;
- a description of the basic legal documents, such as the authorizing resolution, indenture, and trust agreement;
- the security backing the bonds;
- a description of the bonds;
- a description of the issuer, including organization and management, area economy, and a financial summary;
- the construction program;
- the project feasibility statement;
- any regulatory matters;
- any specific provisions of the indenture or resolution, including funds and accounts, investment of funds, additional bonds, insurance, and events of default;
- any accompanying legal proceedings;
- the tax status;
- any appropriate appendices, including consultant reports, the legal opinion, and financial statements; and
- any credit enhancements.

With competitive bid underwritings, a municipality publishes an invitation to bid. Investment bankers respond in writing to the issuer's attorney or other designated official requesting information on the offering. How do the potential underwriters know about the new issue? Through an official notice of sale.

Official Notice of Sale

The official notice of sale to solicit bids for the bonds is usually published in *The Bond Buyer* and local newspapers and includes

- date, time, and place of sale;
- name and description of issuer;
- type of bond;
- bidding restrictions (usually requiring a sealed bid);
- interest payment dates;
- dated date (interest accrual date) and first coupon payment date;
- maturity structure;
- call provisions (if any);
- denominations and registration provisions;
- expenses to be borne by purchaser or issuer;
- amount of good-faith deposit that must accompany bid;
- paying agent or trustee;
- name of the firm (the **bond counsel**) providing the legal opinion;

- details of delivery;
- issuer's right of rejection of all bids;
- criteria for awarding the issue; and
- issuer's obligation to prepare the final OS and deliver copies to the successful bidder.

The bond's rating and the underwriter's name are not included in a notice of sale because they have yet to be determined.

The investment bankers prepare bids for the securities based on information in the notice of sale, comparable new issue supply and demand, and general market conditions. As we have discussed, the winner is the underwriter whose bid represents the lowest cost to the issuers (either NIC or TIC).

New Issue Worksheet

To acquire relevant details about a new issue, the syndicate manager typically orders the New Issue Worksheet from *The Bond Buyer*. This worksheet provides—in an organized format—all information presented in the official notice of sale. It shows a schedule of year-by-year maturities and their corresponding dollar amounts and a computation of bond years.

PRACTICE QUESTION

11. An investor purchases a new issue municipal bond. A copy of the official statement (OS)
    A. must precede the delivery of the bonds.
    B. need only be delivered if requested in writing by the investor.
    C. need not be delivered because an OS is not a prospectus.
    D. must accompany or precede the delivery of the bonds.

    Answer: D. The OS is the municipal industry's disclosure document. It is most similar to the prospectus used in corporate underwritings. MSRB rules require that a copy of the OS must accompany or precede the delivery of the bonds.

LESSON 20.4: SEC AND FINRA RULES ON NEW ISSUES

LO 20.e Distinguish exempt transactions rules and rules regarding restricted securities.

Exempt Transactions

Securities offered by corporations may qualify for exemption from the registration statement and prospectus requirements of the Securities Act of 1933 under one of the following exclusionary provisions:

- Regulation A+: Small and medium corporate offerings
- Regulation D: Private placements
- Rule 147: Securities offered and sold exclusively intrastate
- Regulation S: Offers and sales made outside the United States by U.S. issuers
- Other exempt transactions, including Rule 144, Rule 144A, and Rule 145

Regulation A+: Small and Medium Offerings

With the passage of the Jumpstart Our Business Startups Act, a capital formation scheme was called for that would further ease the requirements for small- and medium-sized companies to raise capital. Previously known as *Regulation A*, the new rule is *Regulation A+*.

Regulation A+ provides two offering tiers for small- and medium-sized companies that will allow the companies to raise capital in amounts substantially more than the $5 million previously allowed under Regulation A:

- Tier 1. Securities offerings up to $20 million in a 12-month period will be allowed. Of the $20 million, no more than $6 million can be sold on behalf of existing selling shareholders. The offering would be subject to a coordinated review by individual states and the SEC.
- Tier 2. Securities offerings up to $50 million in a 12-month period will be allowed. Of the $50 million, no more than $15 million can be sold on behalf of existing selling shareholders. These offerings are subject to SEC review only and none at the state level. Tier 2 offerings are still subject to rigorous disclosure requirements to the SEC, including audited financial statements, annual, semiannual, and current reports.

Offerings under both tiers are open to the public and general solicitation is permitted for both tiers. However, Tier 2 investors must be qualified investors, and there are two ways to qualify:

- Be an accredited investor as defined in Rule 501 of Regulation D.
- Limit the investment to a maximum of the greater of 10% of the investor's net worth or 10% of the investor's net income per offering. Note that self-certification for Tier 2 as to net worth and income is all that is required with no burdensome filings. Tier 1 has no investment limits.

Finally, remembering that the new Regulation A+ is intended for small- and medium-sized companies, the regulation specifically excludes investment companies (i.e., private equity funds, venture capital funds, and hedge funds).

In a Regulation A+ offering, the issuer files an abbreviated **notice of sale**, or **offering circular**, with the regional SEC office. Investors are provided with this offering circular rather than a full prospectus.

The cooling-off period is 20 days between the filing date and effective date, and the issuer need not provide audited financial information. Individuals buying securities in a Regulation A+ offering must receive a final offering circular at least 48 hours before confirmation of sale.

PRACTICE QUESTION

12. ABC, Inc., will be using Regulation A+ to offer $8 million of its common stock in its home state and in three other states. For the offering to be cleared for sale by the SEC, ABC must file
    A. an offering circular.
    B. a standard registration statement.
    C. a letter of notification.
    D. nothing.

    Answer: A. In a Regulation A+ offering, the issuer files an abbreviated notice of sale, or offering circular, with the regional office of the SEC instead of with the SEC in Washington, D.C. It is this offering circular that is distributed to investors rather than a prospectus.

Regulation D: Private Placements

In a major effort aimed at facilitating the capital formation needs of small businesses, the SEC adopted Regulation D, the private placement exempt transaction. Securities offered and sold in compliance with Regulation D are exempt from registration with the SEC and are considered federal covered securities exempt from registration on the state level as well. Our primary concern is with **SEC Rule 506,** a private placement where there is no dollar limit on the amount sold.

The Jumpstart Our Business Startups Act of 2012, or **JOBS Act**, made several important changes to Rule 506 of Regulation D. Rule 506 consists of two sections, 506(b) and 506(c). A company seeking to raise capital through a private placement under Rule 506(b) can sell the offering to an unlimited number of accredited investors (definition following) and up to 35 nonaccredited investors. In addition, no advertising may be done on behalf of the offering.

On the other hand, Section 506(c) permits the offering to be advertised. There are two primary (and interrelated) requirements to do this:

- All purchasers are accredited investors, or the issuer reasonably believes that they are accredited investors.
- The issuer takes reasonable steps to verify that all purchasers are accredited investors, which could include reviewing documentation, such as W-2s, tax returns, bank and brokerage statements, credit reports and so forth.

An issuer can elect to make a typical Rule 506 offering without general solicitation or advertising under Section 506(b) to include up to 35 nonaccredited investors in the offering or to avoid the heightened verification procedures.

The JOBS Act also included a provision that an issuer is disqualified from using Rule 506 under their *bad actor* provisions. Simply, if the issuer or other relevant persons (such as underwriters, directors, officers, or significant shareholders of the issuer), have been convicted of securities fraud or certain other securities violations, an offering under Rule 506 may not take place.

SEC Rule 501 Accredited Investors

SEC Rule 501 classifies an accredited investor for the purposes of Regulation D into several categories. Investors are considered to be accredited under the rule only if the issuer or any person acting on the issuer's behalf has reasonable grounds to believe, and does believe after reasonable inquiry, that the investors are included in one of the categories in the definition.

The separate categories of accredited investors under Regulation D include

- a bank, insurance company, or registered investment company;
- an employee benefit plan if a bank, insurance company, or registered investment adviser makes the investment decisions, or if the plan has total assets in excess of $5 million;
- a charitable organization, corporation, or partnership with assets exceeding $5 million;
- directors, executive officers, and GPs of the issuer;
- any natural person whose individual net worth, or joint net worth with that person's spouse, excluding the net equity in his primary residence, exceeds $1 million at the time of his purchase;
- any natural person who had an individual income in excess of $200,000 in each of the two most recent years or joint income with that person's spouse in excess of $300,000 in

each of those years and has a reasonable expectation of reaching the same income level in the current year; and

- entities made up of accredited investors.

The term *accredited investor* applies only to private placements. A favorite phrase of the regulators is, "eligibility does not equal suitability." Therefore, just because one meets the financial requirements of an accredited investor does not mean that suitability standards are ignored.

TEST TOPIC ALERT

Can assets in an account or property held jointly with another person who is not the purchaser's spouse be included in determining whether the purchaser satisfies the net worth test in Rule 501?

Answer: Yes, assets in an account or property held jointly with a person who is not the purchaser's spouse may be included in the calculation for the net worth test, but only to the extent of her percentage ownership of the account or property.

Purchasers must have access to the same type of information they would receive if the securities were being sold under prospectus in a registered offering. The amount of capital that can be raised is unlimited.

A private placement investor must sign a letter stating that she intends to hold the stock for investment purposes only. **Private placement stock** is called **lettered stock** because of this investment letter. The certificate may bear a legend indicating that it cannot be transferred without registration or exemption; therefore, private placement stock is also called **legend stock**. There will be more on this when we cover Rule 144.

What is Form D, and when does it have to be filed? Under Rule 503 of Regulation D, an issuer that is issuing securities in reliance on Regulation D must file Form D electronically with the SEC no later than 15 days after the first sale of securities in the offering.

The SEC also specifies instances when an amended Form D should be filed, such as to correct a mistake of fact or error or to reflect a change in information.

TEST TOPIC ALERT

Sometimes it is difficult to identify private placement stock in a question because of the many terms that can be used to describe it. Recognize all of the following terms as being synonymous with private placement stock:

- Restricted (because it must be held for a six-month period)
- Unregistered (no registration statement on file with the SEC)
- Letter stock (investor agreed to terms by signing an investment letter)
- Legend stock (bear a restrictive legend on the certificate)

PRACTICE QUESTION

13. Sales made under the provisions of Rule 506(b) of Regulation D must be reported on
    A. Form D.
    B. Form U4.
    C. Form 506.
    D. Form 13F.

Answer: A. Form D is the form that must be filed electronically with the SEC no later than 15 days after the first sale of securities in the offering.

Rule 147: Intrastate Offerings

Under **Rule 147**, offerings that take place entirely in one state are exempt from registration when

- the issuer has its principal office and receives at least 80% of its income in the state, or
- at least 80% of the issuer's assets are located within the state, or
- at least 80% of the offering proceeds are used within the state, or
- a majority of the issuers' employees are based within the state, and
- all purchasers are residents of the state.

TAKE NOTE

To qualify under the Rule 147 exemption, only one of the three 80% tests or the majority of employees test noted earlier must be met. However, the 100% residents rule always applies.

TEST TOPIC ALERT

Purchasers of an intrastate issue may not resell the stock to any resident of another state for at least six months after the purchase.

Regulation S

Offers and sales made outside the United States by both U.S. and foreign issuers are excluded from the registration provisions of the Securities Act of 1933. Because securities distributed offshore by issuers need not be registered with the SEC, they are therefore restricted for the purposes of Rule 144. To avoid registration under Regulation S

- the offer and sale must be made in an offshore transaction and
- there can be no directed selling efforts in the United States in connection with the offering.

To be an offshore transaction, offers and sales cannot be made to any person or entity in the United States. However, U.S. citizens residing outside the United States could purchase these securities. All sales made under Regulation S must be reported to the SEC on Form 8-K.

TAKE NOTE

Regulation S addresses the sale of unregistered securities by U.S.-based issuers to non-U.S. residents. A holding period on Regulation S securities is necessary to prevent flow back into the United States. There is a holding period of either six months or one year depending on the reporting status of the issuer. However, sales may be made immediately to any SEC-designated offshore securities market.

TAKE NOTE

Regulation S applies to United States issuers. Foreign issuers are not subject to this regulation if certain requirements are met. To be a foreign issuer, no more than 50% of its voting securities and no more than 20% of its debt securities can be owned by persons with a U.S. address. If a foreign issuer does not meet these requirements, it will be subject to the provisions of Regulation S (no sales to entities in the United States).

LO 20.f Determine the rules and regulations pertaining to the new issues market.

Shelf Registration (Rule 415)

Rule 415 of Regulation C of the Securities Act of 1933 permits issuers to quickly raise money in the capital markets when needed or when market conditions are just right. The FINRA exam outline refers to this as a "delayed or continuous offering and sale of securities." For example, if a company files a shelf registration statement with the SEC, there is no intention to immediately sell the securities. However, when the right time arrives, such as interest rates are at a low point, or funds are needed to complete the final phase of a large factory, the company can take down the securities from the shelf without the delay of an SEC review. Just keep it simple. Think about putting some canned goods on a shelf. They are there when you need them without having to go to the store.

EXAMPLE

An issuer wants to sell $300 million of five-year AA/Aa2-rated notes, but only when market interest rates allow the sale to be made on a 6.40 basis. The current market shows that rates for five-year investment-grade notes are about 6.55. If the issuer waits for rates to fall 15 basis points and then files a registration statement with the SEC, rates may move back up before the registration is effective. To address this type of situation, an issuer files a shelf registration statement with the SEC, which, once effective, is good for two years. Therefore, as soon as rates fall, the issuer has an effective registration statement in place and can sell the five-year notes with little delay. This permits issuers to match financing needs with market conditions. For certain well-known issuers, the two-year period is extended to three years.

Rule 144

Rule 144 regulates the sale of control and restricted securities, stipulating the holding period, quantity limitations, manner of sale, and filing procedures.

For purposes of Rule 144, **control securities** are those owned by directors, officers, or persons who own or control at least 10% of the issuer's voting stock. These are commonly referred to as **insiders**.

TAKE NOTE

If an unaffiliated individual owns 7% of the voting stock of XYZ, that person is not a control person. However, if that person's spouse owns 4% of the voting stock, then both would be considered control persons. In other words, if there is a 10% or more interest held by immediate family members, then all those family members owning voting stock might be control persons. Please note that combining interests only applies to family members residing in the same home or being supported by or supporting the other family member.

Restricted securities are those acquired through some means other than a registered public offering. A security purchased in a private placement is a restricted security. Restricted securities may not be sold until they have been held fully paid for six months. According to Rule 144, after holding restricted stock fully paid for six months, an affiliate may begin selling shares by submitting Form 144 but is subject to the volume restriction rules as enumerated as follows. In any 90-day period, an investor may sell the greater of

- 1% of the total outstanding shares of the same class at the time of sale or
- the average weekly trading volume in the stock over the past four weeks on all exchanges or as reported through Nasdaq.

There is a de minimis exemption under Rule 144. Form 144 need not be filed if 5,000 or fewer shares are sold and the dollar amount is $50,000 or less. The de minimis rule applies to sales in any 90-day period.

After the six-month holding period, affiliated persons are subject to the volume restrictions for as long as they are affiliates. For unaffiliated investors, the stock may be sold completely unrestricted after the six-month holding period has been satisfied.

Selling shares under Rule 144 effectively registers the shares. In other words, buyers of stock being sold subject to Rule 144 are not subject to any restrictions if they choose to resell.

Figure 20.4: Rule 144

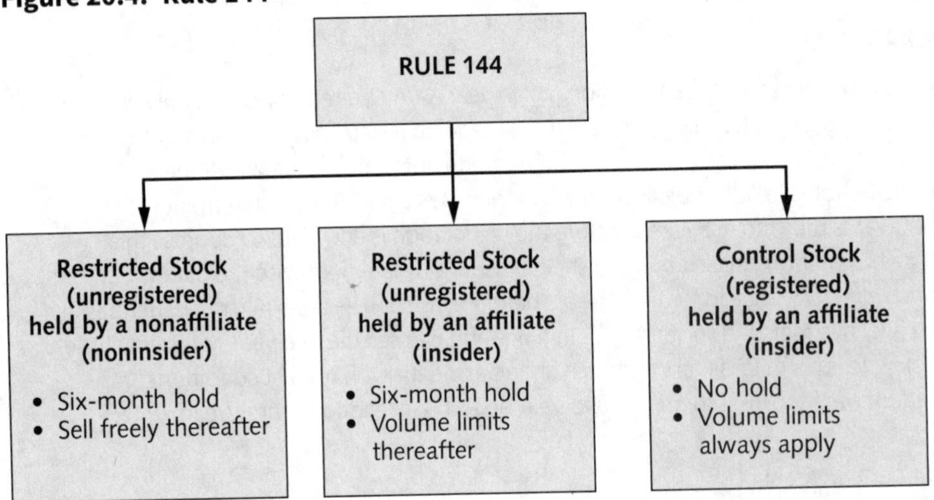

TEST TOPIC ALERT

When you encounter a Rule 144 question, always look for two things:

- What kind of stock is being sold? (Restricted or control)
- Who is selling it? (Insider or noninsider)

Only restricted stock has a holding period. Control stock, unless it is restricted, can be sold immediately, but volume limits always apply.

TAKE NOTE

If an affiliate sells control stock for a profit without holding it at least six months, this is called a *short swing profit*. If a short swing profit occurs, the affiliate must disgorge the profit. This is an SEC rule that is not related to Rule 144, but applies to those people who are control persons.

The term *disgorged* can certainly show up on an exam question. In this case, it means the profit is returned to the issuer.

Rule 144A

Rule 144A allows nonregistered foreign and domestic securities to be sold to certain institutional investors in the United States without holding period requirements. To qualify for this exemption, the buyer must be a **qualified institutional buyer** (QIB). A QIB must have a minimum of $100 million invested on a discretionary basis and cannot have any affiliation with the entity selling the securities.

PRACTICE QUESTION

14. Which of the following persons is subject to the holding period provisions of Rule 144?
    A. A corporate insider who has held restricted stock for two years
    B. A nonaffiliate who has held registered stock for three years
    C. A nonaffiliate who has held control stock for six months
    D. A nonaffiliate who has held restricted stock for three months

Answer: D. Only restricted stock is subject to the six-month holding period for both affiliates and nonaffiliates. Neither registered shares nor control stock are subject to this holding period. The nonaffiliate who has only held the shares for three months will be subject to the holding period until the six-month requirement is met.

Protecting the Public and Restricted Persons Prohibitions (FINRA Rule 5130)

FINRA Rule 5130 is designed to protect the integrity of the public offering process by ensuring that

- members make a bona fide public offering of securities at the POP;
- members do not withhold securities in a public offering for their own benefit or use such securities to reward persons who are in a position to direct future business to the member; and
- industry insiders, such as members and their associated persons, do not take advantage of their insider status to gain access to new issues for their own benefit at the expense of public customers.

The rule applies only to a new issue, which is defined to mean any IPO of equity securities. The rule does not apply to additional issue offerings, debt securities, restricted or exempt securities, convertible securities, preferred stock, investment company securities, offerings of business development companies, direct participation companies, and real estate investment trusts (REITs). Essentially, the rule applies to IPOs of common stock.

The rule prohibits member firms from selling a new issue to any account where restricted persons are beneficial owners. Restricted persons are defined as follows:

- Member firms
- Employees of member firms
- Finders and fiduciaries acting on behalf of the managing underwriter, including attorneys, accountants, financial consultants, and so forth
- Portfolio managers, including any person who has the authority to buy or sell securities for a bank, savings and loan association, insurance company, or investment company
- Any person owning 10% or more of a member firm

Furthermore, any immediate family member of any person in bullet points two through five is also restricted. Immediate family includes parents, in-laws, spouses, siblings, children, or any other individual to whom the person provides material support. Unlike control stock, residence is not a requirement. Giving or receiving support is a requirement, and living in the same home generally would make a family member restricted.

There is an important exemption. The prohibitions on the purchase and sale of new issues must not apply to securities that are specifically directed by the issuer. When a company goes public, it is good business practice to make shares available to employees, many of who would not normally be able to purchase new issues. However, these shares may not be directed to restricted persons.

Finally, there is a de minimis exemption. If the beneficial interests of restricted persons do not exceed 10% of an account, the account may purchase a new equity issue. In other words, restricted persons will be able to have an interest in an account that purchases new equity issues as long as no more than 10% of the account's beneficial owners are restricted persons.

Spinning is the practice of allocating highly sought after IPO shares to individuals who are in a position to direct securities business to the firm. This is why portfolio managers are categorized as restricted persons. These individuals are in a position to direct business to a firm and may be willing to do so on the basis of the size of their allocation.

Before selling an IPO to any account, representatives are required to obtain a written representation from the account owner(s) that the account is eligible to purchase a new common stock issue at the POP. All representations must be obtained within the 12-month period before the sale of the new issue and must be retained for at least three years following the new issue sale.

MUTUAL FUND CUSTOMER SUITABILITY QUIZ

Joe Smith is a registered representative with ABC Investments, Inc. Last week, Joe opened accounts for 10 new customers. Each customer wants Joe to recommend the best mutual fund that he can find.

Joe knows that the best mutual fund for one customer is not necessarily the best choice for every customer. Before he makes a recommendation, he collects important information about the customers' needs, goals, and financial status. For example, Joe asks each customer:

- What is your income?
- How stable is your income?
- What plans do you have for the money you invest?
- What kinds of risks are you comfortable taking?
- How liquid must your investments be?
- How important are tax considerations?
- Are you seeking long-term or short-term investments?
- What is your investment experience?

After Joe has noted a customer's financial status and investment objectives, he can begin to search for the most appropriate mutual fund. Joe has prepared a brief description of each of his 10 new customers, and this is followed by a list of top-performing mutual funds in 10 categories.

Which mutual fund would you recommend to each of Joe's customers? After you have read the descriptions of the customers and the funds, answer each question based on which fund best meets the customer's objectives. Fund descriptions are listed after the questions.

The Customers

1. Andy Jones, 52, and Patty Jones, 56, have a large investment portfolio concentrated in stocks and stock mutual funds, including an international fund. They maintain their cash reserves in a money market account at their local bank. Andy is employed as a consultant, where he earns a $400,000 a year salary. The Joneses are seeking a safe investment because they will need to liquidate a portion of their portfolio when Andy retires in about five years. They also recognize the need for additional diversification of their portfolio.
   A. Spencer Cash Reserve Fund
   B. MacDonald Balanced Fund
   C. Spencer Tax-Free Municipal Bond Fund
   D. MacDonald Stock Index Fund

2. Sarah Davis, 30, and Jim Davis, 32, have been married four years. Both work and they have no children, so their disposable income is relatively high. They live in the suburbs and plan to buy a condominium downtown so they can enjoy some of their favorite activities on the weekends. They need a safe place to invest the amount they have saved for their down payment for about six months while they shop for the perfect unit.
   A. ATF Biotechnology Fund
   B. ATF Capital Appreciation Fund
   C. Spencer Cash Reserve Fund
   D. Laramie Equity Income Fund

3. Adam Garcia is 26 and earns $45,000 a year as an advertising executive. He already has accumulated $5,000 in a savings account and is seeking a secure place to invest the amount and begin a periodic investment plan. He knows his long-term time frame means he should be willing to take some risk, but he is uncomfortable with the thought of losing money. Adam would prefer moderate overall returns rather than high returns accompanied by high volatility.
   A. Spencer Tax-Free Municipal Bond Fund
   B. MacDonald Balanced Fund
   C. XYZ Government Income Fund
   D. MacDonald Stock Index Fund

4. Mark Blair is a retired widower, 72, seeking a moderate level of current income to supplement his Social Security benefits and his company pension plan. Mark is a Depression-era grandfather of six with a conservative attitude toward investments. An equally important goal for him is capital preservation.
   A. MacDonald Stock Index Fund
   B. Spencer Tax-Free Municipal Bond Fund
   C. XYZ Government Income Fund
   D. ATF Overseas Opportunities Fund

5. Helen Wong is 29 and is seeking a long-term growth investment. She is concerned about the loss of purchasin power as a result of inflation and often complains about high commissions and charges that reduce her investment returns. When she was in college, she took a few economics courses and firmly believes that securities analysts cannot consistently outperform the overall market.
   A. MacDonald Balanced Fund
   B. MacDonald Stock Index Fund
   C. Spencer Cash Reserve Fund
   D. ATF Biotechnology Fund

6. Gina and Peter Stout, both 42, have two children, ages 14 and 12. The Stouts have spent the past 10 years accumulating money to provide for their children's education. Their oldest child will enter college in four years and they are not willing to take risks with the money they worked hard to accumulate. They need a safe investment that provides regular income to help them meet tuition payments.
   A. Laramie Equity Income Fund
   B. ATF Capital Appreciation Fund
   C. Spencer Cash Reserve Fund
   D. MacDonald Investment-Grade Bond Fund

7. Pat Long, 60, and Sadie Long, 58, are married and have raised three children. Both have decided to retire this year and are looking forward to an active retirement. They have accumulated a nest egg of about $1 million, which they plan to use to travel the world, pursue their hobbies, and care for their health. Both are concerned about rising inflation and are comfortable with a reasonable level of risk.
   A. Spencer Tax-Free Municipal Bond Fund
   B. XYZ Government Income Fund
   C. Laramie Equity Income Fund
   D. MacDonald Stock Index Fund

8. Amy Cain, 50, and Eric Cain, 48, have a combined annual income of more than $200,000. Their portfolio consists of common stocks and bonds that offer a wide range of safety and return potential. The Cains are becoming even more concerned about the effects of rising inflation in the U.S. economy. They are seeking to invest a small percentage of their portfolio in a fund that will provide additional diversification.
   A. ATF Biotechnology Fund
   B. XYZ Government Income Fund
   C. MacDonald Stock Index Fund
   D. ATF Overseas Opportunities Fund

9. Mike and Mary Cole are both 34 and employed in their computer software business. They have one daughter, age four. The Coles want to begin accumulating the money required to send their daughter to one of the nation's top universities in 14 years. In addition, they have not yet begun to accumulate money for their retirement.
   A. MacDonald Balanced Fund
   B. Laramie Equity Income Fund
   C. ATF Capital Appreciation Fund
   D. Spencer Tax-Free Municipal Bond Fund

10. Liz Scott, 45, is single and in search of maximum capital appreciation. She inherited a substantial amount of money a few years ago and has taken an active interest in managing her investments. Her portfolio is diversified among common stocks, tax-exempt bonds, international investments, and limited partnerships. She has a long-term time frame and is not averse to risk.
   A. Laramie Equity Income Fund
   B. ATF Capital Appreciation Fund
   C. MacDonald Balanced Fund
   D. ATF Biotechnology Fund

The Mutual Funds (Listed Alphabetically)

ATF Biotechnology Fund. The fund seeks maximum capital appreciation through investment in stocks of companies providing innovative products in the biotechnology sector, including pharmaceutical developers and medical equipment suppliers. Fund management seeks to evaluate emerging economic and political trends and to select individual companies that may benefit from technological advances.

ATF Capital Appreciation Fund. The fund seeks to achieve maximum capital appreciation with little or no pursuit of current income. The fund invests in stocks of small- and medium-size companies that demonstrate significant long-term growth potential. The fund's management believes that despite year-to-year fluctuations, the strategy of investing in companies that show strong earnings growth can result in superior investment returns.

ATF Overseas Opportunities Fund. The fund seeks maximum capital appreciation by investing in common stocks of companies located outside the United States. The management selects well-established companies that are listed on their native stock exchanges and that have demonstrated high earnings potential. Although the fund may be affected by fluctuations in currency exchange rates, over the long-term it may provide protection against downturns in U.S. markets.

Laramie Equity Income Fund. The fund seeks primarily current income, with secondary objectives of capital growth and growth of income. Its portfolio consists of common stock, preferred stock, and convertible securities of large, well-established companies with a history of paying high dividends. Its equity concentration can help protect against the loss of purchasing power owing to inflation.

MacDonald Balanced Fund. The fund seeks to preserve capital, to generate current income, and to provide long-term capital growth. Its strategy is to invest 60% of its portfolio in common stocks and 40% in bonds and fixed-income securities. Through diversification, the fund intends to provide protection against downturns in the market. In its endeavors to produce positive returns during market decline, the fund may not participate fully in rising stock markets.

MacDonald Investment-Grade Bond Fund. The fund seeks high current yield (CY) accompanied by reasonable risk. It invests most of its portfolio in corporate bonds having one of the top three ratings according to Moody's and Standard & Poor's. It seeks to reduce the risk associated with interest rate fluctuations by investing a portion of its assets in short-term corporate debt.

MacDonald Stock Index Fund. The fund seeks to duplicate the price and yield performance of Standard & Poor's Composite Index of 500 stocks. The fund invests in each of the index's 500 stocks in approximately the same composition as the index. The portfolio is not actively traded and therefore features a low turnover ratio.

Spencer Cash Reserve Fund. The fund's objectives are to maintain a stable net asset value and to provide current income. The fund invests in high-quality, short-term obligations, including U.S. Treasury bills, commercial paper certificates of deposit, and repurchase agreements. Check-writing privileges are available.

Spencer Tax-Free Municipal Bond Fund. The fund seeks to maximize tax-exempt CY. It invests in a portfolio of high-quality municipal debt obligations. The portfolio is diversified among securities issued by many different state and municipal taxing authorities. Income distributions provided by the fund are exempt from federal income tax.

XYZ Government Income Fund. The fund seeks to maximize safety of invested principal while providing current income. By investing in a broad range of debt securities issued by the U.S. Treasury, as well as by government agencies such as the Government National Mortgage Association, the fund provides reduced risk. It aims for a CY higher than the yield of short-term debt instruments and money market instruments.

MUTUAL FUND CUSTOMER SUITABILITY QUIZ ANSWERS

C. **Spencer Tax-Free Municipal Bond Fund** The Joneses are almost entirely invested in the stock market. As they approach retirement, they should shift some of their portfolio to bonds. Because they are in a high tax bracket, a municipal bond fund best meets their objectives of diversification and safety.

C. **Spencer Cash Reserve Fund** Jim and Sarah Davis are preparing to make a major purchase within the next six months. They require a highly liquid investment to keep their money safe for a short time. The money market fund best matches this objective.

B. **MacDonald Balanced Fund** Adam Garcia is a young investor who is at the beginning of his investment cycle. For other investors in his situation, an aggressive growth fund might help achieve maximum capital appreciation over a long-term time frame. However, Adam is risk averse and has not had any experience investing in the securities markets. A balanced fund is a good place to begin investing for moderate return and low volatility.

C. **XYZ Government Income Fund** Mark Blair requires maximum safety and current income. While all fixed-income funds aim to provide current income, the U.S. government bond fund offers the best combination of safety and a higher yield than a money market fund.

B. **MacDonald Stock Index Fund** Helen Wong requires a mutual fund that offers the potential for long-term capital growth. She believes money managers cannot consistently outperform the overall market; this indicates that an index fund that attempts to match the performance of the stock market is the most appropriate investment for her.

6. D. **MacDonald Investment-Grade Bond Fund** The Stouts' investment goal of providing for their children's education is about four years away. They cannot afford to take a risk that a downturn in the stock market will occur within that time. A safe alternative that also provides additional returns is the high-quality corporate bond fund.

7. C. **Laramie Equity Income Fund** The Longs are preparing for retirement. They want to maintain a comfortable standard of living, which means staying ahead of inflation. A combined fund that offers both current income and growth potential is the best choice for this couple.

8. D. **ATF Overseas Opportunities Fund** The Cains' substantial portfolio is diversified between equity and debt investments. However, to counteract the effects of the U.S. economy on their portfolio returns, they should invest a portion of their assets in the international stock fund.

9. C. **ATF Capital Appreciation Fund** The Coles require maximum capital appreciation. Their long-term time frame enables them to ride out the fluctuations of the stock market. The best investment for them is the stock market fund that concentrates solely on achieving long-term growth rather than on generating current income.

10. D. **ATF Biotechnology Fund** Liz Scott has a high net worth and substantial investment experience. She is capable of assuming the higher risk-and-return potential of a speculative investment such as the biotechnology sector fund.

COMMON ABBREVIATIONS

ABS asset-backed security

ADR/ADS American depositary receipt (share)

AGC Assured Guaranty Corporation

AIR assumed interest rate

AMBAC AMBAC Indemnity Corporation

ARS auction rate security

BA banker's acceptance

BD broker-dealer

BDC business development (growth) company

CAPM capital asset pricing model

CD certificate of deposit

CDO collateralized debt obligation

CEO chief executive officer

CMO collateralized mortgage obligation

CMV current market value

COA code of arbitration

COP Code of Procedure

CPI Consumer Price Index

CQS Consolidated Quotation System

CY current yield

DBCC District Business Conduct Committee

DEA designated examining authority

DJIA Dow Jones Industrial Average

DMM designated market maker

EE Series EE savings bonds

ELN equity-linked note

EPS earnings per share

ERISA Employee Retirement Income Security Act of 1974

ETF exchange-traded fund

FAC face-amount certificate

Fed Federal Reserve System

FDIC Federal Deposit Insurance Corporation

FGIC Financial Guaranty Insurance Company

FIFO first in, first out

FINRA Financial Industry Regulatory Authority

FMV fair market value

FNMA Federal National Mortgage Association

FOMC Federal Open Market Committee

FRB Federal Reserve Board

GDP gross domestic product

GNMA Government National Mortgage Association

GO general obligation

GOs general obligation bonds

HH Series HH savings bond

HSA health savings account

IDR/IDB industrial development revenue bond

IPO initial public offering

IRA individual retirement account

IRC Internal Revenue Code

IRS Internal Revenue Service

JTIC joint tenants in common

JTWROS joint tenants with right of survivorship

LIFO last in, first out

LOI letter of intent

MIG Moody's Investment Grade

MPT modern portfolio theory

MSRB Municipal Securities Rulemaking Board

NASAA North American Securities Administrators' Association

Nasdaq National Association of Securities Dealers Automated Quotation system

NAV net asset value

NHA New Housing Authority

NL no-load

NMS National Market System

NYSE New York Stock Exchange

OSJ office of supervisory jurisdiction

OTC over-the-counter

PAC planned (programed) amortization class

P/E price-to-earnings ratio

PHA Public Housing Authority

POP public offering price

PPN principal-protected note

REIT real estate investment trust

RR registered representative

SAI statement of additional information

SEC Securities and Exchange Commission

SEP simplified employee pension plan

SIPC Securities Investor Protection Corporation

SLMA Student Loan Marketing Association

SRO self-regulatory organization

STRIPS Separate Trading of Registered Interest and Principal of Securities

T+3 trade date plus three business days settlement

TAC targeted amortization class

TCPA Telephone Consumer Protection Act

TSA tax-sheltered annuity

UGMA/UTMA Uniform Gift (Transfers) to Minors Act

UIT unit investment trust

UPC Uniform Practice Code

VIX volatility market index

VL variable life insurance

VRDOS variable-rate demand obligations

YLD yield

YTC yield to call

YTM yield to maturity

ZR zero-coupon

CALCULATIONS

To Calculate...	Use Formula...
Dividend yield	$\frac{\text{Annual dividend}}{\text{Current market price}}$
Current yield	$\frac{\text{Annual interest}}{\text{Current market price}}$
Number of shares for conversion	$\frac{\text{Par value}}{\text{Conversion price}}$
Parity	$\frac{\text{Bond market value}}{\text{Number of shares}}$
Tax-free equivalent yield	Corporate rate × (100% – tax bracket)
Tax-equivalent yield	$\frac{\text{Municipal rate}}{\text{(100\% – tax bracket)}}$
NAV of mutual fund share	$\frac{\text{Fund NAV}}{\text{Number of shares outstanding}}$
Sales charge percentage	$\frac{\text{POP – NAV}}{\text{POP}}$
Public offering price (POP)	$\frac{\text{NAV per share}}{\text{(100\% – sales charge percentage)}}$
Dollar cost average	$\frac{\text{Total dollars invested}}{\text{Number of shares purchased}}$
Average market price	$\frac{\text{Share price total}}{\text{Number of investments}}$
Number of outstanding shares	Issued shares – treasury shares
Shareholders' equity	Assets – liabilities

GLOSSARY

acceptance ratio *See* placement ratio.

acceptance, waiver, and consent A form of plea bargaining under the Code of Procedure. FINRA's Enforcement Department brings disciplinary actions against a respondent and, if the respondent agrees, the proposed settlement is accepted, all rights to a hearing are waived, and the respondent consents to the penalty submitted.

account executive *See* registered representative.

accredited investor Any institution or individual meeting minimum requirements for the purchase of securities qualifying under the Regulation D registration exemption.

accretion of bond discount An accounting process whereby the initial cost of a bond purchased at a discount is increased annually to reflect the basis of the bond as it approaches maturity.

accrual accounting A method of accounting where ncome is reported when it is earned (instead of when the ayment is received) and expenses are reported when they re incurred (instead of when they are paid).

ccrued interest The interest that has accumulated ince the last interest payment, up to but not including he settlement date, and that is added to the contract price f a bond transaction. *See also* flat.

ccumulation stage The period during which ontributions are made to an annuity contract. *See also* ccumulation unit.

ccumulation unit An accounting measure used to etermine an annuitant's proportionate interest in the isurer's separate account during a variable annuity's ccumulation (deposit) stage. *See also* accumulation stage, nnuity unit, separate account.

cid-test ratio A measure of a corporation's liquidity, lculated by adding cash, cash equivalents, and accounts d notes receivable, but not inventory, and dividing the sult by total current liabilities. It is a more stringent test liquidity than current ratio. *See also* current ratio.

CT *See* Automated Confirmation Transaction Service.

ljusted (cost) basis Adjusted basis is used to mpute the gain or loss on the sale or other disposition the asset or security.

adjusted gross income (AGI) Gross income from all sources minus certain adjustments to income, such as deductible contributions to an IRA and net capital losses. It is the amount of income that will be subject to tax. *See* tax liability.

administrator (1) The official or agency administering the securities laws of a state. (2) A person authorized by a court of law to liquidate an intestate decedent's estate.

ADR *See* American Depositary Receipt.

advance refunding Refinancing an existing municipal bond issue before its maturity or call date by using money from the sale of a new bond issue. *See also* defeasance; refunding.

advance/decline line A technical analysis tool representing the total of the differences between advances and declines of security prices. The advance/decline line is considered the best indicator of market movement as a whole. *See also* breadth-of-market theory.

advertisement Any promotional material where the firm has little control over the type of individuals being exposed to the material.

affiliated person Anyone in a position to influence decisions made in a corporation, including officers, directors, principal stockholders, and members of their immediate families. Their shares are often referred to as *control stock*.

agency basis *See* agency transaction.

agency issue A debt security issued by an authorized agency of the federal government. Such issues are backed by the issuing agencies themselves, not by the full faith and credit of the U.S. government (except GNMA and Federal Import Export Bank issues). *See* government security.

agency transaction A transaction in which a broker-dealer acts for the accounts of others by buying or selling securities on behalf of customers. *Syn.* agency basis. *See also* agent; broker; principal transaction.

agent (1) An individual or firm that effects securities transactions for the accounts of others. (2) A securities salesperson who represents a broker-dealer or issuer when selling or trying to sell securities to the investing public; this individual is considered an agent whether he actually receives or simply solicits orders. *See* broker; broker-dealer; dealer; principal.

aggregate exercise price The strike price expressed in total dollars. The aggregate exercise price for a standard July 40 call contract is $4,000 (100 shares at $40 per share).

aggressive investment strategy A method of portfolio allocation and management aimed at achieving maximum return. Aggressive investors pursue aggressive policies, including margin trading, arbitrage, and option trading. *See also* balanced investment strategy, defensive investment strategy.

agreement among underwriters (AAU) The agreement that sets forth the terms under which each member of an underwriting syndicate will participate in a new issue offering and states the duties and responsibilities of the underwriting manager. *See* syndicate; underwriting manager.

agreement of limited partnership The contract that establishes guidelines for the operation of a direct participation program, including the roles of the general and limited partners.

AIR *See* assumed interest rate.

all-or-none order (AON) An order that instructs the firm to execute the entire order. Firm does not have to execute immediately.

all-or-none underwriting (AON) A form of best efforts underwriting in which the underwriter agrees that, if it is unable to sell all the shares (or a prescribed minimum), the issuer will cancel the offering.

alpha The risk-adjusted returns that a portfolio manager generates in excess of the risk-adjusted returns expected by the capital asset pricing model (CAPM).

alternative minimum tax (AMT) An alternative tax computation that adds certain tax preference items back into adjusted gross income. If the AMT is higher than the regular tax liability for the year, the regular tax and the amount by which the AMT exceeds the regular tax are paid. *See* tax preference item.

alternative order An order to execute either of two transactions (e.g., placing a sell limit [above the market] and a sell stop [below the market] on the same stock). If one order is executed, all other linked orders are canceled. *Syn.* either/or order, one cancels other order.

AMBAC Assurance Corporation (AMBAC) A corporation that offers insurance on the timely payment of interest and principal obligations of municipal securities.

American Depositary Receipt (ADR) Facilitate trading in foreign securities in the U.S. domestic markets. Sometimes these are shown as ADS (American Depositary Shares) and are similar to a GDR (Global Depositary Receipt), which is traded outside the United States.

amortization (1) The paying off of debt in regular installments over a period of time. (2) The ratable deduction of certain capitalized expenditures over a specified period of time.

amortization of bond premium An accounting process whereby the initial cost of a bond purchased at a premium is decreased to reflect the basis of the bond as it approaches maturity. *See also* accretion of bond discount.

annual compliance review An annual meeting that all registered representatives and principals must attend, the purpose being to review compliance issues.

annual return on investment (ROI) For example, the annual return on a bond investment, which equals the annual interest and either plus the prorated discount or minus the prorated premium.

annuitant A person who receives an annuity contract's distribution.

annuitize To change an annuity contract from the accumulation (pay-in) stage to the distribution (pay-out) stage.

annuity A contract between an insurance company and an individual. Upon annuitization, it guarantees lifetime income to the individual on whose life the contract is based in return for either a lump sum or a periodic payment to the insurance company.

annuity unit An accounting measure used to determine the amount of each payment during an annuity's distribution stage. *See also* accumulation unit; annuity; distribution stage.

anti-money laundering A program required to be instituted by all FINRA member firms under NASD Rule 3011. All personnel are to be trained to identify the different stages of money laundering and how to combat it.

AON *See* all or none order; all or none underwriting.

AP *See* associated person of a member.

appreciation The increase in value of an asset.

approved plan *See* qualified retirement plan.

arbitrage (1) The simultaneous purchase and sale of the same or related securities to take advantage of market inefficiency (a discrepancy in prices between markets). *See also* international arbitrage, market arbitrage, security arbitrage, special arbitrage account. (2) The difference between the interest paid on tax-exempt bonds and the interest earned by investing the proceeds in higher-yielding taxable securities. Federal law restricts arbitrage earnings in connection with tax-exempt bonds. *See* arbitrage rebate.

arbitrageur One who engages in arbitrage.

arbitration The arrangement whereby FINRA's Board of Arbitration or a designated arbitration association hears and settles disputes between members, allied members, member organizations, and their employees. Nonmembers in dispute with members or employees may submit voluntarily to arbitration. Once both parties agree to the process, there is no appeal. *See also* simplified arbitration.

ascending triangle On a technical analyst's trading activity chart, a pattern indicating that the market has started to move back up; considered to be a bullish indicator. *See also* descending triangle.

ask An indication by a trader or dealer of a willingness to sell a security or a commodity; the price at which an nvestor can buy a security. *Syn.* offer; POP.

ssessed value The value of a property, as appraised by taxing authority, for the purpose of levying taxes. Assessed alue may equal market value or a stipulated percentage of narket value. *See also* ad valorem tax.

ssessment An additional amount of capital that participant in a direct participation program may be alled upon to furnish beyond the subscription amount. ssessments may be mandatory or optional and must be alled within 12 months.

sset A balance sheet item expressing what a corporation wns.

sset allocation fund A mutual fund that splits its ivestment assets among stocks, bonds, and other vehicles, ith a view to provide a consistent return for the investor.

sset-backed security (ABS) One whose value and come payments are backed by the expected cash flow om a specific pool of underlying assets. Pooling the sets into financial instruments allows them to be sold to vestors more easily than selling them individually. This ocess is called securitization.

signee of record A person who has acquired a neficial interest in a limited partnership and whose terest has been recorded on the books of the partnership d is the subject of a written instrument of assignment.

assignment (1) A document accompanying, or part of a stock certificate signed by the person named on the certificate for the purpose of transferring the certificate's title to another person's name. (2) The act of identifying and notifying an account holder that an option held short in that account has been exercised by the option owner. *See also* stock power. (3) Transferring an investment advisory contract to another firm. This may not be done without written consent of the customer. A change in the majority interest in an investment advisory firm organized as a partnership is also considered assignment.

assignment Transferring an investment advisory contract to another firm. This may not be done without written consent of the customer. A change in the majority interest in an investment advisory firm organized as a partnership is also considered assignment.

associated person of a member (AP) An individual who solicits customers, orders, or funds on behalf of a futures commission merchant (FCM) and is controlled by that member or an introducing broker (IB).

assumed interest rate (AIR) (1) The net rate of investment return that must be credited to a variable life insurance policy to ensure that at all times, the variable death benefit equals the amount of the death benefit. The AIR forms the basis for projecting payments, but it is not guaranteed. (2) The rate that a variable annuity separate account must earn to keep annuity payments level. If the account earns more than the AIR, the next payment will increase; if it earns less, the next payment will decrease.

at the money The term used to describe an option when the underlying stock is trading precisely at the exercise price of the option. *See also* in the money; out of the money.

at-the-opening order An order that specifies it is to be executed at the opening of the market of trading in that security or else be canceled. The order will be executed at the opening price. *See also* market-on-close order.

auction market A market in which buyers enter competitive bids and sellers enter competitive offers simultaneously. The NYSE is an auction market. *Syn.* double auction market.

auction rate securities (ARS) Issued by municipalities, nonprofit hospitals, utilities, housing finance agencies, and universities, auction rate securities are long-term variable rate bonds tied to short-term interest rates.

audited financial statement A financial statement of a program, a corporation, or an issuer that has been examined and verified by an independent certified public accountant.

authorized stock The number of shares of stock that a corporation may legally issue. This number is stipulated in the corporation's state-approved charter and may be changed by a vote of the corporation's stockholders.

authorizing resolution The document enabling a municipal government to issue securities.

Automated Confirmation Transaction Service (ACT) Compares OTC trade information provided by market participants and submits locked-in trades for clearance and settlement. Also disseminates last sale information to the public. The FINRA/Nasdaq TRF operates on the ACT technology platform.

automatic exercise A procedure initiated by Options Clearing Corporation (OCC) to automatically exercise in-the-money options upon their expiration.

average A price at a midpoint among a number of prices. Technical analysts frequently use averages as market indicators. *See also* index.

average basis An accounting method used when an investor has made multiple purchases at different prices of the same security; the method averages the purchase prices to calculate an investor's cost basis in shares being liquidated. The difference between the average cost basis and the selling price determines the investor's tax liability.

BA *See* banker's acceptance.

BABs *See* Build America Bonds.

back away The failure of an over-the-counter market maker to honor a firm bid and asked price; this violates Conduct Rules. *Syn.* backing away.

back-end load A fee that is charged when mutual fund shares or variable annuity contracts are redeemed. It is typically found with Class B shares (and for one year with Class C shares). It declines annually, decreasing to zero over an extended holding period—up to eight years—as described in the prospectus. *Syn.* contingent-deferred sales load.

balance of payments (BOP) An international accounting record of all transactions made by one particular country with others during a certain time period; it compares the amount of foreign currency the country has taken in with the amount of its own currency it has paid out. *See also* balance of trade.

balance of trade The largest component of a country's balance of payments; it concerns the export and import of merchandise (not services). Debit items include imports, foreign aid, domestic spending abroad, and domestic investments abroad. Credit items include exports, foreign spending in the domestic economy, and foreign investments in the domestic economy. *See* balance of payments.

balance sheet A financial statement showing the assets, liabilities, and shareholder's equity at a particular moment.

balance sheet equation A formula stating that a corporation's assets equal the sum of its liabilities plus shareholders' equity.

balanced fund A mutual fund whose stated investment policy is to have, at all times, some portion of its investment assets in bonds and preferred stock, as well as in-common stock, in an attempt to provide both growth and income. *See also* mutual fund.

balanced investment strategy A method of portfolio allocation and management aimed at balancing risk and return.

balloon maturity A balloon maturity refers to a large number of an issuer's bonds that become due at the same time. Compare term bonds.

BAN *See* bond anticipation note.

bank guarantee letter The document supplied by a commercial bank in which the bank certifies that a put writer has sufficient funds on deposit at the bank to equal the aggregate exercise price of the put; this releases the option writer from the option margin requirement.

banker's acceptance (BA) A money market instrument used to finance international trade. A banker's acceptance is a time draft drawn on a bank by an importer or exporter of goods, and it represents the bank's conditional promise to pay the face amount of the note at maturity (normally less than three months).

bar chart A tool used by technical analysts to track the price movements of a commodity over several consecutive time periods. *See also* moving average chart; point-and-figure chart.

basis point A measure of a bond's yield, equal to 1/100 of 1% of a yield. A bond whose yield increases from 5.0% to 5.5% is said to increase by 50 basis points. A basis point is equal to 10 cents.

BD *See* broker-dealer.

bear An investor who acts on the belief that a security or the market is falling or is expected to fall. *See* bull.

ar market A market in which prices of a certain group securities are falling or are expected to fall. *See* bull ırket.

arer bond *See* coupon bond.

st efforts underwriting A securities underwriting which the underwriter acts as an agent for the issuer and ts forth its best efforts to sell as many shares as possible of ɔse available. The underwriter has no liability for unsold ıres, unlike in a firm commitment underwriting. *See also* derwriting, *see* firm commitment.

ta coefficient *See* beta.

d (1) An indication by an investor, a trader, or a dealer a willingness to buy a security or commodity; the price at ich an investor can sell to a broker-dealer. (2) The price which an investor can redeem shares of a mutual fund. also offer; public offering price; quotation.

d form A document, generally included with the tice of sale, to be completed by underwriters interested submitting a bid on a new issue of municipal securities be sold competitively. A bidding underwriter will state the bid form its proposed interest rate(s) for the issue d the price it would be willing to pay for the new issue ıbject to any conditions stated by the issuer in the notice sale), and may be asked to propose a structure for the w issue.

ind pool (1) A company that sells stock without ecifying how invested money will be spent. (2) A direct rticipation program that does not state in advance all the specific properties in which the general partners ll invest the partnership's money. At least 25% of the ɔceeds of the offering are kept in reserve for the purchase nonspecified properties. *Syn.* nonspecified property ɔgram.

ock trade A large trading order, defined as an order at consists of 10,000 or more shares of a given stock or at otal market value of $200,000 or more. *Syn.* block sale.

ue-chip stock The equity issues of financially stable, ll-established companies that have demonstrated their ility to pay dividends in both good and bad times.

ue-sky To register a securities offering in a particular ıte.

ue-sky laws The nickname for state regulations verning the securities industry.

ard of directors Individuals elected by stockholders establish corporate management policies. A board directors decides, among other issues, if and when vidends will be paid to stockholders.

bona fide quote An offer from a broker-dealer to buy or sell securities; it indicates a willingness to execute a trade under the terms and conditions accompanying the quote. *See* firm quote; nominal quote; subject quote; workout quote.

bond A legal obligation of an issuing company or government to repay the principal of a loan to bond investors at a specified future date. Corporate bonds are usually issued with a par or face value of $1,000, and municipal bonds with a par of $5,000, representing the amount of money borrowed. The issuer promises to pay a percentage of the par value as interest on the borrowed funds. The interest payment is stated on the face of the bond or its description at issue.

bond anticipation note (BAN) A short-term municipal debt security to be paid from the proceeds of long-term debt when it is issued.

bond attorney *See* bond counsel.

Bond Buyer indexes Indexes of yield levels of municipal bonds published daily by The Bond Buyer. The indexes are indicators of yields that would be offered on AA- and A-rated general obligation bonds with 20-year maturities and revenue bonds with 30-year maturities.

bond counsel An attorney retained by a municipal issuer to give an opinion concerning the legality and tax-exempt status of a municipal issue. *Syn.* bond attorney. *See* legal opinion of counsel.

bond fund A mutual fund whose investment objective is to provide stable income with a minimal capital risk. It invests in income-producing instruments that may include corporate, government, or municipal bonds.

bond interest coverage ratio An indication of the safety of a corporate bond. It measures the number of times by which earnings before interest and taxes exceeds annual interest on outstanding bonds. *Syn.* fixed charge coverage ratio; times fixed charges earned ratio; times interest earned ratio.

bond laddering A fixed income investment strategy that involves purchasing several smaller bonds, each with a different maturity date spread over months or years, rather than one larger bond maturing on a single date.

bond quote Quotes for corporate, municipal, and government bonds are percentages of the bonds' face values (usually $1,000). Corporate bonds are quoted in increments of 1/8. Government bonds are quoted in increments of 1/32. Municipal bonds may be quoted on a dollar basis or on a yield-to-maturity basis. *See* quotation; stock quote.

bond rating An evaluation of the possibility of a bond issuer's default, based on an analysis of the issuer's financial condition and likelihood of meeting all obligations. Standard & Poor's, Moody's Investors Service, and Fitch Investors Service, among others, provide bond rating services. Ratings of municipal bonds may be found on the EMMA System operated by the Municipal Securities Rulemaking Board.

bond ratio One of several tools used by bond analysts to assess the degree of safety offered by a corporation's bonds. It measures the percentage of the corporation's capitalization that is provided by long-term debt financing, calculated by dividing the total face value of the outstanding bonds by the total capitalization. *Syn.* debt ratio.

bond swap The sale of a bond and the simultaneous purchase of a different bond in a like amount. The technique is used to control tax liability, extend maturity, or update investment objectives. *Syn.* tax swap. Related item wash sale.

bond yield The annual rate of return on a bond investment. Types of yield include nominal yield, current yield, yield to maturity, and yield to call. *See* current yield, nominal yield.

book value per share A measure of the net worth of each share of common stock. It is calculated by subtracting intangible assets and preferred stock from total net worth, then dividing the result by the number of shares of common outstanding. *Syn.* net tangible assets per share.

book-entry security A security sold without a certificate. Evidence of ownership is maintained on records kept by a centralized service such as the Depository Trust Corporation. For example, the U.S. Treasury Department keeps records of purchasers of Treasury bills. Transfer of ownership is recorded by entering the change on the books or electronic files. *See also* coupon bond, registered, registered as to principal only.

branch office Any location identified to the public, by any means, as a place where a registered broker-dealer conducts business. *See* office of supervisory jurisdiction (OSJ); satellite office.

breadth-of-market theory A technical analysis theory that predicts the strength of the market according to the number of issues that advance or decline in a particular trading day. *See also* advance/decline line.

breakeven point The point at which gains equal losses.

breakout In technical analysis, the movement of a security's price through an established support or resistance level. *See also* resistance level; support level.

breakpoint The schedule of sales charge discounts a mutual fund offers for lump-sum or cumulative investments. Breakpoints are available to any person. Investment clubs or associations formed for the purpose [illegible] investing do not qualify for breakpoints.

breakpoint sale The sale of mutual fund shares in an amount just below the level at which the purchaser woul[illegible] qualify for reduced sales charges. This violates the Condu[illegible] Rules.

broad-based index An index designed to reflect the movement of the market as a whole. Examples include th[illegible] S&P 100, the S&P 500, the AMEX Major Market Index and the Value Line Composite Index.

broker (1) An individual or firm that charges a fee or commission for executing buy and sell orders submitted [illegible] a customer. (2) The role of a firm when it acts as an agent for a customer and charges the customer a commission fo[illegible] its services. *See also* agent; broker-dealer; dealer.

broker fail *See* fail to deliver.

broker-dealer Person or firm in the business of buyin[illegible] and selling securities. A firm may act as both broker (age[illegible] or dealer (principal) but not in the same transaction. Broker-dealers normally must register with the SEC, the appropriate SROs, and any state in which they do busine[illegible]

broker's broker (1) A municipal securities broker acting as an agent or riskless principal in the purchase or sale of securities for broker-dealers, sophisticated municip[illegible] securities professionals (SMMPs), and institutions when those market participants are seeking liquidity or to adjus[illegible] an inventory position. (2) A designated market maker executing orders for a commission house broker or anoth[illegible] brokerage firm. (3) A floor broker on an exchange or a broker-dealer in the over-the-counter market executing a trade as an agent for another broker.

broker's loan Money loaned to a brokerage firm by a commercial bank or other lending institution to finance customers' margin account debit balances. *See also* call loa[illegible] rehypothecation.

bucketing Accepting customer orders without executi[illegible] them promptly, thereby looking to fill the order later at a[illegible] improved price and showing the customer the price at the time the order was placed, then pocketing the difference. Bucketing is illegal.

Build America Bonds Issued by municipalities under the American Recovery and Reinvestment Act of 2009, Build America Bonds (BABs) make interest payments that are taxable to bondholders. Some types of BABs offer tax credits to the issuer (Tax Credit or Issuer BABs), and others offer tax credits to the bondholder (Direct Payment BABs). BABs are no longer issued, but those previously issued are actively traded.

bull An investor who believes that a security, a commodity, or the market overall is likely to rise. *See also* bear.

bull market A market where prices of a certain group of commodities or securities are rising or are expected to rise. *See also* bear market.

bulletin board *See* OTC Bulletin Board.

business cycle A predictable long-term pattern of alternating periods of economic growth and decline. The cycle passes through four stages: expansion, peak, contraction, and trough.

business day A day on which financial markets are open for trading. Saturdays, Sundays, and most legal holidays are not considered business days.

buy stop order An order to buy a security that is entered at a price above the current offering price and that is triggered when the market price touches or goes through the buy stop price.

buy-in A procedure that the buyer of a security follows when the seller fails to complete the contract (fails to deliver the security). The buyer closes the contract by buying the security in the open market (buy-in) and charges the account of the seller for transaction fees and any loss caused by changes in the markets (if any). *See* sell-out.

buyer's option A settlement contract that calls for delivery and payment according to a number of days specified by the buyer. *See* regular way; seller's option.

buying power The amount of securities a margin client can buy using the special memorandum account balance and without depositing additional equity. Buying power = 2 × SMA. For pattern day traders, buying power is 4 × maintenance margin excess.

calendar spread *See* horizontal spread.

call (1) An option contract giving the owner the right to buy a specified amount of an underlying security at a specified price within a specified time. (2) The act of exercising a call option. *See also* put.

call date The date, specified in the prospectus of every callable security, after which the security's issuer has the option to redeem the issue at par or at par plus a premium.

call feature *See* call provision.

call loan A collateralized loan given by a brokerage firm, having no maturity date, that may be called (terminated) at any time and has a fluctuating interest rate recomputed daily. The loan is payable on demand. If not called, the loan is automatically renewed for another day. *See also* broker's loan.

call loan rate The rate of interest a brokerage firm charges its margin account clients on their debit balances.

call price The price, usually a premium over par value, at which a bond or preferred stock may be redeemed at the discretion of the issuer.

call protection A provision in a bond indenture stating that the issue is noncallable for a certain period (e.g., 5 or 10 years) after the original issue date. *See* call provision.

call provision The written agreement between an issuer and its bondholders or preferred stockholders giving the issuer the option to redeem the securities at a specified price before maturity and under certain conditions. *Syn.* call feature.

call risk The potential for a bond to be called before maturity, leaving the investor without the bond's current income. Because this is more likely to occur during times of falling interest rates, the investor may not be able to reinvest the principal at a comparable rate of return. This risk applies to callable preferred shares, as well.

call spread An option investor's position in which the investor buys a call on a security and writes a call on the same security but with a different expiration date, exercise price (strike), or both.

capital Accumulated money or goods available for use in producing more money or goods.

capital appreciation A rise in the market price of an asset.

capital asset All tangible property, including securities, real estate, and other property, held for the long term.

capital asset pricing model (CAPM) A securities market investment theory that attempts to derive the expected return on an asset on the basis of the asset's systematic risk.

capital contribution The amount of a participant's investment in a direct participation program, not including units purchased by the sponsors.

capital gain The profit realized when a capital asset is sold for a price higher than the purchase price. *See* also capital loss; long-term gain.

capital loss The loss incurred when a capital asset is sold for a price lower than the purchase price. *See* capital gain; long-term loss.

capital market The segment of the securities market that deals in instruments with more than one year to maturity—that is, long-term debt and equity securities.

capital risk The potential for an investor to lose all money invested owing to circumstances unrelated to the financial strength of the issuer. For example, derivative instruments such as options carry risk independent of the changing value of the underlying securities.

capital stock All of a corporation's outstanding preferred and common stock, listed at par value.

capital structure The composition of long-term funds (equity and debt) a corporation has as a source for financing. *See* capitalization.

capital surplus *See* paid-in capital.

capitalization (1) The sum of a corporation's long-term debt, stock, and surpluses. *Syn.* invested capital. *See* capital structure. (2) The number of outstanding shares multiplied by share price. (3) The costs to acquire an asset expensed over the life of the asset.

capitalization ratios Indicators of a company's capital structure (e.g. debt-equity ratio), long-term debt-to-capitalization ratio, and total debt-to-capitalization ratio.

capped index option A type of index option issued with a capped price at a set interval above the strike price (for a call) or below the strike price (for a put). The option is automatically exercised once the underlying index reaches the capped price. *See also*: index option.

capping An illegal form of market manipulation that attempts to keep the price of a subject security from rising. It is generally used by those with a short position. *See* pegging.

carried interest A sharing arrangement in an oil and gas direct participation program whereby the general partner shares the tangible drilling costs with the limited partners but pays no part of the intangible drilling costs. *See also* sharing arrangement.

cash account An account in which the customer is required by the Fed's Regulation T to pay, in full, for securities purchased no later than two days after the standard payment period set by the Uniform Practice Code. *Syn.* special cash account. *See also* margin account; Regulation T.

cash assets ratio A test of liquidity, calculated by dividing the sum of cash and cash equivalents by total current liabilities. *See also* acid-test ratio; current ratio.

cash dividend Money paid to a corporation's stockholders out of the corporation's current earnings or accumulated profits. The board of directors must declare all dividends.

cash equivalent A security that can be readily converted into cash. Examples include Treasury bills, certificates of deposit, and money market instruments and funds.

cash flow The money received by a business minus the money paid out. Cash flow is also equal to net income plus depreciation or depletion.

cash market Transactions between buyers and sellers of commodities that entail immediate delivery of and payment for a physical commodity. *Syn.* cash-and-carry market; spot market.

cash trade *See* cash transaction.

cash transaction A settlement contract that calls for delivery and payment on the same day the trade is executed payment is due by 2:30 p.m. EST (or within 30 minutes of the trade if made after 2:00 p.m. EST). *Syn.* cash trad; cash settlement. *See also* regular way; settlement date.

catastrophe call The redemption of a bond by an issuer owing to disaster (e.g., a power plant built with proceeds from an issue is destroyed by a hurricane). *See* mandatory call; partial call.

certificate of accrual on Treasury securities (CATS) A zero-coupon bond issued by brokerage firms and collateralized by Treasury securities. Obsolete. *See also*: Treasury receipt.

certificate of deposit (CD) A debt instrument issued by a bank that pays a fixed interest rate over a specific time period. CDs are insured up to $250,000 by the FDIC. *See* negotiable certificate of deposit.

chartist A securities analyst who uses charts and graphs of the past price movements of a security to predict its future movements. *Syn.* technician. *See* technical analysis.

CHB *See* commission house broker.

Chicago Board Options Exchange (CBOE) The first nationally recognized securities exchange listing and trading options. The self-regulatory organization with jurisdiction over all writing and trading of standardized options and related contracts listed on that exchange.

Chicago Stock Exchange (CHX) A nationally recognized stock exchange that provides a listed market for smaller businesses and new enterprises. The CHX was acquired by the Intercontinental Exchange in 2018.

churning Excessive trading in a customer's account with the view to generate commissions. *Syn.* overtrading.

class Options of the same type (i.e., all calls or all puts) on the same underlying security. *See also* series; type.

Class A share (1) A class of mutual fund shares issued with a front-end sales load. (2) Shares of a company that have differing characteristics from other classes of stock (e.g., Class A shares in a company offering multiple share classes may offer super voting privileges of many times the number of votes Class B shares may offer).

Class B share A class of mutual fund shares issued with a back-end load. A mutual fund offers different classes of shares to allow investors to choose the type of sales charge they will pay. *See* also back-end load; Class A share; Class C share.

lass C share A class of mutual fund shares issued with a evel load. A mutual fund offers different classes of shares to llow investors to choose the type of sales charge they will ay. *See* also Class A share; Class B share.

lass D share A class of mutual fund shares issued with oth a level load and a back-end load. A mutual fund offers ifferent classes of shares to allow investors to choose the ype of sales charge they will pay. *See also* back-end load; lass A share; Class B share; Class C share; level load.

lassical economics The theory that maximum conomic benefit will be achieved if government does not ttempt to influence the economy (i.e., if businesses are lowed to seek profitable opportunities as they see fit).

earing agency An intermediary between the buy d sell sides in a securities transaction that receives and elivers payments and securities. Any organization that fills is function, including a securities depository [such as the ational Securities Clearing Corporation (NSCC)] but not cluding a Federal Reserve Bank, is considered a clearing ency.

earing broker-dealer A broker-dealer that clears its vn trades as well as those of introducing (correspondent) okers. A clearing broker-dealer can hold customers' curities and cash. *Syn.* carrying broker.

CLN *See* construction loan note.

close (1) The price of the last transaction for a particular commodity or commodity option on a particular day. (2) The midprice of a closing trading range. *See also* closing range.

closed-end covenant A provision of a bond issue's trust indenture stating that any additional bonds secured by the same assets must have a subordinated claim to those assets. *See also* junior lien debt; open-end covenant.

closed-end management company An investment company that issues a fixed number of shares in an actively managed portfolio of securities. The shares may be of several classes, and they are traded in the secondary marketplace, either on an exchange or over the counter. The market price of the shares is determined by supply and demand. *Syn.* publicly traded fund.

closing purchase An options (or futures) transaction in which the seller buys back an option in the same series; the two transactions effectively cancel each other out, and the position is liquidated. *See* opening purchase.

closing range The relatively narrow range of prices at which transactions take place in the final minutes of the trading day. *See also* close.

closing sale An options transaction in which the buyer sells an option in the same series; the two transactions effectively cancel each other out, and the position is liquidated. *See also* closing purchase; opening sale.

CMO *See* collateralized mortgage obligation.

CMV *See* current market value.

COD Type of securities transaction in which the recipient makes payment at the time of delivery, usually in electronic form, check, or cash. Cash on delivery in modern terms means collect on delivery. *See* RVP vs. DVP.

Code of Arbitration Procedure FINRA's formal method of handling securities-related disputes or clearing controversies between members, public customers, clearing corporations, or clearing banks. Any claim, dispute, or controversy between member firms or associated persons is required to be submitted to arbitration. The MSRB has no arbitration rules except to say its members are subject to FINRA's Code of Arbitration.

Code of Procedure (COP) FINRA's formal procedure for handling trade practice complaints involving violations of the Member Conduct Rules. FINRA's Department of Enforcement is the first body to hear and judge complaints. Appeals and review of Department of Enforcement decisions are handled by the National Adjudicatory Council.

coincident indicator A measurable economic factor that varies directly and simultaneously with the business cycle, thus indicating the current state of the economy. Examples include nonagricultural employment, personal income, and industrial production. *See* lagging indicator; leading indicator.

collateral Certain assets set aside and pledged to a lender for the duration of a loan. If the borrower fails to meet obligations to pay principal or interest, the lender has claim to the assets.

collateral trust bond A secured bond backed by stocks or bonds of another issuer. The collateral is held by a trustee for safekeeping. *Syn.* collateral trust certificate.

collateral trust certificate *See* collateral trust bond.

collateralized mortgage obligation (CMO) A mortgage-backed corporate security. Unlike pass-through obligations issued by FNMA and GNMA, its yield is not guaranteed, and it does not have the federal government's backing. These issues attempt to return interest and principal at a predetermined rate.

collect on delivery (COD) *See* delivery versus payment.

collection ratio (1) For corporations, a rough measure of the length of time accounts receivable have been outstanding, calculated by multiplying the receivables by 360 and dividing the result by net sales. (2) For municipal bonds, a means of detecting deteriorating credit conditions; it is calculated by dividing taxes collected by taxes assessed.

combination a blanket term for a number of options strategies involving a put and a call on the same stock at different strike prices, expirations, or both.

combination fund An equity mutual fund that attempts to combine the objectives of growth and current yield by dividing its portfolio between companies that show long-term growth potential and companies that pay high dividends.

combination privilege A benefit offered by a mutual fund whereby the investor may qualify for a sales charge breakpoint by combining separate investments in two or more mutual funds in the same family of funds.

combined account A customer account that has long and short margin positions in different securities. *Syn.* mixed account.

combined distribution *See* split offering.

commercial bank A lending institution in the business of accepting deposits and making business loans. Commercial banks may not underwrite corporate securities or most municipal bonds. *See also* investment banker.

commercial paper (CP) A short-term, unsecured debt instrument primarily issued by corporations and banks, typically for the funding of short-term liabilities such as payrolls, accounts payable, and inventories and normally priced at a discount and redeemed at face value. Maturities are 270 days or less.

commingling (1) The combining by a brokerage firm of one customer's securities with another customer's securities and pledging them as joint collateral for a bank loan; unless authorized by the customers, this violates SEC Rule 15c2-1. (2) The combining by a brokerage firm of customer securities with firm securities and pledging them as joint collateral for a bank loan; this practice is prohibited. *See also* cross lien; segregation.

commission A service charge assessed by an agent in return for arranging the purchase or sale of a security. A commission must be fair and reasonable, considering all the relevant factors of the transaction. *Syn.* sales charge.

commission house broker (CHB) A member of an exchange who is eligible to execute orders for customers of a member firm on the floor of the exchange. *Syn.* floor broker.

commissioner The state official with jurisdiction over insurance transactions and licensure.

Committee on Uniform Securities Identification Procedures (CUSIP) A committee that assigns identification numbers and codes to all securities, to be used when recording all buy and sell orders. Each broker-dealer who acquires a new issue of municipal securities, or financial advisor in a competitive offering, must apply for a CUSIP number(s) to be applied to the applicable bonds.

common stock A security that represents ownership in a corporation. Holders of common stock exercise control by electing a board of directors and voting on corporate policy. *See also* equity; preferred stock.

common stock ratio A measurement of the percentage of the corporation's total capitalization that is contributed by the common stockholders. It is calculated by adding the par value, the capital in excess of par, and the retained earnings, and then dividing the result by the total capitalization. *See also* bond ratio.

communications with the public As defined by FINRA, there are three categories of communications: retail communications, correspondence, and institutional communications. *See* retail communications, correspondence, and institutional communications.

competitive bid underwriting A firm commitment underwriting in which rival syndicates submit sealed bids for underwriting the issue. Competitive bidding is often used to select the underwriters for issues of general obligation municipal bonds and may be required by law in some states. *See also* negotiated underwriting.

compliance department The department within a brokerage firm that over sees the firm's compliance with all applicable laws, rules, and regulations of federal and state regulators and its designated examining authority such as FINRA, NFA, MSRB, et cetera.

Composite Average *See* Dow Jones Composite Average.

concession The amount of payment the selling broker-dealer retains from the sale of a newly issued security.

Conduct Rules Rules written to ensure that FINRA member firms and their representatives follow just and equitable principles of trade. The rules complement and support the Securities Act of 1933, the Securities Exchange Act of 1934, and all other securities laws.

conduit theory A means for an investment company to avoid taxation on net investment income distributed to shareholders. If a mutual fund acts as a conduit for the distribution of net investment income, it may qualify as a regulated investment company and be taxed only on the income the fund retains. *Syn.* pipeline theory.

confidence theory A technical analysis theory that measures the willingness of investors to take risks by comparing the yields on high-grade bonds to the yields on lower rated, more speculative debt securities.

confirmation (securities trade) Written notification disclosing details of a customer securities transaction. It is used to verify that trades were carried out according to instructions. It may be mailed or paperless, as the customer wishes. It must be sent on or before the completion of the transaction.

congestion (futures) A situation where shorts are unable to find an adequate supply of longs willing to liquidate or new sellers willing to enter the market, except at markedly higher prices.

Consolidated Quotation System (CQS) A quotation system only providing last-sale reporting service for exchange-listed equity securities.

consolidation The technical analysis term for a narrowing of the trading range for a commodity or security that may be interpreted as a mark indecisiveness.

constant dollar plan A formula method of investing that attempts to maintain a fixed dollar amount, rather than ratio, in a specific asset class. Periodically, the account is reviewed, and the specified asset class is either sold or purchased to get to the fixed dollar level.

constant ratio plan A formula method of investing that contemplates maintaining a fixed ratio, rather than dollar amount, between specific asset classes in the portfolio. Periodically, the account is reviewed, and the specified asset class is either sold or purchased to get to the fixed ratio level.

construction loan note (CLN) A short-term municipal debt security that provides interim financing for new projects.

Consumer Price Index (CPI) A measure of price changes in a "market basket" of consumer goods and services used to identify periods of inflation or deflation.

consumption A term used by Keynesian economists to refer to the purchase by household units of newly produced goods and services.

contemporaneous trader A person who enters a trade at or near the same time and in the same security as a person who has inside information. The contemporaneous trader may bring suit against the inside trader. *See also* Insider Trading and Securities Fraud Enforcement Act of 1988.

contingent deferred sales load *See* back-end load.

contingent order An order that is conditional upon the execution of a previous order and that will be executed only after the first order is filled.

contra-broker The broker on the buy side of a sell order or on the sell side of a buy order.

contractionary policy A monetary policy that decreases the money supply, usually with the intention of raising interest rates and combating inflation.

control (controlling, controlled by, under common control with) The power to direct or affect the direction of the management and policies of a company, whether through the ownership of voting securities, by contract, or otherwise. Control is presumed to exist if a person, directly or indirectly, owns, controls, holds with the power to vote, or holds proxies representing more than 10% of a company's voting securities.

control person (1) A director, officer, or other affiliate of an issuer. (2) A stockholder who owns at least 10% of any class of a corporation's outstanding voting securities. *See also* affiliate; insider.

control security Any security owned by a director, officer, or other affiliate of the issuer or by a stockholder who owns at least 10% of any class of a corporation's voting securities. Who owns a security, not the security itself, determines whether it is a control security. *See also* Rule 144.

conversion parity Two securities—one of which can be converted into the other—of equal dollar value. A convertible security holder can calculate parity to help decide whether converting would lead to gain or loss.

conversion price The dollar amount of a convertible security's par value that is exchangeable for one share of the issuer's common stock.

conversion privilege A feature the issuer adds to a corporate debt security that allows the holder to change the security into shares of the issuer's common stock. This makes the security attractive to investors and, therefore, more marketable. *See also* convertible bond; convertible preferred stock.

conversion rate *See* conversion ratio.

conversion ratio The number of shares of common stock per par value amount that a holder would receive following a conversion of a convertible bond or preferred share. *Syn.* conversion rate.

conversion value The total market value of common stock into which a corporate debt instrument is convertible.

convertible bond A corporate debt security, such as a bond or debenture, that is exchangeable for the equity securities of the issuing corporation at a specified price or rate.

convertible preferred stock An equity security that may be exchanged for common stock at specified prices or rates. Dividends may be cumulative or noncumulative. *See also* cumulative preferred stock; noncumulative preferred stock; preferred stock.

cooling-off period A waiting period between a registration statement's filing date with the SEC and the registration effective date. In practice, the period varies in length. *Syn.* Waiting period.

COP *See* Code of Procedure.

corporate account An account held in a corporation's name specifying which officers are authorized to trade in the account. A corporation must provide a copy of its charter and bylaws authorizing a margin account.

corporate bond A long-term debt security issued by a corporation to finance its capital improvements and operations.

corporation A form of business organization in which its total worth is divided into shares of common stock, with each share representing a unit of ownership. A corporation is characterized by a continuous life span and its owners' limited liability.

correspondence FINRA defines this category of communications with the public as any written (including electronic) communication that is distributed or made available to 25 or fewer retail investors within any 30-calendar-day period.

cost basis The price paid for an asset, including any commissions or fees, used to calculate capital gains or losses when the asset is sold. Also includes any reinvested distributions.

cost depletion A method of calculating tax deductions for investments in mineral, oil, or gas resources. The cost of the mineral-, oil- or gas-producing property is returned to the investor over the property's life by an annual deduction that takes into account the number of known recoverable units of mineral, oil, or gas to arrive at a cost-per-unit figure.

coterminous A term used to describe municipal entities that share the same boundaries. For example, a municipality's school district and fire district may issue debt separately, although the debt is backed by revenues from the same taxpayers. *See also* overlapping debt.

coupon bond A debt obligation with coupons representing semiannual interest payments attached; the coupons are submitted to the trustee by the holder to receive the interest payments. No record of the purchaser is kept by the issuer, and the purchaser's name is not printed on the certificate. Since 1983, federally tax-advantaged bonds may not be issued in bearer form, with the exception of obligations maturing in a year or less. *Syn.* bearer bond. *See also* book-entry security; registered; registered as to principal only.

coupon yield *See* nominal yield.

covenant A promise made to bondholders found in a debt issue's trust indenture that identifies bondholders' rights and other provisions. Examples include rate covenants that establish a minimum revenue coverage for a bond; insurance covenants that require insurance on a project; and maintenance covenants that require maintenance on a facility constructed by the proceeds of a bond issue.

coverage ratio A measure of the safety of a bond issue, based on how many times earnings (EBIT) cover debt service plus operating and maintenance expenses for a specific period.

covered call writer An investor who sells a call option while owning the underlying security or some other asset that guarantees the ability to deliver if the call is exercised.

covered put writer An investor who sells a put option while owning an asset that guarantees the ability to pay if the put is exercised (e.g., cash in the account).

CPI *See* Consumer Price Index.

CQS *See* Consolidated Quotation System.

CR Credit record. *See* credit balance.

credit agreement A component of a customer's margin account agreement, outlining the conditions of the credit arrangement between the brokerage firm and customer.

credit balance (CR) The amount of money remaining in a customer's account after all commitments have been paid in full. *Syn.* credit record; credit register. *See also* debit balance.

credit department *See* margin department.

credit risk The degree of probability that the issuer of a debt security will default in the payment of either principal or interest. Securities issued by the U.S. government are considered to have little credit risk. *Syn.* default risk; financial risk. *See* Moody's; Standard & Poor's; Fitch Ratings.

creditor Any broker or dealer, member of a national securities exchange, or person associated with a broker-dealer involved in extending credit to customers.

rossed market The situation created when one market naker bids for a stock at a price higher than another market naker is asking for the same stock, or when one market naker enters an ask price to sell a stock at a price lower han another market maker's bid price to buy the same ock. This violates the Conduct Rules. *See also* locked narket.

rossover point The point at which a limited artnership begins to show a negative cash flow with a xable income. *See also* phantom income.

TR *See* currency transaction report.

um rights A term describing stock trading with rights. erived from the Latin cum, meaning, with. *See also* rights; -rights.

umulative preferred stock An equity security that fers the holder any unpaid dividends in arrears. These vidends accumulate and must be paid to the cumulative eferred stockholder before any dividends may be paid to e common stockholders.

cumulative voting A voting procedure that permits stockholders to either cast all of their votes for any one candidate or to cast their total number of votes in any proportion they choose. This results in greater representation for minority stockholders.

currency transaction report (CTR) A report filed by financial institutions to the IRS for deposits of any currency of more than $10,000 on a single day.

current assets Cash and other assets that may be converted into cash within the next 12 months. Examples include such liquid items as cash and equivalents (T-bills), accounts receivable, inventory, and prepaid expenses.

current liabilities A corporation's debt obligations due for payment within the next 12 months. Examples include accounts payable, accrued wages payable, and current long-term debt.

current market value (CMV) The worth of the securities in an account. The market value of listed securities is based on the closing prices on the previous business day. *Syn.* long market value.

current ratio A measure of a corporation's liquidity—that is, its ability to transfer assets into cash to meet current short-term obligations. It is calculated by dividing total current assets by total current liabilities. *Syn.* working capital ratio.

current yield The annual rate of return on a security, calculated by dividing the interest or dividends paid by the security's current market price. *See also* bond yield.

CUSIP Committee on Uniform Securities Identification Procedures. A CUSIP number is a unique alphanumeric code assigned to that specific security by the CUSIP Global Services. The CUSIP number is used to expedite and reduce the risks associated with timely clearance and settlement.

custodial account An account in which a custodian enters trades on behalf of the beneficial owner, who is often a minor. A custodian cannot delegate away fiduciary responsibility but can grant trading authority and investment decisions to a qualified third party.

custodian An institution or person responsible for making all investment, management, and distribution decisions in an account maintained in the best interests of another. For example, mutual funds have custodians responsible for safeguarding certificates and performing clerical duties.

customer Any person who opens an account with a broker-dealer. A customer may be classified in terms of account ownership, trading authorization, payment method, or types of securities traded.

customer agreement (margin agreement) A document that a customer must sign when opening a margin account with a broker-dealer. It allows the firm to liquidate all or a portion of the account if the customer fails to meet a margin call.

customer ledger The accounting record that lists separately all customer cash and margin accounts carried by a firm. *See also* general ledger; stock record.

customer account statement A document showing a customer's trading activity, positions, and account balance. The SEC requires that customer statements be sent at least quarterly.

cyclical industry A fundamental analysis term for an industry that is sensitive to the business cycle and price changes. Most cyclical industries produce durable goods, such as raw materials and heavy equipment.

dated date The date on which interest on a new bond issue begins to accrue—usually the issue date, although the bonds may be delivered at a later date.

day order An order that is valid only until the close of trading on the day it is entered. If it is not executed by the close of trading, it is canceled.

day trader A trader in securities or commodities who opens all positions after the opening of the market and offsets or closes out all positions before the close of the market on the same day.

dealer (1) An individual or firm engaged in the business of buying and selling securities for its own account, either directly or through a broker. (2) The role of a firm when it acts as a principal and charges the customer a markup or markdown. *Syn.* principal. *See also* broker; broker-dealer.

dealer paper Short-term, unsecured promissory notes that the issuer sells through a dealer rather than directly to the public.

debenture A debt obligation backed by the issuing corporation's general credit. *Syn.* unsecured bond.

debit balance (DR) The amount of money a customer owes a brokerage firm. *Syn.* debit record; debit register. *See* credit balance.

debit spread An option strategy where the premiums paid for buying the long options are more than the premiums received for the short options—a net debit to the customer's account. A debit call spread is bullish, and a debit put spread is bearish.

debt financing Raising money for working capital or capital expenditures by selling bonds, bills, or notes to individual or institutional investors.

debt per capita *See* net debt per capita.

debt ratio *See* bond ratio.

debt security A security representing a loan by an investor to an issuer such as a corporation, municipality, the federal government, or a federal agency.

debt service The schedule for repayment of interest and principal (or the scheduled sinking fund contribution) on an outstanding debt. *See also* sinking fund.

debt service ratio An indication of the ability of an issuer to meet principal and interest payments on bonds.

debt service reserve fund The account that holds enough money to pay one year's debt service on a municipal revenue bond. *See also* flow of funds.

debt trend A method of tracking whether certain municipal debt ratios are rising or falling in order to predict a municipality's or community's financial position in the coming years.

debt-to-equity ratio The ratio of total long-term debt to total stockholders' equity. It is used to measure leverage.

declaration date The date on which a corporation announces an upcoming dividend's amount, payment date, and record date.

decreasing debt service A schedule for debt repayment whereby the issuer pays principal in installments of equal size over the life of the issue. Therefore, the amount of interest due decreases, and the amount of each payment becomes smaller over time. *See also* level debt service.

deduction An item or expenditure subtracted from adjusted gross income to reduce the amount of income subject to tax.

default (1) The failure to pay interest or principal promptly when due. (2) The failure to perform on a future contract as required by an exchange.

default risk *See* credit risk.

defeasance The termination of a debt obligation. A corporation or municipality removes debt from its balance sheet by issuing a new debt issue and setting funds aside to call in the older debt in government securities by creating a trust that generates enough cash flow to provide for the payment of interest and principal. *See also* advance refunding; SLGS.

defensive industry A fundamental analysis term for an industry that is relatively unaffected by the business cycle. Most defensive industries produce nondurable goods for which demand remains steady throughout the business cycle. Examples of this include the food industry and utilities.

defensive investment strategy A method of portfolio allocation and management aimed at minimizing the risk of losing principal. Defensive investors place a high percentage of their investable assets in bonds, cash equivalents, and stocks that are less volatile than average.

deferred annuity An annuity contract that delays payment of income, installments, or a lump sum until the investor elects to receive it. *See also* annuity.

deferred compensation plan A nonqualified retirement plan whereby the employee defers receiving current compensation in favor of a larger payout at retirement (or in the case of disability or death).

deficiency letter The SEC's notification of additions or corrections that a prospective issuer must make to a registration statement before the SEC will clear the offering for distribution. *Syn.* bedbug letter.

defined benefit plan A qualified retirement plan that specifies the total amount of money that the employee will receive at retirement.

lefined contribution plan A qualified retirement plan hat specifies the amount of money that the employer will ontribute annually to the plan.

leflation A persistent and measurable fall in the general evel of prices. *See also* inflation.

lelivery A change in ownership or control of a security n exchange for cash. Delivery takes place on the settlement ate.

elivery vs. payment (DVP) A transaction settlement rocedure in which securities are delivered to the buying stitution's bank in exchange for payment of the amount ue. *Syn.* RVP (receipt vs. payment); collect on delivery COD).

emand A consumer's desire and willingness to pay for a od or service. *See also* supply.

emand deposit A sum of money left with a bank r borrowed from a bank and left on deposit) that the epositing customer has the right to withdraw at any time.

emand-pull inflation An excessive money supply that creases the demand for a limited supply of goods that is lieved to result in inflation. *See* Keynesian

depletion A tax deduction that compensates a business for the decreasing supply of the natural resource that provides its income (oil, gas, coal, gold, or other nonrenewable resource). *See also* cost depletion; percentage depletion.

depreciation (1) A tax deduction that compensates a business for the cost of certain tangible assets. (2) A decrease in the value of a particular currency relative to other currencies.

depreciation expense A bookkeeping entry of a noncash expense charged against earnings to recover the cost of an asset over its useful life.

depression A prolonged period of general economic decline. Specifically, the GDP declines for at least six quarters in a row and is accompanied by high unemployment.

derivative An investment vehicle, the value of which is based on the value of another security. Futures, forwards, swaps, and options are among the most common types of derivatives. Derivatives are generally used by institutional investors to increase overall portfolio return or hedge portfolio risk.

descending triangle On a technical analyst's trading activity chart, a pattern indicating that the market has started to fall; considered to be a bearish indicator. *See also* ascending triangle.

designated market maker (DMM) A registered trader that is obligated to maintain a fair and orderly market for specific securities assigned to the firm. Formerly known as specialists, they provide NBBO quotes, facilitate liquidity, open and close securities and furnish trading feedback to brokers.

designated order In a municipal bond underwriting, a customer order that is submitted by one syndicate member but specifies more than one member to receive a percentage of the takedown. The size of the order establishes its priority for subscription to an issue. *See also* group net order; member-at-the-takedown order; presale order.

devaluation A substantial fall in the value of a currency as compared to the value of gold or the value of another country's currency. *See also* revaluation.

developmental drilling program A limited partnership that drills for oil, gas, or minerals in areas of proven reserves or near existing fields. *See also* exploratory drilling program; income program; step-out well.

diagonal spread An option position established by the simultaneous purchase and sale of options of the same class but with different exercise prices and expiration dates. *See also* spread.

dilution A reduction in earnings per share of common stock. Dilution occurs through the issuance of additional shares of common stock and the conversion of convertible securities.

direct debt The total of a municipality's general obligation bonds, short-term notes, and revenue debt.

direct paper Commercial paper sold directly to the public without the use of a dealer.

direct participation program (DPP) A business organized so as to pass through all income, gains, losses, and tax benefits to its owners (partners), the investors; the business may be structured as a limited partnership. Examples include oil and gas programs, real estate programs, agricultural programs, motion pictures, and cattle programs. An interest in a DPP is a security. *Syn.* program.

discount The difference between the lower price paid for a security and the security's face amount at issue. *See also* premium.

discount bond A bond that sells at a lower price than its face value. *See also* par value; premium bond.

discount rate The interest rate charged by the 12 Federal Reserve Banks for short-term loans made to member banks.

discretion The authority given to someone other than an account's beneficial owner to make investment decisions for the account. *See also* limited power of attorney.

discretionary account An account in which the principal (beneficial owner) has given the registered representative authority to enter transactions at the representative's discretion. The registered representative may, if so directed by the customer, use the discretion about price (buy or sell), time, and choice of securities (bought or sold).

disintermediation The flow of money from low-yielding accounts in traditional savings institutions to higher yielding investments. Typically, this occurs when the Fed tightens the money supply and interest rates rise.

disposable income The sum that people divide between spending and personal savings. *See also* personal income.

disproportionate sharing A sharing arrangement whereby the sponsor in an oil and gas direct participation program pays a portion of the program's costs but receives a disproportionately higher percentage of its revenues. *See also* sharing arrangement.

distribution Any cash or other property distributed to shareholders or general partners that arises from their interests in the business, investment company, or partnership.

distribution stage The period during which an individual receives distributions from an annuity account. *Syn.* payout stage. *See also*: accumulation stage; accumulation unit.

diversification A risk management technique that mixes a wide variety of investments within a portfolio, thus minimizing the impact of any one security on overall portfolio performance.

diversified common stock fund A mutual fund that invests its assets in a wide range of common stocks. The fund's objectives may be growth, income, or a combination of both. *See also* growth fund; mutual fund.

diversified management company As defined by the Investment Company Act of 1940, a management company that meets certain standards for percentage of assets invested. These companies use diversification to manage risk. *See also* management company; nondiversified management company; 75-5-10 test.

dividend A distribution of the earnings of a corporation. Dividends may be in the form of cash, stock, or property. All dividends must be declared by the board of directors. *See also* cash dividend; stock dividend.

dividend department The department within a brokerage firm that is responsible for crediting client accounts with dividends and interest payments on client securities held in the firm's name.

dividend disbursing agent (DDA) The person responsible for making the required dividend distributions to the broker-dealer's dividend department.

dividend exclusion rule An IRS provision that permit a corporation to exclude from its taxable income 50% of dividends received from domestic preferred and common stocks.

dividend payout ratio A measure of a corporation's policy of paying cash dividends, calculated by dividing the dividends paid on common stock by the net income available for common stockholders. The ratio is the complement of the retained earnings ratio.

dividend yield The annual rate of return on a common or preferred stock investment. The yield is calculated by dividing the annual dividend by the stock's purchase price. *See also* current yield; dividend.

dividends per share The dollar amount of cash dividends paid on each common share during one year.

DJIA *See* Dow Jones Industrial Average.

DK *See* don't know.

DNR *See* do not reduce order.

do not reduce order (DNR) An order that stipulates that the limit or stop price should not be reduced in response to a stock price adjustment due to a cash dividend.

doctrine of mutual reciprocity The agreement that established the federal tax exemption for municipal bond interest. States and municipalities do not tax federal securities or properties, and the federal government reciprocates by exempting local government securities and properties from federal taxation. *Syn.* mutual exclusion doctrine; reciprocal immunity.

dollar bonds Municipal revenue bonds that are quoted and traded on a basis of dollars rather than yield to maturity. Term bonds are dollar bonds.

dollar cost averaging A system of buying mutual fund shares in fixed dollar amounts at regular fixed intervals, regardless of the share's price. The investor purchases more shares when prices are low and fewer shares when prices are high, thus lowering the average cost per share over time.

donor A person who makes a gift of money or securities to another. Once the gift is donated, the donor gives up all rights to it. Gifts of securities to minors under the Uniform Gifts to Minors Act provide tax advantages to the donor. *See also* Uniform Gifts to Minors Act.

double-barreled bond A municipal security backed by the full faith and credit of the issuing municipality as well as by pledged revenues. *See also* general obligation bond; revenue bond.

Dow Jones averages The most widely quoted and oldest measures of change in stock prices. There are four averages, each based on the prices of a limited number of stocks in a particular category.

Dow Jones Composite Average (DJCA) A market indicator composed of the 65 stocks that make up the Dow Jones Industrial, Transportation, and Utilities averages. *See also* average; Dow Jones Industrial Average; Dow Jones Transportation Average; Dow Jones Utilities Average.

Dow Jones Industrial Average (DJIA) The most widely used stock market indicator, composed of 30 large, actively traded issues of industrial stocks. Futures contracts and futures option contracts trade on the Chicago Board of Trade.

Dow Jones Transportation Average (DJTA) A market indicator composed of 20 transportation stocks. *See also* average; Dow Jones Composite Average; Dow Jones Industrial Average; Dow Jones Utilities Average.

Dow Jones Utilities Average (DJUA) A market indicator composed of 15 utilities stocks. *See also* average; Dow Jones Composite Average; Dow Jones Industrial Average; Dow Jones Transportation Average.

Dow Theory A technical market theory that long-term trends in the stock market may be confirmed by analyzing the movements of the Dow Jones Industrial Average and the Dow Jones Transportation Average.

down tick *See* minus tick.

DPP *See* direct participation program.

DR Debit register. *See* debit balance.

dry hole A well that is plugged and abandoned without being completed or that is abandoned for any reason without having produced commercially for 60 days. *See also* productive well.

dual-purpose fund A closed-end investment company that offers two classes of stock: income shares and capital shares. Income shares entitle the holder to share in the net dividends and interest paid to the fund. Capital shares entitle the holder to profit from the capital appreciation of all securities the fund holds. *See also* closed-end management company.

due bill A printed statement showing the obligation of a seller to deliver securities or rights to the purchaser. A due bill is also used as a pledge to deliver dividends when the transaction occurs after the record date.

due diligence The careful investigation by the underwriting participants necessary to ensure that all material information pertinent to an issue has been disclosed to prospective investors.

due diligence meeting A meeting at which an issuing corporation's officials and representatives of the underwriting group present information on, and answer questions about, a pending issue of securities.

duplicate confirmation A copy of a customer's confirmation that a brokerage firm sends to a party other than the customer.

DVP *See* delivery vs. payment; receipt vs. payment

earned income Income derived from active participation in a trade or business, including wages, salary, tips, commissions, and bonuses. *See* portfolio income; unearned income.

earned surplus *See* retained earnings.

earnings per share (EPS) A corporation's net income available for common stock divided by its number of shares of common stock outstanding. *Syn.* primary earnings per share.

Eastern account A securities underwriting in which the agreement among underwriters states that each syndicate member will be responsible for its own allocation, as well as for a proportionate share of any securities remaining unsold. *Syn.* undivided account. *See also* syndicate; Western account.

EE *See* excess equity.

effective date The date the registration of an issue of securities becomes effective, allowing the underwriters to sell the newly issued securities to the public and confirm sales to investors who have given indications of interest.

efficient market theory Theory based on the premise that the stock market processes information efficiently. It postulates that, as new information becomes known, it is reflected immediately in the price of stock, and therefore, stock prices represent fair prices.

Employee Retirement Income Security Act of 1974 (ERISA) The law that governs the operation of most corporate pension and benefit plans. *Syn.* Pension Reform Act.

endorsement The signature on the back of a stock or bond certificate by the person named on the certificate as the owner. Owners must endorse certificates when transferring them to another person. *See also* assignment.

EPS *See* earnings per share.

EQ *See* equity.

equipment bond *See* equipment trust certificate.

equipment leasing limited partnership A direct participation program that purchases equipment for leasing to other businesses on a long-term basis. Tax-sheltered income is the primary objective of such a partnership.

equipment trust certificate A debt obligation, generally issued by transportation companies such as railroads, that is backed by equipment (rolling stock). *Syn.* equipment bond; equipment note.

equity (1) The ownership interest of common and preferred stockholders in a corporation. (2) In a margin account, equity equals what is owned less what is owed. *See also* common stock; margin account.

equity financing Raising money for working capital or capital expenditures by selling common or preferred stock to individual or institutional investors. In return for the money paid, the investors receive ownership interests in the corporation.

equity option A security representing the right to buy or sell common stock at a specified price within a specified time. *See also* nonequity option; option.

equity security A financial instrument representing proportional ownership interest held in a corporation, company, or other enterprise recognized in the form of shares (e.g., common stock, preferred stock, convertible bonds, rights, warrants, and options).

ERISA *See* Employee Retirement Income Security Act of 1974.

escrow agreement The certificate provided by an approved bank that guarantees that the indicated securities are on deposit at that bank. An investor who writes a call option and can present an escrow agreement is considered covered and does not need to meet margin requirements.

eurobond A long-term debt instrument of a governmen or corporation that is denominated in the currency of the issuer's country but issued and sold in a different country.

eurodollar U.S. currency held in banks outside the United States.

ex-date The first date on which a security is traded without entitling the buyer to receive distributions previously declared. *Syn.* ex-dividend date; ex-warrants; ex-rights; ex-distribution.

ex-dividend date *See* ex-date.

ex-legal A municipal issue that trades without a written legal opinion of counsel from a bond attorney. An ex-legal issue must be designated as such at the time of the trade.

ex-rights Stock trading without rights. *See also* cum rights.

ex-rights date The date on or after which stocks will b traded without subscription rights previously declared.

excess equity The value of securities in a margin account that is in excess of the federal requirement. *Syn.* margin excess; Regulation T excess.

cess margin securities The securities in a margin count that are in excess of 140% of the account's debit lance. Such securities are available to the broker-dealer r debit balance financing purposes, but they must be gregated and earmarked as the customer's property.

change Any organization, association, or group of rsons that maintains or provides a marketplace in which curities can be bought and sold. An exchange does not ve to be a physical place, as several strictly electronic changes do business around the world.

change Act *See* Securities Exchange Act of 1934.

change market All of the exchanges on which listed curities are traded.

change privilege A feature offered by a mutual fund owing an individual to transfer an investment in one nd to another fund under the same sponsor without curring an additional sales charge. *Syn.* conversion ivilege.

change traded fund (ETF) An investment company gally classified as an open-end company or unit vestment trust (UIT), but differing from traditional en-end companies (mutual funds) and UITs. An ETF ues shares in large blocks that are known as *creation its*. Those who purchase creation units are frequently ge institutional traders or investors. The creation units n then be split up and sold as individual shares in e secondary markets, allowing individual investors to rchase shares.

change-listed security A security that has met rtain requirements and has been admitted to full ading privileges on an exchange. The NYSE, NYSE merican, Nasdaq, and all other exchanges set their listing quirements for volume of shares outstanding, corporate rnings, and other characteristics. Exchange-listed curities can also be traded in the third market.

ecutor/executrix A person given fiduciary thorization through a valid will to manage the affairs of a cedent's estate.

empt security A security that need not be in formal mpliance with a given piece of legislation, such as the curities Act of 1933 or the Uniform Securities Act as lopted by a state. Examples include U.S. government d municipal securities. No security is exempt from the tifraud provisions of any securities legislation.

empt transaction (federal) Transactions that do not igger a federal registration. Examples include Regulation + offerings, Regulation S offerings, Regulation D ferings, and Rule 147/147A offerings.

exempt transaction (state) Transactions that do not trigger a state's registration and advertising requirements under the Uniform Securities Act. Examples of exempt transactions include transactions with financial institutions, unsolicited transactions, and private placement transactions.

exercise To effect the transaction offered by an option, right, or warrant. For example, an equity call holder exercises a call by buying 100 shares of the underlying stock at the agreed-upon price within the agreed-upon time period, or the use of a right granted under a contract. For example, a futures call holder exercises by buying the underlying futures at the agreed-upon ("exercise") price within the agreed-upon time period.

exercise price The cost per share at which the holder of an option or warrant may buy or sell the underlying security. *Syn.* strike price.

expansion A period of increased business activity throughout an economy; one of the four stages of the business cycle. *Syn.* recovery. *See* business cycle.

expansionary policy A monetary policy that increases the money supply, usually with the intention of lowering interest rates and combating deflation.

expense ratio A ratio for comparing a mutual fund's efficiency by dividing the fund's expenses by its net assets.

expiration cycle A set of four expiration months for a class of listed options. An option may have expiration dates of January, April, July, and October (JAJO); February, May, August, and November (FMAN); or March, June, September, and December (MJSD).

expiration date The specified date on which an option buyer no longer has the rights specified in the option contract.

exploratory drilling program A limited partnership that aims to locate and recover undiscovered reserves of oil, gas, or minerals. *Syn.* wildcatting. *See also* developmental drilling program; income program.

exploratory well A well drilled in search of either an undiscovered pool of oil or gas, or with the hope of substantially extending the limits of an existing pool of oil or gas.

FAC *See* face-amount certificate company.

face value *See* par value.

face-amount certificate company (FAC) An investment company that issues certificates obligating it to pay an investor a stated amount of money (the face amount) on a specific future date. The investor pays into the certificate in periodic payments or in a lump sum.

fail to deliver A situation in which the broker-dealer on the sell side of a transaction or contract does not deliver the specified securities to the broker-dealer on the buy side. *Syn.* broker fail; fails; fails to deliver; failure to deliver.

fail to receive A situation in which the broker-dealer on the buy side of a transaction or contract does not receive the specified securities from the broker-dealer on the sell side. *Syn.* fails; fails to receive; failure to receive.

Fannie Mae *See* Federal National Mortgage Association.

Farm Credit Administration (FCA) The government agency that coordinates the activities of the banks in the Farm Credit System. *See also* Farm Credit System.

FCO *See* foreign currency option.

FCS *See* Farm Credit System.

FDIC *See* Federal Deposit Insurance Corporation.

Fed *See* Federal Reserve System.

Fed call *See* margin call.

Federal Deposit Insurance Corporation (FDIC) A federal government agency that insures deposits in banks and thrifts for up to $250,000 per depositor.

federal funds Known as *fed funds*, these are immediately available funds representing excess reserves of commercial banks held at Federal Reserve banks. Federal funds are the primary payment mode for government securities and are often used to pay for new issues of municipal securities and secondary market transactions in certain types of securities.

federal funds rate The interest rate charged by one institution lending federal funds to another.

Federal Home Loan Bank (FHLB) A government-regulated organization that operates a credit reserve system for the nation's savings and loan associations.

Federal Home Loan Mortgage Corporation (FHLMC) A publicly traded corporation that promotes the nationwide secondary market in mortgages by issuing mortgage-backed pass-through debt certificates. *Syn.* Freddie Mac.

FICB *See* Federal Intermediate Credit Bank.

fictitious quotation A bid or offer published before being identified by source and verified as legitimate. A fictitious quote may create the appearance of trading activity where none exists.

fidelity bond Insurance coverage required by the self-regulatory organizations for all employees, officers, and partners of member firms to protect against employee fraud. *Syn.* Surety bond.

fiduciary A person authorized, in good faith, to hold assets for another person and manage those assets for the benefit of that person.

filing date The day on which a securities issuer or broker-dealer submits a statement to a regulatory body.

fill or kill order (FOK) An order that instructs the broker to fill the entire order immediately. If the entire order cannot be executed immediately, it is canceled.

final prospectus The legal document that states a new issue security's price, delivery date, and underwriting spread, as well as other material information. It must be given to every investor who purchases a new issue of registered securities. *Syn.* prospectus. *See* preliminary prospectus; red herring.

financial risk An unsystematic risk. Generally, the concern is that an issuer will be unable to meet its debt obligations as they come due. *See* credit risk.

firewall A descriptive name also referred to as an information barrier for the division within a brokerage firm that prevents insider information from passing from corporate advisers to investment traders, who could then make use of the information to reap illicit profits. *See also* Insider Trading and Securities Fraud Enforcement Act of 1988. *See* Chinese wall.

firm commitment underwriting A type of underwriting commitment in which the underwriter agre to sell an entire new issue of securities. The underwriter a as a dealer, pays the issuer a lump sum for the securities, and assumes all financial responsibility for any unsold shares. *See also* underwriting.

firm quote The sure price at which a trading unit of a security may be bought or sold. All quotes are firm quote unless otherwise indicated.

first in, first out (FIFO) An accounting method, used to assess a company's inventory, in which it is assumed that the first goods acquired are the first to be sold. The same method is used by the IRS to determine cost basis f tax purposes. *See also* average basis; last in, first out; share identification.

fiscal policy The federal tax and spending policies set by Congress or the president. These policies affect tax rates, interest rates, and government spending in an effort to control the economy. *See also* monetary policy.

fixed annuity An insurance contract in which the insurance company makes fixed-dollar payments to the annuitant for the term of the contract, usually until the annuitant dies. The insurance company guarantees both earnings and principal.

fixed asset A tangible, physical property used in the course of a corporation's everyday operations. It includes buildings, equipment, and land.

fixed-charge coverage ratio *See* bond interest coverage ratio.

fixed-dollar annuity *See* fixed annuity.

fixed-unit investment trust An investment company that invests in a portfolio of securities in which no changes are permissible. *See* also nonfixed unit investment trust; unit investment trust.

flat A term used to describe bonds traded without accrued interest. They are traded at the agreed-upon market price only. *See also* accrued interest.

flat yield curve A chart showing the yields of bonds with short maturities as equal to the yields of bonds with long maturities. *Syn.* even yield curve. *See also* inverted yield curve; normal yield curve; yield curve.

floor broker A member of an exchange who executes transactions only on an agent-only basis for the member's firm's customers and the customers of other members firms.

floor trader An exchange member who executes transactions from the floor of the exchange only for his own account.

flow of funds The schedule of payments disbursed from the proceeds of a facility financed by a revenue bond. The flow of funds determines the order in which the operating expenses, debt service, and other expenses are paid.

flow-through A term that describes the way income, deductions, and credits resulting from the activities of a business are applied to individual taxes and expenses, as though each incurred the income and deductions directly. *See also* limited partnership.

FNMA *See* Federal National Mortgage Association.

FOK *See* fill-or-kill order.

FOMC *See* Federal Open Market Committee.

forced conversion Market conditions created by a corporation to encourage convertible bondholders to exercise their conversion options. Conversion may be forced by calling the bonds when the market value of the stock is higher than the redemption price offered by the corporation. *See also* redemption.

forced sellout The action taken when a customer fails to meet the deadline for paying for securities and no extension has been granted: the broker-dealer must liquidate enough securities to pay for the transaction.

foreign currency Money issued by a country other than the one in which the investor resides. Options and futures contracts on numerous foreign currencies are traded on U.S. exchanges.

foreign currency option (FCO) A U.S. dollar-settled option security representing the right to buy or sell a specified amount of a foreign currency. *See also* option; FX options.

foreign exchange rate The price of one country's currency in terms of another currency. *Syn.* exchange rate.

foreign fund *See* sector fund; specialized fund.

Form 10-K An annual audited report that must be submitted by reporting companies to the SEC. The form is due within 90 days of year end.

Form 10-Q A quarterly report containing a corporation's unaudited financial data and certain nonrecurring events that arise during the quarterly period, such as significant litigation, must be reported. A Form 10-Q must be submitted to the SEC no later than 45 days after the end of each of the first three fiscal quarters.

forward pricing The basis of computation of mutual fund purchases and redemptions in relation to the next calculated NAV.

fourth market The direct trading of large blocks of securities between institutional investors through a computer network.

fractional share A portion of a whole share of stock most commonly found with mutual funds.

fraud The deliberate concealment, misrepresentation, or omission of material information or the truth, so as to deceive or manipulate another party for unlawful or unfair gain.

FRB *See* Federal Reserve Board.

Freddie Mac *See* Federal Home Loan Mortgage Corporation.

free credit balance The unencumbered cash funds in customer accounts.

freeriding Buying and selling securities prior to the payment due date without making payment. This practice violates the SEC's Regulation T.

freeriding and withholding The failure of a member participating in the distribution of a hot issue to make a bona fide public offering at the public offering price. *See* hot issue.

front-end fee The expenses paid for services rendered during a direct participation program's organization or acquisition phase, including front-end organization and offering expenses, acquisition fees and expenses, and any other similar fees designated by the sponsor.

front-end load A mutual fund commission or sales charge that is included in the purchase price. *See also* back-end load; Class A share

frozen account An account requiring cash in advance before a buy order is executed and securities in hand before a sell order is executed. The account holder has violated Regulation T.

full power of attorney A written authorization for someone other than the beneficial owner of an account to make deposits and withdrawals and execute trades in the account. *See also* limited power of attorney.

full trading authorization A legal power given to a third party to trade an account and add or withdraw funds.

fully registered bond A debt issue having the bondholder's name on the certificate. Principal and interest are paid directly to the investor. *See also* registered; registered as to principal only.

functional allocation A sharing arrangement whereby the investors in an oil and gas direct participation program are responsible for intangible costs, and the sponsor is responsible for tangible costs. Revenues are shared. *See also* sharing arrangement.

fundamental analysis The study of the business prospects of an individual company within the context of its industry and the overall economy. *See also* technical analysis.

funded debt All long-term debt financing of a corporation or municipality (i.e., all outstanding bonds maturing in five years or more).

fungibility Interchangeability resulting from standardization. Options listed on national exchanges are fungible. Nonstandardized OTC options are not.

fungible A term referring to the interchangeability of financial instruments having effectively identical features. Cash is fungible, as are most securities.

GAN *See* grant anticipation note.

GDP *See* gross domestic product.

general account The account that holds all of an insurer's assets other than those in separate accounts. The general account holds the contributions paid for traditional life insurance contracts. *See also* separate account.

general obligation bond (GO) A municipal debt issue backed by the full faith, credit, and taxing power of the issuer for payment of interest and principal. *Syn.* full faith and credit bond. *See also* revenue bond.

general partner (GP) An active party in a direct participation program who is personally liable for all debts of the program and who manages the business of the program. *See also* limited partner.

general securities principal *See* Series 24.

general securities representative *See* Series 7.

generic advertising Communications with the public that promote securities as investments but do not refer to particular securities.

Ginnie Mae *See* Government National Mortgage Association.

Glass-Steagall Act of 1933 Federal legislation that forbids commercial banks from underwriting securities and forbids investment bankers from opening deposit accounts or making commercial loans. *Syn.* banking act.

GNMA *See* Government National Mortgage Association.

GNP *See* gross national product.

GO *See* general obligation bond.

good delivery (form) A term describing a security that is negotiable, in compliance with the contract of the sale, and ready to be transferred from seller to purchaser. *See also* uniform delivery ticket.

good delivery (time) Delivery of the certificate by the seller and payment by the buyer on settlement date—currently T+2 for the regular way.

good faith deposit A deposit contributed by each syndicate involved in a competitive bid underwriting for a municipal issue. It ensures performance by the low bidder

od-til-canceled order (GTC) An order that is left on ꞉ specialist's book until it is either executed or canceled. *n.* open order.

odwill An intangible asset that represents the value ıat a firm's business reputation adds to its perceived value.

›vernment National Mortgage Association (NMA) A wholly government-owned corporation that ues pass-through mortgage debt certificates backed by the ll faith and credit of the U.S. government. *Syn.* Ginnie ae.

vernment security A debt obligation of the U.S. vernment, backed by its full faith, credit, and taxing wer, and regarded as having no risk of default.

› *See* general partner; general partnership.

ant anticipation note (GAN) A short-term municipal bt security issued in anticipation of receiving a funding ant, typically from a government agency.

een shoe option A provision of an issue's registration ıtement that allows an underwriter to buy extra shares ›m the issuer (thus increasing the size of the offering) public demand proves exceptionally strong. The term rives from the Green Shoe Manufacturing Company, ıich first used the technique.

oss domestic product (GDP) The total value of ods and services produced in a country during one ar. It includes consumption, government purchases, vestments, and exports minus imports.

oss income All income of a taxpayer derived from hatever source.

oss proceeds The total of the initial invested capital a direct participation program contributed by all of the iginal and additional limited partners.

oss revenue pledge The flow of funds arrangement a municipal revenue bond issue pledging that all venues received will be used for debt service prior to ꞉ductions for any costs or expenses. *See also* net revenue edge.

ross revenues All money received by a business from ; operations. The term typically does not include interest come or income from the sale, refinancing, or other sposition of properties.

roup net order In a municipal bond underwriting, an der received by a syndicate member that is credited to e entire syndicate. Takedowns on these orders are paid to embers according to their participation in the syndicate. *e also* designated order; member-at-the-takedown order; esale order.

growth fund A diversified common stock fund that has capital appreciation as its primary goal. It invests in companies that reinvest most of their earnings for expansion, research, or development.

growth industry An industry that is growing faster than the economy as a whole as a result of technological changes, new products, or changing consumer tastes.

growth stock A relatively speculative issue that is believed to offer significant potential for capital gains. It often pays low dividends and sells at a high price/earnings ratio.

GTC *See* good-till-canceled order.

guaranteed bond A debt obligation issued with a promise from a corporation other than the issuing corporation to maintain payments of principal and interest.

guardian A fiduciary, generally appointed by a court, who manages the assets of a minor or incompetent for the benefit of that person. *See also* fiduciary.

HALT A message on the Consolidated Tape indicating that trading in a particular security has been stopped. *See also* trading halt.

head and shoulders On a technical analyst's trading chart, a pattern that has three peaks resembling a head and two shoulders. A head and shoulders typically indicates a market reversal.

hedge An investment made to reduce the risk of adverse price movements in a security. Derivatives are a common way to hedge.

HH savings bond *See* Series HH bond.

high The highest price a security or commodity reaches during a specified period of time. *See also* low.

holder The owner of a security, futures option, or futures contract. *See also* long.

holding company A company organized to invest in and manage other corporations that is not considered an investment company.

holding period A time period signifying how long the owner possesses an asset. It starts the day of the purchase and ends on the day of the sale.

horizontal spread The purchase and sale of two options on the same underlying security and with the same exercise price, but with different expiration dates. *Syn.* calendar spread; time spread. *See also* spread.

hot issue A foreign stock fund that invests in pre-emerging economies.

house maintenance call *See* margin maintenance call.

house maintenance requirement *See* margin maintenance requirement.

Housing Authority bond *See* New Housing Authority bond.

HR-10 plan *See* Keogh plan.

hypothecation The practice of pledging securities as collateral for a loan. This is most commonly done when purchasing on margin. *See* margin account.

IDB *See* industrial development bond.

IDC *See* intangible drilling cost.

IDR *See* industrial development bond.

immediate annuity An annuity contract that provides for monthly payments to begin immediately (generally in no more than 60 days) after deposit of the invested funds. *See also* deferred annuity.

immediate family A person who is supported financially by a person associated with the securities industry, including a parent, mother- or father-in-law, husband or wife, child, and any other individual to whom the person provides material support.

immediate-or-cancel order (IOC) An order that instructs the floor broker to execute immediately, in full or in part. Any portion of the order that remains unexecuted is canceled.

income bond A debt obligation where the coupon interest is paid only if the corporation's earnings are sufficient to meet the interest payment. *Syn.* adjustment bond. *See also* flat.

income fund A mutual fund that seeks to provide stable current income by investing in securities that pay interest and/or dividends.

income program A limited partnership program that invests in producing oil or gas wells for the purpose of generating income and taking advantage of the depletion allowance. *See also* depletion; developmental drilling program; exploratory drilling program.

income statement A financial statement spanning a period showing the accounting profit or loss for the period.

index *See* security market index.

index option A security representing the right to recei in cash, the difference between the underlying value of a market index and the strike price of the option. *See also* capped index option.

indication of interest (IOI) An investor's expression of potential interest in buying a security currently in registration.

individual retirement account (IRA) A retirement investing tool for employed individuals that allows an annual contribution of 100% of earned income up to an indexed dollar maximum.

industrial development (revenue) bond (IDB) In general, securities issued by a state, local government, or development agency used to finance the construction or purchase of industrial, commercial, or manufacturing facilities that are to be purchased by or leased to a private user.

industry fund *See* sector fund.

inflation A persistent and measurable rise in the gener level of prices. *See* deflation.

inflation risk *See* purchasing power risk.

information barrier An ethics screen that prevents insider information from passing from, for example, a capital markets division of an investment bank to the bank's traders, who could make use of the information to reap illicit profits. *See also* Insider Trading and Securities Fraud Enforcement Act of 1988. *See* Chinese wall.

initial margin requirement The amount of equity a customer must deposit when making a new purchase in a margin account. *See also* margin; margin call.

initial public offering (IPO) The first sale of common stock by a corporation to the public. *See also* new issue market; public offering.

inside information Material nonpublic information (MNPI) a person obtained or used for the purpose of trading in securities. *See also* material fact.

inside market The best price at which a stock can be bought and sold. The best ask price is the lowest. The best bid price is the highest. The difference between the two prices is also called the *spread*.

insider Any person who possesses or has access to material nonpublic information about a corporation. An insider includes directors, officers, and stockholders who own at least 10% of any class of equity security of a corporation.

nsider Trading Act *See* Insider Trading and Securities raud Enforcement Act of 1988.

nsider Trading and Securities Fraud Enforcement ct of 1988 Legislation that defines what constitutes the licit use of nonpublic information in making securities ades and the liabilities and penalties that apply. *Syn.* nsider Trading Act. *See also* contemporaneous trader; nsider.

nstitutional account Any account opened by a ank, savings and loan, insurance company, or registered nvestment company; an investment adviser registered ther with the SEC or with a state; or any corporation, ust, natural person, et cetera, with total assets of at least 50 million.

nstitutional communication FINRA-defined category f communications, written or electronic, distributed or nade available to institutional investors only. It does not nclude a member's internal communications (i.e., internal nemos).

nstitutional investor A person or organization hat trades securities in larger share quantities or dollar mounts. Institutional investors are covered by fewer rotective regulations because it is assumed that they are nore knowledgeable and better able to protect themselves. xamples would be member firms, banks and savings and oan associations, insurance companies, mutual funds, overnment entities, any entity with $50 million or more n total assets, or any person acting solely on behalf of an nstitutional investor.

nsurance covenant A provision of a municipal revenue ond's trust indenture that helps ensure the safety of the ssue by promising to insure the facilities built. *See also* naintenance covenant; rate covenant.

ntangible asset A property owned that is not physical, uch as a formula, a copyright, or goodwill. *See also* oodwill.

ntangible drilling cost (IDC) In an oil and gas limited artnership, a tax-deductible cost. Usually this is for a onphysical asset, such as labor or fuel, that does not epreciate. *Syn.* intangible drilling development expense.

ntangible drilling development xpense *See* intangible drilling cost.

nterbank market An unregulated, decentralized nternational market in which the various major currencies f the world are traded.

terest The charge for the privilege of borrowing noney, usually expressed as an annual percentage rate.

interest coverage ratio *See* bond interest coverage ratio.

interest rate option A security representing the right to buy or sell government debt securities.

interest rate risk The systematic risk associated with investments, relating to the sensitivity of price or value, to fluctuations at the current level of interest rates.

Internal Revenue Code (IRC) The legislation that defines tax liabilities and deductions for U.S. taxpayers.

Internal Revenue Service (IRS) The U.S. government agency responsible for collecting most federal taxes and for administering tax rules and regulations.

intrastate offering An issue of securities exempt from SEC registration that are available to companies that do business in one state only and sell their securities only to residents of that same state.

intrinsic value The potential profit to be made from exercising an option. A call option is said to have intrinsic value when the underlying stock is trading above the exercise price. *See also* time value.

inverted yield curve A chart showing long-term debt instruments having lower yields than short-term debt instruments. *Syn.* negative yield curve. *See also* flat yield curve; normal yield curve.

invested capital *See* capitalization.

investment adviser A person in the business of giving advice on securities for compensation.

Investment Advisers Act of 1940 Federal legislation requiring certain investment advisers to register as such with the SEC.

investment banker An institution in the business of raising capital for corporations and municipalities. An investment banker may not accept deposits or make commercial loans. *Syn.* investment bank.

investment banking business A broker, dealer, or municipal or government securities dealer that underwrites or distributes new issues of securities as a dealer or that buys and sells securities for the accounts of others as a broker. *Syn.* investment securities business.

investment company A company engaged in the business of pooling investors' money and investing and reinvesting in securities. Examples include face-amount certificate companies, unit investment trusts, and management companies.

Investment Company Act of 1940 Federal legislation setting forth the regulatory requirements for investment companies.

investment grade The broad credit designation given to bonds that have a high probability of being paid and minor, if any, speculative features. Bonds rated BBB or higher by Standard and Poor's or Baa or higher by Moody's Investors Service are deemed by those agencies to be investment grade.

investment objective Any goal a client hopes to achieve through investing. Examples include current income, capital growth, and preservation of capital.

investment pyramid A portfolio strategy that allocates investable assets according to an investment's relative safety. The pyramid base is composed of low-risk investments, the middle portion is composed of growth investments, and the top is composed of speculative investments.

invitation for bids A notice to securities underwriters soliciting bids for the issuing of a bond issue. These notices are published in The Bond Buyer, newspapers, and journals.

IOC *See* immediate-or-cancel order.

IOI *See* indication of interest.

IPO *See* initial public offering.

IRA *See* individual retirement account.

IRA rollover The reinvestment of assets that an individual receives as a distribution from a qualified tax-deferred retirement plan into an individual retirement account.

IRA transfer The direct reinvestment of retirement assets from one qualified tax-deferred retirement plan to another, or to an individual retirement, without ever passing through the investor's hands.

IRC *See* Internal Revenue Code.

irrevocable stock power *See* stock power.

issued stock Equity securities authorized by the issuer's registration statement and distributed to the public. *See also* outstanding stock; treasury stock.

issuer (1) The entity, such as a corporation or municipality, that offers or proposes to offer its securities for sale. (2) The creator of an option. The issuer of an over-the-counter option is the option writer, and the issuer of a listed option is the Options Clearing Corporation.

joint account An account in which two or more individuals possess some form of control over the account and may transact business in the account.

joint life with last survivor An annuity payout option that covers two or more people, with annuity payments continuing as long as one of the annuitants remains alive.

JTWROS *See* joint tenants with right of survivorship.

junior lien debt A bond backed by the same collateral backing a previous issue and having a subordinate claim to the collateral in the event of default. *See also* closed-end covenant; open-end covenant.

Keogh plan A qualified tax-deferred retirement plan for persons who are self-employed. *Syn.* HR-10 plan. *See also* individual retirement account; nonqualified retirement plan; qualified retirement plan.

Keynesian economics The theory that active government intervention in the marketplace is the best way to ensure economic growth and stability.

Know Your Customer Rule Regulation requires that every member must use reasonable diligence, in regard to the opening and maintenance of every account, to know (and retain) the essential facts concerning every customer and concerning the authority of each person acting on behalf of such customer.

lagging indicator A measurable economic factor that changes after the economy has started to follow a particular pattern or trend. Lagging indicators are believed to confirm long-term trends. Examples include average duration of unemployment, corporate profits, and labor cost per unit of output. *See also* coincident indicator; leading indicator.

last in, first out (LIFO) An accounting method used to assess a corporation's inventory in which it is assumed that the last goods acquired are the first to be sold. The method is used to determine cost basis for tax purposes. The IRS designates last in, first out as the order in which sales or withdrawals from an investment are made.

leading indicator A measurable economic factor that changes before the economy starts to follow a particular pattern or trend. Leading indicators are believed to predict changes in the economy. Examples include new orders for durable goods, slowdowns in deliveries by vendors, and numbers of building permits issued. *See also* coincident indicator; lagging indicator.

LEAPS *See* Long-term Equity Anticipation Securities.

lease rental bond A debt security issued by a municipal authority to raise funds for new construction, with the understanding that the finished structure will be rented to the authority and the rental payments will finance the bond payments.

legal list The selection of securities determined by a state agency (usually a state banking or insurance commission) to be appropriate investments for fiduciary accounts.

legal opinion The statement by a bond attorney affirming that the interest from an issue of municipal bonds is exempt from federal income tax. Municipal bonds that trade without a legal opinion are ex-legal, meaning without a legal opinion. *See also* ex-legal; qualified legal opinion; unqualified legal opinion.

legislative risk The potential for an investor to be adversely affected by changes in investment or tax laws.

letter of intent (LOI) A nonbinding agreement between a purchaser of mutual funds and the fund underwriter that allows the investor up to 13 months to reach a specified dollar purchase. *See* breakpoint.

Level 1 The basic level of Nasdaq service. Through a desktop quotation service, it provides registered representatives and public subscribers with up-to-the-minute inside bid and ask quotations on over-the-counter stocks.

Level 2 The second level of Nasdaq service. Through a desktop quotation service, it provides up-to-the-minute inside bid and ask quotations and the bids and asks of each market maker for a security. *See also* National Association of Securities Dealers Automated Quotation System.

Level 3 The broadest level of Nasdaq service. It provides real time inside bid and ask quotations, supplies the bids and asks of each market maker for a security, and allows each market maker to enter new and updated quotations. *Syn.* market maker level.

level debt service A schedule for debt repayment whereby principal and interest payments remain essentially constant from year to year over the life of the issue. *See also* decreasing debt service.

level load A mutual fund sales fee charged annually based on the net asset value of a share. A 12b-1 asset-based fee is an example of a level load. *See also* back-end load; Class C share; front-end load.

leverage Using borrowed capital to increase investment return.

liability A legal obligation to pay a debt. Current liabilities are debts payable within 12 months. Long-term liabilities are debts payable over a period of more than 12 months.

LIBOR *See* London Interbank Offered Rate.

life annuity/straight annuity An annuity payout option that pays over the annuitant's lifetime.

life annuity with period certain An annuity payout option that guarantees the annuitant a monthly check for the longer of a certain period or the annuitant's death. If the annuitant dies before the period expires, the payments go to the annuitant's named beneficiary for the duration of the certain period.

LIFO *See* last in, first out.

limit order An order that instructs the trader to buy a specified security below a certain price or to sell a specified security above a certain price (e.g., "Buy 100 IBM at 120 or better [lower]"). *Syn.* or better order. *See also* stop limit order; stop order.

limited liability An investor's right to limit potential losses to no more than the amount invested. Equity shareholders, such as corporate stockholders and limited partners, have limited liability.

limited partner (LP) An investor in a direct participation program who does not participate in the management or control of the program and whose liability for partnership debts is limited to the amount invested in the program. *See also* general partner; participant; passive investor.

limited partnership (LP) A business, formed by filing a partnership agreement with a state, that consists of a general partner and one or more limited partners.

limited partnership agreement The contract between a partnership's limited and general partners that provides the guidelines for partnership operation and states the rights and responsibilities of each partner.

limited power of attorney A legal authorization for someone other than the beneficial owner of an account to make investment decisions in the account.

limited tax bond A general obligation municipal debt security issued by a municipality whose taxing power is limited to a specified maximum rate.

limited trading authorization *See* limited power of attorney.

liquidation priority In the case of a corporation's liquidation, the order that is followed for paying off creditors and stockholders.

liquidity The ease with which an asset can be converted to cash in the marketplace.

liquidity ratio A measure of a corporation's ability to meet its current obligations. The ratio compares current assets to current liabilities. *See also* acid-test ratio; current ratio.

liquidity risk The potential that an investor might not be able to sell an investment when desired without adverse price disruption. *Syn.* marketability risk.

listed option An option contract that may be bought and sold on a national securities exchange in a continuous secondary market. Listed options carry standardized strike prices and expiration dates. *Syn.* standardized option. *See also* OTC option.

listed security A stock, bond, or other security that satisfies certain minimum requirements and is traded on a regional or national securities exchange such as the New York Stock Exchange. *See also* over-the-counter.

LMV *See* current market value.

loan consent agreement An optional contract between a brokerage firm and a margin customer that permits the firm to lend margin securities to other brokers. The contract is part of the margin agreement. *Syn.* consent to lend agreement.

locked market The trading situation where there is no spread between the bid and the ask on the security being displayed on a quotation system—that is, the bid for a stock is the same price as the ask. This may happen with a manual quotation, and with certain exceptions, is deemed a violation of FINRA quote display rules.

LOI *See* letter of intent.

London Interbank Offered Rate (LIBOR) The world's most widely used benchmark for short-term interest rates.

long The term used to describe the owning of a security, contract, or commodity. For example, an owner of common stock is said to have a long position in the stock. *See also* short; short against the box.

long market value (LMV) *See* current market value.

long straddle An option investor's position of purchasing a call and a put on the same underlying security with the same exercise price and expiration month. The investor is looking for either a rise or fall in the price of the underlying security or futures contract and hopes to avoid a flat market. *See also* short straddle.

long-term capital gain The profit earned on the sale of a capital asset that has been owned for more than 12 months. *See also* capital gain; capital loss; long-term capital loss; short-term capital gain.

long-term capital loss The loss realized on the sale of a capital asset that has been owned for more than 12 months. *See also* capital gain; capital loss; long-term capital gain; short-term capital loss.

long-term equity option *See* Long-term Equity Anticipation Securities (LEAPS).

loss carryover A capital loss incurred in one tax year that is carried over to the next or later years for use as a capital loss deduction. *See also* capital loss.

low The lowest price a security or commodity reaches during a specified time period. *See also* high.

LP *See* limited partner; limited partnership.

M1 A category of the money supply that includes all coins, currency, and demand deposits (i.e., checking accounts and NOW accounts). *See also* M2; M3; money supply.

M2 A category of the money supply that includes M1, in addition to all time deposits, savings deposits, and noninstitutional money market funds. *See also* M1; M3; money supply.

M3 A category of the money supply that includes M2, in addition to all large time deposits, institutional money market funds, short-term repurchase agreements, and certain other large liquid assets. *See also* M1; M2; money supply.

maintenance call *See* margin maintenance call.

maintenance covenant A provision of a municipal revenue bond's trust indenture that helps ensure the safety of the issue by promising to keep the facility and equipmen in good working order. *See also* insurance covenant; rate covenant.

maintenance requirement *See* margin maintenance requirement.

Major Market Index (Symbol XMI) NYSE Arca Major Market Index. A price-weighted market indicator based on 20 well-known industries.

make a market To stand ready to buy or sell a particular security as a dealer for its own account. *See also* market maker.

management company An investment company, either open-end or closed-end, that trades various types of securities under the direction of its portfolio manager, in accordance with specific objectives stated in the prospectus. *See* investment company.

management fee (1) The payment to the sponsor of a direct participation program for managing and administering the program. (2) Fees that are paid out of fund assets to its investment adviser for investment portfolio management. (3) The portion of the underwriting spread paid to the managing underwriter.

mandatory call The redemption of a bond by an issuer authorized in the trust indenture and based on a predetermined schedule or event. *See also* catastrophe call; partial call.

margin The amount of equity contributed by a customer as a percentage of the current market value of the securities held in a margin account. *See also* equity; initial margin requirement; margin call; Regulation T.

margin account An account with a broker-dealer where the firm lends money to the client to purchase securities. *See* cash account; hypothecation.

margin call The Federal Reserve Board's demand that a customer deposit a specified amount of money or securities when a purchase is made in a margin account; the amount is expressed as a percentage of the market value of the securities at the time of purchase. The deposit must be made within one payment period. *Syn.* Fed call; federal call; federal margin; Reg T call; T call. *See also* initial margin requirement; margin.

margin deficiency *See* margin maintenance requirement.

margin department The department within a brokerage firm that monitors and computes the amount of money clients must deposit in margin and cash accounts. *Syn.* credit department.

margin excess *See* excess equity.

margin maintenance call A demand that a margin customer deposit money or securities when the customer's equity falls below the margin maintenance requirement set by the broker-dealer or FINRA. *Syn.* house maintenance call; maintenance call; FINRA maintenance call; minimum maintenance call.

margin maintenance requirement The minimum equity that must be held in a margin account, determined by the broker-dealer and FINRA. The amount of equity required varies with the type of security bought on margin, and the broker-dealer's house requirement is usually higher than that set by FINRA. *Syn.* house maintenance requirement; maintenance requirement; FINRA maintenance requirement.

margin security A security that is eligible for purchase on margin. A firm is permitted to lend money to help customers purchase securities, using them as collateral for margin purchases. *Syn.* eligible security. *See also* nonmargin security; OTC margin security.

mark to market To adjust the value of the securities in an account to the current market value of those securities. It is used to calculate the market value and equity in a margin account.

markdown The difference between the highest current bid price among dealers and the lower price that a dealer pays to a customer.

market letter A publication that comments on securities, investing, the economy, or other related topics and is distributed to an organization's clients or the public.

market maker A dealer willing to accept the risk of holding a particular security in its own account to facilitate trading in that security. *See also* make a market.

market NH *See* not held order.

market not held order *See* not held order.

market order An order that is to be executed immediately at the best available price. A market order is the only order that guarantees execution. *Syn.* unrestricted order.

market risk The potential for an investor to experience losses owing to day-to-day fluctuations in the prices at which securities can be bought or sold. *See* systematic risk.

market value The price at which investors buy or sell a share of common stock or a bond at a given time. *See also* current market value.

market-out clause The standard provision of a firm commitment underwriting agreement that relieves the underwriter of its obligation to underwrite the issue under circumstances that impair the investment quality of the securities.

marketability The ease with which a security can be bought or sold; having a readily available market for trading.

markup (1) The profit made by a dealer when selling a security to a customer. Dealers purchase at one price and sell to their clients at a higher price. That difference is the markup. (2) The difference between the lowest current offering price among dealers and the higher price a dealer charges a customer. *See* markdown.

married put The simultaneous purchase of a stock and a put on that stock specifically identified as a hedge.

material fact Information that a knowledgeable investor would deem significant in making an investment determination. *See also* inside information.

maturity date The date on which a bond's principal is repaid to the investor and interest payments cease. *See* balloon maturity; principal; serial bond; term maturity.

maximum loan value The percentage of market value a broker-dealer is permitted to lend a margin customer for the purchase of securities. Loan value is equal to the complement of the Regulation T requirement: if Reg T were 65%, the maximum loan value would be 35%. *Syn.* loan value.

maximum market value The market value to which a short sale position may advance before a margin maintenance call is issued. Maximum market value is set by the SRO that the broker-dealer reports to and currently equals the credit balance divided by 130%. *Syn.* maximum short market value.

member firm A broker-dealer registered with a self-regulatory organization such as the New York Stock Exchange, the Chicago Board of Exchange, FINRA, Municipal Securities Ruling Board, et cetera.

member order *See* member-at-the-takedown order.

member-at-the-takedown order In a municipal bond underwriting, a customer order submitted by one syndicate member who will receive the entire takedown. Member-at-the-takedown orders receive the lowest priority when the securities of the issue are allocated. Syn. member order. *See also*: designated order; group net order; presale order.

mini-max underwriting A form of best efforts underwriting in which the issuer sets a floor and a ceiling on the amount of securities to be sold. *See also* underwriting.

mini options Option contracts that overlay only 10 shares of the underlying security instead of 100 shares, as is the case for standard options contracts.

minimum increment price rule SEC Regulation NMS sets the minimum price increments for trading stoc depending on their current price and prohibits brokers from displaying any fractional increment. *See also* subpen price.

minor rule violation (MRV) In instances where FINRA's Enforcement Department considers a violation minor and the respondent does not dispute the allegation, the department may prepare and request that the respondent sign an MRV letter, accepting a finding of violation. Once the respondent signs an MRV letter, the settlement is final with no appeal possible.

minus tick A security transaction's execution price that below the previous execution price by a minimum amoun A short sale may not be executed on a minus tick. *Syn.* down tick. *See also* plus tick; plus tick rule; short sale; zero minus tick.

modern portfolio theory (MPT) A formal mathematical approach designed to reduce risk and increa performance of an investment portfolio by using different classes of securities that don't always move in the same direction at the same time.

monetarist theory An economic theory holding that the money supply is the major determinant of price levels and that, therefore, a well-controlled money supply will have the most beneficial impact on the economy.

monetary policy The Federal Reserve Board's actions that determine the size and rate of the money supply's growth, which, in turn, affect interest rates. *See also* fiscal policy.

money laundering The act of cleaning money from illegitimate enterprises through three stages known as placement, layering, and integration for the purpose of hiding the money's origin in anticipation of its later use fo legitimate and illegitimate purposes.

money market The securities market that deals in shor term debt, such as debt maturing in less than one year (e.g Treasury bills, commercial paper).

money market fund A mutual fund that invests in short-term debt instruments. The fund's objective is to ear interest while maintaining a stable net asset value of $1 pe share. Usually sold with no load, the fund may also offer draft-writing privileges and low opening investments. *See also* mutual fund.

money supply The total stock of bills, coins, loans, credit, and other liquid instruments in the economy. It is divided into four categories—L, M1, M2, and M3—according to the type of account in which the instrument kept. *See also* M1; M2; M3.

Moody's Investors Service A nationally recognized statistical rating organization (NRSRO) by the Securities and Exchanges Commission. Moody's rates bonds, commercial paper, preferred and common stocks, and municipal short-term issues. *See* bond rating; Fitch Ratings; Standard & Poor's Corporation.

moral obligation bond A municipal revenue bond for which a state legislature has the authority, but no legal obligation, to appropriate money in the event the municipal issuer defaults.

mortgage bond A debt obligation secured by a property pledge. It represents a lien or mortgage against the issuing corporation's properties and real estate assets.

moving average chart A tool used by technical analysts to track the price movements of a commodity. It plots average daily settlement prices over a defined period (e.g., over three days for a three-day moving average). *See also* bar chart; point-and-figure chart.

MSRB *See* Municipal Securities Rulemaking Board.

multiplier effect The expansion of the money supply that results from a bank being able to lend substantially more money than it receives in deposits.

municipal bond A debt security issued by a state, municipality, or other subdivision (such as a school, park, sanitation, or other local taxing district) to finance its capital expenditures. Such expenditures might include the construction of highways, public works, or school buildings. *Syn.* municipal security.

municipal bond fund A mutual fund that invests in municipal bonds and operates as either a unit investment trust or an open-end fund, with the view to maximize federally tax-exempt income. *See also* mutual fund; unit investment trust.

municipal note A short-term municipal security issued in anticipation of funds from another source. *See also* municipal bond.

Municipal Securities Rulemaking Board (MSRB) A self-regulatory organization that adopts rules with regard to the unique municipal bond market covering professional qualifications, fair practices, uniform practice, and market transparency and places administrative burdens on brokers and dealers.

municipal security Debt security issued by a state or local government, or an authority other than the federal government, to raise money for a public project. Interest payable on these instruments may be free of federal income tax.

mutual fund An investment company that continuously offers new equity shares in an actively managed portfolio of securities. *Syn.* open-end investment company; open-end management company.

mutual fund custodian A national bank, stock exchange member firm, trust company, or other qualified institution that physically safeguards the securities a mutual fund holds. It does not manage the fund's investments; its function is solely clerical.

naked *See* uncovered.

naked call writer *See* uncovered call writer

narrow-based index Commodity Futures Trading Commission defines an index with nine or fewer components designed to reflect the movement of a market segment, such as a group of stocks in one industry or a specific type of investment, as narrow-based. Examples include the Technology Index and the Gold/Silver Index. *See also* broad-based index; index.

Nasdaq *See* National Association of Securities Dealers Automated Quotations, a stock exchange.

Nasdaq Capital Market Of the three Nasdaq market tiers, has the least stringent listing requirements.

Nasdaq Global Market One of three Nasdaq market tiers. Global Market is mid cap, second in hierarchy behind the Global Select Market, and higher than Nasdaq Capital Market.

Nasdaq Global Select Market Market tier with initial listing standards that rank among the highest of any market.

Nasdaq-100 An index of the largest 100 nonfinancial stocks on Nasdaq, weighted according to capitalization.

National Association of Securities Dealers Automated Quotations (Nasdaq) A U.S.-based cash equities stock exchange.

National Market System (Regulation NMS) A broad, sweeping SEC regulation designed to bring trading and reporting uniformity to U.S. securities markets. *See also* order protection rule; minimum increment price rule.

National Public Finance Guarantee A public corporation offering insurance as to the timely payment of principal and interest on qualified municipal issues. Nonrated issues with insurance are implied to be rated AAA.

National Securities Clearing Corporation (NSCC) An organization that acts as a medium through which member brokerage firms, banks, and exchanges reconcile accounts with each other. Provides clearance and settlement functions as well as ACATS. *See* qualified service representative.

NAV *See* net asset value.

NAV of fund The net total of a mutual fund's assets and liabilities. It is used to calculate the price of new fund shares.

NAV per share The value of a mutual fund share, calculated by dividing the fund's total net asset value by the number of shares outstanding.

negotiable certificate of deposit (CD) An unsecured promissory note issued with a minimum face value of $100,000. It evidences a time deposit of funds with the issuing bank and is guaranteed by the bank. *Syn.* Jumbo CD.

negotiated underwriting A form of underwriting agreement in which a brokerage firm consults with the issuer to determine the most suitable price, timing, and call provisions of a forthcoming securities offering. *See also* competitive bid underwriting. *Syn.* negotiated sale.

net asset value (NAV) The daily computation of the value of a mutual fund that is reached by deducting the fund's liabilities from the closing market value of all of its shares and then dividing by the number of outstanding shares.

net change The difference between a security's closing price on the trading day reported and the previous day's closing price. In over-the-counter transactions, the term refers to the difference between the closing bids.

net debt to assessed valuation A measure of the financial condition of a municipality. It compares the municipality's debt obligations to the assessed value of its property.

net direct debt A method a municipality uses to calculate its bonded debt by taking the direct debt, less sinking fund accumulations and self-supporting debt. *Syn.* net bonded debt.

net income to net sales *See* net profit ratio.

net interest cost (NIC) The valuation that an issuer of bonds uses to compute the overall interest expense based on the average coupon rate, weighted to years of maturity, and is adjusted for discounts or premiums. *See also* true interest cost.

net investment income (NII) The source of an investment company's dividend payments.

net investment return Pretax income received from investment assets (e.g., bonds, stocks, mutual funds, and other investments less related expenses).

net operating profits interest A sharing arrangement in an oil and gas direct participation program whereby the general partner bears none of the program's costs but is entitled to a percentage of profits after all royalties and operating expenses have been paid. *See also* sharing arrangement.

net proceeds The amount of money received from the sale an asset, less expenses incurred, such as selling commissions.

net profit ratio A measure of a corporation's relative profitability. It is calculated by dividing after-tax income by net sales.

net revenue pledge The flow of funds arrangement in a municipal revenue bond issue pledging that operating and maintenance expenses will be paid before debt service. *See also* gross revenue pledge.

net tangible assets per share *See* book value per share

net total debt The sum of the debt obligations of a municipality, calculated by adding the municipality's net direct debt to its overlapping debt. *See also* net direct debt; overlapping debt.

net worth The amount by which assets exceed liabilities *Syn.* owners' equity; shareholders' equity; stockholders' equity.

Network A A Consolidated Tape reporting system that provides subscribers with information on transactions in NYSE-listed securities. *See also* Consolidated Tape.

new account form The form that must be filled out for each new account opened with a brokerage firm. The form specifies, at a minimum, the account owner, trading authorization, payment and delivery method, and types of securities appropriate for the customer.

new construction program A real estate direct participation program that aims to provide capital appreciation from building new property.

New York Stock Exchange Composite Index An index of the common stocks, ADRs, REITs, and tracking stock listed on the NYSE.

NH *See* not held order.

NHA A public housing agency whose bonds are backed by the U.S. government.

NIC *See* net interest cost.

no-load The term used to describe a mutual fund whose shares are offered without a sales charge.

nominal owner The person in whose name securities are registered if that person is someone other than the beneficial owner (e.g., the brokerage firm when customer securities are held in street name).

nominal quote A quotation for a security that does not represent an actual offer to buy or sell but is given for informational purposes only. *See* workable indication.

nominal yield The interest rate stated on the face of a bond that represents the percentage of interest the issuer pays on the bond's face value. *Syn.* coupon rate; stated yield. *See also* bond yield.

nonaffiliate A person, who is not an executive officer, a director, or large shareholder, in a relationship of control with an issuer.

nonaccredited investor An investor not meeting the income or net worth requirements of Regulation D. Nonaccredited investors are counted for purposes of the 35-investor limitation for Regulation D private placements.

noncompetitive bid An order placed by smaller investors for Treasury bills in which the investor agrees to pay stop-out price and, in return, is guaranteed that the order will be filled. *Syn.* noncompetitive tender.

noncumulative preferred stock An equity security that does not pay any dividends in arrears to the holder. *See also* convertible preferred stock; cumulative preferred stock; preferred stock.

nondiscrimination In a qualified retirement plan, a formula for calculating contributions and benefits that must be applied uniformly so as to ensure that all employees receive the same treatment. *See also* qualified retirement plan.

nondiversification A portfolio management strategy that concentrates investments in a particular industry or geographic area in hopes of achieving higher returns. *See also* diversification.

nonequity option A security representing the right to buy or sell an investment instrument other than a common stock at a specified price within a specified period. Examples include foreign currencies, indexes, and interest rates. *See also* equity option; foreign currency option; index option; interest rate option; option.

nonmargin security A security that does not have loan value that must be paid for in full and that may not be used as collateral for a loan. *See also* margin security.

nonqualified retirement plan A corporate retirement plan that does not meet the standards set by the Employee Retirement Income Security Act of 1974.

nonrecourse financing Debt incurred for a partnership that does not hold the limited partners personally liable. *See also* recourse financing.

nonsytematic risk Company-specific risk that can be reduced through diversification. *Syn.* unsystematic risk. *See* systematic risk.

normal yield curve A chart showing long-term debt instruments having higher yields than short-term debt instruments. *Syn.* positive yield curve. *See* flat yield curve; inverted yield curve; yield curve.

note A short-term debt security, usually maturing in five years or less. *See* municipal note; Treasury note.

NSCC *See* National Securities Clearing Corporation.

numbered account An account legally titled with something other than the customer's name. The title might be a number, symbol, or special title. The customer must sign a form designating account ownership.

NYSE *See* New York Stock Exchange.

NYSE Composite Index *See* New York Stock Exchange Composite Index.

OBO *See* order book official.

OCC *See* (1) Options Clearing Corporation or (2) Office of the Comptroller of the Currency.

OCC Disclosure Document *See* options disclosure document.

odd lot An amount of a security that is less than the normal unit of trading for that security. Generally, an odd lot is fewer than 100 shares of stock or five bonds. *See also* round lot.

odd-lot theory In technical analysis, a theory that assumes small investors are nearly always wrong. Therefore, if odd-lot sales are up, signifying that small investors are selling, it is a good time to buy.

offer (1) Under the Uniform Securities Act, any attempt to solicit a purchase or sale in a security for value. (2) An indication by an investor, trader, or dealer of a willingness to sell a security; the price at which an investor can buy from a broker-dealer. *See* bid.

offering circular Similar to a prospectus used by corporations issuing securities under a safe harbor from the Securities Act of 1933 (e.g., small offerings, such as a Regulation A, that offer no more than $50 million).

official notice of sale The invitation to bid on a municipal bond issue. The invitation is sent to prospective underwriters and specifies, among other things, the date, time, and place of sale; description of the issue; maturities; and call provisions, as well as the amount of good faith deposit required.

official statement (OS) A disclosure document distributed to purchasers of municipal securities. The OS is the responsibility of the issuer and must be prepared for issues greater than $1 million. *See* SEC Rule 15c2-12.

OID *See* original issue discount bond.

oil and gas direct participation program A direct participation program formed to locate new oil and gas reserves, develop existing reserves, or generate income from producing wells. *Syn.* oil and gas limited partnership.

oil depletion allowance An accounting procedure that reduces the taxable portion of revenues from the sale of oil to compensate for the decreased supply of oil in the ground. Depletion is the natural resource counterpart of depreciation.

omnibus account An account opened in the name of an investment adviser, broker-dealer, or futures commission merchant for the benefit of its customers. The firm carrying the account does not receive disclosure of the individual customers' names or holdings and does not maintain records for the individual customers, thus protecting identity. *Syn.* special omnibus account.

open order *See* good-till-canceled order.

open-end covenant A provision of a bond's trust indenture allowing the issuer to use the same collateral backing for a bond as collateral for future bond issues, resulting in new creditors having equal claim with existing creditors. *See also* closed-end covenant; junior lien debt.

open-end investment company *See* mutual fund.

open-market operations The buying and selling of government or agency debt securities by the Federal Reserve Board's Federal Open Market Committee to control the money supply.

operating expenses The day-to-day costs incurred in running a business, such as out-of-pocket expenses for labor, materials, supplies, and so forth.

operating income The profit realized over a period of business operation.

operating ratio The ratio of operating expenses to net sales. The complement to the margin of profit ratio.

operations and maintenance fund The account from which current operating and maintenance expenses on a facility financed by a municipal revenue bond are paid. *See* flow of funds.

operator The person who supervises and manages the exploration, drilling, mining, production, and leasehold operations of an oil and gas or mining direct participation program.

option A contract that represents the right to buy or sell a security or futures contract at a specified price within a specified time. The purchaser acquires a right, and the seller assumes an obligation.

option agreement The document a customer must sign within 15 calendar days of being approved for options trading. In it, the customer agrees to abide by the rules of the options exchanges and not to exceed position or exercise limits.

Options Clearing Corporation (OCC) The organization that issues options, standardizes option contracts, and guarantees their performance.

order book official (OBO) An employee of the Chicago Board Options Exchange who is responsible for maintaining a fair and orderly market.

order department The department within a brokerage firm that transmits orders to the proper market for execution, as well as returns confirmations to the appropriate representative. *Syn.* order room; wire room.

order memorandum The form completed by a registered representative that contains customer instructions regarding the placement of an order. *Syn.* order ticket.

order protection rule Requires that traders receive an execution price equivalent to the best that is offered on all venues for that security. Under SEC Regulation NMS, prohibits trade-throughs.

order room *See* order department.

order ticket *See* order memorandum.

ordinary income Mainly wages, salaries, commissions, and interest income (as from bonds) taxed at the individual's marginal rate tax bracket.

organization and offering expense The cost of preparing a direct participation program for registration and subsequently offering and distributing it to the public. The cost includes sales commissions paid to broker-dealers

original issue discount bond (OID) A debt security issued at a discount from face value. The discount on an OID bond is accreted annually for the purpose of calculating cost basis. *See also* zero-coupon bond.

OTC Bulletin Board (OTCBB) A regulated interdealer quotation system that displays real-time quotes, last-sale prices, and volume information for OTC equity securities not listed or traded on an exchange.

OTC margin security A security that is not traded on a national exchange but has been designated by the Federal Reserve Board as eligible for trading on margin.

OTC market A negotiated market in which broker-dealers deal directly with one another rather than through an auction on an exchange floor. *Syn.* second market.

OTC Market Group, Inc. The publisher of compiled quotes from market makers in over-the-counter stocks and bonds.

OTC option An option contract that is not listed on an exchange. All contract terms are negotiated between the buyer and seller. *Syn.* nonstandard option. *See also* listed option.

out-of-the-money The term used to describe an option that has no intrinsic value (e.g., a call option when the stock is selling below the exercise price, or a put option when the stock is selling above the exercise price). *See also* at-the-money; in-the-money; intrinsic value.

outstanding stock Equity securities issued by a corporation and in the hands of the public. Issued stock that the issuer has not reacquired. *See also* treasury stock.

overbought When the appetite for an asset pushes its price to levels not supported by the fundamentals.

overlapping debt A municipal issuer's proportionate share of the debt of other local governmental units that overlap it geographically, either in whole or in part.

overriding royalty interest A sharing arrangement whereby a person with a royalty interest in an oil and gas direct participation program takes no risks but receives a share of the revenues. The share is carved out of the working interest without liability for any costs of extraction. *See also* sharing arrangement.

oversold A technical analysis term for a market in which more and stronger selling has occurred than the fundamentals justify. *See also* overbought.

paid-in capital The money a corporation receives in excess of the stated value of the stock at the time of first sale.

par value The dollar amount assigned to a security by the issuer. Par for common stock usually bears no relationship to the market price. Par for debt security is usually $1,000, while par for preferred is usually $100. *Syn.* face value; principal; stated value.

parity (convertible securities) When a convertible security (bond or preferred stock) is selling at the same price as the value of the converted common stock.

parity (options) Describes an in-the-money option trading at its intrinsic value (i.e., an option trading at parity with the underlying security). *See* intrinsic value.

parity (trading priority) In an exchange market, a situation in which all brokers bidding have equal standing, and the winning bid is awarded by a random drawing. *See also* precedence; priority.

participant (1) A person who advises stockholders in a proxy contest. (2) The holder of an interest in a direct participation program. (3) An individual covered by an ERISA plan.

participating preferred stock Preferred stock offering the owner a share of corporate earnings remaining after all senior securities to it have been paid. The payment is made in addition to the fixed dividend stated on the certificate and may be cumulative or noncumulative. *See also* convertible preferred stock; cumulative preferred stock; noncumulative preferred stock; preferred stock.

partnership A form of business organization requiring a minimum of two participants.

partnership account Empowers individual members to act on behalf of the partnership as a whole.

partnership management fee The amount payable to the general partners of a limited partnership or to other persons for managing the day-to-day partnership operations. *Syn.* program management fee; property management fee.

pass-through certificate A security representing an interest in a pool of conventional, Veterans Administration, Farmers Home Administration, or other agency mortgages. The pool receives the principal and interest payments, which it passes through to each certificate holder. *See* Federal National Mortgage Association; Government National Mortgage Association.

passive investment An interest in, for example, rental property, limited partnership, or other enterprise in which the individual is not actively involved. Passive income, therefore, does not include earnings from wages or active business participation, nor does it include income from dividends, interest, and capital gains. *See also* passive loss; unearned income.

passive loss A loss incurred through a rental property, limited partnership, or other enterprise in which the individual is not actively involved. These losses may be used to offset passive income only, not wage or portfolio income. *See also* passive income.

pattern A repetitive series of price movements on a chart used by a technical analyst to predict future movements of the market.

payment date The day on which a declared dividend is paid to all stockholders owning shares on the record date. *See* record date; ex-date.

payout stage *See* distribution stage.

payroll deduction plan An employer's withholding of money for certain purposes, such as benefits and taxes, or for retirement plans, such as a payroll deduction IRA. These plans are not qualified under ERISA.

PE ratio *See* price-earnings ratio.

peak The stage of the business cycle that signals the end of a period of increasing business activity throughout the economy. *Syn.* prosperity. *See also* business cycle.

person As defined in securities law, an individual, corporation, partnership, association, fund, joint stock company, unincorporated organization, trust, government, or political subdivision of a government.

personal income (PI) An individual's total earnings derived from wages, passive business enterprises, and investments. *See also* disposable income.

phantom income Taxable income that is not constructively received but taxed as if it were. *See also* crossover point.

pipeline theory *See* conduit theory.

placement ratio A ratio compiled by The Bond Buyer indicating the number of new municipal issues amounting to $10 million par value or more that have sold within the past week. *Syn.* acceptance ratio.

plan custodian An institution retained by an investment company to perform clerical duties, including the safeguarding of plan assets, sending out customer confirmations, and issuing shares. *See also* custodian; mutual fund custodian.

point A measure of a securities price. (For example, a bond's price of 1 point is equal to 1% of the par value of $1,000, or $10. In stock, 1 point is $1 per share.) *See also* basis point.

point-and-figure chart A tool used by technical analysts to track the effects of price reversals or changes in the direction of prices of a commodity. See also bar chart; moving average chart.

POP *See* public offering price.

portfolio income Earnings from interest, dividends, and all nonbusiness investments. *See* earned income; passive income; unearned income.

portfolio manager The entity (i.e., the adviser) responsible for investing a mutual fund's assets, implementing its investment strategy, and managing day-to-day portfolio trading. *Syn.* fund manager.

position The amount of a security either owned (a long position) or owed (a short position) by an individual or a dealer.

position limit (1) The rule established by options exchanges that prohibits an investor from having a net long or short position of more than a specific number of contracts on the same side of the market. (2) The CFTC rule that prohibits a commodity speculator from having a net long or short position of more than a specific number of futures or futures option contracts on the same side of the market.

positive yield curve *See* normal yield curve.

power of substitution *See* power of attorney.

precedence In an exchange market, the hierarchy of bid and offer ranking according to the number of shares involved. *See also* parity; priority.

preemptive right A stockholder's legal right to maintain a proportionate ownership by purchasing newly issued shares before the new stock is offered to the public. *See also* right.

preferred dividend coverage ratio A measurement of a corporation's ability to make preferred dividend payments. It is computed by dividing preferred dividends by net income.

preferred stock An equity security that represents nonvoting ownership in a corporation. Preferred stock is senior to common and junior to debt. *See also* callable preferred stock; convertible preferred stock; cumulative preferred stock.

preferred stock fund A mutual fund whose investment objective is to provide stable income with minimal capital risk by investing in income-producing instruments such as preferred stock. *See also* bond fund.

preliminary prospectus An abbreviated prospectus that is distributed while the SEC is reviewing an issuer's registration statement. It contains all of the essential facts, but it does not contain pricing or the effective date.

premium (1) The amount of cash that an option buyer pays to an option seller. (2) The difference between the higher price paid for a debt security and the security's face amount at issue. *See also* discount.

premium bond A bond that sells at a higher price than its face value. *See* discount bond; par value.

prerefunding *See* advance refunding.

presale order A presale order is obtained before formation of the underwriting bid of a new municipal bond issue. If the syndicate wins the bid, the order takes the highest priority when orders are filled. *See also* designated order; group net order; member-at-the-takedown order.

price risk The potential that the value of a currency or commodity will change between the signing of a delivery contract and the time delivery is made. The futures markets serve to manage price risk.

price spread *See* vertical spread.

price-earnings (P/E) ratio A tool for comparing the prices of different common stocks by dividing the current market price of the stock by the earnings per share.

primary dealer Large bank or brokerage firm designated by the Federal Reserve Board to bid at Treasury auctions.

primary distribution *See* primary offering.

primary market The issuance of securities that fund municipality, sovereign government, or company to nvestors. See secondary market.

rimary offering An offering in which the proceeds of he underwriting go to the issuing corporation, agency, or unicipality. The issuer seeks to increase its capitalization ither by selling shares of stock, representing ownership, or y selling bonds, representing loans to the issuer.

prime rate The interest rate that commercial banks charge their prime or most creditworthy customers—generally large corporations.

principal (1) A supervisory employee at a broker-dealer. (2) A party in a transaction who is trading for the party's own account.

principal transaction A transaction in which a broker-dealer either buys securities from customers and takes them into its own inventory or sells securities to customers from its inventory. *See also* agency transaction; agent; broker-dealer; principal.

prior lien bond A secured bond that takes precedence over other bonds secured by the same assets. *See also* mortgage bond.

priority In an exchange market, the ranking of bids and offers according to the first person to bid or offer at a given price.

private label CMO Collateralized mortgage obligations issued by investment banks or their subsidiaries, financial institutions, or home builders.

private placement An offering of new issue securities under Regulation D that is not available to the public as a whole, but rather, select investors. *See also* Regulation D.

productive well An oil or gas well that produces mineral resources that may be marketed commercially. *See also* dry hole.

profit-sharing plan An employee benefit plan established and maintained by an employer whereby the employees receive a share of the business's profits.

profitability The ability to generate a level of income and gain in excess of expenses.

profitability ratio One of several measures of a corporation's relative profit or income in relation to its sales. *See* margin of profit ratio; return on equity.

progressive tax A tax that takes a larger percentage of income from high-income earners than that of low-income earners (e.g., the graduated income tax). *See* regressive tax.

prospectus The disclosure document required in conjunction with primary securities offerings and commodity limited partnerships (pools) that must register with the Securities Exchange Commission (SEC). *See* preliminary prospectus; statutory prospectus; summary prospectus; final prospectus.

proxy A limited power of attorney from a stockholder authorizing another person to vote on stockholder issues according to the stockholder's instructions. To vote on corporate matters, a stockholder must either attend the annual meeting or vote by proxy.

proxy department The department within a brokerage firm that is responsible for sending proxy statements to customers whose securities are held in the firm's name, and for mailing financial reports received from issuers to their stockholders.

prudent investor rule Legally known as the Uniform Prudent Investors Act of 1994 (UPIA). A modern adaptation of the prudent man rule, which, as a result of the development of modern portfolio theory, applies the standard of prudence to the entire portfolio rather than to individual investments. It requires the fiduciary to measure risk with respect to return.

Public Housing Authority bond (PHA) *See* New Housing Authority bond.

public offering price (POP) (1) The price of new shares that is established in the issuing corporation's prospectus. (2) The price to investors for mutual fund shares, equal to the net asset value plus the sales charge. *See also* ask; bid; mutual fund; net asset value.

public purpose bond A municipal bond that is exempt from federal income tax, as long as no more than 10% of the proceeds benefit private entities.

Public Securities Association (PSA) An organization of banks and broker-dealers that conducts business in mortgage-backed securities, money market securities, and securities issued by the U.S. government, government agencies, and municipalities.

publicly traded fund *See* closed-end investment company.

purchasing power risk The potential that, because of inflation, a certain amount of money will not purchase as much in the future as it does today. *Syn.* inflation risk.

put (1) An option contract giving the owner the right to sell a specified amount of an underlying security at a specified price within a specified time. (2) The act of exercising a put option. *See also* call.

put bond A debt security requiring the issuer to purchase the security at the holder's discretion or within a prescribed time. *Syn.* tender bond.

put buyer An investor who pays a premium for an option contract and receives, for a specified time, the right to sell the underlying security at a specified price.

put spread An option investor's position in which the investor buys a put on a particular security and writes a put on the same security but with a different expiration date, exercise price, or both.

put writer An investor who receives a premium and takes on, for a specified time, the obligation to buy the underlying security at a specified price at the put buyer's discretion.

pyramiding A speculative strategy whereby an investor uses unrealized profits from a position held to increase the size of the position continuously, but by ever-smaller amounts.

qualification *See* registration by qualification.

qualified legal opinion The statement of a bond attorney affirming the validity of a new municipal bond issue but expressing reservations about its quality. *See* legal opinion of counsel; unqualified legal opinion.

qualified retirement plan A corporate retirement plan that meets the standards set by the Employee Retirement Income Security Act of 1974. Contributions to a qualified plan are tax deductible.

quick assets A measure of a corporation's liquidity that takes into account the size of the unsold inventory. It is calculated by subtracting inventory from current assets, and it is used in the acid-test ratio. *See also* acid-test ratio.

quick ratio *See* acid-test ratio.

quotation The price being offered or bid by a market maker or broker-dealer for a particular security. *Syn.* quote. *See also* ask; bid; bond quote; stock quote.

quote *See* quotation.

RAN *See* revenue anticipation note.

random walk theory A market analysis theory that the past movement or direction of the price of a stock or market cannot be used to predict its future movement or direction.

range A security's low price and high price for a particular trading period, such as the close of a day's trading, the opening of a day's trading, or a day, month, or year. *Syn.* opening range.

rate covenant A provision of a municipal revenue bond's trust indenture that helps ensure the safety of the issue by specifying the rates to charge the user of the facili *See* maintenance covenant.

rating An evaluation of a corporate or municipal bond's relative safety, according to the issuer's ability to repay principal and make interest payments. Bonds are rated by various organizations such as Standard & Poor's and Moody's. Ratings range from AAA or Aaa (the highest) to C or D (company in default).

rating service A company, such as Moody's or Standard & Poor's, that rates various debt and preferred stock issues for safety of payment of principal, interest, or dividends. The issuing company or municipality pays a fee for the rating. See also rating.

ratio writing An option hedge position in which the investor writes more than one call option for every 100 shares of underlying stock the investor owns. As a result, the investor has a partly covered position and a partly naked position.

raw land program A real estate direct participation program that aims to provide capital appreciation by investing in undeveloped land.

real estate investment trust (REIT) A corporation or trust that uses the pooled capital of many investors to invest in direct ownership of either income property or mortgage loans. REITs that are traded on exchanges or OTC are considered very liquid. Real estate is not.

real estate limited partnership A direct participation program formed to build new structures, generate income from existing property, or profit from the capital appreciation of undeveloped land.

realized gain The amount earned by a taxpayer when an asset is sold for a profit. *See also* unrealized gain.

reallowance A portion of the concession available to firms that sell shares in an offering but are not syndicate or selling group members.

recapitalization Changing the capital structure of a corporation by issuing, converting, or redeeming securities.

recapture The taxation as ordinary income of previously earned deductions or credits. Circumstances that may cause the IRS to require this tax to be paid include excess depreciation, premature sale of an asset, or disallowing of a previous tax benefit.

recession A general economic decline lasting from 6 to 18 months (at least two consecutive quarters of declining or negative GDP growth).

reciprocal immunity *See* doctrine of mutual reciprocity.

reclamation Reclamation occurs when a buyer, after accepting securities as good delivery, later discovers that the certificates were not in good deliverable form. The securities can be sent back to the selling dealer with a Uniform Reclamation Form attached.

reclassification The exchange by a corporation of one class of its securities for another class of its securities.

record date The date a corporation's board of directors establishes that determines which of its stockholders are entitled to receive dividends or rights distributions.

recourse financing (loan) Debt incurred for the purchase of an asset and that which holds the borrower personally liable for the debt. *See also* nonrecourse financing.

recovery *See* expansion.

red herring *See* preliminary prospectus.

redeemable security A security that the issuer redeems upon the holder's request. Examples include shares in an open-end investment company and Treasury notes.

redemption The last payment made by the issuer of a debt security. It would represent the principal amount plus the last interest payment (six months of interest).

redemption notice A published announcement that a corporation or municipality is calling a certain issue of its bonds.

regional exchange A stock exchange that serves the financial community in a particular region of the country. These exchanges tend to focus on securities issued within their regions, but also offer trading in NYSE-listed securities.

registered The term that describes a security that prints the name of the owner on the certificate. The owner's name is stored in records kept by the issuer or a transfer agent.

registered as to principal only The term used to describe a bond that prints the name of the owner on the certificate but that has unregistered coupons payable to the bearer. *Syn.* partially registered. *See* coupon bond; fully registered bond.

registered options principal (ROP) A principal at a member firm that supervises options accounts, transactions, and options-related communications.

registered principal An associated person of a member firm who manages or supervises the firm's investment banking or securities business. This includes persons who train associated persons. Unless the member firm is a sole proprietorship, it must employ at least two registered principals.

registered representative (RR) An associated person engaged in the investment banking or securities business. This includes any individual who supervises, solicits, or conducts business in securities or who trains people to supervise, solicit, or conduct business in securities.

registrar The independent organization or part of a corporation responsible for accounting for all of the issuer's outstanding stock and certifying that its bonds constitute legal debt.

registration by coordination A process that allows a security to be sold in a state. It is available to an issuer who files for registration of the security under the Securities Act of 1933 and files duplicates of the registration documents with the state administrator. State registration becomes effective at the same time the federal registration statement becomes effective.

registration by qualification A process that allows a security to be sold in a state. It is available to an issuer who files for registration of the security with the state administrator; meets minimum net worth, disclosure and other requirements; and files appropriate registration fees. The state registration becomes effective when the administrator so orders.

regressive tax A tax that takes a larger percentage of the income of low-income earners than that of high-income earners. Examples include gasoline and cigarette tax.

regular way settlement The time when standard securities transactions are settled. The Uniform Practice Code sets the standard payment period. The type of security being traded determines the amount of time allowed for regular way settlement. *See also* cash transaction; settlement date.

regulated investment company An investment company to which Subchapter M of the Internal Revenue Code grants special status that allows the flow-through of tax consequences on a distribution to shareholders.

Regulation A+ Provides two offering tiers for small- and medium-sized companies that will allow them to raise capital in amounts substantially more than the $5 million previously allowed under Regulation A. There are two tiers: tier 1 for offerings of up to $20 million and tier 2 for offerings of up to $50 million.

Regulation D The provision of the Securities Act of 1933 that exempts from registration offerings sold in private placements. *See* private placement.

Regulation NMS An SEC regulation that fosters competition between markets/exchanges and competition among orders.

Regulation S-P An SEC regulation covering privacy rules promulgated under the Gramm-Leach-Bliley Act. A broker-dealer must provide customers with a notice of its privacy policies and practices and must not disclose nonpublic personal information about a consumer to nonaffiliated third parties unless it provides certain information to the consumer and the consumer has not opted out of the disclosure. Rigorous standards to protect privacy are also required under the regulation.

Regulation T The Federal Reserve Board regulation that governs customer cash accounts and the amount of credit that brokerage firms and dealers may extend to customers for the purchase of securities. Regulation T currently sets the loan value of marginable securities at 50% and the payment deadline at two days beyond regular way settlement. *Syn.* Reg T. *See also* Regulation G; Regulation U.

Regulation U The Federal Reserve Board regulation that governs loans by banks for the purchase of securities. Call loans are exempt from Regulation U. *See also* broker's loan; call loan; Regulation T.

rehypothecation The pledging of a client's securities as collateral for a bank loan. Brokerage firms may rehypothecate up to 140% of customer debit balances to finance margin loans to customers. *See also* hypothecation.

reinstatement privilege A benefit offered by some mutual funds allowing an investor to withdraw money from a fund account and then redeposit the money without paying a second sales charge.

REIT *See* real estate investment trust.

rejection The right of the buyer of a security to refuse to accept delivery in completion of a trade because the security does not meet the requirements of good delivery.

renewal and replacement fund The account that is used to fund major renewal projects and equipment replacements financed by a municipal revenue bond issue. *See also* flow of funds.

reoffering price The price or yield at which a municipal security is sold to the public by the underwriters.

eorganization department The department within brokerage firm that handles transactions that represent a ange in the securities outstanding, such as trades relating tender offers, bond calls, preferred stock redemptions, d mergers and acquisitions.

po *See* repurchase agreement.

purchase agreement A sale of securities with an tendant agreement to repurchase them at a higher price n an agreed-upon future date. The difference between the le price and the repurchase price represents the interest rned by the investor. Repos are considered money market struments and are used to raise short-term capital and as struments of monetary policy. *Syn.* repo. *See also* reverse purchase agreement.

serve maintenance fund The account that holds oney that supplements the general maintenance fund of a unicipal revenue bond issue. *See also* flow of funds.

serve requirement The percentage of depositors' oney that the Federal Reserve Board requires a mmercial bank to keep on deposit in the form of cash or its vault. *Syn.* reserves.

sidual claim The right of a common stockholder to aim corporate assets in the event that the corporation ases to exist. A common stockholder may claim assets ly after the claims of all creditors and other security olders have been satisfied.

sistance level A technical analysis term describing the p of a stock's historical trading range. *See also* breakout; pport level.

stricted account A margin account in which the uity is less than the Regulation T initial requirement. *See so* equity; initial margin requirement; margin account; tention requirement.

stricted security An unregistered, nonexempt curity acquired either directly or indirectly from the suer—or an affiliate of the issuer—in a transaction that es not involve a public offering.

tail communication Any written (including ectronic) communication that is distributed or made ailable to more than 25 retail investors within any)-calendar-day period. A retail investor is any person other an an institutional investor, regardless of whether the rson has an account with the member.

tained earnings The amount of a corporation's net come that remains after all dividends have been paid to eferred and common stockholders. *Syn.* earned surplus; invested earnings.

retention requirement The provision of Regulation T that applies to the withdrawal of securities from a restricted account. The customer must deposit an amount equal to the unpaid portion of the securities being withdrawn in order to reduce the debit balance. The retention requirement is the reciprocal of the initial margin requirement. *See also* restricted account.

retirement account A customer account established to provide retirement funds.

retiring bonds Ending an issuer's debt obligation by calling the outstanding bonds, purchasing bonds in the open market, or paying bondholders the principal amount at maturity.

return on common equity A measure of a corporation's profitability, calculated by dividing after-tax income by common shareholders' equity.

return on equity A measure of a corporation's profitability, specifically its return on assets, calculated by dividing after-tax income by tangible assets.

return on investment (ROI) The profit or loss resulting from a security transaction, often expressed as an annual percentage rate.

revenue anticipation note (RAN) A short-term municipal debt security issued in anticipation of revenue to be received.

revenue bond A municipal debt issue whose interest and principal are payable only from the specific earnings of an income-producing public project. *See also* double-barreled bond; general obligation bond; municipal bond; special revenue bond.

reverse churning The unsuitable practice of placing a client who trades infrequently in a fee-based account rather than a commission-based account that would be more appropriate. *Related item* churning.

reverse repo *See* reverse repurchase agreement.

reverse repurchase agreement A purchase of securities with an attendant agreement to resell them at a higher price on an agreed-upon future date. The difference between the purchase price and the resale price represents the interest earned by the investor. The purchaser initiates the deal. *Syn.* reverse repo. *See also* repurchase agreement.

reverse split A reduction in the number of a corporation's shares outstanding that increases the par value of its stock or its earnings per share. The market value of the total number of shares remains the same. *See also* stock split.

reversionary working interest A sharing arrangement whereby the general partner of a direct participation program bears none of the program's costs and does not share in revenues until the limited partners receive payment plus a predetermined rate of return. *Syn.* subordinated interest; subordinated reversionary working interest. *See also* sharing arrangement.

right (1) A legal guarantee. (2) A security representing a stockholder's entitlement to the first opportunity to purchase new shares issued by the corporation at a predetermined price (normally less than the current market price) in proportion to the number of shares already owned. Rights are issued for a short time only, after which they expire. *Syn.* subscription right; subscription right certificate.

right of accumulation A benefit offered by a mutual fund that allows the investor to qualify for reduced sales loads on additional purchases according to the fund account's total dollar value.

rights agent An issuing corporation's agent who is responsible for maintaining current records of the names of rights certificate owners.

rights offering An issue of additional shares of stock accompanied by the opportunity for each current stockholder to maintain a proportionate ownership by purchasing additional shares before the stock is offered to the nonshareholders.

risk arbitrage A form of arbitrage that has some risk associated with it. Commonly refers to potential takeover situations where the arbitrageur buys the stock of the company about to be taken over and sells the stock of the company that is effecting the takeover. *See also* dividend arbitrage.

riskless and simultaneous transaction The buying or selling by a broker-dealer of a security for its own account so as to fill an order previously received from a customer. Although the firm is technically acting as a principal in the trade, the transaction is relatively riskless because the purchase and sale are consummated almost simultaneously.

ROI *See* return on investment.

round lot A security's normal unit of trading, which is generally 100 shares of stock or five bonds. *See also* odd lot.

royalty interest The right of a mineral rights owner to receive a share in the revenues generated by the resource if and when production begins. The royalty interest retained is free from production costs.

Rule 144 An SEC rule that sets the requirements for selling or purchasing restricted, unregistered, or control securities.

Rule 145 An SEC rule that permits the sale of certain securities acquired through a merger, acquisition, or reclassification to be sold without having to first register with the SEC.

Rule 147 SEC rule that provides exemption from the registration statement and prospectus requirements of the Securities Act of 1933 for securities offered and sold exclusively intrastate.

Rule 15c2-11 SEC rule requiring prospective market makers in non-Nasdaq stocks to file Form 211 with FIN at least three business days prior to quotation entry. In signing Form 211, the firm agrees to maintain a file on th issuer that contains financial and operations information *See* piggyback exception.

Rule G-1 MSRB rule that classifies as municipal securi dealers any separately identifiable departments of banks that engage in activities related to the municipal securitie business. *See* separately identifiable department or divisio

Rule G-10 MSRB rule requiring that once every calen year, each municipal broker-dealer must provide to each customer a statement that it is registered with the SEC a MSRB, the MSRB website address, and the availability o an investor brochure outlining the protections that may afforded by the board's rules and how to file a complaint. Electronic delivery is acceptable.

Rule G-11 MSRB rule governing the priority given to orders received for new issue municipal securities and oth primary offering practices.

Rule G-12 MSRB rule governing the uniform practice for settling transactions between municipal securities firm

Rule G-13 MSRB rule requiring broker-dealers to publish only bona fide quotations for municipal securitie unless the quotations are identified as informational.

Rule G-15 MSRB rule governing the confirmation, clearance, and settlement of customer municipal securiti transactions.

Rule G-16 MSRB rule requiring examinations by a member firm's designated examining authority (DEA) to be conducted at least every four calendar years to verify compliance to board rules. Each municipal securities dea that is a bank or a subsidiary of a bank is required to be examined at least every two years.

Rule G-17 MSRB rule that sets ethical standards for conducting municipal securities business.

Rule G-18 MSRB best-execution rule requiring a deal to use reasonable diligence to ascertain the best market a to buy or sell in that market so the price to the customer as favorable as possible.

Rule G-19 MSRB rule governing discretionary accounts and the suitability of municipal securities recommendations and transactions.

Rule G-2 MSRB rule that sets professional qualification standards.

Rule G-20 MSRB rule that sets a limit on the value of gifts and gratuities given by municipal securities firms.

Rule G-21 MSRB rule governing the advertising of municipal securities.

Rule G-22 MSRB rule requiring disclosures to customers of control relationships between municipal firms and issuers.

Rule G-23 MSRB rule that seeks to minimize conflicts of interest arising out of the activities of financial advisers who also act as municipal underwriters to the same issuer.

Rule G-24 MSRB rule prohibiting the misuse of confidential information about customers obtained by municipal securities firms acting in fiduciary capacities.

Rule G-25 MSRB rule prohibiting the improper use of assets by municipal securities firms and their representatives.

Rule G-27 MSRB rule requiring each municipal securities firm to designate a principal to supervise its municipal securities representatives.

Rule G-28 MSRB rule governing employee accounts held at other municipal securities firms.

Rule G-29 MSRB rule governing the availability of MSRB regulations.

Rule G-3 MSRB rule governing the classification of municipal securities principals and representatives.

Rule G-30 MSRB rule requiring that prices and commissions charged by municipal securities firms be fair and reasonable.

Rule G-31 MSRB rule prohibiting a municipal securities professional from soliciting business from an investment company portfolio in return for sales of that fund to its customers. *Syn.* Antireciprocal rule.

Rule G-32 MSRB rule requiring that customers receive a copy of the preliminary or final official statement when purchasing a new municipal issue. *See* EMMA.

Rule G-33 MSRB rule governing the calculation of accrued interest on municipal bonds using a 360-day year.

Rule G-37 MSRB rule prohibiting municipal securities dealers from underwriting securities issued under the authority of a public official to whom an associated person of the dealer has contributed money.

Rule G-39 MSRB rule requiring telemarketers calling on behalf of a firm to limit calls to between 8:00 am and 9:00 pm in the called person's time zone. The caller must disclose his name, the firm's name, the firm's telephone number or address, and the fact that he is calling to solicit the purchase of municipal bonds or investment services. The rule does not apply if the person called is an established customer.

Rule G-41 MSRB rule requiring that municipal securities dealers establish and implement an anti-money-laundering compliance program designed to achieve and monitor ongoing compliance with the requirements of the Bank Secrecy Act.

Rule G-6 MSRB rule governing the fidelity bond requirements for member broker-dealers.

Rule G-7 MSRB rule governing the documentation that must be kept on each associated person and the length of time such records must be maintained. *See* Form U4.

S&P *See* Standard & Poor's Corporation.

S&P 100 *See* Standard & Poor's 100 Stock Index.

S&P 500 *See* Standard & Poor's Composite Index of 500 Stocks.

sale To convey ownership of a security or another asset for money or value.

sales literature Any written material distributed to customers or the public by a firm in a controlled manner. Examples include circulars, research reports, form letters, market letters, performance reports, and text used for seminars. *See also* advertisement, form letter, market letter.

sales load The amount added to a mutual fund share's net asset value to arrive at the offering price. *See also* mutual fund; net asset value; no-load fund.

SAR *See* suspicious activity report.

savings bond A government debt security that is not negotiable or transferable and may not be used as collateral. *See also* Series EE bond; Series HH bond.

scale A list of each of the scheduled maturities in a new serial bond issue. *See also* writing a scale.

SEC *See* Securities and Exchange Commission.

secondary distribution (offering) (1) A distribution, with a prospectus, that involves securities owned by major stockholders (typically founders or principal owners of a corporation). The sale proceeds go to the sellers of the stock, not to the issuer. *Syn.* registered secondary distribution. (2) A procedure for trading very large blocks of stock shares whereby the trade is executed off the floor of an exchange after the market closes.

secondary market An aftermarket where investors buy and sell to each other apart from the issuer. Exchanges, such as Nasdaq, NYSE, and NYSE American, facilitate the secondary market.

sector fund A mutual fund whose investment objective is to capitalize on the return potential provided by investing primarily in a particular industry or sector of the economy. *Syn.* industry fund; specialized fund.

secured bond A debt security backed by identifiable assets set aside as collateral. In the event the issuer defaults on payment, the bondholders may lay claim to the collateral. *See also* debenture.

Securities Act of 1933 Federal legislation requiring the full and fair disclosure of all material information about the issuance of new securities. Syn. Act of 1933; Full Disclosure Act; New Issues Act; Prospectus Act; Trust in Securities Act; Truth in Securities Act.

Securities Acts Amendments of 1975 Federal legislation that established the Municipal Securities Rulemaking Board. *See also* Municipal Securities Rulemaking Board.

Securities and Exchange Commission (SEC) Commission created by Congress to regulate the securities markets and protect investors. The SEC enforces, among other acts, the Securities Act of 1933, the Securities Exchange Act of 1934, the Trust Indenture Act of 1939, the Investment Company Act of 1940, and the Investment Advisers Act of 1940.

Securities Exchange Act of 1934 Federal legislation that established the Securities and Exchange Commission and aims to protect investors by regulating the exchanges, over-the-counter market, extension of credit by the Federal Reserve Board, broker-dealers, insider transactions, trading activities, client accounts, and net capital. *Syn.* Act of 1934; Exchange Act.

Securities Investor Protection Corporation (SIPC) A nonprofit membership corporation created by an act of Congress to protect clients of brokerage firms that are forced into bankruptcy. Its membership includes all brokers and dealers registered under the Securities Exchange Act of 1934, all members of national securities exchanges, and most FINRA members.

securitization Pooling assets that may be smaller or less liquid into financial instruments, allowing them to be sold more easily to investors.

security Generally, an instrument evidencing debt of, or equity in, a common enterprise in which an investment is made with the expectation of financial return.

segregation Holding customer-owned securities separate from securities owned by other customers and the brokerage firm. *See also* commingling.

selection risk The potential for loss on an investment due to the chosen security's poor performance, in spite of good overall market or industry performance.

self-regulatory organization (SRO) An organization accountable to the SEC for the enforcement of federal securities laws and the supervision of securities practices within an assigned field of jurisdiction.

sell stop order An order to sell a security that is entered at a price below the current market price and that is triggered when the market price touches or goes through the sell stop price.

seller's option A settlement contract that calls for delivery and payment according to a number of days agreed to by the buyer. The earliest delivery can be made is settlement date plus 1 business day.

selling away An associated person engaging in private securities transactions without the knowledge and consent of the employing broker-dealer. This violates FINRA rules.

selling concession *See* concession.

selling dividends Prohibited practice of inducing customers to buy shares by implying that an upcoming distribution will benefit them.

selling group Selected broker-dealers who contract to act as selling agents for underwriting syndicate members and who are compensated by a portion of the spread called the selling concession on newly issued securities. They assume no financial liability to the issuer, as opposed to a syndicate member.

sellout When a customer buying securities has not delivered the required funds by two business days after the settlement date, the broker-dealer must sell the securities (the sellout), charge the customer for any losses incurred, and freeze the customer's account for 90 days.

senior lien debt A bond issue that shares the same collateral as that which is backing other issues, but which has a prior claim to the collateral in the event of default.

senior security A security that grants its holder a prior claim to the issuer's assets over the claims of another security's holders.

SEP-IRA *See* simplified employee pension plan.

separate account The account that holds funds paid by variable contracts issued by insurance companies. The funds are kept separate from the insurer's general account.

Separate Trading of Registered Interest and Principal of Securities (STRIPS) A zero-coupon bond issued and backed by the U.S Department of Treasury. *See also* zero-coupon bond; Treasury receipt.

separately identifiable department or division A department of a municipal bank dealer that engages in the business of buying or offering municipal securities under the supervision of an officer of the bank. A department classified by the MSRB as a municipal securities dealer must register with the MSRB.

serial bond A debt security issued with a maturity schedule in which parts of the outstanding issue mature at intervals until the entire balance has been repaid. *See also* maturity date; series bond.

series Options of the same class that have the same exercise price and the same expiration date. *See also* class; type.

Series 24 The General Securities Principal License, which entitles the holder to supervise the business of a broker-dealer. A Series 7 qualification is a prerequisite for his license.

Series 6 An Investment Company and Variable Contract Products Limited Representative License, which is required to sell mutual funds and variable contracts and is required by many firms that primarily sell insurance-related products.

Series 63 The Uniform Securities Agent State Law Exam, which entitles the successful candidate to sell securities in those states that require Series 63 registration. *See also* Uniform Securities Act.

Series 7 The General Securities Registered Representative License, which entitles the holder to sell all types of securities products.The Series 7 is the most comprehensive of the FINRA representative licenses and serves as a prerequisite for most principal-level examinations.

series bond Bonds issued in a series over a given period. All the bonds in the series have the same priority claim against assets. *See also* serial bond.

Series EE bond A nonmarketable, interest-bearing U.S. government savings bond issued at a discount from par. Interest on Series EE bonds is exempt from state and local taxes. *See also* savings bond; Series HH bond.

Series HH bond A nonmarketable, interest-bearing U.S. government savings bond issued at par and purchased only by trading in Series EE bonds at maturity. Interest on Series HH bonds is exempt from state and local taxes. See also savings bond; Series EE bond.

settlement The completion of a trade through the delivery of a security or commodity and the payment of cash or other consideration.

share identification An accounting method that identifies the specific shares selected for liquidation in the event an investor wishes to liquidate shares.

sharing arrangement A method of allocating the responsibility for expenses and the right to share in revenues among the sponsor and limited partners in a direct participation program. *See also* carried interest; disproportionate sharing; functional allocation; net operating profits interest; overriding royalty interest; reversionary working interest.

shelf registration (offering) Under Rule 415, an SEC provision allowing issuers to register a new issue security without selling the entire issue at once. The issuer can sell limited portions of the issue over a two-year period, and for WKSI companies, a three-year period without reregistering the security.

short (1) The term used to describe the state of not possessing a certain asset. For example, an operations person working in a "cage" cannot locate a security in the vault is said to be short. (2) An investor who borrows shares of stock from a broker-dealer and sells them is said to have a short position in the stock. (3) A producer of a commodity may short (short sell) a futures contract to hedge the commodity. *See also* long; short sale; short against the box.

short against the box The term used to describe the selling of a security, contract, or commodity that the seller owns but prefers not to deliver. Frequently, this is done to defer taxation.

short interest The total number of shares in the stock that are reflected on the books and records of a reporting firm as short as of the current reporting period's settlement date. FINRA requires member firms to report short interest positions in all customer and proprietary accounts in all equity securities twice monthly. *See* short; short sale.

short sale The sale of a security that the seller does not own, or any sale consummated by the delivery of a security borrowed by or for the account of the seller.

short straddle An option investor's position that results from selling a call and a put on the same stock with the same exercise price and expiration month. *See also* long straddle; spread; straddle.

short-term capital gain The profit realized on the sale of an asset that has been owned for 12 months or less. *See also* capital gain; capital loss; short-term capital loss.

short-term capital loss The loss incurred on the sale of a capital asset that has been owned for 12 months or less. *See also* capital gain; capital loss; short-term capital gain.

simplified arbitration A FINRA program applying to arbitrations involving $50,000 or less, exclusive of interest and expenses.

simplified employee pension plan (SEP) A qualified retirement plan allowing employers to contribute to traditional IRAs (SEP-IRAs) set up for employees.

sinking fund An account established by an issuing corporation or municipality into which money is deposited regularly so that the issuer has the funds to redeem its bonds, debentures, or preferred stock.

SIPC *See* Securities Investor Protection Corporation.

SLD A message on the Consolidated Tape indicating that the sale being reported was not reported on time and is therefore out of sequence.

SLMA *See* Student Loan Marketing Association.

SMA *See* special memorandum account.

solvency The ability of a corporation to both meet its long-term fixed expenses and have adequate money for long-term expansion and growth.

special assessment bond A municipal revenue bond funded by assessments only placed on property owners who benefit from the services or improvements provided by the proceeds of the bond issue. *See also* revenue bond.

special memorandum account (SMA) A notation on a customer's general or margin account indicating that funds are credited to the account on a memo basis. The account is used much like a line of credit with a bank. *Syn.* special miscellaneous account.

special revenue bond A municipal revenue bond issued to finance a specific project. Examples include industrial development bonds, lease rental bonds, and special tax bonds. *See also* revenue bond.

special situation fund A mutual fund whose objective is to capitalize on the profit potential of corporations in nonrecurring circumstances, such as those undergoing reorganizations or being considered as takeover candidates.

special tax bond A municipal revenue bond payable only from the proceeds of a tax on certain items, rather than an ad valorem tax. *See also* revenue bond.

specialist An NYSE American Exchange member who stands ready to provide automatically updated two-sided market quotations with size in all the appointed option series. The specialist's role is to maintain a fair, orderly, and competitive market. Formerly used on the NYSE. *Syn.* eSpecialist; specialist unit. *See* Designated Market Maker.

specialized fund *See* sector fund.

speculation Trading a commodity with a higher-than-average risk in return for a higher-than-average profit potential. The trade is effected solely for the purpose of profiting from it and not as a means of hedging or protecting other positions.

speculator One who trades a commodity or security with a higher-than-average risk in return for a higher-than-average profit potential. *See also* speculation.

spin-off A type of divestiture where a parent company sells all of the shares of a subsidiary or distributes new shares of a company or division it owns to create a new company.

split offering A public offering of securities that combines aspects of both a primary and a secondary offering. A portion of the issue is a primary offering, the proceeds of which go to the issuing corporation. The remainder of the issue is a secondary offering, the proceed of which go to the selling stockholders. *Syn.* combined distribution. *See also* primary offering; secondary offering.

sponsor (1) A person who is instrumental in organizin selling, or managing a limited partnership. (2) A term for the underwriter of a mutual fund. Another is *distributor*.

spousal account A separate individual retirement account (arrangement) established for a nonworking or low-income spouse. Contributions to the account made b the working spouse grow tax deferred until withdrawal.

spread (1) In a quotation, the difference between the bid and the ask prices. (2) An options position establishe by purchasing one option and selling another option of t same class but of a different series. (3) The price differenc between two futures contracts. It involves holding a long and a short position in two or more related futures contracts, with the objective of profiting from a change i the price relationship.

read order (1) A option position having both long tions and short options of the same type on the same derlying security. (2) A customer order specifying two tion contracts on the same underlying commodity and a ice difference between them.

RO *See* self-regulatory organization.

abilizing Bidding at or below the public offering price a new issue security. Underwriting managers may enter bilizing bids during the offering period to prevent the ice from dropping sharply. *See also* fixing; pegging.

agflation A period of high unemployment in the onomy accompanied by a general rise in prices. *See also* flation; inflation.

andard & Poor's 100 Stock Index (S&P 100) A arket-value-weighted index composed of 100 leading .S. stocks. The index is a subset of the S&P 500. *See also* dex; Standard & Poor's Corporation; Standard & Poor's omposite Index of 500 Stocks.

andard & Poor's Composite Index of 500 Stocks &P 500) (SPX) A market-value-weighted index at offers broad coverage of the securities market. is composed of 400 industrial stocks, 40 financial ocks, 40 public utility stocks, and 20 transportation ocks. The index is owned and compiled by Standard Poor's Corporation. *See also* index; Standard & Poor's orporation; Standard & Poor's 100 Index.

andby underwriter An investment banker that agrees buy any part of an issue that has not been purchased by rrent stockholders through a rights offering. The firm ercises the remaining rights, maintains a trading market the rights, and offers the stock acquired to the public.

ated yield *See* nominal yield.

atutory disqualification A person may be subject to statutory disqualification (not permitted to work in the curities industry) if the person is enjoined temporarily permanently from violating securities laws by a urt of competent jurisdiction; is barred or suspended om association with a broker-dealer by the SEC, the ommodities Futures Trading Commission (CFTC), a self-gulatory organization (SRO), or foreign equivalent; or s been convicted of any felony or certain misdemeanors ithin the past 10 years. See Securities Exchange Act of 934.

atutory voting A voting method that permits ockholders to cast one vote per share owned for each sition. This method of voting benefits majority ockholders. *See also* cumulative voting.

step-out well An oil or gas well or prospect adjacent to a field of proven reserves. *See also* developmental drilling program.

stock ahead The term used to describe the inability to fill a limit order at a specific price because other orders at the same price were entered previously.

stock broker (stockbroker) *See* registered representative. *Syn.* financial advisor; account executive.

stock certificate Printed evidence of ownership in a corporation.

stock dividend *See* dividend.

stock loan agreement The document that an institutional customer must sign when the broker-dealer borrows stock from the customer's margin account. The document specifies the terms of the loan and the rights of both parties.

stock power A standard form that duplicates the back of a stock certificate and is used for transferring the stock to the new owner's name. *Syn.* irrevocable stock power; power of substitution.

stock quote A list of representative prices bid and asked for a stock during a particular trading day. Stocks are quoted in points, where one point equals $1. *See also* bond quote.

stock split An increase in the number of a corporation's outstanding shares, which decreases its stock's par value. The market value of the total number of shares remains the same.

stop limit order A customer order that becomes a limit order when the market price of the security reaches or passes through a specific (stop) price. *See also* limit order; stop order.

stop order (1) A directive from the SEC that suspends the sale of new issue securities to the public when fraud is suspected or filing materials are deficient. (2) A customer order that becomes a market order when the market price of the security reaches or passes a specific price. *See also* limit order; market order; stop limit order.

straddle An option investor's position that results from buying a call and a put or selling a call and a put on the same security with the same exercise price and expiration month. *See also* long straddle; short straddle; spread; strangle.

straight-line depreciation An accounting method used to recover the cost of a qualifying depreciable asset, whereby the owner writes off the cost of the asset in equal amounts each year over the asset's useful life.

strike price *See* exercise price.

stripped bond A debt obligation that has been stripped of its interest coupons by a brokerage firm, repackaged, and sold at a deep discount. It pays no interest but may be redeemed at maturity for the full face value. *See also* zero-coupon bond.

stripper well An oil well that produces no more than 15 barrels or 90,000 cubic feet of gas per day over a 12-month consecutive time period.

STRIPS See Separate Trading of Registered Interest and Principal of Securities.

Student Loan Marketing Association (SLMA) A publicly owned corporation that purchases student loans from financial institutions and packages them for sale in the secondary market, thereby increasing the availability of money for educational loans. *Syn.* Sallie Mae.

subject quote A securities quotation subject to some condition requiring confirmation by the dealer. *See also* bona fide quote; firm quote; nominal quote; workout quote.

subordinated debenture A debt obligation backed by the good faith and credit of the issuing corporation that has claims to interest and principal subordinated to ordinary debentures and all other liabilities. *See also* debenture.

subordinated debt financing A form of long-term capitalization used by broker-dealers in which the claims of lenders are subordinated to the claims of all other creditors. Subordinated financing is considered part of the broker-dealer's capital structure. It receives advantageous treatment under the net capital rules by being permitted to add the borrowed amount to net worth when computing its net capital. *See* subordinated loan.

subordinated interest *See* reversionary working interest.

subordinated loan A loan to a broker-dealer in which the lender agrees to subordinate its claim to all the claims of the firm's other creditors. Temporary subordinated debt is permitted under certain conditions for limited reasons such as underwriting where a substantial deposit is required.

subordinated reversionary working interest *See* reversionary working interest.

subscription agreement A statement signed by an investor indicating an offer to buy an interest in a direct participation program. In the statement, the investor agrees to grant power of attorney to the general partner and abide by the limited partnership agreement. The sale is finalized when the subscription agreement is signed by the general partner.

subscription amount The total dollar amount that a participant in a direct participation program has invested.

suitability A determination made by a registered representative as to whether a particular security matches a customer's objectives and financial capability. The representative must have enough information about each customer to make a reasonable judgment.

supplemental liquidity provider (SLP) An off-the-trading-floor (upstairs) market maker who is incented by the NYSE to add liquidity. The SLP trades only for its proprietary account and may compete with the on-floor Designated Market Maker in a stock listed on the NYSE. The SLP must maintain a bid or an offer in an assigned stock at least 10% of the trading day.

supply The total amount of a good or service available for purchase by consumers. *See also* demand.

supply-side theory An economic theory contending that a sharp reduction in tax rates will stimulate productive investment by companies that benefit the entire society.

support level A technical analysis term describing the bottom of a stock's historical trading range. *See also* breakout; resistance level.

suspicious activity report (SAR) Financial institutions, such as broker-dealers, banks, thrifts, casinos, must file a suspicious activity report (SARs) with the Treasury Department's Financial Crimes Enforcement Network (FinCEN) whenever customer activity appears out of the ordinary or illegal.

syndicate A group of investment bankers (broker-dealer and banks) formed to distribute a security on behalf of the issuer. Each syndicate member is responsible for the sale and distribution of a portion of the issue. *Syn.* underwriting syndicate. *See* selling group; underwriting.

syndicate manager *See* underwriting manager. *Syn.* Bookrunner; main underwriter.

systematic risk The potential for a security to decrease in value, owing to its inherent tendency to move together with all securities of the same type. Neither diversification nor any other investment strategy can eliminate this risk. *See also* market risk.

T-bill *See* Treasury bill.

T-bond *See* Treasury bond.

T-call *See* Regulation T; margin call.

Tape *See* Consolidated Tape.

tax and revenue anticipation note (TRAN) A short-term municipal debt security to be paid off from future tax receipts and revenues.

tax anticipation note (TAN) A short-term municipal or government debt security to be paid off from future tax receipts.

tax basis *See* cost basis.

tax credit An amount that can be subtracted from a tax liability, often in connection with real estate development, energy conservation, and research and development programs. Every dollar of tax credit reduces the amount of tax due, dollar for dollar. *See also* deduction.

tax liability The amount of tax payable on earnings, usually calculated by subtracting standard and itemized deductions and personal exemptions from adjusted gross income, then multiplying by the tax rate. *See* adjusted gross income.

tax preference item An element of income that receives favorable tax treatment. The item must be added to taxable income when computing alternative minimum tax. Tax preference items include accelerated depreciation on property, research and development costs, intangible drilling costs, tax-exempt interest on municipal private purpose bonds, and certain incentive stock options. *See also* alternative minimum tax.

tax-deferred annuity *See* tax-sheltered annuity.

tax-equivalent yield The rate of return a taxable bond nust earn before taxes in order to equal the tax-exempt arnings on a municipal bond. This number varies with the nvestor's tax bracket.

ax-free bond fund *See* tax-exempt bond fund.

ax-exempt bond fund A mutual fund whose nvestment objective is to provide maximum tax-free ncome. It invests primarily in tax-free municipal debt. *Syn.* ax-free bond fund.

ax-sheltered annuity (TSA) An insurance contract hat entitles the holder to exclude all contributions from ross income in the year they are made. Tax payable on he earnings is deferred until retirement. *Syn.* tax-deferred nnuity.

axability The risk of the erosion of investment income rough taxation.

axable gain The portion of a sale or distribution of, for ample, mutual fund shares that is subject to taxation.

axes per capita *See* taxes per person.

taxes per person A measure of the tax burden of a municipality's population, calculated by dividing the municipality's tax receipts by its population. *Syn.* taxes per capita.

technical analysis A method of evaluating securities by analyzing statistics generated by market activity, such as past prices and volume. Technical analysts do not attempt to measure a security's intrinsic value. *See also* chartist; fundamental analysis.

tenants in common (TIC) A form of joint ownership of an account whereby a deceased tenant's fractional interest in the account is retained by his estate. *See* joint tenants with right of survivorship.

tender offer A limited-period SEC-registered offer to acquire a substantial portion of a company's securities (equity or debt). When a company seeks to acquire its own securities, it is referred to as an issuer tender offer. A filing is required to disclose the terms of the offering and information about the bidders, known as the Offer to Purchase, along with SEC Form TO.

term bond *See* term maturity.

term maturity A repayment schedule for a bond issue in which the entire issue comes due on a single date. *Syn.* term bond. *See* maturity date.

testimonial A statement in an advertisement or other promotional release, usually by a client, indicating great satisfaction with the provider of goods or services. Testimonials may never be used by investment advisers or their representatives.

Third Market A trading market in which exchange-listed securities are traded over-the-counter.

third-party account A customer account for which the owner has given power of attorney to a third party.

tick A minimum upward or downward movement in the price of a security.

ticker tape *See* Consolidated Tape.

TIGR *See* Treasury Investors Growth Receipt.

time deposit A sum of money left with a bank (or borrowed from a bank and left on deposit) that the depositing customer has agreed not to withdraw for a specified time period or without a specified amount of notice. *See* demand deposit.

time spread *See* horizontal spread.

time value The amount an investor pays for an option above its intrinsic value. It reflects the amount of time left until expiration. The amount is calculated by subtracting the intrinsic value from the premium paid. *See also* intrinsic value.

timing risk The potential for an investor to incur a loss as a result of buying or selling a particular security at an unfavorable time.

tombstone A printed advertisement that solicits indications of interest in a securities offering. The text is limited to basic information about the offering such as the name of the issuer, type of security, names of the underwriters, and where a prospectus is available. *See* omitting prospectus.

total capitalization The sum of a corporation's long-term debt, stock accounts, and capital in excess of par.

TRACE *See* Trade Reporting and Compliance Engine.

trade confirmation A printed document that contains details of a transaction, including the settlement date and amount of money due from or owed to a customer.

trade date The date on which a securities transaction is executed.

Trade Reporting and Compliance Engine (TRACE) FINRA-approved trade reporting system for corporate bonds trading in the OTC secondary market.

trade-through Generally, any time an order is executed through the price limit of another order that would have represented a better execution. Trade-throughs are generally prohibited under the order protection rule of Regulation NMS.

trading authorization *See* full trading authorization; limited trading authorization.

trading halt A pause in the trading of a particular security on one or more exchanges, usually in anticipation of a news announcement or to correct an order imbalance.

TRAN *See* tax and revenue anticipation note.

tranche One of the classes of securities that forms an issue of collateralized mortgage obligations. Each tranche is characterized by its interest rate, average maturity, risk level, and sensitivity to mortgage prepayments. Neither the rate of return nor the maturity date of a CMO tranche is guaranteed. *See also* collateralized mortgage obligation.

transfer agent A trust or bank engaged by a company to maintain records of investors.

transfer and hold in safekeeping A securities buy order settlement and delivery procedure whereby the securities bought are transferred to the customer's name but are held by the broker-dealer. *See also* hold in street name; transfer and ship.

transfer and ship A securities buy order settlement and delivery procedure whereby the securities bought are transferred to the customer's name and are sent to the customer. *See* hold in street name; transfer and hold in safekeeping.

Transportation Average *See* Dow Jones Transportation Average.

Treasury bill A marketable U.S. government debt security with a maturity of 52 weeks or less. *Syn.* T bill.

Treasury bond A marketable, fixed-interest U.S. government debt security with a maturity of more than 10 years.

Treasury Bond Receipt (TBR) One of several types of zero-coupon bonds and notes "stripped" of their coupons and issued by brokerage firms and collateralized by Treasury securities. *See also* Treasury receipt.

Treasury Investors Growth Receipt (TIGR) One of several types of zero-coupon bonds and notes "stripped" of their coupons and issued by brokerage firms and collateralized by Treasury securities. *See also* Treasury receipt.

Treasury note A marketable, fixed-interest U.S. government debt security with a maturity of between 2 and 10 years. *Syn.* T-note.

Treasury receipt The generic term for a zero-coupon bond issued by a brokerage firm and collateralized by the Treasury securities a custodian holds in escrow for the investor.

Treasury stock Equity securities that the issuing corporation has issued and repurchased from the public at the current market price. *See also* issued stock; outstanding stock.

trendline A tool used by technical analysts to trace a security's movement by connecting the reaction lows in an upward trend or the rally highs in a downward trend.

triangle On a technical analyst's trading activity chart, a pattern that shows a narrowing of the price range in which a security is trading. The left side of the triangle typically shows the widest range, and the right side narrows to a point. *Syn.* pennant. *See also* ascending triangle; descending triangle.

trough The end of a period of declining business activity throughout the economy, and one of the four stages of the business cycle. *See* business cycle.

true interest cost (TIC) A means of evaluating the competitive bids of prospective bond underwriting syndicates. Each syndicate provides a calculation of the coupon interest to be paid by the issuer over the life of the bond, taking into account the time value of money. *See also* net interest cost.

Trust Indenture Act of 1939 The legislation requiring that all publicly offered, nonexempt debt securities be registered under the Securities Act of 1933 and be issued under a trust indenture that protects the bondholders.

trustee (1) A person legally appointed to act as a fiduciary and make decisions in the best interests of the beneficiary. (2) A bank designated by an issuer of municipal debt as the custodian of funds and representative of bondholders appointed to ensure compliance with the bond contract.

Truth in Securities Act *See* Securities Act of 1933.

two-dollar broker An exchange member (broker) that executes orders for other member (broker-dealer) firms when their floor brokers are especially busy. Two-dollar brokers charge a negotiated commission for their services.

UGMA *See* Uniform Gifts to Minors Act.

UIT *See* unit investment trust.

uncovered The position of an option investor who writes a call on a security they do not own (or put options without a short position in the underlying asset).

uncovered call writer An investor who writes a call option without owning the underlying stock or other related assets that would enable the investor to deliver the stock, should the option be exercised. *Syn.* naked call writer.

underlying securities The futures or securities that are bought or sold when an option, right, warrant, or convertible bond is exercised.

underwriter An investment banker who works with an issuer to help bring a security to the market and sell it to the public.

underwriting The procedure by which investment bankers channel investment capital from investors to corporations and municipalities that are issuing securities.

underwriting compensation The amount paid to a broker-dealer firm for its involvement in offering and selling securities.

underwriting discount *See* underwriting spread.

underwriting manager *See* managing underwriter.

underwriting spread The difference in price between the public offering price and the price an underwriter pays to the issuing corporation. The difference represents the profit available to the syndicate or selling group. *Syn.* underwriting discount; underwriting split.

underwriting syndicate *See* syndicate.

undivided account *See* Eastern account.

unearned income Income derived from investments and other sources not related to employment services. Examples of unearned income include interest from a savings account, bond interest, and dividends from stock. *See also* earned income; passive income; portfolio income.

Uniform Gifts to Minors Act (UGMA) Legislation that permits a gift of money or securities to be given to a minor and held in a custodial account that an adult manages for the minor's benefit. Income and capital gains transferred to a minor's name are usually taxed at the minor's rate. However, if the child is under a specified age and has unearned income above a certain level, those earnings are taxed at the parent's rate. *See* Uniform Transfers to Minors Act.

Uniform Securities Act (USA) Template legislation written by the NCCUSL to serve as the basis for a state's securities legislation if the state wished to adopt it. It regulates securities, persons (broker-dealers and their agents and investment advisers and their representatives), and transactions in the securities markets within the state.

Uniform Transfers to Minors Act (UTMA) Legislation adopted in most states that permits a gift of money or securities to be given to a minor and held in a custodial account that an adult manages for the minor's benefit until the minor reaches a certain age (not necessarily the age of majority). *See* Uniform Gift to Minors Act.

unit investment trust (UIT) An investment company that sells redeemable shares in a professionally selected portfolio of securities. *See* fixed unit investment trust; nonfixed unit investment trust; unit of beneficial interest.

unit of beneficial interest A redeemable share in a unit investment trust, representing ownership of an undivided interest in the underlying portfolio. *Syn.* share of beneficial interest. *See also* unit investment trust.

unit refund annuity An annuity payout option that guarantees that all of the money in the contract (at minimum) at the time of annuitization is distributed to the annuitant/beneficiary.

unqualified legal opinion The statement of a bond counsel affirming the compliance of a new municipal bond issue with municipal statutes and tax regulations, and expressing no reservations about its validity. *See also* legal opinion of counsel; qualified legal opinion.

unsecured bond *See* debenture.

U.S. government and agency bond fund A mutual fund whose investment objective is to provide current income while preserving safety of capital through investing in securities backed by the U.S. Treasury or issued by a government agency.

USA *See* Uniform Securities Act.

UTMA *See* Uniform Transfers to Minors Act.

Value Line An investment advisory service that rates the safety, timeliness, and projected price performance of hundreds of stocks. *See also* Value Line Composite Index.

Value Line Composite Index A market index composed of 1,700 exchange and over-the-counter stocks. *See also* index; Value Line.

variable annuity An insurance contract used to fund retirement. Cash values vary with the performance of a portfolio of investments. An insurance and securities license is required to present variable contracts.

variable-rate demand obligation Municipal bonds issued with variable, or floating, rates of interest. These securities offer interest payments tied to the movements of another specified interest rate.

variable-rate municipal note A short-term municipal debt security issued when either general interest rates are expected to change or the length of time before permanent funding is received is uncertain. *Syn.* variable-rate demand note.

vertical spread The purchase and sale of two options on the same underlying security and with the same expiration date but with different exercise prices. *Syn.* money spread; price spread. *See also* spread.

vesting (1) An ERISA guideline stipulating that an employee must be entitled to all his retirement benefits within a certain period of time, even if he no longer works for the employer. (2) The amount of time that an employee must work before retirement or before benefit plan contributions made by the employer become the employee's property without penalty.

visible supply (1) The disclosure, published in The Bond Buyer, of the total dollar amount of municipal securities known to be coming to market within the next 30 days. (2) All supplies of goods and commodities that are readily deliverable.

VIX The volatility market index, known as the *fear index*, that measures investor expectation of implied volatility in the S&P 500.

volatility The magnitude and frequency of changes in the price of a security or commodity within a given time period.

volume The amount of trading activity, expressed in shares or dollars, experienced by a single security or the entire market within a specified period, usually daily, monthly, or annually.

voluntary accumulation plan A mutual fund account where the investor commits to depositing amounts on a regular basis, in addition to the initial sum invested.

voting right A stockholder's right to vote for members of the board of directors and on matters of corporate policy—particularly the issuance of senior securities, stock splits, and substantial changes in the corporation's business.

warrant (1) A security that gives the holder the right to purchase securities from the warrant issuer at a stipulated subscription price. Warrants are usually long-term instruments with expiration dates years in the future. (2) A debt security, usually a small amount, issued in certain municipal jurisdictions to pay project costs as they are incurred.

wash sale Selling a security at a loss for tax purposes and, within 30 days before or after, purchasing the same or a substantially identical security. The IRS will disallow the claimed loss. *See* bond swap.

Western account A securities underwriting in which the agreement among underwriters states that each syndicate member will be liable only for the sale of the portion of the issue allocated to it. *Syn.* divided account. *See also* Eastern account; syndicate.

when-, as- and if-issued security *See* when issued security.

when-issued A trade agreement regarding a security that has been authorized but is not yet physically available for delivery. The issuer makes delivery as soon as the security is ready, and the contract includes provisions for marking the price to the market and for calculating accrued interest.

when-issued securities (WI) Securities shares (such as Treasury notes) from a stock split and new issues of stocks and bonds that have been authorized but are not yet physically available for delivery. The issuer makes delivery as soon as the security is ready, and the contract includes provisions for marking the price to the market and for calculating accrued interest.

WI *See* when-issued security.

wildcatting *See* exploratory drilling program.

Wilshire 5000 Composite Index A market cap–weighted market indicator composed of about 3,500 exchange-listed and over-the-counter common stocks. It is the broadest measure of the market. *See also* index.

wire room *See* order department.

workable indication The price at which a municipal securities dealer is willing to purchase securities from another municipal dealer. The price may be revised if market conditions change. *Syn.* Nominal quotation.

working capital A measure of a corporation's liquidity—that is, its ability to transfer assets into cash to meet current short-term obligations. It is calculated by subtracting total current liabilities from total current assets.

working capital ratio *See* current ratio.

working interest An operating interest in a mineral-bearing property entitling the holder to a share of the income from production and carrying the obligation to bear a corresponding share of all production costs.

workout quote A qualified quotation whereby a broker-dealer estimates the price on a trade that will require special handling owing to its size or to market conditions. *See also* bona fide quote; firm quote; nominal quote; subject quote.

writer The seller of an option contract.

writing a scale The process by which a syndicate establishes the yield for each maturity in a new serial bond issue in order to arrive at its competitive bid. *See* scale.

yield The rate of return on an investment, usually expressed as an annual percentage rate. *See* current yield; dividend yield; nominal yield.

yield curve A graphic representation of the actual or projected yields of fixed-income securities in relation to their maturities. *See* flat yield curve; inverted yield curve.

yield to call (YTC) The rate of return on a bond that accounts for the difference between the bond's acquisition cost and its proceeds, including interest income, calculated to the earliest date that the bond may be called by the issuing corporation. *See also* bond yield.

yield to maturity (YTM) The rate of return on a bond that accounts for the difference between the bond's acquisition cost and its maturity proceeds, including interest income. *See also* bond yield.

yield-based option A security representing the right to receive, in cash, the difference between the current yield of an underlying U.S. government security and the strike price of the option.

YTC *See* yield to call.

YTM *See* yield to maturity.

zero-coupon bond A corporate or municipal debt security traded at a deep discount from face value. The bond pays no interest; rather, it may be redeemed at maturity for its full face value.

INDEX

W

Z

Notes

Notes

Notes

Notes

Notes

Notes

Notes

Notes